A Concise Introduction to

World Religions

A Concise Introduction to
World Religions

Edited by

Willard G. Oxtoby & Alan F. Segal

OXFORD
UNIVERSITY PRESS

OXFORD
UNIVERSITY PRESS

70 Wynford Drive, Don Mills, Ontario M3C 1J9
www.oup.com/ca

Oxford University Press is a department of the University of Oxford.
It furthers the University's objective of excellence in research, scholarship,
and education by publishing worldwide in

Oxford   New York
Auckland   Cape Town   Dar es Salaam   Hong Kong   Karachi
Kuala Lumpur   Madrid   Melbourne   Mexico City   Nairobi
New Delhi   Shanghai   Taipei   Toronto

With offices in
Argentina   Austria   Brazil   Chile   Czech Republic   France   Greece
Guatemala   Hungary   Italy   Japan   Poland   Portugal   Singapore
South Korea   Switzerland   Thailand   Turkey   Ukraine   Vietnam

Oxford is a trade mark of Oxford University Press
in the UK and in certain other countries

Published in Canada
by Oxford University Press

Copyright © Oxford University Press Canada 2007

The moral rights of the author have been asserted

Database right Oxford University Press (maker)

First published 2007

Library and Archives Canada Cataloguing in Publication

A concise introduction to world religions / edited by Willard G. Oxtoby, Alan F. Segal.

Includes bibliographical references and index.
ISBN 978-0-19-542207-8

1. Religions—Textbooks.   I. Oxtoby, Willard G. (Willard Gurdon), 1933-
II. Segal, Alan F., 1945-

BL80.3.C65 2007   200   C2007-901484-4

Cover Image: Ryan Fox / Getty Images
Cover Design: Brett Miller
Text Design: Sonya Thursby / OPUS House Inc.

2 3 4 – 10 09 08 07
Printed in the United States of America

Contents

Maps

Contributors

ROY C. AMORE has extensive research experience in Asia. His books include *Two Masters, One Message*, comparing the lives and teachings of Christ and Buddha, and *Lustful Maidens and Ascetic Kings: Buddhist and Hindu Stories of Life*. He is Professor in the Department of Political Science at the University of Windsor and is currently writing a book on religion and politics.

MAHMOUD M. AYOUB, Professor of Islamic Studies at Temple University in Philadelphia, wrote the chapter on Islam in *World Religions: Western Traditions*. His books include *Redemptive Suffering in Islam, The Qur'an and its Interpreters*, and *Islam: Faith and Practice*.

ROBERT M. BAUM is Associate Professor of Religious Studies at the University of Missouri where his focus is indigenous religions, especially in West Africa. The author of the award-winning book *Shrines of the Slave Trade: Diola Religion and Society in Precolonial Senegambia*, as well as numerous articles, he is currently working on a history of Diola prophetic movements.

The late JULIA CHING taught at the University of Toronto, where she achieved the distinguished rank of University Professor. Among her many books are *To Acquire Wisdom, Confucianism and Christianity, Probing China's Soul, The Religious Thought of Chu Hsi*, and a personal memoir, *The Butterfly Healing: A Life Between East and West*.

AMIR HUSSAIN is Associate Professor in the Department of Theological Studies at Loyola Marymount University in Los Angeles, where he teaches courses on Islam and world religions. A Canadian of Pakistani origin, he is the author of *Oil and Water: Two Faiths, One God*, an introduction to Islam for North Americans.

VASUDHA NARAYANAN is Distinguished Professor in the Department of Religion and Director of the Center for the Study of Hindu Traditions at the University of Florida. She is the author or editor of six books and has written more than a hundred articles and chapters in books. Her latest book, *A Hundred Autumns to Live*, will be published in 2008.

The late WILLARD G. OXTOBY, the editor of the two-volume *World Religions: Eastern Traditions* and *Western Traditions*, was Professor Emeritus at the University of Toronto, where he launched the graduate program in the study of religion. His books include *Experiencing India: European Descriptions and Impressions* and *The Meaning of Other Faiths.*

ALAN F. SEGAL is Professor of Religion and Ingeborg Rennert Professor of Jewish Studies at Barnard College, Columbia University. He has written extensively in the fields of comparative religion, Judaism, and early Christianity. His books include *Rebecca's Children, Paul the Convert,* and *Life After Death: A History of the Afterlife in Western Religions.*

Introduction

ALAN F. SEGAL | WILLARD G. OXTOBY

Not so long ago, intellectuals regarded religion as a cultural fossil. Aesthetically rich, anthropologically intriguing? Yes. But relevant to today's hard-nosed world of business and politics? Hardly at all. When Will Oxtoby said that he studied religion, he was often asked why he was wasting his life on something so far removed from the concerns of the real world.

No one has asked that question since 1979. In that year the Shah of Iran was deposed in an Islamic revolution. A nation of 40 million people was apparently ready to put lives and livelihoods on the line in defence of their religious values—values utterly alien to Western cultures whose understanding of economic development and politico-military strategy was entirely secular. Not only in Iran but elsewhere, Muslims were saying an emphatic 'no' to the modern West. In increasing numbers, Muslims from Algeria to Zanzibar were re-embracing cultural traditions that earlier generations had abandoned.

Meanwhile, Christian fundamentalism was becoming more important in the political life of the Americas, particularly in the United States. The politicization of the religious right can be understood as the key to the popularity of George W. Bush and perhaps the principal reason for his narrow and incomplete electoral victories in 2000 and 2004. Is this a new religious re-awakening or the last gasp of dying faith? It will be a long time before anyone knows for sure.

To understand the modern world, we now realize, we need to take into account the meanings that traditional religions have for their adherents. Another breathtaking year was 1989, when the communist order of eastern Europe and the Soviet Union began to crumble. There were high hopes for democracy, peace, and progress. But experience soon showed that when the restraints of the socialist order were loosened, old passions and identities resurfaced—passions that many had assumed to have died out. Ethno-religious divisions in the Balkans, the Caucasus, the Middle East, and Central Asia erupted into bitter conflict. In the secular intellectual climate of the modern world, some philosophers and even theologians might assert that God is dead; but in the practical ethno-political climate of the modern world, religion is very much alive.

The Invitation

We invite you to share our fascination with religion. It is not our mandate to make you more religious (or less). Rather, we want you to be better informed *about* religion—regardless of your own investment in any of its particular forms.

Many people consider religion the loftiest, most profound expression of the human spirit. Many others see it as a blight on civilization, the source of superstition, ignorance, hatred, repression, even genocide. There is evidence to support both views, for the history of religion is a mixture of spectacular successes and abject failures.

Many who take a favourable view regard all or most of the world's religious traditions as more or less equal in value. Religions teach that there is order and purpose in the universe, and promote order and benevolence in society. Some who hold a largely positive view of religion would go so far as to say that all the world's religious traditions teach essentially the same things. If you are among them, we invite you to explore those diverse traditions in greater detail, to better understand where they converge and where they differ. On the other hand, many in the modern world do not identify themselves with any traditional religion. The reasons vary. Some consider their own beliefs regarding purpose and value in the universe to be a private matter. Some find that ritualized traditional forms of religion do not resonate with them. Some are simply appalled by the misery that humans have inflicted on one another in the name of God.

Both the positive and the negative assessments of religion we have just sketched are characteristically modern. Both have come to the fore in Western civilization in the last 300 years. And both take humanity as the common denominator of the various religions—as a measure of their achievement and sometimes also as an explanation of their nature and function.

Before the modern era, however, most people in the West clearly differentiated between the positive and the negative in religion, seeing their own way as truth and all others as error. That view is not uncommon even today, especially among those who are religiously committed. For many people the faith and practice commanded by their own traditions are desirable, while the faith and practice of others are at best a waste of time. Comparisons are odious, we are told, and comparison of religions may be among the more odious of activities. Yet it is an irresistible human impulse to compare. Are there any guidelines?

One point that our observations may bear out is that any effort to compare religious traditions should be based on uniform standards. Enthusiasts have often seen only the ideals that religion in general represents, while critics have tended to concentrate on the harm caused by the actions undertaken in its name. Apologists for a particular religious tradition have often praised its ideals while denouncing the way followers of other traditions live out their beliefs in the world. We tend to notice what we were looking for in the first place. Those who seek grounds for contention in religion will find it in ample measure, and those who seek generosity of spirit may be pleasantly surprised at how much of it can be seen.

Insider And Outsider

One of the abiding issues in the academic study of religion is the conscious role of the observer. 'Objectivity' is a value we are taught early in school. Yet theorists today tell us that objectivity is in practice impossible to achieve. Some even say that there is no such thing as objective truth. Certainly we should recognize that every attempt at a historical account necessarily involves selection and interpretation. Even if it were theoretically possible to describe something 'objectively', the simple decision to describe that thing rather than something else can hardly be described as objective.

The study of religion wrestles perpetually with the difference between 'insider' and 'outsider' perspectives. The religious participant can presumably speak from first-hand experience. One of the most famous statements of this view was formulated by the German theologian and philosopher of religion Rudolf Otto, in the opening of his 1917 book known in English as *The Idea of the Holy*:

> The reader is invited to direct his mind to a moment of deeply-felt religious experience, as little as possible qualified by other forms of consciousness. Whoever cannot do this, whoever knows no such moments in his experience, is requested to read no farther; for it is not easy to discuss questions of religious psychology with one who can recollect the emotions of his adolescence, the discomforts of indigestion, or, say, social feelings, but cannot recall any intrinsically religious feelings (Otto 1923:8).

Over the generations that have passed since Otto wrote those words, the argument has often been made that there is no substitute in religion for the faith of the adherent. Often, however, the discussion has confused information and analysis. Testimony is one thing and cross-examination is another. A participant may, but also may not, be able to identify the assumptions on which a tradition rests, or the transitions it has undergone. An adherent may, but also may not, be able to describe fairly the various interpretations of his or her tradition offered by different sectors within the community.

At the opposite pole from Otto are those who maintain that the only hope for scholarly credibility is to be found in the outsider's 'objective' detachment from religion and its claims. At the extreme, to say anything positive about religion is to lose that credibility. In fact, it is not uncommon for scholars of religion to be people who have become profoundly alienated from the faith communities in which they were raised. And in the study of the major traditions of Asia, many significant findings have been arrived at by outsiders—Westerners—some of whom never set foot in the lands about which they wrote. An outsider may not, but also may, have something important and useful to say about a religious tradition.

The insider–outsider question can also be framed in terms of institutional accountability. In the Middle Ages, theology was the 'queen of the sciences' in European universities, many of which were directly linked to the Christian Church. In eighteenth-

and nineteenth-century North America, many colleges and universities were explicitly connected with some particular Christian denomination.

With the secularization of older schools and the establishment of new secular ones, studies in the area of religion have tended to be differentiated depending on whether the source of their funding is religious or secular. Studies supported by religious groups are now generally referred to as 'theological', while studies undertaken by publicly funded institutions are termed 'secular'. But there is a considerable overlap, and many scholars have worked in both areas, sometimes simultaneously.

As a result, the distinction between the 'religious' and 'secular' study of religion is much easier to draw in the context of institutional financial support than of individual perspectives. Many of us, particularly in historical studies, have become semi-spectators on our own traditions even as we have continued to identify with and participate in them. Thus many of us have come to approach our own traditions from the same kind of disciplined (scientific?) viewpoint that we adopt when observing other people's traditions. At the same time, we have come to take a more empathetic (theological?) approach towards traditions other than our own.

In this text we speak as disinterested scholars but also in some sense for our own particular religious identities. Vasudha Narayanan is Hindu, Roy Amore identifies with Buddhism and Christianity, and the late Julia Ching's Chinese family includes Confucians, Buddhists, Muslims, Christians, and Marxists among its members. Willard G. Oxtoby was a Christian and a clergyman of the Presbyterian denomination. Alan F. Segal is a Reform Jew whose family now includes Orthodox Jews and believing Christians as well. Robert Baum is culturally an American Jew who was initiated into Diola dance shrines during his fieldwork in Senegal. None of us is a Sikh, a Jain, or a follower of Shinto. Still, we hope that in all our descriptions we have been able to walk the tightrope of disciplined empathy without falling into the abyss either of advocating or of debunking.

East and West

If one is to separate the world's religious traditions into two groups, where and how does one draw the line? Borderlines, arbitrary or otherwise, produce borderline cases, and to use the pigeonholes we create, we may have to cut some birds in half. When Professor Oxtoby was planning the two volumes on which this concise text is based, it was critical to decide where on the round globe one group of traditions stopped and the other began. His answer was that the conventional distinction between East and West was historically important, even though it reflected a longstanding bias and despite the fact that some regional traditions—notably those in Africa and Australia—fell outside both categories. For this single-volume text, finished three years after Professor Oxtoby's death, the East–West question was no longer so important; but the distinction is still interesting precisely because it draws attention to the West's historic misperception of Asian religions and helps to explain some of the negative responses that Western religions—especially Christianity—have experienced among adherents of other traditions.

There was a time when the concept of 'the East' made sense to Europeans. Well into the twentieth century, the East was everything to the east of Europe. 'The Orient' began where the Orient Express ended, in Istanbul. For some purposes, it even included North Africa.

A century ago Islam was considered an Eastern religion, and Westerners who studied it were called orientalists, even though Islam shares its historic and theological roots with Judaism and Christianity, and virtually all its classic structures developed in the Mediterranean and Persian-speaking world. Today scholars regard Islam as a religion of the West even though the majority of Muslims now live in the Indian subcontinent, Malaysia, and Indonesia—lands where the boundary between East and West is blurred at best.

With this new ordering, some contend that the Western religions are linked by a common focus on prophetic and scriptural revelation from a single God, whereas the Eastern religions are linked by a common focus on human insight gained through disciplined reflection under the guidance of a wise teacher or sage. Prophecy is a kind of religious communication in which someone claims (or is claimed) to transmit a message from a divine source. The message is the word of God, whether dictated verbatim by the deity or formulated in language by the human prophet. Much of the most important insight in the Western religious traditions has come in the form of the prophet's declaration: 'Thus says the Lord.' In the 'wisdom' traditions, by contrast, insight is attained by an individual through his or her own reflection. The product of that insight may be presented as an eternal or cosmic divine truth, but what the sage says is 'I have meditated and reflected, and this insight has come to me.' When the Oxford scholar R.C. Zaehner was editing *The Concise Encyclopedia of Living Faiths* (1959)—an advanced introductory survey that was a landmark work in the field—he used 'prophecy' and 'wisdom' as his two main divisions, rather than 'West' and 'East'. Even so, it is hard to believe that these categories can be absolute. There are wisdom traditions in the West mixed in with the prophetic ones, and there are notions of revelation and scriptural authority here and there in the East. Just as there is only limited truth in the East-West dichotomy, so too there is only limited truth in the prophecy-wisdom contrast. The latter can sometimes be a useful basis of comparison and review—but only *after* one has studied the individual traditions in the specific detail of their development and teachings; if it is adopted beforehand and allowed to structure what the observer sees, it is likely to be misleading.

We can speak in a fairly coherent fashion about the West and its role in the world. Since the end of the fifteenth century, European (eventually Euro-American) civilization has achieved world dominance. This civilization's science and technology have spread worldwide, as have its political and philosophical traditions. Its dominant religion, Christianity, has been carried to the 'four corners' of the globe. And with Christianity's influence have gone particular notions of what 'religion' is in relation to other spheres of life—notions not necessarily shared by the indigenous cultures of those lands. Christianity may be the most obvious instance of a tradition that has transcended its geographical origins; but other religions—notably Buddhism and Islam—have also spread around the world. And though Judaism has been far less likely to proselytize, the diaspora has taken Jews to every continent.

The East, for its part, is hugely diverse. An inventory of the cultural differences between southern and eastern Asia could fill volumes. Is there any common thread? We could even go so far as to suggest that 'the East' as a coherent entity exists only in the mind of the West. The ancient Chinese, for instance, termed their land the 'Middle' kingdom, not the Eastern one. In that, they were not unlike the Westerners who named a sea Mediterranean simply because it happened to be at the middle of their world. In India, the aggregate indigenous heritage, which we in modern times term 'Hinduism', was also the milieu in which Buddhism arose and with which Buddhism shares some (but by no means all) of its own outlooks and practices. Carried then to East Asia, Buddhism interacted with various other indigenous traditions, including Confucianism and Daoism in China, and Shinto in Japan. With this perspective, a historical case can be made for seeing the principal Eastern religious traditions as a constantly changing mixture. Religions are so integrated in much of Asia that one would be hard-pressed to say which one predominates in any single place.

The East–West dichotomy not only skewed the perception of Asian religions: it also left out large sections of the religious world. Prehistoric, archaic, and abandoned religions were simply left unexplored. It is not adequate to think of Egyptian, ancient Near Eastern, classical, Zoroastrian, Hellenistic, Manichean, or Gnostic religions—or Judaism for that matter—as abandoned Western religions, essentially preparation for Christianity. Nor does the East–West dichotomy take into account the indigenous, ethnic, and tribal religions of Africa, Australia, the Americas, Asia, or even Europe. Today the vocabularies of comparative religion are as likely to come from anthropological and historical study of these religions as the scriptural religions of Judaism, Christianity, Islam, Hinduism, and Buddhism.

Will Oxtoby planned this project before his wife Julia Ching lost her long battle with cancer. He himself succumbed only two years later. His impending death made it impossible for him to complete the project, but he wished it to continue under the direction of Alan F. Segal and with the collaboration of the original contributors. Roy Amore reworked all the material on Buddhism, Confucianism, Daoism, and the varied religious life of Korea and Japan. When Mahmoud Ayoub was unable to edit his chapter on Islam, Amir Hussain agreed to step in. Vasudha Narayanan, in addition to revising her own chapters on the Hindu and Jain traditions, edited Will Oxtoby's chapter on Sikhism. Finally, Robert Baum wrote an entirely new chapter on indigenous religions. Unfortunately, not all the traditions covered in the original work could be treated in any depth here; one notable example is Zoroastrianism. Readers are encouraged to consult the two-volume *World Religions* whenever questions arise.

Many people have worked behind the scenes to bring this project to fruition. It was first envisioned by Laura McLeod and Will Oxtoby. Rachael Cayley and Lisa Proctor saw the manuscript through the initial development phase. Wendy Dockray, Meryl Segal, and Heather Trobe helped me in the early stages of the editorial process. And Sally Livingston spent countless hours with each of us on the line-by-line editing. We are also grateful for the assistance of Euan White and Phyllis Wilson.

Further Reading

Bowker, John, ed. 1997. *Oxford Dictionary of World Religions*. Oxford: Oxford University Press. An alphabetically arranged single-volume desk reference.

Brandon, S.G.F., ed. 1970. *A Dictionary of Comparative Religion*. London: Weidenfeld & Nicolson. Excellent historical articles; still valuable.

Eliade, Mircea, ed. 1987. *The Encyclopedia of Religion*. 16 vols. New York: Macmillan. The standard multi-volume library reference, with good articles especially on thematic topics and on developments in particular geographical regions.

al-Faruqi, Ismail R., and Donald E. Sopher, eds. 1974. *Historical Atlas of the Religions of the World*. New York: Macmillan. Contains useful survey text as well as maps.

Hastings, James, ed. 1908–26. *Encyclopaedia of Religion and Ethics*. 13 vols. Edinburgh: T. & T. Clark. Truly a landmark work: three generations old, but hardly superseded on account of the wealth of detail it offers.

Smart, Ninian, ed. 1999. *Atlas of the World's Religions*. Oxford: Oxford University Press. Well illustrated, in colour.

Smith, Jonathan Z., ed. 1995. *The HarperCollins Dictionary of Religion*. [New York]: Harper SanFrancisco. Concise but sophisticated entries. Probably the best single-volume desk reference for purchase.

Young, Serenity, ed. 1999. *Encyclopedia of Women and World Religions*. 2 vols. New York: Macmillan Reference. A place to turn for material relevant to feminist interests.

References

Otto, Rudolf. 1923. *The Idea of the Holy: An Inquiry into the Non-rational Factor in the Idea of the Divine and Its Relation to the Rational*. London: Oxford University Press.

Zaehner, R.C. 1959. *The Concise Encyclopedia of Living Faiths*. London: Hutchinson.

Indigenous Religions

ROBERT M. BAUM

Today most scholars define an indigenous religious tradition as one that was created by a particular community or nation, is closely related to that group's sense of identity, and has remained uniquely associated with that group (that is, its adherents have not attempted to spread it to other communities). The fact that indigenous religions reinforce a sense of cultural identity does not preclude borrowing from other traditions, but the borrowed elements—rituals, deities, ideas—are integrated into the indigenous system. Adherence to that system is often an essential aspect of membership in the community.

Introduction

In the past, scholars often described indigenous religions as '**primitive**', conjuring images of savagery, superstition, and childish simplicity even though such traditions typically involve extensive instruction and complex rituals. More recently some scholars have preferred terms like 'tribal', 'small-scale', 'oral', or 'traditional'. But these terms too are problematic. Why should the **Yoruba** tradition of West Africa, with some twenty million practitioners on four continents, be labelled 'tribal' or 'small-scale' when the traditions of far smaller communities, such as Jews, Baha'is, and Zoroastrians, are recognized as world religions?

'Primal', for its part, suggests either infancy and raw emotion (as in 'primal scream') or the earliest stage in an evolutionary model of development leading towards some preconceived notion of what a religion ought to be. As for 'oral', it is true that most indigenous religious traditions have been transmitted orally. But to characterize them as 'oral' or 'preliterate' is to ignore the fact that some indigenous peoples have had written traditions for over a thousand years—not to mention the important oral dimensions of 'world' religions.

Finally, even the term 'traditional' is unsatisfactory, since many other kinds of religion have existed for millennia. Thus 'indigenous religion' has come to be the preferred term for the particular type of tradition created by a particular group of people for whom that tradition is part of what defines them as a distinct community.

Until roughly 3,500 years ago, all the world's religions were 'indigenous' in this sense. The development of religions like Judaism and Hinduism drew adherents away from earlier traditions, some of which disappeared as distinct entities. Still, even those older traditions exerted important influences on the new dominant religions.

Even at the beginning of the twenty-first century, indigenous religious traditions command significant followings around the world, although reliable statistics in many cases do not exist, and official sources tend to exaggerate the numbers of adherents to 'official' religions. For example, indigenous traditions continue to be practised by indigenous peoples throughout the Americas. Some of their practices show clear signs of influence from religions not native to the Americas, notably Christianity; in effect, new traditions have developed that integrate ideas and practices from both indigenous and foreign traditions. Known as **syncretism**, this amalgamation process is common wherever different religions have interacted over a long period of time.

Religious syncretism has taken place throughout history and in all parts of the world. The Africans transported to the Americas as slaves brought with them traditions, either African religions and/or Islam, that interacted with indigenous American Indian religions and European-American Christianity to create new religious traditions such as Vaudou, Santeria, Candomblé, and Umbanda. In Africa itself, indigenous religions still flourish despite centuries of proselytizing by Muslims and Christians. Even among those who do not practise indigenous traditions, many have found ways of reconciling the religious duties and understandings of Christianity or Islam with their own religious traditions and knowledge. Indigenous and newer religions have influenced each other and produced distinctively African syncretic traditions.

Indigenous religions remain important in Australasia as well. Southeast Asia, Malaysia, and Indonesia have been influenced by Hindu and Buddhist traditions for nearly two millennia, by Islam for nearly a thousand years, and by Christianity for nearly five hundred. In this region indigenous religions, which tend to be stronger in rural than in urban areas, still exert significant influence on the local practice of world religions. In Australia and the Pacific Islands—Malaysia, Indonesia, New Guinea, Melanesia, Polynesia, and Micronesia—contact with outside communities came later. In Australia British colonization caused radical declines in Aboriginal populations and religions alike. In the Pacific Islands, however, where the European occupation was less harsh, population declines were less dramatic and conversion to other religious traditions less widespread.

Indigenous religious communities in northeast Asia have coexisted with Buddhism for well over a thousand years, with Islam for about 800 years, and with Christianity for about 500 years. In Mongolia, southern Siberia, Tibet, and Japan, the interaction between Buddhism and indigenous religions has been so prolonged that it is difficult to separate the one from the other. Japanese Shinto is closely integrated with Buddhist traditions received from Korea and China. In fact, it was under the influence of Buddhist teachers that Japanese scholars recorded the oral traditions of early Japan in what became the sacred texts of Shinto religion. For most Japanese the ritual calendar includes both Buddhist and Shinto holidays. In Siberia many people converted to Russian Orthodox Christianity in the eighteenth and nineteenth centuries, but others continued to practise indigenous religious traditions. For most of the twentieth century indigenous religions throughout the Soviet Union were somewhat insulated against active missionary work of any kind—Christian, Muslim, or Buddhist—by the Soviet authorities' suspicion of institutionalized religion.

With the exception of some groups in northeast Asia and North America that shared cultural origins and maintained limited contact, indigenous religious clusters generally developed in isolation until the nineteenth century. It was only with the expansion of the Islamic and Christian worlds, when they were forcibly integrated into a Western-dominated world trade system and Western (or Western-inspired) colonial systems, that they were exposed to other religious traditions. Efforts to win indigenous peoples over to Islam, Christianity, and (to a lesser extent) Buddhism have often been aggressive. And even in places where independence movements have succeeded in returning formal sovereignty to the indigenous people, the new political leadership has often been dominated by adherents of world religions who marginalize indigenous traditions. The experience of foreign domination and marginalization within their own countries is one common thread in the religious histories of indigenous peoples. Still, every indigenous religious tradition has its own rich and distinctive history.

Indigenous Religions and Western Scholarship

Interestingly, the comparative study of religion has focused particular attention on indigenous religions. In the nineteenth century, when religious studies was struggling to break free of theology and establish itself as an independent academic field, Western libraries were beginning to accumulate accounts, by explorers and other travellers, of unusual customs and practices from around the world. These accounts provided a wealth of information for scholars seeking to develop 'scientific' theories of society and religion, who—at a time when most universities were affiliated with state-sponsored churches—did not dare put Western traditions under the microscope for fear of losing their jobs.

As a result, many of the key terms used in the comparative study of religion were derived from indigenous religions, indigenous languages, or both. Scholars would take a word like '**totem**'—a Canadian Ojibwa (Anishinaabe) term for a spiritual kinship between a particular animal or species and a particular individual, family, or clan—and apply it to cultures as different as the Zulu, Hopi, and Maori. In the same way the Melanesian word '**mana**', denoting a free-flowing power in the universe capable of either enhancing or diminishing life, was applied to religious traditions all over the world, and the Polynesian word *tapu*, referring to a sacred prohibition, was borrowed to form '**taboo**'. Perhaps the best-known example is the Siberian Tungus word '**shaman**': the term for the primary ritual specialists in that culture, whose souls could leave their bodies and travel into other realms to encounter spirits. 'Shaman' has become a general term for the visionaries in many cultures who use ecstatic trances and out-of-body experiences to communicate with spiritual beings on behalf of the community.

Terms such as these were rarely applied to the scholars' own religious traditions, however. The dietary laws of Islam and Judaism were not identified as taboos; neither Elijah's ascent to heaven in a whirlwind nor Muhammad's ascent on the angelic steed Buraq is described as a shamanic journey. At the same time local customs or ideas were reshaped in the scholar's study to fit a foreign terminology. Accounts of indigenous religions often exaggerated their 'exotic' aspects, minimizing their similarities to the dominant world religions and presenting them as fundamentally different. In the nineteenth and twentieth centuries, scholars tended to perceive indigenous religions as living replicas of the traditions their distant ancestors followed before embracing Judaism or Christianity.

Underlying this view was the assumption that religions developed in stages, beginning at the 'primitive' level and rising until they either reached their 'highest' form (usually monotheism) or withered away into atheism. In comparative religion textbooks, it is still not uncommon to see indigenous religion described as if that term were merely another way of referring to **Paleolithic** or **Neolithic** religion. This perspective reflects a stereotype of indigenous peoples as 'natural' and unchanging. Yet in fact scholarly research is now finding that every indigenous religion has its own history, and that some of them have experienced more changes over time—in concepts of deities, rituals, ethics, social organization—than some world religions.

It is important to keep in mind that most of the information available about indigenous religions has not come from adherents of those traditions. Most informants have been outsiders, and not many of them have been trained and objective observers. By contrast, most texts describing world religions have been the work of believers. Many of the primary sources on indigenous religions have been explorers, traders, and missionaries—people whose primary attention was focused elsewhere. Accounts written by indigenous people themselves are rare, and those that do exist often reflect the influence of earlier writings grounded in Western theories of religion.

It is also important to remember that most of the descriptions we have were written after the period of initial contact with Europeans, when the political, economic, cultural, religious, and environmental changes initiated by that contact were already well underway. Most accounts of indigenous religions in the Americas, for example, were recorded well after Aboriginal populations had been devastated by European diseases. Most descriptions of African religions were written by people of European origin some time after the establishment of the Atlantic slave trade, which generated a unique set of power dynamics between black and white in the Atlantic world. Furthermore, such descriptions were usually the work of traders, missionaries, and scholars who depended on the support of Western authorities, and so were produced in a situation of power inequality between the observers and the observed. Typically, the means of communication have been the monopoly of Westerners, while indigenous people themselves have been marginalized.

Many early accounts of indigenous religions were written by explorers and traders who did not stay long enough to learn the local languages and therefore relied on interpreters unschooled in religious concepts and terminology. Making their way to universities in Britain, France, and Germany—far from the actual practitioners who could have corrected any misrepresentations—these reports were then interpreted by 'arm-chair' anthropologists who often imposed on them theoretical frameworks that had little or nothing to do with the traditions in question. The quality of missionaries' reporting was usually much higher because they stayed longer, had some knowledge of local languages, and were specifically concerned with religious issues. Nevertheless, missionaries' desire to convert indigenous peoples tended to limit their empathy and influence their interpretations.

It was not until the late 1800s that professional ethnographers began to undertake extensive field research based on participant observation (in which researchers live among the people they are studying and take part in community activities) and interviews. Interviews allow indigenous people to explain their own interpretations of religious activities and the roles they play in daily life. They can also provide access to historical source materials in the form of **oral traditions**—narratives, legends, fables, proverbs, riddles—that are passed down from generation to generation and that, like the scriptures of literate religions, serve to make important religious ideas accessible to the general public.

Some cultures emphasize exact memorization of these oral texts; others are more free-flowing. Still, oral traditions depend on individuals' memories, and people living in different circumstances may emphasize different aspects of a shared tradition. In other words, oral traditions are dynamic, subject to change, and this means that other sources may be needed to assist in the interpretation of such data.

Archaeological evidence is also important, especially for the more distant past. Ruins of temples or ritual sites, tombs, images of gods or ancestors carved in wood or stone, paintings, frescoes or carvings of religious activities or ideas, all provide valuable insights. Even the debris found at ritual sites, such as bone fragments or seeds, can offer clues to sacrificial practices. Sometimes recognizable features of the local environment, such as waterfalls, grottos, or unusual trees, can assist in the interpretation of traditional narratives.

The study of indigenous religions, therefore, requires a multi-faceted approach based on written and oral texts, field research, and archaeological evidence. Scholars must be familiar with all the available information—historical, anthropological, and archaeological. Interestingly, scholars of the dominant world religions today are applying a similar multiplicity of approaches to their discipline, which in the past focused almost exclusively on sacred texts and commentaries on them.

The rest of this chapter will focus on five major clusters of indigenous religions—African, American Indian, Asian, and Australasian—and how each of them experienced the challenges of European domination.

Africa

If archaeologists are correct in believing that the first human beings came from Africa, then it stands to reason that the first religions also originated there. For decades, a succession of archaeological finds in East Africa, between Ethiopia and Tanzania, has been pushing back the date for the earliest human presence in the region. But evidence regarding religion is scanty at best. Excavations of Paleolithic burial sites, dating back as far as 100,000 years, have revealed that bodies were placed in the ground with faces turned towards the setting sun, and were often painted with ochre. These practices suggest that early humans valued their dead and may have linked their passage out of life to the setting of the sun, while the personal items (such as hunting weapons, tools, or food) often placed in the grave with the body suggest a belief in some form of afterlife. Graves from the end of the Paleolithic Age, approximately 10,000 years ago, sometimes contain animal bones that appear to have been heated until they cracked—perhaps so that a **diviner** could study the patterns and use them to foresee the future or understand the causes of current problems. Discoveries such as these suggest that the earliest humans were concerned with making an uncertain world more predictable and controllable.

As early as 10,000 years ago, Saharan and southern African rock paintings depicted people hunting various types of animals. Some of these scenes include images of figures

NUMBERS

There are no reliable statistics on the numbers of people who practise indigenous African religions. Estimates run as high as 200 million, or slightly more than twenty-five per cent of the continent's total population.

DISTRIBUTION

Mainly south of the Sahara desert, especially in the forest areas of West and Equatorial Africa and a range of ecological zones in East and southern Africa.

PRINCIPAL HISTORICAL PERIODS

616 CE	First Muslims arrive in Ethiopia
1444	Portuguese begin exploring sub-Saharan Africa
c. 1480	Beginning of Atlantic slave trade
1885	Africa partitioned by European powers at Congress of Berlin; intensive missionary efforts begin in non-Muslim areas
1956–65	Beginning of post-independence era

FOUNDERS AND LEADERS

Some traditions mention a founder, but most do not. Many notable leaders have emerged in times of crisis. Examples include Kinjikitile and Alinesitoué Diatta.

DEITIES

Most African religions recognize a supreme being who began the process of creation, is the ultimate source of lesser deities' power, gives or withholds rain, and judges human beings on their behaviour before they enter the afterlife. This deity can be male, female, both male and female (androgynous), or neither. The lesser spirits and ancestors are often the primary focus of ritual activity because they are more approachable than the supreme being. Trickster deities are common.

AUTHORITATIVE TEXTS

African religions are fundamentally oral. Most traditions include accounts of the creation of the world and the settlement of particular regions. Recently, indigenous scholars have written down some oral traditions, and these texts are used for religious guidance.

NOTEWORTHY TEACHINGS

The supreme being is the ultimate source of all life and all spiritual power, and determines the fate of people when they die. Reincarnation is an important part of most African religions. The most favourable afterlife is that of ancestors who can continue to help their descendants before being reborn, often within their original lineage. A communitarian ethic is central to all African religious systems.

with rays coming out of their heads. Commentators have suggested that the latter represent a freely circulating spiritual power that some powerful individuals were able to tap. But we cannot know what these images meant for the people who painted them. Even if the culture in question has an oral tradition explaining the origins of the world, for example, it may provide little information on religious practices or the nature of the deities, spirits, or powers that were active in the formative period. It is also possible that, as the earliest humans slowly migrated to other areas of Africa and other continents of the world, they carried with them religious ideas and practices that originated in quite different places.

Africa is the world's second largest continent, stretching from the Mediterranean Sea in the north to the southern reaches of the Atlantic Ocean. Through most of its history, the area north of the Sahara Desert had close connections with the Mediterranean and Middle Eastern cultural regions, and most of its peoples were converted to either Christianity or Islam during the first eight centuries of the Common Era. The Saharan and sub-Saharan regions, however, had relatively little contact with the Mediterranean world. Today the sub-Saharan region is home to the world's largest concentrations of indigenous practitioners—perhaps as many as 200 million.

The first Europeans to visit sub-Saharan Africa were Portuguese navigators who explored the western coastline in their search for a sea route to India and the Spice Islands during the Age of Discovery. Some explorers recorded vivid descriptions of African rituals, though their lack of a shared language and the brevity of their visits made their interpretations questionable. With the beginning of the Atlantic slave trade in the late fifteenth century, European accounts of Africa became increasingly lurid, describing 'brutal' rituals that made the idea of slavery more palatable to Europeans. Some claimed that Africans had no religion at all and maintained that the rituals described by early travellers were only 'superstitions'. The German philosopher Georg Friedrich Hegel (1770–1831) described Africa as a land without history, a place of sorcery and superstition.

By the late 1800s European scholars were developing evolutionary theories that traced the origins of religion to Africa. Such theories typically saw humanity as progressing in stages from 'primitive' African beliefs in multiple gods and spirits to the final flowering of Western monotheism. Thus Edward Tylor saw Africans as **animists**, believing that there were souls in all things. Charles de Brosses and James Frazer thought that Africans worshipped objects endowed with special powers; these objects they called **fetishes**. Others suggested that Africans were polytheists, worshippers of many gods who were often represented by statues and masks. These images filtered into Western popular culture. The ballet *Petrouchka* (1911) includes a character called the Blackamoor who worships a coconut, and more recent notions of African religions have been shaped by Hollywood movies, from the Tarzan series to Jim Carrey's *When Nature Calls*. The anthropologist E.E. Evans-Prichard described the standard 'recipe':

> A reference to cannibalism, a description of Pygmies (by preference with a passing reference to Herodotus), a denunciation of the inequities of the slave trade, the need for the civilizing influence of commerce, something about rain-makers and other superstitions, some sex (suggestive though discreet), add snakes and elephants to taste; bring slowly to the boil and serve (Evans-Prichard cited in Ray 1976:3)

| Map 1.1   Selected African cultural areas

These were my first images of African religions as well. They reflected the long history of slave trading, colonization, and Western ethnocentrism, which tended to minimize the creative genius of African peoples.

African Religious Thought

So what are African religions really like? First, it is important to recognize that the continent is home to more than a thousand distinct religious traditions. Their diversity reflects the diversity of the communities in which they developed, each of which has its own history, patterns of contact with other cultures, ecological environment, and economic system. One thing they have in common, however, is a focus on life in this world, on human communities and their immediate environments. Reflecting that focus, they are strongly instrumental in emphasis, seeking direct assistance from deities, spirits, or ancestors who might be able to ease the difficulties of daily life.

African religions also share a focus on a supreme being, what English-speakers would call God, who is seen as the source of all life. Individual traditions differ on whether the supreme being actually created the world or delegated that task to subordinates. The Yoruba of Nigeria and Benin maintain that Olodumare, the lord of the heavens, delegated the creation to lesser gods called *orisha*, while the Dogon of Mali believe that their supreme being, Amma, began the task of creating the world but left it to be completed by spirits known as Nummo, also created by Amma. The Nuer and Dinka of the southern Sudan, the BaMbuti of Congo, and the Khoisan of South Africa, for their part, all emphasize that the supreme being alone was responsible for creation. The fact that almost every African ethnic group already had a term for the supreme being made it relatively easy for nineteenth-century missionaries to translate the Christian idea of 'God'.

Different traditions also differ in their views of the role that the supreme being plays in the daily affairs of their communities. The Yoruba tradition suggests that Olodumare reigns but does not rule—just as the Yoruba kings are sacred symbols of the townships that they oversee but do not rule their city-states. Similarly, the Igbo of southeastern Nigeria have a saying—'God is like a rich man, you approach him through his servants'—that suggests their supreme being is far removed from human beings and has created lesser spirits, divine servants, to handle specific types of problems. In both cases, the implication is that humans should avoid appealing to the supreme being except in matters of great importance or when appeals to lesser spirits have repeatedly failed. To ask the supreme being for help with minor concerns like getting a job or winning a football game would be to show an arrogance bordering on blasphemy.

Most African religious communities do not have specific shrines for the worship of the supreme being, though they have many shrines dedicated to the lesser spirits or deities whose job it is to assist humans in daily life. This pattern has created the false impression in the West that the supreme being is not central to African religious life. On the contrary, it shows both the people's reverence for the supreme being, who has no need of sacrificial offerings, and their recognition of how insignificant their concerns are in the context of the universe. (Sometimes the supreme being is male, sometimes female, sometimes both, but there are no gendered pronouns in West African languages.)

The matters that are controlled by the supreme being are the most critical ones: the life transitions of birth and death, and the precious, life-sustaining resource that is water. Many traditions maintain that the supreme being is the source of the vital force that enters into a woman's womb to create life. For the Dogon of Mali and Burkina Faso, that force—*nyama*—originates with the supreme being, Amma, and flows throughout the universe. For the Yoruba, conception occurs when the supreme being Olodumare allows the spirit of an ancestor seeking rebirth to enter a woman and assigns the unborn infant a fate that determines the broad outlines of his or her life. Particularly in regions where rainfall is scarce, the supreme being also gives or withholds rain depending on the community's ethical conduct and fulfillment of ritual obligations. In most African religions, the supreme being judges people after death and assigns them to an afterlife of either punishment or reward, depending on their conduct in life. Most people, however, are eventually reincarnated and return to the living community in a never-ending cycle of life and death.

The precise nature of the lesser gods and spirits varies. The Nuer people of Sudan regard them as emanations of the supreme being and use the same term for both: the supreme being is called Kwoth Nhial, while lesser spirits are known simply as 'kwoth'. Among the Yoruba, lesser spirits have distinct personalities, extraordinary independence, and rich bodies of sacred traditions or myths describing their activities. By contrast, the Bantu-speaking peoples of Equatorial, East, and southern Africa tend to emphasize the importance of ancestors, people who, having led basically good lives, have passed into the realm of the dead but continue to influence the lives of their living descendants. Eventually, they may be reborn within their own lineages or extended families. In societies with traditions of kingship, like the Buganda of Uganda and the BaKongo of Angola and Congo, royal ancestors have major shrines dedicated to their memory.

In much of West Africa the lesser deities have their own elaborate mythologies. The Yoruba recognize 401 *orisha*, each of which has a unique personality and history, a distinct set of duties, and special preferences for ritual offerings and behaviour by followers. Oduduwa, for example, is an *orisha* who completed the creation of the world after his brother Obatala got drunk and fell asleep. Oduduwa eventually became the king of Ile-Ife, the place where the world was created and the oldest of the Yoruba cities. His sister Oshun is associated with women's fertility, sexuality, and beauty, and has acquired the additional powers of her male husbands or lovers. The *orisha* can possess their devotees, mounting them as if they were horses and using their bodies to make themselves present and communicate necessary information. The *orisha* continue to develop new functions in community life. Thus Ogun, the god of iron and war, has come to be associated with the protection of metal workers, car mechanics, and chauffeurs. Shopona, a goddess traditionally associated with smallpox, became linked with HIV–AIDS when smallpox was eradicated and AIDS became a grave threat. At the same time Yoruba religion reserves a vital role for ancestors, people who have crossed over into the realm of the spirit and who continue to assist their living descendants. Throughout most of Yorubaland, the ancestors can become physically present in masked dances.

Trickster deities are particularly important in West Africa. The trickster is not a force for evil, but one who loves chaos and disorder. He encourages impulsive behaviour in humans and often acts impulsively himself, disrupting any kind of social order. For instance, tricksters often serve as messengers for the other gods and purposely make minor changes in their messages so that they can enjoy the resulting confusion. In Dogon religion the Pale Fox or Jackal, a sibling of the Nummo, not only disrupts earthly existence but also possesses the power to see into the future and discern the causes of disorder in the distant past.

The Yoruba trickster, Eshu, is the messenger god who summons the other *orisha* to attend all major rituals in Yoruba religion. Eshu delights in forgetting parts of messages or changing them in small ways, just to see what will happen. He loves to play tricks on human beings, whose greed, laziness, or desire makes them easy to fool. He is also described as a kind of perpetual adolescent, over-sexed and promiscuous.

Christian missionaries, who saw good and evil as locked in eternal conflict, often associated tricksters like Eshu with Satan, but for the Yoruba the forces that enhance life and detract from it are commingled. These radically different world views are often described as '**conflict**' and '**complementary**' **dualism**. African religions (like most indigenous religions) generally tend towards the 'complementary' model.

Ritual

The purpose of rituals such as prayer, animal sacrifice, offerings of grain and libations of palm wine, water, or milk is to communicate with gods or spirits. Such ceremonies release life forces that nourish the gods and spirits, who then return those life forces to those seeking assistance. In turn, the participants in the ritual commit themselves to the purpose of the ceremony by consuming the food and libations after they have been offered to the gods. In this way the ritual nourishes all the participants, divine and human. Sacrifices may be offered for fertility (of crops, livestock, or humans), for adequate rain, for healing, for protection against dangerous tasks or witchcraft, or to ensure a successful transition from one life stage to another.

The rituals associated with life transitions—events such as puberty, marriage, birth, and death—are often referred to as rites of passage. Many of these rituals have a three-stage structure. In the first stage the initiates are separated from their familiar world; for example, boys entering puberty may eat a last meal with their mothers before attending a ceremony in which they prepare to separate from the community for a time. The second stage is often described as one of liminality (from the Latin for 'threshold'). It is during this marginal stage, when initiates are between life phases, that much of the work of the transition or passage takes place. Initiates are instructed in their new religious and social responsibilities, and develop a feeling of solidarity with other initiates that the anthropologist Victor Turner has called 'communitas'. Finally they are reintegrated into their communities, with the added powers and responsibilities of their new status.

Throughout Africa, special containers are used to hold ritual libations, and special spears and knives are used for animal sacrifices and preparation of the ritual meals that follow. Of all the material objects used in rituals, however, the ones that have attracted the most attention are images of gods and ancestors in the form of statues and masks. Non-Africans have dismissed such images as idols—objects of worship in themselves—based on the erroneous assumption that the image contains the god. In some cases statues of gods are ritually prepared with special medicines to summon the presence of the god, but the god can be present in many places at once and is never contained by an object.

There has been a similar confusion about the masks used in ritual dances. Activation of the dancers' spiritual power may allow them to receive the presence of the gods, spirits, or ancestors represented by the masks they wear, but the dancer's body is merely a temporary dwelling place. The masks bring the god, spirit, or ancestor into the community, sometimes symbolically, sometimes by displacing the conscious mind of the dancer so that the deity or ancestor may speak through him or her, but the mask is only a vehicle that allows the spiritual power to manifest itself.

The design of masks and statues is highly symbolic. Thus spirits associated with women's fertility tend to be depicted with faces that represent idealized forms of beauty, and their bodies have large hips and breasts that evoke the ability to bear and nourish children. Masks of spirits that protect against malevolent forces, such as witches, often emphasize their power to terrorize spirits and humans alike.

Witchcraft

In many African traditions witchcraft serves to explain the presence of evil and suffering in the world. Witches are believed to be people whose souls travel outside their bodies to attack and consume other people's souls or objects that are considered valuable. There is no material evidence for witchcraft. It takes place entirely in the realm of the soul. For evidence, witch-finders typically look to dreams, visions, or divination, though sometimes suspects will be forced to drink special witch-finding beverages believed to be capable of making the guilty fall ill or die. Witchcraft is also used to explain chance misfortune—the sort of thing that Westerners call 'bad luck'. For example, Azande elders told the anthropologist Evans-Pritchard of a man who took a nap under a corn crib and was crushed to death when the crib collapsed. While the immediate cause of death did not need explaining, the fact that the crib collapsed while the victim was sleeping under it was attributed to witchcraft.

In many instances the society of witches is envisioned as the exact opposite of ordinary existence. Diola witches, for instance, organize in hierarchical and authoritarian groups, in stark contrast to ordinary Diola society, which emphasizes egalitarianism and opposes any concentration of authority in a single person or group. Similarly among the Yoruba, in ordinary society women are subordinate, but female witches can wield extraordinary power over men. Although most societies recognize witches of both sexes, some believe that witchcraft is restricted to either women or men. These variations may reflect tensions between the sexes, or competition between various social groups.

Five Major Traditions

The rest of this section will take a closer look at the traditions of five peoples in different geographical regions of the continent: the Diola of southern Senegal, the Dogon of

Mali, the BaKongo of the central (equatorial) region, the Nuer of southern Sudan, and the Shona of what is now Zimbabwe.

Diola

The Diola people number about 600,000 and form minority communities in Senegal, Gambia, and Guinea-Bissau. Considered to be the best wet-rice farmers in West Africa, they live close to their rice paddies in large townships that were traditionally self-governing through local assemblies and councils of elders. These institutions continue to operate today, although they are not recognized by national governments. The large majority of Senegambians are Muslim, and the Diola themselves have significant Muslim and Christian communities. But they also have a vital and dynamic indigenous religion.

At the centre of Diola religion is a supreme being called Emitai (literally, 'of the sky'); we know that this name was in use as long as ago as the seventeenth century, since it appears in a slave-trading company's dictionary of the Diola language. In addition to creating life and controlling the rain, Emitai judges individuals' conduct in life and decides what becomes of them in the afterlife. People who have led good lives, who have been generous, honest, and hardworking, become ancestors; their souls live near the Diola communities, so close that you can feel (but not see) their cooking fires. They can advise and guide their living descendants through dreams and visions, and will eventually be reincarnated.

By contrast, people who have led destructive lives—who have harmed others or violated basic community norms—became phantoms, their souls confined to the forest areas or 'bush' beyond the areas of settled habitation. These phantoms cannot speak, but they can trick people wandering alone at dusk, challenging them to wrestling matches that the living will always lose. They too will be eventually reborn, but they will have a dim memory of their misdeeds and will be unable to repeat them in the next life. Finally, some people will die without sufficient grounds for judgment. They will be reborn in a village to the south of where the Diola live now, in an area from which they emigrated centuries ago. It is Emitai who determines the fate of the dead, and Emitai who decides when life will be created.

Emitai may also choose certain individuals to impart some message to the people or to establish a new 'spirit shrine': a term that includes not only the physical shrine dedicated to a particular spirit but that spirit itself and the cult that surrounds it. By the late nineteenth century at least eleven people had been 'sent by Emitai' to assist the Diola. Some founded villages; others introduced lesser spirits, newly created by Emitai, and taught the people how to supplicate them for help in the procurement of rain or in their struggles against European colonization. These people may be considered the equivalent of prophets.

The Diola also have a number of lesser spirits created by Emitai to assist people in specific aspects of life. Thus in many communities there is a spirit shrine dedicated to assisting township elders in their governance role by giving authority to their rulings on matters such as community work, wages, or prices. Similarly, a male initiation shrine helps to ensure proper conduct by men and towards men, while a female fertility spirit is charged with ensuring that women conduct themselves properly and that men respect them. Anyone who does not follow the rules risks punishment in the form of diseases inflicted by the spirits. A man who abuses women, for example, is threatened with developing a disease that gives him a distended belly, resembling pregnancy.

Other spirit shrines are linked to specific economic activities: blacksmithing, hunting, rice farming, fishing, and so on. Some are associated with particular homesteads or extended families. Others protect a certain neighbourhood, village quarter, or township. The large number of shrines, whose priesthoods and councils of elders are open to most adult members of the community, ensures that most people will be able to participate in township governance and serve in a position of religious authority at some stage in their lives. This tendency to provide broad access to leadership roles, together with the idea that the spirits can reveal themselves to people at times of crisis, contributed to an ongoing tradition of innovation that has allowed Diola religion to meet

A Diola boy receives gifts from his maternal relatives in preparation for the circumcision ritual he will undergo a few months later. The rice stalks scattered over him symbolize fertility (Robert M. Baum).

the continuing challenges of missionary Christianity and Islam. Before colonization, male prophets 'sent by Emitai' established a number of new spirit shrines and rituals designed to address the persistent problem of drought, for example. Existing spirits assumed new roles and new spirits were introduced to regulate the slave trade by establishing rules for raiding, trading, and ransoming slaves, and by inflicting horrible diseases on anyone who violated the rules.

The typical Diola ritual consists of libations of palm wine (seen as containing the life force of the palm tree) accompanied by spoken prayer. Offering wine and prayer together reinforces the power of the life forces contained in each. More important rituals may also include offerings of chickens, goats, pigs, or cattle, whose blood further strengthens the force of the appeal to the spirits whose assistance is sought. By eating the sacrificial meat and drinking the wine, the congregation ingests the words of the

Diola women celebrate the initiation of a new priestess of a women's fertility shrine. The priestess, dressed in locally made cotton cloth, carries a cow's tail fly whisk, a symbol of ritual authority. She and two of her associates are dancing across someone's cloth in order to bring its owner good luck (Robert M. Baum).

prayer and lends its support to the ritual activity. In this way ritual sacrifice can be seen as serving a social purpose as well as a religious one.

Though a few shrines are open to both men and women, most are reserved for one or the other. Male spiritual power is distinct from female power, but both are important. Thus men control the rituals of the hunt, the blacksmithing forge, war, and death, while women control the rituals of female fertility and childbirth. Females are excluded from the cemetery until the day they die, and males are not allowed into the maternity houses from the time they leave as infants. The most important rites of passage are the male circumcision ritual, male initiation into the rites for the dead, girls' puberty rituals, and women's initiation into the congregation of mothers.

In most Diola communities, male circumcision ceremonies are held only once every twenty years; thus each group of initiates forms a distinct generation, sharing not only the ordeal of the operation but one or two months of ritual seclusion during which they receive an intensive religious and social education. Girl's initiation, which does not involve any kind of surgery, is held in small groups, whenever several girls are approaching the onset of menstruation. Members of the group attend special festive meals at one another's homes and their mothers and other older women introduce them to some of the religious and social responsibilities they will encounter as adolescents. Full instruction in those responsibilities, however, is not provided until after the delivery of the first child, at which time women are initiated into the fertility cult of Ehugna.

Dogon

The Dogon people of Mali and Burkina Faso number roughly 300,000 and live along the semi-arid ridges south of the Niger River, farming crops such as millet and onions. Like the Diola, the Dogon associate the supreme being with the sky and life-giving rain. However, their lesser spirits have more distinct personalities and a greater degree of independence. In addition—and in sharp contrast to the Diola—the Dogon have a rich tradition of representational art in the form of masks and statues.

The Dogon also possess an extraordinarily complex body of creation myths. According to the oral traditions collected between the 1930s and the 1950s by the French anthropologist Marcel Griaule and his associates, the supreme being, Amma, created the world because he was lonely. Accounts differ as to how he did so, but according to one he transformed himself into a womb, within which he created four spirit beings called Nummo. Two of the Nummo were predominantly male, but also female; the other two were predominantly female, but also male. They were supposed to stay in the womb for sixty years, but one of the males—the Pale Fox—was impatient to be with his sister/wife. Amma, anticipating this breach of the natural order, had hidden the sister in another part of the womb, and the Pale Fox was unable to find her. In the course of his search he tore away part of the womb, and that part became the earth. To purify the world, Amma sacrificed the sister and then life began.

While their impatient brother continued to wander in search of his mate, the two remaining Nummo clothed their mother Earth with a simple loincloth of living vegetation moistened with the creative power known as the First Word, which emanated from Amma and became the *nyama*: the creative life force that circulates throughout the universe.

But the Pale Fox, anxious for company, stole the loincloth from his mother and, in touching her genitals, committed incest. This pollution led to the first menstruation, from which the Earth had to be purified before she could nurture life. The Pale Fox acquired the simple speech associated with the First Word, an imprecise way of speaking, which became the language of divination. To purify the Earth, the Nummo created a Second Word, a more complex type of clothing.

Then Amma and the Nummo created and placed on the Earth eight beings who were to become the ancestors of humans. Lured into the genitals of Mother Earth, they ascended to the heavens, where they were directed to eight different chambers and given different types of grain, one of which—a small grain that was difficult to prepare, a millet called fonio—they all vowed never to eat. But in time they became lonely in their isolated rooms, and when their food ran out they gathered together and cooked the fonio. As a result all eight were expelled from the heavens in a Celestial Granary—a model of the universe containing symbols of all the animals, plants, ethnic groups, and seeds of this world, as well as the Third Word, a more elaborate and refined type of cloth and the word that bore the full complexity of speech. When the Granary crashed to the Earth, its contents were released, and at that moment human life began.

Dogon communities are organized around four major ritual societies, each of which was organized by one of the four ancestral fathers. The oldest of these, Amma Seru, is associated with the supreme being, and the oldest member of each extended family performs rituals in his honour. Beyond the extended family are lineages or clans, each with its own priest of the Binu cult, which links the clans to particular animal species with whom they share certain powers and spiritual ties. These organizations have shrines specially painted to depict important events in the agricultural year. The Binu cult is particularly associated with water.

A third cult is associated with a man named Lebe who was sacrificed to preserve the Third Word after the descent of the Celestial Granary and was reborn as a large snake. Lebe is closely associated with Mother Earth; his priest is the oldest man in the community and serves as its political leader as well. Known as a Hogon, this priest serves as the judge in local disputes and ensures the proper operation of the village market. Because his duties on behalf of his community were seen as exhausting, Dogon tradition held that Lebe, in the form of a snake, would appear to the Hogon on a nightly basis and lick his body, imparting life-enhancing *nyama* and enabling the priest to carry out his duties for another day.

Finally, the fourth cult, linked to a man named Dyongu, controls the transition from life into death. Its members are in charge of funeral rituals, the masks associated with them, and a ritual called Sigi, which commemorates the origins of death itself in the disobedience of Dyongu, who as a deceased ancestor used the speech of humans to express anger at the misconduct of some living people.

Nuer

The Nuer people of the southern Sudan number more than 300,000 and inhabit the marshy area known as the Sudd and the surrounding plains. Historically, they earned their livelihood as cattle herders and governed themselves through clan elders and 'leopard skin' priests, who mediated disputes between clans. For most of the past fifty years, however, Nuer life has been severely disrupted by the Sudanese civil war.

The Nuer call their supreme being Kwoth Nhial. Lesser spirits are seen as emanations of Kwoth Nhial, who is omnipotent and omniscient, but physically distant. According to at least two oral traditions, at one time Kwoth Nhial lived closer to humanity; the divine realm of the sky was connected to earth by a rope. One myth says that the connection was broken after a girl who lived in the sky used the rope to descend to the earth, where she fell in love with a man; when she refused to return to the sky, Kwoth Nhial withdrew the rope and the two realms became separate. Another story blames a prank by a trickster god in the form of a jackal. In any case, following the separation of heaven and earth, Kwoth Nhial either created or extended himself into a host of lesser spirits (*kwoth*), sometimes referred to as Spirits of the Above (celestial spirits) and Spirits of the Below (spirits on Earth).

Increasing contact with a closely related group called the Dinka, together with the disruption caused by the northern Sudanese slave trade, led to a dramatic increase in both the numbers of Spirits of the Above and their activity in the nineteenth century. Today many such spirits are openly acknowledged to be of Dinka origin. From the 1850s until the 1930s, a number of 'prophets'—people possessed by the spirits—emerged who played important roles in the Nuer resistance against Sudanese slave raiders as well as British colonizers.

Today Spirits of the Above continue to seize people with illness: sometimes to summon them to the priesthood, sometimes as punishment for moral infractions or neglect of community obligations. In the latter case, a healing ceremony is held that includes public discussion of the social problems that could be responsible for pollution and illness; then the community is cleansed through an animal sacrifice and ritual meal.

Spirits of the Below, for their part, include totemic spirits representing spiritual ties between particular Nuer clans and individuals and particular animal species. Other Spirits of the Below are associated with various natural forces and places that evoke a sense of awe and spiritual power.

In the absence of formal political structures, leopard-skin priests play a crucial role as arbitrators in disputes between clans and lineages. Their charismatic authority and ability to cleanse people of the polluting effects of misconduct allows them to insist that the various parties make a genuine effort to resolve their disagreements.

BaKongo

The BaKongo number almost five million people in what are now Congo, the Democratic Republic of Congo, and Angola. Although today they are involved in every aspect of Congolese life, urban and rural, historically they were farmers who supplemented their root crops with hunting and fishing. When the Portuguese arrived in the fifteenth century, Kongo was a highly centralized kingdom with its capital in northern Angola.

The BaKongo king, Alfonso I, invited Portuguese missionaries to his court to teach their religion and share their knowledge of Western technology. To pay for the missionaries' assistance with the establishment of missions and schools, however, the Portuguese

| Box 1.1   Ngundeng Bong: A Nuer Prophet

Until the mid-nineteenth century, Nuer and Dinka engaged in intermittent warfare over the pasturelands that both needed for their large herds of cattle. Conflict increased in the 1840s, however, with the arrival of Egyptian slave-traders who, in addition to raiding both groups for slaves themselves, incited the Nuer and Dinka to raid one another for slaves to sell. As this warfare escalated, new religious leaders emerged in both communities, men claiming to have received revelations or experienced possession by Spirits of the Above. These 'prophets' claimed the power to lead their people in battle and to renew the strength of their communities in the face of various threats to their well-being.

The most famous Nuer prophet was Ngundeng Bong, who claimed to have received revelations from a spirit named Deng. One of the many new cults adopted by the Nuer in response to the increasing turmoil in the region, the cult of Deng had originated among the Nuer's Dinka neighbours. In 1878 Ngundeng used the spiritual powers he received from Deng to lead Nuer warriors into battle against a Dinka group that was raiding the Nuer for slaves. As he led his forces into battle, speared a special ox, which died with its head facing their opponents—a good omen. Then Ngundeng raised a large root in the air. Rain and lightning fell from the skies, and many Dinka were said to fall dead, even before the battle. After the battle he built an earthen pyramid, surrounded by elephant tusks, in which he ritually deposited many of the destructive powers that were held responsible for the threats to the Nuer.

Warfare between Nuer and Dinka eased thereafter, but slave raiding continued unabated until 1902, when the British arrived and established a colonial administration in the area. Ngundeng conceded that he could not defeat them, and in 1906 he died. His son Gwek, who claimed similar powers, assumed the religious leadership of his community. In 1929 he too speared an ox in an effort to inspire a group of warriors confronting British forces, but he failed to kill it. He died in battle and the British destroyed the pyramid that his father had constructed.

Nevertheless, Ngundeng's prophecies of renewed warfare and eventual liberation helped to inspire the southern Sudanese secessionist movement that began in the 1950s. In the 1990s a young male prophet of the supreme being, Kwoth, Wutnyang Gataker, raised an army that fought alongside southern Sudanese forces, and his support of their common cause made him an effective mediator between different ethnic and lineage groups in the region.

crown insisted that the BaKongo provide slaves for sale. The Atlantic slave trade sharply reduced the population, and in the seventeenth century the BaKongo lost control of their kingdom to the Portuguese. The massive disruption brought on by the slave trade, increasing Portuguese intervention in BaKongo affairs, and the presence of an influential Christian elite make it difficult to establish the early outlines of BaKongo religion.

The high incidence of disease and violence in that period led to a proliferation of healing shrines. Of particular importance were the Nkita and Lemba cults. Dedicated to healing disease and protecting people involved in the slave trade, they continue to play an important role in BaKongo religious life today.

The BaKongo emphasize the role of a supreme being, Nzambi Mpungu, who created the world and continues to create life. Lesser gods are not as important in this region as they are in West Africa. Rather, BaKongo practice focuses on the ancestors who have passed over into the realm of the dead but continue to influence the lives of their descendants through dreams and visions. Matrilineal ancestors are the most important, since ancestry is traced primarily on the mother's side.

The BaKongo conceive of the world as two mountains—the mountain of the living, where one is born in the east and dies in the west, and the mountain of the dead, where one is born in the west and dies in the east—separated by an ocean known as Kalanga. It has been suggested that this worldview may have contributed to the warm welcome the Portuguese received when they arrived in the region: the fact that they came from the Atlantic Ocean (Kalanga), were deathly pale, and seemed uncomfortable on land may have suggested to the BaKongo that the newcomers were actually ancestors returning from the land of the dead.

In the event of illness or misfortune, a ritual specialist called a *nganga* will identify the spirit or source of power that must be contacted in order to correct the problem. This power is often manifested in consecrated ritual objects known as *minkisi*: carved objects in which the *nganga* conceals powerful medicines. Though normally used to heal the sick or protect people from misfortune, they can be used for malevolent purposes. In that case they are associated with *kindoki* (witchcraft). Witches are often depicted with a special organ in the digestive tract that both empowers them with witchcraft and creates the appetite to consume the spiritual power of others. In BaKongo thought, *kindoki* is closely associated with unusual wealth and success, and it is possible that this association dates from the time of the slave trade (1480–1880), when a few people profited at the expense of many others. Even when the immediate cause of a misfortune is clear—when someone is struck by lightning, for example—the fact that it happened to that particular person is often attributed to witchcraft. The destructive power of witchcraft as a force circulating through the world also serves to explain the persistence of evil and suffering.

Because of the region's long involvement in the slave trade, BaKongo accounted for a large proportion of the slaves taken to the Americas. Their traditions have had a profound influence on the religions that developed in the African diaspora, from the southern United States to the south of Brazil.

Shona

The Shona are the largest ethnic group in the high plateau area of present-day Zimbabwe, numbering more than eight million. Until the colonial occupation by the British South African Company, at the end of the nineteenth century, most Shona were farmers raising corn and cattle on scattered homesteads under the authority of local chiefs.

The supreme being of Shona religion, Mwari, receives prayer and ritual offerings at various shrines. Like the supreme beings of the Diola and Dogon, Mwari is associated with rainfall, a vital resource in a region where drought is common. At Mlanjeni, a major oracle site, female spirit mediums make the wishes of Mwari known. The medium sits inside a cave and goes into a state of possession, during which a voice speaks that is said to be the voice of Mwari. Male priests interpret Mwari's message to pilgrims seeking advice. Messengers and priests of Mwari were seen as playing a vital role in the Shona revolt against British colonization in 1896.

Shona ritual life focuses on the spirits of the dead: not only individual families' ancestors, but culture heroes: people from the distant past who taught the people the basic tasks and obligations of their communities. There are also spirits associated with the chieftaincy and with strangers whose souls cannot settle in a particular location. These spirits communicate with the living through dreams, visions, and the persons of the individuals they choose to serve as their mediums. Those so chosen are identified when they are stricken with illness and a diviner determines that the cause is spirit possession. Then the chosen person is initiated into the cult, trained to control his or her spirit possession, and instructed in how to perform divination rituals. These cults are often described as shrines of affliction, because the disease itself becomes a summons to spirit-mediumship. Ancestors continue to offer advice and guidance to their living descendants, just as they did when they were alive. When the living ignore this advice or neglect their obligations to the ancestors, the latter may punish them with illness or problems such as infertility.

The spirits of dead chiefs are known as *mhondoro* ('lion spirits'). They play a particularly influential role in their former domains, and their spirit mediums are among the most powerful people in Shona society. *Mhondoro* from the people's early days in the region can facilitate the distribution of rain and enhance the fertility of the land, while those from more recent chiefly lineages tend to concern themselves with matters related to the social and political structure of their former territories, including the selection of new chiefs. Two of the most powerful *mhondoro*, Chaminuka and Nehanda, played central roles in uniting Shona communities, first against incursions by the Ndebele people (a Ngoni group based on the coast) and then against British settlers.

Summary

Even the brief overview above reveals important similarities among the religious traditions in different parts of Africa. All the religions surveyed focus on a supreme being who is generally seen both as the source of life (and often rain) and as the judge who determines humans' fate in the afterlife. These beings make their wishes known through prophets and mediums, as well as dreams and visions. Most ritual sites, however, are dedicated to lesser gods or spirits. These lesser beings are often gendered, male or female, and their powers are described in gender-specific terms. They too communicate with humans through dreams, visions, and prophetic revelation. Among peoples such as the Yoruba and Dogon they often have distinct personalities and bodies of myth. Some are tricksters who, although they are not evil, enjoy disrupting the orderly and predictable operation of the universe. Other traditions focus more on spirits that are associated with particular types of religious issues such as fertility or hunting, or that serve the needs of particular groups within a community. Thus the Diola have spirits associated specifically with women's fertility, blacksmithing, or male initiation. Finally, ancestors play important roles in many traditions, advising and if necessary punishing their living descendants. In some religions these lesser spirits are sometimes represented by masks or statues that serve as a focus for community ritual or for the transmission of spiritual power. The supreme being, however, is never represented in physical form.

On the other hand, it is important to recognize how these traditions differ. While many African religions involve ritual worship of the supreme being, some do not. Nor do all have traditions of spiritual possession. Some actively seek to communicate with the supreme being through prophets or mediums, or to receive divine communications through dreams or visions; but others regard the deity as too powerful to concern Itself with the problems faced by humans in their daily lives.

The impact of European conquest on these peoples will be examined in more detail later in the chapter.

North and Central America

When many people think of Native Americans, they imagine Plains people on horseback wearing feathered headdresses and either hunting buffalo or vigorously resisting European settlement—the image emphasized in movies and on TV. Ironically, this image itself is largely a product of the European presence. The domesticated horse was not introduced to the Americas until the sixteenth century, when Spanish settlers arrived in Mexico. Before the first horses made their way to the Great Plains, hunters would stampede buffalo herds over cliffs or corner them in canyons in order to kill them. The increased mobility offered by the horse allowed a number of mountain and woodland peoples to establish themselves on the Plains and develop a new economy based on the buffalo hunt.

A number of new cultural practices soon developed that reflected the Plains environment. Central to an emerging cluster of Plains religions was the **Sun Dance**, which focused on the most powerful deity, the god of the Sun. Held near the summer solstice, when the sun appeared to be most powerful, it required elaborate preparations. Those who pledged to perform the dance itself offered their bodies to the sun god, either in hope of receiving extraordinary powers or in gratitude for powers already received. Military and religious leaders such as Sitting Bull and Crazy Horse performed the Sun Dance on numerous occasions to empower and guide their leadership.

The details of the Sun Dance vary from people to people; the following description comes from the **Lakota** Sioux. First, to purify the participants, a sweat lodge would be constructed of branches and animal skins with an opening toward the East—the source of all life power. Stones heated over a fire to the east of the lodge were then taken into the lodge to create a dry heat that cleansed the participants' bodies.

To bind themselves to their common purpose, participants also smoked a ceremonial pipe modelled on one given to the Lakota by the goddess Whope (White Buffalo Cow Woman). The pipe was a model of the universe, with a red stone bowl symbolizing the presence of Inyan (the first god, the God of Stone) and Maka, Mother Earth. The wooden stem of the pipe linked these earthly realms to the heavenly realms of Skan, the Sky God, and Wi, the Sun God, while eagle feathers attached to the stem reinforced the association with the celestial powers.

Before the pipe was smoked, the master of ceremonies offered tobacco to the four directions, to the above and below, inviting all the beneficent powers of the universe to be present. Mingling with the smoke of the pipe, the words of prayer were inhaled by the participants and disseminated throughout the universe. The purification ritual of the Sweat Lodge was a common preliminary to most major ceremonies of the Lakota and other Plains Indians.

Following purification, male elders searched out a tall cottonwood tree to serve as the focus of the Sun Dance ritual. The chosen tree was then cut down by young girls who had not yet married or engaged in sexual relations. The girls carried the tree to the ritual site—already purified by the burning of sweet grass—and erected it in the centre of a circle. After four days and four nights of fasting and dancing, those who had pledged to make the sacrifice would have the skin of their chests pierced through with ropes, which were tied to the central pole. While dancing until the ropes broke through their skin, they sought visions from the sun god, Wi, which they could use on behalf of their communities.

The Lakota conceived of a universe permeated by a life-enhancing power known as *wakan*. In nineteenth and twentieth century cosmologies, the supreme being was named Wakan Tanka ('Great Spirit' or 'Great Mystery'), but earlier cosmologies envisioned four primary gods. In the beginning there was Inyan, the Rock. In order to have companions, Inyan sacrificed himself by cutting into his body. The blood that flowed out created Maka, Mother Earth; Skan, the Sky God and god of justice; and Wi, the Sun God. After giving up so much blood to create the other gods, Inyan was left as hard and dry as rock.

The four gods then created partners for themselves: Inyan, for example, created Wakinyan, the Thunderbird who controls rain and storms, while Wi created Hanwi, the Moon. Together each pair created a new generation of deities, including tricksters who worked to disrupt the cosmic order. The sacrifice of Inyan, which led to the creation of the three other gods of the first generation, provided a model for the Sun Dance: the offering of one's own body in order to enhance life.

Another important Lakota ritual is the vision quest. Following purification in the Sweat Lodge, a young man goes into seclusion, often on a hilltop, to fast and await a vision that will shape the rest of his life. For a maximum of four days, he cries out for a vision in which a special relationship will be established with a deity or an animal guardian spirit. In some societies girls are also permitted to undertake a vision quest, but it is more often required of boys as part of their passage to adulthood.

Visions can take many forms. Sometimes they will identify the seeker as having specific gifts to share with the community. Sometimes they will empower him to become a healer, hunter, or warrior. Sometimes a vision will invite the seeker to take up the life of a *winkte*: a biological man who lives as a woman. In the past, such men were not uncommon in Native societies (another common name for them is *berdaches*), which considered them sacred because of their ability to tap into the distinctive spiritual powers of both men and women. Some communities consider biological women who live as men to be sacred as well, though this is less common. The majority of Aboriginal cultures in North America regard the vision quest as an powerful indicator of the roles that young people will assume in their societies.

NUMBERS

By the year 2000 the number of Aboriginal people in Canada and the United States had reached nearly five million (a small fraction of the indigenous population when Columbus established a permanent link between Europe and the Americas). There are no reliable statistics for the number of people who practise indigenous religions today.

DISTRIBUTION

Although many Aboriginal people are Christian, indigenous traditions are still practised in some areas. Some more recent traditions that developed in the wake of Euro-American expansion also continue to have significant followings. The Handsome Lake religion has adherents among the Iroquois of Quebec and New York, and the Native American Church is influential in many communities in both the United States and Canada.

PRINCIPAL HISTORICAL PERIODS

c. 1500–1800	First contacts with Europeans
c. 1500–1900	European colonization and Christian missionary activity
1799	Handsome Lake's vision
1880s	US Congress bans the Sun Dance
1889	Wovoka revives the Ghost Dance
1890	More than 300 Ghost Dancers killed at Wounded Knee
1930–60	Governments begin to reduce restrictions on Aboriginal life
c. 1960	Aboriginal population numbers begin to recover
1960s–	Revival of indigenous religious traditions

FOUNDERS AND LEADERS

Few of the pre-conquest traditions trace their origins to a particular founder, but the new religious movements that developed in response to colonization are usually closely associated with a particular individual (for example, the Iroquois leader Handsome Lake).

DEITIES

Most Native American religions do not see any single deity as the source of all life and power. Rather, they attribute creation to a series of gods, and often the most important deity is one of the second or third generation.

AUTHORITATIVE TEXTS

The earliest 'texts' are oral traditions, most of which involve the creation of the present world and the beginnings of the community in question. Meso-Americans, however, did have written sacred texts early in the Common Era. More recent religions often have their own sacred texts (for instance, the *Gaiwiio* of Handsome Lake).

NOTEWORTHY TEACHINGS

Native American religions are theistic, but do not necessarily worship the original creator deity. Many emphasize the spiritual powers of the natural world and the ability of religious specialists or visionaries to use these powers on behalf of their communities.

First Contacts

Most Native American creation myths describe the world as beginning somewhere in the Americas, if not in the place where the people now live, then in one they migrated from or were removed from by conquest. The majority of scholars, however, believe that the earliest ancestors of 'indigenous' people originated outside the Americas. The dominant theory is that they arrived on the continent from northeastern Asia approximately 30,000 years ago, crossing the Bering Strait in several waves during periods when the sea level was low enough to expose a 'land bridge' between what are now Siberia and Alaska. The first encounters between Europeans and Native Americans took place along the eastern coast of North America, in the Caribbean, and in coastal areas of Latin America.

Early European accounts of North America sparked intense debate about the nature of Native people. Did they have souls? Did they have religions? Should they be treated as human beings or as brutish savages? Did they have rights that Europeans were obliged to respect? Could they be enslaved? Should they be converted to Christianity? Just two months after arriving in the New World, Columbus wrote that the peoples he encountered had no religion, but were 'very gentle and ignorant of evil' and would readily accept Christianity. Those who shared his view recommended a paternalistic colonial policy in which European governments and missionaries would protect the 'noble savages' from exploitation by less scrupulous newcomers. Others favoured harsher treatment, including enslavement of those who resisted.

The Native societies of North America varied widely in environment, language, economic activity, and social organization, and their religions reflected this diversity. There are some broad similarities, however. Most Native American traditions include a creator god (or series of gods), but they do not generally consider a single deity to be the source of all life and power. Rather, they tend to classify deities in different groups, either by generation (as in the Lakota myth outlined above) or by type. In many instances it is a deity of the second or third generation that is the primary object of veneration. The Swedish historian of religion Ake Hultkranz has argued that Native American deities can be classified according to their primary abode. Thus he describes sky gods (associated with the sun, stars, moon, etc.); atmospheric spirits (the four winds, rain spirits, Thunderbirds); earth spirits (the Buffalo Spirit, the Maize Spirit); and underworld beings (Mother Earth, underwater beings).

Creation Myths

The Tewa of New Mexico belong to the group of peoples that the Spanish called 'Pueblo' because—unlike the hunter-gatherer peoples to the north—they lived in settled villages. According to Alfonso Ortiz, the Tewa believed that the area where their six communities were located was the spiritual centre of the world, surrounded by four mountains, one in each of the four cardinal directions. Closer to the pueblo, on small hills on the outskirts of town, altars were constructed where the people could perform rituals honouring the powers of the north, south, east and west. Their most important rituals, however, were performed in the centre of the pueblo, where the power from all four directions was concentrated. The Zuni and Hopi similarly believed in what the historian of religion Mircea Eliade called the *axis mundi*: the central point where the spiritual realms of the heavens and the underworld intersected with the earth. In many Pueblo communities, the place of transition between worlds was represented by a ritual centre known as a *kiva*.

In Pueblo creation myths it is the younger gods that are commissioned to create life and left to control it; therefore they are the focus of worship. A Hopi account traces the beginning of life to a third-generation goddess named Kokyangwuti or Spider Woman, who creates two gods from saliva and earth, covers them with a white cape embodying wisdom, and sings the Creation Song. These two gods in turn are entrusted with continuing the process of creation, one of them solidifying the earth and the other filling it with sound. Spider Woman also creates all the plants and animals on the earth; human beings are formed from four different colours of earth, mixed with saliva. For the Hopi, the life essence is embodied in Spider Woman's saliva; songs and wisdom are the forces of creation.

Many creation myths, particularly among the peoples of the Eastern Woodlands, suggest that in the beginning all was water and without form; then an animal or a god dives under the water and brings back earth to begin building dry land. These accounts (which also recall shamanic journeys into other realms) are often referred to as Earth Diver myths. The same motif can be seen in an **Iroquois** creation account. In this story the first two animals to try bringing earth from under the water are a duck and a fish, both of which fail. Finally a muskrat—well-adapted to life both in water and on land— succeeds and the creation of the land can begin.

Similarly, the Muskogee people of the southeastern United States have a myth in which the gods decide to create dry land so that they can obtain food. First they send Dove out to find land, but all he finds is water. Then they send Crayfish. For three days he too fails, but on the fourth day he returns with a small ball of dirt; from it Eagle fashions a plot of land on which the gods live until the remaining waters recede. Similar motifs are found in early Japanese and other northeast Asian traditions, reinforcing the idea that the human populations of the Americas originated in Asia.

Animals and the Spiritual Order

Across the Americas, indigenous religious traditions reflect the peoples' careful observation of animal behaviours and powers. In many cases, particular gods and humans were said to share in the skills of particular species. Animals were seen as spiritually powerful, both individually and collectively. They played crucial roles in the creation of the lands where humans live. They appeared to individuals on vision quests, offering specific types of powers associated with their particular characteristics. They voluntarily gave up their lives to hunters so that people could live. In turn, humans were expected to offer prayers of thanksgiving for successful hunting or fishing, to treat the deceased animals with respect, and to recognize the relationship between hunter and hunted.

Such rules were enforced by deities known as 'Keepers of the Game'. For example, the **Inuit** required that a hunter who killed a polar bear place the body facing the direction from which the bear had come, so that its spirit could return. Hunters gave fresh water to the whales and seals they had killed, so that their souls would return to the sea reinvigorated and ready to be reborn. The Algonquian and Iroquoian peoples of the Eastern Woodlands had similar views regarding the animals they killed. When rules were violated, the Keepers of the Game could remove the animals from the area where the offending people lived, depriving the community of an essential food source.

| Map 1.2 | Native culture groups and missionary activity in North America

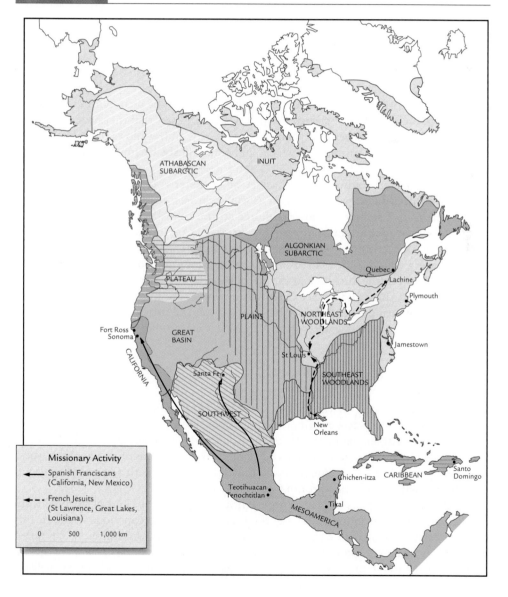

Missionary Activity

— Spanish Franciscans (California, New Mexico)

- - - French Jesuits (St Lawrence, Great Lakes, Louisiana)

0   500   1,000 km

A particular individual, clan, or extended family might also have a spiritual relationship with a particular animal species. Sharing certain characteristics, abilities, or sensibilities with that species, those people would be expected to treat it with special respect: they would not hunt it, nor would they ordinarily be harmed by it. Such a relationship is described as 'totemic' (from the Ojibwa word for 'family'), and its most familiar expression is probably the Northwest Coast totem pole. It would be a mistake, however, to assume that relationships between humans and the spirit world were always harmonious. There are many accounts of monstrous spirits who devour human beings or drive them to madness, and the world of the animal spirits themselves was sometimes imagined as no less violent than that of humans.

In an Inuit myth recorded by Franz Boas, for instance, the goddess Sedna is initially married to a bird who mistreats her. Her father rescues her and kills her husband, but the husband's kin, a group of sea birds, chase Sedna and her father as they try to escape by boat. The birds stir up a massive storm and Sedna is swept overboard. She clings to the side of the boat, but her father, afraid that it will capsize, chops off her fingers. Once the storm subsides, her father lets her back into the boat, but in revenge she sets her dogs on him while he sleeps. When he awakes and sees that they have gnawed off his feet and hands, he curses her. Then the earth opens and swallows them up. Sedna's fingers become the various types of whales and seals and she becomes the keeper of the animals of the sea.

Other sacred traditions emphasize the trickster roles of animal deities like Coyote, Wolf, and Raven, which are seen as wily creatures. Many of the sorrows of this world—death, disease, hunger—are attributed to the chaos-loving nature of trickster deities. Like their African counterparts, these tricksters are forces not of evil, but of disorder. Evil and suffering can come from the actions of trickster gods, but so can creative ways of dealing with disorder. For example, the Shoshone and Paiute of the Great Basin (the region between the Rockies and the Sierra Nevada) consider the trickster Coyote to be the creator of the world. Other Great Basin peoples see him as the creator both of death and of mourning rituals (since his own son was the first to die), as well as sexual reproduction, which became necessary after death was introduced.

The Eastern Woodlands

Like the Yoruba, many of the Algonquian and Iroquoian peoples of the Eastern Woodlands saw the universe in complementary dualist terms, with life-enhancing power (*manitou* for the Algonquians, *orenda* for the Iroquoians) circulating through the world in opposition to life-destructive powers (*windigo, utgo*). The origins of this dualistic world view can be traced to an Iroquoian creation myth that begins with a human-like group of divinities living in a celestial realm illuminated by a giant tree.

As in the Iroquois society of eighteenth-century Quebec and New York, so in this divine society, dreaming is the way the soul speaks to the conscious mind. In this celestial realm, a young man has dreams about a young woman with whom he has fallen in love. He is unable to communicate his feelings to her and is unable to eat. In a dream, he is instructed to tell his brothers of his feelings and ask them to tell her how he feels.

| Box 1.2 | Hiawatha

According to Iroquois oral traditions, Hiawatha lived in the fifteenth century. Devastated by the death of his wife and family in one of the many wars dividing the Iroquoian-speaking peoples of the Eastern Woodlands, he retreated to the forest where he lived alone as a thief— some say a cannibal— ambushing isolated travellers and hunters. When he reached his lowest point, he saw a face reflected in a pot of water. Assuming that it was his own, he thought it did not look like the face of a cannibal. In fact it was not his face but that of the god Dekanawidah.

At that moment Dekanawidah revealed himself and told Hiawatha that he was must persuade the Onondaga, Oneida, Cayuga, Mohawk, and Seneca nations to unite into the Long House Confederation. Hiawatha abandoned his anti-social behaviour, rejoined his community, and set out on this mission. Eventually, he persuaded 49 chiefs to gather at Onondaga to establish the confederation. They committed the five nations (who were eventually joined by the Tuscarora) to stand together as one extended family, a longhouse. They forbade all blood feuds within the League and established a Condolence Council to console mourners and mediate disputes about the deaths of family members. This confederation, initiated by a visionary experience, and consecrated by ritual, united the Iroquois peoples for nearly three and a half centuries. The story of Hiawatha's visionary experience at a time of moral and physical crisis provided a model for later prophetic figures, including Handsome Lake (see p. 51).

They do so and she marries him. Shortly thereafter, he has another dream in which he is instructed to tell his brothers to uproot the celestial tree that provides light and warmth. Reluctantly, the brothers do so, leaving a huge hole in sky, but with continued light from the stars. One day, as his wife sits with her feet dangling over the edge of the hole, she is impregnated by the Wind. Angered by this turn of events, the young man pushes his wife through the hole, but her fall is broken by birds and eventually she comes to rest on dry earth that has been gathered on the back of a turtle.

There she establishes a home and gives birth to a daughter who, when she is grown, defies her mother's order not to swim in the nearby lake and becomes pregnant in the waters. She conceives twin boys: the first, Tarachiawagon, embodies the life-enhancing power of *orenda*; the second, Tawiskaron, embodies the life-destructive powers of *utgo*. (The fact that they could trace their ancestry only on their mother's side formed the basis for Iroquoian societies' emphasis on matrilineal descent and matrilocal marriage.)

Tarachiawagon is born first, in a normal birth, but his brother chooses a short-cut through his mother's armpit, which results in her death. As she is dying, the mother tells Tarachiawagon how to bury her and reveals that corn will grow out of her breasts in the grave. (Corn, grown primarily by women, was the Iroquois' agricultural staple, nourishing the community just as mother's milk nourished an infant.) Using the power of *orenda*, Tarachiawagon creates human beings out of soil and breathes life into them. He creates rivers in which canoeists can travel with the current, along with edible plants and a variety of animals and other objects that can be used by human beings.

Tawiskaron, however, uses the power of *utgo* to create rapids in the streams, along with weeds, insect pests, dangerous animals, and diseases.

It is here that the meaning of complementary dualism becomes clear, for the *utgo* that Tawiskaron uses to create disease is the same power that is used to cure it. Thus it is Tawiskaron who empowers the most important of the Iroquois healing societies, the False Face Society. In sharp contrast to conflict dualist religions, the Iroquois tradition sees destructive powers as capable of enhancing life. Healing rituals involving the telling of dreams, the confessing of misconduct, and ritual offerings are an important part of the Iroquois ceremonial cycle, beginning with the Midwinter festival and continuing through the Green Corn Festival of the summer and the fall harvest ceremony.

Healing and the Afterlife

Medicine societies—often composed of people who had survived similar illnesses—were an important part of life in many Native American communities. As in Africa, contracting a particular disease was often interpreted as a summons to take on the responsibilities of a healer. Initiation took place in stages over the course of one's adult years. Each stage of initiation was linked to a particular type of animal, beginning with water mammals like beaver and muskrat, continuing with birds, then land animals like snakes or bobcats, and culminating with the animal most closely associated with healing, the bear. The Ojibwa-Anishinaabe Medewewin society was slightly different in that its members were led to become healers as a result of a dream or vision; this society developed in the early days of the fur trade, before the French and English began taking over Aboriginal lands, and may have represented a way of coping with the devastating epidemics of smallpox, measles, and other diseases that arrived with the Europeans.

Some traditions believed that individual healers or shamans could travel into the realms of the gods and bring back healing powers. Shamans could be either men or women. While their bodies remained in a deep trance, their souls were believed to travel under the seas or into the heavens to learn the causes of their patients' illnesses and the appropriate cures (often herbal remedies). Shamans also could use various rituals to divine the causes of illness or to predict the future. Shamanic healing was particularly important among the Inuit, the peoples of the Northwest Coast, and the various communities of the Great Basin.

Disease and calamity could also be interpreted as punishment for violation of community rules or as the result of witchcraft. Witchcraft also figures in many creation myths. According to Hopi and Navajo traditions, for example, humans began to practise witchcraft in the lower world before they emerged into the present world.

Funeral rituals varied dramatically. Some peoples buried their dead in the ground; some practised cremation; and others constructed scaffolds to offer the bodies of the dead to the powers of the celestial realm. In most cases the purpose of funeral rituals was to ensure the safe journey of the soul to the land of the dead while discouraging the spirit from lingering. There were exceptions, however. The Lakota suggested that a portion of the soul could stay with the family while the rest travelled south to the land of the dead. Other peoples, especially on the Northwest Coast, believed that the souls of the dead would be reborn among the living. Some, especially on the Great Plains, believed that the dead could reveal themselves to their living descendants. Others, including the Pueblo and Navajo in the southwest and the Inuit in the far north, feared the souls of the dead.

Meso-America

Urban civilizations dominated large areas of Meso-America, beginning with the Olmecs some 2,000 years ago and continuing with the Mayans, Toltecs, and Aztecs until the Spanish conquest in the early sixteenth century. In sharp contrast to the popular image of indigenous traditions, these were literate cultures with elaborate spiritual practices organized according to a calendar based on complex astronomical calculations. Rituals were conducted at special ritual centres such as the Mayan Chichen Itza and the Aztec Tenochtitlan. Deities associated with corn played a particularly important role in Meso-American religions. In addition, however, the Aztecs offered human sacrifices to their war god, Huitzilopochtli, in return for protection, and to the sun god who ensured the continuing vitality of the world.

Just beyond the area of the great urban civilizations lived a number of Chicimec hunter-gatherer groups, among them the Huichol Indians. Although they had originated in the northern desert, they settled in the Sierra Mountains, near Guadalajara, to escape attacks by their more powerful neighbours. Struggling to growing corn, beans, and squash in a physical environment that was not suited to agriculture, they envisioned the corn goddesses as delicate deities who required careful attention and longed to return to Wirikuta, where their gods continued to live. Led by a shamanic priest, small groups of Huichol made annual pilgrimages to their original homeland to gather parts of the peyote cactus, which were used to induce visions and reunite the people with their gods. Beautiful images made of coloured yarn record some of the visions experienced by the Huichol under the influence of peyote (see p. 42).

Summary

Native American religious traditions have many elements in common. Like their African counterparts, they are primarily theistic, centred on divinities rather than abstract forces (as in some schools of Hinduism, Jainism, and Buddhism). Their principal concerns are the concerns of this world: ensuring adequate food, fertility, health, and protection from enemies. Still, as we have seen with the Iroquois and the Hopi, different traditions have different visions of the origins of the world, the nature of the gods, and human relationships both with the environment and with the ancestors who have died before them. Many of the traditions described here are still practised in many areas, but newer traditions developed in response to the massive disruption caused by European settlement. These will be discussed later in this chapter.

Detail from 'Pilgrimage to Wirikuta', a 3-metre-long yarn painting by Emeteria Rios Martinez. In this final section the pilgrims gather the peyote cactus that they believe to be a gift sent by the gods to allow the people to communicate with them (photo courtesy of Eugene Garfield).

Northeast Asia and Australasia

Northeast Asian and Australasian religions are extremely diverse, but can be divided into a number of clusters within which interaction and mutual influence were significant: Inner Asia, from Afghanistan and Tibet in the south to Mongolia and Siberia in the north; Southeast Asia, from southern China to Indonesia; Aboriginal Australia; Melanesia; Polynesia; and Micronesia. Indigenous traditions continue to be practised in all these areas, but the great missionary religions of Christianity, Islam, and Buddhism have had a significant impact as well. Similarities in religious practice can probably be attributed to migration from the Asian mainland, but thereafter the various clusters were largely isolated from one another until the period of European expansion that began in the sixteenth century. Japanese Shinto, Korean shamanism, and Chinese folk religion will be discussed in Chapter 10.

Siberia

Siberia, the vast and sparsely populated eastern region of Russia, extends from northern forests to the Arctic tundra. Until the Russian empire expanded into the region, beginning in the seventeenth century, it was largely populated by hunter-gatherers and fisherfolk who spoke Paleo-Siberian, Tungus, or Turkic languages. Siberian religious traditions centred on a supreme being, closely associated with the sky, rain, and storms, who created the world in which people live. A second generation of gods, both male and female, were given the tasks of mediating between humans and the sky god and of ensuring the maintenance of the world. Although the term 'shaman' (or 'saman') originated with the Tungus people of Siberia, it could be applied to many of the most important ritual specialists of Siberia.

Farther south, in Mongolia, indigenous religious traditions developed that have co-existed with Buddhist traditions for over a thousand years. This area, adjacent to the ancient trade routes that linked eastern and western Asia (and Europe), was also influenced by early contact with Zoroastrians, Christians, and Muslims, producing a rich syncretic tradition. Like their Siberian neighbours, Mongolians associated their supreme being (Atagha Trigri) with the sky and placed a strong emphasis on shamanism. Unlike the Siberians, however, they also envisioned ancestors as playing an important role. Ancestors together with many lesser deities communicated their needs and desires through the shamans' trance journeys. Some of these deities, such as Bisnu Trigri (the Indian Vishnu) and Qormusta Trigri (the Zoroastrian Ahura Mazda), reflected the influence of other religions.

Australia

Australian Aborigines had little contact with the outside world before the beginning of British colonization in the late eighteenth century. Until then they controlled the entire Australian continent, from the well-watered and temperate southeast to the tropical northern regions and the desert interior. Hunting, fishing, and gathering wild foods were the primary economic activities, and there was little if any political organization beyond the authority exercised by clan elders. Massive violence against Aborigines, including women and children, together with imported European diseases drastically reduced their numbers. Today they account for less than three per cent of the total population of Australia. Before European settlement, there were nearly five hundred different Aboriginal tribes, each with its own language or dialect and its own particular religious ideas and practices; now there are fewer than one hundred. Written accounts begin with European contact, and most oral traditions were collected after the colonization process had begun.

In sharp contrast to most of the world's peoples, Australian Aborigines had no creation myths: for them the world had always existed. The supreme being was associated with the sky and was the source of all power in the universe, but was not the focus of worship. Rather, ritual practices focused on a number of spirits who were believed to sleep within the earth and periodically emerge to transform it. These earth spirits were envisioned as capable of assuming either human or animal form and were considered to be the 'totemic ancestors' of particular Aboriginal clans.

The term 'Dream Time' was coined by nineteenth-century anthropologists to refer to a primordial era that plays a central part in Australian Aboriginal myths. In fact, though, different groups envisioned that era in different ways. Among the Aranda of central Australia, a more accurate term might be 'uncreated time', the period when the first ancestors shaped the world and established the traditions that their descendants

The gigantic sandstone formation called Uluru (known in English as Ayers Rock), in the central interior of Australia, is sacred to the local Aboriginal peoples. It is as tall as the Empire State Building and covers an area larger than New York's Central Park (Willard G. Oxtoby).

must follow. The actions of these earth spirits or ancestors were thought to be imprinted on the land, in distinctive physical landscapes such as Uluru (Ayers Rock), or in unusual water holes, or in the particular characteristics of animals and plants. The Dream Time was the physical landscape of the universe and the sacred traditions that describe it. The Dream Time was the foundation of Aboriginal thought and religious practice and its power was regarded as ongoing. Many ritual practices focused on re-enacting the formative events of that primordial era.

The Western Pacific Islands

The islands of the western Pacific Ocean are usually grouped in three clusters: Polynesia, Micronesia, and Melanesia. The easternmost, Polynesia, in turn embraces three widely separated island groups: New Zealand, Tahiti, and Hawaii.

Polynesia

In Polynesian religions the supreme being and creator of the universe, Tangaroa or Kanaloa, was most closely associated with the ocean rather than the sky; in island societies it is not surprising that the sea would be a central force in people's lives. Two other important deities throughout Polynesia were Tane or Kane, the god associated with life-giving fresh water, which he found by plunging a digging stick into the earth, and Lono or Rongo, the deity associated with the fertility of the land, healing, and peaceful relations among people. In addition there was a group of deities, collectively known as Tu or Ku, that assisted humans in daily life and were also invoked in times of crisis, such as famine or epidemic disease.

The gods entered this world from the spirit realm in order to shape natural forces and make their wishes known. Their priests not only performed rituals on behalf of the community, but also advised kings and local chiefs. Both rituals and priests were subject to rules known as *tapu* (the source of the English 'taboo'), the violation of which would provoke negative spiritual consequences. The term is now applied to many sorts of rules enforced by fear of pollution or spiritual retribution.

Micronesia

Micronesia is a series of archipelagos in the western Pacific, formed largely from coral reefs. In the early nineteenth century Micronesians relied mainly on fishing and farming (taro, sweet potatoes, coconuts). But colonization and the establishment of Christian missions created new opportunities for employment in European-dominated sectors of the economy.

Religious life focused on ancestral spirits who made their presence known either through dreams or by entering the body of a living person ('spirit possession'). Shaking and a trance-like state were interpreted as signs that an ancestral spirit had come to tell the people something about the future or advise them on some current problem. Ancestors who were particularly well remembered or who possessed a spirit medium came to be closely associated with specific extended families or lineages. Some of these 'great ghosts' became the subjects of myth and were assumed to have extraordinary powers to influence the world.

Several deities associated with the creation of the world were also important, as were the trickster gods who, although they provoked disruption and amorality, were also seen as the providers of necessities such as fire. The Micronesian tradition had no counterpart to the wholly evil forces found in many Western religions.

Melanesia

Melanesia consists of the large islands of New Guinea and Fiji together with nearby archipelagos such as the Solomon Islands and New Caledonia. Before the European conquest, most of the peoples of this region supported themselves by hunting, fishing, raising pigs, and farming yams and taro.

It was from Melanesia that scholars borrowed the term 'mana', used to refer a life-enhancing power emanating from deities. Although early anthropologists incorrectly assumed that Melanesian religion was pre-theistic—lower down the evolutionary scale than even polytheistic traditions—in fact its sacred myths describe the roles played by various gods in creating the world and endowing it with mana. It is true, however, that ritual attention tended to focus less on the gods than on the ancestors who sometimes assisted and sometimes punished their living descendants.

Male religious leaders in Melanesia tended to be deeply suspicious of women's powers and enforced an elaborate system of menstrual avoidance; sexual intercourse was regarded as causing a dangerous loss of male power, even within the institution of marriage. In some areas of central New Guinea, boys were required to ingest the semen of older men so that they would be strong enough to weather the dangers of sexual intercourse with women once they reached adulthood, and married men induced monthly nosebleeds to remove the 'pollution' caused by sexual contact with their wives—the ritual equivalent of menstruation.

Indigenous Responses to European Colonialism

Until the fifteenth century, Europe was a relatively weak and isolated region on the western fringes of the Eurasian land mass. Then the voyages of the great Portuguese and Spanish navigators launched a process of expansion that by the early twentieth century had made Europe the centre of the world economy and the dominant force in global culture, including religion. Most indigenous communities lost their independence, came under the domination of European powers, and were challenged by the new religion of Christianity.

Africa

With a few exceptions—in Algeria, South Africa, Rhodesia, and Kenya—the European powers that colonized Africa were not trying to create settler societies like the ones they established in the Americas and Australia. Thus in most regions of Africa there was no need to remove the indigenous populations from the land to make way for European immigrants. Rather, the colonial powers used African soldiers to establish and maintain their empires.

Disease may help to explain why the imperial enterprise took a different form in Africa. In the Americas and Australia the job of establishing European control had been greatly facilitated by the vulnerability of indigenous populations to Old World diseases like smallpox, pneumonia, measles, and tuberculosis. In Africa, however, the situation was reversed. Here Europeans were vulnerable—to endemic diseases like malaria, yellow fever, and dysentery—while most indigenous peoples had already developed resistance to the diseases that accompanied European expansion, since they had links to Europe and Asia going back thousand of years.

Europeans first explored the African coast in search of a sea route to South and East Asia, but by the late fifteenth century the Atlantic slave trade had become a central part of their activities. By the time it ended, between ten and twenty million people had been forcibly taken from Africa and enslaved in the New World. Many more died, either on the way to the coast or in the inter-African wars fuelled by competition in the trade. The consequences for West African and Central African societies were profound, shifting the balance of power from the interior toward coastal areas and increasing the violence and frequency of warfare. As the slave trade was gradually suppressed in the nineteenth century, European traders moved into buying tropical products for export and selling manufactured goods in Africa. Under the influence of economic theories that advocated controlling the sources of raw materials and protecting markets for manufactured goods, the European powers moved towards formal colonization. The partition of Africa was largely completed in the later nineteenth century.

The success of the colonization project sparked a crisis of confidence in indigenous religious systems. Several factors contributed to the loss of confidence, including the close association of political and religious authority in African societies, the tradition of relying on religious ritual to secure military success, and the Europeans' disdain for African religious practices. Some people adopted the religion of the European conquerors in the hope of understanding the spiritual basis of their power. Some looked to Christian missionaries for protection against the abuses of colonial rule. Some wanted to succeed in the new colonial order and saw a missionary education as the essential first step on the path to success.

Some people, however, experienced a profound conversion, seeing Christianity as a new source of religious authority and a way of understanding the spiritual basis of the Europeans' power. Today approximately one-quarter of Africa's people are Christian; most conversions took place during the colonial era or since independence, when European dominance persisted in more subtle forms. Ironically, Islam also experienced its most rapid growth following the colonial conquest, perhaps because it represented a new way of explaining the world and offered a connection to a global religious system that did not entail embracing European ways.

Many people continued to rely on indigenous religious systems to explain the meaning of the European occupation, contain its influence, and preserve their communities. But those systems themselves were also affected by the experience of colonial rule. Reform movements emerged with charismatic leaders claiming privileged communication with the spirit world. Some of these **revitalization movements** sought to purify African religious practices, seeing the European conquest as punishment for lax observance of indigenous traditions. Finally, some regarded their own time of sorrows as a prelude to a golden age in which the Europeans would leave and the ancestors would return, bringing peace and prosperity for Africans.

South Africa: Nongqawuse and the Xhosa Cattle-Killing

In 1856, in the region that is now South Africa, a young Xhosa woman named Nongqawuse had a vision in which her ancestors told her that the military defeats her people had suffered at the hands of Europeans were their punishment for practising

| Box 1.3 | Alinesitoué Diatta

In 1941, in a crowded market in Dakar, Senegal, a young Diola woman named Alinesitoué Diatta had the first in a series of visions of the supreme being. Emitai commanded her to return to her village and tell the people that one of the reasons for the prolonged drought they were suffering was that many had abandoned the religious traditions of their ancestors in favour of Islam or Christianity.

But that was not Alinesitoué's only message. Equally important, she said that Emitai was withholding the rain in protest against the changes in Diola agricultural practices that had taken place under French colonial rule: in particular, the replacement of traditional African rice with higher-yield (but less hardy) Asian varieties, and the introduction of groundnuts (peanuts) as a cash crop, which not only required that forests be cut to create fields but led many men to grow the new crop and leave the job of growing rice for the family to their wives. In effect, Alinesitoué explained that the recent agricultural disasters were directly connected to French intervention in the people's daily lives.

To restore her community's relations with Emitai, Alinesitoué introduced a new cult, centred on the annual sacrifice of a black bull, which was adopted by Diola throughout the region. The priests of this cult, called Kasila, were to be chosen by divination and could be rich or poor, male or female, young or old. Challenging the power of a religious elite that had become established during the era of the slave trade, Alinesitoué's new cult made it possible for women, young people, and the poor to become community leaders.

The Kasila ritual lasted six days and six nights, during which the participants slept outside in the public square, ate all their meals together, and sang and danced songs of the ancestors, reaffirming the sense of community that Alinesitoué saw as the basis of Diola society. She also insisted that all members of the Diola community participate, regardless of their individual religious affiliations, and that the former Diola practice of observing a day of rest every six days be restored—contrary to the rules of both Christianity and Islam.

Finally, amid growing unrest, French authorities ordered Alinesitoué's arrest. Convicted in 1943 of obstructing colonial authorities and causing embarrassment to colonial officials, she was exiled to Timbuktu, where she starved to death a year later, at the age of 23. But the movement that Alinesitoué started did not end with her arrest. Within a year, two other Diola women claimed that they too had been sent by Emitai to offer guidance to their communities, and since then more than twenty other people, mostly women, have come forward to teach in the tradition of prophetic authority associated with Alinesitoué. They remain active today, emphasizing the close relationship between the supreme being, agricultural practices, and adequate rainfall. Her prophetic tradition is a major factor in the continued vitality of Diola religion in a region that is otherwise overwhelmingly Muslim.

witchcraft. She relayed this message to her uncle and guardian, a chief named Mhlakaza, telling him that it was because many Xhosa had used witchcraft to enrich themselves and harm others that Europeans had been allowed to take over their land and steal their cattle. In order to cleanse themselves of this spiritual pollution, the ancestors demanded that the people destroy their remaining cattle and If they did so, the Europeans would disappear; the Xhosa's ancestors would return from the dead, and their property would be restored to them in greater quantities than they had ever known.

Following Nongqawuse's instructions, many people killed their cattle and burnt their granaries to demonstrate their faith in the ultimate beneficence of their tradition's celestial beings. The result was a devastating famine in which thousands of Xhosa lost their lives. Those who survived lost their independence, the Xhosa resistance to the British collapsed, and many people sought asylum with missionaries, with the result that Christianity made enormous inroads within the Xhosa community. Meanwhile, those who had not agreed to destroy their lands and livelihoods were blamed for the failure of Nongqawuse's prophecy.

How could people put their faith in such a vision? One factor might be desperation after more than century of military defeats. Another might have to do with the tendency of indigenous religious systems to understand catastrophe as punishment: much as the ancient Hebrews considered the Babylonians and Assyrians to be scourges sent by God to punish them for violating his laws, so the Xhosa appear to have seen the Europeans as instruments used by a supreme being to punish and remind them of their religious obligations. As Nongqawuse emphasized, for the Xhosa to regain control over their lives and restore a prosperous and independent community, they had to forsake witchcraft and put their faith entirely in the hands of the ancestors and the supreme being.

When the prophecies failed, Xhosa resistance to the British ended. Many Xhosa sought out Christian missionaries, who offered assistance with the necessities of life and a way of understanding a world in which their own religious resources had failed to provide effective answers. Still, a significant minority—known as 'Red Xhosa' for the red ochre they used to paint their bodies in certain rituals—remained faithful to their Xhosa religious traditions. Moreover, within thirty years of their emergence as the majority among their people, Xhosa Christians began raising issues that reflected those indigenous traditions, such as healing and witchcraft, while asserting their right to protect their distinctive cultural practices. By the late nineteenth century Xhosa Christians began breaking away and forming their independent churches, many of which called themselves Zionist because they looked forward to the liberation of their promised land. This blending of indigenous and foreign traditions is an example of syncretism.

Tanganyika: The Maji-Maji Revolt of 1905–7

By the end of the nineteenth century Germany too had established several colonies in Africa, among them Tanganyika (now the largest portion of Tanzania). This region was home to several ethnic groups, and in 1905 a visionary named Kinjikitile tried to unite them in an effort to regain their independence. Some three years earlier, Kinjikitile claimed to have experienced a kind of shamanic journey in which he disappeared into a river and emerged several days later, completely dry. In the course of this journey he met a water god called Bokero and a spirit of considerable regional importance, known as Hongo, and learned of a powerful medicine called Maji-Maji (Swahili for 'water-water') that would render those who bathed in it invulnerable to German guns. Calling on the diverse peoples of the Matumbi hills region to unite behind his leadership, he built a pilgrimage site at Ngarambe and said that the ancestors were waiting there to return to life once the Germans had been driven away and witchcraft had been suppressed. He used divination to expose witches and get them to stop their attacks, while emphasizing regional spirit cults rather than ethnically specific religious rituals. Although Kinjikitile himself was captured and executed in the early stages of the rebellion, it dragged on for more than two years, with disastrous consequences for the people of the region. Estimates of the death toll range between 75,000 and 130,000.

The African Diaspora

African religious traditions were carried to the Americas through the Atlantic slave trade. Particularly in the Caribbean and South America, where slaves greatly outnumbered Europeans or free people of mixed ancestry, slave societies developed new syncretic religions that combined African (especially Yoruba), and Native American traditions with elements of Christianity. In these African diaspora religions, saints were identified with specific African deities, initially as a way of concealing African religious practices that were seen as posing a threat to slave-based societies. Gradually, however, the characteristics of African gods and European saints blended into one another and new syncretic practices developed that were neither European nor African.

Candomblé, Macumba, and Umbanda in Brazil; Vaudou in Haiti; and Santeria or Lucumi in Cuba, all emphasized spirit possession and healing. In Macumba, Candomblé, and Santeria, gods known by the Yoruba term *orisha* were said to ride their followers much as people ride horses. In Haitian Vaudou, African deities and violent local gods known as Petro spirits (often associated with slave masters) possessed believers. Saints and gods acquired new roles and new forms of religious community emerged in response to the trauma of slavery and the continuing struggle to live in societies beset by poverty and political uncertainty.

Since emancipation, these traditions have also gained some adherents among people of European descent and have been carried by immigrants to Europe as well as Canada and the United States. In recent years, local governments in Florida have sought to limit Santeria and Vaudou practices by prohibiting animal sacrifice, but the United States Supreme Court ruled that such a ban was an unconstitutional threat to freedom of religion.

The Americas

The disruptions that came with European expansion in the Americas were particularly severe. According to some estimates, a total population of perhaps eighty million was reduced by three-quarters within a century of Columbus's arrival, primarily as result of European diseases against which the indigenous peoples had no natural immunity. For central Mexico, some scholars have suggested a 95 per cent loss during the sixteenth century. Entire nations died out, and those that survived in many cases had to join forces with others in order to form sustainable communities. By 1890, when the North American frontier was generally considered to have closed, more than ninety per cent of the land in the United States had been taken from Native Americans and given to newcomers, primarily of European origin. Meanwhile, the animal populations that Native peoples depended on had been devastated by the fur trade, settlement, and (especially in the case of buffalo), 'sport' hunting.

The Eastern Woodlands: Handsome Lake Religion

The Iroquois Confederacy was a group of five (six after 1720) Iroquoian nations that dominated the Eastern Woodlands area from Quebec in the east through New York and southern Ontario to the midwestern US in the seventeenth and eighteenth centuries. Through alliances and military force, the Cayuga, Mohawk, Oneida, Onondaga, Seneca, and, eventually, Tuscarora controlled the fur trade in this region, and they were quite effective in playing off the imperial ambitions of the French, Dutch, and British against one another.

But their bargaining power was severely compromised after the fall of New France in 1760, when the British gained exclusive control over most of North America. When the United States won their independence from Britain, in 1783, the 'Indian Territory' to the west of the thirteen colonies lost its British protection. By 1800 the fur trade was no longer viable and the once mighty Iroquois were confined to several small reserves in northern New York, southern Quebec, and southern Ontario, where many eventually succumbed to disease, alcoholism, and despair.

Among them was a Seneca named Ganioda'yo or Handsome Lake (c. 1735–1815). As a young man he witnessed the devastating impact of American land annexations, the decline of the fur trade, and the spread of disease, and when his people were confined to small reservations in western New York he sank into despair and chronic alcoholism. Finally in 1799 he fell into a coma-like state and his family thought he had died. They were beginning to prepare for his funeral when he regained consciousness and described a vision of three angels sent by the Creator, Tarachiawagon, that led him to reform his life and begin teaching a new form of Iroquois religion.

As a result of that vision, Handsome Lake taught that the Iroquois should worship only Tarachiawagon—not his destructive twin, Tawiskaron. Two months later, a fourth angel took him on what became known as the 'Sky Journey', a trip to heaven and to hell. In hell he saw a jail containing handcuffs, a whip, and a rope knotted into a hangman's noose—symbols of the Euro-American penal system—and a church without exit doors or windows, filled with people wailing. He encountered George Washington and Jesus on the road to heaven; both of them he saw as good white men.

In further teachings, eventually recorded in a book that became known as the *Gaiwiio*, 'the good word', Handsome Lake emphasized a new, radical division between good and evil. He urged his people to avoid the 'four evils' (whiskey, witchcraft, love magic, and abortion or anti-fertility medicines), renew themselves, and restore their proper relationship with Tarachiawagon. Although he did not succeed in banning the medicine societies that relied on Tawiskaron's power of *utgo*, he effectively shifted the Iroquois worldview from complementary dualism to conflict dualism along the lines of the Christian model. Tawiskaron became identified as the Evil Twin, as the Punisher who, like the Christian Satan, tormented souls in hell.

Handsome Lake also advocated the public confession of sin, sought to simplify mourning ceremonies, and identified witches as sources of sin and internal enemies of

Iroquois communities. As part of his social program he preached accommodation with the economic organization of Euro-Americans, encouraging agricultural work by men as well as women, individual land-holding, and houses, and patrilineal, patrilocal social organization (as a result, Iroquoian women lost some of the influence they had enjoyed when woman's family was the primary kinship unit).

With the assistance of his half-brother, Chief Cornplanter, Handsome Lake's teachings gained a significant following. Many Iroquois abandoned the practices he condemned as evil, such as witchcraft and alcohol consumption. At the same time, his encouragement of farming helped to ease the transition to a new way of life within the new nation-states of Canada and the United States. Today approximately one-third of the Iroquois people continue to gather to study the Gaiwio and practise what has come to be known as the Handsome Lake or Longhouse religion.

The Ghost Dance

Almost a century later, the Lakota of the northern Plains experienced a similar loss of land. In 1874, just six years after the US Congress had approved a treaty promising the Lakota a vast territory for 'as long as the grass is green and streams flow', it allowed gold prospectors into the sacred territory of the Black Hills. The resistance that followed reached its climax in the Battle of the Little Big Horn (1876), in which General George Armstrong Custer suffered the worst military defeat in the history of the American Indian wars. Pursued relentlessly by Custer's replacement, a number of Sioux led by Chief Sitting Bull took refuge across the border in the territory that would become Saskatchewan.

Four years later, forced by food shortages to accept the confines of reservation life, they returned to the US and surrendered. What they found was not what they had been promised in the 1860s. Parents were pressured to send their children to residential schools where they were forbidden to speak their language and were forcibly instructed in Euro-American Christianity and concepts of labour. In the 1880s the US Congress passed legislation forbidding traditional healers to practise their craft and banning the Sun Dance as well as a custom called Keeping of the Soul, in which a ritual bundle containing a small portion of a deceased relative's scalp was prepared and kept in the house. These laws effectively stripped the Lakota of their primary ways of coping with disease, invoking the sun god, and remaining in contact with their ancestors.

In 1889 a man named Wovoka revived a short-lived movement started nearly twenty years earlier by a close relative among the Paiute named Wodziwob. Like Wodziwob, Wovoka had experienced a vision in which he was told that his people could hasten the restoration of their old way of life if they performed a certain dance for their ancestors that came to be known as the Ghost Dance. Urging his people to embrace hard work and honesty, and put an end to warfare and feuding, he prophesied that the white people would be removed, the ancestors would return, and the lost buffalo and other game would be restored. As news of these teachings spread, the Lakota were particularly drawn to the Ghost Dance as a replacement for their outlawed rituals.

In 1889, Lakota pilgrims travelled to Nevada to hear Wovoka's teachings. That same year the Lakota performed the Ghost Dance, wearing colourfully painted Ghost

Shirts that were supposed to permit them entry to the new world and carrying bows and arrows in anticipation of the buffalo herds' return. Seeing the weapons, a young Indian agent named D.F. Royer, nicknamed Young-Man-Afraid-of-Indians, panicked and called in the cavalry, which in December 1890 attacked a group of Ghost Dancers at a place called Wounded Knee, killing more than three hundred men, women, and children.

This ended the Ghost Dance among the Lakota, though it continued among some other Indian communities. The prohibitions on the Sun Dance and the Ghost Dance were lifted in the 1930s, and since then these traditions have been revived.

Australasia and the Western Pacific

In describing religious responses to conquest in East Asia and Australasia, it is important to distinguish between the Asian mainland on the one hand and Australia and the Pacific Islands on the other. After centuries of commercial and religious contact, the former were not unprepared for dealing with foreigners. They had had time to develop some degree of immunity to foreign diseases, and in most cases their territories were not particularly attractive for settlement. Despite the loss of their political independence, therefore, the peoples in those regions were generally able to adapt to the changes that came with colonialism.

In sharp contrast, the peoples of the Pacific Islands had little experience of large imperial states or missionary religions prior to European expansion. They also had far less resistance to foreign diseases. In the case of Polynesia and Australia in particular, the land was considered suitable for European settlement, and the people therefore suffered massive losses of territory. Throughout the region, new religious movements emerged to explain and contain the destabilizing forces associated with European colonization.

Melanesia: Cargo Cults

The peoples of Melanesia first encountered Europeans in the mid-nineteenth century. A highly distinctive form of religious movement emerged in response to those first contacts, especially in coastal regions. The development of these **cargo cults** reflected the enormous differences in economic organization and manufacturing capability that shaped the Melanesians' early encounters with Europeans.

Seeing ships arrive carrying manufactured goods for European military, traders, administrators, and missionaries, some Melanesians began to envision a day when similar cargoes of canned goods, iron tools, and firearms would arrive for them, provided by their ancestors rather than the Europeans who were seeking commercial ties and political control. When that day came, they said, Melanesians would no longer have any need for Europeans. During the Second World War cargo cult prophecies would expand to include deliveries on island airstrips or wharves built by Allied militaries. Although similar cults continued to be reported into the 1980s, this discussion will focus on two earlier examples.

One of the first such movements emerged in Fiji. The Tuka Cult began in 1885, when a man named Ndungumoi claimed that his soul could leave his body and communicate with spirits. He predicted that a revolutionary new world was coming in which Europeans would serve Fijians, ordinary people would rise to positions of authority over their former chiefs, and Fijians would have trade goods—especially cloth and canned food—in abundance. Among the rituals he created was one that involved anointing his followers with sacred water, for which he charged a small fee; then he would use the proceeds to host elaborate feasts. Those who refused to take part in Ndungumoi's rituals were told that they would have to serve his followers or suffer a terrible fate in the afterlife.

When the date of the transformative event drew near, Ndungumoi instructed his followers to place all their faith in his prophecy. The movement came to an end, however, when he began to speak out against European planters and administrators, who arrested him along with his chief aides and exiled them to a nearby island.

Another cargo cult developed in the New Guinean community of Tangu in the late 1930s when a prophet named Mambu began teaching that white Europeans and black Melanesians were descended from two brothers. The white brother was given a greater share of material goods and was expected to share them with his brother, but had failed to do so. Mambu claimed that the gods who had created these commodities had also sent them to the people of New Guinea, but that Europeans had intercepted them. He established a ritual centre near the coast and encouraged his followers to be 'baptized' with sacred water on their genitals and to wear European-style clothes so that they would be prepared for the cargo's arrival. In the meantime, however, they should avoid all contact with European government officials or missionaries. Mambu was arrested by colonial officials before his prophecy could be fulfilled.

New Zealand: The Pai Marire Movement

The Pai Marire ('Good and Peaceful') movement was established during a period of increasing tension between the Maori and British settlers. Its founder, Te Ua Haumene Horopapera Tuwhakararo, had been captured by English travellers as a child in the 1820s and been taken to a Wesleyan Methodist mission station, where he was baptized, studied the Bible, and worked for missionaries. When war broke out in 1860 he sided with the Maori king and served him as an adviser during the early campaigns. Two years later, however, he experienced a vision of the angel Gabriel, who commanded him to work for the unification of the Maori and a peaceful separation between them and the British settlers.

Te Ua's teachings reflected Maori understandings of Christian doctrine, focusing on the ancient Hebrews' longing for a messianic leader through whom their land might finally be liberated. His followers rejected what they regarded as missionary paternalism and insisted on their own right to interpret the Bible. Te Ua introduced two new deities alongside the Trinity: Riki and Rura. Rura was associated with the angel Gabriel; Riki was a war god, associated with the angel Michael, who would protect the Maoris against all invaders. Te Ua also emphasized the imminence of Judgment Day; those who followed him would enter heaven and those who refused would be judged harshly. Rituals

A sculpture at the Maori traditional site named Whakarewarewa in Rotorua, New Zealand (Willard G. Oxtoby).

focused on ceremonial poles, with four carved wooden heads, inserted in the ground, around which dances and songs were performed. Although the movement did not survive for long after Te Ua's death in 1866, it inspired a number of later Maori nationalist movements. By relating Christian teachings to the spiritual predicament in which Maori found themselves, it created an opening for Maori interpretations of Christianity and the development of other Maori syncretic movements.

Summary

Indigenous religions were profoundly affected by the experience of conquest and colonization. New religious leaders came forward offering new teachings and practices based on divine revelations. Some urged direct resistance to European expansion. Some focused on reforming their own societies—by eliminating witchcraft, reducing dependence on European trade goods, restoring economic self-sufficiency—and renewing their commitment to their own traditions. Others predicted the coming of a new age when the ancestors would return, depleted animal populations would be restored, and diseases would be eliminated; these movements have often been labelled millennial or millenarian (after the Christian idea that God would establish his kingdom on earth a thousand years after the death of Jesus).

All these movements sought to redress the sudden and traumatic loss of autonomy suffered by indigenous peoples under colonial rule. Those that were able to make sense of that loss and restore a sense of order to the world helped to revitalize their communities and continued to gain adherents after their founders had died; the movements founded by Handsome Lake and Alinesitoué Diatta are examples of successful revitalization movements. The resistance movements of Nongqawuse, Kinjikitile, and Wovoka (the Ghost Dance) proved less successful because they directly challenged the European presence (or were perceived by colonial administrators to do so) and therefore were quickly suppressed.

Conclusion

Despite their diversity, the indigenous religions examined in this chapter share a number of characteristics. First, they have all focused on the worship of personal deities (as opposed to impersonal forces) and assumed that these deities play an active role in the world. Second, they have been profoundly oriented towards this world (as opposed to the next) and the well-being of the community. Ritual specialists seek to invoke the spiritual powers of the universe to improve the human situation, not just for individuals but for the communities in which they live. Third, they have strong ethical systems: actions are judged to be righteous or destructive on the basis of their impact on the life of the community. Finally, they are capable of dramatic transformation in response to changing political, economic, social, or environmental conditions. This chapter has focused on the changes associated with European colonialism, but equally dramatic changes have taken place in response to other situations, such as disease pandemics or prolonged drought.

For most of human history, all religious traditions conformed to the indigenous model. It was only in the second millennium before the Common Era that a new kind of religion began to emerge in which members of the community defined themselves in terms of shared knowledge and practice rather than shared descent. In the early twenty-first century, indigenous traditions persist in some regions, but their practitioners generally make up only a minority of the population. Nowhere do they have the government representation they would need to counteract the assimilationist pressures exerted by institutions such as schools and social service agencies. Furthermore, in sharp contrast to practitioners of world religions like Christianity, Islam, and Buddhism, they are not members of an international community and therefore cannot look to other countries for either moral or financial support. Preserving those perspectives will be an even greater challenge in the future, as globalization gives renewed impetus to cultural homogenization.

Glossary

animism The belief that natural phenomena, including plants and inanimate objects, have souls; term coined by E.B. Tylor in 1871.

axis mundi A place believed to be the spiritual centre of the world, where the celestial world and the underworld meet the earth and it is possible to travel between realms; term coined by Mircea Eliade.

cargo cult One of several Melanesian religious movements centred on the belief that one day ships would arrive bringing supplies of food and manufactured goods for the local people, rather than Europeans, and ushering in a new age of peace and prosperity.

complementary dualism The concept (common to many indigenous religions) that the universe contains life-enhancing and life-diminishing forces that can work together and are equally necessary to its survival.

conflict dualism The concept (common to the Abrahamic or Western religious traditions) that the universe contains good and evil forces that are wholly separate and in constant opposition.

diviner A ritual specialist who uses various mechanical techniques to 'see' into the realm of spiritual forces.

fetish Originally, a valued object in the Portuguese African trade; the term was eventually applied to any object believed to be endowed with spiritual powers. Fetishism is the worship or use of such objects in ritual.

Inuit 'True human beings'; the preferred name for the people that Europeans called 'Eskimo'.

Iroquois A confederacy of five (eventually six) Iroquoian-speaking nations, formed sometime before the arrival of Europeans, that dominated the Eastern Woodlands area of North America from Quebec and New York to the northern Great Lakes.

Lakota The largest of the Siouan-speaking peoples in the Great Plains region of North America.

mana A Melanesian term for a life-enhancing power that can be concentrated in people or objects; widely used by anthropologists in theories about the origins of religions.

Neolithic Age The 'New' Stone Age; the stage in world history when humans first began to develop agriculture and animal husbandry.

oral traditions Narratives, myths, histories, legends, fables, proverbs, and riddles that are transmitted verbally from generation to generation within a community and are seen as authoritative sources of knowledge.

orisha The 401 lesser gods in the Yoruba traditions of West Africa.

Paleolithic Age The 'Old' Stone Age; the stage of world history that preceded the Neolithic.

revitalization movement A religious movement, sparked by a social crisis, that seeks to reform and give new life to a particular tradition.

shaman A ritual specialist trained in the use of visions, ecstatic trances, and out-of-body travel to communicate with the gods on behalf of the community; the term was borrowed from the Tungus people of Siberia.

Sun Dance One of the most important rituals practised by First Nations of the Great Plains and northern Rockies.

syncretism The blending of elements from two or more religious traditions; use of the term is often negative, suggesting contamination of a 'pure' religion under the influence of a different tradition.

taboo A Polynesian term for an action or object that is prohibited; any violation of a taboo is regarded as having dire spiritual consequences.

totem An Ojibwa term for an animal that is believed to share a spiritual connection with a particular clan or lineage.

Yoruba A West African ethnic group, one of the largest on the continent; because a large proportion of the slaves sent to the Americas were Yoruba, their traditions had the most visible influence on the religions of the African Diaspora.

Further Reading

Baum, Robert M. 1993. 'Homosexuality and the Traditional Religions of the Americas and Africa'. In Arlene Swidler, ed. Pp. 1–46 in *Homosexuality in World Religions*. Valley Forge, PA: Trinity Press, International.

Baum, Robert M. 1999. *Shrines of the Slave Trade: Diola Religion and Society in Precolonial Senegambia*, New York: Oxford University Press.

Bell, Diane. 1993. *Daughters of the Dreaming*. Minneapolis: University of Minnesota Press.

Bockie, Simon. 1993. *Death and the Invisible Powers: The World of Kongo Belief*. Bloomington: Indiana University Press.

Brown, Joseph Eppes. 1971. *The Sacred Pipe*. Harmondsworth, England: Penguin Books

Burridge, Kennelm. 1986. *New Heaven, New Earth: A Study of Millenarian Activities*. Oxford: Basil Blackwell.

Clark, Paul. 1975. *"HauHau': The Pai Marire Search for Maori Identity*. Auckland: Auckland University Press.

Daneel, M.L. 1970. *God of the Matopos Hills*. The Hague: Mouton.

Durkheim, E. 1965 (1915). *The Elementary Forms of the Religious Life*. New York: Free Press.

Evans-Prichard, E.E. 1956. *Nuer Religion*. London, Oxford University Press, 1956.

Griaule, Marcel. 1972. *Conversations with Ogotemmeli: An Introduction to Dogon Religious Ideas*, London, Oxford University Press, 1972.

Heissig, Walther. 1980. *The Religions of Mongolia*, London: Routledge and Kegan Paul.

Herdt, Gilbert H., ed. 1982. *Rituals of Manhood: Male Initiation in Papua New Guinea*. Berkeley: University of California Press.

Hultkrantz, Ake. 1987. 'North American Religions: An Overview. Pp. 526–35 in Mircea Eliade, ed. *The Encyclopedia of Religion*. Vol. 10. New York: Macmillan.

Hussein, Ebrahim. 1970. *Kinjeketile*. Nairobi: Oxford University Press.

Iliffe, John. 1979. *A Modern History of Tanganyika*. Cambridge: Cambridge University Press.

Janzen, John, and Wyatt MacGaffey. 1974. *An Anthology of Kongo Religion*. University of Kansas Publications in Anthropology, #5. Lawrence: University of Kansas Press.

Lessa, William. 1966. *Ulithi: A Micronesian Design for Living*. New York: Holt, Rinehart, & Winston.

Martin, Calvin. 1978. *Keepers of the Game: Indian-Animal Relationships and the Fur Trade*, Berkeley: University of California Press, 1978.

Martin, Joel W. 2001. *The Land Looks After Us: A History of Native American Religion*. New York: Oxford University Press.

Mooney, James. 1970 (1896). *The Ghost Dance Religion and the Sioux Outbreak of 1890*. Chicago: University of Chicago Press.

Myerhoff, Barbara. 1974. *Peyote Hunt: The Sacred Journey of the Huichol Indians*. Ithaca: Cornell University Press.

Neihardt, John. 1988 (1932). *Black Elk Speaks: Being the Life Story of a Holy Man of the Oglala Sioux*. Lincoln: University of Nebraska Press.

Ortiz, Alfonso. 1969. *The Tewa World: Space, Time, and Becoming in a Pueblo Society*. Chicago: University of Chicago Press.

Peires, J.B. 1989. *The Dead Will Arise: Nongqawuse and the Great Cattle-Killing Movement of 1856-1857*. Johannesburg: Raven Press.

Pelton, Robert. 1989. *The Trickster in West African Religion: A Study of Mythic Irony and Sacred Delight*. Berkeley: University of California Press.

Wallace, A.G. 1972. *The Death and Rebirth of the Seneca*. New York: Random House.

Waters, Frank. 1963. *Book of the Hopi*. New York: Ballantine Books.

Williams, Walter. 1986. *The Spirit and the Flesh: Sexual Diversity in American Indian Culture*. Boston: Beacon Press.

Worsley, Peter. 1968. *The Trumpet Shall Sound: A Study of 'Cargo' Cults in Melanesia*. New York: Schocken Books.

References

Ray, Benjamin. 1976. *African Religions: Symbol, Ritual, and Community*. Englewood Cliffs, NJ: Prentice Hall.

Turner, Victor. 1969. *The Ritual Process*. Ithaca: Cornell University Press.

The Jewish Tradition

ALAN F. SEGAL

Judaism is quintessentially a historical religion. It sees human history as a reflection of the desires and demands of God, and understands itself to have been founded at Mount Sinai more than 3,200 years ago, when a divine revelation was given through Moses to the people Israel. The covenant (agreement) with God that was sealed at Mount Sinai established a set of moral and ritual obligations that continue to govern Judaism today.

A Ritual Initiation

These obligations are reaffirmed at the synagogue every Saturday in the ceremonies that mark the coming of age of 13-year-olds. The details of the ceremony in which a young person becomes a 'bar mitzvah' (Aramaic for 'son of the commandments') or 'bat mitzvah' ('daughter of the commandments') reflect a number of the features that Jews regard as most significant in their tradition generally.

The **Bar Mitzvah** ceremony is a regular part of a congregation's weekly worship. Saturday for Jews is the day of rest, called the **Sabbath**. It is a day for prayer and public assembly in the **synagogue**, the house of worship and community meeting. In the Bar Mitzvah ceremony, the teenager reads two selections from the Bible: one from the **Pentateuch** (the five books of Moses, which constitute the first section of the Bible) and one from a later section called *The Prophets*.

For the first time, the young person reads publicly from the **Torah**, the scripture that Jews are expected to read and study throughout their lives. In the broadest sense, the Torah (i.e., the religious law) consists of the Hebrew Bible itself and all the commentaries on it, but the term also refers specifically to the first five books of the Bible, which are handwritten on parchment scrolls. Typically, the young person chants from one of the Torah scrolls, having learned the traditional melodies and the special skills necessary to read the ancient calligraphy.

Next the candidate recites a series of special blessings that reflect the community's values, and the community responds by reaffirming the blessings. He or she then gives thanks for the scripture that has served as a guide for the people Israel. Jerusalem and the dynasty of David are mentioned, and the Sabbath itself is extolled for the beauty and quietude it brings. In the benediction the congregation notes that the only way in which Jews differ from anyone else is that they have been given the special responsibility of studying and observing the Torah.

In other respects Bar Mitzvah ceremonies can vary widely. Some synagogues conduct their services almost entirely in the local language (English, French, etc.). Others prefer a service largely or even wholly in Hebrew. Some insist that the child preparing for the Bar Mitzvah learn the traditional chants and melodies for reading from the scrolls. Others substitute essay-writing, social action, and good works for some of the

c. 1280 BCE	Moses leads the Exodus from Egypt
c. 1000 BCE	David takes Jerusalem and makes it his capital
922 BCE	Northern kingdom separates following Solomon's death
722 BCE	Assyrians conquer northern kingdom and disperse its people
621 BCE	Josiah centralizes worship at the temple in Jerusalem in Deuteronomic reform
586 BCE	Babylonians conquer Jerusalem and deport its leaders
538 BCE	Persians conquer Babylon, permitting exiles to return
164 BCE	Rededication of the temple after Maccabean uprising
70 CE	Romans lay siege to Jerusalem and destroy the temple
c. 220	The *Mishnah* of Rabbi Judah ha-Nasi
c. 500	The Babylonian *Talmud*
882	Birth of Saadia, *gaon* in Babylonia (d. 942)
1040	Birth of Rashi, commentator on Bible and *Talmud* (d. 1105)
1135	Birth of Moses Maimonides, author of *Guide of the Perplexed* (d. 1204)
1250	Birth of Moses of León, author of the *Zohar* (d. 1305)
1492	Jews expelled from Spain
1666	Sabbatai Zvi is promoted as the messiah
1698	Birth of Israel ben Eliezer, the Baal Shem Tov, in Poland (d. 1759)
1729	Birth of Moses Mendelssohn, pioneer of Reform in Germany (d. 1786)
1881	Severe pogroms in Russia spur Jewish emigration
1889	Conservative Judaism separates from Reform in the United States
1897	Theodor Herzl and the first Zionist Congress
1938	German synagogues vandalized in prelude to the Holocaust
1948	Establishment of the state of Israel

traditional Hebrew skills. The majority of North American synagogues today also call each young woman to the Torah as a bat mitzvah, and those that do still limit the honour to boys will frequently offer an alternative ceremony for girls.

After the ceremony, the family usually holds a luncheon or dinner for relatives and friends, to celebrate the young person's success and the family's good fortune. These events may be simple, focused on the religious dimensions of the day, but they can be almost as lavish as wedding receptions, with a catered feast and a dance orchestra. For most of its history, the Bar Mitzvah had far fewer of the festive elements that are so widespread today. These are modern developments, reflecting the Jewish community's achievement of legal rights in European society and participation in European intellectual life.

Defining Judaism

In the course of its historical development, Judaism gave rise to two other world religions: Christianity and Islam. Judaism is by far the smallest of the three; the world's Jewish population is only 1 to 2 per cent the size of its Christian and Muslim populations. Historically, however, the influence of the Jewish people has been far greater than their numbers would suggest, for it was with them that the belief in one God originated.

Is the Jewish heritage by definition religious? The answer is yes and no. Many people do identify themselves as Jews on the basis of religious participation. It is possible to join the Jewish community through conversion, and many have done so. Nevertheless, the tradition is far more commonly inherited as part of the identity of one's ancestors, and for this reason Judaism is frequently considered an 'ethnic' religion.

Some Jews have said yes to their ethnic identity while saying no to the religion. A substantial number of North Americans, Europeans, and Israelis identify themselves as Jews and think of themselves as belonging to a Jewish family, but do not participate in the religious tradition. Rather, they see themselves as part of a culture with distinct literary and artistic traditions, folkways, and roles in various social and historical milieus. Religion, for them, is a part of their culture, but not the defining part.

On the other hand, the idea that the Jews constitute a genetic race, which was one of the bases for their persecution in the twentieth century, simply cannot be substantiated. Ever since the ancient Hebrew kingdoms, people of diverse origins have converted or married into the community. Jews today exhibit a vast range of physical characteristics: eastern in eastern countries, African in Africa, European in Europe. Judaism can be identified as a religion, Jews think of themselves as a family, and Jews around the world have an identifiable culture; but identification on the basis of biology is fraught with error.

In all, Jews number about 14 million worldwide today. Half of that total—more than 7 million—live in the Americas, mostly in the United States and Canada. More than a quarter, 3 million, live in Asia, most of them in Israel. Fewer than a quarter remain in Europe, mainly in Russia and the other lands controlled until 1989 by the Soviet Union, though Russian Jews have been immigrating to Europe, the United States, and Israel in large numbers in recent years. The world population of Jews in the early twenty-first

NUMBERS
Approximately 14 million.

DISTRIBUTION
7 million in the Americas (mostly US, Canada, and Buenos Aires, Argentina); 3 million in Asia (mostly in Israel); 4 million in Europe (mostly in Russia, Ukraine, France, and England).

PRINCIPAL HISTORICAL PERIODS
170 BCE–70 CE	Biblical
c. 70–700	Talmudic
700–1700	Medieval
1700–present	Modern

PRINCIPAL FOUNDERS
The patriarchs and matriarchs: Abraham and his wife Sarah (legendary, c. 1700 BCE); Isaac (their son) and his wife Rebecca; Jacob (their son; also called Israel) and his wives Leah and Rachel) (father and mothers, with Bilhah and Zilpah, of the children of Israel).

Also Moses (legendary prophet who received the Ten Commandments on Mount Sinai, c. 1200 BCE); Saul, David, and Solomon (semi-legendary kings, c. 1000–900 BCE).

LEADERS
Ezra helped build the second temple, 515 BCE. Yohanan ben Zakkai founded the first rabbinic academy, 70 CE. Judah the Prince produced the *Mishnah*, 220 CE. David Ben Gurion became the first prime minister of the state of Israel, 1948.

DEITY
One God, called 'Lord' or 'God' in English. His name is never spoken in Hebrew.

AUTHORITATIVE TEXTS
The Hebrew Bible, the *Talmud*, and the *Midrash* (commentaries).

NOTEWORTHY DOCTRINES
All the righteous of the world can be saved; God has commanded the Jews to observe special laws, including dietary and dress codes.

century is almost one-third smaller than it was in 1939. In that year the Second World War began, and by the time it ended, in 1945, approximately 6 million Jews had been put to death by the Nazis, the political party that ruled Germany, in what today is known as the **Holocaust**.

Israel aside, the main centres of Jewish culture today are the large cities of eastern North America, together with a few cities elsewhere, especially in Europe. About half of all Jews are unaffiliated with any synagogue. The other half represent a broad range from liberal to intensely traditional. In Canada and the United States the three major groupings are Reform, Conservative, and Orthodox. To understand Judaism it is important to recognize that its major divisions are based more on differences in ritual and practice than in belief or doctrine. By contrast, in Christianity belief and doctrine are the defining issues that distinguish one denomination from another.

Jews understand that God expects all human beings to observe a fundamental moral code that was revealed to Noah after the primeval flood and is accessible to the entire human race through reason. They also understand that Jews are obliged to observe a number of additional rules, laid down in the covenant between God and Moses at Sinai, that set them apart from all other peoples. In a later covenant this God also promised explicitly: 'I shall be your God and you shall be my people.' Jews understand themselves to be God's special people not in the sense that they are preferred above any other, but in the sense that they have been elected to a special responsibility: to serve as God's priests in the world.

Origins

The Biblical Period

The history of Israel is contained in the Torah, but it is history written from a special perspective. It is the history of a people as they understand and follow a God who has chosen them as his instrument. Some of that history is well known because the first set of Jewish religious writings, the Hebrew Bible, is scripture for Christians and Muslims as well. Interpretations of that scripture differ not only between those three communities but also within Judaism.

The liberal wing of Judaism accepts modern historical principles and reserves the right to question aspects of the accuracy and historicity of the biblical text, just as most Christian and some Muslim scholars today do. They distinguish between myth, legend, and history in the biblical text. On the other hand, members of the traditional wing of Judaism believe every word in the text to be literally true, often in a historical sense, and take the scripture to have been transmitted to the prophets, beginning with Moses, by divine inspiration. In short, there are many opposing perspectives on the same events.

The earliest known reference to the Israelites by another people has been dated to roughly 1230 BCE. It was found on an Egyptian stela (monumental stone) inscribed with a hymn describing the victories of the Egyptian pharaoh Merneptah: 'Israel is laid waste, his seed is not' (Arnold and Beyer, 2002:160). Although the hieroglyph referring to Israel designates a migratory people rather than a nation with a land and fixed borders, the Hebrews were clearly recognized by their neighbours by the end of the thirteenth century BCE—the period of the Biblical book of *Judges*.

Creation in Genesis

The first eleven chapters of *Genesis* describe the primeval history of the universe. In Chapter 1 God creates heaven and earth. Interestingly, the text does not actually claim that the universe was created from nothing. What it says is that God created different things on each 'day' of creation, culminating with humanity, male and female, on the sixth day. On the seventh day God rests, establishing the pattern of a weekly Sabbath. Because the text describes the order of time as moving from evening to morning, Jews celebrate the Sabbath starting at sundown Friday night and ending at sundown on Saturday. This first creation story emphasizes that humans should never worship created objects like the sun, the moon, and the stars.

Chapter 2 of *Genesis* suggests a different beginning, with God causing a mist to rise from the ground, out of which vegetation sprouts. He plants a garden in Eden and populates it with animals and the primal human couple.

The Primal Couple

Genesis 2 ends with God's creation of man and woman. 'Adam' is the Hebrew word for 'man' in the sense of humanity, but here it is also used as the proper name of the individual created. Adam therefore connotes 'Everyman' in English. 'Eve', according to the biblical text and most interpreters, is derived from the word for 'living'.

In *Genesis* 2 Adam and Eve are naively innocent, standing without shame in their nakedness. It is only in *Genesis* 3—when, tempted by a snake, they defy God's order not to eat from Tree of the Knowledge of Good and Evil—that the peace and harmony of their existence is broken and they are expelled from the garden. Adam and Eve do not lack intelligence before they eat the forbidden fruit; what they lack is moral sense—the knowledge 'of Good and Evil'. In short, the story is about how humans learned to make moral distinctions.

The Eden story explains the conditions of human life through narrative rather than philosophical argument. Pain and evil have come about through human disobedience. Banished from the immediate presence of God, Adam and Eve must live at a distance from him, though God still shows loving care even while expelling them. The narrative purports to explain everything from why snakes crawl on the ground to why the sexes are different, why they feel sexual attraction to one another, why women have pain in childbirth, why we have to work for a living, why we wear clothes, and why we die. Some of these matters are natural, some are cultural, and some are ultimate issues of human existence. Explanatory myths of this kind are called etiological (from the Greek meaning 'cause' or 'reason').

Jewish interpretations of the Eden story are largely positive, emphasizing humans' moral capacity to choose good over evil and to obey God's laws. By contrast, the dominant Christian interpretation of the same material emphasizes inescapable 'original sin' and insists on a deep and sinister relationship between sexuality, evil, and death.

The Israelite Narratives

The first eleven chapters of *Genesis* provide the background that explains why God had to choose a specific people to convey his ideas to the human race. In this sequence of narratives, humans left free to follow their own conscience repeatedly fail to make the right choices. In fact, they so foul the earth with violence and corruption that God must destroy their evil society.

The story of the flood was virtually universal in the ancient Near East. In the dominant Mesopotamian accounts, the gods cause the flood because they are disturbed by the din of human life (some scholars have suggested that this story points to overpopulation). In the Hebrew version of the story, however, God acts to punish the evil that humans have perpetrated. In order to make a fresh start, God floods the earth, killing all its inhabitants except for the few that he has arranged to preserve aboard Noah's ark. Afterwards, God establishes his 'covenant' with the survivors, promising never again to destroy the earth by flood.

But human judgment is no better after the flood than before it. Within a few generations, the king of Babylon attempts to approach God's level by building a tower to heaven. God responds by confounding human language.

The Covenant

The central organizing concept in the Israelites' religion was the idea of the 'covenant' (*berith* in Hebrew): an agreement or contract specifying exactly what human behaviour is acceptable to God and giving a divine mandate to the Israelites' societal laws. The second covenant that God makes is with Abraham, who is introduced at the beginning of Chapter 12. God promises Abraham that his descendants will inhabit the land of Canaan. The Hebrews' own narratives make it clear that they knew the land was not originally theirs: they take it over from various groups already living there, whose behaviour they condemn as sinful. The Bible treats the Hebrews' right to possess the land as a promise from God. But it is not a free gift. Both parties to the covenant must live according to specific obligations.

The Hebrews' legendary ancestors—Abraham, his son Isaac and grandson Jacob, and finally Moses—are all pictured as making covenants with God. These legendary events parallel the ceremonial covenant-making of such historical figures as the Hebrew kings David, Solomon, and Josiah, and the scribe Ezra, each of whom re-enacted the covenant between themselves, their people, and their God.

The important benefits of offspring and homeland will accrue to the descendants of Abraham as long as they keep faith with God. Abraham himself is rewarded for his deep faith by being allowed to live into old age and be buried with his ancestors, but there is no suggestion of a reward after death. This society understands ultimate rewards in concrete terms: an easy death after a long and comfortable life, with many descendants to carry on afterward. Historical events are the result of God's intervention in response to the nation's behaviour.

In the shadow of Mount Sinai (Andrew Leyerle). There is no archaeological proof that this peak on Egypt's Sinai Peninsula is the one where Moses received the Ten Commandments, but it has been associated with the event since at least the fourth century.

Moses and the Exodus

The narratives of the patriarchs as national ancestors in *Genesis* are followed by a dramatic account in *Exodus* of Moses as leader and lawgiver. Whereas the patriarchs represent a migration from Mesopotamia into the land of Canaan, the traditional accounts of Moses place him at the head of a migration from the other centre of ancient Near Eastern civilization, Egypt. These two migrations seem historical and may in fact have overlapped, some of the Hebrew ancestors coming from the direction of Egypt via the Sinai Peninsula and others from the east and north, in the direction of Mesopotamia.

In any event, the compilers of the biblical text have put the two stories in strict chronological and historical sequence, using the Joseph narratives of *Genesis* 37–50 to send the descendants of Abraham to Egypt, from whence Moses will lead them into the promised land. The form in which the story is told emphasizes the linearity of Hebrew thought and its doggedly historical approach, in which God is seen as the author of every step in the sequence of events.

The Divine Name

Chapter 3 of *Exodus* relates an encounter that Moses has with God during a visit to the wilderness before his people's escape from Egypt. Moses sees a vision of God's presence as a flame in a bush that burns without being consumed. God then declares his identity as the God of the patriarchal lineage Abraham–Isaac–Jacob and gives his personal name, represented in Hebrew by the four letters YHWH. This name of God, the most holy of all, is sometimes referred to by the Greek term the Tetragrammaton.

No one today knows exactly what vowels are to be pronounced between those consonants, but the text of *Exodus* 3:14, 'I am who I am,' associates their meaning with the Hebrew verb *hayah*, 'to be'. Biblical scholars conventionally render the name 'Yahweh', partly because Hebrew personal names that incorporate it as a component often end in *-yahu*. Its original meaning may have been 'He who causes to be.' Thus 'I am who I am' may mean 'I am the one who causes things to happen'—'I am the author of all events.'

Over time, partly because of the commandment not to take God's name in vain, it became the practice not to pronounce the name at all. In traditional Judaism, to pronounce it was considered blasphemy. Without changing the Hebrew text, therefore, Jews reading aloud would either substitute *adonay*—a Hebrew word resembling the title 'Lord'—wherever the written text used 'YHWH', or respectfully alter the Hebrew word for God, 'Elohim', to 'Elokim'.

Other conventions have evolved over the centuries. Some Jews will not even write the four consonants, and simply use a double *y*, or *h* with an apostrophe. In spoken usage the Hebrew expression *ha-Shem*, 'the Name', is a frequent substitution. A further extension of piety found in Orthodox circles today is to avoid writing the term 'God' even in English, substituting 'G-d' or 'L-rd'.

The Exodus

The Hebrews in the Exodus story are working as labourers on Egyptian construction projects in the eastern part of the Nile Delta. The work amounts to slave labour, and God tells Moses to request their release from the pharaoh. When Pharaoh refuses, God sends plagues on the Egyptians but spares the Hebrews, and they are able to escape across the Yam Suf—literally, the 'Reed Sea', though it came to be known as the Red Sea. The sea swamps Pharaoh's pursuers, allowing the Hebrews to reach the barren Sinai Peninsula.

In time all Jewish people, whatever their individual origins, would come to identify with the Exodus as a metaphor of the transition from slavery to the status of a people with a destiny and a purpose. The Passover festival commemorates their participation in that historic event.

The Ten Commandments, found in *Exodus* 20:2–17 and again in *Deuteronomy* 5:6–21 (etymologically, 'Deuteronomy' means 'second law'), are stipulations of a covenant that all the people, not just the patriarchal ancestor, make a communal vow to obey. The foundations of Israelite ritual life can also be seen in the wilderness narratives. Moses' brother, Aaron, becomes the archetypal priest. In the absence of a permanent temple, worship is instituted in an elaborate tent called the Tabernacle. Kept in the Tabernacle as the central cult object is a chest called the Ark of the Covenant, which serves as the throne of God's invisible presence. But no image is placed on this base, for the Hebrews' God is not to be represented by any three-dimensional image. This prohibition marks a sharp contrast to the image-rich traditions of all the Hebrews' neighbours.

Box 2.1	The Ten Commandments, Exodus 20:2–17

I am the Lord your God who brought you out of Egypt, out of the land of slavery.

You shall have no other god to set against me.

You shall not make a carved image for yourself nor the likeness of anything in the heavens above, or on the earth below, or in the waters under the earth. You shall not bow down to them or worship them; for I, the Lord your God, am a jealous god. I punish the children for the sins of the fathers to the third and fourth generations of those who hate me. But I keep faith with thousands, with those who love me and keep my commandments.

You shall not make wrong use of the name of the Lord your God: The Lord will not leave unpunished the man who misuses his name.

Remember to keep the sabbath day holy. You have six days to labour and do all your work. But the seventh day is a sabbath of the Lord your God; that day you shall not do any work, you, your son or your daughter, your slave or your slave-girl, your cattle or the alien within your gates; for in six days the Lord made heaven and earth, the sea, and all that is in them, and on the seventh day he rested. Therefore the Lord blessed the sabbath day and declared it holy.

Honour your father and mother, that you may live long in the land which the Lord your God is giving you.

You shall not commit murder.

You shall not commit adultery.

You shall not steal.

You shall not give false evidence against your neighbour.

You shall not covet your neighbour's house; you shall not covet your neighbour's wife, his slave, his slave-girl, his ox, his ass, or anything that belongs to him.

The Israelite Kings

The Israelites proceed from nomadic to settled life under Moses' successors, beginning with Joshua. The book of *Joshua* recounts some spectacular conquests as the Israelites enter the land of Canaan. But the following book, *Judges*, suggests a less triumphant view.

The Canaanite civilization was well established and not easily displaced. The Israelites are even tempted to join the Canaanites in their worship of a fertility god named Ba'al. But Yahweh abhors the Canaanite religion, which includes ritual prostitution and child sacrifice. He demands that the Israelites keep apart from the Canaanites and repudiate their practices, promising them progeny and long life if they obey.

In this period the Israelites had a loose tribal confederation ruled by informal chieftains called *shofetim* (often translated as 'judges'). Their leadership was charismatic, meaning that it was based entirely on divine designation and popular acceptance, though their election was confirmed by the Shilonite priesthood. According to the book of *Judges*, each of these leaders—Deborah, Samson, Shamgar, Jephthah, Ehud, and many more—is chosen by God to save the Israelites from a specific threat of foreign domination.

The shift to a centralized monarchy took place over two generations shortly after 1000 BCE. Kingship was a new institution that emerged in response to the threats posed by the Philistines—a people of Aegean origins who arrived in the land of Israel at the same time as the Israelites and who had mastered the art of iron smelting, which gave them a great technological advantage over the latter. As the story is narrated in *1* and *2 Samuel*, God chooses first Saul, then David, and finally David's successors to preserve the Israelites from the Philistine menace.

We first meet David as a boy so young and inexperienced that he is fit only to look after the sheep. But God strengthens David's hand to the point that he is able to unify the Israelite people and defeat the Philistines. David captures the town of Jerusalem from the Jebusites and makes it his capital.

David is succeeded by Solomon—his son by Bathsheba, his favourite wife. Solomon builds a temple to Yahweh on a hill called **Zion**, on the northern side of Jerusalem (the identification of the hill on the southern side of the city as Mount Zion comes from a much later time) and undertakes a number of ambitious construction projects around the kingdom. But his emphasis on centralized government and his use of conscript labour alienate the ten northern tribes, leaving only the two southern tribes—Judah and Benjamin—in the kingdom of Judah, whose capital remained Jerusalem.

On Solomon's death, about 921 BCE, the kingdom broke up. The northern tribes, centred on Samaria, seceded and used the name Israel for themselves until they were overrun and dispersed by the Assyrians in 722 BCE, after which they were referred to as the 'ten lost tribes'. The southern tribes, centred on Jerusalem, called themselves Judah and continued until they were defeated by Babylonian invaders in 586 BCE.

The Composition of the Bible

For centuries, tradition attributed the composition of the first five books of the Bible to Moses, acting under divine inspiration or dictation. Faced with a discrepancy or difficulty in the received text, a traditional commentator would resolve the seeming contradiction by asking what God intended the text to mean. Modern scholars, by contrast, have tended to approach such problems from a different perspective, asking who would have chosen to make a particular statement, and why. From this perspective, discrepancies are not challenges to faith but clues for investigation. At the root of this approach is a theory, developed in the latter half of the nineteenth century, called the **documentary hypothesis**, which proposes that the Pentateuch is a composite text consisting of four major blocks.

The documentary hypothesis has been vehemently criticized by traditional Jews, Christians, and Muslims alike, who reject its humanizing assumptions. It has also been criticized by many liberal and radical scholars, who may share those assumptions but differ on the details of composition and compilation. Still, the broad outlines of the documentary hypothesis continue to shape much contemporary scholarship and serve as a basis for further exploration. In that sense, it stands as one of the great intellectual achievements of the nineteenth century.

But the early theory has needed continuous refinement. Nineteenth-century Bible scholars imagined individual persons writing specific documents at specific times. Now we know that the source materials originated with a variety of groups or institutions in the society—including the royal bureaucracy and the priesthood—and that in each case the process of composition continued in oral and written form over several generations.

For example, the material that uses the name 'Yahweh' is thought to be the product of an author (or school) called the Yahwist. This material is referred to as J, because in German—the language of the scholars who first suggested the hypothesis—the name Yahweh is spelled with a 'J'. The Yahwist, who emphasized southern localities and the role of Abraham, wrote in the southern kingdom of Judea, probably beginning before the division of the kingdoms late in the tenth century BCE.

The second source, E, is the work of an author or school termed the Elohist for its use of the generic term 'Elohim' to refer to God. E wrote in the northern kingdom after its separation, probably starting during the ninth century BCE, and emphasized northern local traditions. E's usage calls the sacred mountain Horeb, not Sinai; and refers to the people displaced by the Hebrews as Amorites rather than Canaanites. God is a more remote and figure for E than for J, and the covenant relationship is less nationalistic.

Nevertheless, the two strands, J and E, were woven together in many places. The result is a great Hebrew epic in a voice—JE—that can be recognized by its use of the term 'the LORD God' to speak of the divinity. The Garden of Eden story beginning in *Genesis* 2 is a good example of JE, whereas *Genesis* 1 represents a priestly prologue to the whole story.

During the reign of Josiah, in 621 BCE, a copy of the law was reportedly found in the course of repairs to the temple in Jerusalem (*2 Kings* 22:8). On the authority of that document, Israelite altars elsewhere were suppressed and worship was centralized at the Jerusalem temple for the first time. Since *Deuteronomy* 12:13 restricts worship to one location only, and since there is little sign of complaint in earlier times about the worship of Yahweh at many sites, it is assumed that the document found in Jerusalem was *Deuteronomy* and that it, the D source, was a new production.

Ostensibly *Deuteronomy* is a sermon by Moses, which would place its setting 600 years earlier. But its vocabulary and concerns are those of Josiah's day, when the prophet Jeremiah was active. Indeed, Moses speaks of himself as a prophet in *Deuteronomy* 18:15 and describes his role in terms typical of the prophetic movement as it existed in the eighth and seventh centuries BCE, but hardly earlier. Central to the D source is a rewards-and-punishments theology of national morality, not unlike that of the prophetic books.

In some ways the most striking aspect of the documentary hypothesis is its postulation of P, the priestly source, as a late contribution to the Pentateuchal corpus. Thought to come from 586–539 BCE—the period following the Babylonian invasion, when the Jerusalem temple was destroyed and the Judean leadership sent into exile—it includes detailed descriptions and measurements of the temple and its furnishings. As long as the temple stood, these details would not have been necessary; but with the temple in ruins, P offers a literary blueprint for its restoration. It is now clear that many of the P legal traditions predate *Deuteronomy*. We have to distinguish between the time when the P document was edited and the times when the traditions within it originated. Though priestly materials can be very old, they are the most recent additions to the document.

The Prophets

Alongside the echoes of priestly and legal voices in the Hebrew Bible there is another and perhaps even more important voice: that of the prophets. Since both Christianity and Islam also claim to be founded in prophetic insight, the prophetic movement may be said to have influenced more people than any other religious movement in human history.

The great prophetic books that constitute the section of the Bible called the *Prophets—Isaiah, Jeremiah,* and *Ezekiel,* along with *Amos, Hosea,* and *Micah*—date from about 750 BCE onwards. But the prophetic tradition began much earlier, in the period of Hebrew settlement of the land and during the early monarchy, with figures such as Micaiah ben Imlah, as well as Elijah and Elisha perhaps. Later ecstatic visions and utterances from God are recorded in the books of *Zachariah, Zephaniah, Joel, Habbakuk, Haggai, Obadiah, Malach,* and *Nahum.*

The Exile

In 586 BCE the Judean kingdom fell, Solomon's temple was razed, and the society's leaders were exiled to Babylonia. As much as any single event, the Exile marks the transition from the national cult of an ancient kingdom to the religious heritage of a widely dispersed people. From the sixth century BCE on, we speak of Jews (i.e., 'Judeans') and Judaism, rather than of Hebrews or Israelites and Hebrew or Israelite religion.

The transition did not happen overnight. But the Babylonian invasion disrupted many ancient Israelite institutions, while the Exile gave focus and impetus to a number of significant social and religious changes. The heritage was now more that of a subject or minority population than of a national state. Especially among Jews dispersed abroad, life became more urban than agricultural, so that many of the old agriculturally based laws and rituals needed to be rethought. At some time during the Exile, the institution known as the synagogue was born, and even after the ruined temple was rebuilt, three generations later, congregational life gained in emphasis over temple worship. Aramaic gradually replaced Hebrew as the vernacular language, moving Hebrew into a ritual and antiquarian role. Yearning for the restoration of Yahweh's sovereignty manifested itself in a variety of forms, including visions of a deliverer king (messianism) and an overhaul of the cosmos in battle and judgment at the end of the age (apocalyptic literature).

The destruction of the temple caused a crisis of confidence. The problem was not that Yahweh's dominion was limited to a particular region, for he was lord of all creation. It was that he had been worshipped in a single place for so long. Did the destruction of that building mean that Yahweh had abandoned his people? As the author of *Lamentations* 5:20–2 put the question:

> Why dost thou forget us for ever, why dost thou so long forsake us?
> Restore us to thyself, O LORD, that we may be restored! Renew our days
>   as of old!
> Or hast thou utterly rejected us? Art thou exceedingly angry with us?

The Second Commonwealth

In 538 BCE Cyrus the Persian conquered Babylon. Although the Israelites living there saw his victory over their oppressors as part of God's plan to bring a new order to the world (see *Ezra* 1:1; *Isaiah* 41:2, 44:28, 45:1), Cyrus saw himself as the champion of all the old gods and ancient regimes destroyed by the Babylonians. He allowed the traditional priesthood of Babylonia's god Marduk to practise their own religion. And he allowed the Jews who had been captive in Babylon to return home and re-establish their temple.

Not everyone wanted to return, however. Many prospering artisans and aristo-crats stayed behind in Babylon, where they laid the foundations of a community that was eventually to play a major role in the writing of the *Talmud*.

With prophetic rhetoric, a postexilic author of later chapters in *Isaiah* announced the theme of homecoming, declaring that God was about to deliver his people once again. A new heaven and a new earth would be created, and this new Israelite common-wealth marked a fresh beginning: 'Arise, shine; for your light has come, and the glory of the Lord has risen upon you' (*Isaiah* 60:1).

Isaiah's words are among the most stirring passages in the Bible. Unfortunately, archaeological evidence indicates that the conditions the former exiles returned to were far from glorious. In fact, the beginnings of the postexilic community, known as the 'second commonwealth', were so meagre that it is hard to reconstruct the events of that period.

The fate of the Davidic royal line is not known for certain. A Davidic king who adopted the Babylonian name Sin-Ab-Usuru (Sheshbazzar in Hebrew) arrived in Jerusalem shortly after the return began. But thereafter the descendants of David were called *nasi* ('prince') rather than *melekh* ('king'), perhaps in deference to the country's Persian rulers. Zerubbabel, another descendant of David, apparently arrived in Judea to succeed Sheshbazzar. The second temple was then completed in 515 BCE. After that, nei-ther Zerubbabel nor the kingship is mentioned again.

Ezra and Nehemiah, who established a stable government in Judea, went there as court officials of the Persian Empire. The dates of their administrations are not certain, but the government they set up was explicitly based on the covenantal formula used in the first temple period.

| Box 2.2 | Isaiah 2:2–4 |

In the days to come the mountain of the Lord's house shall be set over all other mountains, lifted high above the hills. All the nations shall come streaming to it, and many peoples shall come and say, 'Come, let us climb up on to the mountain of the Lord, to the house of the God of Jacob, that he may teach us his ways, and we may walk in his paths.' For [Torah] issues from Zion, and out of Jerusalem comes the word of the Lord; he will be judge between nations, arbiter among many peoples. They shall beat their swords into mattocks and their spears into pruning-knives; nation shall not lift sword against nation nor ever again be trained for war.

An inhabitant of this region, the former tribal territory of Judah, was known as a *yehudi*, a Judean. This is the source for the English word 'Jew'. Although the term did not gain its modern religious sense until the first and second centuries CE, when the New Testament was being written, ethnicity already had religious overtones in the Persian period.

In the absence of a king, most affairs of state were handled by the priests. This system is often described as a 'theocracy', but in fact God did not rule directly. Rather, the ruling priests claimed to be carrying out God's purposes, though some of them operated mainly as political bureaucrats.

The Torah became the foundation document of the nation in the second commonwealth period in somewhat the same way that the collected body of British law serves as Britain's constitution. However, the Hebrew constitution came complete with cosmogonic (world-constructing) myth, epic, and narrative history because of the conventions in which covenants were written.

The Hellenistic–Hasmonean Period (331 BCE–65 BCE)

The Persian Empire was conquered by Alexander the Great in 331 BCE. We call the age that followed 'Hellenistic' to distinguish it from the earlier Hellenic age of the city states in classical Greece (the word *hellenizo* in Greek means literally 'I speak Greek' or 'I learn to speak Greek'). Greek was adopted by many peoples of the eastern Mediterranean and remained the major language of trade even after the Romans moved into the region.

Yet the common culture of the period had little to do with the values of ancient Athens. Trade and cultural contact had fostered a cosmopolitan outlook that eroded the Judeans' formerly automatic assent to the traditions of their forefathers. Judaism had to evolve new ways of understanding and explaining itself. This was true especially for the members of the **Diaspora** (from the Greek for 'sowing of seed', hence 'dispersal'): the people living outside the ancient land of Israel, in the Mediterranean region and Mesopotamia, who now constituted the majority of Jews. The Jewish community of Alexandria in Egypt, for example, adopted Greek styles of architecture and dress as well as Greek names. By the early third century BCE, reading knowledge of Hebrew had become so rare that the Bible had to be translated into Greek. The **Septuagint** translation brought the Bible to a community with a new set of cultural expectations. Jews in Alexandria regarded their Greek Bible more as an object of meditation or literary study than as the covenant charter of the Hebrew state.

In the fourth century BCE the Greek philosopher Theophrastus described the Jews as 'a race of philosophers' because they 'discourse[d] on the divine . . . observe[d] the stars at night . . . and call[ed] to them in their prayers'. Not all pagan responses to Judaism were so positive, however. Most anti-Jewish comments by Greek and Roman writers in the Hellenistic period merely expressed a general dislike of foreigners. But in the case of Apion in the first century, xenophobia crossed the line into anti-Semitism. According to the first-century Jewish historian Flavius Josephus, Apion—a Hellenistic educator who wanted to keep Jews out of the great schools of Alexandria—had 'the effrontery' to claim that the Jews in Jerusalem worshipped a golden ass's head in the temple.

The Maccabean Revolt

Competition between two Greek dynasties descended from Alexander's generals, the Ptolemies of Egypt and the Seleucids of Syria, had an impact on the history of Judea. When Antiochus III the Great, who came to the Seleucid throne in 223 BCE, won a decisive victory over the Ptolemaic rulers of Egypt, control of ancient Israel passed from the Ptolemies to the Seleucids.

Identifying the Hebrews' Yahweh with the supreme god of the Hellenized world, the Seleucids transformed Jerusalem's temple into a cult place of Zeus in 168 BCE. Antiochus IV raided it for its riches, then moved troops into the temple area and suspended the local Torah constitution. He may not have intended specifically to crush the Judeans' religion; his motives may have been primarily economic and political. But from the Judeans' perspective any threat to their community amounted to an attack on their religion.

In 166 BCE a general revolt broke out, led by a group of resistance fighters called the Maccabees ('hammer', the Hebrew nickname for their leader Judah). Though its immediate objective was to expel the Seleucids, this action also reflected a dispute within the Jewish community between traditionalists and a faction that favoured assimilation to the new Hellenistic culture. In *1 Maccabees* the traditionalists accuse the Hellenizers of 'abandon[ing] themselves to evil ways': repudiating the covenant, intermarrying with gentiles, and 'remov[ing] their marks of circumcision'(*1 Maccabees* 1:11–15). The latter involved a painful plastic surgery, which could not have been undertaken lightly. This suggests that the motives of those who had their circumcisions reversed were not cosmetic but symbolic, signifying willful apostasy from the religion of the forefathers.

Those who favoured assimilation probably thought it would advance political and economic interests of Jerusalem. In the less Hellenized rural areas, however, they were seen as undermining the religious basis of Judean life and violating the Torah constitution. Worse yet, the main proponents of Hellenization were the priests.

The moderately traditionalist Maccabees prevailed, recapturing Jerusalem in 164 BCE. The rededication of the temple following its desecration by the Seleucids brought the divided community together and is commemorated in the minor holiday called Hanukkah (see p. 106 below). The Maccabees succeeded in restoring the Jewish state to its pre-exilic boundaries. Thereafter, however, the rebels set themselves up as client kings and readily adopted Hellenistic culture. Known as the Hasmonean dynasty, they ruled in shaky independence for more than a century, from 165 BCE until 64 BCE, when the Roman general Pompey took Jerusalem and brought Judea under the control of Rome.

First-Century Jewish Sects and Parties

Hellenistic society was not merely cosmopolitan but individualistic, and Hellenistic culture encouraged opposing concepts of truth. These qualities were reflected in Hellenistic Judaism, which comprised a variety of sects. Any attempt to impose a single orthodoxy would have led to wholesale defections, but accommodating diversity promoted stability. As in North American party politics today, power was effectively balanced between two major groups—the Sadducees and Pharisees—who together ran the Sanhedrin, a communal council with juridical functions. Representing the upper and middle classes respectively, both these groups faced challenges from two smaller, more radical sects: the Essenes and the Zealots.

Sadducees
The Sadducees represented the upper stratum of Judean society—the aristocracy that embraced Hellenization. The upper class both politically and occupationally, they were also the party of the priestly establishment. The temple was the centre of their power, and they read the laws literally. They also denied that there was life after death.

Pharisees
The Pharisees were the most popular sect, representing the middle classes. Some were landowners, some were skilled workers (tent-makers, carpenters, glass-blowers), and many were professional scribes serving the aristocratic Sadducees. From time to time the Pharisees also achieved power in the temple, but they were more at home in the synagogues of Judea.

In contrast to the Sadducees, the Pharisees were disposed to interpret the scriptural text broadly, and in time their influence came to prevail in the Sanhedrin. Unlike the more radical Essenes, however, the Pharisees tried to establish principles and procedures for scriptural interpretation—principles that would eventually be developed in the rabbinic period beginning around 200.The Pharisees were also punctilious about rules of purity and tithing, which distinguished members in good standing from the general populace. Special groups called *havuroth* ('brotherhoods') that formed among them were even more strict about these matters and preferred to live near their fellowship brothers within the general population. Disdaining the Sadducean priests as purely cultic functionaries, they considered themselves to be the proper custodians of the law.

The Christian writers of the New Testament, not surprisingly, were critical of the Pharisees, depicting them as hypocrites, more interested in the outward forms of ritual than in the inner substance of righteousness. From the Pharisees' own perspective, however, assigning priorities to the various commandments, and focusing on the intention with which they were observed, was a way of making the law humane and livable.

Essenes
Widely believed to have been the authors of the Dead Sea Scrolls—the collection of manuscripts from the Maccabean and early Roman period discovered in 1947 near the Dead Sea at Qumran—the Essenes were a group of rigorously observant priests under the leadership of a man they called the Teacher of Righteousness, or Righteous Teacher. When a candidate they disapproved of was appointed high priest, they left Jerusalem and retired to the desert. There they established a centre of priestly purity in preparation for what they believed to be the coming **apocalypse**: the final battle between the forces of darkness and light at the end of time.

Zealots
At the far end of the political spectrum were several groups that rejected Roman authority under any circumstances. Most of what we know about these groups comes from

Josephus, who from his perspective describes them as bandits. But in fact their motives appear to have been purely political.

The most famous of these revolutionaries were the Zealots (also known as the Fourth Philosophy), who came together expressly to liberate Judea from Roman control. John of Gischala was an important figure in this movement, from the beginning of the revolt in the northern region called Galilee, in 66 CE, until the final destruction of Jerusalem in 70, when he was captured. Eleazar ben Yair was another Zealot leader who oversaw the Jewish defence of the fortress **Masada**.

Masada was a natural high mesa near the Dead Sea, fitted out by Herod the Great as a self-sufficient fortified palace, which the Zealots captured from the Romans shortly after the Revolt began. It remained the almost impregnable headquarters for the Zealot movement until the rest of Judea had fallen. But after a four-year siege, it too was finally conquered in 73. Tradition says that when the Romans entered the fortress they found all the remaining defenders—men, women, and children—dead by their own hands. According to Josephus, Eleazar made a stirring speech, recommending death over slavery, before the Zealots' mass suicide:

> But since we had a generous hope that deluded us, as if we might perhaps have been able to avenge ourselves on our enemies . . . let us make haste to die bravely. Let us pity ourselves, our children, and our wives, while it is in our own power to show pity to them; for we were born to die, as well as those were whom we have begotten. . . . But certainly our hands are still at liberty, and have a sword in them. Let them then be subservient to us in our glorious design; let us die before we become slaves of our enemies, and let us go out of the world, together with our children, and our wives, in a state of freedom (Whiston 1802, 3:471–2).

The emergence of the Zealots upset the first-century Sadducee–Pharisee balance described above. The revolt against Rome left Jerusalem and the temple in ruins and also destroyed Qumran. It was from the ashes of these disasters that the rabbinic movement would emerge to carry on the traditions of Pharisaism.

Samaritans

Descendants of the northern Israelite tribes and the peoples who perhaps started mixing with them during the Assyrian period (eighth century BCE), Samaritans became distinguished from Jews by the Hellenistic period, in part by their corpus of scripture. They rejected the *Prophets* and *Writings* of the Hebrew Bible, accepting only the first five books of Moses as canonical. In addition, their version of the *Pentateuch* differs from the Hebrew Bible in that it contains several references to a messianic figure who is to be a prophet like Moses.

Christians

Christianity also began as a sect within Judaism, and it is the only Jewish sect of its day whose origins are well known. If we understand Christianity better by considering it as a first-century Jewish sect, then, we also understand the first-century Jewish sects better by considering Christianity as one of them.

The Christian message that, with repentance, all are equal before God was typical of all sectarian apocalypticism in first-century Judea. The Christian practices of public repentance, purification through baptism, and chaste communal living were likewise typical of the other contemporary apocalyptic groups. Yet these similarities only emphasize the striking difference between Christianity and Essenism, for example. Essenism was limited to a priestly elite and preoccupied with the cultic purity rules that allowed priests to approach God's holy places. Christianity, by contrast, was primarily interested in converting the distressed or sinful. This emphasis began in the teaching of John the Baptist, a Jewish apocalyptist opposed to the Herodian house.

Jewish Thought in the Hellenistic Period

The Concept of God

Contact with Greek culture challenged Judaism's concept of God. Most philosophical Greeks had already abandoned the traditional pantheistic cosmology (theory of the universe). Now they saw the universe as depending on a single principle (such as love, beauty, or the good) and regarded the traditional gods as allegorical figures representing the virtues. For the Greeks, change of any kind necessarily implied imperfection, and since creation implied change, the ultimate good could not be a creator. Rather, creation had to take place at some level below that of the divine, through the action of a semi-divine intermediary or 'demiurge'.

It was in this cultural context that Jews in the Hellenistic period tended to understand their Judaism. Under the influence of Greek thought, Jewish philosophers like Philo—a first-century Alexandrian whose views reflect those current among Hellenized Jews in Judea as well as the Diaspora—reasoned that there must be intermediaries of some kind to carry out Yahweh's actions on earth. For Philo, the principal mediator was the *logos*: a kind of instrumental divine intelligence.

The notion of the *logos* as an intermediary between the divine and the human was taken up by Christianity in the Gospel of John. It allowed Christians to present Jesus as having a double nature, divine and human at the same time. Modifying the Jewish conception of a unitary divinity to encompass both a son and a father, Christianity presented Judaism with the strongest theological challenge of the Hellenistic period.

At the same time Christians presented the Israelites with a competing claim for the role of God's chosen people—with a significant difference. Whereas Judaism emphasized the responsibility entailed by the covenant, Christianity emphasized the fulfillment of the promises made at Mount Sinai, without the obligation to obey the specific ordinances of Jewish law.

Resurrection for the Righteous

The Jewish Bible abounds in predictions about the fate of the world at the end of this age. It says virtually nothing about the fate of the individual at the end of his or her earthly existence.

Doctrine concerning the end of the age is termed '**eschatology**', from the Greek for 'study of the end'. A genre of Jewish literature that developed in the later prophetic books and flourished in the Hellenistic era is termed 'apocalyptic', from the Greek for 'unveiling' (the Latin equivalent is 'revelation'). Not only is most apocalyptic literature eschatological in nature, but it is visionary in its expression. Whereas the prophets claimed to report what Yahweh said, the apocalyptists were more likely to describe their own visions: 'I saw, and behold . . . '.

Regarding the individual, the ancient Hebrews were not preoccupied with an existence after death—perhaps in part because they made no strict distinction between body and soul. The original answer to the question of where personality goes after death was Sheol, an underground place (like the Greek Hades) where the person resides in greatly attenuated form. Sheol is not equivalent to heaven or hell; rather it is a pit, a place of weakness and estrangement from God, to which all the dead go and from which their spirits issue on the rare occasions when they can be seen on the earth. Occasionally, the psalmists and prophets appear to say that the righteous live in God's presence (*Psalm* 139:7–8, 11–12; *Psalm* 90:9–10, 12).

What mattered was not to continue as a spirit but to live on in one's descendants. We have seen that progeny were an important part of the covenant promise to Abraham. A litany of curses in *Psalm* 109:13 includes the wish that the adversary's line be blotted out. Nothing in the Hebrew Bible anticipates the idea of paradise or resurrection as a reward for a righteous life. There is no difference between humans and other animals in this respect. Consider *Ecclesiastes* 3:19: 'For the fate of the sons of men and the fate of beasts is the same; as one dies, so dies the other. They all have the same breath, and man has no advantage over the beasts; for all is vanity.'

On the other hand, Judaism did develop a doctrine of resurrection after death specifically for martyrs. The concept of martyrdom—choosing to die rather than renounce one's faith—appears to date from the Maccabean revolt (166 BCE). And the first indisputable reference to resurrection in biblical literature comes from the book of *Daniel*, which—although it is set during the Babylonian captivity—is now generally believed to have been written during the years of oppression leading to that revolt. *Daniel* 12:2 prophesies that

> many of those who sleep in the dust of the earth shall awake, some to everlasting life, and some to shame and everlasting contempt. And those who are wise shall shine like the brightness of the firmament; and those who turn many to righteousness, like the stars for ever and ever.

The Messiah

The term 'messiah' was originally used with reference to current kings, prophets, and priests. Like the doctrine of resurrection, the concept is one whose development can be located historically within the experience of Israel. As we have seen, in Hellenistic times the term 'messiah' came to mean an ideal king who is expected to arrive at some unspecified time in the future, to lead Israel to victory, demonstrating God's power and vindicating God's reputation.

A doctrine of the end-time—the belief in an end-purpose and plan to human life—appears in the biblical prophets, but in those books the end of time does not necessarily entail a messiah. The earliest apocalyptic writings, such as the book of *Daniel*, do not specify a messiah at all, rather suggesting that an angel (a military-style 'messenger') will lead the final battle against the wicked nations that have scorned the laws of God.

'Messiah' comes from the Hebrew *mashiah*, meaning 'anointed one' (anointing—pouring oil over the head—was a standard Hebrew ritual signifying divine sanction). Before the Exile, a few passages in the prophets express the expectation that God will raise up a king who will rule with justice and righteousness. The idea of an ideal king probably reflected experience with less-than-perfect rulers, as well as foreign influence. Still, as long as a Hebrew king reigned, he—not some future ideal king—was the anointed one. The expected king is sometimes called the son of David (*Isaiah* 11; *Ezekiel* 34; *Micah* 5) or the 'branch' (*Jeremiah* 23), a new shoot on the Davidic family tree.

It was during the Persian period after the Exile, when the last heir to the Davidic throne disappeared without a historical trace, that the idea of a future king took on a new significance. The promise, in *2 Samuel* 7, that Israel should never fail to have a king of the Davidic line became the foundation of hope for the line's restoration. Not until the advent of Christianity was there any suggestion that the messiah would suffer, let alone die, for humanity's sins. In fact, the messiah was the one expected finally to bring God's justice to the world. However supernatural his actions, then, the messiah was also a political figure.

The disastrous wars against Rome and the spread of Christianity made the rabbinic community wary of messianic movements, for they exposed the community to Roman retaliation. The rabbis told the people never to give up faith that the messiah would come, but they also advised that if one were ploughing a field and heard that the messiah had arrived, one should 'finish ploughing and then go to see whether the messiah has come'. Clearly, while it is important not to give up hoping for the messiah's arrival, it would be foolhardy to trust too easily in someone who could be fomenting rebellion or heresy.

Crystallization

The Rabbinic Movement

The collapse of Jerusalem in 70 marked a turning-point in Judaism comparable to the Exile of the sixth century BCE. Once again the temple was destroyed, and this time it was not rebuilt. Institutions and practices associated with temple worship—such as animal sacrifice—disappeared from Jewish life.

It fell to the Pharisees to preserve the Jewish tradition as the other principal first-century movements lost their bases of power. The temple that had been the centre of the Sadducees' power was no more; the Essenes' base at Qumran had been razed by the Romans on their way to besiege the desert fortress of Masada; and the Zealots had been wiped out. More than half a century later, a second attempt at independence, launched by Simon Bar Cochba in 132, also failed.

The Pharisees too disappeared. But Pharisaic traditions, refurbished and trans-formed for a new national purpose, lived on in the institutions of rabbinic Judaism. In a real way, the rabbis are successors of the Pharisees. Etymologically, the Hebrew term *rabbi* means 'great one', 'leader', or, as it appears to mean in the New Testament, 'master'. Later, it comes to have the implied sense of 'teacher', since the rabbis were legal special-ists and teachers, not ministers.

By the end of the second century the Romans had granted local autonomy in Galilee to the Jews and, in many cases, to the Jewish communities in major Roman cities. Tradition has it that while Jerusalem remained in ruins, Yochanan ben Zakkai received Rome's permission to move a circle or academy of rabbinical study down to the town of Yavneh near the Mediterranean coast. It was in Rome's interest to encourage the devel-opment of a unified Jewish authority in order to prevent further rebellion and guaran-tee the collection of taxes and duties.

The rabbinic movement was not a hereditary priesthood: anyone with the requi-site education was entitled to interpret the law. A man had only to study at the school-house, later called a **yeshiva** ('sitting', 'session'), and when he had completed his studies to the satisfaction of the teachers, he was ordained a rabbi.

The rabbis directed a new attention to religious observance in daily life, and in so doing provided the new structure that Jewish society needed if it was to survive the loss of the temple. By emphasizing formal laws, rituals, and rules of conduct, they gave the Jewish community a new way of living its part of the covenant with God. The sense of the sacred that had been concentrated in the temple, where sacrifice provided atonement with God, was relocated at the table of every Jew who observed the rules of purity, and the faithful found another means of reconciliation with God in performing good deeds or 'acts of lovingkindness'. At the same time, the rabbis' emphasis on close textual analy-sis ensured that the community's traditions were carefully recorded and preserved. The Judaism that we know today is founded on the Judaism practised by the early rabbis in late antiquity.

The Synagogue

The locus of public worship was no longer the temple but the synagogue (the Greek root means 'assembly' or 'gathering'—the congregation rather than the building). Jews con-tinued to pray three times a day, as dictated by the Bible and the conventions of temple service, and added special services in commemoration of the special services in the tem-ple. But Jewish worship never again revolved around a central temple. Nor was it restricted to synagogues: Jews may follow the traditional order of prayer at home or at work if no synagogue is available.

The first synagogues may have been established following the destruction of the first temple in 586 BCE. They certainly existed in the Diaspora, serving as places of assembly, study, and prayer for those without access to the second temple. After 70, many of the temple's functions and much of the liturgy were transferred there and aug-mented by prayers, poems, and psalms written by rabbinic Jews.

By the second and third centuries, synagogues were beginning to evolve the specific architecture that now characterizes them. The congregation prayed facing

A boy reads from a Torah scroll during his Bar Mitzvah at a synagogue in Jerusalem (Sherwood Burton/Ponkawonka.com).

Jerusalem, the site of the temple. Cut or painted in the wall in front of the worshippers was a niche in which the Torah was placed during the service. Thus most synagogues in Western countries today face east, and for prayer at home, many Jews mark the direction with a plaque reading '*Mizrah*' ('east' in Hebrew).

Eventually, the Torah niche became an elaborate piece of furniture: the holy ark permanently houses the Torah scrolls at the front of the synagogue. In later tradition there is a lamp above the ark, the *ner tamid* ('eternal lamp'), which is tended continuously in imitation of the lamps in the temple. Also part of synagogue architecture is the *bema* (Greek for 'rostrum'), from which the Torah is read. When placed in the centre of the congregation, this rostrum makes worship a kind of theatre in the round. When placed at the front with the ark containing the Torah, it forms a kind of stage.

The use of the seven-branched *menorah* ('candlestick' or 'lamp stand') in both ancient and modern synagogues dates back to the days of the temple (the nine-branched Hannukah menorahs have one branch for every night of the festival plus one to light the others.).

Scripture and Commentary

After the biblical corpus became fixed or closed, it continued to be the subject of commentary in the early centuries CE. The rabbis collected and added to a growing body of

Bible commentary known as *midrash* ('interpretation'). Most Midrashic commentaries are line-by-line interpretations following the sequence of the biblical text, although they may also be ordered by the lectionary cycle (the weekly schedule of biblical readings) traditionally used in the synagogue.

The early *midrashim* contain a great many legal discussions. In the first and second centuries the Pharisees made imaginative use of exegetic principles to derive rulings about contemporary customs from the written text of the Bible. Then they claimed that their interpretations reflected oral traditions passed down from the very beginning.

These few books—the *Mekhilta* for *Exodus*, and *Sifra* for *Leviticus*, and *Sifre* for *Numbers* and *Deuteronomy*—contain a wealth of information about the contexts in which the legal discussions were held. But the process of commenting continued for several centuries before the books were published separately, and as a result the dating of some traditions has been open to dispute. The rabbinic writers of *midrash* took it as their task not to write the Bible— they considered its text unalterable—but rather to understand the significance of what the text contained. Often with remarkable ingenuity, they attempted to resolve contradictions implicit in particular biblical narratives or between one biblical passage and another.

The Mishnah

A major achievement in the rabbis' restructuring of the religion was their elaboration of the heritage of law. Forms that had been passed down orally by the Pharisees were now ordered and codified in writing. This basic literature of rabbinic Judaism consisted of first the *Mishnah* and then the *Talmud*.

As was noted above, rabbinic biblical commentary follows the sequence and structure of books already extant in the Hebrew canon at the end of the first century. By contrast, the *Mishnah* was a new production with its own topical arrangement. It is organized in six 'orders' or divisions: Seeds (agriculture), Festivals, Women, Damages (torts), Holy Things (ritual), and Purifications. The *Mishnah* summarizes the application of the traditional law as the Pharisaic–rabbinic movement interpreted it. It is the oldest datable rabbinic document, having been produced shortly before 220 by Rabbi Judah, who was known as ha-Nasi ('the prince'). Although the *Mishnah* of Rabbi Judah the Prince is highly honoured and is quoted as authoritative, it is not the only repository of the commentary produced by the early rabbis (often called the **Tannaim**—Aramaic for 'repeaters' or 'teachers'). Alternative Tannaitic traditions are also found in a book called the *Tosefta* (Aramaic for 'addition'), and they provide precedents of equal value in rabbinic discussions.

Claims for the authoritative nature of the *Mishnah* were based on the notion of the 'oral law'—the idea that, alongside the five books traditionally ascribed to Moses, there was another body of precedent and interpretation that had been passed down from Moses in a direct line of oral tradition. This doctrine allowed the rabbis to claim that their own interpretations were just as authoritative as the doctrines written explicitly in the Torah.

The development of Pharisaic traditions is reflected in two first-century schools of interpretation, one led by Hillel and the other by his contemporary Shammai. The earliest stages may well have involved the codification of laws on the issues of greatest interest to the Pharisees—Sabbath law, purity, and tithing. However, the early rabbis also paid close attention to marriage and divorce, for rules of personal status contributed to the definition of membership in the Jewish community.

The Talmud

By about 200, the formerly open and growing body of interpretation claimed by the Pharisees to have come orally from Moses had, like the Bible, become a fixed, written text. And, like the Bible, the *Mishnah* of Rabbi Judah now became the subject of passage-by-passage commentary. The structure of the *Mishnah* in its six orders, subdivided into a total of 63 tractates (treatises), became the skeleton around which developed a very large body of commentary known as the *Talmud*.

There is one *Mishnah* and it is about the length of a desk dictionary. Commenting on the *Mishnah* are two different *Talmud*s, each closer to the size of a multi-volume encyclopedia. Each *Talmud* consists of the Hebrew *Mishnah* of Rabbi Judah together with one of the two bodies of commentary, known as a *gemarah* (plural *gemaroth*, 'completion').

One *gemarah* is from the Jewish community living in the land of Israel, the other from the Jewish community living in Babylonia. The *Mishnah* and the Palestinian *Gemarah* form the *Palestinian Talmud*; this material is also often referred to as the *Jerusalem Talmud*, though it was likely produced in the Galilee area of northern Palestine, not in Jerusalem. The same *Mishnah* and the other *Gemarah*, produced in Babylonia, form the *Babylonian Talmud*.

The *Mishnah* is in Hebrew, which was a language of the past, of tradition, liturgy, and scholarly study, just as Church Latin became for Christians in the European Middle Ages. The *gemaroth*, by contrast, are in Aramaic, the vernacular of the day. Typically, the text of the *Talmud* starts with a short passage from the *Mishnah* and then continues with the text of the related *Gemarah*, which could be many times longer. The nature of the commentary tradition is graphically evident in printed editions such as the standard Vilna edition of 1880-6, in which the *Mishnah* and *gemarah* appear in a narrow column in the centre of the page, with columns on either side carrying later additions, later commentaries, and various other study aids like cross-references.

The Palestinian or *Jerusalem Talmud* is an interesting source of historical records, lore, and tradition in Judaism at a time when the situation of its producers was deteriorating. Not only was the economy in decline, but—worse for Jews—the Roman Empire was in the process of Christianization; discriminatory laws were being enacted; and about 425, the Christian emperor Theodosius II abolished the office of the patriarch, the head of the leading Palestinian academy.

Meanwhile in Babylonia the ruling Sasanian Persians (224–641 CE) were more tolerant of the Jewish community. The legal discussions in the *Babylonian Talmud* were more incisive than their Palestinian counterparts, and it became the authoritative version for the Babylonian Jews. In the seventh century Muslims succeeded the Sasanians as rulers of the Mesopotamian or Babylonian region, which they called Iraq.

At first Palestine was in charge of the ritual calendar. Only Palestine had the authority to declare the arrival of a new month (determined by direct observation of the moon), and it then transmitted this information to other lands by a system of signal fires, runners, and rams' horns. Once the calendar came to be calculated mathematically, however, the Babylonian community embarked on an independent ritual life. This change formalized the primacy of the Babylonian Talmudic academies, which had been gaining in talent and prestige for generations.

The *Gemarah* records the arguments of more than 2,000 sages concerning specific ways to resolve issues by referring to the *Mishnah*. In contrast to the ordered discussion of the *Mishnah*, the discussions of the *Gemarah* are quite complex and far-ranging, indeed often free-associational. Even so, the text is written in a kind of Aramaic shorthand that uses brief technical terms to signal the formal characteristics of the specific arguments that are about to be mounted.

Since the text of the *Mishnah*, the core of the *Talmud*, is a document of law, a considerable amount of the *Gemarah* is strictly legal. Sometimes a legal discussion ends with a specific prescription, called a *halakha* ('the way' or 'procedure'; more specifically, the proper legal procedure for living life). For this reason, any legal discussion can be loosely described as halakhic.

There is another style of discussion that is more anecdotal; it is referred to as *aggada* ('narrative'). Whereas *halakha* is characterized by legal analysis and explicit directives, *aggada* teaches a moral lesson by telling a story.

Jews conventionally regard the *halakha* of the *Talmud* and the *aggada* of the *Midrash* as two separate genres, but both collections contain both kinds of teachings, though in vastly different proportions. As a result, the terms *halakha* and *aggada* may be used to refer to either a particular type of teaching (legal or narrative/anecdotal) or the particular text (*Talmud* or *Midrash*) dominated by each type.

The Status of Torah

The same elasticity of definition characterizes rabbinic and Jewish understandings of the term *torah*. At the time of the first temple, *torah* apparently referred only to laws governing priestly behaviour. Starting with the book of *Deuteronomy*, however, it was used to refer first to a written book of law, and then to all five books of the *Pentateuch*.

In biblical times books were written on scrolls. This form has been retained for the copy of the sacred text used in synagogues. Called a *sefer Torah* ('book of the Torah'), it is written by hand on parchment and mounted on wooden rollers. For private study one would use a copy of the *Pentateuch* bound as a book (the form that replaced scrolls in late antiquity). That is called a *Humash*, from the Hebrew word for 'five'.

In an extended sense, the Torah is the entire Hebrew Bible or *Tanakh*: an acronym for 'Torah', *Nebi'im* (prophets), and *Ketuvim* (sacred writings). And even the books of the oral law—*Midrash*, *Mishnah*, and *Talmud*—can be called Torah. That is because every discussion of holy law and procedure, whether moral, ritual, or ceremonial, was considered part of the same divine revelation, continuing over the millennia. Thus 'Torah' can refer to any revelatory or canonical literature. In rabbinic parlance, the *Talmud* and later commentaries on it, produced by various experts in various lands over the centuries, are part of Torah, although they are also called *Torah she ba'al peh*, 'oral Torah'.

The study of Torah continued unabated as the *Talmud* was completed. The two principal rabbinic academies of Babylonia, in the towns of Sura and Pumbeditha, were the intellectual centre of the Jewish world from the fourth to the ninth centuries and even after. There the leader of the yeshiva, known by the honorific term **gaon** ('excellency'), often enjoyed greater power and respect than the ostensible head of the Jewish community, the exilarch. This was because the *gaon* supervised the legal interpretation that constituted the principal locus of authority for most Jews.

Further Development of Jewish Law

With the *Talmud* compiled and undergoing no further additions by the seventh century, the ongoing development of Jewish law took three principal forms: passage-by-passage commentary on the Talmudic text, which now included the *Gemarah* as well as the *Mishnah*; rabbinic rulings on specific questions; and the development of legal codes. Perhaps the most famous commentator on the *Talmud* was Rabbi Shlomo ben Yitzhak (1040–1105) of Troyes, north of Paris. As is common with rabbinic writers, he is known by the acronym of his title and name: Rashi (R–Sh–Y). His commentaries are invaluable aids to understanding the simple sense of difficult passages. (Rashi also wrote biblical commentaries that are landmarks in the history of Jewish scriptural interpretation. Because he often translated difficult words into medieval French, Rashi is also consulted by scholars of French language and literature for his evidence on eleventh-century French.)

In addition, great lights among the various rabbis commented on individual problems in the *Talmud*. A selection of these later annotations appears on a printed *Talmud* page. They are known as *Tosafot* (Hebrew for 'additions' or 'footnotes') and are not to be confused with the *Tosefta* (Aramaic for 'the Addition'), the early third-century collection of the sayings of the first rabbis, the Tannaim, which accompanies the *Mishnah*.

The second form of development, the corpus of rabbinical rulings, took shape as individual communities wrote to the acknowledged experts of their time for advice on specific issues. This *Teshuvah* ('return', i.e., response) literature, which always took the form of a public letter, is also known as **responsa** (Latin for 'answers'; singular, *responsum*) literature. Orthodox rabbis today still issue *responsa* and are often called on to extend Talmudic reasoning to questions on issues raised by modern technology, such as the use of birth control and new medical procedures.

Finally, the law codes developed in the medieval period served to clarify complicated legal material and explain what had been done in similar situations. Two influential medieval codes were the **Mishneh Torah** ('A Copy of the Torah') of Moses Maimonides (1135–1204; see p. 93) and the *Arba'a Turim* ('Four Rows') of Jacob ben Asher (1269?–1340?). Following the outline of that work, Joseph Karo (1488–1575), a Spanish Jew living in Palestine, brought diverse legal opinions together in a massive compilation entitled *Bet Yosef* ('House of Joseph'), which he condensed in 1565 under the title *Shulhan Arukh* ('Spread Table', an allusion to *Psalm* 23). Omitting the intricacies of legal discussion in the original work, the *Shulhan Arukh* is still used today as a guide to the simplest and most practical ways of carrying out the Torah's instructions.

Applying Legal Principles

Originally the civil law of the Israelites, the Torah became the religious law of rabbinic Judaism, the guide to moral conduct for Jews far removed in space and time from the ancient state. For such a law to remain relevant, a healthy tradition of study and commentary was essential.

Rabbinic Judaism emphasized the fatherhood of God and the brotherhood of Israel under God's revealed law. It gave enormous emphasis to proper ethical conduct. In detailing Jewish law, the rabbis were outlining an ethical program for Jews. The tradition called for numerous specific actions of both a ritual and a moral nature, but the basic approach was to analyze each situation to determine proper conduct. Since no two circumstances were fully identical, study of the *Talmud* essentially meant learning how to analyze every situation as minutely as possible and from every conceivable perspective.

'An eye for an eye, a tooth for a tooth' says the book of *Exodus*, implying a principle of rigorous compensation for damages. As harsh as this sounds today, it may have been unusually humane in the second millennium BCE: in other cultures at that time, a serf who injured his master might well be put to death. 'An eye for an eye' limits punishment to the extent of the injury. By the rabbinic period, however, this principle was considered too severe—what the Romans called a *lex talionis* ('law of retaliation'). After very little debate, the rabbis concluded that the Bible meant to limit compensation to the payment of a financial price for the victim's loss.

For centuries Jewish exegetes have applied the principles of Torah to contemporary problems. In the Hellenistic period, for instance, many people were reluctant to lend money when a sabbatical year (the year fields lie fallow) was approaching, for fear that they would lose their capital. Even though the Torah does not speak specifically about this problem, the rabbis were confident that the solution could be found in scripture. In this case the answer was derived from the principle (attributed to Hillel) of *takkanah* ('remediation'), which lets the court itself take over debts for the sabbatical year. Thus lenders could feel confident that they would recover their principal, and debtors could arrange the loans they needed.

Rabbinic law was hardly unanimous or monolithic. For example, it offers no single answer on whether a woman may seek an abortion. The biblical precedent is found in *Exodus*, where a rule on accidental miscarriage is stated: 'When men fight, and one of them pushes a pregnant woman and a miscarriage results, but no other damage ensues, the one responsible shall be fined according as the woman's husband may exact from him, the payment to be based on reckoning' (*Exodus* 21:22). Rabbinic interpretation takes this to mean that the destruction of a fetus is a tort but is not in itself a capital crime. If the life of a mother is endangered, it is certainly permissible to abort the pregnancy.

Whether a particular abortion may be performed, however, depends on subtle distinctions in rabbinic law. To avoid any danger of overstepping the rules, many Jews would never perform an abortion. Others would do so only if the mother faces an acute physical emergency. Still others, interpreting more broadly, might perform an abortion for a woman who reports that she is psychologically unfit for motherhood. Reform Jews would say that, although it is important to consult the rabbinic opinions of the past, those opinions are not automatically binding on contemporary life. They might extend one principle or another discussed by the rabbis, coming to a decision that is never actually attested by rabbinic opinion and justifying their decision on the basis of what a rabbi operating under similar principles might do today.

Purity and Community

Some of the most arcane laws of the Torah involve ritual purity. When the rabbis turned their attention to these, they were codifying a complex symbolic system. Purity laws have been viewed in modern times as serving a hygienic purpose for primitive societies, because they tend to prohibit the eating of harmful substances, such as corpses or human excreta. Sometimes, however, completely harmless substances are taboo, while harmful ones are central to ritual events. Similarly, Hebrew rules do not always have obvious medical value.

Hebrew society, like many non-Western societies, had a series of food taboos. Of these the best known is the commandment not to eat the meat from pigs (pork, ham, bacon), or even to touch it. Others included not eating blood or predatory birds or mammals. Shellfish such as clams, shrimp, and lobsters are also prohibited.

One rabbinic ruling forbids eating meat and milk together, but this prohibition is not biblical. What the Bible says is not to eat a young goat boiled in its mother's milk; it says nothing about keeping meat and milk strictly separate. The rabbis introduced this rule as a safeguard against violating the biblical injunction. This illustrates what the rabbis described as 'making a fence around the Torah': establishing rules to prevent inadvertent violations.

Another series of rulings rooted in the Bible forbade contact with various polluting substances—corpses, reptiles, menstrual blood, or semen. Touching these substances was not a sin in itself, for people regularly come into contact with them in the normal course of life. On the other hand, the product of such contact was uncleanness, which had to be removed by a visit to a *mikveh*, a ritual bathhouse, where a total-immersion baptism was performed regularly for the purpose of purification. These purity laws prevented husband and wife from engaging in sexual intercourse for approximately the first two weeks of every menstrual cycle, and a ritual immersion was required for both each time they had intercourse thereafter. In Orthodox Judaism women and men still visit ritual baths to ensure family purity.

Purity laws were symbolic boundary markers. They separated the ritually pure from the less pious, and Jews from the host society, imposing a high degree of group coherence. Although Jews were permitted to eat with gentiles, the proliferation of dietary and purity laws tended to limit contact.

In biblical society, the priests who served at the temple in Jerusalem came from a special class that maintained a high degree of ritual purity. But there was no need for a ritually pure priesthood once the temple had been destroyed. Instead, maintaining ritual purity became a personal obligation for every member of the Jewish community in its priestly role among the nations of the world.

Repentance

The rabbis put great emphasis on the concepts of forgiveness and repentance. But they did not design a 'scoreboard' religion in which good deeds could be totalled against bad. Rather, they constantly preached that repentance (Hebrew *teshuvah*, literally 'turning' or 'returning') is the purpose of human life, which it is supremely able to transform.

Everyone is asked to imagine his or her life as constantly balanced between good and evil deeds. Thus everyone constantly needs to repent in order to be received by God.

The rabbis even suggested that without repentance, rites of atonement amount to nothing more than attempts at magic. Although sacrifices were offered in the temple, and the holiday of Yom Kippur granted atonement for communal sin, no ritual could be effective unless there was sincere repentance on the part of each person.

There are several stages to repentance. First, the person admits to having done wrong. The rabbis acknowledged that most sin is not committed deliberately by evil people. Rather, it is committed by people who know right from wrong and seek to do the right, but who tend to rationalize their behaviour and fail to recognize the evil of their ways.

The next stage in repentance should be true and honest sorrow for the action. One must promise never to repeat the sin and take steps to fulfill that undertaking. But feeling sad and promising to change one's behaviour is not enough. Repentance also requires appropriate compensation for anyone whom one has injured.

If God forgives the sincere penitent, humans should do the same. A person who has suffered damages from another may seek repentance and restitution, but thereafter is obliged to respond with forgiveness. One must seek the forgiveness of the person one has wronged, and if the wrongdoer is sincerely penitent the person wronged must not unfairly withhold forgiveness. Only then—when forgiveness and restitution have been accomplished—may the sinner expect that God will accept the repentance offered on Yom Kippur, the annual Day of Atonement.

Some damage cannot be repaired. In the case of murder, for example, nothing can bring back the life of the victim. Therefore compensation may require the death of the perpetrator. A murderer who truly repents and is willing to accept death may enter God's presence as a forgiven sinner. Although the rabbis had no authority to impose the death penalty, the Bible clearly prescribed it for murder, and therefore they had to admit capital punishment as a possibility. But they imposed so many legal strictures on capital punishment that there was virtually never a situation sufficiently clear-cut to justify the death penalty. The rabbis developed a very sophisticated notion of intention or *kavvanah*. Just as English common law recognizes several degrees of intention in murder cases, the rabbis recognized that to understand the significance of any action, subtle differences in intention must be recognized. In practice, to find someone guilty of murder, they usually require a degree of intentionality that would be very difficult to prove in court under open testimony. Ultimately, because the rabbis believe that God knows the intentions of every human and is present at any action, they leave it to him to find an equitable solution. Thus even if lack of evidence makes it impossible for human justice to sentence someone to death, the rabbis assume that God will ensure the correct punishment is administered. God will punish the wrongdoer, and human courts have no business intervening.

This leads us to a subtle but important distinction. Although rabbinic law resembles a national law code, covering civil and criminal situations, it is distinctive in that it assumes God to be a participant throughout the process. Thus rabbinic literature may express a religious law, but there is nothing legalistic about rabbinic literature. It might be more accurately described as a very theological system of law.

Commandments for Jews and Gentiles

Rabbinic thought had a clear notion of the Torah, both written and oral, as God's distinctive gift to the Jews. The next logical question for the rabbis to answer was what God intended for the gentile nations (in Hebrew, *goyim*). Did they have privileges and responsibilities in a divine plan? By what standards should their conduct be judged?

In the biblical account, Yahweh's transactions with Abraham and Moses establish specific privileges and responsibilities for the people of Israel. The Ten Commandments given to Moses are at the heart of the law, but, in the classic rabbinic interpretation of Torah, the people Israel must also obey the 613 commandments (*mitzvoth*) given orally at Sinai. (The number is conventional; the rabbis of the Middle Ages delighted in enumerating exactly 613 of them.)

Before the covenant with Abraham and the formation of a distinct Israelite people, however, God had already made a covenant with Noah after the primeval flood, a covenant sealed with the rainbow. The rabbis linked the salvation of the gentiles explicitly to this covenant, in which God promised mercy and deliverance to all humanity. The rabbis saw God as giving the non-Israelite nations a set of specific laws prohibiting blasphemy, idolatry, bloodshed, incest, theft, and the eating of flesh from living animals (often added to these is recognition of the true God). In medieval Judaism these Noahide Commandments were used to understand God's plan for Christianity and Islam—newer religions seemingly founded on biblical and Jewish principles.

The rabbis came to acknowledge Islam as consonant with the intent of the Noachic commandments because of Islam's strict monotheism and its prohibition of images. They took the same position on Christianity, even though they thought that the Christian veneration of images came dangerously close to idolatry. The rabbinic justification was that

---

| Box 2.3 | **The Rabbis on Gentiles in the World to Come**

The rabbis argued over the status of gentiles, but eventually decided that the righteous of all nations have a place in the world to come.

Rabbi Eliezer said: 'All the nations will have no share in the world to come, even as it is said, "The wicked shall go into Sheol, and all the nations that forget God" [Psalm 9:17]. The wicked shall go into Sheol—these are the wicked among Israel.' Rabbi Joshua said to him: 'If the verse had said, "The wicked shall go into Sheol with all the nations," and had stopped there, I should have agreed with you, but as it goes on to say "who forget God," it means there are righteous men among the nations who have a share in the world to come' (Tosefta Sanhedrin 13:2).

Rabbi Jeremiah said: 'Whence can you know that the gentile that practises the law is equal to the high priest? Because it is said, "which, if a man do, he shall live through them" [Leviticus 18:5]. And it says, "This is the Torah of man" [2 Samuel 7:19]. It does not say, "the law of the priests, Levites, Israelites," but "This is the law of man, O Lord God." And it does not say, "Open the gates and let the priests and Levites and Israel enter," but it says: "Open the gates that the righteous may enter" [Isaiah 26:2]. And it says, "This is the gate of the Lord, the righteous shall enter it." It does not say, "The priests and the Levites and Israel shall enter it," but it says, "The righteous shall enter it" [Psalm 118:20]. And it does not say, "Rejoice ye, priests, Levites, and Israelites," but it says, "Rejoice ye righteous" [Psalm 33:1]. And it does not say, "Do good, O Lord, to the priests and the Levites and the Israelites," but it says, "Do good, O Lord, to the good" [Psalm 124:4]. So even a gentile, if he practises the Torah, is equal to the high priest (Sifra 86b; b. Baba Kamma 38a).

Christians worshipped the same God as Jews and Muslims. Although it is forbidden for Jews to worship the one God with images, it was not forbidden for gentiles.

Jews accept converts to Judaism willingly. But they do not believe that conversion is necessary, since salvation is available to all righteous people. Rather, conversion is reserved for those who want to join their fate with that of the people Israel.

Differentiation

The Medieval Period

European and Eastern Judaism

The Jews of the premodern world were divided geographically into two groups: Sephardim to the south, in the Mediterranean region, and Ashkenazim to the north, in central and eastern Europe.

By the medieval period Sepharad was identified with Spain, which with Portugal became the centre of Sephardic intellectual life. European Jewish settlement in the New World began with Sephardim from Spain, Portugal, and Italy, the pioneering lands of exploration and colonial empire-building. There have also been important Sephardic centres in Italy and the Turkish Empire, and Jews from Morocco to Iraq and the Yemen are also included among the Sephardim.

Ashkenaz was identified with Germany. The Ashkenazim include the Jews of Germany, Poland, Hungary, Romania, and Russia. Over the centuries, some also settled in France and England, and many Ashkenazim from across Europe eventually migrated to North America. Living as a minority under Christian domination, all Ashkenazim were subject to treatment that varied from ignorance and insensitivity at best to repression and persecution.

Medieval Jewish Philosophy

Medieval Jewish philosophy flourished primarily in Muslim-controlled lands, where intellectual life was deeply influenced by Greek philosophy.

Saadia
The earliest notable Jewish philosopher of the medieval period was Saadia (882–942), who became the *gaon* or principal of the major rabbinic academy of Sura in Babylonia. He translated the Hebrew Bible into Arabic and defended rabbinic Judaism against the Karaites—a popular movement that held only the Bible to be authoritative and rejected the *Talmud*.

Saadia's most important philosophical work was *The Book of Beliefs and Opinions* (*Sefer Emunoth veDeoth*), in which he maintained that Judaism alone is the divinely revealed truth. Although human beings have the inherent power to derive truth by means of their rational faculties, revelation is a gift from God that shortens the time needed to reason out a moral or cosmological problem. Thus revelation and reason are in complete agreement, but revelation is preferable.

Yehuda Ha-Levi

Yehuda Ha-Levi (1075–1141) was born in the Spanish city of Toledo shortly after it had fallen under Christian control. He is known for his poetry as well as his philosophy. His prose work *The Kuzari* was based on a famous legend according to which the Khazars, a Tatar people living near the Caspian Sea, had converted to Judaism sometime in the eighth century. In Ha-Levi's version of the story, the conversion of the Khazars takes place after the monarch has listened to representatives of the three great religions—Islam, Christianity, and Judaism. Ha-Levi suggests that both Islam and Christianity are appropriate preparatory faiths for naïve nations. When the nations of the world mature in their faith, they will be ready for Judaism.

Maimonides

Moses Maimonides, or Moses ben Maimon, was born in Córdoba, Spain, in 1135, lived in Egypt, and is by all accounts the most famous and most impressive of all Jewish philosophers. In religious texts he is usually known as 'Rambam': R–M–B–M, the acronym of 'Rabbi Moses ben Maimon'.

Maimonides was thirteen when the Almohads, a Muslim fundamentalist group from North Africa, took control in Spain. He fled to Morocco and then to Palestine, which was under the control of the European Crusaders, and finally to Egypt, where he found employment, and the freedom to practise his religion, as the court physician for the Muslim sultan Salah al-Din (Saladin). In that connection he wrote several important medical treatises.

Maimonides' accomplishments were truly prodigious. He wrote the famous code of Jewish law, *Mishneh Torah*, in Hebrew. He also wrote a treatise on logic and several *responsa* advising Jewish communities around the world on matters such as false conversion, the concept of resurrection, and the arrival of the messiah. His most important philosophical treatise, *The Guide of the Perplexed*, was composed in Arabic rather than Hebrew—perhaps to mark a broadening of his concern from technical issues in Judaism to religious thought generally—but it was quickly translated into Hebrew. Ostensibly a letter of advice to a single student, the *Guide* was aimed at the considerable number of cosmopolitan and philosophically sophisticated Jews who had begun to question the truth of their own religion.

Maimonides had a deep knowledge of Aristotelianism, which put him at the forefront of the intellectual life of his day. It afforded more scope than Judaism did for analytic observation of physical phenomena and human behaviour, but was suspect because it offered a more mechanistic explanation of the universe. Provisionally accepting Aristotle's principles of physics for the purpose of proving the existence of God, Maimonides set out to demonstrate that the world is God's free creation out of nothing, as he thought the Bible maintains. Opposing the Platonist view of the world as an eternal and necessary emanation of God through the heavenly spheres, Maimonides suggested that when one believes the Bible, one needs no further proof, but he used Greek philosophy to show that biblical religion is true.

Rambam's greatest contribution was his effort to resolve the tension between faith and knowledge. He saw no contradiction between reason and revelation. Like most Jewish philosophers before him, he suggested that the Bible speaks a special analogical and metaphoric language and is not to be taken literally where it appears to say something unflattering or untrue about God. The Bible's anthropomorphisms—characterizations of the divine with human forms and feelings—are meant to be systematically reinterpreted as allegory.

Indeed, he tried to demonstrate that the revelations of the prophets represent the perfection of both the intellectual and imaginative faculties, since the prophets received their truths as visions. For Maimonides, the commandments were all rational in principle, even if humans could not understand the reasoning behind them.

The last part of *The Guide of the Perplexed* discusses the meaning of the commandments and also tackles difficult questions regarding God's providence. How can God's sovereignty be perfect if individual humans have free choice? The rabbis were content to recognize the paradox and express it in formulations such as 'All is foreseen yet free will is given', or 'All is in the hands of heaven except for the fear of heaven', meaning that God controls everything except individual humans' responses to him. Maimonides asked the question about divine providence in a traditional scholastic way: 'How far does God's knowledge extend into our imperfect world?

For the Arabic Aristotelian philosophers, God's knowledge extended only to the level of the species. In the case of sparrows, for instance, God knows the species—he brought it into existence—but his thinking does not extend to the fate of any individual bird. Whether a particular sparrow dies or survives is not part of God's general providence. Maimonides accepted that description up to point; but he suggested that humans represent the unique exception to the rule.

In his view, the capacity for thought means that individual humans also have the benefits of God's special providence. To the extent that humans use their rational facilities, God is able to perceive them as individuals and guide their actions. Prophets, because they have perfected their rational and imaginative facilities, are the models for human behaviour. Because true morality is truly rational, the more we train and use our rational faculties, the more moral we become—and the more we can be guided by God's special providence.

| Box 2.4 | Maimonides' Twelfth Principle of Faith

In his commentary on the Mishnah, *called the* Mishneh Torah, *Maimonides included a summary of Judaism under the heading 'Thirteen Principles of Faith'*

I believe in perfect faith that the Messiah will come, and we should not consider him as tardy: 'Should he tarry, wait for him' [*Habakkuk* 2:13]. No date may be fixed for his appearance, nor may the Scriptures be interpreted in such a way as to derive from them the time of his coming.

| Box 2.5 | The Memoirs of Glueckl of Hamelin |

Glueckl (1646–1724) married Hayyim of Hamelin at the age of fourteen. She bore twelve children, became his adviser in business, and, after his death in 1689, carried on the business alone. Her memoir is both touching and historically important.

In my great grief and for my heart's ease I begin this book in the year of creation 5451 [1690–1]—God soon rejoice us and send us His redeemer!

I began writing it, dear children, upon the death of your good father, in the hope of distracting my soul from the burdens laid upon it, and the bitter thought that we have lost our faithful shepherd. In this way, I have managed to live through many wakeful nights, and springing from my bed shortened the sleepless hours.

This, dear children, will be no book of morals. Such I could not write, and our sages have already written many. Moreover, we have our holy Torah, in which we may find and learn all that we need for our long journey through this world to the world to come. It is like a rope which the great and gracious God has thrown to us as we drown in the stormy sea of life, that we may seize hold of it and be saved.

The kernel of the Torah is 'Thou shalt love thy neighbour as thyself.' But in our days we seldom find it so, and few are they who love their fellowmen with all their heart—on the contrary, if a man can contrive to ruin his neighbour, nothing pleases him more (Lowenthal 1977).

For Maimonides this meant that the truly rational person is the truly moral and good person. It did not mean that the truly rational human will never experience sorrow or misfortune: rather, it meant that the moral person's misfortunes and setbacks are specifically known by God and are somehow part of a divine plan. For the ignoramus, however, the converse was true. The ignoramus is both intellectually and morally insensitive and therefore whatever happens to him is accidental, in the same way that it is accidental whether a particular bird hits a building or flies free.

All those who study and follow the law are, in fact, training to be prophets. We participate in prophecy to the extent that we perfect our intellectual potentialities. Greek philosophy, Christianity, and Islam also necessarily partake in this truth, but to a lesser degree because each of them has fallen victim to error in one way or another. For Maimonides, then, reason and revelation were identical processes, and they were both identical with the power by which God creates and preserves the universe.

Rambam's great accomplishment was to promote a thoroughly rational understanding of Judaism. A view of Judaism as rational had existed even among the ancient rabbis, but the intellectual structure that Maimonides forged has characterized Jewish self-understanding to this day. Yet it cannot be said that Jews universally admired or adopted his system. Maimonides wrote for an elite among the Jews of his day in the Islamic world, speakers of Arabic who were in step with the Aristotelianism of medieval Islamic thought. The situation of Jews was very different in Christian lands such as France, where his writing set off a century of fierce dispute within Judaism—punctuated by book burnings and edicts of ostracism—which historians term the Maimonidean controversy.

On the whole, Maimonides' emphasis on reason has served the Jewish community well in times of peace and prosperity, when an intellectual tradition could flourish. In times of trial and tribulation, however, those in need of consolation have often turned to mysticism instead.

The Early Modern Period

Three centuries after Maimonides, the Islamic regime that had allowed Jewish thought to flourish in Spain was replaced by the Christian regime of Ferdinand (r. 1479–1516) and Isabella (r. 1474–1504). In 1492—a full ten years before they expelled the Moors from

| Map 2.1   Expulsion and migration of Jews from Europe, eleventh to fifteenth centuries CE

Town from which Jews were expelled

Town, at the time under Christian ruler, providing Jews with refuge

Town, at the time under Muslim ruler, providing Jews with refuge

Direction and date of major migration of Jews following expulsion

Dates accompanying name of town or region refer to expulsion of Jews

Source: I.R. al Fārūqi and D.E. Sopher, *Historical Atlas of the Religions of the World* (New York: Macmillan, 1974):148–9.

Spain—Ferdinand and Isabella expelled all the Jews. Evidently the Jews had been considered helpful as go-betweens and translators in a culture shared with Arab Muslims, but no longer served any useful purpose once Spain had been returned to Christian control. When Columbus set out on his celebrated voyage for the New World, he could not leave from any of Spain's larger ports because the trade routes were clogged by ships carrying Jews expelled from their Spanish homes.

Ferdinand and Isabella were not the first Christian monarchs in western Europe to expel their Jewish populations. But the Iberian Peninsula contained an enormous number of Jews who were both affluent and highly cultured. While the previous expulsions had been tragic for the individuals affected, the Iberian expulsion was devastating for Jewish culture as well.

In the course of the Reconquista, numerous Spanish Jews had already converted to Christianity, and many others converted once the expulsions began. But some of them continued to practise their old religion in secret. To root out the 'heretics' among the 'New Christians'—also known as *conversos* or, derisively, Marranos ('pigs')—the Spanish Inquisition was established in 1478.

Most of the Jews expelled from Spain found their way to the Ottoman Empire, which was ruled from Istanbul. When Sultan Bayazid II (r. 1481–1512) heard of the Jews' expulsion from Spain, he mocked the Spanish monarchs for their lack of wisdom and suggested that Turkey would recover the squandered 'wealth' of Spain. He thereafter encouraged the dispossessed Jews to take shelter in his empire.

Jewish Mysticism

The spiritual crisis generated by the expulsion sparked a renewed interest in mysticism. For mystics, the most interesting biblical passages are the ones where God manifests himself to his people in some physical form known as the *shekhinah* ('presence') or *kavod* ('glory of God'). The earliest and longest phase of Jewish mysticism, stretching from the prophecy of *Ezekiel* and the apocalyptic visions in *Daniel* through the twelfth century, is known as Merkabah ('chariot') mysticism. Its central characteristics were (1) an anthropomorphic concept of God and a keen interest in questions such as his size, as in the Shiur Koma ('measurement of the body') literature, (2) heavenly ascents, (3) theurgic (magical) spells and motifs, and (4) apocalyptic and revelatory writings.

The central experience in the Merkabah tradition was the ecstatic journey of the adept to the heavenly throne room. Although the figure seated on the throne was usually referred to by some angelic name (such as Metatron or Zoharariel), it was understood to represent 'the king in his glory'. The texts, called the *Hekhaloth* ('Palaces') texts, were edited and re-edited throughout the first millennium of Jewish mysticism. In the form in which we have them, they display many of the characteristic concerns of the Hasidei Ashkenaz, a group of Jewish pietists who flourished in fourteenth-century Germany.

The gradual diminution of Merkabah mysticism can probably be traced to the rise of the teaching called **Kabbalah** ('received tradition') in the twelfth century. In Kabbalah, the heavenly journey of the Merkabah mystics became a journey into the self. In place of the heavenly palaces, Kabbalah developed a notion of ten *spherot* ('countings' or 'spheres'), which are emanations of God and objects of meditation. By correctly aligning these *spherot* through rituals, pious deeds, and mystical meditation, the Kabbalist gains access to the divine and can affect the future course of events and so participate in the divine plan for the universe.

The Zohar

The principal text of Kabbalah is known as the *Zohar*. Although it purports to be the work of Rabbi Simeon bar Yohai, a famous early third-century rabbi, its real author was likely Moses ben Shemtov of León (1250–1305), a kabbalist who lived in Granada, Spain. The *Zohar* describes God as an unlimited divine principle, En Sof ('without end'), who produces the universe indirectly as the series of emanations called the *spherot*, and it has a special mystical agenda.

At some points the *spherot* recall the heavenly spheres of philosophical discourse; but at others times they seem more like imaginative configurations of the different powers of God. They can be envisioned as forming a tree of life or even a kind of cosmic man that may be connected to the earlier notion of God's principal angelic mediator, who is gigantic in size and somehow embodies the name of God. The correct alignment of the *spherot* will bring about the most harmonious balance of divine forces.

The *Zohar* believes that this insight is implied in the biblical text. In form, then, it is a Midrashic interpretation of scripture:

> He who desires to understand the wisdom of holy unity, let him contemplate the flame which rises from coal or from a candle for the flame rises only when it is attached to a material thing. Come and see: in the rising flame there are two lights, one a white shining light, and the other a dark bluish light that holds on directly to the candle. . . . Come and see: there is no stimulus for the kindling of the blue light that it might provide the basis for the white light save through the people of Israel who . . . unite with it from below and continue in their endurance (*Zohar* III, 290a; Caplan and Ribalow 1952:161–2).

In this passage the blue light is symbolic of the *spherah* known as Malkut ('kingship') or Shekhinah ('God's indwelling'), which in turn is identified with the spiritual presence of the people Israel. This particular *spherah*, or aspect of divinity, is not only grammatically feminine in Hebrew but explicitly feminine in nature, and is seen as engaging in sexual congress with the masculine aspects of God.

The white light conventionally symbolizes the higher *spherah* of *hesed*, God's aspect of 'lovingkindness'. Thus even a simple flame embodies a secret about how God and Israel interact. The existence and behaviour of Israel are deeply and integrally related to God's lovingkindness in the world. The purpose of these manifestations of God's various aspects in the world is to ensure the correct flow of divine effulgence (*shefa*), which is usually considered to be best balanced when the upper *spherah* (usually Tiferet, 'beauty') is properly related through *yesod* ('foundation') to the *spherah* Malkut or Shekhinah, the feminine aspect of God that signifies Israel.

The mystic tradition maintains that this balance is affected by human behaviour, ritual and otherwise, and often envisions it in terms of sexual intercourse. Thus mystical practice often centres on sexual relations within marriage. When a kabbalistically sophisticated married couple has sexual relations with the proper intentions and meditation, they help to align the heavenly dimensions of God. But properly completed ritual actions like the blessing over wine (Kiddush, part of the grace before meals) can have the same effect.

The system seemed irrational and even polytheistic to many Jewish intellectuals steeped in the rational systems of the philosophers and legal specialists, and even ordinary Jews could see the threat it posed to monotheism. Nevertheless, it appealed to many people troubled by the distress that Jews suffered and the continuing presence of evil in the world. Kabbalah explained evil by reference to a misalignment of divine effulgence and the necessity of human action to help the divinity in his progress towards the goal of cosmic perfection:

> The story of Jonah may be construed as an allegory of the course of a man's life in this world. Jonah descends into the ship: this is parallel to man's soul descending to enter into his body in this world. Why is the soul called Jonah [whose name literally means 'aggrieved']? For the reason that she becomes subject to all manner of vexation when once she enters into partnership with the body. Thus, a man in this world is as in a ship crossing the vast ocean and like to be broken, as it is written 'so that the ship was like to be broken' (*Zohar* on *Jonah* 1:4; Scholem 1949:103).

In this view, the 'vexation' of the earthly body is intended precisely to motivate the soul to work towards perfection.

Luria and Sabbatai Zvi

Until Isaac Luria (1534–72), Kabbalah was largely a private, individual, contemplative discipline. Luria, who lived in the century after the expulsion from Spain, had settled in the hilltop town of Safed in the Galilee region, making Safed a special place for mystics and eventually, in our time, artists and tourists. It is in Luria's mysticism that the consequences of the expulsion from Spain are most clearly seen.

Luria explains the tragedy of Jewish life in terms of a cosmic split in the Godhead. Before God can begin the creation, he must contract himself (*tsimtsum*) to make room for the world. But in that process God removes his perfection from the area that is to become the universe. When creation begins, the vessels that God designates to carry the divine sparks fracture and the sparks become mixed with the gross and evil material of creation. The human counterpart of this cosmic process is the historical exile (*galut*) of Israel.

Mystics, then, seek to help God return the divine sparks to their correct place. Humans can contribute to this *tikkun* ('rectification' or 'fixing') of the universe through meditation, magic, and pious acts, including rituals. The community that Isaac Luria founded in Safed practised asceticism and observed the rules of Judaism with special intensity, hoping that this would help God in the enterprise of redemption and hasten the coming of the messiah.

These mystical notions also quickened messianic expectations. In 1666 an adept of Lurianic Kabbalah named Sabbatai Zvi (1626–76), from Izmir (Smyrna), Turkey, was proclaimed the messiah by Nathan of Gaza and attracted a varied following of mystically oriented Jews. Influenced by the quickening of millennialist expectations (triggered by the date) among Christians, the followers of the mystical messiah marched on the sultan in Istanbul. At first the sultan was not greatly worried; but in time he became aware of the danger of this rag-tag army camped outside the walls. He had Sabbatai Zvi imprisoned, and when this did not completely stifle the messianic expectations of Sabbatai's followers, he offered Zvi a choice between conversion to Islam and death. Faced with a stark alternative, Zvi converted, and most of his followers gave up in despair.

Those who did not repudiate him saw in Zvi's actions a deeper meaning, namely, that the commandments could be fulfilled by the messiah's taking on the evil world directly and conquering it. This gave further impetus to the aspects of mysticism termed 'antinomian': counter to rule or law. Many of the most devoted followed Sabbatai Zvi into Islam, where they became a group of crypto-Jews, continuing to practise their ancestral tradition in secret. There are still some members of this sect in modern Turkey, called in Turkish the Dönmeh ('returners').

From the point of view of Orthodox Judaism, the Sabbatians resemble Christians in that they are a mystical and antinomian messianic group that originated in Judaism but abandoned it over issues having to do with Jewish law. A similar group in Podolia (western Ukraine) became outwardly Christian under the influence of a later Sabbatian, Jacob Frank (1726–91).

Hasidism

The founder of the Hasidic movement was Israel ben Eliezer (1698–1759), known as the Baal Shem Tov ('master of the Good Name'; often abbreviated to 'the Besht'). During his youth in Romania and Moldavia, he was known for his delight in telling stories to children. What seems to have impressed everyone who met him was his humility. He wandered from community to community in Podolia (western Ukraine) and Walachia (southern Romania), meeting ordinary people and attracting disciples. He appears to have received the title 'Baal Shem' as a result of his success at healing. Sometimes he organized impromptu retreats where he taught through informal conversations and humble lessons.

The common people who were the Besht's principal audience knew enough Hebrew to say their prayers but were largely uneducated. As a result, the scholars produced by the rigorous and elitist Talmudic academies of eastern Europe had little of relevance to say to them. By contrast, the Baal Shem Tov proclaimed a simple and accessible message: the best way of communing with God is through humility, good deeds, prayer (ecstatic and otherwise), and joy. He preached the importance of virtues such as forbearance and mutual help. He himself became the model for a Hasidic leader, a *zaddik* ('righteous person'). He sought the presence of God in everyday life. As one famous Hasidic story points out, the student learns about the divine from watching the master tie his shoes. The stories told by the Hasidic masters often recall the paradoxical wisdom of a Zen koan.

The pietistic Judaism of the Besht became very popular in eighteenth-century eastern Europe, where his adherents were called **Hasidim** ('pious ones'). After his death, the leadership of the movement was taken up by one of his primary disciples, Rabbi Ber of Mezeritz (1710–72), known also as the Maggid ('preacher'). It was during the Maggid's life that the theory of leadership under the *zaddikim* was first articulated. According to this doctrine, all the leaders of Hasidism after the Baal Shem Tov were to be called Zaddik and could pass on their authority to their children. Thus a *zaddik* ('Rebbe' in Yiddish) was both the holder of a hereditary office and a kind of intermediary between the people and God. The popular appeal of Hasidism provoked the opposition of the rabbinic community, who were characterized as Misnogdim ('opponents') by the Hasidim in Ashkenazic Hebrew.

When Hasidism spread to Latvia and Lithuania, the centre of rabbinic rationalism in eastern Europe, it changed character again. In those communities Talmudic training was quite common, and in order for Hasidism to spread there, it had to acquire a level of formal expertise that until then it had lacked. When a respected Talmudist named Shneur Zalman (1746–1812) of Lyadi, Belorussia, joined the movement, he began the process of synthesizing the scholarly tradition with Hasidic pietism. He wrote a tract known as *Tania* ('It Is Taught'). Known as Habad, Zalman's movement was centred in the Belorussian town of Lubavitch, and his followers came to be commonly known as Lubavitcher Hasidim (see p. 114).

Practice

Prayer

Prayer can be private or public. Public prayer continues to follow the order of the temple service, which was performed three times a day. In addition, Jews characteristically pray privately after rising and before retiring. For convenience some of the prayers may be combined, and the three prayers during the day may also be performed in private. But Jews try to find a *minyan*, a group of ten persons, usually in a synagogue, as a quorum for their daily prayers.

Jews may also address additional prayers to God at any time. One may pray virtually anywhere, as long as the place does not detract from the dignity of the prayer and as long as the proper *kavvanah* (spiritual intention) can be achieved.

The Content of Prayer

It is permissible to ask for God's special favour, but only if the advantage sought would not cause harm to anyone else. Thus someone who sees a plume of smoke in the distance is not allowed to pray, 'Let it not be my house,' because to do so would amount to praying for the fire to be in someone else's house. Jews are not even allowed to pray for the fall of their enemies (*Avoth* 4:19). Rather, prayer for the benefit of others is constantly encouraged.

| Box 2.6 | The Shema (Deuteronomy 6:4–9) |

In Jewish liturgy this passage is called the Shema, after its first word in the Hebrew. It is the watchword of Israel's faith, repeated morning and evening, as the text specifies.

Hear O Israel, the Lord our God, the Lord is One. You shall love the Lord your God with all your heart and with all your soul and with all your strength. These words which I command you this day are to be kept in your heart. You shall repeat them to your children, speaking of them indoors and outdoors, morning and night. You shall bind them as a sign upon your hand and wear them as signs upon your forehead; you shall write them on the doorposts of your houses and on your gates.

The rabbis took a lively interest in the content of prayer. The very first tractate of the *Mishnah*, and hence of the *Talmud*, is *Berachoth* (Blessings), which specifies the form of public prayer. Indeed, most formal Jewish prayers begin as blessings, thanking God for his protection, guidance, and sustenance. The fact that the rabbis inserted this tractate at the beginning of the *Talmud*, in the section devoted to agricultural laws (*Zera'im*, 'Seeds'), indicates the importance they attributed to it. In this way they ensured that prayer would be the very first subject a young person encounters when beginning to study the texts. The most common formula is 'Blessed are you, O Lord our God, king of the universe . . .'. Private prayer, of course, is more like a conversation with God, encouraged at any time.

The particular kinds of prayers offered and their specific wording have developed over millennia. Traditionally, prayers are said in Hebrew; and even though the prayer books used by Sephardic and Ashkenazic Jews differ somewhat, on the whole the order of Hebrew prayer is the same the world over.

Many prayers end with the word *amen* ('in truth' or 'in faith'), meaning 'so be it'.

Items Worn in Prayer

When praying, Jewish men may choose to wear special garments, derived from the dress described in the Bible, to help them attain the proper *kavvanah*.

Among those garments is the **tallith** or prayer shawl. This is a large rectangle of fabric that originated during the Hellenistic period as an ordinary outer garment. The Jewish version contained the correct fringes at the corners, as specified by biblical law (*Numbers* 15:37–41). It is now worn when praying and at ceremonial functions. Today a *tallith* is a specially designed shawl, usually striped in blue and white (though other colours are also possible) with long fringes at the corners. Orthodox Jews also wear a short *tallith*, called the *hatzi tallith* (half *tallith*), an undershirt that has the fringes of the longer garment, under their street clothes. At the other extreme, Reform Jews generally do not use even a prayer shawl.

Jewish males always cover their heads when they pray, including at meals. For this reason, more traditional Jews today wear a skullcap called the **kippah** (Hebrew for 'cap') or **yarmulke** (the equivalent in Yiddish) all the time. Reform Jews may pray bareheaded, however.

On weekdays traditional Jews use *tefillin* in prayer. These are two cube-like black boxes about 5 cm (2 in.) high, tied by leather thongs, one to the forehead and one to the upper arm. Inside the boxes are specific passages from scripture explaining their purpose and use. The usual English name for these boxes is **phylacteries**. Literally fulfilling the biblical commandment to bind the words of Torah 'upon the hand and as frontlets between the eyes', pious Jews put on *tefillin* every morning except Saturday, when the work involved would violate the Sabbath. One box is looped to the forehead by a thong; the other is lashed to the arm, facing the heart. The leather thong is wrapped around the arm and around the fingers in a special pattern. Reform Jews have suspended the use of *tefillin* almost entirely.

Blessings

Jews take care to bless all the gifts that God provides. Most blessings follow a formula designed by the early rabbis: beginning 'Blessed art Thou, O Lord our God, King of the Universe [or king forever] ', it then continues with the appropriate words of thanks, specific to the occasion. Jews normally pronounce short blessings over wine and bread whenever they are served, and after a meal, a fairly long doxology (series of blessings and praises to God) is recited or—if there are enough people—sung communally.

The daily round of Jewish prayer is both a comfort and an expression of joy for God's creation. Even Reform Jews and Reconstructionists, who sometimes question whether God answers prayer, suggest that the constant round of prayer throughout the day, and even more the prayers for forgiveness as the high holidays approach, helps to concentrate attention on the ethical goals of life.

Sabbath Observance

The Sabbath (Shabat) begins at sunset on Friday and continues to Saturday evening. On Friday night Jews may attend synagogue services. Orthodox services tend to be short and close to sunset. Conservative and Reform Judaism currently favour a longer service, in the evening after the Sabbath dinner.

Even though it occurs every week, the Sabbath is surely the holiest day in the Jewish calendar. The Sabbath prayers consecrate the day as a sacred time of quiet and rest, reserved for song, prayer, and contemplation.

Jews return home early on Friday afternoon so that they can prepare for the Sabbath meal—cleaning, cooking, lighting candles—before sundown, when all work must cease. The meal itself includes customary graces or prayers over bread and wine, with special additions celebrating God's work of creation as well as psalms, hymns, and special Sabbath songs. Typically the Sabbath dinner is a particularly fine one, served with the best silver and china. Specially braided breads called *halloth* or *challoth*—after the showbread of the temple—are blessed, together with the wine. The meal is dedicated to celebrating rest and thanking God for the Sabbath.

On Saturday the men in the family normally spend the morning at the synagogue while the women often stay home to prepare another special meal. Then the afternoon may be spent in study or quiet contemplation.

| Box 2.7 | A Techina (Devotional Prayer) for Women |

This the woman says when she puts the Sabbath loaf into the oven:

Lord of all the world, in your hand is all blessing. I come now to revere your holiness, and I pray you to bestow your blessing on the baked goods. Send an angel to guard the baking, so that all will be well baked, will rise nicely, and will not burn, to honour the holy Sabbath (which you have chosen so that Israel your children may rest thereon) and over which one recites the holy blessing—as you blessed the dough of Sarah and Rebecca our mothers. My Lord God, listen to my voice; you are the God who hears the voices of those who call to you with the whole heart. May you be praised to eternity (Umansky and Ashton 1992:55).

At the end of the Sabbath, many Jews return to synagogue for a service called Havdalah that marks the distinction between the Sabbath and the rest of the week. Using wine, a braided candle, and a spice box (symbolizing the sweetness of the Sabbath), the service also highlights the promise of the new week, blessing it until the next Sabbath. Songs wish everyone a good week. The service mentions the prophet Elijah, presumably in the hope that he will come during the following week and mark the arrival of the messianic age.

Dietary Laws

Jewish dietary laws (*kashrut*) specify what is and is not permitted in three areas: (1) the species of animals that may be consumed, (2) the special requirements for food preparation, and (3) the various foods that may be combined at the same meal.

Animals that are not **kosher** (ritually acceptable) may not be eaten. The pig is not to be touched or used for any purpose. In addition, all animals and birds that prey on others are excluded, though fish are permitted. Land animals must have a split hoof and chew the cud; hence beef is a frequent Jewish meat dish, prepared by stewing or braising to keep it tender. In North America chicken has become the typical Sabbath evening meal; in fact, kosher chicken soup with matzoh balls (in Yiddish *knaydelach,* 'dumplings') is the quintessential Ashkenazic ethnic dish.

Sea creatures must have both scales and fins, a rule that excludes sharks, all shellfish, all invertebrates, and a variety of lower marine forms. North American Jews who share north European culinary traditions eat lox (smoked salmon) with cream cheese on a bagel ('little ring'), usually with herring or other smoked fish for Sunday brunch.

Kosher slaughtering practice respects the prohibition against eating the blood of animals or birds. Thus every piece of meat is drained, and any remaining blood is removed by washing and salting. Animals must be slaughtered in such a way that they die immediately, without feeling pain. In practice this means one quick stroke from a very sharp knife with no nicks in it. The animal may not be stunned or hurt before the slaughter—contrary to the common practice in other slaughterhouses. The carcass is then inspected for a variety of impairments, any of which can disqualify the animal. The meat must also be cut in specific ways so as to remove parts considered unfit for Jewish consumption.

At Passover, a time of 'spring cleaning' and new beginnings (see p. 107), all the equipment used to prepare food must be either brand-new or thoroughly cleaned. In addition, all the food eaten during the eight-day holiday must be free of any yeast or leaven.

Many Jews take elaborate care not to combine milk and meat at the same meal. These rules are based on the injunction (*Exodus* 23:19) not to eat a kid boiled in its mother's milk. The rabbis expanded this regulation in significant ways. In order not to transgress the rule inadvertently, observant Jews will wait a specified period of time after eating meat, for example, before consuming any kind of milk product. Ashkenazim will never eat chicken with cheese. Observant Jews will never put milk in tea or coffee following a meat meal, or have ice cream for dessert. Nor will they ever eat cheeseburgers. Cheese itself—normally made from milk or cream curdled with rennet from a cow's stomach—must be made in a special way in order to be kosher. Many Jews keep two complete sets of dishes, silverware, pots and pans, and cooking utensils for use with milk and with meat. Some even insist on two different dishwashers, sinks, and ovens as well. European Jews classify foods using terms in Yiddish: *flaischich* (meat), *milkich* (dairy), *pareve* or *parve* (neither), and *kosher lepaysach* (kosher for Passover).

Some Reform Jews do not observe dietary laws at all, some observe them symbolically by abstaining from shellfish and pork only, and some observe them in full. Conservative Jews do usually try to observe the rabbinic ordinances, and will eat in a restaurant only if there is a fish dish on the menu. Orthodox Jews, on the other hand, avoid any restaurants without a certificate of *kashrut* ('fitness') and may not necessarily consider the *kashrut* certificates of certain restaurants trustworthy. The care with which people observe the dietary laws is taken as an indicator of their piety, and the distinctions between degrees of care can be quite subtle.

Synagogue Services

The chanting in the synagogue reaches a crescendo with the reading of the Torah scrolls, which traditionally happens on Mondays, Thursdays, the Sabbath, and special holidays. As in antiquity, so today, the synagogue service is conducted by laypersons rather than rabbis, who are viewed as jurists or even judges in various capacities; rabbis may offer sermons or legal opinions during services, however.

The basic order of formal service in the synagogue follows the pattern established at the ancient temple in Jerusalem, which consisted of song, musical accompaniment, and sacrifice. The tradition of sacrifice was abandoned after the destruction of the temple, but the other aspects of the temple service—including music, when appropriate—were transferred to the synagogue and incorporated into individual piety.

In time, services came to include professional singers, known as *hazanin* or '**cantors**', who sing various lines from the prayer books as members of the congregation pray quietly (but audibly) at their own pace. Reform congregations at first chose to recite the prayers in unison, but are now reinstituting a few more traditional aspects of Jewish prayer.

Most North American synagogues today continue to serve as houses of study, with libraries and classroom wings. In addition, they often include a large social hall for weddings and Bar Mitzvah celebrations.

The Annual Festival Cycle

The Jewish calendar is lunar rather than solar. Each month starts with the new moon, which is a time for special prayers, and the fourteenth day of every month coincides with the full moon. Since twelve lunar months add up to only 354 days, an extra month, Adar Sheni ('second Adar'), is periodically added as a 'leap' month in the calendar in the early spring. Thus the Jewish calendar never gets more than a few weeks out of step with the Western one. It is common to hear Jews say, 'The High Holidays are early [or late] this year.'

Most annual festivals had their origins in ancient agricultural practices, which the early rabbis then associated with specific events in the history of the Israelites.

New Year and the Day of Atonement

Rosh Hashanah (New Year) and Yom Kippur (the Day of Atonement) come at the autumn harvest, always the first and tenth of the month of Tishri, and traditionally were marked by the blowing of the ram's horn or *shofar*. In rabbinic observance, the *shofar* allegorically wakes up the congregation from its moral slumber with a reminder to consider carefully the deeds of the past year. On the Day of Atonement, the most solemn day of the year, the liturgy evokes the imagery of the shepherd counting his sheep or the commander counting his troops to describe God's final judgment of his people.

Sukkoth

At Sukkoth (booths or 'tabernacles'), an eight-day festival that marks the end of the autumn harvest, many Jews still build a *sukkah* (a small temporary shelter) outside the house and sleep in it for the duration of the festival, or at least eat in it when possible. This festival probably originated in the ancient farmers' practice of camping out in the fields to protect the ripening crops, but the rabbinic interpretation associates it with the Israelites' flight from Egypt under Moses' leadership, when they needed temporary shelter.

Hanukkah

Hanukkah is a relatively recent festival dating from the Hellenistic period. It celebrates the victory of the Maccabean Jews over their oppressors in the mid-second century BCE. and the purification and rededication (*hanukkah*) of the temple after it had been pro-faned. The miraculous eight-day duration of one day's supply of oil is symbolized by the Hanukkah *menorah*.

Purim

Another minor festival is Purim, which falls in the month of Adar (usually March). Its narrative, drawn from the book of *Esther*, recalls the deliverance of the Jews in Persia from destruction at the hands of Haman, an evil member of the court of Shah (King) Ahashuerus. Purim celebrations are reminiscent of the North American Hallowe'en, with costume parties, merrymaking, and gifts of candy.

Passover (Pesach)

The important festival of Passover comes in the spring, the season of agricultural rebirth and renewal, at the full moon in the Hebrew month of Nissan. The Passover liturgy, called the Haggadah ('narrative'), recounts the Exodus from Egypt, which is celebrated at home with a special family meal called a Seder. Matzah (flat, unleavened bread) is eaten in memory of the Israelites' hasty departure from Egypt, when they had to leave before the bread they were making could be baked. The liturgy tells every Jew that, through the Seder, he or she too has experienced the divine deliverance of the Exodus: 'In every generation, each of us should feel as though we ourselves had gone forth from Egypt, as it is written: "And you shall explain to your child on that day, it is because of

The Passover Seder recalls the last meal that the Israelites ate before fleeing Egypt (Bill Aron/Ponkawonka.com).

what the LORD did for me when I, myself, went forth from Egypt.'" The Passover Seder is a great favourite of Jews around the world.

Shavuoth

Shavuoth ('weeks'), in late spring, was originally the winter grain harvest, and eventually came to be observed with the eating of dairy foods as well as cereals. It is known to Christians as Pentecost (Greek, 'fiftieth') because it comes fifty days after Passover. The early rabbis associated the festival with the giving of the Torah on Mount Sinai.

The Ninth of Ab

Towards the middle of summer, a fast-day called Tisha B'av (the ninth day of the Hebrew month of Ab) is observed. This date is said to be the historical anniversary of the destruction of the first and second temples. In addition to fasting from sunset to sunset,

Students on an Israeli kibbutz (collective farm) re-enact the bringing of the first fruit on the eve of Shavuoth (Rahaf Merkine/Ponkawonka.com).

observant Jews avoid all luxurious display on this day; they will not wear leather, for example, because it was considered a luxury item in rabbinic times.

Life-Cycle Rituals

Birth

The most characteristic ritual associated with birth is circumcision of the male foreskin. Unless the infant's health is endangered or some other circumstance makes it undesirable, the operation is performed on the eighth day of life, usually by a ritual circumciser called a *mohel*. These days, the *mohel* may also be a physician, but there are still many 'paramedical' people who have been trained to do the operation according to the rabbinic procedure.

Circumcision normally takes place in the home and is the occasion for a family celebration. The liturgy of the ritual centres on a commitment to give the child a Jewish education, stressing learning, good deeds, marriage, and a life within the community.

Marriage

Marriage is universally encouraged in Judaism. Though some great scholars are forgiven for remaining single, everyone else is enjoined to marry and raise children. Sexuality within the sanctified bounds of marriage is encouraged not only for procreation but for the pleasure it brings to the couple. Indeed, it is considered a man's responsibility to give his wife sexual pleasure and fulfillment. Thus a Jewish marriage is a joyous event that usually involves both religious seriousness and a certain degree of indulgence.

A marriage can be celebrated in a home, a hotel, or a catering establishment as well as in a synagogue. A rabbi is present more in a legal than a liturgical capacity; he makes sure that the marriage contract is properly prepared and also that the proper procedures are followed. Official witnesses to the legal proceedings must also be present. The same is true for a Jewish divorce. In North America today, rabbinic specifications are rarely followed exactly, but Orthodox Jews will observe Orthodox marriage and divorce customs in addition to the legal formalities required by the state.

Divorce

The Jewish marriage contract provides a number of safeguards for women that were not always available to women in the surrounding cultures. Judaism also accepts divorce as a legal institution. It is mentioned several times in the Bible and treated explicitly in *Deuteronomy* 24:1–4. The actual use of divorce as a remedy for a family crisis is infrequent, however. The divorce decree (called a *get* in Hebrew) is presented to the wife by the husband and normally includes a financial settlement and provision for the return of properties that rightfully belong to the wife.

The most famous *takkanah* on the subject of marriage is the repeal of polygamy, often attributed to Rabbenu Gershom (Gershom ben Judah Me'or Ha-Golah, c. 960–1028), to whom is also ascribed a *takkanah* prohibiting a husband from divorcing his wife against her will. This *takkanah* essentially outlaws polygamy for Jews in Christian cultures though it continues occasionally in the Muslim world even today. Also transformed by rabbinic rulings was the biblical institution of levirate marriage, which required a man to marry the wife of his childless deceased brother so as to produce heirs in his name. Although this institution still exists in theory, absolution from the practice is now standard. The rabbinic practice today, even in polygamous cultures, is to use another biblical procedure (*halitsah* or 'unbinding') to release the woman from this legal obligation.

Death

Jews believe that death should be faced resolutely and without illusion. Funerals can even be conducted in the home, although that is extremely rare in North America today. The funeral liturgy is meant to console the grieving family. It explicitly says that God will resurrect the righteous, that they will shine as the brightness of the firmament, and that they will be bound up into the bonds of life. But even at these moments Judaism is relatively non-specific about how God will fulfill the prophecies that the dead will live again. In modern Judaism, the body is always placed in a plain coffin, without embalming. Hence interment always takes place as quickly as is practical after the death, though no funerals are held on the Sabbath or during festivals.

When a death occurs, community members band together to cook and do whatever else they can to free the bereaved family from ordinary affairs for a time. The family announces that it will receive visitors during certain hours every day for a week after the burial, a custom known as 'sitting Shiva' (from the Hebrew for 'seven'). Mirrors are covered, while family members wear sombre colours and either rip their clothing or wear a short black ribbon with a cut in it to symbolize ripping. All these customs are meant to free the family from the vanity of everyday life. The children, by tradition especially the sons, honour the memory of the dead by reciting a special prayer, the Kaddish, every day for a year.

Religious Education

Traditionally, a Jewish boy's religious education began around the age of five. There were often ceremonial parades displaying the new students to the community. The first subject of study, during the school years, was the Bible. Then students would progress to the medieval Bible commentators Abraham ibn Ezra (c. 1090–1164) and Rashi. Advanced education took place in a yeshiva, where the young men worked under the direction of acknowledged Talmudic masters to understand the refractory pages of the text. Between lessons, they prepared pages of the *Talmud* together in study groups. Young rabbinic sages also consulted a variety of commentaries.

Today, of course, education is no longer restricted to boys. Growing numbers of Jewish parents in North America are now sending their children to private Jewish day schools, which normally devote roughly half the day to Jewish subjects and the other half to the standard curriculum. In other cases girls and boys attend special classes three or four days a week, after regular school hours, where they study. Jewish literature, history, customs, and ceremonies, and often Hebrew. In addition, more traditional families ensure that boys are taught at least the rudiments of Jewish law. The end of this 'elementary school' phase of religious education is marked by the Bar Mitzvah or Bat Mitzvah, which serves as a kind of graduation ceremony.

But the Bar Mitzvah need not mark the end of the young person's religious education. Many young people continue their Jewish studies, and Reform Judaism has instituted an additional graduation ceremony known as confirmation, held several years after Bar Mitzvah. It is celebrated in late spring at the time of the Shavuoth holiday, which roughly coincides with the end of the school year in North America.

Interaction and Adaptation

The Reform Movement

The Reform movement in Judaism was a product of eighteenth-century Europe and reflected the progressive ideas of the Enlightenment. Until that time, the Ashkenazim tended to live as semi-autonomous groups within the various countries of Europe. Those who left the ghetto usually converted to Christianity and simply disappeared into the mainstream of European society. Others, however, wanted to reform Judaism in such a way that it could take an active part in modern European life. This movement reached its most significant form in Germany in the late eighteenth and early nineteenth centuries.

The first and most influential advocate of reform, Moses Mendelssohn (1729–86), may be seen as the father of modern Orthodoxy as well, because his formula for the relationship between Jewish identity and European nationality became the basis for modern Jewish life almost everywhere. Mendelssohn was born in a ghetto in Dessau, Germany, and educated in traditional Judaism both at home and in Berlin.

In his treatise *Jerusalem*, published in 1783, Mendelssohn argued that the Jews of Germany, instead of resisting German culture, should absorb as much of it as they could. Enjoying the same intellectual freedom as other Germans, he argued, would in no way affect the essence of Judaism, which Mendelssohn argued is a religion of reason combined with a revealed law. Mendelssohn separated Jewishness from personhood, in effect, suggesting that Jews could be Germans in the same way that Protestants and Catholics were Germans. Progress towards equal rights was slow, but by the time Hitler came to power in the 1930s most German Jews were fully assimilated members of German society.

Even as the movement towards participation in secular life was gaining strength, however, some questioned whether Jews were really prepared to give up their rights as a semi-autonomous people within Europe. In 1807 Napoleon called for an assembly of rabbis and Jewish laymen, modelled on the ancient Sanhedrin, to determine whether the Jews of France were truly committed to French citizenship. The delegates' answers suggested they were anxious to enjoy the privileges of French nationality. It was not long before the fears of more traditional thinkers in the Jewish community were confirmed: as Jews' freedom to participate in secular society increased, so did the numbers of Jews converting to Christianity. One response to the weakening of the Jewish community was religious reform.

The Reform movement, centred in Germany, sought to counter the temptations of Christianity by offering Jews a religious life that suited the time. They reformed Jewish worship to resemble church services by introducing Western musical instruments, more vernacular prayer, and sermons in the vernacular. They abbreviated the services by cutting out numerous repetitions, and even adopted the Christian custom of holding Sabbath services on Sunday rather than Saturday. Although the latter change has been largely abandoned, Reform groups in the United States today continue to adapt to the times: in recent years, for instance, they have begun referring to the matriarchs as well as the patriarchs in prayer, and addressing God in feminine as well as masculine terms.

The Reform movement's emphasis on the present over the past is evident in the following extracts from the platform of American Reform rabbis meeting at Pittsburgh in 1885:

- The Bible reflects primitive ideas of its own age, clothing conceptions of divine Providence in miraculous narratives.
- The laws regulating diet, priestly purity and dress do not conduce to holiness and obstruct modern spiritual elevation
- We are no longer a nation but a spiritual community and therefore expect no return to Palestine.

| Box 2.8   **From American Reform Platforms**

Pittsburgh, 1885

We recognize in every religion an attempt to grasp the Infinite One, and in every mode, source or book of revelation held sacred in any religious system the consciousness of the indwelling of God in man. We hold that Judaism presents the highest conception of the God-idea as taught in our holy Scriptures and developed and spiritualized by the Jewish teachers in accordance with the moral and philosophical progress of their respective ages. We maintain that Judaism preserved and defended amid continual struggles and trials and under enforced isolation this God-idea as the central religious truth for the human race.

Columbus, 1937

In view of the changes that have taken place in the modern world and the consequent need of stating anew the teaching of Reform Judaism, the Central Conference of American Rabbis makes the following declaration of principles. It presents them not as a fixed creed but as a guide for the progressive elements of Jewry.

Judaism is the historical religious experience of the Jewish people [and] . . . its message is universal, aiming at the union and perfection of mankind under the sovereignty of God. Reform Judaism recognizes . . . progressive development in religion and consciously applies this principle to spiritual as well as to cultural and social life. . . . (Alexander 1984:137–8).

Reform Jews often refer to their congregations as 'temples', suggesting that the central place of worship is where they now live, and that restoration of the first-century temple is no longer expected or even desired.

Conservative Judaism

Some reformers, however, preferred a more conservative approach. Among them was Leopold Zunz (1794–1886), who in 1819 founded the *Jüdische Wissenschaft* ('science of Judaism') movement. Zunz and his colleagues tended to look for historical justification before making an innovation. Similarly, Zecharias Frankel (1801–75) attended many of the meetings called by the reforming rabbis of Germany but stopped short of accepting all the reforms proposed by the modernizers, arguing that some apparently irrational rituals had legal and aesthetic justifications.

These scholars captained what has become Conservative Judaism in the United States and Canada. Conservative Judaism takes an intermediate position between Reform and Orthodoxy. The justification for change is usually historical precedent—not, as in Reform Judaism, rational procedure. If a particular custom can be shown to be fairly recent, then there is a precedent for further change. Since the black caftans worn by Hasidim, for example, did not become customary until the fifteenth century or later, they are not obligatory. On the other hand, the order of prayers in the Jewish service goes back to the temple service in the first century, if not before, and therefore should not be changed.

Orthodox Judaism

Orthodox Judaism emphasizes the preservation of Jewish tradition. Although many Orthodox Jews in North America have adopted modern dress, they still conduct services in Hebrew and observe Sabbath obligations based on the ancient rules found in the

---

| Box 2.9 | Solomon Schechter on the Faith of Catholic Israel

Another consequence of this conception of Tradition is that it is neither Scripture nor primitive Judaism, but general custom which forms the real rule of practice. Holy Writ as well as history, Zunz tells us, teaches that the law of Moses was never fully and absolutely put into practice. Liberty was always given to the great teachers of every generation to make modifications and innovations in harmony with the spirit of existing institutions. Hence a return to Mosaism would be illegal, pernicious, and indeed impossible. The norm as well as the sanction of Judaism is the practice actually in vogue. Its consecration is the consecration of general use—or, in other words, of Catholic Israel. It was probably with a view to this communion that the later mystics introduced a short prayer to be said before the performance of any religious ceremony, in which, among other things, the speaker professes to act 'in the name of all Israel' (Schechter 1896:xix).

| Box 2.10 | From S.R. Hirsch, 'The Dangers of Updating Judaism'

But, above all, what kind of Judaism would that be, if we were allowed to bring it up to date? If the Jew were actually permitted at any given time to bring his Judaism up to date, then he would no longer have any need for it; it would no longer be worthwhile speaking of Judaism. We would take Judaism and throw it out among the other ancient products of delusion and absurdity, and say no more about Judaism and the Jewish religion!

If the Bible is to be for me the word of God, and Judaism and the Jewish law the revealed will of God, am I to be allowed to take my stand on the highway of the ages and the lands and ask every mortal pilgrim on earth for his opinions, born as they are between dream and waking, between error and truth, in order to submit the word of the living God to his approval, in order to mould it to suit his passing whim? And am I to say: 'See here modern, purified Judaism! Here we have the word of the living God, refined, approved and purified by men!' (Grunfeld 1956, 2:215-6)

Bible; they insist on kosher meals; and they maintain the traditional distinctions in gender roles, restricting the leadership in worship and ritual to males.

Rejecting even moderate reform programs such as *Jüdische Wissenschaft* as a betrayal of authentic Judaism, Orthodox Jews nevertheless have to live in the modern world. Therefore they have tried to find a modern idiom for traditional Judaism. Among the most effective spokespersons for this perspective was Rabbi Samson Raphael Hirsch (1808–88). Instead of merely condemning the reformers, he outlined a positive program for modern Orthodoxy. Essentially he gave credence to both the modern world and the traditional sources of Jewish identity, calling for both Torah (law, used here in the sense of 'Jewish religious truth') and *Derekh Eretz* (literally 'the way of the land'; here referring specifically to European life).

The Hasidim outwardly resemble strict Orthodox Jews. But they are not Orthodox in their beliefs and practices. One sect within the movement, known as Lubavitcher Hasidim, has even moved towards messianism since its last *Zaddik*, Rabbi Menachem Schneerson, died in 1994 without a male heir. Many Lubavitchers have declared Rabbi Schneerson to be the messiah and are expecting his return.

These and other Hasidic sects, founded by other early pupils of the Baal Shem Tov, have often been in sharp competition both with one another and with the Orthodox mainstream, which remains quite hostile to most of the Hasidic program.

Twentieth-Century Theology

Periods of acculturation and assimilation have stimulated Jewish theological and philosophical inquiry. In the twentieth century, as during the multicultural Hellenistic period and, later, the heyday of Arab–Jewish cooperation in Muslim Spain, Judaism again entered a period of rich theological expression.

Franz Rosenzweig (1886–1929) is perhaps a good example of the kinds of forces in European and North American life that helped to stimulate Jewish philosophical speculation. Rosenzweig was born into a cultured and affluent, assimilated, and not very religiously committed family that wanted him to become a physician. Instead he embarked on a career in philosophy, and at a crucial point in his life decided that he could be the kind of Liberal Christian described by the philosopher G.W.F. Hegel (1770–1831). Before converting, however, Rosenzweig determined that he should approach Christianity 'not as a pagan but a Jew'. To that end, he had first to deepen his experience of Judaism. After attending a Yom Kippur service in a small Orthodox synagogue in Berlin, he decided that Judaism was preferable to Christianity because Jews are already with 'the Father' and therefore have no need to apply to 'the Son' for mediation.

Drafted into the German army in the First World War, he wrote his first and only systematic work, *Der Stern der Erlösung* ('The Star of Redemption') in correspondence to his mother while he was in the trenches. In it he takes an incipiently existentialist stance, declaring all truth to be subjective. He suggests that both Judaism and Christianity are true in the subjective sense. He sees the politically powerful countries of Christendom as constantly projecting the purposes of God into the world and so helping to convert and transform it.

Judaism, on the other hand, he sees as politically powerless but clear-sighted in its ritual and liturgical concerns. Jews are eternally with God, communicating with him through the eternally repeated rituals of Judaism. For Rosenzweig, the Jews' covenant with God is eternal and timeless because the rules governing Jewish life have served to insulate Judaism and prevent any dilution of its spiritual power. Christianity, by contrast, has had the job of bringing the word of God to other nations, and through its engagement in the world risks the dilution that Judaism has avoided.

Tragically, Rosenzweig developed amyotrophic lateral sclerosis ('ALS' or 'Lou Gehrig's disease') in the early 1920s and for several years before his death was able to communicate only through his wife. Nevertheless, his understanding of the value of traditional Judaism from the standpoint of liberal and secular thought has gained him a following across the broad spectrum of modern Judaism. His concept of Judaism as standing outside history quickly became unsustainable, however, given the events of the 1930s and after. Like it or not, Jews have fully re-entered history.

Another person whose theological work has been significant to Judaism and to religious people everywhere is Martin Buber (1878–1965). Buber was a student of two important German intellectuals—Wilhelm Dilthey and Georg Simmel—but he also felt the influence of Hasidism through his family and especially his grandfather, Solomon Buber, who was a famous scholar of *midrash*. Buber and Rosenzweig were not only associates in Das jüdische Lehrhaus ('The Jewish School'), an institute of Jewish learning in Frankfurt, and co-translators of a German translation of the Bible, but close personal friends.

In 1923 Buber published his most famous work, *Ich und Du* (translated as *I and Thou*), which generations of religiously concerned thinkers have studied, admired, scrutinized, and critiqued. The book is not so much a treatise as a poem suggesting that all human beings have two ways of relating to the world. Most of those interactions are functional, focused on manipulation and control; Buber calls these 'I–It' experiences. But there are also moments of epiphany, or 'I–Thou' experiences, in which the divine presence can be felt and true dialogue is possible.

The founder of Reconstructionism, Mordecai Kaplan (1881–1983), felt that belief in God was traditionally important to Jews' self-understanding but was not essential to the definition of the group. Attempting to redefine Judaism as a religious civilization—in today's terms, a religious culture—he translated 'God' and 'Lord' with terms like 'The Eternal'.

Founded in the 1930s, Reconstructionism was for many years a kind of ideological position that found a considerable intellectual following across the spectrum of movements within North American Judaism. In the 1960s, however, Reconstructionism became a separate entity with its own rabbinical seminary in Philadelphia. Today there are several Reconstructionist synagogues in North America, but they represent a very small segment of the community. Ideologically, many Jews who think of themselves as an ethnic group espouse Reconstructionist ideals but continue as members of Reform or Conservative synagogues.

Zionism

It was in the mid- nineteenth century, when nationalism became a powerful cultural and political force, that European Jews began to explore the idea of returning to their ancient homeland in the Near East. To be sure, medieval Jewish literature had often referred to the sense of absence from the land of Israel. Yehuda Ha-Levi wrote poetically of his sadness to be in the West (Spain) when his heart was in the East. The words of the Passover Seder, 'next year in Jerusalem', attest to the ongoing spiritual longing to return, whether now or in the messianic age. And some Jews had continued to live in the land of Israel throughout history. But the nineteenth century introduced several other currents that flowed together to give modern Zionism its impetus. The modern movement to return to the ancient land of Israel, to found a nation there on the modern European model, is called Zionism.

Among those currents was the desire to revive the Hebrew language as an important aspect of national identity. The movements for the unification of Italy and Germany, hitherto politically fragmented into various principalities, both derived momentum from the fact that the peoples involved spoke the same language. Hebrew, which was still widely used in prayer and for literary and intellectual purposes but rarely spoken, was the only language that all Jews had in common, and so its revival became an important part of the Zionist impulse.

The principal founder of the movement was Theodor Herzl (1860–1904), a Viennese Jew who became committed to the goal of Jewish statehood after covering the Dreyfus trial in France as a foreign correspondent. Alfred Dreyfus, a French army captain assigned to the war ministry, was charged in 1894 with selling secret information to the German military attaché. It was clear to all that Dreyfus had been unfairly accused and convicted and that anti-Semitism in the French armed forces had played the deciding role in the proceedings.

Although Herzl himself had grown up in an assimilated home, he came to believe that the only chance for Jews to lead a normal existence, free of persecution, would be as a people in their own land, and that they would have to have a political state or something approximating it. His Zionistic ambitions were thus entirely secular and nationalistic; indeed, for a time Herzl flirted with the notion of locating the new Jewish national homeland in some place other than in the land of biblical Israel.

In the twentieth century, although the Zionist movement coalesced around Herzl's leadership, a number of intellectuals suggested that a Jewish homeland could represent more than a haven from persecution. Asher Ginsberg (1856–1927), for example, a Russian intellectual who wrote under the *nom de plume* Ahad Ha-'Am ('one of the people'), thought that a Jewish national homeland should be a spiritual centre for the development of the world and the Jewish people. For him, Jewish nationalism meant pride in the moral virtues that the Jewish people had always valued. He pointedly defined his concept of Jewish life over against the concept of the *Übermensch* ('superior being') proposed by the German philosopher Friedrich Nietzsche.

Some Orthodox Jews believed that human intervention in the return to Zion was a sin. They would not work for the creation of the modern state, and after it came into being, in 1948, they refused to acknowledge its existence. A legitimate Jewish state, some of them said, would have to await the coming messianic age. Many settled in Israel

Praying at the Western Wall in Jerusalem. The lower part of the wall dates from Roman times, when it stood as the enclosure of the temple precincts (Andrea Pistolesi/Ponkawonka.com).

anyway, whether because it housed many of the important sites of Jewish history or because it was the only asylum available to them after the Second World War. They continue to live as if the state did not exist, though they accept its subsidies for household life and education.

There has also been a religious Zionist movement, which accepts and supports the existence of a Jewish state. This movement is quite strong today; indeed, most of North American immigrants to Israel in recent decades have been religiously motivated Zionists. Several political parties in contemporary Israel are composed of religious Zionists.

But the notion of Jewish peoplehood also evokes other kinds of loyalties. Jews who cherish no religious sentiments at all may still feel ethnically or nationally attached to Israel and may consider its continued existence to be important to their Jewish identity. Furthermore, many Reform Jews who initially felt estranged from Zionism because they were completely at home in Germany, or the United States, or Canada, have become more sympathetic towards it, even if they have no intention of moving to Israel themselves.

The decades since Israeli statehood in 1948 have seen a number of shifts in attitude on the part of North American Jews. Many supported Israel at the time of the Six-Day War in 1967, when it was surrounded by hostile nations led by Egypt. These sentiments were underscored in 1973 when Israel was attacked by surprise on Yom Kippur, the holiest day of the Jewish calendar. In the end Israel won the Yom Kippur War, but the threat to its survival galvanized Jewish sympathy and support around the world. By contrast, opinion has been quite sharply divided concerning Israel's invasion of Lebanon in 1982, its policies in the West Bank and Gaza, and its war against the Hezbollah militia in 2006.

Judaism in the Americas

Jews from different European countries have quite different understandings of their Jewish identities. The first wave of Jewish immigrants to the Americas—mainly South America, the Caribbean islands, and the United States—were Sephardim from Spain and Portugal who arrived between the sixteenth and eighteenth centuries. They established the Jewish community in Curaçao and were responsible for the founding of several synagogues in the United States, including the famous Touro Synagogue in Newport, Rhode Island, and the Spanish-Portuguese Synagogue in Manhattan. Sephardim in North America include Jews of Spanish descent who had settled in England and Holland before crossing the Atlantic. A few Jews with Spanish names like Costas, Gomez, and Seixas remain, but this wave assimilated long ago.

German Jewish immigration began in the 1840s after the failure of liberal political reforms in Germany. Many of these people reflected the influence of the Reform movement, considering themselves to be Germans of the Mosaic persuasion—German nationals who happened to be Jewish in religion. They settled mostly in the United States, often in the same areas where other German immigrants settled, especially in the midwest. But they tended to be peddlers and shopkeepers rather than farmers. It was this second wave of Jewish settlement in the Americas, at the end of the nineteenth century, that produced the great mercantile families like the Bambergers (who owned the department stores Macy's and Bamberger's and helped found the Institute for Advanced Studies at Princeton) and the Guggenheims (American mining entrepreneurs who founded the Guggenheim Museum and the Guggenheim Fellowship). They arrived with many German customs, including Christmas trees (*Tannenbäume*, 'fir trees', a term with no explicitly Christian connotation in German).

The largest wave of Jewish immigration to America, however, came from the *shtetlach* (singular *shtetl*, Yiddish for 'little town') and the urban Jewish quarters of eastern Europe. The three million Jews living in areas controlled by Russia had not been touched by the social forces that allowed for Jewish liberation in western Europe and the Americas. Jews did make some political and economic gains during the relatively benign rule of Czar Alexander II (r. 1855–81), but his successor Alexander III (r. 1881–94) openly encouraged pogroms (massacres) and deportations of Jews.

His policies were directly responsible for the enormous wave of Jewish immigrants who landed mostly on the eastern coast of the United States and in eastern Canada. At first most of them went to New York. The German Jews, while they donated massively to help these indigent immigrants, were not particularly friendly towards these *Ostjuden* ('eastern Jews'), who were not literate in German or English and who quickly found jobs in the tobacco and clothing sweatshops on the lower East Side of Manhattan.

In Russia each ethnic group had been treated as a separate nationality, and even today the passports of Russian Jews identify their nationality as 'Jewish'. Thus Jews arriving from eastern Europe have tended to think of themselves as Jewish by nationality as well as religion. Ironically, some thought they had sacrificed their religion in crossing the Atlantic, because Orthodox rabbis in Europe warned against North America as a land of non-kosher iniquity.

In 1922 new immigration quotas stopped the flow of Jewish immigration to the United States, but they continued to arrive in Canada, Cuba, Mexico, and South America. In Canada Jewish immigrants settled primarily in urban Quebec and Ontario, but also in Winnipeg. French-speaking Jews from North Africa and the French possessions tended to favour the Montreal area. English-speaking Jews settled in Montreal, Toronto, and farther west.

The doors of the United States remained largely shut to Jews fleeing Nazi oppression in the 1930s, and Canada too refused most Jewish refugees during the Second World War. Most of the Jews who arrived in Canada and the United States after 1945 were Holocaust survivors.

The Holocaust

No event since the expulsion from Spain has so affected the Jewish people as the Holocaust in Europe. Adolf Hitler (1889–1945), whose National Socialist ('Nazi') party came to power in 1933, was able to convince a majority of the German people that the source of their economic problems was not the German state's disastrous economic policies, or the reparations it had to pay after the 1914–18 war, but the country's Jewish population.

The Nazis, fearing that the Jewish presence among them would sully their 'racial' superiority, passed a series of laws that were ever more cruel to Jews. First they stripped

Jews of German nationality. Then they looted Jewish stores and prevented Jews from practising their livelihoods. They sent Jews to concentration camps to work as slaves. Finally, they erected gas chambers and crematoria to kill the Jews, a program the Nazis called the *Entlösung*—'the Final Solution' to the Jewish Problem.

Of course, Hitler could not have succeeded in this effort without Europe's 2,000-year-long tradition of vilifying the Jews. The tradition had its roots in the New Testament, whose compilers painted Jews in an extremely bad light for their own theological reasons. Through the centuries, images of Jewish perfidy were readily available to anyone who wished to exploit hatred against the Jews for his or her own purposes.

It can be argued that Hitler's war against the Jews was the most successful of all his endeavours. For whatever reasons, the Allies did not strike back strongly enough even when they clearly understood what he was doing. There were no Allied raids on the railway tracks that daily took tens of thousands of Jews to their deaths. Worse still, Hitler found some ready accomplices for his work in eastern Europe, especially Poland.

Yet there were also many individual Christians who risked death to hide Jews or help them escape, and many who met the same fate. The 6 million Jewish deaths in the Second World War amount to between one-third and one-quarter of the total death toll in Europe, sometimes estimated at 22 million. The Holocaust killed roughly one-third of world Jewry—men, women, and children—in the space of a few years.

Jews shuddered when the enormity of the crime became known. They had always assumed that, although they might sin, the eternity of the people Israel was a sign of God's continuing favour. That God could have allowed the wholesale killing of so many innocent and non-combatant men, women, and children raised questions that may never be answered. For many Jews, the only possible response is to continue to interpret historical events as the unfolding of God's design, in which their people have a special role.

Nevertheless, some have attempted to formulate answers. Among them is the writer Elie Wiesel (b. 1928). Wiesel was a traditional *yeshiva* student in the town of Sighet in Romania when the Nazis arrived. His first novel, *Night*, is the chronicle of the murder of his family and his survival of the extermination camps. Since then he has written movingly in fiction and non-fiction of the predicament of modern Jews. He has articulated an ambivalent and often tentative faith, but his mixture of doubt and grudging affirmation of Jewish and human values, in the face of the absurdity of existence, seems to speak to the complex feelings with which many Jews and gentiles alike contemplate the horrors of the modern world.

'Jews must continue to live so as not to grant to Hitler a posthumous victory,' said Emil Fackenheim (1916–2003), a German rabbi and professor who immigrated to Canada in 1938 and to Israel after 1981. In this regard, Fackenheim spoke for a wide spectrum of Jews who feel that Hitler's near-success in exterminating the Jewish people must be remembered, and that the world can never again allow any people to be targeted for genocide. The Holocaust has given Jewish identity a new significance and Jewish people a new responsibility in the world. In Fackenheim's view, Jews are no longer permitted to undergo martyrdom (which had been judged honourable starting in the Hellenistic era), no matter how good the reasons, because the people must survive. To the traditional 613 commandments, God has added a 614th: you must never again allow yourselves to be helpless.

The State of Israel

For most Jews, the foundation of the state of Israel is closely associated with the terrible tragedy of the Holocaust. Although in no sense a compensation for the lives that were lost, Israel represented the promise that there would be a place in the world where Jews might at last be safe. In the years following the Second World War, the Zionist campaign for a haven from persecution enlisted the support of non-Jewish leaders. The United Nations voted to partition Palestine and create two states, one Jewish and one Arab. The creation of Israel did a great deal to resolve the problem of Jewish refugees in Europe. But the proposed Arab state has not yet come into being and, as a result, peace and security are not yet a reality.

For many years, the neighbouring Arab states of Egypt, Jordan, Syria, and Lebanon vied with each other as well as Israel for control of all the area. But they were unable to defeat Israel militarily and eventually ceded to Palestinians the right to control their own territory. The Palestinians, however, have not been able to agree on a policy to deal with Israel's occupation of the lands gained in the 1967 war. Many seem willing to negotiate a state in the land of Israel and Palestine. Others refuse to negotiate and have taken up arms against civilians in the Israeli state. Israel, claiming its own need to defend its citizens, has imposed very strenuous controls on the civilian population, to try to prevent bombings, suicide actions, and rocket launches. Nearly six decades after its creation, Israel still has not managed to resolve some problems fundamental to accommodating an emerging Palestinian nationality. The question of sovereignty and control over the old city of Jerusalem, for example, has been a constant and so far insoluble difficulty.

One can hope that peace negotiations will eventually resume, after all hostilities have shown themselves to be pointless. But it does not lie in the hands of Israel alone to bring this about.

Assimilation

For many years American culture has assumed that assimilation should be the goal of every immigrant, and that all ethnic groups should blend together in one 'melting pot'. Yet the range of immigrants that the American pot has succeeded in blending is actually quite small, consisting mainly of a few northern European groups (English, Irish, Scottish, Scandinavian). Other European groups have remained largely separate, as have 'visible minorities' such as Blacks and Asians.

One could argue that it is to the advantage of Jews to stay out of the melting-pot. Jewish leaders have traditionally railed against intermarriage. And for two generations, most American Jews did marry within their own community. Since 1985, however, 55 per cent of all marriages involving Jews have included one non-Jewish partner. If enough people were to convert to Judaism, especially in the context of marriage, perhaps that would help to stabilize the Jewish population. On the other hand, some predict that within a few generations the community will consist only of those Jews most resistant to inter-marriage, the Orthodox.

The situation in Canada is slightly different. Like the United States, Canada is a country built on immigration, but Canadians tend to see their society as a mosaic rather than a melting-pot. For centuries Canada has accommodated at least two distinct cultural communities, French and English, and the nation itself was founded on the idea that the two should have equal rights to live their own lives. Even before 'multicultural-ism'—a type of cultural pluralism—became official policy in the 1970s, new Canadians of other ethnic backgrounds may have experienced somewhat less pressure to assimilate than their counterparts in the US.

In any event, the future of Jewish communities in North America is hardly less certain that that of the Israeli state, though the threats to their survival lie not in a hostile environment but rather in an attractive and tolerant one. To survive these challenges, Jews are going to have to think very carefully about the sources of their identity.

Hope for the Future: A Jewish Wedding

Nowhere are hopes for the future of Judaism more clearly expressed than at a Jewish wedding. Whatever the setting—a home, a synagogue, a hotel ballroom—the marriage ceremony is conducted under a *huppah*: a special canopy reminiscent of a tent. Often the bride and groom are escorted to the *huppah* by their parents, although the bride may enter in a procession, as in a Christian wedding. At an Orthodox wedding she will circle the groom seven times before the ceremony begins with the bride and groom drinking from a consecrated cup of wine.

After the legal formalities have been completed and the ring given (or rings exchanged), seven blessings are recited over a second cup of wine. The blessings thank God for his creation of the world and human life, and recall the joy that ancient Judah took in the celebration of marriages. In fulfillment of the last blessing, which prays for the sound of joy in Judah and Israel, the wedding usually concludes with an enormous feast.

The wedding ceremony in many ways encapsulates the Jewish people's hopes for their community's survival. In consecrating the union of two young Jews, members of the community thank God for creation and sustenance, remember the long history of their people, pledge their responsibilities publicly, and pray for the continuation of the people Israel. These themes are particularly poignant today, when the future looks so uncertain.

In ancient times the prophet Hosea likened the covenant between Israel and its God to a wedding. Just as the wedding ceremony, in uniting two people, continues to unite them with their community's destiny even today, so the covenant between God and Israel continues to mediate the sense of Jewish purpose in the world.

Mount Sinai The place where *Exodus* 20–31 says the children of Israel received the Ten Commandments and the subsequent Book of the Covenant. The landform called Mount Sinai today may or may not be the same one.

Jerusalem A fortress of the Jebusites that was conquered by David around the year 1000 BCE (2 *Samuel* 5:5–10); also known as 'The City of David'.

Samaria The capital city of the Northern Kingdom.

Alexandria A city in Egypt, founded by Alexander the Great, which became the home of an important Greek-speaking Jewish community.

Masada The mountain fortress where Jewish Zealots made their last stand against the Romans in 73 CE, three years after the destruction of the Temple in Jerusalem.

Yavne (also known as Jamnia). A small town west of Jerusalem, where the early rabbinic movement fled for safety during the revolt against Rome (70 CE).

Okop, Podolia A small village in the Polish Russian pale of settlement where the founder of the Hasidic movement, Israel ben Eliezer, the Ba'al Shem Tov, was born in 1698.

Cincinnati, Ohio The capital of the Reform movement in the United States and location of the principal Reform seminary.

New York City The home of the largest Jewish population in the Americas and headquarters of the (Conservative) Jewish Theological Seminary.

Glossary

aggadah Anecdotal or narrative material in the *Talmud*; see also *halakha*.

apocalypse From the Greek for 'unveiling' (the Latin equivalent is 'revelation'); the final battle between the forces of darkness and light expected at the end of time. Apocalyptic literature flourished in the Hellenistic era.

Ashkenazim Jews of northern and eastern Europe, as distinguished from the Mediterranean **Sephardim**.

Bar Mitzvah 'Son of the commandments'; the title given to a thirteen-year-old boy when he is initiated into adult ritual responsibilities; some branches of Judaism also celebrate a Bat Mitzvah for girls.

berith Hebrew term for covenant, the special relationship between God and the Jewish people.

cantor The liturgical specialist who leads the musical chants in synagogue services.

Diaspora 'Dispersal', the Jewish world outside the land of ancient Israel; it began with the Babylonian Exile, from which not all Jews returned.

documentary hypothesis The theory (1894) that the **Pentateuch** was not written by one person (Moses) but compiled over a long period of time from multiple sources.

eschatology Doctrine concerning the end of the age, from the Greek for 'study of the end'.

Exile The deportation of Jewish leaders from Jerusalem to Mesopotamia by the conquering Babylonians in 586 BCE; disrupting local Israelite political, ritual, and agricultural institutions, it marked the transition from Israelite religion to Judaism.

Exodus The migration of Hebrews from Egypt under the leadership of Moses, understood in later Hebrew thought as marking the birth of the Israelite nation.

gaon Title of a senior rabbinical authority in Mesopotamia under Persian and Muslim rule.

Gemarah The body of Aramaic commentary attached to the Hebrew text of the *Mishnah*, which together with it makes up the *Talmud* (both the Jerusalem *Talmud* and the Babylonian *Talmud*).

Haggadah The liturgy for the ritual Passover supper.

halakha Material in the *Talmud* of a legal nature; see also *aggada*.

Hasidim 'Pious ones'; applied to two unrelated groups of loyal or pious Jews: those who resisted Hellenism militarily in second-century-BCE Palestine, and the mystically inclined followers of the Baal Shem Tov in eighteenth-century Poland and their descendants today.

hesed Hebrew term for the loyal conduct, sometimes translated as 'mercy' or 'loving-kindness', incumbent on God and on humans as parties to the covenant relationship.

Holocaust 'burnt offering' or 'burnt sacrifice'; one of the ancient sacrifices mandated in the Hebrew Bible. The term has more recently been applied to the persecution and murder of 6,000,000 European Jews by the Nazis before and during the Second World War (1939–45).

Humash The first five biblical books, the Pentateuch, when bound in book form for private study; in synagogue worship the same text is read from a scroll (see *Sefer Torah*).

Kabbalah The medieval Jewish mystical tradition; its central text is a commentary on scripture called the *Zohar*, compiled by Moses ben Shemtov of León (d. 1305) but attributed to Rabbi Shimon bar Yohai, a famous second-century rabbinic mystic and wonder-worker.

Karaites 'Scripturalists', an eighth-century anti-rabbinic movement that rejected the *Talmud* and post-biblical festivals such as Hanukkah, taking only the Bible as authoritative.

kippah 'Dome' or 'cap'; the Hebrew word for skullcap or *yarmulke*.

kosher Term for food that is ritually acceptable, indicating that all rabbinic regulations regarding animal slaughter and the like have been observed in its preparation.

logos 'Word'; a kind of divine intelligence thought to mediate between God and humanity and carry out God's intentions on earth.

Masada The fortress whose Jewish defenders are said to have committed suicide rather than surrender to Rome.

menorah The seven-branched candlestick, a Jewish symbol since ancient times, well before the widespread adoption of the six-pointed star; the nine-branched menorah used at Hanukkah is sometimes called a *hanukiah*.

midrash Commentary on scripture.

minyan The quorum of ten required for a prayer service in the synagogue.

Mishnah The Hebrew summary of the oral law—inherited from Pharisaism and ascribed to Moses—arranged by topic; edited by Rabbi Judah ha-Nasi before 220 CE, it has an authority paralleling that of the written Torah.

Mishneh Torah A topically arranged code of Jewish law written in the twelfth century by Moses Maimonides.

mitzvah A commandment; in the Roman era, the rabbinic movement identified exactly 613 specific commandments contained within the Torah.

Passover The major spring festival of agricultural rebirth and renewal, given a historical dimension by association with the hasty departure of the Israelites from Egypt under Moses' leadership.

patriarchs and matriarchs Ancestors of the Israelite nation in the Hebrew Bible's narratives of origins; 'patriarch' was also a title given to the head of the Jewish community in early rabbinic times.

Pentateuch The first five books of the Hebrew Bible, ascribed by tradition to Moses but regarded by modern scholars as the product of several centuries of later literary activity.

phylacteries The usual English term for *tefillin*.

rabbi A teacher, in Roman times an expert on the interpretation of Torah; since priestly sacrifices ceased with the destruction of the temple, the rabbi has been the scholarly and spiritual leader of a Jewish congregation.

responsa literature From the Latin for 'answers' (singular, *responsum*); accumulated correspondence by medieval and recent rabbinical authorities, consisting of rulings on issues of legal interpretation. Also known as *Teshuvoth*.

Rosh Hashanah The new year festival, generally occurring in September.

Sabbath The seventh day of the week, observed by Jews since ancient times as a day of rest from ordinary activity.

seder 'Order'; the term used for the ritual Passover supper celebrated in the home; the six divisions of the *Mishnah* are also called orders or *seders*.

Sefer Torah 'Book of the law'; a special copy of the first five books of Moses, hand-lettered on parchment for use in synagogue rituals (see also *humash*).

Sephardim The Jews of the premodern Mediterranean and Middle Eastern world, as opposed to the Ashkenazim of northern and eastern Europe.

Septuagint The Greek translation of the Hebrew scriptures, made in Alexandria in Hellenistic times.

shekhinah The divine presence or 'dwelling', often described in visionary terms by ancient commentators on Ezekiel and by medieval mystics.

sukkah A temporary booth or shelter, originally constructed in autumn to protect ripening crops and given a historical interpretation recalling the migration experience of the Exodus.

synagogue The local place of assembly for congregational worship, which became central to the tradition after the destruction of the Jerusalem temple.

takkanah 'Remediation'; a principle (attributed to Hillel) that facilitated borrowing by allowing the court to take over farmers' debts in years when their fields were fallow.

tallith A shawl worn for prayer, usually white with blue stripes and with fringes at the corners.

Tanakh The entire Hebrew Bible, consisting of Torah or law, *Nebi'im* or prophets, and *Ketuvim* or sacred writings, and named as an acronym of these three terms.

Tannaim The rabbinic authorities whose opinions are recorded in the *Mishnah*, as distinguished from the rabbis (Amoraim) whose opinions appear in the *Gemarah* material of the Talmud.

tefillin Small black leather boxes, also termed phylacteries, containing words of scripture, tied to the forehead and forearm by leather thongs.

Teshuvoth Also called *shealoth veteshuvoth*; see *responsa* literature.

Torah A word meaning 'teaching' or 'instruction'; applied most specifically to the the Law of Moses (the Pentateuch) but may also refer to the entire scripture, including commentaries, and even the entire spiritual thrust of Jewish religion.

yarmulke The Yiddish word for the *kippah* or skullcap worn by Orthodox Jewish males.

yeshiva A traditional school for the study of the scriptures and Jewish law.

Yiddish The language spoken by many central and eastern European Jews in recent centuries; though it is written in Hebrew characters and contains some words derived from Hebrew, it is essentially German in its basic structure and vocabulary.

Yom Kippur The day of atonement, ten days after **Rosh Hashanah**; the day for the most solemn reflection and examination of one's conduct.

Zaddik 'Righteous person', a title conveying the Hasidic ideal for a teacher or spiritual leader.

Zion In biblical times, the hill in Jerusalem where the temple stood as God's dwelling place; by extension, the land of the Israelites as the place of God's favour; in modern times the goal of Jewish migration and nation-state settlement.

Further Reading

Barnavi, Elie, ed. 1992. *A Historical Atlas of the Jewish People: From the Time of the Patriarchs to the Present*. New York: Knopf. Excellent on the diaspora in medieval and modern times.

Baskin, Judith, ed. 1998. *Jewish Women in Historical Perspective*. 2nd edn. Detroit: Wayne State University Press. An anthology of essays on the role of women in Jewish history.

Biale, David, ed. 2002. *Cultures of the Jews*. New York: Schocken Books. A recent scholarly examination of the various periods of Jewish history.

Encyclopedia Judaica. 1971. 16 vols. Jerusalem: Encyclopedia Judaica; New York: Macmillan. The basic reference book for Judaism. Some of the articles, such as the one on Jerusalem, are almost books in themselves.

Gaster, Theodor H. 1952. *The Festivals of the Jewish Year*. New York: William Sloane Associates. Explains how agricultural festivals came to be associated with specific events in biblical history.

Hertzberg, Arthur. 1972. *The Zionist Idea: A Historical Analysis and Reader*. New York: Atheneum. An anthology of standard sources on the Zionist movement.

Montefiore, Claude G., and Herbert Loewe, eds. 1938. *A Rabbinic Anthology*. London: Macmillan. A good collection of basic rabbinic texts.

Newman, Louis I., ed. 1934. *The Hasidic Anthology: Tales and Teachings of the Hasidim*. New York: Scribner. Contains many of the most frequently cited Hasidic texts.

Segal, Alan F. 1986. *Rebecca's Children: Judaism and Christianity in the Roman World*. Cambridge, MA: Harvard University Press. Treats the Christian and early rabbinic movements as parallel developments.

Steinsaltz, Adin. 1989. *The Talmud, the Steinsaltz Edition: A Reference Guide*. New York: Random House. Valuable explanations of technical rabbinic terminology and usage.

Yerushalmi, Yosef. 1982. *Zakhor: Jewish History and Jewish Memory*. Seattle: University of Washington Press. A sophisticated appraisal of the use of history in traditional Judaism.

References

Alexander, Philip, ed. 1984. *Textual Sources for the History of Judaism*. Manchester: Manchester University Press.

Arnold, Bill T., and Bryan E. Beyer. 2002. *Readings from the Ancient Near East*. Grand Rapids, MI: Baker.

Grunfeld, Isidor, trans. 1956. *Judaism Eternal: Selected Essays from the Writings of Rabbi Samson Raphael Hirsch*. 2 vols. London: Soncino Press.

Herzl, Theodor. 1946. *The Jewish State*. New York: American Zionist Emergency Council.

Lowenthal, Marvin, trans. 1977. *The Memoirs of Glückel of Hameln*. New York: Schocken.

Kohn, H., ed. 1962. *Nationalism and the Jewish Ethic: Basic Writings of Ahad Ha-Am*. New York: Herzl Press.

Marcus, Ralph, trans. 1961. *Josephus, Antiquities XII–XIV*. Cambridge, MA: Harvard University Press.

Schechter, Solomon. 1896. *Studies in Judaism*. 1st series. New York: Macmillan.

Thackeray, H. St. J., trans. 1927. *Josephus in Nine Volumes*. Cambridge, MA: Harvard University Press.

Umansky, Ellen, and Dianne Ashton, eds. 1992. *Four Centuries of Jewish Women's Spirituality: A Sourcebook*. Boston: Beacon.

Whiston, William, trans. 1802. *The Genuine Works of Flavius Josephus*. Edinburgh: Thomas and John Turnbull.

The Christian Tradition

ALAN SEGAL | WILLARD G. OXTOBY

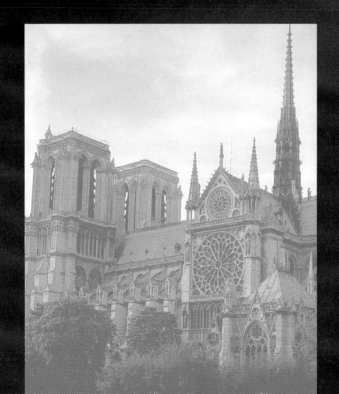

Throughout the Christian world, the year reaches a climax in late December, when the Christmas season marks the birth of Jesus in Israel approximately 2,000 years ago. Christians see Jesus as the manifestation of divine nature and purpose in a human life and believe that in him God has reached out to conquer humanity's weaknesses.

To identify oneself as a Christian is to declare Jesus lord and saviour of the world. The heavy emphasis that Christians place on this declaration is crucial for understanding Christianity's function as a religious tradition. To be a Christian involves making a commitment of faith—expressed not only in one's conduct but also as affirmation of doctrine. Christians 'confess' or 'believe' Jesus to be the incarnate son of God and saviour of the world.

Celebrating a Birth

The word 'Christmas' means 'the **mass** of Christ'. The mass or **Eucharist** is Christianity's central rite: a symbolic meal, offered at worship services throughout the year, that recalls or re-enacts Jesus' self-sacrificing death. Its solemnity figures as a theme even amid the optimism of Christmas, pointing towards the death and resurrection that will be commemorated at Easter, the central Christian festival. For Christians, the reports of Jesus' followers that they saw him risen from the dead confirm his divine lordship.

Christians recognize that many of the cultural trappings around Christmas are secular rather than religious. In theory, they distinguish between the sacred and the secular—a distinction that reflects the early Christians' experience as a minority movement before Christianity became the established religion of any state. In practice, however, the distinction has not always been easy to apply; separating the spheres of church and state was a problem in the European Middle Ages and remains one today.

Christians are found in every part of the world. Persons identified as Christian, whether or not they are observant, constitute the world's largest religious community. Estimates place their number at a billion and a half—roughly one-quarter of the global population. They are the majority in Europe, throughout the Western hemisphere, and in Australia and New Zealand.

Origins

The Gospels

The gospels are four biographies of Jesus believed to have been written by four of his disciples: Mark, Luke, Matthew, and John. The word **gospel** (*evangelion* in Greek, the

c. 30	Death of Jesus
c. 65	Death of Paul
312	Constantine's vision of the cross
325	First Council of Nicaea
337	Constantine is baptized on his deathbed
c. 384	Augustine's conversion experience
451	Council of Chalcedon
529	Benedict establishes monastery
842	Iconoclastic controversy ends
862	Cyril and Methodius in Moravia
c. 1033	Birth of Anselm (d. 1109)
1054	Break between Rome and Constantinople
1095	Urban II calls for the first crusade
1187	End of the Latin Kingdom of Jerusalem
c. 1225	Birth of Thomas Aquinas (*Summa Theologiae*) (d. 1274)
1517	Luther posts his 95 theses
1534	Henry VIII becomes head of the Church of England
1536	Calvin's *Institutes*
1563	Council of Trent concludes
1738	John Wesley's conversion experience
1781	Immanuel Kant's *Critique of Pure Reason*
1830	Book of Mormon
1859	Charles Darwin, *On the Origin of Species*
1870	First Vatican Council concludes
1910	Publication of *The Fundamentals*
1948	First assembly of the World Council of Churches
1965	Second Vatican Council concludes

language of the New Testament's composition) means 'good news'—the news of redemption that the Hebrew prophets had promised.

In Mark's gospel, when Jesus gasps his last breath on the cross, a Roman soldier is moved to observe: 'Truly this was a son of God.' It is fitting that Mark attributes this comment to a Roman soldier rather than one of Jesus' followers, for the Christian movement soon grew beyond its initial base as a Jewish sect. Within a generation of his death, the Christians decided that their message was not for the Jews alone—that anyone could be a Christian. In that decision lay the seeds of Christianity's development as a missionary religion.

More than three centuries later, when Christianity became the established religion of the Roman empire, Church leaders made a list of the writings they acknowledged to be scripture. That standard list, or **canon**, of books and letters is what Christians know as the New Testament. It includes the four gospels that had achieved universal acceptance throughout Christendom. But in the late first and early second centuries, when these and a number of other gospels were first written and circulated, the situation was much more fluid.

Mark

Although Mark's gospel comes second in the New Testament, it is considered to be the earliest of the four gospels that were eventually accepted as canonical. Certainly it is the simplest and most straightforward. Mark says nothing about Jesus' life before the beginning of his mature ministry. Instead, his account begins with John the Baptist, the leader of a desert-based movement, who performs the ritual of **baptism** on Jesus. Jesus then withdraws into the desert himself. After a forty-day retreat during which he wrestles with Satan, God's arch-enemy, Jesus launches his ministry in the region of Galilee, proclaiming that the kingdom of God is at hand. His local reputation spreads as he performs healing miracles. When he is challenged for picking grain and healing the sick on the Sabbath, he takes the notion of Jewish legal authority into his own hands and declares that the Sabbath is made for people rather than people for the Sabbath. It is in response to this apparent arrogance, Mark suggests, that the Jewish priests conspire to do away with him.

Jesus selects from those who follow him a group of twelve (a significant figure in the Jewish tradition, the size of a complete set of months, tribes, and prophetical books, among other things) to form an inner circle of disciples. Accompanied by them, he continues to heal and teach and to challenge the priorities of religious authority. Eventually he goes to Jerusalem, arriving with a crowd that shouts 'Hosanna' (a cry for divine deliverance in Hebrew prayer) and proclaims the coming of the messiah: a king in the line of the dynastic founder, David, who brings deliverance. During the course of a week in Jerusalem, he disputes with the religious authorities, celebrates the Passover with his disciples, is betrayed by one of them (Judas), is arrested, and is brought to trial before Pontius Pilate, the Roman governor. When he does not deny that he is the king of the Jews, and offers no defence, he is sentenced to crucifixion.

At the height of his suffering on the cross, Jesus cries out, 'My God, my God, why have you forsaken me?' He expires and, before the beginning of the Sabbath, his body is

NUMBERS
1.5 billion around the world.

DISTRIBUTION
Christians constitute the majority of the population in Europe and the Americas, Australia, New Zealand, and the Philippines; approximately half the population of Lebanon; and almost a third of the population of South Korea.

PRINCIPAL HISTORICAL PERIODS

c. 3 BCE– c. 30 CE	Lifetime of Jesus
c. 30–c. 120	The New Testament or Apostolic age
c. 120–451	The early Church
451–1517	Medieval Christianity
1517–c. 1600	The Protestant Reformation
17th century–present	The modern period

FOUNDERS
Founded by the followers of Jesus of Nazareth, called the Christ, on the basis of his teachings and resurrection. Among the early founders, the apostles Peter and Paul were especially important.

DEITY
One God, called 'God' or 'Lord', who exists in three persons: as Father, Son, and Holy Spirit.

AUTHORITATIVE TEXTS
The Christian Bible consists of the Old Testament (the Hebrew Bible) and the New Testament. The Roman Catholic and Orthodox churches include as part of the Old Testament a number of books from the Septuagint that Protestants set apart as *Apocrypha*. In addition, Roman Catholics hold the teaching office (magisterium) of the Church to be authoritative.

NOTEWORTHY DOCTRINES
Jesus is the second person of the Trinity, truly God as well as truly man, and his resurrection is the sign that those who believe in him will have eternal life. The authority of the Church has been passed down from the apostles.

placed in a tomb that is sealed with a large stone. The day after the Sabbath, when three women from among his following go to the tomb, they find the stone rolled away and the body missing.

Luke

Luke's biography of Jesus includes two chapters of material not found in Mark. In addition to recounting events in Jesus' life before his baptism, this material includes visions and portents anticipating the birth of John the Baptist as well as that of Jesus. Luke tells how Jesus was born in Bethlehem, how angels (divine messengers) announced the birth to shepherds in the fields, and how the shepherds went to pay their respects to the newborn messiah. Although Luke does not mention any wise men from the East (the *magi*, Persian for 'priests', are in Matthew), he does say that, at a new-born-purification ceremony in the temple, a devout man also proclaims the infant to be the messiah.

Luke also provides more detail than Mark regarding the trial and crucifixion of Jesus. In his version, the charge is that by claiming kingship, Jesus has incited rebellion. Here Pilate himself declares Jesus innocent of any crime, but yields to mob pressure to have him executed anyway. Luke's Roman centurion declares that Jesus is innocent, not that he is a son of God. Finally, Luke tells how, after the discovery of the empty tomb, Jesus appears among his followers and speaks to them.

| Box 3.1 | Sayings of Jesus

From the body of teachings of Jesus in Matthew *conventionally known as the 'Sermon on the Mount'. The translation is that of the* New English Bible: The New Testament *(Oxford University Press and Cambridge University Press, 1961).*

If, when you are bringing your gift to the altar, you suddenly remember that your brother has a grievance against you, leave your gift where it is before the altar. First go and make your peace with your brother, and only then come back and offer your gift (5:23–4).

You have learned that they were told, 'Eye for eye, tooth for tooth.' But what I tell you is this: Do not set yourself against the man who wrongs you. If someone slaps you on the right cheek, turn and offer him your left. If a man wants to sue you for your shirt, let him have your coat as well. If a man in authority makes you go one mile, go with him two. Give when you are asked to give; and do not turn your back on a man who wants to borrow (5:38–42).

Pass no judgment, and you will not be judged. For as you judge others, so you will yourselves be judged, and whatever measure you deal out to others will be dealt back to you. Why do you look at the speck of sawdust in your brother's eye, with never a thought for the great plank in your own? Or how can you say to your brother, 'Let me take the speck out of your eye,' when all the time there is that plank in your own? First take the plank out of your own eye, and then you will see clearly to take the speck out of your brother's (7:1–5).

Matthew

Matthew's account includes much of the same material as Luke's, but his focus is noticeably different. As a writer, Matthew has clearly designed his narrative to persuade a Jewish audience of the truth of Jesus' claim to be the messiah. For example, it has been suggested that his account of Jesus' escape from the slaughter of infants by King Herod was specifically intended to echo the *Exodus* account of the Israelites' escape from the wrath of the Egyptian pharaoh. Though Herod was a tyrant, no other source records this barbarity.

Matthew opens his gospel by giving a genealogy of Jesus as the descendant of King David, in a lineage that runs through Joseph, husband of Mary. However, Matthew then bypasses this genealogy by telling how Mary conceived the child—by the Holy Spirit—before her marriage to Joseph. Apparently it was part of Matthew's purpose to show that the birth of Jesus exactly fulfilled a prophecy in the seventh chapter of *Isaiah*: 'Behold, a virgin shall conceive and bear a son, and his name shall be called Emmanuel (which means, "God with us").'

Although the Hebrew of *Isaiah* mentions only a 'young woman', the Greek version is ambiguous and can be read as 'virgin'. The stage is thus set for one of Christianity's more problematic teachings: the virgin birth. Luke and Matthew are the only New Testament sources for this doctrine.

John

Despite their differences, Mark, Luke, and Matthew have much more in common with one another than any of them does with the fourth gospel. For this reason scholars often refer to the first three as the 'synoptic gospels', underlining the similarity of their perspectives in comparison with the very different perspective of John.

John's purpose is not simply to recount Jesus' life or (as in the case of Matthew) to show how it fulfilled the Hebrew scriptures. Rather, he is expressly concerned to assert the cosmic significance of that life and declare Jesus' identity as messiah and saviour. John is candid at the end of his twentieth chapter: 'these are written that you may come to believe that Jesus is the Messiah, the Son of God, and that through believing you may have life in his name' (*John* 20:30–1). John's theoretical reflection developed over some decades after the composition of the synoptic gospels.

In his opening passage, called by scholars the prologue, John shows his theological interest at once. 'In the beginning,' he writes (echoing the opening words of *Genesis* in the Hebrew scriptures), 'was the *logos*, and the *logos* was with God, and the *logos* was God; all things were made through him.' As we saw in Chapter 2, *logos* is a Greek term with an important range of meaning in the philosophy and religion of the Hellenistic world at the time of Jesus. Although translated as 'word', it signifies far more—a divine blueprint or pattern or divine intelligence.

A few verses later in the prologue, John declares Jesus to be the **incarnation** of that divine Word. 'The *logos* became flesh and dwelt among us, full of grace and truth; we have beheld his glory, glory as of the only Son from the Father.' For John, the eternal

---

| Box 3.2 | Sources of the Gospel Narratives |

Much of the Gospel material consists of Jesus' teachings. Some of these take the form of parables: narrative stories designed to teach a moral lesson. Others take the form of short sayings that could stand alone, apart from any narrative, as universally applicable proverbs or maxims. In chapters 5 through 7 of his account, Matthew describes Jesus as delivering a collection of these on a mountain in northern Palestine; the material is thus known as the Sermon on the Mount. Luke presents the same material—though in his gospel it is delivered on a plain.

In general, Luke and Matthew overlap to a considerable extent, and it has been assumed that both of them used Mark's narrative as a source for their accounts. Yet some of the material they both include is not found in Mark.

These discrepancies led German scholars in the nineteenth century to postulate that the material not in Mark must have come from a different source, one that both Luke and Matthew used and that has since been lost. This hypothetical document has come to be known as 'Q', from the initial letter of *Quelle*, the German word for 'source'.

---

divine purpose has now become a personal presence in human form, and this incarnation took place only a short while ago, in the community's recent experience.

John is in step here with Paul, an early convert who probably contributed as much as anyone to the shaping of the early Christian message. John, like Paul, is now using the title '**Christ**' (the Greek translation of the Hebrew word for messiah, 'anointed') practically as a second personal name for Jesus. John's view of the significance of Jesus is encapsulated in a frequently quoted passage: 'For God so loved the world that he gave his only Son, that whoever believes in him should not perish but have eternal life' (*John* 3:16).

From Sect to Church

The handful of Jesus' disciples who were left at the time of his execution were peasants from rural Galilee whose teacher had stirred in them the hope that low-status and marginalized people—the poor, sinners, Samaritans, women—had a place in God's plan. As a group, they amounted to a minor Jewish sect that expected the end of the age and the glorious return of their teacher at any moment.

Various explanations have been offered for how that small group of people transformed itself into an independent missionary religion that within four centuries had become the state church of the Roman Empire. Not surprisingly, the New Testament book *Acts of the Apostles*, which is Luke's sequel to his gospel, describes a miraculous event. In *Acts* 2 the disciples are gathered on Shavuoth, the festival held seven weeks after the Passover during which Jesus was executed (Luke uses the Greek word **Pentecost** for this holiday). Experiencing the Holy Spirit as a rush of wind and fire, they begin to speak—and be understood—in diverse languages, thus enabled to preach to all people.

Paul

The principal influence on the direction of the early Church was not one of Jesus' band of twelve, but an educated and sophisticated convert who took the name Paul. He was a cosmopolitan person with the privileged status of a Roman citizen. According to Luke, Paul was a Pharisee from the diaspora Jewish community in Tarsus, a large ancient city located on the southern coast of contemporary Turkey, who had gone to Jerusalem for religio-legal study.

Paul had not known Jesus himself. Rather (by Luke's account), while on the way to Damascus to persecute Christians there, he experienced a personal encounter with the post-resurrection Jesus that reoriented his life. This reorientation would today be called a **conversion**. For the next quarter-century he travelled tirelessly around the eastern Mediterranean, initially directing his message to the diaspora Jewish communities, but eventually preaching that Jews and gentiles (non-Jews) alike were heirs in Christ to the promises of God.

Paul carried on a correspondence with the scattered communities of Christian converts in places like Corinth and Rome in letters whose content ranged from personal greetings and liturgical blessings to essays on questions of theology. Paul's letters, which come from a time before the gospels were written, are the earliest Christian literature, and their formative effect on Christian theology can hardly be overestimated.

In his letters Paul refers to himself as the apostle to the gentiles. He opposes the view that in order to follow Jesus one must first become a Jew, be circumcised (if male), and follow the dietary regulations and other commandments of Pharisaism. For Paul, it is not through observance of ritual laws or even correct moral conduct that salvation is attained, but rather through faith in Jesus and the divine grace that comes through him.

In addition, Paul introduces what will become a pervasive theme in subsequent Christian theology, contrasting life 'in the spirit'—life centred on lasting religious values such as faith, hope, and love—with life 'in the flesh', the pursuit of what passes away, including worldly ambition or pleasure.

Thanks to Paul's voyages, Christian communities were established in many of the port cities of the Roman Empire by the time he died, about the year 65. At the beginning of his involvement with Christianity, Paul had assisted the people who stoned the apostle Stephen to death, by holding their coats. Now Paul was to become a martyr (etymologically, a 'witness') himself, executed in Rome as part of the emperor Nero's persecution of Christians.

Marcion

If Paul was the principal architect of the early Church, then we might describe Marcion (d. c. 160) as a draughtsman whose blueprint was rejected. Marcion lived a century after Paul. The son of a bishop, he was a wealthy shipowner from Sinope, on the south shore of the Black Sea. He made his way to Rome, the capital, where his teachings led to his **excommunication** (formal expulsion) from the Church in 144, but this did not deter him from his views, which he continued earnestly to advocate.

In his theology, Marcion takes Paul's ideas to astonishing lengths. Paul's contrast between law and gospel becomes for Marcion a contrast not only between the Old and New Testaments but between two distinct deities. For Marcion the creator God of the

Hebrew scriptures, the one who gives the law to Moses, is what he calls the 'Demiurge': a stern and fearsome deity, capricious, despotic, and cruel. The coming of Jesus reveals an utterly different God of love and mercy, whose purpose is to overcome the Demiurge. The God revealed by Jesus should replace the God of the Hebrew scriptures. Thus, Marcion reasoned, the Christian scriptures should not include any Old Testament book; in fact, he rejected almost all Christian scriptures as well, except for an abridged version of the Gospel of Luke and some of Paul's letters.

After much dispute, Marcion's canon itself was rejected, largely because the Church needed the prophecies of the Old Testament to justify its claims to historicity. But it took the notion of a canon from Marcion and set out to create its own.

The Gnostics

Another spiritual and doctrinal challenge for the early Christian Church was **Gnosticism**: a school of thought that probably originated sometime in the early Christian era. The Gnostics claimed to have privileged, secret knowledge (the Greek word *gnosis* means 'knowledge'). To their Christian adherents they offered an inner meaning of Christianity (and to Jewish Gnostics, of Judaism). At first they were not a separate community, but rather a school of interpretation within the network of the Christian churches.

The Gnostic philosophical narrative is dualistic: the divine powers of good are opposed by demonic forces of evil, and spirit is in a cosmic struggle with matter. In the beginning, the material world was created through the entrapment or fall and fragmentation of spirit into matter. Although accounts differ on the details—in some, spirit falls victim to temptation; in others, to treachery or attack—all agree that there will be a long struggle before spirit is restored to its proper place.

The Christian Gnostics saw Jesus as an emissary from the realm of the spirit who appeared in human form but did not take on full material existence. For this reason critics within the Church objected that gnosticism robbed the religion of the benefits accruing from the doctrine of incarnation.

In the mid-twentieth century there was a major discovery of Gnostic manuscripts on papyrus at Nag Hammadi, an up-river site on the Nile in Egypt. Consequently a more sympathetic view of Gnostic ideas has been available to historians in recent decades. Among the Nag Hammadi texts is the *Gospel of Thomas*, one of many writings, Gnostic and otherwise, that did not gain ratification as scripture by the Church at large. Although it was probably written after Jesus' death, it presents his sayings as though he were still alive and does not describe his death.

Crystallization

The Early Church

In its earliest years the Christian movement had no formal organization. With the Easter story as their model, Christians simply gathered in one another's homes on Sundays to pray and affirm their faith. Various individuals emerged as teachers, and some became evangelists, spreading the word and forming new groups. Eventually a process of ordination was established whereby certain individuals were qualified to perform ritual and administrative functions. The most basic grade was deacon, and women as well as men were so designated in the early Church. The ranking priest in a political jurisdiction was the **bishop** (from the Greek *episkopos*, 'supervisor'). By the third century four episcopal jurisdictions or 'sees' had gained prominence because of the importance of their cities: Jerusalem, Rome, Alexandria in Egypt, and Antioch in Syria. The bishops of these cities came to be known as **patriarchs**. A fifth patriarch was added in the fourth century, when Constantinople replaced Rome as the imperial capital.

The Ascetic Tradition

Jesus was not the first religious figure to withdraw from his society into the desert for contemplation. John the Baptist and his followers are associated with the desert, and the Essenes had a well-established community near the Dead Sea until it was destroyed by the Romans in the first century. During the anti-Christian campaigns of the second and third centuries, life in the desert also offered some security from persecution. In less dangerous times, however, exchanging the comforts of normal life in society for the harsh and austere discipline of life in the desert was a way of repudiating the laxity and complacency of the broader Christian community, especially after Christianity won the official sanction of Rome.

The earliest Christian ascetics or 'desert fathers' were hermits such as Antony (c. 251–356), whose solitary life in Egypt became the model for the monastic tradition. Another was Simeon Stylites (c. 390–459) in northern Syria. After having already been a hermit for ten years, in his mid-twenties Simeon built a pillar and sat on top of it for the rest of his life, using a basket to haul up the supplies provided by his admirers. Simeon's dedication attracted converts and pilgrims, and set an example that other 'stylites' (pole-sitters) copied. As the Greek root *monos* ('one', 'alone') suggests, monasticism entailed a life apart from the wider society; but in time various hermits took up locations near one another for safety and mutual support. Such groupings were at first informal, but by the mid-fourth century nine monasteries for men and two for women had been established in Egypt alone. Basil (c. 330–79), bishop of Caesarea in east-central Turkey, drew up regulations for such communities that included poverty and chastity, specified hours of prayer, and assigned manual tasks. Monasticism was becoming formalized as a corporate discipline.

Roman Persecution

Roman society had civic gods and rituals that the population at large was supposed to support. But the Christians stood aloof from the public religion, which they considered idol worship. From the biblical point of view, they were faithful to the Hebraic tradition of monotheism. From the Roman point of view, however, they were guilty of insubordination.

The emperor Decius (r. 249–51), seeking to revitalize his shaky regime, commanded public sacrifices to the Roman civic gods, with the penalty of death or imprisonment for anyone who would not comply. Throughout the empire, in the years 250–1, Christians were systematically persecuted as a matter of policy, and in 257–9 Valerian conducted another widespread campaign of official persecution.

Many Christians were put to death for their faith. Modelling their conduct on the self-sacrificing death of their lord, they accepted martyrdom in the expectation that their reward would be a life in the next world in fellowship with him.

The last and fiercest persecutions of the Christians began in 303 under the emperor Diocletian. For the next nine years, Christians were killed, Church properties destroyed, and Christian sacred writings burned. But the 'Great Persecution' was no more successful than its predecessors.

'The blood of the martyrs is the seed of the church,' said Tertullian (c. 160–c. 220), who came from Carthage in North Africa and was the first theologian to write in Latin. The Roman policy of persecution had the unintended effect of helping Christians to establish a reputation for bravery and fidelity that attracted many new converts.

Constantine

A shift of policy under Diocletian's successor forever changed Christianity's place in the world. Constantine (r. 306–37) gradually abandoned the persecution policy and in 313 gave them liberty to practise their religion.

Eusebius (c. 260–c. 340), bishop of Caesarea in Palestine, lived through the transition. According to his *Life of Constantine*, the emperor's conversion was sparked by a vision he experienced—on the eve of a decisive battle in 312—of a cross in the heavens and the words 'conquer in this sign'. The following day his troops won the battle and gave him control of the western half of the empire.

Modern historians have speculated about Constantine's motives and sincerity. The allegedly sudden vision does not square with the gradual pace of policy change. Christian symbols appeared on Constantine's coinage alongside pagan symbols for several years; Sunday did not become a public holiday until 321 and even then it coincided with popular worship of the sun. Finally, Constantine was not baptized a Christian until he was on his deathbed. Some rationalize his delay by arguing that, at a time when baptism was considered a once-only total cleansing from sin that guaranteed salvation, people postponed it in order to enter heaven with as clean a slate as possible.

Whatever his religious motives (his mother was a Christian), Constantine must have been a shrewd enough politician to recognize that the Church could help to stabilize his regime. The Church was dispersed throughout the entire empire. It had a system of regional government supervised by bishops. It seemed to be arriving at a coherent sense of its teaching, in response to doctrinal challenges. And it had remarkable discipline, at both institutional and personal levels.

Still, Christianity did not replace paganism overnight. The etymology of the word 'pagan' hints at the process; like 'peasant', it comes from the Latin word meaning 'rural'. Christianity spread in the towns and along the trade routes, while in more remote areas the old ways remained. (Similarly, what survived on the remote heaths of northern Europe is called 'heathen'.) In intellectual circles, Christianity faced competition from other movements. The emperor Julian (r. 361–3) attempted unsuccessfully to bring back pagan worship and teaching, though he stopped short of reintroducing persecution of Christians. It was only with Theodosius I (r. 379–95) that the empire became officially Christian.

Doctrinal Issues

By the fourth century the Church had formulated at least two formal statements of belief called **creeds** (from the Latin for 'belief'). The importance attributed to such statements has had a lasting influence on Christians' understanding of themselves and of others. Because Christians have defined themselves by their beliefs about Jesus and God and the world, they have often mistakenly expected other traditions to be formulated in terms of belief as well.

Perhaps as early as 150 but certainly by the early third century, a formulation known as the Apostles' Creed was coming into use, especially in the Latin-speaking western part of the Mediterranean. Named for the first generation of Jesus' followers, the Apostles' Creed is still widely used. A somewhat more detailed formulation is the Nicene Creed, named for the Council of Nicaea in 325 but ratified in its present form in 381. It is still recited in Eucharistic services in the Catholic tradition.

The Trinity

The Nicene creed reflects the emergence of the explicit doctrine of the **Trinity**: that God has three manifestations or 'persons': father, son, and Holy Spirit. Christians today often

---

| Box 3.3 | **The Nicene Creed**

We believe in one God, the Father almighty, maker of heaven and earth, and of all things visible and invisible; and in one Lord Jesus Christ, the only-begotten Son of God, begotten of the Father before all worlds, God of God, light of light, very God of very God, begotten not made, being of one substance with the Father, by whom all things were made, who for us men and for our salvation came down from heaven, and was incarnate by the Holy Spirit of the Virgin Mary, and was made man, and was crucified for us under Pontius Pilate. He suffered and was buried, and the third day he rose again according to the scriptures, and ascended into heaven, and sits on the right hand of the Father, and he shall come again with glory to judge both the living and the dead; whose kingdom shall have no end. And we believe in the Holy Spirit, the Lord and giver of life, who proceeds from the Father (and the Son), who with the Father and Son together is worshipped and glorified, who spoke by the prophets. And we believe in one holy catholic and apostolic church. We acknowledge one baptism for the remission of sins. And we look for the resurrection of the dead, and the life of the world to come.

assume that this doctrine has been part of the tradition from the beginning, but it has not: although the New Testament speaks of God as father and of Jesus as son, and of God's spirit, it almost never puts the three together in an explicit list.

In fact, the Trinity was the subject of intense controversy at the time of Constantine. In Alexandria, a presbyter ('elder') named Arius (c. 250–c. 336) proposed that the son of God was not eternal, but was created within time by the father as part of the creation of the world; in other words, 'there was an existence when the Son was not'. This meant that the son was not eternal by nature but was subject to change. This view was opposed by another Alexandrian, Athanasius (c. 296–373), who asserted the coeternity and coequality of father and son. One of the arguments for this interpretation was that it emphasized the power of the son to be a saviour. The conflict has been termed a battle over a Greek diphthong, the Athanasians calling the son *homoousion* (of the same substance) in contrast to the Arian *homoiousion* (of similar substance).

Hoping that a unified Church would promote stability in his empire, Constantine called the bishops to meet at the Council of Nicaea, not far from Constantinople, in 325. The dispute between Arius and Athanasius was part of the agenda, and the decision went against Arius. But Arian views continued to enlist support, and for half a century they surfaced in various attempts at compromise formulas, even prevailing for a time, before being rejected at the Council of Constantinople in 381.

No sooner had the Athanasian position become orthodoxy, however, than a corollary to it cried out for attention. If the eternal son is coequal with the father, then how does the eternal divinity of Jesus relate to his historical humanity? There were three principal options, around which regional divisions emerged. The incarnate Christ could be:

- Two separate persons, one divine and one human, as the **Nestorian** churches, stretching eastward across Asia, held;
- One person, with only a divine nature, as the **Monophysites**, from Ethiopia and Egypt to Syria and Armenia, held; or
- One person, but with both a divine nature and a human one, as the Greek- and Latin-speaking churches held.

Each of these fifth-century options has continued to command adherents to the present day. In a sense, these theological debates gave intellectual justification to the desire of local, regional, and national churches for more independence from Rome. The Roman Church, however, affirms a theology in which God is one simple, single divine essence, which has eternally had three distinct persons, one of whom is the Christ, who was both truly God and truly man. This formula is a synthesis that reflects the Church's desire to appeal to the widest possibly clientele, though it glosses over many intellectually interesting solutions to this intractable problem.

Two Christian Worlds: Byzantium and Rome

The Council of Chalcedon in 451 was composed almost exclusively of eastern bishops, but in response to the Monophysite challenge it arrived at a Christological formulation that accommodated Rome as well as Constantinople.

| Box 3.4 | Christianity in Egypt, Ethiopia, and Armenia

The indigenous Christians of Egypt, the Copts, believe that their faith was taken to Egypt by the gospel writer Mark, and that their ancestors were early pioneers in the development of monasticism. After the Islamic conquest in the seventh century, Egyptians who remained Christian were a minority, but a significant one. The Copts have retained a sense of cultural pride as 'original' Egyptians.

By the fourth century Christian influence had extended to Ethiopia. Although Ethiopia gave asylum to Muslim emigrants, it was not subjugated by Islam. It remained Christian, recognizing the authority of the Coptic patriarch in Cairo and maintaining a window on the world through its own priests and monks in Jerusalem. The Ethiopian church has remained essentially Coptic, though it has been formally independent of Cairo since the mid-twentieth century.

In Armenia as in Egypt, legend traces the introduction of Christianity to the missionary activity of the apostles, in this case Thaddeus and Bartholomew. Armenian Christians maintain that their king Tiridates III, who was baptized by Gregory the Illuminator around 301, was the first to establish Christianity as a state religion.

Chalcedon steered a middle course between the Nestorians, who compromised the eternal deity of Jesus, and the Monophysites, who compromised his humanity. But the middle position—that the incarnate Christ was one person but with both a divine and a human nature—was still ambiguous. And so the debate continued.

In the early seventh century there was what amounted to a rerun of the Monophysite controversy. In an attempt to win back the Monophysite Christians, it was proposed that Christ had two natures, divine and human, but only one will (in Greek, *thelema*); hence the name Monothelite for this view. But this effort was soon repudiated, and by now much of the region that had been home to the Monophysites was moving to Islam anyway.

Greek and Latin Christianity grew further and further apart. The underlying reasons were differences in language and culture, but once again a theological formulation provided the rallying point for rival factions whose differences were primarily political. At issue was a single word, *filioque* (Latin, 'and from the son'). Did the Holy Spirit 'proceed' from God the father, as the Greek Church had maintained in the Nicene Creed, or from the father and the son, as the Latin Church came to hold? In 867 Photius (c. 810–93), patriarch of Constantinople, denounced both the intrusion of Latin missionaries into Bulgaria, which he considered Greek territory, and the insertion of *filioque* into the creed. For the next two decades, one party in Constantinople repudiated the term and condemned the pope, while another supported the term and condemned Photius.

Behind the theological niceties lay the basic issue of authority, for Rome had added *filioque* to the creed without the consent of a universal Church council. This action pitted Rome's claim to be the single centre of authority against the Greek understanding of Rome as one among five equally important patriarchates. It set the Roman notion of authority as vested in the **pope**—the bishop of Rome—against the Greek notion of authority as vested in a council of bishops. The result was a break between Rome and

Constantinople that is conventionally dated to 1054, though it was in the making before then and various attempts were made after that date to heal it.

The Greek Orthodox Tradition

Christianizing the Slavs

It was the Greek Orthodox form of Christianity that was spread from Byzantium to various peoples in eastern Europe. Orthodox missions to the Slavic peoples made significant headway in the ninth century. Language played a role in their success. Though the language of the Byzantine empire was Greek, missionaries used local vernaculars in their work beyond the imperial frontier. This encouraged the development of independent local churches with a strong sense of national identity based on language.

The missionary effort was sparked by two brothers, Cyril (826–69) and Methodius (c. 815–85). In 862 they went to Moravia (the region of the modern Czech Republic), where they preached in the vernacular and produced Slavonic translations of the Bible and liturgy. After Cyril's time a new alphabet, a modification of the Greek, was devised for Slavic languages such as Bulgarian, Serbian, Ukrainian, and Russian, and named 'Cyrillic' in his honour.

On the floor of a Byzantine church in Madaba, Jordan, a mosaic map depicts Jerusalem before the arrival of Islam (Kevin Unger/Ponkawonka.com).

The early centre of Russian Orthodoxy was Kiev, in the Ukraine. There, in about 987, the fearsome pagan ruler Vladimir married the sister of the Byzantine emperor, who was a Christian, and through her influence became a vigorous promoter of Christianity. According to some, his new faith made him a more gentle ruler, but other accounts suggest that he continued to rely on coercion even in his promotion of Christianity. Kiev suffered a Mongol invasion in 1237, after which Moscow replaced it as the centre of Russian religion and politics.

Romania, which was originally colonized by Rome as the province of Dacia, was Christian from the fourth century, although its Church later came into the eastern Orthodox orbit. As a Romance language, Romanian is written using Latin characters.

Slavic peoples in other regions, such as Croatia, Slovakia, Poland, and Lithuania, were converted by Roman Catholic missionaries and adopted the Latin alphabet. Roman Catholicism also became the dominant form of Christianity among Hungarians and they also adopted the Latin alphabet, although their language is entirely separate from both the Slavic and Romance groups.

Rome's efforts to recruit Christians in the Eastern Orthodox world eventually led to the formation of several **Uniate Churches**. The name (first used by those who disapproved of the connection) was derived from the Union of Brest-Litovsk (1595), in which a Ukrainian community allied itself with Rome. Other affiliations with churches of the Byzantine rite included the Ruthenians of Hungary in 1595, Serbs in 1611, Romanians in about 1700, Melkites in the Levant in 1724, and Bulgars and Greeks in 1860.

The Iconoclastic Controversy

The Byzantine Church developed a distinctive form of portraiture for depicting religious figures. An **icon** (from the Greek word for 'image') might be an entirely two-dimensional painting, often on a piece of wood, or it might be overlaid in low relief, in wood or precious metal, and ornamented with jewels. While the robes clothing the figure were executed in relief, the hands and face characteristically remained two-dimensional, so that the parts of image representing flesh appeared as openings in the relief. In the seventh and eighth centuries these images became the subject of a heated dispute known as the iconoclastic controversy.

Pitting a faction called the iconoclasts ('icon breakers') against one called the iconodules ('icon worshippers'), the debate served in part as a vehicle for political and other disagreements. But points of principle were nonetheless at stake, and Byzantine intellectuals engaged in serious theological discussions concerning the justification for and role of images in worship. In the end the Second Council of Nicaea in 787 decided that icons were permissible and could be venerated, as long as the faithful did not actually worship them.

Today in Orthodox sanctuaries a massive screen in front of the altar shields it from the main portion of the sanctuary. The screen is called an iconostasis ('place for icons') and is designed to hold a number of icons, each one the size of a newspaper page. Smaller icons are hung in private homes; some, as small as a pocket diary, are equipped with folding covers so that they can be carried on the person, especially when travelling.

A Coptic priest lights candles at an altar holding icons in the Church of the Holy Sepulchre in Jerusalem (Richard Nowitz/Ponkawonka.com). This church is the site of a spectacular ritual on the eve of Easter, when hundreds of Greek Orthodox worshippers watch as a priest is ritually searched to ensure that he is carrying no matches. He then enters the chamber at the centre of the rotunda—the traditional site of Jesus' tomb. After a time he extends his arm with a miraculously burning taper. The people nearest light their candles from his and share the fire with others, so that within moments the rotunda is a sea of flame. Runners then carry the fire to other congregations, symbolizing the spreading of the Easter light and the gospel message.

The Latin Tradition

The Papacy

The Church centred in Rome thought of itself as 'catholic', that is, universal. Its interaction with political regimes in the Latin world (the western Mediterranean and northern Europe) produced the synthesis of religion, culture, and governmental and social structure often referred to as Christendom (the 'domain' of Christianity).

The bishop of Rome had unchallenged ecclesiastical authority in the Latin-speaking western part of the empire, parallel to that of the bishops of Greek-speaking centres such as Alexandria and Antioch. His office was considered important not only because Rome was the capital but also because of Jesus' punning remark to the disciple that Catholics believed to have been the first bishop of Rome: 'You are Peter [from a word meaning 'stone' or 'rock'], and upon this rock I will build my church.' (*Matthew* 16:18). In that account Jesus clearly sees Peter's faith as foundational, but Christians of other traditions did not accept the Roman claim that Peter's successors as bishops of Rome inherited a special status on that account. Nevertheless, by the third century the popes (from *papa*, 'father') were claiming theological primacy as successors of Peter. And their practical influence in matters of government increased dramatically after the fifth century, when government in the western part of the empire collapsed under Germanic invasions. In those chaotic times the Church was the principal source of organization and continuity. Rome might have lost the military struggle, but on the cultural and religious levels Latin Christianity would conquer the Germanic victors.

A remarkable leader, Pope Gregory I 'the Great' (r. 590-604) performed ecclesiastical and imperial administrative duties simultaneously. His reputation was such that the collecting and editing of a repertory of ancient musical melodies, which took place after his death, in the seventh and eighth centuries, was attributed to him. Gregorian chant was not the only such collection, but it was the most influential religious source for the later development of European music.

Augustine

A landmark figure in the evolution of Christianity in this period was Aurelius Augustine (354-430), who was born in what is now Algeria. In his dramatic and passionate life several currents flow together. The son of a pagan father and a Christian mother, he studied classical philosophy and rhetoric as well as Neoplatonism, the mystical interpretation given to Plato's philosophy by Plotinus (205-70). His mother, Monica, had attempted to raise him as a sincere Christian. But he sowed his wild oats in his student years, even having a child by his common-law companion. Between the ages of twenty and thirty he turned to **Manichaeism**—an intensely dualistic religion that grew out of Gnosticism—but in 386 he experienced a dramatic conversion and embraced Christianity. He became a priest and a prolific theological writer and, as bishop of Hippo in North Africa, campaigned actively against heresy: beliefs or practices considered unacceptable by the central Roman authority.

The questions that preoccupied Augustine while he was a Manichaean—the struggle between good and evil, spirit and matter—remained in his Christian writing. Augustine's ideas concerning human dependence on divine grace shaped medieval Christianity's view of the human self and personality, and his sense of guilt about the body's appetites was reflected in the medieval Church's central concern with liberation from sin.

Augustine's best-known book is probably his *Confessions*. Relating his own spiritual struggles, the tension between his conscience and his will, he tells how he came to the Christian faith and how it is in principle possible for anyone to follow the same path.

A lay monk from Britain named Pelagius (c. 360–418) disputed Augustine's views regarding human frailty. Quoting Jesus' words, 'Be therefore perfect as your heavenly father is perfect,' Pelagius argued that it was possible for humans to achieve perfection through their own moral efforts. Pelagius did not actually deny the grace of God, but his

| Box 3.5 | Augustine's Conversion

I was greatly disturbed in spirit, angry at myself with a turbulent indignation because I had not entered thy will and covenant, O my God, while all my bones cried out to me to enter. . . . It was I who willed and I who was also unwilling. In either case, it was I. . . . Suddenly I heard the voice of a boy or a girl—I know not which—coming from the neighbouring house, chanting over and over again, 'Pick it up, read it'. . . . In silence I read the paragraph on which my eyes first fell: 'Not in revelling and drunkenness, not in lust and wantonness, not in quarrels and rivalries. Rather, arm yourselves with the Lord, Jesus Christ; spend no more thought on nature and nature's appetites' (Outler 1955:170–6).

critics, including Augustine, charged that he did not give adequate weight to the importance of divine grace in overcoming human frailty.

Medieval Christianity

The Middle Ages are generally considered to stretch from the collapse of the western Roman Empire, around 500, to the beginning of the Renaissance, around 1500. It was during this period that many Christian doctrines and practices became established.

The Monastic Tradition

Monks played an important role in both Greek and Latin Christianity. Technically, monks were laymen rather than priests, but they made a demanding schedule of prayer and worship part of their practice. A distinction was drawn between 'religious' or 'regular' clergy, who followed a monastic rule, and 'secular' clergy, who worked in the world. The Greek Church permitted its secular clergy to marry, but the Latin Church did not.

For Latin Christianity the Rule of St Benedict is fundamental to the definition of monastic life. Benedict (c. 480–550) came from Nursia, east of Assisi in Italy. In about 529 he moved with a small band of monks to Monte Cassino, a summit overlooking the route between Rome and Naples. The instructions for community religious life that he established concerned spiritual discipline as well as such practical matters as economic self-sufficiency. Benedict's sister Scholastica (c. 480–c. 543) established a convent for women nearby. Many Benedictine monasteries were founded in western Europe. For several centuries they were individually self-governing, each following Benedict's Rule.

A 'religious'—a monk or a nun—in the Catholic tradition has taken a vow to follow the spiritual discipline and live by the rule of a religious community. Daily living in the Middle Ages involved many menial tasks, since monasteries and convents had to support themselves, often through the sale of the products of their own fields and vineyards.

The discipline of the community also included both prayer services at specified hours and serious scriptural study. In their cultivation of learning, the medieval monasteries became the custodians of culture, and their libraries preserved many ancient texts that might have otherwise been lost.

Cluniac Fathers

Cluny, north of Lyon in France, was the site of one of the most influential monasteries, founded in 910 by William the Pious, Duke of Aquitaine. Over the next two and a half centuries the Cluniac order founded more than 300 satellite religious houses across Europe. Like the Church itself in Constantine's day, the order served as a stabilizing force at a time of political fragmentation and turbulence. Cluny's abbey church, which was begun in 1080 and completed in 1231, was the largest church in Europe at the time.

Cistercians

In reaction against the opulence of Cluny, Robert of Molesmes in 1098 founded the Cistercian order, called after the Latin name for its centre, Cîteaux (north of Cluny near Dijon). The Cistercians wore simple undyed wool habits, ate no meat, and worshipped in sparely decorated churches.

One group of Cistercians in particular became known for their austere silence. The Cistercians of the Strict Observance, or Trappists, were founded in the 1600s by Armand de Rancé, abbot of the monastery of La Trappe in Normandy. Trappist ideals have been made known in modern times partly through the writings of the mystic Thomas Merton (1915-68), who became interested in Asian spirituality and active in social protest in the 1960s.

Carthusians

Also influenced by Robert was a German named Bruno (c. 1032-1101), who turned to the religious life in his mid-forties and followed Robert's spiritual direction before founding his own order in 1084. Named the Carthusian order (after its base at La Grande Chartreuse, near Grenoble in France), it too demanded a vow of silence and considerable austerity from its members. Like the Benedictine abbey of Fécamp, near the English Channel, the abbey at Chartreuse supported itself in part by making and selling a famous liqueur, in this instance the brilliant green one that gave its name to the colour chartreuse.

Mendicant Orders

Urban poverty was becoming a serious problem in the growing towns and cities of Europe by the thirteenth century. In response, a new type of religious order emerged. Instead of turning their backs on the world and withdrawing to monasteries, members of these 'mendicant' orders were dedicated to serving the people, and worked or begged for their living.

Franciscans

Francis of Assisi (1182-1226) grew up as the son of a wealthy cloth merchant in central Italy, but rethought his priorities during an illness in his twenties. On a pilgrimage to Rome he was so moved by the beggars outside St Peter's cathedral that he changed

| Box 3.6 | The Prayer of St Francis

This prayer, which is cherished by many Christians, is not found in the writings of St Francis of Assisi (c. 1181–1226), but has been attributed to him by Franciscan oral tradition.

Lord, make me an instrument of your peace. Where there is hatred let me sow love; where there is injury, pardon; where there is doubt, faith; where there is despair, hope; where there is darkness, light; and where there is sadness, joy.

O divine master, grant that I may not so much seek to be consoled as to console; to be understood as to understand; to be loved as to love. For it is in giving that we receive; it is in pardoning that we are pardoned; and it is in dying that we are born to eternal life.

places and clothing with them for a day, which he spent begging. Returning to Assisi, he began ministering to lepers and repaired a run-down church. Francis's rule of life, which emphasized poverty, received papal approval in 1209. Clara of Assisi formed a Franciscan women's order, the Poor Clares, about 1212.

Among other things, the Franciscans were assigned the custody of Latin sites in the Holy Land. The simple sandals and rope belt worn by Francis and his associates became distinctive features of the Franciscan habit. Often the habit is brown, but in England Franciscans are called 'Grey **Friars**'. An offshoot of the Franciscans called the Capuchins drew up their own separate rule in 1529 under the leadership of Matteo di Bassï.

Dominicans
In 1216–17 a priest from northern Spain named Dominic Guzmán (1170–1221) received a papal mandate to establish a preaching order dedicated to combatting Albigensianism (named for the city of Albi in southwestern France). The so-called Albigensian heresy was a dualistic doctrine, not unlike Manichaeism, centred on a view of existence as a struggle between light and darkness, and was highly critical of Roman Catholicism. Dominicans like Thomas Aquinas (1225–74) rapidly established their influence as itinerant preachers of doctrine in university towns such as Paris. In England they became known as 'Black Friars' for the black mantle worn over their white habits.

Carmelites
The Carmelites (hermits of Mount Carmel) were organized in Palestine in 1154, during the Crusades, and given a rule by the patriarch of Jerusalem. As the numbers of crusaders in the Holy Land declined, the Carmelites established themselves in Europe and in England, where they were termed 'White Friars'. Another mendicant order, the Hermits of St Augustine ('Austin Friars'), is the one to which Martin Luther belonged.

The Crusades

Arab Muslims had captured Jerusalem in 637. The minority of local populations that remained Christian were formally tolerated, and Christians from outside the Islamic world were still free to make pilgrimages to Jerusalem.

In the eleventh century, however, such pilgrimages were interrupted by a series of events that included the burning of the Church of the Holy Sepulchre in 1010, the split between Rome and Constantinople in 1054, and the capture of Jerusalem in 1071 by the Seljuq Turks, who—as recent converts to Islam—were less accommodating than the Arabs. The Byzantine emperors felt threatened and appealed for Western help.

In 1095, when Pope Urban II called for an expedition to the east, thousands of French, Norman, and Flemish knights responded by 'taking the cross' in a public act signifying their commitment to the cause. The crusaders won some bloody victories, capturing Antioch and Jerusalem (1099) and even Edessa in northeastern Syria.

The crusaders formed two military orders, the Knights Templar and Knights Hospitaller, and to hold on to the conquests, small crusader states such as the Latin kingdom of Jerusalem were organized along the Syro-Palestinian coast. The crusaders held Jerusalem for roughly a century, until their power was broken by Salah al-Din (Saladin) in 1187, after his victory at the Horns of Hattin in the Galilee.

Three more expeditions eventually set out from Europe to bolster the crusader enterprise, but their energies were often dissipated before they reached Jerusalem. The second crusade, for instance, was diverted in 1148 to the unsuccessful siege of Damascus, a city that had been at peace with the kingdom of Jerusalem. In the third crusade, Richard I ('the Lion-hearted') of England took Cyprus from the Byzantines in 1192. Troops of the fourth crusade in 1204, bound for Egypt, went instead to Constantinople, which they looted and burned and on whose throne they placed a ruler from Flanders. In 1261 the Byzantines recaptured the city, but relations between Western and Eastern Christians did not recover.

Beliefs and Doctrine

Sainthood

Over the centuries the Church developed a canonical list of saints, criteria for sainthood (including the performance of attested miracles), and a rigorous procedure for screening new nominees for the title. The first person to become a saint under these papal regulations was a German bishop, in 993.

The saints collectively came to be thought of as a kind of heavenly senate or honour society composed of meritorious individuals whose personal credit could be drawn on by believers who wanted them to intercede with God on their behalf. By praying to the saints, or making pilgrimages to their shrines, believers might win release both from punishment in the next existence and from guilt in this one. In short, the saints could be powerful allies in the quest for spiritual benefit.

Particular saints are honoured on particular days, and many European explorers named places in the New World for the saints on whose days they were 'discovered'. St John's, Newfoundland, for example, was so named by John Cabot because he first entered its harbour on the feast of St John the Baptist (24 June).

The Figure of Mary

Early Christianity, both Greek and Latin, accorded a pre-eminent place among the saints to Mary, the mother of Jesus. The development of that place has roots in the biblical record, but it began to flower after Constantine.

From scanty biblical details, Christian regard for Mary developed along two parallel lines. She became the focus of popular devotion, both as the principal feminine point of access to the Trinity and as a model of sorrow-enduring love in her own right. Among the holidays, recalling events in her biography, that developed in the Greek east and spread elsewhere were the Annunciation (when the angel Gabriel announced to her that she had been chosen to bear the Son of God), the Purification (the ritual following childbirth), and the Dormition ('falling asleep').

At the same time Mary was the subject of theological speculation. According to the doctrine of the virgin birth, she remained a virgin before, during, and after the birth of Jesus, while the doctrine of the **assumption** maintained that her body was taken up into heaven, where she now reigns with her son and mediates between him and the faithful. The doctrine of the **immaculate conception**, according to which she herself was born without the 'stain' of original sin, was the subject of a centuries-long debate, but was finally proclaimed official doctrine in 1854. As the 'Mother of God' in the Roman tradition and *theotokos* ('bearer of God') in the Eastern, Mary also came to be regarded as the mother of the Church itself.

Pilgrimages and Relics

In the early Church, the bodies of saints and martyrs were interred in churches. This practice marked a break from Jewish tradition, which viewed the dead as unclean and required that they be promptly buried in cemeteries. By the fourth century it had become customary for the altar cloths used in Eucharistic services to have fragments of saints' bones sewn into their hems. And the Second Council of Nicaea declared it mandatory for every church sanctuary to contain a relic—part of the body or personal paraphernalia of a venerated individual.

The function of relics in medieval popular piety can hardly be overestimated. As tangible things, they were easy for people with little or no schooling to understand, and the practice of making pilgrimages to see them became common in the Middle Ages. The only opportunity that most people ever had to travel beyond the fields and towns where they worked, a pilgrimage was an experience to look forward to. The fourteenth-century English pilgrims travelling to the shrine at Canterbury in Geoffrey Chaucer's *Canterbury Tales* represent a variety of social types (including one who is ready to make a quick profit by producing fraudulent relics).

The most treasured relics were naturally those associated with Jesus himself, especially with his suffering and death. Chips or slivers of wood and assorted nails, purporting to be from the 'True Cross', were highly prized, as were spines from the Crown of Thorns worn by Jesus on the cross. A piece of cloth known as Veronica's veil was believed to carry an impression of Jesus' face en route to the crucifixion, and a linen shroud that turned up in France in the fourteenth century was said to bear an impression of his entombed body; now kept in Turin, Italy, it is known as the Shroud of Turin.

The Problem of Evil

Does the devil exist? Today many Christians who are quite ready to talk about God in personal terms are very reluctant to suppose that a comparable being exists as his adversary. In 1999 Pope John Paul II advised the faithful to think of hell not as a place but as a condition of spiritual estrangement. Things were different in the Middle Ages. Not only did God have an angelic host, but the devil—Satan, or the Antichrist—commanded a corresponding host of demons. Satan is still a reality to a huge number of Protestant Christian evangelicals.

The Hebrew Bible contains little evidence for an independent evil creature. The word 'satan'—Hebrew for 'adversary'—is found in the Hebrew Bible, but does not refer to a fallen angel. At most this figure is one of God's courtiers (as in the book of Job), dependent on God's command. The term 'antichrist' originally referred to a false teacher in the New Testament letters of John. But notions of a supernatural opponent to God emerged in Apocalyptic Judaism near the birth of Christianity.

A view common since the early Christian writers is that the devil started as an angel, but through pride tried to take over God's role and so fell from grace. This is the implication of the name Lucifer ('bearer of light'): a star that has fallen from heaven, based on a tendentious interpretation of the 'day star' in Isaiah 14:12. Christian theology identified the snake in the garden of Eden with Satan, and this story is central to its notion of the **'original sin'** innate in humanity.

In Christian tradition, Lucifer falls to the realm of hell, which is the destiny of the wicked. The medieval imagination depicted in gory detail the torments that the wicked suffered there, far from the divine light; images of hell often showed the damned prodded by pitchforks, speared, and boiled in cauldrons.

Sin, Heresy, and Witchcraft

To the modern mind, the Latin Christianity of the Middle Ages seems obsessed with sin. Referring to the first New Testament letter of John (*1 John* 5:16), medieval theologians identified two kinds of sin. A 'mortal' sin deprived the soul of God's grace: only an act committed both knowingly and willfully and concerning a 'grave matter' qualified as a mortal sin. The Church required that such act be reported in private confession to a priest, who had to prescribe penance and absolve the offender before he or she could receive the Eucharist. Lesser sins were termed 'venial' and did not require confession.

For moral edification, the Church also warned the faithful against the Seven Deadly Sins: pride, covetousness or avarice, lust or lechery, envy, gluttony, anger or wrath, and sloth. A list of seven was established as early as the beginning of the seventh century by Pope Gregory I, although his seventh sin was despair rather than sloth.

During the eleventh century it became increasingly common for secular authorities to execute those convicted of heresy by burning them alive at the stake. Groups considered heretical, such as the Albigensians or the Waldensians (a similar group in northwestern Italy) tended to seek refuge in regions where the risks of apprehension were relatively low. In the twelfth century Church councils prescribed a range of penalties for heresy that included expulsion from the Church, imprisonment, and confiscation of property but stopped short of death.

By the beginning of the thirteenth century, however, the Church was prepared to take more severe action against heretics. Bishops were instructed to carry out 'episcopal inquisitions' in their dioceses and turn offenders over to secular authorities for punishment. And in the 1230s a special institution was established specifically to identify and prosecute heretics. Staffed mainly by Dominicans, the papal Inquisition was particularly active in southwestern France, where the trial procedures it established set a pattern that would be followed for centuries. In 1252 Pope Innocent IV stipulated that torture could be used and that heretics handed over to secular authorities should be executed within five days.

The Inquisition was at its most brutal in Spain, where Ferdinand and Isabella used it specifically to target those Jews and Muslims who converted to Christianity in order to avoid expulsion. The Grand Inquisitor Tomás de Torquemada (c. 1420–98) ordered more than two thousand executions.

The efforts of religious authorities to root out heresy combined with peasant superstition to encourage the medieval belief in witches as agents of the devil, practitioners of malevolent magic who were said to have intimate sexual relations with him. The standard handbook for Christian witch-hunting was the *Malleus Maleficarum* ('Hammer of Witches'), published in 1486 by two Dominicans authorized by Pope Innocent IV to eradicate witchcraft from Germany. In reality, however, records of sixteenth- and seventeenth-century witchcraft trials in England suggest that accusations of witchcraft were often inspired either by personal grudges, or by fear of non-conforming behaviour. Widows and women with knowledge of herbal cures were particularly likely to attract accusations of witchcraft. It is also possible that the symptoms of 'demonic possession' suffered by some accusers may have been physiological; records of the witchcraft trials of 1692 in Salem, Massachusetts, have suggested to some modern researchers that the accusers were accidentally poisoned by ergot—a grain fungus that produces a hallucinogen quite similar to LSD. People who ingest ergot-infected grain often die, but those who survive report strange experiences and wild visions.

Scholastic Philosophy

As the first European universities developed in cities like Paris, Bologna, and Oxford, theology became a central subject in the curriculum. Scholasticism was the school of thought devoted to understanding scripture through reason.

John Scotus Erigena was a ninth-century scholastic philosopher who was born in Ireland and taught in Paris. For him, scripture was authoritative, but it was the duty of reason to examine and expound it. Early scholastic teaching was based on the reading of scripture. At this early stage the scholastics were seeking to distill and summarize scripture and arrive at a rational grasp of its meaning.

Anselm

As time went on, scholastic teaching developed a dialectical, thesis-and-objections structure in which a proposition of doctrine was stated, objections were raised, and then the objections were dealt with. Anselm (c. 1033–1109), a native of the Italian Alps who became archbishop of Canterbury in England, moved away from the principle of scriptural authority, asserting that faith itself has a kind of rationality. One of his best-known formulations is the statement 'I believe so that I may understand.'

The most tantalizing of the medieval proofs for the existence of God is Anselm's **ontological argument** ('ontology' is the study of being or existence). Unlike later thinkers who inferred God's existence from inspection of the universe (the 'cosmos'), Anselm found it implied in the idea of God itself. Characterizing God as 'a being greater than which nothing can be conceived', Anselm argues (in a treatise called the *Proslogion*) that such a being must exist, not only in the mind but in reality, since if it did not exist, some other being that did exist would be greater. Anselm then pursues the argument in a second and more substantial form: a being that cannot be conceived not to exist is greater than one that can. In philosophical terms, all other being is contingent, whereas God's being is necessary.

Thomas Aquinas

The greatest of the Aristotelian scholastics was Thomas Aquinas ('of Aquino', a town near Naples; c. 1225–74), a Dominican who taught in Paris. In his *Summa Theologiae* ('Summation of Theology') and other writings Thomas sharpened the distinction between reason and faith. For him a number of Christian faith assertions, such as the doctrines of the Trinity and the incarnation of God in Christ, lie beyond reason (although that does not mean they are contrary to reason). Other Christian affirmations, however, such as the existence of God, he did believe to be provable by reason.

Thomas identified five 'ways' of proving God's existence. The first three are variations on what philosophers term the '**cosmological argument**' for God's existence; that is, they are based on observation of the universe. First, change or motion in the universe is evidence that there must be a Prime Mover to sustain the process. Second, the pattern of cause and effect points to God as the First Cause. Third, things have the possibility of existing or not existing, being generated or corrupted, but in order for there not to have once been nothing at all, there must have been some being that existed out of necessity, and that is God.

Aquinas's fourth argument is that there are gradations of goodness, truth, and nobility in what we experience, and that therefore there must be a being that is supremely good, supremely true, and supremely noble; in a sense, this is also a type of cosmological argument. Finally, Aquinas's fifth 'way' consists in the idea that the plan observable in the universe is evidence of a divine planner; this is an example of the '**teleological argument**' (from Greek *telos*, 'end' or 'purpose').

Three years after Thomas died, the archbishop of Paris formally condemned a list of propositions close to those that Thomas had taught. But later generations appreciated the comprehensive nature of Thomas's system. In 1567, at the time of the Catholic Reformation, Pope Pius V declared him 'Doctor of the Church'. In 1879 Pope Leo XIII opened a modern era for Thomism when, in an effort to counteract modern thinking, he made Thomas required reading for theology students.

Mysticism

Today the word 'mysticism' often suggests something unclear, uncertain, or mysterious. In the context of Christianity, however, **mysticism** is defined as *scientia dei experimentalis*: the knowledge of God from (personal) experience. The certainty of God that a mystic has is based not on logical proof but on a moment of vivid, intense awareness. At such a moment one may experience ecstasy (from Greek, 'standing outside oneself') or displacement from one's ordinary mode of awareness. Characteristic of that experience is a sense of union with, or a vision of, the divine—a temporary dissolving or bridging of the gulf that separates the human person from God.

In medieval Europe the most formidable systematizer of mystical thought was the German Dominican Johannes ('Meister') Eckhart (c. 1260–1327). For Eckhart, human life is as an image of God, but it is finite and creaturely and therefore obscures the divine. The mind of the spiritual person permits an actualization of the divine nature that the human soul contains. The individual mystic becomes aware of the divinity of his or her being. Eckhart's religious experience is usually called 'unitive' mysticism because it tends towards dissolving distinctions between self and God.

In Bonaventure (1221–74), an Italian Franciscan who taught at Paris and wrote a text entitled *Journey of the Mind to God*, it is meditation on the humanity of Christ that leads to experiential contact with the divine. Several centuries later, St John of the Cross (1542–91), a Spanish Carmelite, wrote of how the soul seeks to purify itself, and the 'dark night' in which, purged of its attachments, the soul rises to God in a union described in a language of pure flame.

A striking feature of late medieval mysticism is the scope it afforded for women. Though women were prevented from participating fully in clerical activities and limited to supporting roles in their religious orders, there was no limit to the experiential depth they could attain in their devotion. Hildegard of Bingen (1098–1179) was a Benedictine abbess who had a rich creative life in writing and music. She was also involved in politics, and became known as the 'Sybil of the Rhine' among the clergy and nobles who sought her advice. When she became abbess in 1141, she had a vision of tongues of flame from the heavens settling on her, and over the next ten years she wrote a book of visions called *Scivias* ('Know the ways [of God]').

Catherine of Siena (1347–80 or 1333–80) was a member of the Dominican lay order in Italy. She was actively involved in the religious politics of the day, but her *Dialogue* records her mystical visions.

Julian of Norwich (c. 1342–c. 1413) was an English mystic who experienced visions one day during a five-hour state of ecstasy, and another vision the next day. At fifty, after two decades of reflection, she wrote a description and analysis of her visions in her *Sixteen Revelations of Divine Love*. To her, evil is a distortion introduced by the human will, serving to reveal by contrast all the more clearly the divine love of God.

Teresa of Avila (1515–82), a Spanish Carmelite living in the same spiritual milieu as John of the Cross, decided at the age of forty to seek spiritual perfection. Some time later she experienced her first mystical ecstasy, and over the next fifteen years, while

---

| Box 3.7 | Mysticism

From Book II, section 2.6, of Hildegard of Bingen's Scivias *('Know the ways [of God]').*

On the Trinity: Just as the flame contains three essences in the one fire, so too, there is one God in three persons. How is this so? The flame consists of shining brightness, purple vigour and fiery glow. It has shining brightness so that it may give light; purple vigour so that it may flourish; and a fiery glow so that it may burn.

In the shining brightness, observe the Father who, in his fatherly devotion, reveals his brightness to the faithful. In the purple vigour contained within it (whereby this same flame manifests its power), understand the Son who, from the Virgin, assumed a body in which Godhead demonstrated its miracles. And in the fiery glow, perceive the Holy Spirit which pours glowingly into the minds of believers.

But where there is neither shining brightness, nor purple vigour, nor fiery glow, there no flame is seen. So too, where neither the Father nor the Son nor the Holy Spirit is honoured, there God is not worthily revered.

And so, just as these three essences are discerned in the one flame, so too, three Persons are to be understood in the unity of Godhead (Bowie and Davies 1990:53, 75).

From Chapter 18 of Teresa of Avila's autobiography.

Previously, . . . the senses were permitted to give some indication of the great joy they feel. But now the soul enjoys incomparably more, and yet has still less power to show it. For there is no power left in the body—and the soul possesses none—by which this joy can be communicated. At such a time anything of the sort would be a great embarrassment, a torment and a disturbance of its repose. If there is really a union of all the faculties, I say, then the soul cannot make it known, even if it wants to—while actually in union I mean. If it can, it is not in union.

How what is called union takes place and what it is, I cannot tell. It is explained in mystical theology, but I cannot use the proper terms; I cannot understand what mind is, or how it differs from soul or spirit. They all seem one to me, though the soul sometimes leaps out of itself like a burning fire that has become one whole flame and increases with great force. The flame leaps very high above the fire. Nevertheless it is not a different thing, but the same flame which is in the fire (Happold 1963:321).

---

actively working to establish religious houses, she deepened her spiritual life until in 1572 it reached the state of 'spiritual marriage'.

A woman who was not a contemplative mystic but nonetheless experienced intense spiritual visions was Joan of Arc (1412–31), who in 1492 led a military expedition to relieve the French forces under siege by the English at Orléans, south of Paris. Captured the following year, she was convicted of witchcraft and heresy, and burnt at the stake in 1431. On a review of her trial in 1456 she was posthumously found innocent, and in 1920 she was declared a saint.

Differentiation

The Protestant Reformation

By the early sixteenth century, pressure for change in the Latin Church had been building for decades. Princes north of the Alps were challenging the power of the papacy in
Rome. The period of cultural rebirth known as the Renaissance was well underway, as
was the revival of classical learning central to humanism, exemplified in the Dutch
scholar Desiderius Erasmus (1466–1536). Condemning complicated scholastic theology,
Erasmus urged a return to the simple morality of Jesus through the critical study of
scripture in local languages; he also wrote a scathing satire of Catholic doctrine and
Church corruption called *Encomium moriae* ('The Praise of Folly', 1509). A few years later,
Ulrich von Hutten and Crotus Rubianus published *Letters of Obscure Men* (1513–15),
mocking the intricacy and futility of Church regulations.

Literacy was spreading and local vernacular dialects were developing into regional
languages. But suggestions that the Bible might be translated into the languages of the
people were firmly rejected by the Church, which was well aware of the threat that direct
access to scripture would pose to its authority. When John Wyclif (1329–84) in England
and John Hus (c. 1369–1415) among the Czechs proposed to replace Latin with the vernacular in worship and to translate the Bible into the languages of the people, the
church condemned them as heretics.

Martin Luther

Although the danger signals had been in evidence for decades, it was the stubborn and
uninhibited personality of one man that ultimately enabled the Protestant Reformation
in Germany to erupt as it did. Martin Luther (1483–1546) was an Augustinian monk and
theological scholar at the university in Wittenberg who objected to the Church's practice
of selling **indulgences**: releases from time in **purgatory** (the supposed holding area for
the soul in its passage from death to the next existence).

At that time the standard way of raising a topic for debate was to post a notice
about it on the church door. Thus in 1517 Luther posted a list of 95 propositions or 'theses' criticizing various aspects of Church practice.

In 1521 Luther had to defend himself against charges of political subversion at
an imperial council called the Diet of Worms, held at the German city of Worms. When
he refused to retract his views, he was first censured and eventually excommunicated.
But support for his ideas spread and took on a concrete political form.

Luther was hardly the first to object to the Church's extravagance and corruption.
The core of his challenge, however, was theological. Luther wanted to reform the very
understanding of the nature of sin and redemption. He rejected the idea of redemption
as a transaction in which the individual confesses particular sins and expiates them
through particular acts of penance. Instead, Luther maintained that through Jesus divine

grace reaches out to save and redeem human beings regardless of their merit or deeds. Taking up a key theme in Paul's letter to the Romans, Luther insisted that humans are **justified**—freed from the penalty of sin—not by works, but by faith alone. Like Paul, he based his stand on experiential certainty, which he described as the inner guidance or testimony of the Holy Spirit. For Paul, the works in question were Jewish ritual observances; for Luther, the rituals of confession and penance in Latin Christianity.

From 1517 until 1521 Luther had the opportunity to withdraw his challenges to the Church. Had a settlement been negotiated, the pressure for reform might have dropped off; but Luther stood his ground. Historians doubt that he actually spoke the words attributed to him: 'Here I stand; I can do no other.' But the sentiment is in keeping with what he likely did say at the Diet: 'Unless I am convicted by Scripture and plain reason—I do not accept the authority of popes and councils, for they have contradicted each other—my conscience is captive to the Word of God, I cannot and I will not recant anything' (Bainton 1974, 15:551).

The emperor, Charles V, called Luther a threat to order and banished him. During the few days he was given to leave under safe conduct, Luther was intercepted by some armed men along the highway and disappeared for more than a year. Many thought him dead, but he was actually in hiding under the protection of his patron, Prince Frederick. Luther used this period of seclusion to produce a string of theological writings and to translate the New Testament from the original Greek into a direct, lively German that eventually gave the Luther Bible a profoundly influential place in German literature.

In the form it took, the Protestant Reformation could not have come about much earlier than it did. The technology of printing from movable type had been introduced in Europe only half a century earlier—a Latin Bible came off Johann Gutenberg's press in 1456. Though prohibitively expensive at first, printed materials soon became less costly to produce. Luther's challenges to the Church were rapidly disseminated in pamphlets that reached a wide popular audience. As many as a million pamphlets were reportedly produced between 1521 and 1524. Of Luther's own short tracts or pamphlets there were at least 1,300 different printings by 1523. His very readable translation of the Bible had an impact, too (the New Testament appeared in 1522 and the Old Testament in 1534).

By the mid-1520s Luther's teachings had inspired a dozen nuns to leave the convent in Wittenberg. Three of them went back to their families, but the other nine were now homeless. Luther found husbands for eight and then married the last, Katherina von Bora, himself. In the course of time they had six children and also adopted four orphans. In his writing *Concerning Married Life*, Luther suggests that even such ordinary activities as diaper-washing can be ennobled by faith.

In effect, Luther removed the priesthood from the pedestal it had occupied since the time of Constantine. Replacing institutional tradition with the authority of the Bible and the inner guidance of the Holy Spirit meant that there was no longer any need for an intermediary between Christians and God to transmit human petitions or dispense divine grace. Protestants use the phrase 'the priesthood of all believers' to refer to the egalitarianism of spiritual access that Luther introduced.

In 1524–5, when an uprising broke out among German peasants, Luther refused to endorse all their demands. As a consequence, the more radical among them left Luther to follow a more strident leader, Thomas Müntzer. Eventually they founded the

Anabaptist movement, so-called because it held that baptism should be reserved for adults capable of making make a mature decision for faith, and therefore rebaptized people who had already been baptized as infants.

Luther also broke with the Swiss reformer Huldrych (Ulrich) Zwingli over the interpretation of the Eucharist. Both men rejected the Roman Catholic view of the Eucharist as a literal re-enactment of Christ's self-sacrifice. But whereas Luther continued to believe that Jesus was physically present, if unseen, during the rite, Zwingli insisted that the words 'this is my body' meant only 'this represents': in short, that the rite was purely symbolic.

Branches of Protestantism: Sixteenth Century

From the beginning, the Reformation was marked by division and diversity. Protestants had rejected the central institutional control of Rome, but many early reformers were no less authoritarian than the church they had rejected. Those who disagreed with a particular leader would often break away and establish their own denominations. This tendency towards denominational fragmentation has continued to the present day. This section will provide an overview of the main branches of Protestantism that have emerged since Luther's time.

Three main 'establishments' emerged from the Reformation in the course of the sixteenth century: Lutheran, Anglican, and Calvinist. (Other branches, such as the Anabaptists, are considered non-establishment.)

Lutheranism

Luther's followers became the majority in Germany and Scandinavia. Like him, they stressed the authority of scripture and the guidance of the Holy Spirit. There was ample scope for rational and intellectual argument in the exposition of scripture, but Lutheranism also encouraged a deep sense of personal piety. In Lutheran hymns God is a friend and companion as well as a warrior and judge.

In worship and ecclesiastical organization Lutherans departed in only some respects from the precedents of the Roman Church. They retained a Eucharistic service; but they celebrated it in the vernacular rather than Latin and rejected the doctrine of **transubstantiation**, according to which, at a certain moment during the service of the mass, the wafer and the wine are actually transformed into the body and the blood of Christ. Rather, they held that although Christ's body became present during the ceremony, it was not produced out of the bread and wine. In addition, the Lutheran Church retained a priesthood governed by bishops, but permitted its clergy to marry. (Ordination of women as priests is a recent phenomenon among Lutherans.)

Outside Germany and Scandinavia, Lutheranism has spread through both missionary activity and migration. In the nineteenth century, German immigrants took Lutheranism to regions such as Pennsylvania, Ohio, Missouri, Ontario, and the shores of Lake Michigan, while Scandinavian immigrants took it mainly to Minnesota and Wisconsin. Since then the ethnic character of North American Lutheran churches has generally become diluted over time, except in areas where German and Scandinavian immigration has continued.

| Map 3.1   Christianity: Major spheres of influence

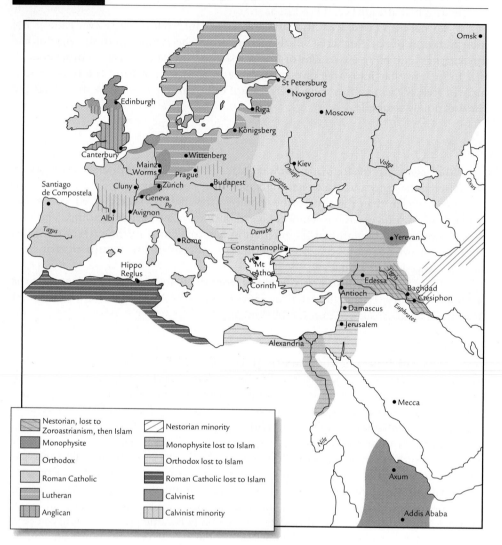

Nestorian, lost to Zoroastrianism, then Islam

Monophysite

Orthodox

Roman Catholic

Lutheran

Anglican

Nestorian minority

Monophysite lost to Islam

Orthodox lost to Islam

Roman Catholic lost to Islam

Calvinist

Calvinist minority

Anglicanism

Whereas in Germany the Reformation had been a popular movement, in England it was royal policy. Henry VIII wanted a male heir, but his queen, Catherine of Aragon, had borne only a daughter. Hoping that Anne Boleyn would produce a son, in 1527 Henry requested an annulment of his first marriage on the grounds that it was invalid because Catherine had previously been married to his deceased brother. Although Pope Clement VII refused the request, Henry found some support in European universities. In 1533, therefore, he secretly married Anne and then had the Archbishop of Canterbury, Thomas Cranmer, annul the first marriage and pronounce the second valid.

At Henry's instigation, the English parliament in 1534 passed an Act of Supremacy, which 'for corroboration and confirmation' proclaimed the king and his successors by authority of Parliament 'the only Supreme Head in earth of the Church of England'. Although the wording implied that the monarch had always held that distinction, in reality he had not; the act itself was the first statement in which the king replaced the pope as head of the English Church.

But divorce and a male successor were not the only things on Henry's mind. While the break with Rome could be interpreted as stemming from a high-minded principle of secularity, it is more likely that Henry was motivated by the desire to expropriate the Church's vast landholdings.

The key Protestant reformer under Henry's successor Edward VI (r. 1547–53; the son of Henry's third wife), was Cranmer, who made an enduring contribution in the 1549 *Book of Common Prayer*. Though it has undergone a number of revisions, it is still a model for Anglican worship.

In the end, even though the English Reformation was often directed from the top down, the church it produced had much in common with the one produced by the grass-roots Lutheran Reformation: an established state church without links to Rome; a traditional mass, but conducted in the vernacular; a hierarchy with bishops, but with clergy who could now marry. The Church of England has remained a state church, with the monarch as its titular head. (When the monarch is in Scotland, however, she or he is head of the Church of Scotland, which is Presbyterian—governed by elders or 'presbyters' rather than bishops.) The ranking bishop of the Church continues to be the archbishop of Canterbury. In most European countries, and in Canada, the established or state churches receive significant financial support from the government.

The tradition of the Church of England is generally called Anglican, although it is known in the United States as Episcopalian, after its form of government by bishops. It has taken root wherever British influence has been strong: not only in Canada, the United States, Australia, New Zealand, and South Africa, but also in the former British colonies and protectorates in East Africa, West Africa, the Caribbean, India, and the Polynesian islands.

The diversity of the human community is reflected among the participating bishops at international meetings of the Anglican communion. In recent years, the relative liberality of the American and English churches in approving homosexual priests and bishops has led to a serious disagreement with the more conservative bishops of the former colonies and protectorates, one that may yet end in schism (a split).

A tension of much longer standing is the one between what came to be called 'high-church' and 'low-church' Anglicanism. The high-church side can approach Roman Catholicism in its emphasis on ritual, whereas the low-church side is more spontaneous and evangelical. Although this tension had existed for centuries, it came to a head in the nineteenth century, when the 'Oxford movement' within the Church of England feared that the church might lose its established status. The response of the Oxford movement was to emphasize that the Anglican Church was not dependent on the state, but instead derived its authority from 'catholic' tradition—by which they meant not the Roman Catholic Church but the tradition that began with the apostles.

From 1833 to 1841 John Keble, John Henry Newman, and others published 90 *Tracts for the Times*, arguing for the continuity of that apostolic tradition. At the same time the Tractarians, as they came to be called, promoted a revival of Anglican interest in the aesthetics of the liturgy and the dignity of priesthood.

Calvinism

From the 1520s to 1560s, the Reformation movement in and around Switzerland departed from Luther's position on several points. While Zwingli in Zürich disputed Luther's Eucharistic theology, Martin Bucer in Strasbourg promoted a more active role for lay people as ministers, elders, deacons, and teachers.

The dominant intellectual leader of the Reformation, however, was John Calvin (1509–64), a lawyer and classical scholar (even a Renaissance humanist) who imposed rigorous norms of doctrine and conduct on the city of Geneva. Calvin's Geneva has been termed a theocracy comparable to Iran under the rule of religio-legal scholars after 1979. Yet to his followers Calvin's trust in God's power and caring providence brought at least as much joy as it did fear.

Calvin's principal theological treatise, published in 1536 (just before he became actively involved in Geneva's civic life) and expanded in later editions, bears a title commonly translated as *Institutes of the Christian Religion*. In form it is a manual of spiritual discipline that might be more aptly titled 'instruction in Christian piety'. Echoing Augustine in his *Confessions*, Calvin maintains that humans are created for communion with God and cannot rest until they arrive at it. The human approach to God is both intellectual and spiritual; Calvin uses the term 'knowledge' almost synonymously with 'faith'. Unlike the writings of Luther, which were usually responses to specific situations, Calvin's *Institutes* has a systematic overall structure,.

For Calvin, God is absolutely sovereign, initiating all actions, both creating and redeeming the world. Two implications of this teaching were given a central place by Calvin's interpreters, and the Reformed tradition has struggled to defend them ever since: first, humans are dependent on divine grace and are utterly sinful and powerless to achieve salvation; second, the sovereign God, who is both omniscient and omnipotent, predestines every person to either salvation or damnation. Strictly speaking, in Calvin's thought, no one could know who was saved or damned. From sixteenth-century Geneva, the ideas of the Swiss Reformation spread to other lands, notably France (where the adherents of the Reformation came to be known as Huguenots), the Netherlands, Hungary, England, and Scotland.

In the Netherlands Calvin's doctrine of **predestination** was challenged by Jacobus Arminius, who believed that God's sovereignty was compatible with human free will. Arminian views were condemned by an assembly in Dordrecht (Dort) in 1518, which sentenced their sympathizer, the scholar and jurist Hugo Grotius, to life imprisonment. Grotius escaped in a box of books being shipped to his wife and settled for a time in Paris, but strict predestinarian doctrine carried the day in Holland.

Calvinist churches in the Netherlands and Hungary are termed **Reformed**. In England the same tradition is called Presbyterian, as is the established state Church of

Scotland. **Reformed churches** do not have bishops; instead, the regional representative assembly, the presbytery, corporately performs the traditional tasks of a bishop, including the supervision, examination, and ordination of candidates for ministry. Presbyterians call a multi-presbytery gathering a synod—the old term for a meeting of bishops.

Presbyterianism has taken root on other continents through migration. Presbyterians from England and Scotland settled in eastern Canada and the middle Atlantic American states, as well as in New Zealand and Australia. Dutch Reformed settlers carried their tradition to South Africa and to New Amsterdam (New York) and Michigan. In the nineteenth and twentieth centuries, Presbyterian missions from Britain and North America reached many parts of Asia and Africa. In most lands the 'younger churches' founded by missionaries remained small, and in the Islamic world they found most of their recruits not among Muslims but among Eastern Orthodox populations. Presbyterians did become a sizable minority in Korea, however.

Anabaptists

All three branches of the Reformation named so far were willing, even eager, to take over the governance of their respective societies and replace established institutions by becoming establishments themselves. The situation was different with the somewhat more diverse and less cohesive group called Anabaptists.

The Anabaptists' emphasis on adult rather than infant baptism reflected their voluntaristic conception of the nature of the Church. In their view, baptism should not be imposed but actively sought on the basis of mature personal commitment. The Church should seek to restore the close-knit sense of community of the apostolic era, and should remain apart from political institutions and structures. Anabaptist groups rely on lay preachers rather than trained clergy and have tended to pacifism in times of war. Anabaptist groups emerged in response to various local causes of dissatisfaction with the pace of change during the first decade of the Reformation. One of the first breaks with the 'establishment' Reformation was a dispute with Zwingli in Zürich in 1525, in which the dissidents administered adult baptism. Essentially, the Anabaptist movement emerged as an antiestablishment, underground movement within central European Protestantism.

In 1533-5, Anabaptist efforts to establish the kingdom of God by force in the northwestern German town of Münster prompted a severe crackdown by Catholic and Protestant authorities. Thereafter a former Dutch priest named Menno Simons (1496-1561) led the movement in a largely otherworldly and non-violent direction. Since there was virtually no chance of removing the authorities, he urged his followers to remove themselves from society. In the course of their withdrawal his followers—the Mennonites—spread eastward through Germany and Austria to the Ukraine.

Some Mennonites escaped hardship or persecution in Europe by migrating to the Americas, particularly Pennsylvania and, later, Ontario and the Canadian prairies. In Pennsylvania, where some arrived as early as 1663, they came to be known as Pennsylvania Dutch (from *Deutsch*, meaning 'German'). While most Mennonites today use modern technology, some branches, such as the Old Order Amish farmers in Pennsylvania and Ontario, prefer traditional modes of dress and conduct. They continue to farm with the draft animals and simple tools of a century ago, resisting more modern machinery and gadgetry as part of the moral temptation and corruption of today's life.

Unitarianism

Unitarianism rejects the doctrine of the Trinity. Thus if Christianity is strictly defined as faith in Jesus as son of God, it is legitimate to ask whether Unitarianism belongs in a survey of Christianity. Historically, however, it is only in the context of traditional Christianity that Unitarianism makes sense, for it emerged as individuals struggled intellectually with the admittedly difficult doctrine of the Trinity and then concluded that they could not affirm the divinity of Jesus.

As early as 1527 in Strasbourg, Martin Cellarius, a pupil of the German humanist Johann Reuchlin, rejected the doctrine of the Trinity and preferred to speak of God as a single person. Subsequently, Unitarian communities emerged in several lands. In Poland an Italian named Giorgio Biandrata launched Unitarian ideas in 1558 and was followed by Fausto Sozzini in 1579; Socinianism, as the teaching was called, was banished from Poland in 1658. In 1553 Biandrata planted Unitarian ideas in Hungary, where he won the support of the king, John II Sigismund Zápolya, but after the end of his reign the movement was persecuted.

In England the figure considered the father of Unitarianism was John Biddle, who began to publish tracts in 1652, but a Unitarian denomination was not organized until 1773–4, when Theophilus Lindsey resigned from the Church of England and opened a Unitarian chapel in London.

In the United States a sermon delivered by the left-wing Congregationalist William Ellery Channing in 1819 is generally taken as a kind of denominational manifesto. But Channing himself did not regard Unitarians as a separate group, and claimed to belong 'not to a sect, but to the community of free minds'.

In the nineteenth and twentieth centuries North American Unitarianism continued to appeal to a humanist and rationalist clientele, often in university circles. In 1961 the Unitarians merged with a kindred group called the Universalists.

Puritanism

Puritanism was not a denomination but a movement in English and colonial American Protestant churches that flourished from the mid-sixteenth to the mid-seventeenth century. It began as an effort to 'purify' the Church of England of the remnants of Catholicism in church vestments, furnishings, and ecclesiastical organization that it retained after the accession of Elizabeth I in 1558, when Protestants exiled during the reign of the Catholic Mary I returned to England from Calvinist Geneva.

Among the influences the exiles introduced from Geneva was the idea of predestination. Individuals who believed themselves to have been chosen by God for salvation tended to display a strict, sometimes smug, sense of moral vocation that was reflected in the Puritan movement. Puritans were morally activist and stressed moderation in behaviour. The poems of John Milton and the *Pilgrim's Progress* of John Bunyan are well-known literary expressions of Puritan ideals.

Puritans and English Presbyterians found themselves in substantial agreement in the Westminster Confession of Faith in 1647, and in the 1650s Oliver Cromwell sought to unite Congregationalists, Presbyterians, and Baptists in a Puritan state church. But the Church of England largely rid itself of Puritanism with the restoration of the monarchy in 1660, and thereafter Puritanism ceased to have a coherent existence as a movement in England. It had a ripple effect, however, in non-conformist (i.e., non-Anglican Protestant) denominations such as the Congregationalists. By the time Puritanism waned in England, it had already spread to the New World, carried by Puritan immigrants to New England.

Protestant Denominations: Seventeenth Century

More reformist denominations emerged and were carried from England to America in the seventeenth century. Though they differed in the details of their beliefs, each in its own way reflected the Reformation's rejection of external human authority. The Congregationalists insisted on autonomy for every local group of believers; the Baptists refused state interference; and the Quakers looked inward for insight.

Congregationalism

The Congregational movement traces its roots to 'separatist' clergy in the time of Elizabeth I, but it did not become a significant force until the era of Cromwell. As far as doctrine is concerned, there is little to distinguish Congregationalists from Presbyterians. Where they differ is in their form of governance. Carrying the notion of the priesthood of all believers to its logical conclusion, Congregationalists reject the idea of elders and accord each individual congregation the ultimate authority to manage its theological and institutional affairs: for them, the only higher power is God.

In England Congregational churches formed a Congregational Union in 1832 and were active in political and missionary causes throughout the nineteenth century. But the stronghold of Congregationalism emerged in Massachusetts, where it included both the Puritans of Massachusetts Bay and the Separatists of Plymouth. Among the educational institutions founded by Congregationalists in the American northeast were both Harvard University (established in 1637 in order not 'to leave an illiterate ministry to the churches, when our present ministers shall lie in the dust') and Yale (est. 1701).

Baptists

Like the Anabaptists on the European continent, the English Baptists practised the baptism of mature believers rather than infants. They had more in common with the English Puritan movement, however, than with the continental Anabaptists. What was important to these Puritan separatists at the beginning of the seventeenth century was that people should choose their religion rather than be born into it, and that this choice ought to be private and beyond any interference by the state. England's non-Calvinist Baptists, called General Baptists because they proclaimed a general redemption for humanity, were augmented in the 1630s by Calvinist or Particular Baptists, so called because they limited redemption to a particular sector of humanity. By that time the Particular Baptists were already practising the ritual of baptism by total immersion rather than by sprinkling of the initiate.

The real growth of the Baptists in the United States began after the revivalist movement of 1740–3 known as the Great Awakening. Though the Baptists were not among its principal protagonists, they made massive numerical gains in its wake. They positioned themselves to become the largest American Protestant denomination in part by appealing to the Black population; by the middle of the twentieth century, two out of every three African-American Christians were Baptists.

Quakers

George Fox (1624–91) was an English dissenter or non-conformist who in 1646, after three years of searching, achieved the spiritual enlightenment he had sought. He began to preach that moral and spiritual peace was to be found not in institutional religion but in the experience of the 'inner light' of the living Christ. He called his followers Friends of the Truth, but in 1650, when Fox was charged with blasphemy, a judge referred to him as a 'Quaker' because Fox had advised him to tremble at the word of the Lord. The name now used, Religious Society of Friends, dates from the nineteenth century.

In 1682 the colony of Pennsylvania was founded by William Penn as a place where Quakers might find religious toleration and free expression. There Fox's initially impulsive group became staid, solid citizens. Quakers at worship combine intellectual and spiritual reflection. Seemingly observing no fixed ritual, they sit silently until moved by the Holy Spirit to speak. Though Quakers number only about 100,000 worldwide, their humanitarian involvement in peace and refugee-relief causes has been significant and has earned the movement great respect. The Quakers are strongest in Pennsylvania and Indiana, and around university towns.

Protestant Denominations: Eighteenth Century

Pietism

Pietism emphasized individual piety, taking as its model the spirituality of the earliest Christians. Although the term 'Pietist' was applied in Lutheran circles to a group led by Philipp Jakob Spener (1635–1705), similar tendencies also emerged in Reformed (Calvinist) circles in the Netherlands. Thus the term designates less a formal denomination than a movement that rippled through several Protestant denominations.

Pietists were dissatisfied with what they perceived as doctrinal and institutional rigidity in the Protestant churches that emerged from the Reformation. Instead, they sought a spontaneous kind of devotion in which the individual believer would experience a kind of rebirth or **conversion**—a complete renewal of faith accompanied by certainty of divine forgiveness and acceptance. For many, the feeling of that certainty was all the evidence they needed—a position that in Germany pitted Pietism against the emerging rationalism of the eighteenth-century Enlightenment, but that found intellectual expansion in the emphasis laid on feeling by Schleiermacher (see p. 181).

Pietism spread in Lutheran circles both in Europe and in the Americas. In the form articulated by the Moravian Brethren—who traced their origins to the early Czech reformer John Hus—it also influenced John Wesley and contributed to the development of Methodism.

Methodism

In the late 1720s a number of Anglican students at Oxford formed a group to study the Bible and attend church together. This methodical approach inspired the nickname 'Methodists'. Among them were John Wesley (1703–91), his brother Charles, and George Whitefield, all three of whom embarked on itinerant preaching careers. In 1735 John and Charles set out on a mission to evangelize Native Americans in Georgia, but their condemnation of slavery made them unwelcome in the American South and they returned to England in 1738. A few months later, after a visit to a Moravian Pietist community, Charles experienced conversion, and three days later John felt his heart 'strangely warmed' in Pietist fashion.

John Wesley began to preach to public gatherings, often of miners and workers, outside the established churches. In the 53 remaining years of his life he preached more than 40,000 sermons, averaging 15 a week, and travelled 320,000 km (200,000 mi.), mainly on horseback. Though he had at first hoped his movement would revitalize the Church of England from within, Wesley eventually oversaw the organization of his following as an independent denomination and personally ordained leaders for it.

Revivalism

By the mid-1700s the Pietist model of spiritual rebirth or conversion had spread to a number of denominations. Efforts to promote a reawakening of spiritual enthusiasm resulted in a wave of revivals, especially in the American colonies. The Great Awakening was a revival that swept New England in 1740–3, sparked by the preaching of the gifted and versatile Calvinist theologian Jonathan Edwards (1703–58).

The influence of the Great Awakening extended well beyond New England, and it altered the shape of American Protestantism as the nation expanded westward after the Revolutionary War. Camp meetings held by itinerant preachers from various denominations would often inspire mass conversions. Although Edwards had preached mainly to Congregationalists and Presbyterians, Methodists and Baptists were more successful in making new recruits. In time the Methodists emerged as the largest Protestant denomination in the American Midwest, and were second only to the Baptists in the American South.

Roman Catholicism after 1500

The Roman Church recognized the need to correct the abuses that Luther had condemned. Beginning with the Council of Trent (1545–63), it undertook a process of renewal that has often been called the Counter-Reformation.

The Catholic (Counter-) Reformation

The Council of Trent

After several delays, the Council of Trent opened in 1545 at the Italian city of Trent, northwest of Venice, and continued on and off until 1563, when it finished with a burst

| Box 3.8 | Major Branches of Christianity

Following are the main divisions within Christianity, with the approximate numbers of adherents for each of the major groups at the beginning of the twenty-first century.

Nestorians (about 200,000)
   'Assyrians' of Iraq, Iran, and Turkey
   Nestorian Malabar Christians in India
Monophysites (about 30 million)
   Copts in Egypt
   Ethiopians
   Jacobites or Syrian Orthodox
   Jacobite Malabar Christians in India
   Armenians
Orthodox (at least 150 million)
   Greek
   Bulgarian, Serbian, and Romanian
   Russian and Ukrainian
Catholics (about 900 million)
   Roman Catholics
   Eastern 'Uniate' churches
   (some Anglicans)
Protestants (about 400 million)
   Sixteenth-century divisions
      Lutherans
      Anglicans
      Reformed (Presbyterian) churches
      Anabaptists
      Unitarians
   Seventeenth- and eighteenth-century divisions
      Congregationalists
      Baptists
      Quakers
      Methodists
   Nineteenth-century divisions
      Disciples
      Seventh-Day Adventists
      Jehovah's Witnesses
      Christian Scientists
      Mormons

of decisive energy. Although participation was restricted to Catholic bishops, some sessions were attended by Protestants as well.

The decrees formulated at Trent—the adjective for them is 'Tridentine'—would stand as the Roman Catholic Church's self-definition for four centuries. They covered the whole range of issues, both practical and theoretical, that had come to a boil in the

Reformation. The council acted to enforce discipline and end the abuses and excesses that had so weakened the Church's credibility as an institution. But it stood its ground against some of the Protestants' theoretical positions. It reiterated the traditional understanding of the mass as a sacrifice, reaffirmed the authority of institutional tradition alongside scripture, and upheld the idea of a distinct status and function for priests as intermediaries. It also reaffirmed the tradition of celibacy for priests and instituted seminaries for training.

The Society of Jesus (Jesuits)

Established shortly before the Council of Trent, in 1540, the Jesuit order or Society of Jesus exemplified three crucial areas of Counter-Reformation renewal: spiritual discipline, education, and missionary expansion. Its founder, Iñigo (c. 1495–1556), of the family of López of the northern Spanish town of Loyola, came to be known by the name Ignatius of Loyola. As a young man he was a soldier who served with bravado in the retinues of various nobles until he was wounded in the leg by a cannonball. The books available during his convalescence included the lives of saints, which may have influenced his decision around the age of thirty to take religious vows of poverty, chastity, and obedience.

While following a regimen of prayer and bodily self-denial, he wrote a short text called *Spiritual Exercises* in 1522–3. A manual for Christian meditation, a theological reflection on Christ's incarnation as a divine intervention in human history, and a call to arms to join a spiritual crusade, it is a classic of Catholic piety; and in 1922 Pope Pius XI named Ignatius, who had been canonized exactly 300 years earlier, the patron saint of spiritual exercises.

As time passed, the Jesuits became important as a teaching order, well known for their methods as well as their schools.

The Ursulines

The most prominent Catholic teaching order of women dates from the same period. The Ursulines were founded in 1535 in Italy by Angela Merici (1474–1540) and received papal approval in 1544. They became particularly influential in France and Canada. One of the most famous Ursulines was the French mystic Marie Guyard (1599–1672), better known as Marie de l'Incarnation. Left a widow before she was twenty, she entrusted her young son to her sister and entered the Ursuline convent at Tours at the age of twenty-seven. Inspired by the Jesuits' accounts of their mission in New France, in 1639 she travelled to the small French settlement at Quebec, where she established a convent, a school, and a 'seminary' for young Aboriginal women. Her numerous letters are an invaluable source of information on early New France. She also wrote of her personal development as a mystic.

Catholic Missions

India

One of Ignatius's original circle, the Spanish Jesuit Francis Xavier was sent by the king of Portugal to evangelize the East Indies. He reached India in 1542, made Goa his base, and began to establish communities of converts elsewhere on the Indian and Sri Lankan coasts as well as the Malay peninsula. Seven years later, despite chronic seasickness, he sailed on to Japan and introduced Christianity there too. He set out for China in 1552 but fell ill and died en route from Goa. The Jesuits have attributed 700,000 conversions to Francis.

Japan

In Japan the first Christian missionaries found remarkable success. The Portuguese priests admired the military discipline of the Samurai class, and the Japanese apparently saw the Jesuits as akin to their own Zen monks in their discipline and learning. An estimated 500,000 Japanese had become Christians by 1615.

But later Japanese rulers saw the Christian and foreign influence as a threat. In 1587 the shogun Hideyoshi Toyotomi ordered the missionaries banished, though he did not enforce the ban until 1597, when he executed nine missionaries and 17 Japanese Christians. The Tokugawa shogun Hidetada intensified the persecution, which reached a peak in the early 1620s, when torture awaited those who would not comply when asked to step on an image of Christ or Mary. The Roman Catholic Church counts 3,125 as martyrs in this period in Japan. Around Nagasaki, where Christianity had been strongest, resentment of the central Tokugawa government prompted an uprising in 1637–8, but the crushing of this resistance marked the end of Japan's 'Christian century'.

China

Three decades after the death of Francis Xavier, a party of missionaries led by the Italian Jesuit Matteo Ricci landed at the southern Chinese port of Macau. The emperor in Beijing was so pleased with their gifts—including mechanical clocks, European maps, and lenses and prisms—that they were invited to stay, and even received a monthly stipend. Ricci spent the remaining nine years of his life in Beijing. This was a time of active cultural exchange, in which Chinese philosophical and religious texts were translated into Latin, and European scientific and mathematical texts were translated into Chinese.

In the latter part of the 1600s, however, Dominicans and Franciscans began to complain to the pope about the Jesuits' willingness to accommodate indigenous cultural traditions. Three issues in particular raised questions about the compatibility of Chinese customs and Christianity. First, the Jesuits allowed Chinese converts to take part in rituals honouring Confucius, presumably endorsing his moral system as compatible with Christianity. Second, they permitted converts to continue practising the rituals sometimes called 'ancestor worship', in which deceased family members were honoured with prostrations, incense, and food offerings. Third was the question of 'terms': whether Chinese terms such as 'Tian' ('heaven') and 'Shangdi' ('the Lord above') meant the same thing as the Christian term 'God'. By the 1740s the Jesuits' ability to present Christianity in indigenous terms had been severely restricted, and with it their ability to attract new converts.

Central and South America

From the very beginning of Spanish and Portuguese influence in the New World, an intimate relationship prevailed between Church and state. Barely a year after Columbus landed at Santo Domingo, a papal bull effectively divided the non-European world between the two powers: Portugal was awarded all the territory east of a certain point west of the Azores, and Spain everything to the west. Thus Portugal received Africa, Asia, and Brazil, while the rest of Latin America went to Spain.

When Hernán Cortés reached Mexico in 1519 and Francisco Pizarro reached Peru in 1532-3, they encountered highly sophisticated social and religious institutions. Yet the great civilizations of the Aztecs and Mayans in Mexico and the Incas in Peru seemed to fall like dominoes before the relatively small Spanish forces. In the past, some historians attributed the collapse of those civilizations to Spain's advantage in weapons, or its use of horses, which the indigenous peoples of the Americas did not have. More recent theories have emphasized the devastating effect of European diseases on populations that had no natural immunity to them.

With the allocation of territory went the responsibility to evangelize its population. The expeditions that followed, therefore, always included missionaries. Some made no effort to learn the local language, relying instead on pictures, symbols, and gestures. Others made it their business not only to learn the people's language but to document their myths, symbols, and rituals. Among the latter was the Spaniard Bernardino de Sahagún, whose *Historia de las cosas de Nueva España* ('History of matters in New Spain') is a valuable ethnographic record of Mexico at the time of its conquest by Hernán Cortés in 1519. Other priests devoted themselves to defending the rights of Native people against European exploitation.

Of these the greatest was Bartolomé de Las Casas (1474–1566), a Spanish priest who had served as a chaplain during the conquest of Cuba in 1513. As a veteran of that campaign he was allotted a parcel of land and a number of local people to work it, effectively as slave labour. But Las Casas soon renounced his allotment of serfs and set out to win a hearing for the rights of the Indians. He eventually joined the Dominican order and wrote a monumental *Historia de las Indias* ('History of the Indies'), which detailed Spanish abuses in Mexico and was published only after his death. Named bishop of Chiapas in Guatemala in 1544, he denied absolution to any slave-holders in his diocese. And in 1550 he defended the Indians' case in a great debate—held at the request of the king of Spain—on the moral justification for European Christian conquest of the peoples of the New World. The issues that Las Casas raised concerning cultural imperialism and the use of force are still relevant today.

In terms of numbers, the missionary effort appears to have been a tremendous success. One Franciscan friar estimated that he had baptized 200,000 Mexicans within ten years of Cortés's arrival, as many as 14,000 in a single day. Today half the world's Roman Catholics live in Latin America, and from Mexico to Tierra del Fuego Catholic Christianity appears to have no serious rivals.

On closer inspection, however, it becomes clear that conquered populations did not necessarily abandon their traditions when they accepted Christianity. Behind the Christian altars in Mexico were pagan images. Inside early Mexican crucifixes are Aztec cult objects. And in coastal Brazil, where West African blacks were taken as slaves, African tribal deities persist in the guise of Catholic saints in the cult or folk religion known as Candomblé.

Across the hemisphere, **syncretism**—the combination of elements from more than one religious tradition—has given local people religious figures that they can identify as their own. The most important of these figures in Mexico is the Virgin of Guadalupe, whose cult goes back to a hill near Mexico City that was sacred to the Aztec goddess Tonantzin, herself a virgin mother of gods. In 1531 a Christian convert named Juan Diego reported an apparition of a beautiful lady who said she was 'one of his own people' and instructed him to gather roses from the hilltop and present them to the bishop. He wrapped them in a piece of cloth, and when he opened the package before the bishop, an image of the Virgin appeared to be visible on the cloth. Preserved in a basilica at the foot of the hill, the cloth is still venerated today, and the cult that surrounds it is reminiscent of popular piety in medieval Europe.

North America

Roman Catholic influences in North America reflect migration as well as missionary activity. Florida was an area of early settlement direct from Spain. Texas and New Mexico were part of Mexico until the mid-nineteenth century. In California the Franciscans established a chain of missions, the last and northernmost of them at Sonoma, north of San Francisco, in 1823. (A short distance to the north, Russian settlers had already established Fort Ross, the site of the first Orthodox chapel south of Alaska. Arguably, the encounter between the Spanish and the Russians in California marked the moment when Christianity's overland spread finally encircled the globe.)

But the Spanish and Portuguese were not the only missionaries to the New World. Farther north were the French. In 1535–6 the explorer Jacques Cartier had sailed up the St Lawrence River as far as the first rapids. Because he was looking for a route to China, he called the spot—near the site of the future Montreal—Lachine. But a permanent French settlement on the St Lawrence had to await the arrival of Samuel de Champlain, who established a fur-trading post at Quebec in 1608 and travelled upstream to the Great Lakes.

Missionaries followed: four Récollet friars in 1615 and five Jesuits in 1625. The Jesuit Jacques Marquette arrived in Quebec in 1666 and two years later founded a mission at Sault Ste Marie, at the northern end of Lake Michigan. With the layman Louis Jolliet, a native of New France, he explored southward along the Mississippi River. French missionary activity among the Iroquois and other Native American peoples was handled largely by the Jesuits. Their respect for Native ways attracted many converts, without eradicating Native traditions.

The other major inroads of European Catholicism in North America were the result of migration. French settlements developed not only along the St Lawrence but in Acadia (Nova Scotia) and along the lower Mississippi (Louisiana), while the colony of Maryland was established in 1632 by George Calvert, Lord Baltimore, as a refuge for English Catholics fleeing persecution in Britain. Other regions, including Atlantic Canada and the future Ontario, also attracted Catholic settlers from the British Isles. From the mid-nineteenth century on, the growth of industrial cities along the east coast of North America attracted large numbers of immigrants from Ireland and, later, Italy. To some extent the ecclesiastical hierarchy of the Catholic Church in North America today mirrors the more recent history of immigration.

Practice

Worship

Prayer

Prayer is reverent and contemplative conversation with the divine. Christians can pray individually as well as in groups; in fact, Jesus tells his disciples not to make a public show, but to pray in private (*Matthew* 6). The prayer he teaches them is known both as the Lord's Prayer and as the 'Our Father' or (in Latin) *Pater noster* (from its opening words). It was already in fairly wide use around the end of the first century, when the gospels were produced, and is common to all branches of Christians. From the beginning, music was also part of Christian worship, for the Church inherited from Judaism the biblical psalms that had been sung in the temple.

The Rosary

A rosary is a string of beads used in prayer, especially by Roman Catholics. It consists of 58 beads arranged in five groups of ten (separated by single beads of a different colour or size) and a small **crucifix**: a cross bearing an image of the suffering Christ. (The English word 'bead' comes from the same origin as the German *beten*, 'to pray'.) The person using the rosary will say one 'Our Father' (the Lord's Prayer) and ten Hail Mary's, following the sequence of the beads. The Hail Mary is a brief prayer: 'Hail, Mary, full of grace, the Lord is with you; blessed are you among women, and blessed is the fruit of your womb, Jesus. Holy Mary, mother of God, pray for us sinners now and at the hour of our death.'

The Eucharist

The central Christian ritual, the Eucharist (from the Greek word for thanksgiving), re-enacts the story of the 'last supper': the Passover supper that Jesus shared with his disciples on the Thursday night of his final week in Jerusalem. In the story, Jesus breaks some bread and passes around a cup of wine, declaring these to be his body and his blood, given for the disciples, and asking them to do the same in remembrance of him.

This **sacrament**, later called the Eucharist, is common to all branches of Christianity, though it goes by a variety of names and is understood in different ways by different denominations. Roman Catholics commonly refer to the Eucharistic service as the **mass**, from the final words of the Latin ritual: *Ite, missa est* ('Go; it has been delivered'), while Eastern Orthodox Christians often call it the Liturgy, from a Greek word meaning 'service'. Many Protestants use the terms Holy Communion or Lord's Supper.

Some Protestant denominations also departed from Rome in their interpretations of the sacrament. Some Anglicans and Lutherans have retained the traditional understanding of the ritual as a sacrifice, believing that the body and blood of Christ are present in or together with the bread and wine of the ceremonial meal. In Switzerland, however, the sacramental theology of reformers such as Zwingli and Calvin led most

Protestants to understand the Eucharist less as a sacrifice than as a memorial in which the bread and wine symbolize Christ's body and blood.

Baptism

Baptism is the ritual in which a person is admitted into the Christian community. It recalls the ritual bathing practised by a number of movements at the time of Jesus (including the one with which Jesus' forerunner, John the Baptist, was associated): a symbolic washing away of prior uncleanness in preparation for beginning a new life. As long as Christianity remained a minority religion, joined at considerable personal risk, baptism was not undertaken lightly. People were initiated into the faith only after a course of instruction called catechism.

The Christian Year

The liturgical year for Christians is calculated largely from the two main festivals of Christmas and Easter. It begins with **Advent**, the series of four Sundays that precede Christmas.

Christmas

We do not know the time of the year when Jesus was actually born. By the fourth century, however, his birth had come to be celebrated around the winter solstice—a season that coincided with a number of Roman festivals, including the celebration of the unconquered sun on 25 December. Apparently the Christian idea of a birth bringing new blessing was readily associated with the annual renewal of the sun's radiance.

Easter

Whereas Christmas has a fixed date because it is related to the solar year, Easter is related to the phases of the moon and therefore has a variable date. The first Easter occurred just after Passover, a spring festival in the Jewish lunar calendar, but in the course of time, Christians diverged from Jewish calendrical calculations. The Latin Church eventually fixed Easter as the first Sunday after the first full moon after the spring equinox. Thus it can fall anywhere in a period of five weeks from late March to late April. The date of Easter in the Greek Church is calculated in a slightly different way, with the result that it coincides with the Latin Easter only about one year in every four.

As the feast of Jesus' resurrection, Easter comes at the conclusion of a period of six and a half weeks known as **Lent**, of which the last and climactic week is called Holy Week. For most Christians Lent is the time of the year for the greatest solemnity, the most serious reflection, and the most stringent discipline, which has often meant abstinence from things such as meat and other pleasures. Accordingly, the last day before Lent has traditionally been a time of wild partying. Shrove Tuesday, as it is called in

English, is Mardi Gras ('fat Tuesday') in French, notably in New Orleans, and Carnival (etymologically 'goodbye, meat'), in the Hispanic culture of the Caribbean.

Lent consists of forty days before Easter, not counting Sundays. The English name is a description of the season, when the days 'lengthen'. Lent begins on Ash Wednesday, so named because in some Christian churches the foreheads of worshippers are daubed with ashes. The ashes come from the dried palm leaves used as church decorations the preceding year on Palm Sunday—the day that inaugurates Holy Week, when churches are often decorated with palm leaves recalling the branches that welcomed Jesus as he entered Jerusalem.

The day of Jesus' last Passover supper with his disciples is called Maundy Thursday in English, for the commandment (*mandatum* in Latin) to love one another that in *John* 13 Jesus gives on that occasion. Friday of Holy Week is known as **Good Friday**. Some think the name refers to the idea that Jesus' self-sacrificing death on the cross was 'good' for humanity, but a more convincing explanation suggests that the original term was 'God's Friday'. This most solemn day of the Christian year is marked by services recalling the **Passion**: Jesus' suffering on the cross.

Easter day itself commemorates the disciples' discovery, on the morning after the Sabbath, that Jesus has risen from the dead. Among the layers of meaning that Christians may find in the story of the resurrection is a sense of cosmic triumph over sin and death.

Like Passover, Easter is a spring festival associated with the renewal of life. Some of the most common Easter symbols in popular Christian culture probably antedate Christianity and connote fertility: the egg, for instance, and the rabbit. The English name 'Easter' itself comes from Eostre, a pagan goddess. In most other European languages, though, the term for Easter is derived from Pesach, the Hebrew name of Passover; in French, for instance, Easter is Pâques.

The fiftieth day counting from Easter is Pentecost, from the Greek for 'fifty'. In England Pentecost is often called Whitsunday, on account of the white garments formerly worn by persons baptized on that day. In Latin countries the day is generally referred to as the feast of the Holy Spirit.

Cultural Expressions

Medieval Church Architecture

In the western Mediterranean, as in Byzantium, the round arch developed by the Romans was the characteristic shape used in the churches. In northern Europe, however, a new pointed arch came into fashion beginning after the eleventh century. This Gothic arch made it possible to achieve greater height, and in the course of the Middle Ages church architects learned to build cathedrals with naves as much as five times as high as they were wide. It has often been suggested that these structures directed the thoughts of worshippers heavenward.

Flying buttresses support the walls of the Cathedral of Notre Dame in Paris, begun in 1163 (Andrew Leyerle).

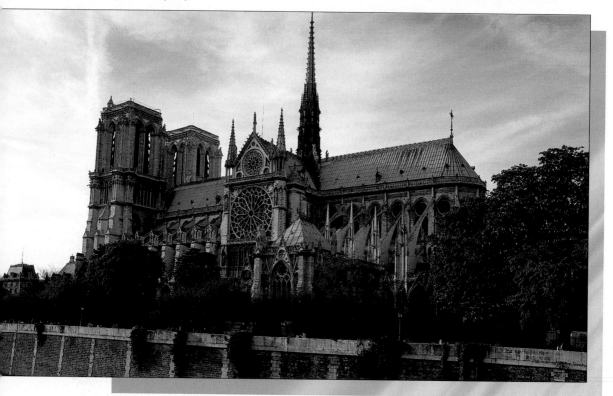

As architects pushed the capacity of their material—stone—to its limits, many Gothic churches had to be supported on the outside to keep the weight of the roof from forcing the upper parts of the walls outward. When these supports stood free of the wall and were bridged to it with half-arches, they were called 'flying buttresses'.

Gothic churches were usually much more elaborately ornamented than their Byzantine or Romanesque counterparts, both inside and out. Carvings in stone and wood, usually brightly painted, depicted events in the life of Christ and the saints. Also developed in the Middle Ages was the stained-glass window made up of thousands of pieces of coloured glass—especially in deep, clear blues and reds—joined by strips of lead. Whether in sculpture, painting, tapestry, or stained glass, scenes from the Bible were often arranged in sequence like the panels of a comic strip, and served as teaching aids in an era when literacy was limited.

Unique to Roman Catholic churches is a feature known as the **stations of the cross**: a sequence of fourteen locations, usually along the side of the nave of the church, recalling the events from Jesus' trial to the placing of his body in the tomb. The stations may be paintings, or plaques, or sculptures, or even, in austerely decorated churches,

Stained-glass windows at the thirteenth-century Cathedral of Notre Dame in Reims in northeastern France (Andrew Leyerle).

simply Roman numerals or crosses. During Lent worshippers move from one station to the next, meditating on Jesus' final suffering.

Protestant Art and Music

Protestant architecture in northern Europe was not markedly distinct from earlier Catholic forms, since in many cases Protestants took over existing churches. In the sanctuary, however, Reformed churches rearranged the furniture to suit their sacramental theology. In place of the traditional altar that the priest faced with his back to the worshippers, Protestants adopted a communion table behind which the minister would stand and face the congregation.

The sixteenth-century reformers strongly disapproved of what they considered image worship, and preferred an empty cross to a crucifix with the suffering Jesus on it. Statues and paintings were destroyed with fanatical zeal, though stained-glass windows were often spared. Some denominations have kept their church interiors bare and austere. Others have at least an aesthetic affection for Renaissance paintings of the Madonna (Mary) with the infant Jesus. Mary does appear in Protestantism at the Christmas season, but is clearly subordinated to Jesus himself and is associated mostly with his infancy.

In music Protestantism made a major cultural contribution, often taking over the tunes of folk songs and using them in worship. Martin Luther himself wrote what is probably the most widely cherished Protestant hymn, and since the 1960s it has been adopted by Catholics as well:

> A mighty fortress is our God, a bulwark never failing;
> Our helper he amid the flood of mortal ills prevailing.
> For still our ancient foe doth seek to work us woe;
> His craft and power are great; and armed with cruel hate, on earth is not
>   his equal.

> Did we in our own strength confide, our striving would be losing,
> Were not the right man on our side, the man of God's own choosing.
> Dost ask who that may be? Christ Jesus, it is he,
> Lord Sabaoth [i.e., Lord of hosts] his name, from age to age the same, and
>   he must win the battle.

Musically, most Protestant hymns are simple, usually consisting of four lines in which the fourth returns to the melody of the first two. But their texts express a wide range of religious concerns—from praise to God as creator to calls for social justice and world peace.

Among the Calvinists in Switzerland and Scotland, the musical repertory consisted mainly of the biblical psalms set to music. The tunes of the sixteenth-century Genevan Psalter include a familiar setting of *Psalm* 100, to which Protestants often sing the doxology (song of praise):

> Praise God from whom all blessings flow;
> Praise him all creatures here below;
> Praise him above, ye heavenly host:
> Praise Father, Son, and Holy Ghost.

From the middle of the eighteenth century to the end of the nineteenth, a frequent theme for hymns was the experience of receiving divine favour. An example is 'Amazing Grace', which is often sung to a familiar early American tune; the words date from 1779:

> Amazing grace—how sweet the sound—
>   that saved a wretch like me!
> I once was lost, but now am found,
>   was blind, but now I see.

Interaction and Adaptation

The Modern Era

Together, the eighteenth-century Enlightenment and the American and French revolutions loosened the official ties between church and state. But the shift towards secularism did not mean that Christian symbols and values ceased to play an important role in Western culture and political life. And the increasing emphasis on reason and scientific investigation—even of scripture—did not necessarily diminish Christians' faith.

Philosophy and Christianity

The eighteenth century was a period of philosophical scepticism about claims for the transcendent. Enlightenment thinkers contended that the objects of religion cannot be substantiated through the operation of reason. Particularly decisive were the critiques of such philosophers as the Scotsman David Hume (1711–76) and the German Immanuel Kant (1724–1804). Aquinas's argument for 'God as First Cause' cannot be proved; as Kant argued, causality is not part of the physical world but part of the framework of thought within which human minds interpret it.

Yet what Kant showed to be in principle unprovable is by the same token undisprovable. Instead of making cognitive assertions about the divine or transcendent, modern philosophers of religion since Kant have generally preferred to speak of experience and feeling—that is, of the dynamics of the human response to the transcendent. The German philosopher Friedrich Schleiermacher (1768–1834), for instance, characterized religion as an 'intuitive sense of absolute dependence': if we cannot prove the existence of what we intuitively feel that we depend on, at least we can describe that intuition. In the same post-Kantian vein, the twentieth-century German philosopher of religion Rudolf Otto (1869–1937) adopted the word 'numinous' to refer to what people sense to be an overpowering yet fascinating mystery.

Schleiermacher also contributed to a 'subjective' understanding of Christ's **atonement**. In the traditional Christian understanding, it is through Christ's sacrifice that humanity is saved and restored to its proper relationship with God. For Schleiermacher, however, Jesus functions above all as a moral example, an embodiment of human awareness of God: salvation comes first as a change in spiritual awareness, and atonement follows in the form of reconciliation between the divine and the human.

Meanwhile, the nineteenth-century Danish philosopher Søren Kierkegaard (1813– 55) pioneered the line of inquiry called existentialism, in which the focus shifted from knowledge (already limited by Kant) to commitment. It is no accident that many modern intellectual defences of religion see it as analogous to love, which likewise depends on commitment rather than argument.

Commitment-based theologies have been influential, but they do not rule out one powerful classic argument against religious faith: the problem of evil and suffering. We find it already in ancient literature (including the biblical book of *Job*): how can one treat as both powerful and good, and hence worthy of worship, a deity that would allow either the evil that results from some human actions or the suffering that results from accident or chaos in nature? Even in a mechanistic theory, where after creation the deity does not intervene in the world, the creator does not escape responsibility. The modern world has in no way eliminated evil and suffering as objections to theistic faith, nor has it come up with any striking new ways of answering them.

Protestantism after 1800

Protestant Missions and Colonialism

The colonial policies of the northern European nations and the missionary efforts of Protestants peaked in the second half of the nineteenth century. In Africa, one of their main targets, the aims of church and state went hand in hand. The British established themselves on large stretches of the African coastline and then moved into the interior of the continent by river, road, and eventually rail. Although formerly active in the slave trade between West Africa and the New World, Britain had outlawed slavery in 1834, and

An Anglican church in Placencia, Belize (Andrew Leyerle).

by mid-century its opposition to the ongoing slave trade in East Africa had become one of the arguments it used to justify its colonization efforts. Even the Scottish missionary David Livingstone (1813–73) made an explicit connection between evangelism and empire; in a speech to a Cambridge audience in 1857, he said: '[Africa] is now open; do not let it be shut again! I go back to Africa to try to make an open path for commerce and Christianity. Do you carry on the work I have begun.' (Livingstone 1858:24).

Elsewhere in the world there were comparable opportunities. A missionary to the southwestern Pacific reported in 1837 that 'at the lowest computation 150,000 persons, who a few years ago were unclothed savages, are now wearing articles of British manufacture.'

New American Denominations

A defining feature of Protestantism is the freedom it allows for individual expressions of faith. The result has been a bewildering diversity, which is illustrated by the new denominations that emerged on the American scene in the nineteenth and twentieth centuries.

Disciples of Christ

Following Presbyterian opposition to a revival in Kentucky in 1804, Barton Stone (1772–1844) left the Presbyterians to become a 'Christian only' and attracted a number of followers. Meanwhile, when Thomas Campbell (1763–1854), a Presbyterian from Northern Ireland, became disaffected with the sectarian character of his church, he and his son Alexander joined Baptist associations, calling themselves Reformers. In 1832 the Stone and Campbell movements merged to form the Disciples of Christ (also called the Christian Church or Churches of Christ).

Seventh-Day Adventists

In 1831 a Baptist lay minister in upstate New York began to preach that the second coming of Christ was imminent. Interpreting the reference to 2,300 days in *Daniel* 8:14 as 2,300 years, William Miller (1782–1849) expected the Advent in or around the year 1843. After the 'great disappointment' of the prediction's failure, the Millerites revised their calculations several times, and eventually gave up making specific predictions.

From the 1840s until her death, the 'gift of prophecy' of Ellen Gould White (1826–1915), who experienced trances and visions, was the spiritual authority of the movement. Seventh-Day Adventists worship on Saturday rather than Sunday.

Jehovah's Witnesses

Growing up near Pittsburgh, Charles Taze Russell (1852–1916) was exposed to forecasts, by Miller and others, of the end of the world and the return of Christ. He was intensely interested in Bible study but largely self-taught. The study group he formed began publishing *Zion's Watch Tower and Herald of Christ's Presence* in 1879 and predicted that the end of the world would come in 1914. When that prediction failed to come true, they maintained that 1914 was the year when Jehovah's Kingdom was inaugurated in anticipation of the end, which was subsequently predicted for 1918, 1920, 1925, 1941, and 1975.

Russell himself died in 1916. It was under his successor, J.F. Russell, that the movement adopted the name Jehovah's Witnesses. Their principal activity is door-to-door missionary work distributing their publications *Awake!* and *The Watchtower.* Witnesses reject the doctrine of the Trinity and regard Jesus Christ as a created being (as Arius did), although they believe that in dying he gave humanity a second chance to choose right-eousness and escape the punishment expected at the end. They also refuse to salute flags or serve in armies, not because they are pacifists but because they see themselves as citi-zens of another kingdom and therefore reject the authority of secular states.

Christian Scientists

The Church of Christ, Scientist, was founded in Boston in 1879 by Mary Baker Eddy (1821–1910), a New England woman who had become interested in spiritual healing after receiving help for her spinal condition from a healer who worked without medi-cines. She began to write about spiritual healing, and her *Science and Health*, published in 1875, came to be regarded by her followers as an inspired text second in authority only to the Bible.

Mrs Eddy departed in many ways from standard Christian views, maintaining that not only disease and suffering but sin, death, and the material world itself are all illusions.

Mormons (Church of Jesus Christ of Latter-day Saints)

The Church of Jesus Christ of Latter-day Saints was founded in 1830 by Joseph Smith, Jr (1805–44), who claimed that in 1820, as a boy in upstate New York, he had had a vision of God and Jesus in which he was told not to join any of the existing denomina-tions. Subsequent visions persuaded him that he had been divinely chosen to restore the true Church of Christ. The authority of that church, Smith claimed, was revealed by apostolic figures to him and his associate Oliver Cowdery (1806–50) in 1829.

As a textual basis for the enterprise, Smith published the *Book of Mormon*: an account of God's dealings with the Western hemisphere paralleling the Bible's account of events in the Eastern hemisphere, which Mormons regard as a scripture. Smith said he had translated the text from gold plates inscribed in 'reformed Egyptian' that had been divinely entrusted to him.

Moving westward from New York state after 1830, Smith's followers established settlements in Ohio, Missouri, and—when they were driven out of Missouri—in Nauvoo, Illinois. By now they were calling themselves the Church of Jesus Christ of Latter-day Saints. In Nauvoo Smith introduced unusual practices including polygamy, and declared himself a candidate for the American presidency. Some of his innovations caused strife between different factions of the Latter-day Saints, and in 1844 Smith and his brother were killed by an anti-Mormon mob. Some traditionalist, anti-polygamy Mormons stayed in the midwest as the Reorganized Church of Latter-Day Saints, with headquar-ters in Independence, Missouri, but the majority moved on to Utah in 1847 under the leadership of Brigham Young (1801–77).

Thereafter the Mormon community adopted a code of behaviour that included not only a rigid sexual morality but strict abstinence from all stimulants, including tea and coffee. Mormons expect their young adults to serve for two years as volunteer mis-sionaries. Among their distinctive doctrines is the idea that as human beings improve, so God himself increases in perfection. Distinctive practices include baptism of the dead as a way of augmenting the spiritual community; as a consequence, some of the world's most energetic genealogical research is conducted in Utah. Mormons have also taken an interest in Western-hemisphere archaeology in hopes of discovering documentation regarding the *Book of Mormon*.

Holiness Churches

In time, the main Methodist bodies in America became more organized and conventional, more sedate and mainline. But new independent churches and movements continued to spring from the revivalist roots of Methodism. Because these congregations emphasized the experience of receiving the gift of holiness, they are often referred to as 'Holiness' churches.

The intensity of feeling associated with that experience can bring striking changes in behaviour. Some people roll in the aisles of the meeting (hence the nickname 'holy rollers'); others speak out ecstatically in an exotic prayer language they have not previously known ('speaking in tongues', technically termed '**glossolalia**'). In either case, the group believes such behaviour to be inspired by the Holy Spirit. The term '**charismatic**', from the Greek word for spiritual gifts, is also used to describe such groups. Though initially a Protestant phenomenon, charismatic activity has also begun to emerge among Catholic Christians since the 1970s.

Pentecostal Churches

Protestant congregations that cultivate the practice of 'speaking in tongues' are called **Pentecostal**. Although the name recalls the Pentecost experience recounted in *Acts* 2:1, the 'tongues' that modern Pentecostals speak are understood not as the native languages of those present, but as the mystical language of heaven.

Many locate the birth of the modern Pentecostal movement in a revival held at a church in Los Angeles in 1906. Its leader was William J. Seymour (1870–1922), whose parents had been slaves. Newspaper coverage described the sounds of Seymour's meetings as a 'weird babble'. At the outset blacks and whites worshipped together, but as Pentecostalism diversified, it developed segregated congregations.

With its emphasis on immediate personal experience rather than any textual or doctrinal tradition, Pentecostalism can take a variety of forms and appeal effectively to people with little formal education. It also has a cross-cultural appeal, and Pentecostal missionaries enjoy remarkable success in Latin America and Africa. Some consider Pentecostalism the fastest-growing segment of Christianity today.

Evangelicals and Fundamentalists

Seen in its broadest compass, twentieth-century Protestant evangelicalism is a movement cutting across the major denominations. It is not a denomination as such, although some denominations are solidly evangelical. It draws on earlier themes, notably the individual conversion experience—the confident assurance of God's grace and acceptance—that characterized Reformation Pietism in continental Europe and the revivalist movements of England and North America. Evangelicals refer to conversion as a spiritual rebirth, an experience of being 'born again' (a phrase that refers to Jesus' injunction in *John* 3:7: 'Ye must be born again'). As the name **evangelical**—which comes from the Greek for gospel or 'good news'—suggests, many evangelicals make it their business to spread their message, and they often do so with the conviction that it, and no other, is valid.

Because Protestantism had put so many of its eggs in the basket of scriptural authority as opposed to the institutional church, critical study of the Bible was bound to provoke a particularly sharp reaction among Protestants. Committed to the literal authority of the scriptures, evangelicals fought a rearguard battle against the findings of modern historical and literary study of the Bible in the late nineteenth and early twentieth centuries and also against the competing Darwinian theory of human evolution.

In 1910 a series of booklets entitled *The Fundamentals* affirmed the inerrancy—that is, the infallibility—of the Bible and traditional doctrines. Three million copies were distributed free to Protestant clergy, missionaries, and students in the United States through the anonymous sponsorship of 'two Christian laymen': William Lyman Stewart and his brother Milton. By 1920 advocates of inerrancy were being called 'fundamentalists'.

The test case for **fundamentalism** was the 1925 trial of a high-school teacher named John T. Scopes (1900–70) for violating a new Tennessee law that banned the teaching of evolution in contradiction to the Bible. Thus began the famous 'Scopes Trial', used by fundamentalists as a demonstration of the truth of their religion. The court found for the prosecution's traditionalist oratory of William Jennings Bryan against the defence of Clarence Darrow and fined Scopes $100. So extensive was the news coverage, however, that in effect fundamentalism itself was put on trial in the court of public opinion. Darwin, Scopes, and Darrow emerged the clear victors among the population at large, although supporters of fundamentalism believed they had been vindicated. Scopes's conviction was overturned in 1927 on appeal, on the technicality that the fine was too high, and the Tennessee law was eventually repealed in 1967.

Fundamentalists (and some evangelicals) often perceive a struggle between good and evil forces in the world. Many believe that evil, personified in Satan, is tangibly manifested in social groups with which they disagree, such as proponents of evolution, defenders of free choice in abortion, or advocates of homosexual rights. They also tend towards the apocalyptic conviction that a final battle between the forces of good and evil is imminent. Though their views on complex social and ethical issues are often criticized as simplistic, evangelicals are generous givers to charitable causes like famine relief.

In the twentieth century, a number of Protestant evangelical preachers—heirs to the revivalist tradition—became famous for their 'crusades', attracting huge audiences and calling on them to make 'decisions for Christ': to convert from a lapsed or inactive form of the faith to a revitalized one. Pioneered by the Southern Baptist Billy Graham (b. 1918), the use of television to take the evangelical message into people's homes gave rise to a succession of 'televangelists' who made the electronic audience their primary 'congregation' and solicited contributions by mail and telephone. Several highly entrepreneurial preachers who operated outside established denominations built what amounted to personal empires. Success could lead to temptation, and did not necessarily deliver from evil. Financial and marital scandals brought a few of the most visible televangelists into disrepute in the late 1980s. But audience ratings remain high, particularly for the success-oriented 'Hour of Power' broadcast from the Crystal Cathedral of Robert Schuller (b. 1926) in southern California.

The Second Vatican Council

In 1958 the Italian cardinal Angelo Giuseppe Roncalli (1881–1963) was elected Pope John XXIII. At the time, few had any inkling of the changes that lay in store for the Roman Catholic Church. Though already in his late seventies, this man of great human warmth proved to have both a vision for his church and a fearless openness to change. Calling for *aggiornamento* ('updating'), John XXIII convoked the Second Vatican Council (1962–65; the First Vatican Council, held in 1869–70, had established the doctrine of papal infallibility).

A major breach developed between the Catholic Church and the laity, however, shortly after Vatican II, when John XXIII's successor, Pope Paul VI, issued an encyclical (letter) entitled *Humanae Vitae* ('On Human Life'; 1968) that prohibited the use of artificial birth control by Catholics. Since then the gap between the Church's official stand on sexuality and the actual practice of many Catholics has continued to widen. Many of the faithful have ceased to take their church's teachings seriously in large areas of their lives.

At the same time *Humanae Vitae* intensified the theological tension between reform and traditionalist wings in the Church's hierarchy. Progressive Catholics saw the document, which was issued by the pope without the consensus of bishops in council, as an attempt to undermine the accomplishments of Vatican II, turn back the clock, and reaffirm the papal authority established in Vatican I.

Ecumenism

One of the principal concerns of Vatican II was to promote reconciliation with other branches of Christianity. For Rome, the ultimate goal was what the Council, in its 1964 decree on **ecumenism** (from the Greek for 'inhabited world'), called 'the restoration of unity among all Christians' within 'one Church and one Church only'.

In fact, ecumenism was by that time a reality within Protestantism, albeit on a more modest scale. The mainline denominations had begun overcoming centuries of separation in the early 1900s, partly as a consequence of their collaboration in mission fields where distinctions between Anglicans and Presbyterians, Baptists and Congregationalists, meant little or nothing. Even if they disagreed on matters such as Eucharistic theology, the different denominations could readily support one another on issues such as social justice.

In Canada, Methodists, Congregationalists, and a majority of the country's Presbyterians merged to form the United Church of Canada in 1925. In the United States, a Congregational–Christian merger with the Evangelical and United Brethren produced the United Church of Christ. In England the Presbyterians and Congregationalists formed the United Reformed Church in 1972. And in Australia a similar group of churches joined to form the Uniting Church in 1977. Meanwhile, most of the major

| Box 3.9 | From Martin Luther King, 'Letter from Birmingham Jail'

In the spring of 1963 the Baptist minister and civil-rights leader Martin Luther King, Jr, was arrested and imprisoned for leading a protest against racial segregation in Birmingham, Alabama. On 16 April he responded to criticism of his activity by eight other clergymen with an open letter that came to be known as the 'Letter from Birmingham Jail'.

So I, along with several members of my staff, am here because I was invited here. I am here because I have organizational ties here.

But more basically, I am in Birmingham because injustice is here. . . . I am cognizant of the interrelatedness of all communities and states. I cannot sit idly by in Atlanta and not be concerned about what happens in Birmingham. Injustice anywhere is a threat to justice everywhere. We are caught in an inescapable network of mutuality, tied in a single garment of destiny. Whatever affects one directly, affects all indirectly. Never again can we afford to live with the narrow, provincial 'outside agitator' idea. Anyone who lives inside the United States can never be considered an outsider anywhere within its bounds. . . .

You express a great deal of anxiety over our willingness to break laws. . . . One may well ask: 'How can you advocate breaking some laws and obeying others?' The answer lies in the fact that there are two types of laws: just and unjust. I would be the first to advocate obeying just laws. One has not only a legal but a moral responsibility to obey just laws. Conversely, one has a moral responsibility to disobey unjust laws. I would agree with St Augustine that 'an unjust law is no law at all'. . . .

I have traveled the length and breadth of Alabama, Mississippi and all the other southern states. On sweltering summer days and crisp autumn mornings I have looked at the South's beautiful churches with their lofty spires pointing heavenward. I have beheld the impressive outlines of her massive religious-education buildings. Over and over I have found myself asking: 'What kind of people worship here? Who is their God? . . . Where were they when Governor Wallace gave a clarion call for defiance and hatred? Where were their voices of support when bruised and weary Negro men and women decided to rise from the dark dungeons of complacency to the bright hills of creative protest?' . . .

There was a time when the church was very powerful—in the time when the early Christians rejoiced at being deemed worthy to suffer for what they believed. In those days the church was not merely a thermometer that recorded the ideas and principles of popular opinion; it was a thermostat that transformed the mores of society. Whenever the early Christians entered a town, the people in power became disturbed and immediately sought to convict the Christians for being 'disturbers of the peace' and 'outside agitators.' But the Christians pressed on, in the conviction that they were 'a colony of heaven,' called to obey God rather than man. . . .

But the judgment of God is upon the church as never before. If today's church does not recapture the sacrificial spirit of the early church, it will lose its authenticity, forfeit the loyalty of millions, and be dismissed as an irrelevant social club with no meaning for the twentieth century. Every day I meet young people whose disappointment with the church has turned into outright disgust. . . .

Yes, they [some clergy] have gone to jail with us. Some have been dismissed from their churches, have lost the support of their bishops and fellow ministers. But they have acted in the faith that right defeated is stronger than evil triumphant. Their witness has been the spiritual salt that has preserved the true meaning of the gospel in these troubled times. They have carved a tunnel of hope through the dark mountain of disappointment.

> I hope the church as a whole will meet the challenge of this decisive hour. . . .
> Let us all hope that the dark clouds of racial prejudice will soon pass away and the deep fog of misunderstanding will be lifted from our fear-drenched communities, and in some not too distant tomorrow the radiant stars of love and brotherhood will shine over our great nation with all their scintillating beauty (King 1964: 76–95).

Protestant and Orthodox churches had come together to establish the World Council of Churches in 1948.

The spirit of reunion was in the air. By the end of the 1960s Protestant and Catholic institutions for the study of theology and the training of clergy were making collaborative arrangements, their students attending the same lectures and reading the same books. A gulf that had divided Western Christendom for four centuries was being bridged.

Twentieth-Century Theology

In the last century a number of Roman Catholic theologians and philosophers have explored the Aristotelian principles and methods of Thomas Aquinas for modern purposes. One of the most innovative and wide-ranging was the German Jesuit Karl Rahner (1904–84). Another influential Jesuit concerned with the theory of knowledge was the Canadian Bernard Lonergan (also 1904–84), who taught in Rome for half his career. Jacques Maritain (1882–1973) was a French neo-Thomist with conservative views on many issues who converted to Catholicism while a student and taught in Paris, Toronto, and Princeton. Widowed at seventy-eight, he joined the Dominicans in a French monastery for his last years.

Tradition-based theologies have also continued to attract adherents among Protestants. A commentary on Paul's letter to the Romans propelled the Swiss theologian Karl Barth (1886–1968) into prominence at the end of the First World War, a time of disillusionment with the idea that human progress was inevitable. Barth's theology is termed 'dialectical' because it draws a sharp distinction between what humans can do or know by themselves and the saving grace given to them by God; the Barthian position has been popular in conservative Protestant circles.

For existentialist thought, the unprovability of religion is irrelevant: what matters is individual commitment and experience. Existentialism has been particularly important among theologians trained in Europe. The German Paul Tillich (1886–1965), who settled in the United States in the 1930s, characterizes the movement of religious awareness not from God downward, as Barth does, but from the human experience upward: religion is, in Tillich's words, 'ultimate concern'. Tillich's formulations were widely influential during the second half of the century.

A distinctly American movement is **process theology**. Drawing on the process thought of Alfred North Whitehead (1861–1947), it has appealed especially to people who associate modernity with change. For its principal thinkers, such as the American

Charles Hartshorne (1897–2000), creation is unfinished and God is a dynamic power open to virtually unlimited possibility.

Recent liberal theology has concentrated on social liberation, feminist empowerment, the global environment, and equality for homosexual, transsexual, and transgendered Christians. In particular, liberal theology has seemed reactive in its relationship to modern life, shifting and rethinking its priorities in response to the demands of the culture.

By contrast, fundamentalism in both its Protestant and Catholic forms is a defensive reaction against modernity that promises a return to the basics of Christian faith. Where the two varieties of fundamentalism differ is in what they look to as the ultimate authority: scripture in one case and the tradition of the church itself in the other.

Women and Gender

The twentieth century, particularly its second half, brought dramatic changes in the status of women in Western society. Traditional notions of females as inferior to, or the property of, males were discredited and the range of roles open to women expanded significantly.

Liberal Protestant denominations in North America were ordaining women as clergy by the middle of the twentieth century, and the Anglican communion did so after mid-century. Barbara Harris (b. 1930) became an Episcopalian bishop in Massachusetts in 1989, and Lois Wilson (b. 1927), a minister and also moderator of the United Church of Canada, served as one of the presidents of the World Council of Churches from 1983 to 1991.

The Roman Catholic and Eastern Orthodox churches, however, do not yet ordain women as priests, let alone admit women to their senior hierarchies. (The Old Catholics, who broke away from the Roman Catholic Church after Vatican I, began ordaining women in 1996.) Both the Greek and Latin churches put special emphasis on historical precedent, and the tradition of women's subordination is so entrenched that it has proven particularly difficult to overturn. Formerly women were not allowed by Rome to take degrees in theology, but in recent decades Catholic women, both lay and religious, have made substantial contributions as scholars in the subject.

Efforts to redress two millennia of patriarchal bias have taken a variety of forms. Some scholars have directed their attention to female figures and symbols in the history and psychology of religion. Comparative studies have suggested parallels between the mother goddesses of various other religious traditions and the function of Mary as the archetypal mother in Roman Catholic piety.

Some theologians suggest that the real problem is the traditional conception of the Christian God as male. They see the deity as equally masculine and feminine, and they address their prayers to 'Our Father and Mother'. Others argue that a gender-balanced God is still anthropomorphic—a deity in human form. For them, the God who transcends the world must necessarily transcend gender.

Bethlehem The traditional birthplace of Jesus.

Nazareth Jesus' home in youth and manhood.

Jerusalem The site of Jesus' crucifixion and centre of the earliest Jewish Christian community; capital of the Latin Christian Kingdom in the Holy Land from 1099 to 1187.

Rome The capital of the Roman Empire, where Peter introduced Christianity and the Roman Catholic Church eventually established its headquarters in Vatican City—the world's smallest independent country.

Anatolia A region (corresponding to modern-day Turkey), evangelized by Paul, that became an important centre of the early Church; the location of the famous councils of Chalcedon, Nicea, and Constantinople.

Constantinople The capital of the Byzantine Empire and headquarters of the Orthodox Church; conquered by the Ottoman Turks in 1453 and renamed Istanbul.

Wittenberg The German town where Martin Luther posted his 95 theses, beginning the Protestant Reformation.

Worms The German city where an imperial council (Diet') tried Luther for political subversion.

Trent (Trentino in Italian) Site of the Council of Trent (1545–63) and centre of the Catholic Church's response to Protestantism, known as the Counter-Reformation.

Geneva The city in which John Calvin attempted to translate his vision of Christianity into a practising community.

Muenster A town in northwestern Germany that became a centre of the Anabaptist movement.

Valladolid City in Spain; the site of a great debate in 1550 in which Bartolomé de Las Casas defended the rights of the indigenous peoples of the New World.

Salt Lake City, Utah Founded by the Mormons in 1847; the headquarters of the Church of Jesus Christ of Latter-day Saints.

Christianity and Pluralism

By the beginning of the third millennium, diversity had become part of the national fabric not only of societies built on immigration—like Canada, the United States, and Australia—but also, increasingly, of European societies where until recently the great majority of citizens shared a common cultural background, including the Christian faith. At the same time those societies have become more and more secular.

Many factors have contributed to the process of secularization. The most obvious is science, but there is good reason to think that Christianity itself has played a part. Certainly the first modern attempts to create secular states took place in Christian societies: England, France, the United States. The distinction between sacred and secular, which was fundamental to Christianity from the beginning, was undoubtedly a factor in the diversification of Protestant Christianity, and it has been reflected in a general recognition of the right to freedom of religion.

Thus Christianity has largely ceased to play a significant official role in the public life of these secular societies. Many Christians remain convinced that the truth of their gospel leaves no room for other beliefs. Nevertheless, Christians have no choice today but to live as one among faith group among many. And even if that were not the case, Jesus' commandment to love our neighbours as ourselves would demand full openness to the identities of our fellow human beings. The plural nature of religious life today is a fact that must be accepted. To see that fact as desirable is to embrace what has come to be known as pluralism.

Pluralism presumes a human community whose common values may yet override the particularism of traditional Christian theology. An early proponent of pluralism was the Canadian scholar of comparative religion Wilfred Cantwell Smith (1916–2000). Smith suggested that to be modern is to be self-conscious about change and to take an active hand in shaping it. This chapter's overview of the Christian tradition makes it clear that change has been a feature of Christian history in every age. One would be ill advised to rule out the possibility of dramatic and creative change in the future.

Glossary

Advent The beginning of the Christian liturgical year, a period including the four Sundays immediately preceding Christmas.

apostles The first generation of Jesus' followers.

atonement Christ's restoration of humanity to a right relationship with God, variously interpreted as divine victory over demonic power, satisfaction of divine justice, or demonstration of a moral example.

baptism Sprinkling with or immersion in water, the ritual by which a person is initiated into membership in the Christian community. Baptism is considered a cleansing from sin.

bishop The supervising priest of an ecclesiastical district called a diocese.

canon A standard; a scriptural canon is the list of books acknowledged as scripture; the list of acknowledged saints is likewise a canon. Canon law is the accumulated body of

Church regulations and discipline. Clergy subject to the rule of a particular cathedral or congregation are also sometimes termed canons.

charismatic Characterized by spiritual gifts such as **glossolalia**.

Christ The Greek translation of the Hebrew word for messiah, 'anointed'.

conversion Spiritual rebirth, accompanied by certainty of divine forgiveness and acceptance.

cosmological argument An argument that infers the existence of God from the fact of creation, based on the assumption that every effect must have a cause and that there cannot be an infinite regress of causes.

creeds Brief formal statements of doctrinal belief, often recited in unison by congregations. The Apostles' Creed was in use by the third century and is widely used in worship services. The Nicene Creed, named for the Council of Nicaea (325 CE), is longer and more explicit and is recited in Catholic Eucharistic services.

crucifix A cross with an image of the suffering Jesus mounted on it.

ecumenism The movement for reunion or collaboration between previously separate branches of Christianity.

Eucharist The ritual re-enactment of Jesus' sacrifice of himself, patterned after his sharing of bread and wine as his body and blood at the final Passover meal with his disciples. Orthodox Christians term it the liturgy, Catholics the mass, and Protestants the Lord's Supper or Holy Communion.

Evangelical In Germany, a name for the Lutheran Church; in the English-speaking world, a description of conservative Protestants with a confident sense of the assurance of divine grace and the obligation to preach it.

excommunication Formal expulsion from the Church, particularly the Roman Catholic Church, for doctrinal error or moral misconduct.

friar A member of a Latin mendicant order such as the Dominicans, Franciscans, or Carmelites.

fundamentalism A twentieth-century reaction to modernity, originally among Protestants who maintained the infallibility of scripture and doctrine. Implying insistence on strict conformity in conduct and militancy in defending tradition against modernity, the term has been used more broadly in recent years; thus traditionalist Roman Catholics, for example, have also been described as 'fundamentalist'.

glossolalia Speaking in 'tongues'; a distinguishing feature of **charismatic** movements.

Gnosticism An ancient movement that believed the material world to be the evil result of a fall from pure spiritual existence. Christian Gnostics viewed Jesus as the bearer of a secret, saving knowledge through which the faithful would be redeemed from this material realm.

Good Friday The solemn holy day, two days before Easter, that commemorates the Passion or suffering and death of Jesus on the cross.

gospel 'Good news' (*evangelion* in Greek); the news of redemption that the Hebrew prophets had promised. The gospels are the accounts of Jesus' life attributed to his disciples Mark, Matthew, Luke, and John.

Holiness Churches Protestant churches that believe their members have already received 'holiness' (spiritual perfection) as a gift from God.

icon From the Greek for 'image'; a distinctive Byzantine form of portraiture used to depict Jesus, Mary, and the saints. The 'iconoclastic controversy' of the seventh and eighth centuries centred on an ultimately unsuccessful attempt to ban the use of icons.

Immaculate Conception The doctrine that the virgin Mary was without sin from the moment she herself was conceived; defined as Roman Catholic dogma in 1854.

incarnation The embodiment of the divine in human form.

indulgences Releases from time in purgatory; the selling of indulgences was one of the abuses that led to the Protestant Reformation.

justification by faith alone The Lutheran belief that humans are saved only by faith, not by 'works'—specifically, the Catholic rituals of confession and penance.

Lent The period of forty days, not counting Sundays, leading up to Easter; the season for the most serious Christian spiritual reflection.

logos 'Word' in the sense of eternal divine intelligence and purpose, an idea prominent in Greek thought at the time of Jesus.

Manichaeism An intensely dualistic religion, founded by Mani in the third century, that grew out of Syrian Christianity under the influence of Gnosticism.

mass The Roman Catholic Eucharistic ceremony, in which bread and wine are eaten as the body and blood of Christ; celebrated in Latin until 1965 and in local languages since then.

mendicant orders Medieval religious orders operating in the cities and towns rather than in monasteries set apart from them. Members worked or begged for a living, originally as a protest against the monasteries' wealth.

Monophysites Fifth-century advocates of the view that Christ's nature was fully divine.

mysticism A tradition cultivating and reflecting on the content of moments of intensely felt spiritual union with the divine.

Nestorians Fifth-century advocates of the view that the incarnate Christ was two separate persons, one divine and one human.

ontological argument The eleventh-century theologian Anselm's argument based on logic holding that God must necessarily exist.

original sin The sinfulness, or tendency towards sin, supposedly innate in human beings as a consequence of Adam's Fall.

Passion The suffering and death of Jesus on the cross.

patriarchs The five bishops who together represent supreme authority in the Eastern Orthodox tradition.

Pentecost The fiftieth day after Easter, commemorated as the dramatic occasion when Jesus' followers experienced the presence of the Holy Spirit and the ability to preach and be understood in different languages.

Pentecostal Churches Modern Protestant groups that emphasize speaking in 'tongues' as a mark of the Holy Spirit's presence and of the individual's holiness or spiritual perfection.

Pietism A movement that originated in late seventeenth-century Lutheran Germany, expressing a spontaneity of devotion and a confident certainty of forgiveness, over against institutional rigidity. It contributed to the emergence of Methodism in eighteenth-century England.

pope From *papa*, 'father'; the bishop of Rome, who represents supreme authority in the Roman Catholic tradition.

predestination The notion, based on faith in God as all-powerful and all-knowing, that God anticipates or controls human actions and foreordains every individual to either salvation or damnation.

purgatory In Catholic doctrine, the realm to which the soul proceeds after death for some unspecified period in preparation for entering heaven; the concept of purgatory developed in the medieval period.

Puritanism A Calvinist-inspired movement (1558–1660) that sought to 'purify' the Church of England of Catholic influences; before running its course in England, it became a major influence in Congregational churches in New England.

Reformed Churches Churches that are Calvinist in doctrine and often Presbyterian in governance; strong in the Netherlands and Scotland and also found in France, Switzerland, Hungary, and other places populated by settlers from those lands.

rosary A string consisting of 58 beads and a small crucifix, used in Catholic devotion to keep count when repeating Our Father and Hail Mary prayers.

sacrament A ritual action seen as signifying divine grace. The most widely accepted sacraments are baptism and the Eucharist, although the Catholic Church also recognizes five others.

Stations of the Cross Fourteen locations marked in the nave of a Catholic church, recalling events along the route in Jerusalem from Jesus' trial to his crucifixion.

syncretism The combination of elements from more than one religious tradition.

teleological argument From Greek *telos*, 'end' or 'purpose'; an argument inferring the existence of God from the perception of purpose or design in the universe; as much a strategy for discussing God as a formal proof of his existence.

transubstantiation The Catholic doctrine that, at the moment of consecration in the Eucharistic service, the bread and wine are miraculously transformed into the body and blood of Christ.

Trinity The concept of God as having three 'persons' or manifestations: as father, as son, and as Holy Spirit; the doctrine of the Trinity emerged in the late third century and was adopted after vigorous debate in the fourth.

Uniate Churches Churches in the Eastern Orthodox world and farther east with which the Roman Catholic Church established relations, recognizing their distinctive rites, conducted in languages other than Latin, and their married clergy.

Further Reading

Allen, E[dgar] L. 1960. *Christianity among the Religions*. London: Allen and Unwin. Still one of the most perceptive discussions of historical and contemporary issues of religious pluralism.

Aulén, Gustav. 1930. *Christus Victor*. London: SPCK; New York: Macmillan. A classic discussion of Christian theories of the atonement.

Barraclough, Geoffrey, ed. 1981. *The Christian World: A Social and Cultural History*. London: Thames and Hudson; New York: Abrams. Combines authoritative text with ample pictorial material.

Barrett, C.K. 1989. *The New Testament Background: Selected Documents*. Rev. ed. San Francisco: Harper & Row. Provides a context for understanding Christian origins.

Barrett, David B., ed. 1982. *World Christian Encyclopedia*. Nairobi: Oxford University Press. Current facts and figures, country by country.

Barbour, Ian G. 1966. *Issues in Science and Religion*. Englewood Cliffs: Prentice-Hall. A perceptive historical account by a scholar with scientific training.

Bettenson, Henry S., ed. 1999. *Documents of the Christian Church*. 3rd edn. London: Oxford University Press. Strong on the early Church and Anglicanism.

Buttrick, George A., ed. 1962. *The Interpreter's Dictionary of the Bible*. 4 vols. New York: Abingdon Press. Authoritative articles on Old and New Testament topics.

Forristal, Desmond. 1976. *The Christian Heritage*. Dublin: Veritas. A uniquely readable survey of Christian literature, art, architecture, and music across the ages.

Gilson, Étienne. 1955. *History of Christian Philosophy in the Middle Ages*. New York: Random House. Magisterial synthesis by one of the leading medievalists of his generation.

Isichei, Elizabeth. 1995. *A History of Christianity in Africa: From Antiquity to the Present*. London: SPCK. Traces the emergence of Christian identities in Africa south of the Sahara.

Küng, Hans. 1976. *On Being a Christian*. London: Collins; New York: Doubleday. A comprehensive review of Christian theology by a leading progressive Roman Catholic thinker.

McManners, John, ed. 1990. *The Oxford Illustrated History of Christianity*. Oxford: Oxford University Press. Comprehensive; well-written chapters by reliable authors.

van der Meer, F., and Christine Mohrmann. 1958. *Atlas of the Early Christian World*. London: Nelson. Illustrated guide to the geographical spread and the monuments of Christianity's first seven centuries.

The New Catholic Encyclopedia. 15 vols. 1967. New York: McGraw-Hill. A good place to start for many medieval and Roman Catholic topics.

Pelikan, Jaroslav. 1985. *Jesus through the Centuries: His Place in the History of Culture*. New Haven: Yale University Press. An erudite, wide-ranging review.

Placher, William C. 1983. *A History of Christian Theology: An Introduction*. Philadelphia: Westminster Press. A lively review of major thinkers, particularly useful for Protestantism since the Reformation. For primary texts, Placher's sourcebook in two volumes (early and modern), *Readings in the History of Christian Theology* (Philadelphia: Westminster Press, 1988) offers what may be the best selection currently available.

Roeder, Helen. 1951. *Saints and Their Attributes*. London: Longmans, Green. A useful guide to Christian iconography.

Ruether, Rosemary R., and Eleanor McLaughlin, eds. 1979. *Women of Spirit: Female Leadership in the Jewish and Christian Tradtions*. New York: Simon and Schuster. One of the best feminist collections.

Zernov, Nicholas. 1961. *Eastern Christendom: A Study of the Origin and Development of the Eastern Orthodox Church*. London: Weidenfeld and Nicolson; New York: Putnam. A comprehensive survey.

References

Bainton, Roland H. 1974. 'Reformation'. In *Encyclopaedia Britannica*, vol.15, 547–57. Chicago: Encyclopaedia Britannica Inc.

Bowie, Fiona, and Oliver Davies, eds. 1990. *Hildegard of Bingen: Mystical Writings*. New York: Crossroad.

Bradford, Ernle. 1967. *The Great Betrayal: Constantinople 1204*. London: Hodder & Stoughton.

Colgrave, Bertram, ed. 1969. *Bede's Ecclesiastical Histoy of the English People*. Oxford: Clarendon Press.

Durkheim, Émile. 1915. *The Elementary Forms of the Religious Life*. London: Allen & Unwin.

Faber, Richard. 1966. *The Vision and the Need: Late Victorian Imperialist Aims*. London: Faber.

Frend, W.H.C. 1965. *The Early Church*. Oxford: Blackwell.

Happold, F.C. 1963. *Mysticism: A Study and an Anthology*. Harmondsworth: Penguin.

King, Martin Luther, Jr. 1964. *Why We Can't Wait*. New York: New American Library.

Livingstone, David. 1858. *Cambridge Lectures*. Cambridge: Deighton.

McManners, John, ed. 1990. *The Oxford Illustrated History of Christianity*. Oxford: Oxford University Press.

Meyendorff, John. 1964. *A Study of Gregory Palamas*. London: Faith Press.

Meyer, Robert T., trans. 1950. *Athanasius, Life of St. Anthony*. Westminster, MD: Newman Press.

New English Bible. 1970. New York: Oxford University Press; Cambridge: Cambridge University Press.

O'Brien, Elmer. 1964. *Varieties of Mystic Experience*. New York: Holt, Rinehart and Winston.

Oliver, Roland. 1957. *Sir Harry Johnston and the Scramble for Africa*. London: Chatto & Windus.

Outler, Albert C., trans. 1955. *Augustine: Confessions and Enchiridion*. Philadelphia: Westminster Press; London: SCM Press.

Pass, Herman L. 1911. 'Demons and Spirits.' In *Encyclopaedia of Religion and Ethics*, ed. J. Hastings, vol. 4, 578–83. Edinburgh: T. & T. Clark; New York: Scribner.

Radice, Betty, trans. 1986. 'Moriae encomium'. In *Collected Works of Erasmus*, vol. 27. Toronto: University of Toronto Press.

Schlesinger, Arthur. 1974. 'The Missionary Enterprise and Theories of Imperialism'. In *The Missionary Enterprise in China and America*, ed. J. K. Fairbank, 336–73. Cambridge, MA: Harvard University Press.

Smith, Wilfred Cantwell. 1963. *The Faith of Other Men*. New York: New American Library.

Stevenson, J., ed. 1957. *A New Eusebius*. London: SPCK.

Stokes, Francis G., trans. 1909. *Epistolae obscurorum virorum*. London: Chatto & Windus.

Whitehead, Albert North. 1929. *Process and Reality*. Cambridge: Cambridge University Press; New York: Macmillan.

The Islamic Tradition

AMIR HUSSAIN | MAHMOUD M. AYOUB

It is Friday afternoon, a few minutes before the start of the weekly congregational prayer. In this mosque in Southern California, perhaps 200 men and 30 women are gathered; the difference in numbers reflects the fact that this prayer is obligatory for men but optional for women. A young man walks to the front of the large men's section (the women are seated in a second-floor gallery), raises his hands to his ears, and begins the call to prayer: 'Allahu akbar, God is greater . . .'. When he has finished, the people behind him line up in rows and wait for the imam—the person who will lead the prayer—to begin.

Were this service in a different location, the call to prayer might already have been sounded in the traditional way, broadcast from minarets (towers) beside the mosque. But there are no minarets here, as the mostly non-Muslim residents of this neighbourhood wanted a building that would 'fit in' with its surroundings. Nor does this mosque have the characteristic dome. Instead it is a two-storey building designed to look more like a school than a mosque. In this non-traditional context, the function of the call to prayer has changed. Instead of being broadcast outside, to let the community know that it is time to pray, the call is broadcast inside to those already assembled for the prayer. This is one of the ways in which the Muslims who come to this mosque have adapted to their surroundings.

The Name and Concept of Islam

Islam is the last of the three historic monotheistic faiths that arose in the Middle East, coming after Judaism and Christianity. Its name means 'submission' in Arabic and signifies the commitment of its adherents to live in total submission to God. A person who professes Islam is called a Muslim, meaning 'one who submits to God'. An older term, rarely encountered today, is 'Mohammedan', which misleadingly—and to Muslims offensively—suggests that Muslims worship the prophet Muhammad himself.

Who is a Muslim? The Qur'an, the Islamic scripture, presents Islam as the universal and primordial faith of all the prophets from Adam to Muhammad and of all those who believe in God, the one sovereign Lord, creator, and sustainer of all things. According to the Qur'an, Islam is God's eternal way for the universe.

Inanimate things, plants and animals, even the angels are all *muslims* to God by nature or instinct. Only human *islam* is an *islam* of choice. Human beings may voluntarily accept or wilfully reject faith, but on the Day of Judgment they will face the consequences of their choice. They can expect to be rewarded for their faith or punished for their rejection of it.

622	Muhammad's *hijrah* from Mecca to Medina
632	Muhammad dies; leadership passes to the caliph
642	Birth of Hasan al-Basri, early Sufi ascetic (d. 728)
661	Damascus established as capital of Umayyad caliphate
680	Death of Husayn at Karbala', commemorated as martyrdom by Shi'a
711	Arab armies reach Spain
762	Baghdad established as 'Abbasid capital
922	Al-Hallaj (born c. 858) executed for claiming to be one with the Truth
1058	Birth of al-Ghazali, theological synthesizer of faith and reason (d. 1111)
1071	Seljuq Turks defeat Byzantines in eastern Anatolia
1165	Birth of Ibn Arabi, philosopher of the mystical unity of being (d. 1240)
1207	Birth of Jalal al-Din Rumi, Persian mystical poet (d. 1273)
1258	Baghdad falls to Mongol invaders
1492	Christian forces take Granada, the last Muslim stronghold in Spain
1529	Ottoman Turks reach Vienna (again in 1683)
1602	Muslims officially expelled from Spain
1703	Birth of Ibn 'Abd al-Wahhab, leader of traditionalist revival in Arabia (d. 1792)
1924	Atatürk, Turkish modernizer and secularizer, abolishes the caliphate
1930	Iqbal proposes a Muslim state in India
1947	Pakistan established as an Islamic state
1979	Ayatollah Khomeini establishes a revolutionary Islamic regime in Iran
2001	Osama bin Laden launches terrorist attacks on America
2004	Madrid train station bombings
2005	London transit bombings

| Box 4.1   The Prophet on Mercy

From Sahih al-Bukhari, Vol. 2, *Hadith* 373 (unless otherwise noted, translations in this chapter are the authors' own).

A dying child was once brought to the Prophet Muhammad (peace be upon him). When, on seeing the child's last breaths, the Prophet began to shed tears, one of his companions asked why he was crying. He replied: 'It is mercy that God has put in the hearts of God's servants, and God is merciful only to those of God's servants who are merciful to others.'

Most Muslims are born into Muslim families. But it is also possible to become a Muslim simply by repeating before two Muslim witnesses the *shahadah*, or profession of faith: 'I bear witness that there is no god except God, and I bear witness that Muhammad is the messenger of God.' Anyone who does this becomes legally a Muslim, with all the rights and responsibilities that this new identity entails.

Origins

Jewish and Christian communities existed in Arabia long before the emergence of Islam in the seventh century. The city of Mecca, where Muhammad was born, was dominated mainly by one tribe, the Quraysh, but it was open to a broad range of cultural and religious influences, including Jewish and Christian moral and devotional ideas. There were desert hermits who practised holiness and healing, and a group of Meccan Arabs known as *hanifs* ('pious ones') who concurred with Jews and Christians in their ethical monotheism. The majority of the society, however, was polytheistic, and many of the images of the gods and goddesses they worshipped were housed in an ancient structure called the Ka'bah, believed to have been built by Abraham and his son Ishmael.

The Life of Muhammad (570–632 CE)

Muhammad was born into the Quraysh tribe around the year 570. His father died before his birth and his mother died a few years later. Muhammad thus grew up an orphan and was cared for first by his paternal grandfather, 'Abd al-Muttalib, and then, after his grandfather's death, by his uncle Abu Talib.

Little is known about Muhammad's youth. He worked as a merchant for a rich widow, Khadijah, whom he married in his mid-twenties. Muhammad is described in the early biographical sources as a contemplative, honest, and mild-mannered young man. He was called al-Amin ('the faithful' or 'trustworthy') because of the confidence he inspired in people.

Once a year, during the month of **Ramadan**, Muhammad spent days in seclusion in a cave on Mount Hira', a short distance from Mecca. Tradition reports that it was

NUMBERS
There are approximately 1 billion Muslims around the world; roughly 600,000 in Canada; and between 7 and 8 million in the United States.

DISTRIBUTION
Although Islam originated in Arabia, the largest Muslim populations today are in Indonesia, Pakistan, India, and Bangladesh. Muslims are the second largest religious community (behind Christians) in many Western countries, including Canada, Great Britain, France, and Germany.

PRINCIPAL HISTORICAL PERIODS
570–632 CE   Lifetime of the Prophet Muhammad
632–661   The time of the four Caliphs
661–750   Umayyad caliphate
750–1258   'Abbasid caliphate
1517–1924   Ottoman caliphate

FOUNDER AND LEADERS
All Muslims place authority in Muhammad as the last prophet. Shi'i Muslims give special authority after Muhammad to his son-in-law 'Ali and to 'Ali's descendents.

DEITY
Allah—Arabic for 'the God'—is the same God worshipped by Jews and Christians. The word is cognate with the Hebrew *eloh* (plural *elohim*), 'deity'.

AUTHORITATIVE TEXTS
The essential text is the Qur'an (literally, 'The Recitation'), believed to have been revealed by God to Muhammad between the years 610 and 632 CE. Second in importance are the sayings of Muhammad, known as the *hadith*.

NOTEWORTHY DOCTRINES
Islam, like Judaism and Christianity, is a faith based on ethical monotheism. Its prophetic tradition begins with the first created human being (Adam) and ends with the Prophet Muhammad. Muslims believe that the first place of worship dedicated to the one true God is the Ka'bah in Mecca, built by Abraham and his son Ishmael.

during one of those retreats he received the call to prophethood and the first revelation of the Qur'an.

As Muhammad was sitting one night in the solitude of his retreat, an angel—later identified as Gabriel (Jibril in Arabic)—appeared. Taking hold of him and pressing him hard, the angel commanded, 'Recite [or read]!' Muhammad answered, 'I cannot read.' After repeating the command for the third time, the angel continued, 'Recite in the name of your Lord who created, created man from a blood clot. Recite, for your Lord is most magnanimous—who taught by the pen, taught man that which he did not know' (Q. 96:1–5). Shivering with fear and apprehension, Muhammad ran home and asked the people of his household to cover him.

Yet the angel returned to him often, saying, 'O Muhammad, I am Gabriel, and you are the Messenger of God.' Khadijah consoled and encouraged him, and eventually took him to her cousin, a Christian savant called Waraqah bin Nawfal. Waraqah confirmed Muhammad in his mission, declaring him to be a prophet sent by God with a sacred law like that of Moses.

The idea of a prophet—*nabi* in both Arabic and Hebrew—was not unfamiliar to Muhammad's people. For twelve years Muhammad the Prophet of Allah preached the new faith in the One God to his people with little success. The Meccans did not wish to abandon the ways of their ancestors, and they feared the implications of the new faith both for their social customs and for the religious and economic status of the Ka'bah. Muhammad's message was not only religious but also moral and social. He admonished the Meccans to give alms, to care for the orphaned, to feed the hungry, to assist the oppressed and destitute, and to offer hospitality to the wayfarer. He also warned of impending doom on the day of the last judgment. The first to accept the new faith were the Prophet's wife Khadijah, his cousin and son-in-law 'Ali b. Abi Talib, his slave Zayd b. Harithah—whom he later freed and adopted—and his faithful companion Abu Bakr.

Muhammad and his followers were often vilified. One group without tribal protection faced such severe persecution that the Prophet advised them to migrate across the Red Sea to the Christian country of Abyssinia (Ethiopia), where they were well received. The Prophet himself lost all support and protection in 619 when both his uncle Abu Talib and his wife Khadijah died within the space of barely two months. It was soon after these losses that he experienced what came to be known as the *mi'raj* or 'night journey', travelling from Mecca to Jerusalem in the course of one night and then ascending to heaven, where he met some of the earlier prophets and then had an audience with God. For Muslims, these miraculous events confirmed that Muhammad was still supported by God.

The First Muslim Community

In 622 the Prophet was invited to arbitrate between two feuding tribes in the city of Yathrib, about 400 km (250 mi.) north of Mecca. His migration (*hijrah*) to Yathrib, which thereafter came to be known as 'the city of the Prophet' or Medina ('the city'), marked the beginning of community life under Islam, and thus of Islamic history. (It also marked the beginning of the dating system used throughout the Muslim world, in which years are counted backwards or forwards from that event and accompanied by the abbreviation AH, from the Latin for 'year of the *hijrah*'. Because Muslims use the lunar year—which is 11 days shorter than the solar year—*hijri* dates gain one year approximately every 33 solar years, reaching 1400 AH in 1979 CE.)

In Medina Muhammad established the first Islamic commonwealth: a truly theocratic state, headed by a prophet believed to be ruling in accordance with the dictates of a divine scripture.

Medina was an oasis city with an agricultural economy. Its social structure was far more heterogeneous than Mecca's, including a substantial Jewish community as well as two hostile tribes, the Aws and the Khazraj, whose old rivalries kept it in a continuous state of civil strife. Muhammad was remarkably successful in welding these disparate elements into a cohesive social unit. In a brief constitutional document known as the covenant of Medina, he stipulated that all the people of the city should henceforth be one Muslim commonwealth. The covenant granted the Jews full religious freedom and equality with the Muslims, on condition that they support the state and not enter into any alliance against it, with the Quraysh or any other tribe.

The Qur'an's narratives and world view are closely akin to the prophetic vision of history laid out in the Hebrew Bible. The Prophet expected the Jews of Medina, recognizing this kinship, to be natural allies, and he adopted a number of Jewish practices, including the fast of the Day of Atonement (Yom Kippur). But the Medinan Jews rejected both Muhammad's claim to be a prophet and the Qur'an's claim to be a sacred book. The resulting tension between the two communities is clearly reflected in the Qur'an's treatment of the Jews, which is sometimes positive (3:113–115) and sometimes negative (5:51). Increasingly, Islam began to distinguish itself from Judaism, so that within two years of the Prophet's arrival in Medina, the fast of Ramadan took precedence over the fast of Yom Kippur and the *qiblah* (direction of prayer) was changed from Jerusalem to the Ka'bah in Mecca.

In the Qur'an the people of Medina are called Ansar ('helpers') because they were the first supporters and protectors of Islam and the Prophet. As the flow of Muslim immigrants from Mecca increased, however, a new social group was added to an already diverse society. The new immigrants, along with those who came with or shortly after the Prophet, were called Muhajirun ('immigrants').

The Conversion of Mecca

Having left all their goods and property behind them in Mecca, the Muslims resorted to raiding Meccan caravans returning from Syria. In response, the Meccans sent an army of roughly a thousand men to Medina in 624. At the well of Badr they were met by a 300-man detachment of Muslims.

Though poorly equipped and far outnumbered, the Muslims were highly motivated, and they inflicted a crushing defeat on the Meccans. Thus the Battle of Badr remains one of the most memorable events in Muslim history. It is celebrated in the Qur'an as a miraculous proof of the truth of Islam: 'You [Muhammad] did not shoot the first arrow when you did shoot it; rather God shot it' (Q. 8:17); 'God supported you [Muslims] at Badr when you were in an abased state' (Q. 3:123).

To avenge their defeat, the Meccans met the Muslims the following year by Mount Uhud, not far from Medina, and this time they prevailed. The Prophet was badly injured in the battle, and it was rumoured that he had been killed.

Following the Battle of Uhud, the Prophet decided to expel the Jews from Medina and its neighbouring settlements. Although the official reason was the Jews' revocation of their covenant of protection with the Muslims, the real motive may have been to free the Muslim state of external influences at this critical stage in its development.

As the Muslims grew in strength and the occasional skirmishes with the caravans of the Quraysh continued, they received word that the Meccans were planning to attack Medina itself. On the advice of Salman the Persian, a former slave, the Prophet had a trench dug around the exposed parts of the city, to prevent Meccan cavalry from entering. Thus when the men of the Quraysh, along with a large coalition of other tribes, attacked Medina in what came to be known as the Battle of the Trench (627), the city was able to withstand the siege, and in 628 the Meccans were impelled to seek a truce.

Two years later, after the Quraysh had breached the truce, the Prophet set out with a large army to conquer Mecca. But instead of fighting, the Meccans capitulated and accepted Islam. Whenever an individual or tribe accepted Islam, all hostility was to cease and enemies were to become brothers in faith; thus the Prophet granted amnesty to all in the city. Asked by the Meccans what he intended to do with them, he answered, 'I will do with you what Joseph did with his brothers. Go; you are free.' Then he quoted Joseph's words to his brothers: 'There is no blame in you today; God forgive you' (Q. 12:92).

Muhammad attributed the conquest of Mecca solely to God. The words on the subject in the Qur'an are not those of a conqueror but of a thankful servant: 'When support from God comes, and victory, and you see men enter into the religion of God in throngs, proclaim the praise of your Lord and seek His forgiveness, for He is truly relenting' (Q. 110). The Prophet returned to Medina, where he died two years later, in 632, after making a farewell pilgrimage to Mecca and its sacred shrine, the Ka'bah.

Muhammad was always known as *rasul Allah* ('the Messenger of God') rather than as a ruler or military leader. But he was all of these. He waged war and made peace. He laid the foundations of a community (*ummah*) that was ideally to be a religious community. He established Islam in Arabia and sent expeditions to Syria. Within 80 years the Muslims would administer the largest empire the world had ever known, stretching from southern France through North Africa and the Middle East into India and Central Asia.

At the time of Muhammad's death, however, no one could have foreseen that future. The majority of Muslims (the **Sunni**, meaning those who follow the *sunnah* or traditions of the Prophet) believed that he had not even designated a successor or specified how one should be chosen. But a minority community, known as the **Shi'a** (from the Arabic meaning 'party'), believed that Muhammad had in fact appointed his son-in-law 'Ali to succeed him. Muhammad's death therefore precipitated a crisis that grew into a permanent ideological rift.

A *khalifah* is one who represents or acts on behalf of another. After Muhammad's death, his comrade Abu Bakr was called the *khalifat rasul Allah*—the 'successor' or 'representative' of the Messenger of God—and Abu Bakr's successor, 'Umar b. al-Khattab, was at first called the 'successor of the successor of the Messenger of God'.

The caliphate had a worldly as well as a religious dimension from the beginning. As a successor of the Prophet, the **caliph** was a religious leader. At the same time, as the chief or administrative head of the community, he was the *amir* or commander of the Muslims in times of war and peace. Perhaps conscious of this temporal dimension of his office, 'Umar is said to have adopted the title 'commander of the faithful' in place of

The Dome of the Rock in Jerusalem, built in 687 by Caliph 'Abd a-Malik b. Marwan on the site of the Hebrew temple destroyed in 70 CE (Zafer Kizilkaya/Ponkawonka.com).

his cumbersome original title. Nevertheless, the caliph continued to function as the chief religious leader (**imam**) of the community. The first four caliphs following Muhammad's death were chosen by the community. The fifth caliph, however, established a dynasty known as the Umayyads, who retained control of the caliphate from 661 to 750, when they were defeated by the 'Abbasids. The latter in turn established their own dynasty, which would continue to rule the Muslim world until 1258.

Crystallization

Prophets and Messengers

According to the Qur'an and Islamic tradition, God operates through prophets and messengers who convey God's will in revealed scriptures and seek to establish God's sacred law in the lives of their communities. From the Islamic point of view, therefore, human history is prophetic history.

| Box 4.2   Abraham Destroys the Idols

From the Qur'an, surah 21, al-Anbiya' (The Prophets), verses 51–73.

When he said to his father and his people, 'What are these idols that you so fervently worship?' they said, 'We found our fathers worshipping them.'

He said, 'Both you and your fathers are in manifest error.' They said, 'Have you come to us with the truth, or are you one of those who jest?'

He said, 'Your Lord is indeed the Lord of the heavens and the earth, for he originated them; and to this I am one of those who bear witness. By God, I shall confound your idols as soon as you turn your backs.'

He thus destroyed them utterly except for the chief one, so that the people might turn to it [for petition].

They said, 'Who did this to our gods? He is surely a wrongdoer.'

Some said, 'We heard a youth called Abraham speaking of them.'

Others said, 'Bring him here in the sight of the people, so that they may all witness.'

They said, 'Did you do this to our gods, O Abraham?'

He said, 'No, it was their chief who did it. Question them—if they could speak.'

The people then turned on one another, saying, 'Indeed you are the wrongdoers!' Then they bowed their heads in humiliation, saying, 'You know well, [O Abraham], that these do not speak.'

He [Abraham] said, 'Would you then worship instead of God a thing that can do you neither good nor harm? Fie on you and on what you worship instead of God; do you not reason?'

They said, 'Burn him and stand up for your gods, if you would do anything.'

We [God] said, 'O fire, be coolness and peace for Abraham!'

They wished evil for him, but We turned them into utter losers. And We delivered him and Lot to a land that We blessed for all beings. We also granted him Isaac and Jacob as added favour, and We made them both righteous. We made them all leaders guiding others by our command. We inspired them to do good deeds, perform regular worship, and give the obligatory alms; and they were true worshippers of Us alone.

Islamic tradition maintains that, from the time of Adam to the time of Muhammad, God sent 124,000 prophets into the world to remind people of every community of their obligation to the one and only sovereign Lord and warn them against heedlessness and disobedience: 'There is not a nation but that a warner was sent to it' (Q. 26:207). The Qur'an mentions by name 26 prophets and messengers. Most are well-known biblical figures, among them Abraham, Moses, David, Solomon, Elijah, Jonah, John the Baptist, and Jesus. It also mentions three Arabian prophets: Shu'ayb, Hud, and Salih.

Islamic tradition distinguishes between prophets and messengers. A prophet (*nabi*) is one who conveys a message from God to a specific people at a specific time. A messenger (*rasul*) is also a prophet sent by God to a specific community; but the message he delivers is a universally binding sacred law (*shari'ah*). The Torah given to Moses on Mount Sinai was an example of the latter: though sent to the ancient Hebrews, it remained binding on all those who knew it, Hebrews and others, until the arrival of the next revelations—the psalms of David and the gospel of Jesus. In other words, every messenger is a prophet; but not every prophet is a messenger. Among the messenger-prophets, five—Noah, Abraham, Moses, Jesus, and Muhammad—are called *ulu al-'azm* ('prophets of power or firm resolve', Q. 46:35). Their special significance lies in their having received universally binding revelations from God.

In the context of Muslim piety, respect for Muhammad is shown by speaking (or writing) the phrase 'peace [and blessings of God] be [up]on him' every time his name or title is mentioned (in writing, the formula is often abbreviated as PBUH). When the prophets as a group, culminating in Muhammad, are mentioned, the formula changes to PBOTA, 'peace be on them all'.

The Qur'an

The Qur'an was revealed (literally, 'sent down') to the prophet Muhammad over a period of 22 years. According to both the Qur'an and Muslim tradition, the angel Gabriel appeared to him, often in human guise, transmitting the verses and *surahs* (chapters) that came to constitute the Qur'an.

The Prophet's role as transmitter of revelation is reflected in the Qur'an's characteristic phrasing as God ('We') instructs the Prophet ('you') to 'say' something to the people (that is, to deliver a particular message to them). The first instruction, however, as we have seen, was the command that Muhammad himself 'recite' or 'read' (*iqra'*). The term Qur'an is derived from the same root: *q–r–'*, meaning 'to read' or 'recite'.

In size the Qur'an is nearly as long as the New Testament. The individual portions revealed to Muhammad vary in length and content from short verses on a single theme or idea to fairly lengthy chapters. The early Meccan *surahs* are generally brief admonitions couched in terse and powerful verses, while the later ones are didactic narratives or illustrative tales of earlier prophets and their communities. Through stories, parables, and exhortations enjoining good conduct and dissuading people from evil and indecent behaviour, the Qur'an aims to create an *ummah*: a 'community' (that is, a society united by faith).

The *surahs* revealed in Medina are fewer in number but longer, presenting didactic arguments, discourses, and legal pronouncements, often in response to questions or situations arising in the life of the community.

| Box 4.3 | **From the Qur'an: The Day of Judgment**

Following is surah 99, al-Zalzalah ('The Earthquake'), in its entirety.

When the earth shall be shaken with a great quake, and the earth yields up its burdens, and man exclaims, 'What has happened to it!' On that day it shall recount its tidings—as your Lord had inspired it.

Whoever does an atom's weight of good shall then see it, and whoever does an atom's weight of evil shall then see it.

The Status of the Qur'an

Muslims believe that the Qur'an is an immutable heavenly book containing the eternal Word of God. In fact, there is an interesting theological parallel with Christ, who in the prologue to John's gospel is proclaimed to be the eternal Word of God made incarnate at a certain moment in history.

Muslims understand the Qur'an to have been revealed specifically in the Arabic language. Hence any translation is considered to constitute an interpretation, not the Qur'an itself. Even in places where few if any Muslims speak the language, the Qu'ran is always recited in Arabic.

The words of the Qur'an are spoken in a newborn child's ear as a blessing. They are also recited to bless and seal a marriage contract or a business deal, to celebrate a successful venture, or to express sorrow and give solace in times of misfortune. Throughout the Muslim world, the Qur'an is recited on most special public occasions and daily on radio and television. Qur'anic recitation is an art of great virtuosity and hypnotic power. For private devotional recitation in the course of a month, the Qur'an has been divided into 30 parts of equal length. The words of the Qur'an, in the form of calligraphy, have also been a central motif in Islamic art, used to decorate Muslim homes, mosques, and public buildings.

Compiling the Qur'an

When the Prophet died in 632, there were many people who had committed the Qur'an to memory. The only physical records, however, consisted of fragments written on stones, bones, palm leaves, and animal parchment, which were held in a variety of private collections. In some cases the same material existed in several versions with different readings of certain words or phrases. These variant readings became identified with specific readers through the generations of Muslim scholars.

The process of producing an official text of the Qur'an was completed under the third caliph, 'Uthman b. 'Affan, within twenty years of the Prophet's death. As an earthly book, the Qur'an has been shaped by Muslim history. Tradition maintains that while the verses of each individual *surah* were arranged by the Prophet at Gabriel's instruction, the order of the *surahs* in relation to one another—roughly in decreasing order of length— was fixed by a committee that 'Uthman appointed to compile an official version. Of the 114 *surah*s, 113 are preceded by the invocation *bism-illahi ar-rahman ar-rahim* ('in the name of God, the All-merciful, the Compassionate'); the exception is the ninth *surah*, which commentators generally believe to be a continuation of the eighth.

Qur'anic Commentary (*Tafsir*)

The term for commentary on the Qur'an, *tafsir*, means 'unveiling', or elucidating the meaning of a text. Any such interpretation is based on one of three authoritative sources: the Qur'an itself, Prophetic *Hadith* (tradition), and the opinions of the Prophet's Companions and their successors. The earliest commentaries, like the Qur'an and the *hadith*, were transmitted orally, but by the tenth century Qur'anic interpretation had developed into a science with several ancillary fields of study.

In fact, every legal or theological school, religious trend, or political movement in Muslim history has looked to the Qur'an for its primary support and justification. The result has been a wide range of interpretations reflecting the diversity of the sects, legal schools, and mystical and philosophical movements that emerged as the Islamic tradition developed.

The Qur'an's Concept of God

The Qur'an presents its view of the divinity in direct and unambiguous declarations of faith in the One and only God, creator, sustainer, judge, and sovereign Lord over all creation. For Muslims it is a sin to associate any other being with God or to ascribe divinity to any but God alone.

'Allah' is not the name of a particular deity but the Arabic word for God, 'the Lord of all beings' (Q. 1:2), who demands faith and worship of all his rational creatures. It was used in the same sense by the pagan Arabs before Islam, and is still used by Arab Jews and Christians today.

Islamic theology holds that God's essence is unknowable, inconceivable, and above all categories of time, space, form, and number. Materiality and temporality cannot be attributed to God. Nor, properly speaking, can masculinity or femininity, although references to God in the Qur'an and throughout Islamic literature use pronouns, verbs, and adjectives that are masculine in form.

God is known through attributes referred to in the Qur'an as the 'most beautiful names' (sometimes translated as 'wonderful names'). These divine attributes are manifested in the creation in power and mercy, life and knowledge, might and wisdom. The Qur'an declares:

> He is God other than whom there is no god, knower of the unknown and the visible. He is the All-merciful, the Compassionate. He is God other than whom there is no god, the King, the Holy One, Peace, the Faithful, the Guardian, the Majestic, the Compeller, the Lofty One (Q. 59:22–3).

Faith and Action

Righteousness as it is expressed in the Qur'an has several components. It includes faith in God, God's angels, books, and prophets, and the judgment of the last day. It includes good works: Muslims should give of their wealth, however cherished it may be, to orphans and the needy or for the ransoming of slaves and war captives. It includes patience and steadfastness in times of misfortune or hardship and war. And it includes integrity in one's dealings with others.

Because all men and women belong ultimately to one humanity, they are all equal before God, regardless of race, colour, or social status. They may surpass one another only in righteousness: 'Humankind, We have created you all of one male and one female and made you different peoples and tribes in order that you may know one another. Surely, the noblest of you in God's sight is he who fears God most' (Q. 49:13).

The Arabic word *iman* means faith, trust, and a personal sense of safety and well-being in God's providential care, mercy, and justice. On this level of inner personal commitment, *iman* is synonymous with *islam*: total surrender of the human will and destiny to the will of God. The opposite of *iman* is *kufr*, rejection of faith. To have faith is to know the truth and assent to it in the heart, profess it with the tongue, and manifest it in concrete acts of charity and almsgiving. *Kufr*, on the other hand, means knowing the truth but wilfully denying or obscuring it by acts of rebellion against the law of God. The word *kufr* literally means covering up, denying, or obscuring.

The Qur'an also makes an important distinction between Islam and faith. Outwardly, Islam is a religious, social, and legal institution, whose members constitute the worldwide Muslim *ummah* or community. *Iman*—faith—is an inner conviction whose sincerity God alone can judge, a commitment to a way of life in the worship of God and in moral relations with other persons. Faith, as a comprehensive framework of worship and moral conduct, is explicitly depicted in the answer that the Prophet is said to have given to the question 'What is faith?': 'Faith is seventy-odd branches, the highest of which is to say "There is no god except God" and the lowest is to remove a harmful object from the road.'

Above Islam and *iman* stands *ihsan* (doing good or creating beauty). On the level of human interrelations, *ihsan* is a concrete manifestation of both Islam and *iman*. On the level of the personal relationship of the man or woman of faith with God, *ihsan* constitutes the highest form of worship, expressed in this *hadith*: 'Ihsan is to worship God as though you see him, for even if you do not see him, he sees you.'

Religious Sciences

In Arabic a learned person is termed an *'alim*. The plural, *'ulama'*, refers to the religio-legal scholars, or religious intellectuals, of the Islamic world as a group. What Muslims call the 'religious sciences' were part of a comprehensive cultural development as Islam expanded geographically far beyond the religio-political framework of its Arabian homeland. Cosmopolitan, pluralistic Islamic cultural centres like Baghdad, Córdoba, and Cairo offered ideal settings for intellectual growth. Beginning in the eighth century, comprehensive achievements in philosophy, theology, literature, and science continued in different parts of the Muslim world well into the seventeenth.

Islam is a religion more of action than of abstract speculation about right belief. Hence the first and most important of the religious sciences, Islamic law, stresses that the essence of faith is right living. The Prophet characterizes a Muslim thus: 'Anyone who performs our prayers [i.e., observes the rituals of worship] and eats our ritually slaughtered animals [i.e., observes the proper dietary laws] is one of us.' For Muslims, inner submission to the will of God is God's way for all of humankind. At both the personal and the societal level, Islam is a faith and a way of life to be realized within the framework of divine law, the *shari'ah*: a way of life or conduct based on moral imperatives.

The Sources of Islamic Law

The Qur'an
The Qur'an and hence the *shari'ah* are centrally concerned with relationships, both among individuals in society and between individuals and God. The most intimate

human relationship is the one between a husband and wife; the second is the relationship between parent and child. The circle then broadens to include the extended family, the tribe, and finally the *ummah* and the world.

Islam has no official priesthood. Every person is responsible both for his or her own morality and for the morality of the entire Muslim *ummah*: 'Let there be of you a community that calls to the good, enjoins honourable conduct and dissuades from evil conduct. These are indeed prosperous people' (Q. 3:104).

The Qur'an places kindness and respect for parents next in importance to the worship of God. Also important is caring for the poor and the needy through alms-giving. Usury is prohibited as a means of increasing one's wealth. But renunciation of material possessions is no more desirable than total attachment to them. Rather, the Qur'an enjoins the faithful to 'Seek amidst that which God has given you, the last abode, but do not forget your portion of the present world' (Q. 28:77).

In short, the Qur'an is primarily concerned with moral issues in actual situations. Of its 6,236 verses, no more than 200 are explicitly legislative.

The Sunnah

The life-example of the Prophet includes not only his acts and sayings but also his tacit consent. His acts are reported in anecdotes about situations or events to which he reacted or in which he participated. In situations where he expressed neither approval nor objection, his silence is taken to signify consent. Thus the *sunnah* of consent became a normative source in the development of Islamic law.

Accounts that report the Prophet's *hadith* (sayings) must go back to an eyewitness of the event. The *hadith* literature is often called 'tradition' in English, in a quite specific sense. 'Islamic tradition' (or 'Prophetic tradition') is the body of sayings traced to the prophet Muhammad through chains of oral transmission. *Hadith* is the most important component of *sunnah* because it is the most direct expression of the Prophet's opinions or judgments regarding the community's conduct.

To qualify as a *hadith*, a text must be accompanied by its chain of transmission (*isnad*), beginning with the compiler or last transmitter and going back to the Prophet. The aim of the study of *hadith* is to ascertain the authenticity of a particular text by establishing the completeness of the chain of its transmission and the veracity of its transmitters.

There are six canonical collections of *hadith*. The earliest and most important collectors were Muhammad b. Isma'il al-Bukhari (810–70) and Muslim b. al-Hajjaj al-Nisaburi (c. 817–75). As their names suggest, the former came from the city of Bukhara in Central Asia and the latter from Nishapur in northeastern Iran. Although the two men did not know each other, they were contemporaries and both spent many years travelling across the Muslim world in search of *hadith* traditions. The fact that their independent quests produced very similar results suggests that a unified *hadith* tradition was already well established.

Both men are said to have collected hundreds of thousands of *hadiths*, out of which each selected about 3,000, discounting repetitions. Their approach became the model for all subsequent *hadith* compilers. Their two collections, entitled simply *Sahih* (literally 'sound') *al-Bukhari* and *Sahih Muslim*, soon achieved canonical status, second in authority only to the Qur'an. Within less than half a century, four other collections—by

Abu Dawud al-Sijistani, Ibn Majah, al-Tirmidhi, and al-Nasa'i—were produced. It is noteworthy that, like Muslim and al-Bukhari, these four also came from Central Asia and Iran. Each of these collections is entitled simply *Sunan* (the plural of *sunnah*).

As legal manuals, all six collections are organized topically, beginning with the laws governing the rituals of worship and then continuing with the laws regulating the social, political, and economic life of the community.

The Scope of Islamic Law

For Muslims God is the ultimate lawgiver. The *shari'ah* is sacred law, 'the law of God'. It consists of the maxims, admonitions, and legal sanctions and prohibitions enshrined in the Qur'an and explained, elaborated, and realized in the Prophetic tradition.

The term *shari'ah* originally signified the way to a source of water. Metaphorically it came to mean the way to the good in this world and the next. It is 'the straight way' that leads the faithful to paradise in the hereafter. Muslims believe the *shari'ah* to be God's plan for the ordering of human society.

Within the framework of the divine law, human actions range between those that are absolutely obligatory and will bring rewards on the Day of Judgment, and those that are absolutely forbidden and will bring harsh punishment. Actions are classified in five categories:

- lawful (*halal*), and therefore obligatory;
- commendable, and therefore recommended (*mustahabb*);
- neutral, and therefore permitted (*mubah*);
- reprehensible, and therefore disliked (*makruh*); and
- unlawful (*haram*), and therefore forbidden.

These categories govern all human actions. The correctness of an action and the intention that lies behind it together determine its nature and its consequences for the person who performs it.

Jurisprudence (*Fiqh*)

Jurisprudence or *fiqh* is the theoretical and systematic aspect of Islamic law, consisting of the interpretation and codification of the *shari'ah* or sacred law. A scholar who specializes in this exacting science is called a *faqih* ('jurist').

Islamic jurisprudence as it was developed in the various legal schools is based on four sources. Two of these, the Qur'an and *sunnah*, are its primary sources. The other two are secondary sources: the personal reasoning (*ijtihad*) of the scholars and the general consensus (*ijma'*) of the community. The schools of Islamic law differed in the degree of emphasis or acceptance that they gave to each source.

Personal reasoning is the process through which legal scholars deduced from the Qur'an and *sunnah* the laws that are the foundations of their various schools of thought. The term *ijtihad* signifies a scholar's best effort in this endeavour, which is based on reasoning from analogous situations in the past (so, for example, modern software piracy is considered analogous to theft).

| Box 4.4 Jurisprudence: Muhammad b. Idris al-Shafi'i

A decisive stage in Muslim jurisprudence came in the ninth century with Muhammad b. Idris al-Shafi'i (767–820). Having travelled widely and studied in various centres of learning across the Muslim world, he spent his last years in Egypt, where he wrote the first systematic treatise on the subject. This work radically changed the scope and nature of Islamic jurisprudence. Rejecting personal opinion in favour of absolute dependence on the two primary sources, the Qur'an and *sunnah*, Shafi'i based his system on a vast collection of *hadith* and legal traditions entitled *Kitab al-Umm*, which he compiled in order to write his work. In opposition to the majority of jurists of his time, he argued that jurists should not base their judgments on the opinions of men, but should rely exclusively on the Book of God and the *sunnah* of his Prophet.

Although Shafi'i's legal system was later adopted as the basis of a school of thought bearing his name, he himself expressly opposed the idea. He saw himself not as the founder of a new legal school, but as the reformer of Islamic law. The Shafi'i school took root early in Egypt, where its founder lived and died. It then spread to southern Arabia and later followed the maritime trade routes to East Africa, and then to Southeast Asia, where it remains the dominant legal school.

Finally, the principle of consensus (*ijma*) is meant to ensure the continued authenticity and truth of the three other sources. In the broadest sense, *ijma* refers to the community's acceptance and support of applied *shari'ah*. More narrowly, it has encouraged an active interchange of ideas among the scholars of the various schools, at least during the formative period of Islamic law. Consensus, moreover, has remained the final arbiter of truth and error, expressed in the Prophet's declaration that 'my community will not agree on an error.'

Yet even this important principle has been the subject of debate and dissension between scholars of the various schools. Among the many questions at issue are whether the consensus of earlier generations is binding on the present one, and whether the necessary consensus can be reached by the scholars alone, without the participation of the community at large.

Islamic Philosophy and Theology

In addition to the religious sciences described above (known as the transmitted sciences), the rational sciences of philosophy and theology are also important. Theology is discourse about God, God's attributes, and God's creation and nurture of all things. It is also concerned with human free will and predestination, moral and religious obligations, and the return to God on the Day of Resurrection for the final judgment. Insofar as theology addresses human faith and conduct, it is part of the science of *fiqh* or jurisprudence.

In time, however, theology also came to concern itself with more philosophical questions about the existence of God, creation, and the problem of evil and suffering. In these areas Islamic theology reflects the influence of Hellenistic philosophy, whose principles and rationalistic methodology it adopted.

The rapid spread of Islam out of Arabia into Syria and Mesopotamia brought Muslims into contact with people of other faiths and ethnic backgrounds, including Hellenized Jews and Christians. With the rise of the 'Abbasid dynasty in the mid-eighth century, interest in Greek philosophy, science, and medicine increased, and Arabic translations of Greek works began to appear.

The quest for knowledge reached its peak under the caliph al-Ma'mun (813–833), whose Bayt al-Hikmah ('House of Wisdom') in Baghdad was the first institution of higher learning not only in the Islamic world but in the West. Christian scholars had already translated many Greek medical, philosophical, and theological treatises into Syriac and commented on them. But they were able to carry on their work with greater support at the House of Wisdom, which housed an impressive library of Greek manuscripts. Families of translators worked in teams, rendering into Arabic the ancient treasures of Hellenistic science and philosophy. Smaller centres of philosophical and medical studies in Syria and Iran also made notable contributions.

The Early Period

Early Islamic philosophy had a distinct character: Aristotelian in its logic, physics, and metaphysics; Platonic in its political and social aspects; and Neoplatonic in its mysticism and theology. Two figures stand out in this early period. The first was the Iraqi theologian-philosopher Abu Yusuf Ya'qub al-Kindi (d. 870), who used philosophical principles and methods of reasoning to defend fundamental Islamic teachings such as the existence and oneness of God, the temporal creation of the universe by God's command out of nothing, the inimitability of the Qur'an, and the necessity of prophets. In his argument for the latter, al-Kindi underlined the distinction between the philosopher who acquires his knowledge through rational investigation and contemplation and the prophet who receives his knowledge instantaneously, through divine revelation.

In sharp contrast to al-Kindi, Abu Bakr Zakariyah al-Razi ('the one from Rayy, Iran'; c. 865–926) was a thoroughgoing Platonist who rejected the doctrine of creation out of nothing. Rather, drawing on the theory that Plato elaborated in his *Timaeus*, al-Razi argued that the universe evolved from primal matter, floating gas atoms in an absolute void. The universe or cosmos came into being when God imposed order on the primeval chaos, but it will return to chaos at some distant point in the future, because matter will revert to its primeval state.

The Flowering of Islamic Philosophy

Abu Nasr al-Farabi (c. 878–950), who moved to Baghdad from Turkestan in Central Asia, was not only a great philosopher but an important musical theorist and an accomplished instrumentalist. His Platonic philosophical system was comprehensive and universal. According to al-Farabi, God is pure intellect and the highest good. From God's self-knowledge or contemplation emanates the first intellect, which generates the heavenly spheres and a second intellect, who then repeats the process. Each subsequent intellect generates another sphere and another intellect.

Agreeing with al-Kindi, al-Farabi held that a prophet is gifted with a sharp intellect capable of receiving philosophical verities naturally and without any mental exertion. He then communicates these truths to the masses, who are incapable of comprehending them on the philosophical level.

Although al-Farabi was called 'the second teacher', after Aristotle, even he was excelled by 'the great master' Ibn Sina (Avicenna, 980–1037). Ibn Sina, who was born in Bukhara, Iran, was a self-taught genius who mastered the religious sciences at the age of ten and became a leading physician, philosopher, and astronomer by the age of eighteen. His encyclopedic manual of medicine, *al-Qanun fi al-Tibb*, and his philosophical encyclopedia, *al-Shifa'* ('The Book of Healing'), were studied in European universities throughout the Middle Ages.

Ibn Sina built on al-Farabi's Neoplatonic ideas to produce a comprehensive system of mystical philosophy and theology. He accepted and developed al-Farabi's emanationism, placing it in a more precise logical and philosophical framework. Although he affirmed the prophethood of Muhammad, the revelation of the Qur'an, and the immortality of the soul, he rejected the Qur'anic traditions of the resurrection of the body, the reward of paradise, and the punishment of hell.

According to a widely accepted Prophetic tradition, at the beginning of every century God raises a scholar to renew and strengthen the faith of the Muslim community. Such a man is known as a *mujaddid* ('renovator') of the faith. Abu Hamid Muhammad al-Ghazali (1058–1111) of Tus in Iran has been regarded as the *mujaddid* of the sixth Islamic century. His work went far beyond theology and philosophy, encompassing mysticism and all the religious sciences.

In 1091 al-Ghazali was appointed a professor of theology and law at the prestigious Niyamiyah college in Baghdad, where he tirelessly defended mainstream Sunni Islam against the innovations of the theologians and the heresies of the philosophers. Four years later, however, he suffered a deep psychological crisis and gave up teaching. After a long quest, he determined that true knowledge could not be attained through either the senses or the rational sciences, but only through a divine light that God casts into the heart of the person of faith. His reason thus enlightened, al-Ghazali produced one of the most ambitious works in the history of Islamic thought. Appropriately entitled *Ihya' 'ulum al-din* ('The Revivification of the Religious Sciences'), this magnum opus examines all religious learning from a deeply mystical point of view.

In his book *The Incoherence* [or 'Collapse'] *of the Philosophers*, al-Ghazali rejected the philosophical view of causality and the necessity of the world for God. Instead he proposed a theory of occasionalism: each time God wills an act by a human being, both the act and its cause are created. Al-Ghazali's critique would itself be the subject of a critique by the Andalusian Aristotelian philosopher Ibn Rushd.

Ibn Rushd (Averroës, 1126–98), who was born in Córdoba, Spain, was the greatest Muslim commentator on Aristotle. He came from a long line of jurists, and was himself a noted scholar of Islamic law. His legal training decisively influenced his philosophy. In his critique of al-Ghazali, entitled *The Incoherence of the Incoherence*, Ibn Rushd methodically criticizes al-Ghazali for misapprehending philosophy and Ibn Sina for misunderstanding Aristotle. Ibn Rushd was the first to construct a true Aristotelian philosophical system.

Ibn Rushd essentially shared his eastern predecessors' belief in the primacy of philosophy over religion. However, he elaborated this view in his famous double-truth theory, maintaining that the two approaches to truth are equal, although religion is meant for the masses, whereas philosophy is meant for the intellectual elite. After him the thirteenth century witnessed the great philosopher-mystic Ibn 'Arabi (see p. 223), and his systematic Aristotelian expositor Ibn Sab'in (d. 1270). A more empirical philosopher was the Tunisian-born 'Abd al-Rahman Ibn Khaldun (1332–1406). Through his extensive travels and the positions he held as a jurist and political theorist, Ibn Khaldun gained insight into the workings both of nations and of political and religious institutions. This led him to write a universal history. The most important part of this work is its introduction (*Muqaddimah*), in which Ibn Khaldun presents the first social philosophy of history in either the Islamic or the Western world.

The ninth through the twelfth centuries, from al-Kindi to Ibn Rushd, constituted a great epoch of philosophical thinking. Islamic philosophy, particularly Aristotelianism, had a lasting influence on medieval and Renaissance thought in Europe. Muslim philosophers were known to Europeans by Latinized forms of their names: Rhazes for al-Razi, Alpharabius or Avennasar for al-Farabi, Avicenna for Ibn Sina, Algazel for al-Ghazali, Avempace for Ibn Bajjah, Averroës for Ibn Rushd.

Hellenistic philosophy did not end with Ibn Rushd. It has continued to grow and prosper, especially in the Shi'i community of Iran.

Differentiation

Shi'ism

As we have seen, the Muslim community was permanently divided soon after the death of the Prophet when a political party (*shi'ah*) formed around his cousin and son-in-law 'Ali in support of his right to succeed Muhammad as leader or imam.

'Shi'ism' is a broad term covering a variety of religio-political movements, sects, and ideologies. What they share is a general allegiance to 'Ali and his descendants, and their right to spiritual and temporal authority in the Muslim community after Muhammad.

For Sunni Muslims, the term 'imam' refers to anyone who serves as the leader of prayer at the mosque, a role that the caliph sometimes performed. For Shi'a, by contrast, 'Imam' is the title given to the one individual held to be the rightful, divinely mandated leader of the Muslim community.

In general, Shi'ism has always been characterized by absolute devotion to the Prophet's household. To Shi'a, the Qur'an underlines the high status of Muhammad's family ('the people of the house'): 'Surely, God wishes to take away all abomination from you, O people of the House, and purify you with a great purification' (Q. 33:33).

Furthermore, Muhammad is prompted to declare that he wishes no reward for his work in conveying God's revelation 'except love for [my] next of kin' (Q. 42:23). The expressions 'people of the house' (*ahl al-bayt*) and 'next of kin' (*al-qurba*) are usually interpreted as referring to the Prophet's daughter Fatimah, her husband 'Ali, and their two sons, Hasan and Husayn.

The foundation of the Shi'i claim is the following *hadith*, according to which the Prophet halted on his way back from Mecca to Medina at a place called Ghadir Khumm. Taking 'Ali by the hand, he addressed a large gathering of Muslims:

> O people, hear my words, and let him who is present inform him who is absent: Anyone of whom I am the master, 'Ali, too, is his master. O God, be a friend to those who befriend him and an enemy to those who show hostility to him, support those who support him and abandon those who desert him.

On the basis of this and other sayings in which they believe the Prophet directly or indirectly designated 'Ali as his successor, Shi'i specialists on the Prophetic oral tradition constructed an elaborate legal and theological system based on the doctrine of *imamah*, according to which the source of all legitimate authority is the office of the Imam.

Ashura

In the year 680 the Prophet's grandson Husayn (the son of 'Ali) was killed at Karbala' in Iraq when he led an uprising against the Umayyad Caliph Yazid. The anniversary date, the Tenth of Muharram, has become a focal point for the Shi'i community's hopes and frustrations, messianic expectations, and highly eschatological view of history.

'Ashura' ('ten'), as the anniversary came to be known, is still commemorated by the Shi'i community throughout the Muslim world. Blending sorrow and merriment, blessing and mystery, it has inspired a rich devotional literature, providing the theme and context for numerous popular passion plays re-enacting the events leading up to the death of Husayn. Above all, it is observed by the Shi'i community as a day of suffering and martyrdom. Its symbolism is expressed in a variety of devotional acts, including solemn processions, public readings or enactments of the story of Husayn's death, and a pilgrimage to the sacred ground of Karbala'. Sunni Muslims commemorate Ashura with a day of fasting.

'Twelver' or Imami Shi'ism

According to the doctrine of *imamah* as elaborated by the Twelver Shi'i tradition, the Prophet appointed 'Ali as his viceregent. 'Ali in turn appointed his son Hasan to succeed him as Imam, and Hasan appointed his brother Husayn. Thereafter, each Imam designated his successor, usually his eldest son.

For Twelver Shi'a, the line of imams descended from Husayn did not stop with Ja'far but continued through his son Musa al-Kazim until 874, when the twelfth Imam, Muhammad b. Hasan al-'Askari, disappeared at the age of four. Twelver Shi'a believe that he went into hiding ('occultation') and thereafter communicated with his Shi'a through four successive deputies until 941. At that point the phase known as the 'lesser occultation' ended and he entered into a 'greater occultation', which will continue until the end of the world. Then, before the Day of Resurrection, he will return as the **Mahdi**, 'the rightly guided one', along with Jesus, to establish universal justice and true Islam on earth.

Imami Shi'a agree with Sunni Muslims on the centrality of the Qur'an and *sunnah* as the primary sources of Islamic law. However, they understand the *sunnah* to include not only the life-example of the Prophet Muhammad and his generation, but the life-examples of the imams—the men they believe to be his rightful successors. Hence the period of the *sunnah* for Twelver Shi'i Muslims extends over three centuries, until the end of the lesser occultation of the twelfth Imam in 941.

'Sevener' or Isma'ili Shi'ism

The majority of Shi'a accepted the line of Husaynid imams down to Ja'far al-Sadiq (d. 765), the sixth in the succession. But a major schism occurred when Ja'far's oldest son and successor, Isma'il, died about ten years before him. Ja'far then appointed a younger son, Musa al-Kazim, as his successor.

Many of Ja'far's supporters considered this appointment irregular and insisted that the seventh Imam should be Isma'il's son Ahmad. For this reason they came to be known as **Isma'ilis** or 'Seveners'. The largest faction, called Nizaris, carried on the line of imams through Ahmad and his descendants down to the present.

Basic to Isma'ili faith and world view is the doctrine of the divine mandate of the Imam and his absolute temporal and religious authority. Over the centuries Isma'ili philosophers and theologians developed this fundamental teaching into an impressive esoteric system of prophetology. The Isma'ilis have played a very conspicuous intellectual and political role in Muslim history.

For centuries they lived as an obscure sect in Iran, Syria, East Africa, and the Indo-Pakistani subcontinent. Since 1818 their leader or Imam has been known as the Aga Khan, an Indo-Iranian title signifying nobility. The third Aga Khan (1877–1957) initiated a process of reconciliation with the larger Muslim community, and this process has continued under his Harvard-educated successor, Karim Aga Khan (b. 1936). In modern times Isma'ilis have migrated in large numbers to the West, where they form a prosperous and well-organized community.

Sufism: The Mystical Tradition

The term *tasawwuf* (Sufism) is derived from the Arabic *suf*, meaning 'wool', because the early Sufi mystics wore a garment of coarse wool over their bare skin in emulation of Jesus, who is represented in Islamic hagiography as a model of ascetic piety. Asceticism was only one element in the development of Sufism, however.

At least as important was the Islamic tradition of devotional piety. Since the ultimate purpose of all creation is to worship God and hymn his praises (see Q. 17:44 and 51:56), the Qur'an enjoins the pious to 'remember God much' (Q. 33:41), 'in the morning and evening' (Q. 76:25), for 'in the remembrance of God hearts find peace and content-ment' (Q. 13:28). The Prophet's night vigils and other devotions, alluded to in the Qur'an (73:1–8) and greatly embellished by hagiographical tradition, have served as a living example for pious Muslims across the centuries. *Hadith* traditions, particularly the 'divine sayings' (*hadith qudsi*), in which the speaker is God, have also provided a rich source of mystical piety. Above all, the Prophet's *mi'raj*, or heavenly journey, has been a guide for numerous mystics on their own spiritual ascent to God.

The early Muslim ascetics were known as *zuhhad*, meaning 'those who shun [the world and all its pleasures]'. One of the earliest champions of this movement was the well-known theologian and traditionist al-Hasan al-Basri, who was born in Medina in 642 and lived through both the crises and the rise to glory of the Muslim *ummah*. In a letter addressed to the pious caliph 'Umar b. 'Abd al-'Aziz, Hasan likens the world to a snake: soft to the touch, but full of venom.

The early ascetics were also called weepers, for the tears they shed in fear of God's punishment and in yearning for his reward. Significantly, this early ascetic movement began in areas of mixed populations, where other forms of asceticism had existed for centuries. These centres were Kufah and Basrah in Iraq (long the home of eastern Christian asceticism), northeastern Iran, particularly the region of Balkh (an ancient centre of Buddhist ascetic piety, now part of Afghanistan), and Egypt (the home of Christian monasticism as well as Gnostic asceticism).

Asceticism for its own sake, however, was frowned on by many advocates of mys-tical piety. Among the critics was the sixth imam, Ja'far al-Sadiq, who argued that when God bestows a favour on his servant, he wishes to see it manifested in the servant's attire and way of life. Ja'far's grandfather 'Ali Zayn al-'Abidin is said to have argued that God should be worshipped not out of fear of hell or desire for paradise, but in humble grati-tude for his gift of the capacity to worship him.

What transformed ascetic piety into mysticism was an infusion of divine love that is exemplified by the woman mystic Rabi'ah al-'Adawiyah of Basrah (c. 713–801). Because of adverse family circumstances, Rabi'ah had been sold into slavery as a child, but her master was so impressed with her piety that he set her free. She lived the rest of her life in mystical contemplation, loving God with no other motive than love itself. Her most famous prayer was:

> My Lord, if I worship you in fear of the fire, burn me in hell. If I worship you in desire for paradise, deprive me of it. But if I worship you in love of you, then deprive me not of your eternal beauty.

Mystics of all religious traditions have used the language of erotic love to express their love for God. Rabi'ah was perhaps the first to introduce this language into Islamic mys-ticism. She loved God with two loves, the love of passion and a spiritual love worthy of him alone.

The love of which Rabi'ah spoke was the devotional love of the worshipful ser-vant for his or her Lord. A more controversial tradition within Sufism, however, pursued absolute union with God. Among the proponents of this ecstatic or 'intoxicated' Sufism was Husayn b. Mansur al-Hallaj (c. 858–922), who was brutally executed by the 'Abbasid

| Box 4.5   Rabi'ah al-'Adawiyah

Rabi'ah al-'Adawiyah (713–801), of non-Arab background, was a slave and a flute player before entering a life of religious contemplation.

The Sufis of Basra urged Rabi'a to choose a husband from among them, rather than continue to live unmarried. She replied, 'Willingly,' and asked which of them was most religious. They replied that it was Hasan. So she said to him that if he could give her the answer to four questions, she would become his wife.

'What will the Judge of the world say when I die? That I have come forth from the world a Muslim, or an unbeliever?'

Hasan answered, 'This is among the hidden things known only to God. . . . '

Then she said, 'When I am put in the grave and Munkar and Nakir [the angels who question the dead] question me, shall I be able to answer them (satisfactorily) or not?' He replied, 'This is also hidden.'

When people are assembled at the Resurrection and the books are distributed, shall I be given mine in my right hand or my left?'. . . 'This also is among the hidden things.'

Finally she asked, 'When mankind is summoned (at the Judgment), some to Paradise and some to Hell, in which group shall I be?' He answered, 'This too is hidden, and none knows what is hidden save God—His is the glory and the majesty.'

Then she said to him, 'Since this is so, and I have these four questions with which to concern myself, how should I need a husband, with whom to be occupied?' [She remained unmarried.] (Smith 1928:11)

authorities for the seeming blasphemy of his theopathic utterances: expressions of sympathy with the divine so intense as to suggest that he made no distinction between God and himself.

Al-Hallaj had been initiated into Sufism early in life and travelled widely, studying with the best-known Sufi masters of his time. But in time al-Hallaj broke away from his teachers and embarked on a long and dangerous quest of self-realization. It began when he went one day to see his teacher Abu Qasim al-Junayd. When the latter, asked who was at the door, al-Hallaj answered, 'I, the absolute divine truth' (*ana al-Haqq*)—calling himself by one of the 99 'wonderful names' of God mentioned in the Qur'an. Al-Junayd reprimanded his wayward disciple and predicted an evil end for him.

The core of al-Hallaj's message was moral and deeply spiritual. But his apparently incarnationist theology (holding that God takes the form of a human person, as Christians believe of Jesus) shocked most Muslims of his time. Whereas a less extreme predecessor, Bayazid Bistami, had preached annihilation of the mystic in God, al-Hallaj preached total identification of the lover with the beloved:

I am He whom I love, and He whom I love is I.
We are two spirits dwelling in one body.
If thou seest me, you see Him; and if thou seest Him, you see us both
(Nicholson 1931:210–38)

| Box 4.6   Farid al-Din 'Attar

Farid al-Din 'Attar lived in Iran at the turn of the thirteenth century. The phrase 'Ask not' echoes one used by theologians to express paradox—bila kayf ('without asking how')— but here it expresses the mystic's sense of ineffability.

His beauty if it thrill my heart
If thou a man of passion art
Of time and of eternity,
Of being and non-entity,
   Ask not.
When thou hast passed the bases four,
Behold the sanctuary door;
And having satisfied thine eyes,
What in the sanctuary lies
   Ask not. . . .
When unto the sublime degree
Thou hast attained, desist to be;
But lost to self in nothingness
And, being not, of more and less
   Ask not.

(Arberry 1948:32–3)

After eight years in prison and much controversy, al-Hallaj danced in his chains to the gallows. He begged his executioners: 'Kill me, O my trusted friends, for in my death is my life, and in my life is my death.' For many Muslims, al-Hallaj lives on as the martyr of love who was killed for the sin of intoxication with the love of God by the sword of the *shari'ah* of God.

The Crystallization of Sufism

The mystical life is a spiritual journey to God. The novice who wishes to embark on such an arduous journey must be initiated and guided by a master who becomes in effect his or her spiritual parent. As Sufism grew, however, many well-recognized masters attracted too many disciples to allow for a one-to-one relationship. Therefore teaching manuals became necessary by the eleventh century to impart the ideas of great masters to eager disciples. A high point in this process of crystallization was al-Ghazali's 'Revivification of the Religious Sciences'.

Roughly half a century after al-Ghazali, Shihab al-Din Suhrawardi (c. 1155–91) became known as the great master of illumination (*shaykh al-ishraq*). He grew up in Iran and eventually settled in northern Syria. Drawing on the Qur'anic Light verse (24:35, in which God is called the light of the heavens and the earth) and al-Ghazali's interpretation of it in his famous treatise *Mishkat al-Anwar* ('The Niche of Lights'), as well as ancient Iranian and Neoplatonic wisdom, Suhrawardi described a cosmos of light and darkness populated by countless luminous angelic spirits.

The most important Sufi master of the thirteenth century was Muhyi al-Din Ibn 'Arabi (1165–1240), who was born and educated in Muslim Spain and travelled widely in the Middle East before finally settling in Damascus. The central theme of Ibn 'Arabi's numerous books and treatises is the doctrine of 'the unity of being' (*wahdat al-wujud*). According to this doctrine, God in his essence remains in 'blind obscurity', but manifests himself in his creation through an eternal process of self-disclosure or manifestation. While human beings need God for their very existence, therefore, God also needs them in order to be known.

Ibn 'Arabi's doctrine of the unity of being had many implications. If God alone really is, then all ways ultimately lead to him. This means that the various religions are mere names, for the reality is one. Ibn 'Arabi says:

> My heart has become capable of every form, a pasture for gazelles, a cloister for monks, a temple for idols, the votary's Ka'bah, the tablets of the Torah, the scroll of the Qur'an. It is the religion of love that I hold: wherever turns its mounts, love shall be my religion and my faith.

He remains one of the greatest mystical geniuses of all time.

Rumi

The most creative poet of the Persian language was Jalal al-Din Rumi (1207–73). Like Ibn 'Arabi, he was the product of a multi-religious and multicultural environment. Rumi was born in Balkh, Afghanistan, but fled with his parents as a child before the advancing Mongols. At last they settled in the city of Konya in central Anatolia (Turkey), a region that had been part of the Roman Empire.

In 1244 Rumi met a wandering Sufi named Shams of Tabriz. The two men developed a relationship so intimate that Rumi neglected his teaching duties, because he could

---

| Box 4.7 | Jalal al-Din Rumi |

The poetry of Jalal al-Din Rumi (1207–73) expresses Islamic mysticism's experience of union with God, using various metaphors for dissolving individual identity, including ardent love and death. From Mathnavi, III.3901, translated by Nicholson (1950:103).

I died as mineral and became a plant
I died as plant and rose to animal,
I died as animal and I was Man.
Why should I fear? When was I less by dying?
Yet once more I shall die as Man, to soar
With angels blest; but even from angelhood
I must pass on: all except God doth perish (Q. 28:88).
When I have sacrificed my angel-soul,
I shall become what no mind e'er conceived.
Oh, let me not exist! for Non-existence
Proclaims in organ tones, 'To him we shall return' (Q. 2:151).

not bear to be separated from his friend. In the end Shams disappeared and Rumi poured out his soul in heart-rending verses expressing his love for the 'Sun' (Shams) of Tabriz.

Rumi's greatest masterpiece is his *Mathnawi* ('Couplets'), a collection of nearly 30,000 verses. The spirit of this vast panorama of poetry is clearly expressed in its opening verses, which portray the haunting melodies of the reed flute telling its sad tale of separation from its reed bed. In stories, couplets of lyrical beauty, and at times even coarse tales of sexual impropriety, the *Mathnawi* depicts the longing of the human soul for God.

Sufi Orders and Saints

The religious fraternity is an ancient and widespread phenomenon. The earliest Sufi fraternities were established in the late eighth century, and by the thirteenth century a number of these groups were becoming institutionalized. Usually founded either by a famous *shaykh* or by a disciple in the *shaykh*'s name, Sufi orders began as teaching and devotional institutions located in urban centres, where they would often attach themselves to craft or trade guilds in the main bazaar.

It became a common custom for lay Muslims to join a Sufi order. Lay associates provided income for the order, participated in devotional observances, and received in return the blessing (*barakah*) of the *shaykh*.

The truth and authenticity of a *shaykh*'s claim to spiritual leadership depended on his spiritual genealogy. By the thirteenth century, Sufi chains of initiation (similar to chains of *isnad* in *hadith* transmission) were established. Such chains began with the *shaykh*'s immediate master and go back in an unbroken chain to 'Ali or one of his descendants, or in some cases to other Companions of the Prophet or their successors.

Through this spiritual lineage, a *shaykh* inherited the *barakah* of his masters, who inherited it from the Prophet. In turn, the *shaykh* bestows his *barakah*, or healing power, on his devotees, both during his life and, with even greater efficacy, after his death.

The *shaykh*s of Sufi orders are similar to the saints of the Catholic Church in that the faithful ascribe miracles or divine favours (*karamat*) to them; unlike Christian saints, however, they are recognized through popular acclaim rather than official canonization.

Devotional Practices

The most characteristic Sufi practice is a ritual called the **dhikr** (remembrance) of God, which may be public or private. The congregational *dhikr* ritual is usually held before the dawn or evening prayers. It consists of the repetition of the name of God, Allah, or the *shahadah*, 'There is no god except God' (*la ilaha illa Allah*). The *dhikr* is often accompanied by special bodily movements and, in some Sufi orders, by elaborate breathing techniques.

Often the performance of the *dhikr* is what distinguishes the various Sufi orders from one another. In some popular orders it is a highly emotional ritual (similar to charismatic practices in some Pentecostal churches) intended to stir devotees into a state of frenzy. By contrast, in the sober Naqshbandi order (founded by Baha' al-Din al-Naqshbandi in the fourteenth century), the *dhikr* is silent, offered as an inward prayer of the heart.

Another distinctly Sufi devotional practice is the *sama'* ('hearing' or 'audition'), which consists of listening to chants, often hypnotically beautiful, of mystical poetry, accompanied by various musical instruments. As instrumental music is not allowed in the mosque, *sama'* sessions are usually held in a hall adjacent to the mosque, or at the shrine of a famous *shaykh*.

Music and dance are vital elements of devotional life for members of the Mevlevi (Mawlawi) order, named after Mawlana ('our master') Rumi and founded by his son shortly after his death. As practised by the Mevlevis—also known as the 'Whirling Dervishes'—the dance is a highly sophisticated art symbolizing the perfect motion of the stars; the haunting melodies of the reed flute and large orchestra accompanying the chants of Rumi's mystical poetry and poetry in praise of the Prophet echo the primordial melodies of the heavenly spheres.

Sufism has always shown an amazing capacity for self-reform and regeneration. It was the Sufis who preserved Islamic learning and spirituality after 1258, when Baghdad fell to Mongol invaders, and Sufis who carried Islam to Africa and Asia. Today in the West it is primarily Sufi piety that is attracting non-Muslims to Islam.

The Spread of Islam

Like Christianity, Islam is a missionary religion. Muslims believe that the message of their faith is intended for all humankind, to be practised in a community transcending geographical, cultural, and linguistic borders.

Islam is ideologically and historically a post-Jewish, post-Christian religion. Ideologically, it sees itself as one of the religions of the Book, one that confirms the scriptures that preceded it, notably the Torah and the Gospel. Historically, Muslims from the beginning responded to and interacted with the communities of other faiths, particularly Christians and Jews. It was therefore necessary for Islam as a religio-political power to regulate its relations with non-Muslim citizens.

The Qur'an regards Jews and Christians as People of the Book. They were promised full freedom to practise their faith in return for a poll tax that also guaranteed them physical and economic protection and exemption from military service. Legally such communities came to be known as *dhimmis* ('protected people'). In the course of time, this designation was expanded to encompass other communities with sacred scriptures, including Zoroastrians in Iran (see Chapter 11) and Hindus in India.

In its first century Islam spread through conquest and military occupation. Much of the Byzantine and Roman world and all of the Sasanian Persian domains yielded to the Arab armies and came under Umayyad rule. In subsequent centuries, especially where Arabs, Persians, and Turks ruled, politico-military regimes continued to contribute to Islam's dominance.

Over time, however, the influence of mystics, teachers, and traders has reached farther and endured longer than the power of caliphs and conquerors. It was principally through the preaching and the living examples of individual Muslims that Islam spread

| Map 4.1   Language and culture in the spread of Islam

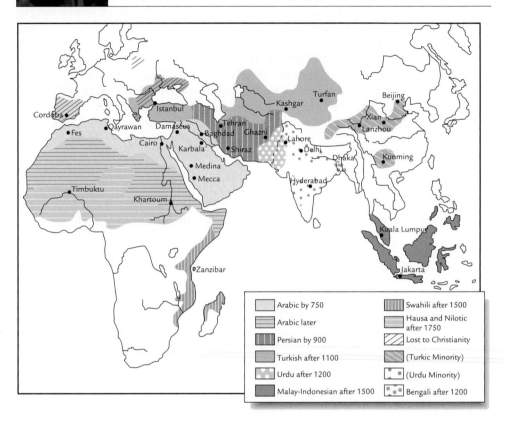

Arabic by 750	Swahili after 1500
Arabic later	Hausa and Nilotic after 1750
Persian by 900	Lost to Christianity
Turkish after 1100	(Turkic Minority)
Urdu after 1200	(Urdu Minority)
Malay-Indonesian after 1500	Bengali after 1200

to China, Southeast Asia, and East and West Africa. In modern times, migration and missionary activity have carried it to the Western hemisphere as well.

North Africa

After the conquest of what came to be the heartland of Islam—Syria, Egypt, and Persia—North Africa was conquered in the second half of the seventh century. Before that time North Africa had been first an important Roman province and then an equally important home of Latin Christianity. With its indigenous Berber, Phoenician, Roman, and Byzantine populations, North Africa was an area rich in cultural and religious diversity, and it has always maintained a distinct religious and cultural identity that reflects its ancient heritage.

The Umayyads had established their capital in Damascus in 661. With the shift of the capital from Damascus to Baghdad under the 'Abbasids in 762, the main orientation of the eastern Islamic domains became more Persian than Arab, more Asian than Mediterranean. Meanwhile, the centre of Arab Islamic culture shifted from Syria to the western Mediterranean: to Qayrawan, the capital of North Africa, in what is today Tunisia; and to Cordoba, Islam's western capital, in Spain, which rivalled Baghdad and Cairo in its cultural splendour. North African mystics, scholars, and philosophers were all instrumental in this remarkable achievement.

In the nineteenth and twentieth centuries North African religious scholars and particularly Sufi masters played a crucial role in the region's struggle for independence from European colonial powers. They helped to preserve the religious and cultural identity of their people and mobilized them to resist Italian and French colonization in Libya and Algeria. Despite the deep influence of the French language and secular culture, North African popular piety still reflects the classical Islamic heritage.

Spain

Before the appearance of Arab conquerors on the Iberian Peninsula in 711, Spain was torn by civil strife. Jews who had lived in Spain for centuries were subjected to harsh restrictions by rulers recently converted to Catholic Christianity, and they assisted the Arabs, whom they saw as liberators.

With astonishing rapidity, Umayyad forces conquered the land of Andalusia or al-Andalus, as the Arabs called southern Spain, and laid the foundations for an extraordinary culture. Arab men married local women, and a mixed but harmonious society developed that was Arab in language and expression and Arabo-Hispanic in spirit. Muslims, Christians, and Jews lived together in mutual tolerance for centuries before fanatical forces on both sides stifled one of the most creative experiments in interfaith living in human history.

In addition to symbiotic creativity, however, the 900-year history of Arab Spain (711–1609) included the tensions and conflicts typical of any multi-religious, multicultural society ruled by a minority regime. In the end, it witnessed the ultimate failure of Islamic faith and civilization not only in Spain but in Europe as well.

Arab Spain produced some of the world's greatest minds, including not only Ibn 'Arabi, Ibn Tufayl, and Ibn Rushd (p. 216 above), but the jurist-littérateur Ibn Hazm (994–1064) and the mystic-philosopher Ibn Masarrah (d. 931). Islamic Spain was the cultural centre of Europe. Students came from as far away as Scotland to study Islamic theology, philosophy, and science in centres of higher learning such as Córdoba and Toledo. It was in these centres that the European Renaissance was conceived, and the great universities in which it was nurtured were inspired by their Arabo-Hispanic counterparts.

In Muslim Spain the Jews enjoyed a golden age of philosophy and science, mysticism, and general prosperity. Jewish scholars, court physicians, and administrators occupied high state offices and served as political and cultural liaisons between Islamic Spain and the rest of Europe. Arab learning did indeed penetrate deeply into western Europe and contributed directly to the rise of the West to world prominence.

Sub-Saharan Africa

Islam may have arrived in sub-Saharan Africa as early as the eighth or ninth century. As in other places where it became the dominant religion, it was spread first by traders and then on a much larger scale by preachers. Finally jurists came to consolidate and establish the new faith as a religious and legal system. Sufi orders played an important part both in the spread of Islam and in its use as a motivation and framework for social and political reform.

Islam always had to compete with traditional African religion. Muslim prayers, for example, had to show themselves to be no less potent than the rain-making prayers or rituals of the indigenous traditions. The Moroccan Muslim traveller Ibn Battutah (1304–68) provided a vivid account of the efforts of Muslims in the Mali Empire of West Africa to adapt the new faith to local traditions.

In East Africa Islam spread along the coast, largely through maritime traffic from Arabia and the Gulf trading in commodities and also in slaves. From the sixteenth century onward, after Portuguese navigators rounded the southern cape of Africa, the cultural and political development of East African Islam was directly affected by European colonialism as well.

Unlike the populations of Syria, Iraq, Egypt, and North Africa, the peoples of East Africa did not adopt the Arabic language. But so much Arabic vocabulary penetrated the local languages that at least one-third of the Swahili lexicon today is Arabic. Until recently, most of the major African languages were written in the Arabic script.

An important element of East African society has been the Khoja community. Including both Sevener (Isma'ili) and Twelver Shi'a, the Khojas immigrated from India to Africa in the mid-1800s. They have on the whole been successful business people with Western education and close relationships with Europe and North America. These relationships have been strengthened by the migration of many Khojas to Britain, the United States, and Canada.

Iran and Central Asia

Central Asia had a cosmopolitan culture before Islam. Buddhism, Zoroastrianism, Judaism, and Christianity existed side by side in mutual tolerance. The Arab conquest of the region took more than a century: beginning in 649, less than two decades after the Prophet's death, it was not completed until 752.

Under the Samanid dynasty, which ruled large areas of Persia and Central Asia in the ninth and tenth centuries, Persian culture flourished, as did classical *hadith* traditionists, historians, philosophers, and religious scholars working in the Arabic language. Particularly important centres of learning developed in the cities of Bukhara and Samarkand, located in what is now Uzbekistan, which owed much of their prosperity to trade with India, China, and the rest of the Muslim domains. With the first notable Persian poet, Rudaki (c. 859–940), Bukhara became the birthplace of Persian literature.

While their contemporaries the Buyids promoted Shi'i learning and public devotions in the region that is now Iraq, the Samanids firmly established Sunni orthodoxy in

Central Asia. Many Sunni theologians and religious scholars lived and worked in Bukhara and Samarkand under Samanid patronage. Among the great minds of this epoch were the theologian al-Maturidi (d. 944), the philosopher Ibn Sina (p. 216) , the great scholar and historian of religion Abu Rayhan al-Biruni (973–1048), and the famous Persian poet Ferdowsi (c. 935–c. 1020). In this intellectual environment Islam was spread by persuasion and enticement rather than propaganda and war.

Early in the eleventh century the Samanids were succeeded by the Seljuq Turks in the Middle East and the Karakhanid Mongols in Persia and Central Asia. The Mongols profoundly altered the situation in that region as they would in the Middle East a century later. The devastating consequences of the Mongol conquest of Persia and Central Asia were compounded by the loss of trade revenues when the traditional caravan routes were abandoned in favour of sea travel to India and China. Central Asia never recovered from the resulting decline in culture and prosperity.

The Turks

As Turkic tribal populations from Central Asia moved into parts of the Middle Eastern Muslim heartland, they were converted to Islam through the activity of Sufi missionaries in particular. They became influential from the tenth century onward in Central Asia, Armenia, Anatolia, and Syria. Mahmud of Ghazna in Afghanistan (r. 998–1030), of Turkish descent, broke away from the Persian Samanid dynasty; his successors, the Ghaznavids, extended Muslim power in northern India. Mahmud was the first person to be called 'sultan', a term that until his time had referred to the authority of the state.

The Seljuqs, another Turkic family, prevailed in Iran and farther west a generation after Mahmud. The second Seljuq sultan, Alp Arslan, inflicted a crushing defeat on the Byzantines at Manzikert, in eastern Anatolia, in 1071. Bit by bit, eastern Anatolia (today's Turkey) fell to the Seljuqs, who ruled until they were conquered by the Mongols in 1243.

The Ottoman Turks took over the caliphate from the 'Abbasids and ruled for more than six centuries, from their dynastic founder Osman I (r. 1299–1326) until 1923. Beginning in the fourteenth century by absorbing former Seljuq territory in eastern Anatolia and taking over western Anatolia from the Byzantines, they reached the height of their power in the sixteenth century, occupying the Balkans as far north as Vienna, the Levant (i.e., the Syro-Palestinian region), and all of northern Africa except Morocco. So widespread was their empire that Christian Europe until the nineteenth century thought of Islamic culture as primarily Turkish.

As their imperial symbol the Ottomans adopted the crescent, an ancient symbol that the Byzantines had also used. Conspicuous on the Turkish flag, the crescent was considered by Europeans and eventually by Muslims themselves to be the symbol of Islam. Turkic languages continue to prevail in much of the region of Central Asia ruled by the Soviet Union for much of the twentieth century. From Azerbaijan to Uzbekistan and Turkmenistan, a dominant element in the population is Turkic. The same is true of Chinese Central Asia, in the vast region of Xinjiang.

China

Islam may have made contact with China shortly after the Prophet's death, although the first written sources referring to Islam in China do not appear till the seventeenth century. For earlier information we have to rely on Chinese sources, which unfortunately focus on commercial activities and have little to say about the social and intellectual life of Chinese Muslims.

The extent of the Muslim presence in an area may often be gauged by the number of mosques. There seem to have been no mosques in the main inland cities of China before the thirteenth century. Along the coast, however, the minaret of the mosque in Guangzhou (Canton) and various inscriptions in the province of Fujian suggest that maritime trade was under way considerably earlier, in 'Abbasid times.

From the beginning, Persian and Arab merchants were allowed to trade freely so long as they complied with Chinese rules. But it was not until the thirteenth century that Muslim traders began settling in China in numbers large enough to support the establishment of mosques. The presence of Islam in China before that time was probably limited.

Muslim communities in China prospered under the Mongol (1206–1368) and Ming (1368–1644) emperors. After the Mongol period Chinese Muslims were assimilated culturally but not religiously. Since it was through trade that they kept in touch with the rest of the Muslim *ummah*, the decline of the overland trade with Central Asia in the 1600s had the effect of isolating the Chinese Muslim community. It became virtually cut off from the rest of the world, so that our information about Muslims in China after the seventeenth century is largely a matter of conjecture.

Unlike Buddhism, centuries earlier, Islam never came to be seen as culturally Chinese, and Muslims remained an identifiable minority in Chinese society. The Muslim Uighurs of Xinjiang (Chinese Turkestan), in the far northwest of the country, are distinguished both by language and by region. Yet even the Chinese-speaking Muslims in the principal eastern cities of 'Han' China are set apart by their avoidance of pork—a staple of the Chinese diet. The presence of *halal* (ritually acceptable) restaurants and butcher shops is a sure sign of a Muslim neighbourhood.

Chinese Muslims have experienced their share of repression under the Communist regime, particularly during the Cultural Revolution of 1966–76. But their situation has improved since then. Today there are approximately 50 million Muslims in China. Like other religious communities in contemporary China, they face an uncertain future, but the ethnic base of the minorities in the country's Central Asian interior is not likely to disappear soon.

South Asia

Islam arrived early in South Asia, carried by traders and Arab settlers, and Umayyad armies began moving eastward in 711. Even so, the Muslim conquest of India was a long process. Mahmud the Ghaznavid and his successors advanced over the Khyber pass onto the North Indian plain beginning around 1000. By the end of the reign of the first Mughal emperor, Babur (1483–1530), most of India had come under Muslim rule, with the exceptions of Tamilnadu and Kerala in the far south.

Because the Muslim rulers of India were of non-Indian ancestry, from Iran and Central Asia, maintaining and expanding Muslim power over a large Hindu population meant continuous warfare. The Muslim regime was undoubtedly repressive for Hindus. Yet Indian Islam developed a rich religious and intellectual tradition, and in time it became an integral part of Indian life and culture.

India was something new in the history of Islam's territorial expansion. For the first time, the majority of the conquered population did not convert to the new faith. In ancient Arabia Islam had been able to suppress and supplant polytheism; but in India it had to learn to coexist with a culture that remained largely polytheistic.

At the same time Islam was something new to India. In a land where people often had multiple religious allegiances, and community boundaries were fluid, Islam's exclusive devotion to the one God and clear delineation of community membership represented a dramatically different way of life.

The Badshahi or Great Mosque in Lahore, Pakistan, built by the Emperor Aurangzeb in 1673–4 (Philip Game, Photographers Direct).

Collectively, the three countries of the Indian subcontinent—India, Bangladesh, and Pakistan—have the largest Muslim population in the world. The Muslims of India alone comprise the third-largest Muslim population (after Indonesia and Pakistan), numbering between 100 and 120 million. Even so, they are a minority whose future appears bleak in the face of rising Hindu nationalism.

Southeast Asia

Southeast Asia, when Islam arrived there, consisted of small kingdoms and settlements that were home to a wide variety of languages and cultures, and its religious life had been strongly influenced by the Hindu and Buddhist traditions. These influences can still be seen in the ancient Hindu culture on the island of Bali and the great Buddhist stupa complex of Borobudur in Indonesia.

There is no evidence for the presence of Islam in Southeast Asia before the tenth century. But Yemeni traders are reported to have sailed into the islands of the Malay archipelago before the time of the Prophet, and this suggests that the Malay people may have been exposed to Islam at an early date. Scattered evidence from Chinese and Portuguese travellers, as well as passing references by Ibn Battutah, indicate that by the fifteenth century Islam had spread widely in Southeast Asia. By the seventeenth century, when British and Dutch trading companies arrived in the region, Islam had become the dominant religion and culture of the Malay archipelago.

By the thirteenth century Muslim communities in small states ruled by sultans are widely reported. The earliest of these was Pasai, a small kingdom on the east coast of northern Sumatra; others appeared in the following centuries. Some of the states that arose in the fifteenth century gained considerable prominence both culturally and economically. In every case, prosperity attracted Muslim religious scholars from India to these states.

In an effort to expand and strengthen his realm, the sultan Iskandar Muda of Acheh (r. 1607–36) became the first Muslim ruler in Southeast Asia to establish alliances with European powers. Acheh also produced noteworthy Islamic scholarship, which is still used in the Malay world today.

In Southeast Asia even more than elsewhere, Sufi orders played a crucial part in the process of Islamization. They were also prominent in later political and social struggles for reform and liberation. In the late nineteenth and early twentieth centuries, modernist reform movements in the Middle East inspired similar movements in Indonesia and other countries of the region. At present Islam is the majority religion in Malaysia, Indonesia, and Brunei, and there are Muslim minorities in all the other countries of Southeast Asia. Most Muslims in the region follow the Shafi'i legal school.

Southeast Asia can claim at least one-third of the Muslims of the world. Indonesia alone has a Muslim population of at least 180 million, making it the largest Muslim country in the world today.

Practice

The Five Pillars of Islam

Individual faith and institutional Islam converge in the worship of God and service to others. A well-attested Prophetic tradition characterizes Islam as built upon five 'pillars'. With the exception of the first (the *shahadah*, the profession of faith through which one becomes a Muslim), the pillars are all rites of worship, both personal and communal. The Five Pillars are:

- to declare, or bear witness, that there is no god except God, and that Muhammad is the Messenger of God;
- to establish regular worship;
- to pay the *zakat* alms;
- to observe the fast of Ramadan; and
- to perform the *hajj* pilgrimage.

The Five Pillars are the foundations on which Islam rests as a religious system of faith and social responsibility, worship, and piety. Acts of worship are obligatory duties for all Muslims. Each of the Five Pillars has both an outer or public obligatory dimension and an inner or private voluntary dimension.

Bearing Witness

The first pillar is the *shahadah*: 'I bear witness that there is no god except God, and I bear witness that Muhammad is the messenger of God.' It consists of two declarations. The first, affirming the oneness of God, expresses the universal and primordial state of faith in which every child is born. The Prophet is said to have declared, 'Every child is born in this original state of faith ; then his parents turn him into a Jew, Christian or Zoroastrian, and if they are Muslims, into a Muslim.'

The second declaration, affirming Muhammad's role as messenger, signifies acceptance of the truth of Muhammad's claim to prophethood, and hence the truth of his message.

Prayer

The second pillar consists of the obligatory prayers (*salat*). These are distinguished from voluntary devotional acts, such as meditation and personal supplicatory prayers (which may be offered at any time), in that they must be performed five times in a day and night: at dawn, noon, mid-afternoon, sunset, and after dark. The *salat* prayers were the first Islamic rituals to be instituted.

The hours of prayer are posted on the door of a small mosque in Paris (Andrew Leyerle).

The *salat* prayers must always be preceded by ritual washing. *Wudu'* ('making pure or radiant') or partial washing involves washing the face, rinsing the mouth and nostrils, washing the hands and forearms to the elbows, passing one's wet hands over the head and feet, or washing the feet to the two heels.

Five times a day—on radio and television, through loudspeakers, and from high minarets), a *mu'adhdhin* chants in a melodious voice the call to prayer inviting the faithful to pray together either in a mosque or at home. Whether a Muslim prays alone or behind an imam in congregation, he or she is always conscious of countless other men and women engaged in the same act of worship. Each phrase of the call to prayer is repeated at least twice for emphasis:

> God is greater. I bear witness that there is no god except God, and I bear witness that Muhammad is the Messenger of God. Hasten to the prayers! Hasten to success or prosperity!
> [Shi'i Muslims add: Hasten to the best action!] God is greater. There is no god except God.

The prayers consist of cycles or units called *rak'ah*s, with bowing, kneeling, and prostration. The dawn prayers consist of two cycles, the noon and mid-afternoon prayers of four each, the sunset prayer of three, and the night prayers of four cycles. Apart from some moments of contemplation and personal supplication at the end of the *salat*, these prayers are fixed formulas consisting largely of passages from the Qur'an, especially the opening *surah* (*al-Fatihah*):

> In the name of God, the All-merciful, the Compassionate:
> Praise be to God, the All-merciful, the Compassionate, King of the Day of Judgment. You alone do we worship, and to you alone do we turn for help. Guide us to the straight way, the way of those upon whom you have bestowed your grace, not those who have incurred your wrath, nor those who have gone astray (Q. 1:1–7).

The *Fatihah* for Muslims is in some ways similar to the Lord's Prayer for Christians. It is repeated in every *rak'ah*—at least 17 times in every 24-hour period.

Unlike Judaism and Christianity, Islam has no Sabbath specified for rest. Friday is the day designated for *jum'ah* ('assembly'), for congregational prayers. In the Friday service the first two *rak'ah*s of the noon prayers are replaced by two short sermons, usually on religious, moral, and political issues, followed by two *rak'ah*s. The place of worship is called *masjid* ('place of prostration in prayer') or *jami'* (literally, 'gatherer'). The English word 'mosque' is derived from *masjid*.

Other congregational prayers are performed on the first days of the two major festivals, **Eid al-Fitr** and **Eid al-Adha**, at the end of Ramadan and the *hajj* pilgrimage respectively.

Faithful Muslims see all things, good or evil, as contingent on God's will. Hence many do not state a future commitment or prediction without prefacing it with the phrase *in-sha' Allah*, 'if God wills'. The hope is that one's plan of action will be accepted by God and guided to completion.

Almsgiving

The close relationship between worship of God and service to the poor and needy is instituted in the third pillar of Islam, the paying of *zakat* alms. The Qur'an frequently couples regular worship and almsgiving (see Q. 2:43, 5:55, and 9:71). The root meaning of the word *zakat* is 'to purify or increase'. Offering alms purifies a person from greed and attachment to material possessions.

Zakat is an obligatory welfare tax to be paid annually by all adult Muslims on all surplus earnings. It consists of 2.5 per cent of the value of all accumulated wealth (savings, financial gains of any kind, livestock, agricultural produce, real estate, etc.) During the early centuries of Islam, when the community was controlled by a central authority, the *zakat* revenues were kept in a central treasury and disbursed for public educational and civic projects, care for orphans and the needy, and the ransoming of Muslim war captives. Now that the Muslim world is divided into so many independent nation-states, most of which have adopted some form of modern Western taxation, the *zakat* obligation has become largely voluntary: many ignore it and others pay through donations to private religious and philanthropic organizations.

Voluntary almsgiving—in addition to the obligatory *zakat* alms—is called *sadaqah*. The Qur'an describes *sadaqah* as a loan given to God, which will be repaid in manifold measure on the Day of Resurrection (Q. 57:11). *Sadaqah* giving is not bound by any consideration of race, colour, or creed: the recipient may be anyone in need.

The Ramadan Fast

The fourth pillar of Islam is the fast of the month of Ramadan. Fasting is recognized in the Qur'an as a universal form of worship, enjoined by scriptures of all faiths. The Prophet appears to have observed a variety of voluntary fasts in Mecca, which are still honoured by many pious Muslims.

While prayers and almsgiving are frequently mentioned by the Qur'an, the Ramadan fast is mandated in just one passage:

> O you who have faith, fasting is ordained for you as it was ordained for those before you, that you may fear God. [. . .] Ramadan is the month in which the Qur'an was sent down as a guidance to humankind, manifestations of guidance and the Criterion. Therefore whosoever among you witnesses the moon, let him fast [the month], but whosoever is sick or on a journey, an equal number of other days (Q. 2:183, 185).

This passage accords Ramadan the honour of being the month in which the Qur'an was revealed to the Prophet.

Ramadan is a month-long fast extending from daybreak till sundown each day. It requires complete abstention from food, drink, smoking, and sexual relations. The fast is broken at sunset, and another light meal is eaten at the end of the night, just before the next day's fast begins at dawn. In the course of elaborating the rules of the Ramadan fast, the Qur'an declares, 'God desires ease for you, not hardship' (Q. 2:185). Therefore the sick, travellers, children, and women who are pregnant, nursing or menstruating are exempted from the fast either altogether or until they are able to make up the missed days.

The Arabs before Islam observed a lunar calendar in which the year consisted of only 354 days. To keep festivals and sacred months in their proper seasons, they (like the Jews) added an extra month every three years. The Qur'an abolished this custom, however, allowing Islamic festivals to rotate throughout the year.

When Ramadan comes in the summer, particularly in the equatorial countries of Asia and Africa, going without water can be a real hardship. But when it comes in winter, as it did in the 1990s in the northern hemisphere, it can be relatively tolerable. Ramadan ends with a happy festival called Eid al-Fitr, a three-day celebration during which people exchange gifts and well-wishing visits. Children receive gifts and wear brightly coloured new clothes, and people visit the graves of loved ones, where special sweet dishes are distributed to the poor. Before the first breakfast after the long fast, the head of every family must give special alms for breaking the fast, called *zakat al-fitr*, on behalf of every member of the household. Those who are exempted from fasting for reasons of chronic illness or old age must feed a poor person for every day they miss.

The fast of Ramadan becomes a true act of worship when a person shares God's bounty with those who have no food with which to break their fast. True fasting means not only giving up the pleasures of food and drink, but also abstaining from slandering others and any idle talk, and turning one's heart and mind to God in devotional prayers and meditations.

Pilgrimage to Mecca

The fifth pillar of Islam is the *hajj* pilgrimage, instituted by Abraham at God's command after he and his son Ishmael were ordered to build the Ka'bah (see Q. 22:26-9 and 2:125-7). Thus most of its ritual elements are understood as re-enacting the experiences of Abraham, whom the Qur'an declares to be the father of prophets and the first true Muslim.

Before the pilgrims reach the sacred precincts of Mecca, they exchange their regular clothes for two pieces of white linen, symbolic of the shrouds in which Muslims are wrapped for burial. With this act they enter the state of consecration. They approach Mecca with the solemn proclamation: 'Here we come in answer to your call, O God, here we come! Here we come, for you have no partner, here we come! Indeed, all praise, dominion, and grace belong to you alone, here we come!'

Once in Mecca, the pilgrims begin with the lesser *hajj* (*'umrah*). This ritual is performed in the precincts of the Great Mosque and includes the *tawaf* (walking counterclockwise around the Ka'bah) and running between the two hills of al-Safa and al-Marwa. In the traditional narrative, Hagar, Abraham's handmaid and the mother of his son Ishmael, ran between these two hills in search of water for her dying child. After the seventh run, water gushed out by the child's feet, and Hagar contained it with sand. The place, according to Islamic tradition, is the ancient well of Zamzam ('the contained water'). The water of Zamzam is considered holy, and pilgrims often take home containers of it as blessed gifts for family and friends.

The *hajj* pilgrimage proper begins on the eighth of Dhu al-Hijjah, the twelfth month of the Islamic calendar, when throngs of pilgrims set out for 'Arafat, a large plain, about 20 km (13 mi.) east of Mecca, on which stands the goal of every pilgrim: the Mount of Mercy (Jabal al-Rahmah). In accordance with the Prophet's *sunnah* (practice), many pilgrims spend the night at Mina, but others press on to 'Arafat. As the sun passes the noon meridian, all the pilgrims gather for the central rite of the *hajj* pilgrimage: the standing (*wuquf*) on the Mount of Mercy in 'Arafat.

Men and women stand in solemn prayers and supplications till sunset, as though standing before God for judgment on the last day. This rite links the present moment to three sacred occasions : the times when Adam and Eve stood on that plain after their expulsion from paradise, when Abraham and his son Ishmael performed the rite during the first *hajj* pilgrimage, and when Muhammad gave his farewell oration, affirming the brotherhood and sisterhood of all Muslims.

The sombre scene of prayers and supplications changes abruptly at sundown, when the pilgrims leave 'Arafat for Muzdalifah, a sacred spot a short distance along the road back to Mecca. There the pilgrims observe the combined sunset and evening prayers and gather pebbles for the ritual lapidation (throwing of stones) at Mina the next day.

The tenth of Dhu al-Hijjah is the final day of the *hajj* season, and the first of the four-day festival of sacrifice ('Id al-Adha). The day is spent at Mina, where the remaining pilgrimage rites are completed.

Tradition tells that on his way from 'Arafat to Mina, Abraham was commanded by God to sacrifice to God that which was dearest to him—his son Ishmael. (For Jews and Christians the son was Isaac, and the attempted sacrifice took place in Jerusalem.) Satan whispered to him three times, tempting him to disobey God's command. Abraham's response was to hurl stones at Satan, to drive him away. Thus at the spot called al-'Aqabah, meaning the hard or steep road, a brick pillar has been erected to represent Satan. Pilgrims gather early in the morning to throw seven stones at the pillar, in emulation of Abraham. Three other pillars in Mina, representing the three temptations, are also stoned.

Following the ritual of stoning, the pilgrims offer a blood sacrifice—a lamb, goat, cow, or camel—to symbolize the animal sent from heaven with which God ransoms Abraham's son (Q. 27:107). After this, to mark the end of their state of consecration, pilgrims ritually clip a minimum of three hairs from their heads (some shave their heads). The *hajj* ends with a final circumambulation of the Ka'bah and the completion of the rites of the lesser *hajj* (*'umrah*) for those who have not done so.

Tradition asserts that a person returns from a sincerely performed *hajj* free from all sins, as on the day when he or she was born. Thus the *hajj* is regarded as a form of resurrection or rebirth, and its completion marks a new stage in the life of a Muslim. Every pilgrim is henceforth distinguished by the title *hajji* before his or her name.

Cultural Expressions

Islamic Architecture

The functions of the mosque include not only prayer, implied in the Arabic *masjid* ('kneeling place'), but other community activities, implied in Arabic *jami'* ('gatherer'). Early mosques functioned as treasuries, where financial records were kept; as law courts, where judges heard cases; and as educational centres where classes and study circles were held. In time these other institutions moved into their own buildings, appropriate to their activities, but the function of public assembly and prayer continued to dictate the architectural form of mosques. Two other types of buildings with religious functions— the *madrasah* or religious school, and the tomb or mausoleum—drew on much the same repertory of styles that mosques did.

Every mosque includes four essential features: a fountain for washing hands, face, and feet upon entering; a large area for kneeling and prostration in prayer; a pulpit (*minbar*) from which the leader of Friday noon worship delivers the sermon; and an imageless niche (*mihrab*) in the middle of the wall closest to Mecca, indicating the *qiblah* (direction of prayer). Not part of the earliest mosques in Arabia but characteristic of Islam in many places is the minaret, the tower from which the *mu'adhdhin* delivers the

The Sultan Ahmet or Blue Mosque in Istanbul, Turkey, built in 1609–16 (Andrew Leyerle).

call to prayer. Beginning in the sixteenth century, the Turks made much use of the dome, an important feature of church architecture among the Byzantines who had preceded them. A high central dome, resting on four semi-dome apses, enclosed the prayer space. Some major Turkish mosques had four or more minarets, marking the corners of the mosque. Central dome architecture, though often simpler and without minarets, is also characteristic of mosques in Malaysia and Indonesia, where the rainy climate dictates that the prayer space must be roofed over.

Ultimately, much in Islamic architecture is specific to geographic regions and their distinctive idioms. The keyhole arch, for instance, though it appears in the great mosque of Damascus, is characteristic mainly of North Africa and Islamic Spain. A shallow pointed arch, similar to the English Tudor arch, emerged in Iraq, predominated in Iran, and spread to Central Asia and India. The bud or onion domes of Indo-Muslim architecture have been picked up in Southeast Asia. In China many mosques are built like Chinese temples, with tiled roofs resting on wooden columns and bracket structures. A number of Chinese minarets are built in the form of East Asian Buddhist pagodas.

Islamic Art

Islamic art is rich, elaborate, even exuberant. Three elements are particularly distinctive: calligraphy (the decorative use of script and units of text); geometrical decoration (particularly the interlaced motifs called arabesques in the West); and floral designs (especially common in Iran). All three are more abstract than pictorial and therefore point beyond themselves in a way that pictorial images may not. Design using these elements captures the viewer's attention and directs it to the larger structure on which the decoration appears, whether a page of the Qur'an, a prayer rug, or the tiled entrance of a mosque. Religious content is most obvious in the decorative use of calligraphy in mosques, where the texts used are often passages from the Qur'an, but even the craft items sold in bazaars are often adorned with some of the 99 'wonderful names' or attributes of God.

Three-dimensional sculpture is prohibited in Islam, but the two-dimensional representation of living creatures is highly developed. Some Persian carpets include animals in their garden scenes. Persian and Indian manuscripts are illustrated with minia-

In the courtyard of the Rustem Pasha Mosque (1560) in Istanbul (Andrew Leyerle).

| Box 4.8   Mohamed Zakariya

Mohamed Zakariya (b. 1942) is the best Islamic calligrapher in the United States. Born in Ventura, California, he moved to Los Angeles with his family and saw Islamic calligraphy for the first time in the window of an Armenian carpet store. Travelling to Morocco in his late teens, he became fascinated with Islam and Islamic calligraphy. On his return to the United States he converted to Islam.

He made other journeys to North Africa and the Middle East, and spent some time studying manuscripts in the British Museum in London. After studying with the Egyptian calligrapher Abdussalam Ali-Nour, Zakariya in 1984 became a student of the Turkish master calligrapher Hasan Celebi. In 1988 he received his diploma from Celebi at the Research Center for Islamic History, Art and Culture in Istanbul, the first American to achieve this honour. He received his second diploma, in the *ta'lik* script, from the master calligrapher Ali Alparslan in 1997.

Zakariya lives with his family in Arlington, Virginia. His work has been displayed in various museums and galleries, and is in a number of private collections. He was the artist commissioned by the United States Postal Service to design its Eid stamp, which debuted on 1 September 2001.

In addition to teaching calligraphy according to the Ottoman method, producing new work, and exhibiting it around the world, Zakariya writes contemporary instructional material and translates classic texts. Mohamed Zakariya's work shows that American Islam has become an integral part of the Muslim world. Now students from that world travel to the United States to study with an American master of an ancient Islamic art.

ture paintings of legendary heroes and current rulers. Among Iranian Shi'a, portraits of 'Ali are a focus of popular piety. While representations of the Prophet himself are avoided, the steed that carried him on his *mi'raj* or heavenly journey, Buraq, is portrayed in popular art as a winged horse with a human head; this is a common motif on trucks and buses in Afghanistan and Pakistan. In addition, Arabic calligraphy has been used ingeniously to create the outlines of birds and animals, as well as crescents, mosques, minarets, and other forms to the present day.

Interaction and Adaptation

Islam and Modernity

Throughout the history of Islam, many individuals and groups have taken it upon themselves to reform the rest of the Muslim community. An external impetus for reform has been Muslim interaction with Western Christendom. The first major Western challenges to Muslim power and Islam's capacity to rally its people in a universal struggle to defend the integrity of its domains were the crusades. Fired by a spirit of Christian holy war for the liberation of Jerusalem from Muslim domination, the armies of the first crusade captured the Holy City in 1099 after massacring its Jewish and Muslim inhabitants. For nearly two centuries, Frankish Christian kingdoms existed side by side with Muslim states along the eastern Mediterranean shores, sometimes peacefully but more often at war.

In the end the crusaders returned home and those who remained were assimilated. But the spirit of the crusades lived on, as did the distorted images of Islam and its followers that the crusaders took back with them. The equally distorted images of Christianity and Western Christendom that the crusades left in Muslim lands have also lived on, and have been reinforced and embellished in response to Western imperialism and its aftermath.

Pre-modern Reform Movements

We shall examine Islam in the modern era from two perspectives: internal reform and the challenge of the West.

Common to all reform movements has been the call to return to pristine *islam*, the *islam* of the Prophet's society and the normative period of his 'rightly guided' successors. Among those who championed this cause was the great Egyptian religious scholar Ibn Taymiyah (1263–1328), a jurist who fought relentlessly against Shi'i beliefs and practices, Sufi excesses, and the blind imitation of established legal traditions, while fighting to revive the practice of *ijtihad*. He exerted a powerful and long-lasting influence on subsequent reform movements.

Some four centuries later, Ibn Taymiyah's ideas became the basis of the reform program advocated by the Wahhabi movement, named for its founder Muhammad Ibn 'Abd al-Wahhab (1703–92). Significantly, this uncompromising and influential revivalist movement began in the highlands of Arabia, the birthplace of Islam. Ibn 'Abd al-Wahhab's long life allowed him to establish his movement on a firm foundation. He allied himself with Muhammad 'Al Sa'ud, a local tribal prince, on the understanding that the prince would exercise political power and protect the nascent movement, which would hold religious authority. This agreement remains operative today: the kingdom of Saudi Arabia is a Wahhabi state, ruled by the descendants of 'Al Sa'ud.

The Wahhabis preached a strictly egalitarian Islam based solely on a direct relationship between the worshipper and God. They repudiated the widely cherished hope that the Prophet and other divinely favoured individuals would intercede with God for the pious to grant them blessing and succour in this life and salvation in the next. The Wahhabis regarded the veneration of saints, including the Prophet, as a form of idolatry. They even advocated the destruction of the sacred black stone of the Ka'bah, on the grounds that it stood as an idol between faithful Muslims and their Lord.

The Wahhabis held all those who did not share their convictions to be in error. They waged a violent campaign aimed at purging Muslim society of what they considered to be its un-Islamic beliefs and practices. They destroyed the Prophet's tomb in Medina and levelled the graves of his Companions. They attacked the Shi'i sacred cities of Najaf and Karbala', massacred their inhabitants, and demolished the shrines of 'Ali and his son Husayn. They also went on a rampage in Arab cities, desecrating the tombs of Sufi saints and destroying their shrines.

The basic ideals of Wahhabism have appealed to many revivalists and played an especially significant role in eighteenth- and nineteenth-century Sufi reforms. In the present day, however, a number of extremist groups influenced by Wahhabi ideology, including al-Qaeda and the Taliban, have transformed the internal struggle to 'purify' Islam into an external war against all perceived enemies, Muslim and non-Muslim alike.

Nineteenth-Century Revivalism

Jihad—Arabic for 'struggle'—has two components. Inner *jihad* is the struggle to make oneself more Islamic; outer *jihad* is the struggle to make one's society more Islamic.

A number of Sufi *jihad* movements arose in the nineteenth century, partly in response to Wahhabi reforms and partly in reaction against European colonial encroachment on Muslim domains. Several of these movements were able to establish short-lived states, such as those of Usman ('Uthman) dan Fodio (1754–1817) in Nigeria, Muhammad al-Sanusi (1787–1859) in Libya, and Muhammad Ahmad al-Mahdi (1844–85) in the Sudan. Common to all these movements was an activist ideology of militant struggle against external colonialism and internal decadence. They also strove for reform and the revival of *ijtihad*.

Because of their broad appeal, these Sufi reform movements exerted a lasting influence on most subsequent reform programs and ideologies. In North Africa in particular, Sufi *shaykh*s and religious scholars not only helped to preserve their countries' religious, linguistic, and cultural identity but in some cases spearheaded the long and bloody struggles for independence from French and Italian colonial rule. The Sufi *shaykh* Abdelkader ('Abd al-Qadir, 1808–83), for example, played an important political role in the campaign for Algeria's independence. King Muhammad V of Morocco (1909–61), who negotiated his country's independence from France, was himself a Sufi *shaykh* and a 'venerable descendant' (*sayyid*) of the Prophet. And the grandson of al-Sanusi, Idris I, ruled Libya as king from independence in 1951 until he was overthrown in a revolution in 1969.

The movement begun by al-Sanusi in Libya promoted reform and Muslim unity across North and West Africa. By contrast, the goal of al-Mahdi's movement in Sudan was more eschatological: its founder saw himself as God's representative on earth and set out to establish a social and political order modelled on that of the Prophet. He regarded the Ottoman-Egyptian occupation of Sudan to be un-Islamic and waged a war of *jihad* against it. In 1885 he triumphed over Egyptian forces and established an Islamic state based on strict application of the *shari'ah* law. Although al-Mahdi himself died within a few months, the regime lasted till 1889, when it was overthrown by British and Egyptian forces.

Ahmadiyah

The career of Mirza Ghulam Ahmad (1835–1908) reflects both the social and the religious diversity of the Punjab in the 1880s, a time of various movements for renewal of Hindu and Muslim identity, as well as a growing emphasis on self-definition among the

Sikhs. To this mix Ghulam Ahmad, from Qadian, near Amritsar, contributed several volumes of commentary on the Qur'an and claims of his own leadership status.

In 1889 he accepted from his followers the homage reserved for a prophet like Muhammad. Ahmadis, as they are known, have also revered him as the *mujaddid* (renewer) ushering in the fourteenth century of Islam, as the Mahdi of Shi'i expectation, as the tenth incarnation of the Hindu deity Vishnu, and as the returning Messiah of Christianity (Ahmadis also maintain that Jesus did not die in Palestine but went to Afghanistan, in search of the ten lost tribes of Israel, and was buried in Srinagar, Kashmir).

Active proselytizers, Ghulam Ahmad and his followers preached in the streets, engaged in debates, and published translations of the Qur'an. The movement has spread widely. Including four million in Pakistan, Ahmadis now total at least ten million, or one per cent of the world's Muslims. Leadership since the founder's death in 1908 has been termed *khilafat al-Masih* (succession of the Messiah). Although the successor is chosen by election, since 1914 the title has stayed in Ghulam Ahmad's family, held first by a son and then by two grandsons. Because they identified themselves as Muslims, on the partition of India in 1947 the Ahmadis were displaced from Qadian and relocated their centre across the border in Rabwah, Pakistan, west of Lahore.

Many Muslims, however, have not accepted the Ahmadis as fellow Muslims. As early as 1891, Ghulam Ahmad's claim to prophethood was rejected by orthodox Muslim authorities. In Pakistan Ahmadis have been the target of riots and demonstrations; in 1984 they were declared to be a non-Muslim minority (hence ineligible for opportunities accorded Muslims); and they have been prohibited from calling themselves Muslims or using Islamic vocabulary in their worship and preaching.

Ahmadiyah's future, therefore, may lie in its diaspora. Missions have been notably successful in lands not historically Islamic, such as West Africa, the Caribbean, and the overseas English-speaking world. The largest mosque in North America, opened in 1992, is the Ahmadi Baitul Islam mosque in the Toronto suburb of Maple.

Modernist Reformers

As the nineteenth century opened, European influence in the Muslim world was growing. Napoleon, who landed on Egyptian shores in 1798, brought with him not only soldiers, but also scholars and the printing press; in this way the Middle East discovered Europe. The great Ottoman Empire, which in the early decades of the sixteenth century had threatened Vienna, had by the nineteenth become 'the sick man of Europe'. Meanwhile the British Empire was extending its rule in India and its control over much of the Muslim world.

Muslim thinkers everywhere were awed by the West and resentful of the political inertia into which the Muslim *ummah* had apparently fallen. Even so, many areas of the Islamic east did experience an intellectual and cultural revival in the nineteenth century. Egypt, for instance, was the home of an Arab intellectual renaissance. Owing to unsettled social and political conditions in the Levant, a number of Western-educated Syro-Lebanese Christians immigrated to Egypt, where they established newspapers and cultural journals and participated actively in the recovery of the Arabo-Islamic heritage.

The Arab renaissance of the nineteenth century was largely stimulated by the cultural and intellectual flowering that was taking place in the West. Undermined first by the Protestant Reformation and then by the Enlightenment, religious faith and institutions were now giving way to secularism and romantic nationalism. These ideas similarly appealed to eastern Mediterranean Muslims, and in the end they led to the rise of Arab nationalism. The same ideas also influenced Muslims in other regions, so that nationalistic identities came to compete with, and in some cases even supersede, Islamic identities.

These and other Western influences were reinforced by the proliferation of Western Christian missionary schools and institutions of higher learning throughout the Muslim world. In short, Islamic reform movements of the nineteenth and twentieth centuries in Asia, Africa, and the Middle East arose in a context of widespread cultural and intellectual ferment.

The Indian Subcontinent

With the demise of the Mughal Empire in the seventeenth century, calls for reform along traditional lines intensified. One of the strongest voices for reform was that of Ahmad Sirhindi (1564–1624), who called for a return to the *shari'ah*, regarded Sufis as deviants, and condemned Ibn 'Arabi in particular as an infidel.

The most important movement of Islamic reform on the Indian subcontinent in modern times was begun by Shah Wali Allah of Delhi (1702–62). Although he was a disciple of Ibn 'Abd al-Wahhab, he was a Sufi himself, and instead of rejecting Sufism he sought to reform it. Shah Wali Allah was a moderate reformer with encyclopedic learning. He rejected the legal principle of blind imitation of earlier jurists (*taqlid*) and called for reopening the door of *ijtihad*. He also attempted to reconcile Shi'i–Sunni differences, which had been (and are still sometimes) a source of great friction on the Indian subcontinent in particular.

Shah Wali Allah's grandson Ahmad Barelwi (1786–1831), however, transformed his program into a *jihad* movement against British rule and the Sikhs. In 1826 he established an Islamic state based on the *shari'ah* and adopted the old caliphal title 'commander of the faithful'. Although he was killed in battle in 1831, his *jihad* movement lived on. For Barelwi, India ceased to be an Islamic domain after the end of Mughal rule, and therefore Muslims should wage a *jihad* to liberate it. If independence from infidel sovereignty was not possible, Muslims should undertake a religious migration (*hijrah*) to an area where Muslims did rule.

The shock that Indian Muslims suffered with the consolidation of British rule was intensified by the fact that the British tampered with Islamic law itself. The result was the interesting code—a mixture of Islamic law and Western humanistic rulings—known as Anglo-Muhammadan law.

At the opposite end of the spectrum of reaction to British rule from *jihad* movements like Barelwi's was the approach of Sayyid Ahmad Khan (1817–98). Like all reformers, Khan called for modern *ijtihad* or rethinking of the Islamic heritage, but unlike most of them he rejected *hadith* tradition as a legitimate basis for modern Islamic living. He founded the Aligarh Muhammadan College (later Aligarh Muslim University), where he attempted to apply his ideas in a modern Western-style program of education.

Muhammad Iqbal

The ideas of Sayyid Ahmad Khan and his fellows culminated in the philosophy of Muhammad Iqbal (1876–1938), the greatest Muslim thinker of modern India. Central to Iqbal's work is the idea of an inner spirit that moves human civilization.

Iqbal argued that Western science and philosophy were rightfully part of the Islamic heritage and should be integrated into a fresh 'Reconstruction of Religious Thought in Islam' (the title of his only major work in English, published in the 1930s). This call for a dynamic rethinking of Islamic faith and civilization is frequently repeated in Iqbal's philosophical or mystical Urdu and Persian poetry.

Twentieth-Century Secularism

Many of the early Muslim reformers were at once liberal modernists and traditional thinkers. For this reason they are known as *salafis*: reformers who sought to emulate the example of 'the pious forebears' (*al-salaf al-salih*). This important ideal of equilibrium between tradition and modernity disappeared by the 1920s. Thereafter, Islamic reform meant either revivalism, apologetics, or secularism.

Following the Ottoman defeat in the First World War, a young army officer named Mustafa Kemal Atatürk (1881–1938) launched a movement for national liberation. After gaining power, he abolished the caliphate in 1924, transforming the Turkish state from a traditional Islamic domain into a modern secular republic of which he became the first president. Although for centuries the caliphate had been a shadowy office without any power, it had nevertheless embodied the only hope for a viable pan-Islamic state. Its disappearance therefore had far-reaching consequences for Islamic political thought.

Atatürk banned Sufi orders, dissolved Islamic religious institutions, replaced the Arabic alphabet (in which Turkish had traditionally been written) with the Latin, and mounted a nationwide campaign for literacy in the new script. His express aim was to westernize the Turkish republic and cut it off from its Islamic past. He encouraged the adoption of Western-style clothing and even went so far as to ban the fez—the brimless conical red hat that, like all traditional Muslim headgear, allowed the faithful to touch their foreheads to the ground during prayer.

Though Atatürk's ideology has remained the official state policy in Turkey, his program largely failed, for the people's Islamic roots were not easily destroyed. Islamic faith and practice remain strong among the people of Turkey, and the country has its own powerful revivalist movements.

Twentieth-Century Islamic Revivalism

Islamic reform movements generally seem to have experienced a loss of nerve after the international upheavals of the First World War and the break-up of the Ottoman empire. Despite their differences, the various reform movements of the nineteenth century shared a dynamic and courageous spirit of progress. The premature stifling of that spirit may have reflected the lack of a coherent program of reform that post-colonialist Muslim thinkers could implement or build upon. In any event, the liberal reform movements of the nineteenth century were transformed in the twentieth into traditional revivalist movements.

On the eve of Atatürk's abolition of the caliphate in 1924, Muhammad Rashid Rida (1865–1935) published an important treatise on the Imamate or Supreme Caliphate in which he argued for the establishment of an Islamic state that would be ruled by a council of jurists or religious scholars. Such a state would recognize nationalistic sentiments and aspirations, but would subordinate them to the religio-political interests of the larger community. Rida's Islamic revivalism and Arab nationalism came to represent a major trend in twentieth-century Muslim thinking, and his political plan for a council of jurists would be implemented in Iran following the revolution of 1978–9.

Contemporary Revivalist Movements

It remains the ideal of Islamic reform to establish a transnational Islamic caliphate. The reality, however, has been a proliferation of local movements reflecting local needs and ideas.

Common to most revivalist movements in the second half of the twentieth century was the ideal of an all-inclusive and self-sufficient Islamic order. This ideal had its roots in the Society of Muslim Brothers (Jam'iyat al-Ikhwan al-Muslimin), founded in 1928 by an Egyptian schoolteacher named Hasan al-Banna (1906–49). The aim of this society was to establish a network of Islamic social, economic, and political institutions through which the total Islamization of society might in time be achieved. Working through social and educational facilities such as schools, banks, cooperatives, and clinics, the Muslim Brothers penetrated all levels of Egyptian society.

The political and militaristic aspects of revivalism also had their beginnings in the Muslim Brothers, particularly after the assassination of the populist and generally peaceful al-Banna in 1949. He was succeeded by hard-line leaders who advocated active *jihad* against the Egyptian state system, which they regarded as un-Islamic. Among the products of the Muslim Brothers' ideology were the young officers, led by Gamal Abdel Nasser, behind the 1952 socialist revolution that abolished monarchical rule in Egypt.

A charismatic proponent of Arab nationalism in the 1950s and 1960s, Nasser nevertheless clashed with the Muslim Brothers, and in the mid-1960s he imprisoned, exiled, or executed most of their leaders. One of those leaders was Sayyid Qutb, who is important as a link to modern Islamist groups. As a theoretician he influenced Islamist ideology; and as an activist whose defiance of the state led to his execution he provided younger militants with a model of martyrdom to emulate. Following the Arab defeat in the six-day Arab–Israeli war of June 1967 and the death of Nasser three years later, the Muslim Brothers were driven underground and superseded by more powerful revivalist movements under Anwar Sadat and his successor Hosni Mubarak, some of which advocated the use of violence to achieve their goals. Although driven underground in Egypt, the Brotherhood has spread in other Arab countries; but in exile, without its social infrastructure, it has been more influential on the level of ideology than of social action. A similar organization, the Jama'at-i Islami (Islamic Society), was established in 1941 by Mawlana Sayyid Abu al-A'la Mawdudi (1903–79). Like Hasan al-Banna', Mawdudi was committed to pan-Islamic unity. But also like al-Banna', he concentrated his efforts on his own community—in this case the Muslims of India and (after 1947) Pakistan. The influence of both organizations spread far beyond their original homes.

While most contemporary revivalist movements, including the two organizations noted above, have been open to modern science and technology, they have rejected many Western values and practices—including capitalist democracy, women's liberation, and the free mixing of the sexes—as decadent. Therefore, unlike the nineteenth-century reformers who looked to the West for ideas and models, contemporary revivalist reformers have insisted on finding Islamic alternatives. Mawdudi, for example, wishing to distinguish his Islamic state model from Western democracies, described it as a 'theo-democracy' based on the broad Qur'anic principle of consultation (*shura*) and the *shari'ah* law.

State Islam and the Islamic Revolution

Following a coup in 1969, Gaafar Mohamed el-Nimeiri (r. 1971–85) made *shari'ah* the law in Sudan. The result was a bloody conflict between the Muslim north and the generally Christian south that has continued for decades, reducing a formerly rich agricultural country to famine. Similarly in Pakistan, which for three decades had been a constitutionally Islamic but modern state, the introduction of *shari'ah*—by General Mohammad Zia-ul-Haq (1924–88) following a coup in 1977—led to violent social and political conflict.

In Egypt and Algeria revivalist movements continue to resort to violent means in their quest to establish Islamic states. Again, the results are social strife and instability.

In almost every Muslim country there is at least one revivalist movement advocating some form of Islamic state. In countries like Malaysia and Indonesia, the governments themselves espouse Islamic national policies in order to silence extremist demands for radical reform. Nevertheless, in most Muslim countries feelings continue to run high between Islamic movements made up of educated middle-class men and women and despotic regimes determined to hold on to power at any cost.

In such highly charged social and political conditions, religion serves as a powerful moral, social, and spiritual expression of discontent—not only for Islamic activists, but for a broad spectrum of the community as well. It was on precisely such mass discontent that Imam Ruhollah Khomeini (1901–89) and his fellow Shi'i mullahs (religio-legal functionaries) built the Islamic republic of Iran, in which social, political, economic, and religious life are all under the control of a religious hierarchy headed by a supreme Ayatollah (*ayat Allah*, 'sign of God').

Throughout the long period of Shi'i secular rule in Iran (1501–1979), the authority of the religious *'ulama'* operated in more or less continuous tension with the secular authorities. This tension was greatly increased during the reign of Shah Mohammad Reza Pahlavi (r. 1941–79), who sought to westernize the country and obscure its Islamic identity by emphasizing Iran's pre-Islamic cultural past. In 1963, during the Muharram observances of Husayn's martyrdom, matters came to a head when the Shah's dreaded secret police ruthlessly put down mass demonstrations led by the *'ulama'*. Khomeini, already a prominent religious leader, was sent into exile, where he elaborated his religio-political theory, according to which the jurist should have all-embracing authority in the community.

In 1979 Khomeini returned to Iran at the head of the Islamic revolution. The Islamic republic he founded has had a turbulent history, including an eight-year war with Iraq (1980–8), out of which it emerged greatly weakened but still intact. The dramatic assassinations and other acts of sabotage that the Mujahidin-i Khalq opposition carried out also had their effect. But in the absence of an alternative program, and with the popular support that the religious establishment in Iran has continued to enjoy, the 'authority of the jurist' remains unchallenged.

Islam in Western Europe

The Islamic presence in western Europe began with the establishment of Umayyad rule in southern Spain in 711. Commercial, political, and cultural relations were initiated with both Latin and Byzantine states, but medieval Europe would not tolerate a permanent Muslim community on its soil. The campaign to drive the Muslims out of Spain succeeded in 1492 with the conquest of Granada. As a result, the Muslim communities in western Europe today are a relatively recent phenomenon.

In the twentieth century some Muslims migrated to Europe from various colonies as students, visitors, and merchants. Many also went as menial labourers and factory workers, especially after the Second World War. The majority of these post-war immigrants were men ranging in age from their teens to their forties.

The ethnic make-up of the Muslim communities in Europe was largely determined by colonial ties. Muslims from the French colonies in North Africa, for example, went to France. Indian and, later, Pakistani and Bangladeshi Muslims tended to go to Britain. Those from Turkey and the former Soviet Turkic republics went to Germany and the Netherlands, while Bosnians went to Austria. These patterns were established in the early decades of the twentieth century and continued in spite of many restrictions.

Muslim communities in Europe tend to reflect ethnic and linguistic rather than sectarian affiliations. In recent years hundreds of mosques and cultural centres have been established in European cities, and Muslim communities have become a dynamic religious and intellectual force in European society. France (where it is expected that Muslims will constitute half the population within a few decades) and Britain no longer confine Muslims to the status of 'guest workers', as most other European countries do. Yet even there, the long histories of European racism, ethnocentrism, and colonialism have ensured that many Muslims continue to be treated as second-class citizens. This has created serious problems.

After the Islamic revolution of 1978–9, many Iranians also immigrated to Europe, adding yet another layer of ethnic and religious diversity to European Muslim society. Likewise, the 15-year Lebanese civil war of 1975–90, as well as the disturbances in other Arab countries, including the Gulf War of 1991, sent many political and economic refugees to the West. Intermarriage and conversion have also infused new blood into the Muslim community in the Western world.

Many European-born Muslims of foreign parentage are assimilating into European society and culture. On the other hand, most European countries have taken legal measures to limit immigration, and since the mid-1980s a number of them have repatriated some of their Muslim immigrants. Such actions may have been prompted in part by economic considerations, but also perhaps by nationalistic fears that Muslim immigrants might alter the social and ethnic character of these countries. At the same time, European discrimination against ethnic minorities and the Islamic awakening precipitated by the Iranian revolution have made Muslims more aware of their own religious and cultural identity.

Islam in North America

When the first Muslims arrived on American shores is a matter of conjecture. Suggestions that Muslims from Spain and West Africa may have sailed to America long before Columbus should not be discounted, but they are far from conclusive. It is very likely that the fall of Granada in 1492 and the harsh treatment imposed on Muslims and Jews by the Inquisition led many to flee to America soon after Columbus's historic voyage. Scattered records point to the presence of Muslims in Spanish America before 1550.

In the sixteenth and seventeenth centuries, hundreds of thousands of Africans were taken as slaves to the Spanish, Portuguese, and British colonies in the Americas. Although the majority were from West Africa, Muslims made up at least 20 per cent of the total. And among the slaves taken from Senegal, Nigeria, and the western Sudan, the majority were Muslims, many of whom were well educated in Arabic and the religious sciences. Some were able to preserve their faith and heritage, and some tried to maintain contacts with Muslims in their home areas, but many others were quickly absorbed into American society, adopting their masters' religion and even family names.

Islamic customs and ideas can still be traced in the African-American community, and today efforts are underway to reconstruct the story behind them from slave narratives, oral history, and other archival materials, including observations by white travellers of some Islamic activities in the mid-1800s.

Beginning in the late nineteenth century, African-Americans made conscious efforts to recover their Islamic heritage. In the early 1930s, Elijah Muhammad (born Elijah Poole, 1897–1975) became a follower of Wallace D. Fard (1877?–1934?) and founded the Nation of Islam in America. He saw Islam as a religion of Black people only, misrepresenting the universalistic and non-racial nature of Islam. However, his sons and successors, after travelling in the Muslim world and observing the international and multiracial character of the *hajj* pilgrimage, have drawn closer to classical Islam. African-American Muslims often refer to themselves as Bilalians, after Bilal, an African companion of the Prophet's time and community. Islam continues to be the fastest-growing religion in America, particularly among African-Americans.

Before the revival of Islam in the African-American community early in the twentieth century, Muslims, mainly from Syria and Lebanon, came to the United States and

Canada in small numbers. These early immigrants were uneducated men who came to North America intending to earn money and then return home. Instead, many married Canadian or American women and were soon completely assimilated.

The first Muslim missionary in America was Muhammad Alexander Webb (d. 1916), a jeweller, newspaper editor, and diplomat who was converted to Islam while travelling in India. On his return, Webb created an Islamic propaganda movement, wrote three books on Islam, and founded a periodical, *The Muslim World* (not to be confused with the academic journal of the same name). He travelled widely to spread the new faith and established Islamic study circles or Muslim brotherhoods in many northeastern and midwestern American cities. When Webb died, however, his movement died with him.

The numbers of Muslim immigrants coming to Canada and the United States increased markedly during the twentieth century. Most were of South Asian origin. Many were students who later chose to stay, or well-educated professionals who immigrated in search of better opportunities. But others came to escape persecution in their homelands on account of their religious or political activities. Interestingly, many recent newcomers have arrived as staunch anti-Western revivalists but soon forgotten their hostility and taken up life as peaceful, responsible, and law-abiding citizens.

Although these and other religiously committed Muslim immigrants may have moderated their political convictions, they retained a high degree of religious zeal, which they put to good use in the service both of their own community and of the society at large. They have played a crucial role in preserving the Islamic identity of fellow immigrants and promoting a better understanding of Islam through media activities and academic meetings.

The first mosque in the United States was built in 1915 by Albanian Muslims in Maine; another followed in Connecticut in 1919. Other mosques were established in the 1920s and 1930s in South Dakota and Iowa. In 1928 Polish Tatars built a mosque in Brooklyn, New York, which is still in use. The first Canadian mosque was built in Edmonton, Alberta, in 1938, and a number of smaller towns in Alberta also have Muslim communities. In Toronto, the first Muslim organization was the Albanian Muslim Society of Toronto, founded in 1956. In 1968 this organization purchased an unused Presbyterian church and converted it into a mosque. Toronto currently has Canada's largest Muslim population.

The exact numbers of Muslims in Canada and the United States are a matter of debate. The 2001 Canadian census counted almost 600,000 Muslims, making Islam the second largest religion in the country. The United States has not had a religious census since 1936, but the current Muslim population there is estimated to be between 6 and 8 million. Whatever the numbers may be, Islam in North America is no longer an exotic rarity: it is the faith of many people's co-workers and neighbours.

Women and the Family

Islam strictly forbade the practice of female infanticide, and required that those who had killed their daughters in pre-Islamic times make expiation for such a heinous act. The Qur'an states that on the Day of Resurrection, it will be asked of the child who was buried alive, 'For what sin was she slain?' (Q. 81:8–9). Victims are to be vindicated and recompensed on the Day of Judgement for the wrong done them in this life.

Marriage under Islam, as before it, is essentially a contractual relationship negotiated between the prospective husband and the woman's father or guardian. But the Qur'an emphasizes that the contract is essentially between the husband and wife, based on mutual consent: the woman's father or guardian, 'he in whose hand is the tie of marriage' (Q. 2:237), is expected to act on her behalf and, ideally, in her interest. Divorce is allowed, but only as a last resort, to be used only after all efforts to save the marriage have been tried and have failed.

The Qur'an allows polygyny (simultaneous marriage to more than one wife). But it places two significant restrictions on such marriages. First, it limits to four the number of wives that a man can have at one time, whereas before Islam the number was unlimited. Second, it demands strict justice and equality in a man's material and emotional support for all his wives. If this is not possible, the Qur'an stipulates, 'then only one'. It also maintains that 'You cannot act equitably among your wives however much you try.' As a result, the vast majority of Muslim marriages are monogamous, not polygamous (Q. 4:3 and 129).

Even more significantly, the Qur'an changes the nature of polygyny from an entitlement to a social responsibility. The verses dealing with this subject open with the proviso, 'If you [men] are afraid that you would not act justly towards the orphans [in your care], then marry what seems good to you of women: two, three, or four' (Q. 4:3). This statement may be interpreted in two ways. It may mean that a man could marry the widowed mother of orphans in order to provide a family for them. It may also mean that a man could marry two, three, or four orphan girls after they have attained marriageable age, again to provide a home and family for them. In either case, marriage to more than one wife is explicitly allowed by the Qur'an as a way of providing for female orphans and widows in a traditional society beset with continuous warfare, where a woman could find the love and security she needs only in her own home.

In addition the Qur'an allows women to own property and dispose of it as they please. Women may acquire property through bequest, inheritance, and bride dowry. To be sure, judged by today's social and economic needs and circumstances, these rights may seem inadequate. Yet, as Muslims regularly assert, the Qur'an undeniably recognizes in women a human dignity and a social and emotional personality that were denied until recently in many societies.

Islamic law and social custom, however, have been not been so generous and forward-looking. In general, they have tended either to restrict the rights laid out in the Qur'an or to render them virtually inoperative. Of the many social and political questions currently at issue in the Muslim community, one of the most important is the age-old question of women's rights, with all its ramifications.

The Qur'an does not refer at all to the *hijab* or veiling of women as we have it today. It only demands that women avoid wearing jewellery and that they dress modestly; and in the very next verse it also demands modesty of males. However, we can see from the *hadith* that the Muslim community adopted the practice of *hijab* during the time of the caliphate, probably under the influence of eastern Christian and ancient Greek usage. An extreme manifestation of the practice has been the seclusion of women, which is also attributable to these non-Arab influences. It became a hallmark of Turkish life especially in the *harim* system of the Ottoman aristocracy and court.

In the twentieth-century Muslim world and in the West, the *hijab* has come to symbolize for some an affirmation of women's Islamic identity and for others a limitation of their rights. The question at issue is whether and to what extent women can be excluded from public life. Increasingly, social and economic conditions throughout the world call for equal participation and equal rights for women and men alike. We can expect that women's rights will continue to be a major topic of debate in the worldwide Muslim community.

Islam and the Future

A major development in the history of Islam is now underway in the West. Muslims who, through migration, have moved from majority to minority status are being spurred to define the priorities of their faith. Their decisions about what to pass on to their Western-born children will shape the contours of Islam in the twenty-first century and beyond. At the same time, the Western emphasis on open discussion calls on Muslims from different cultural and regional backgrounds to work out a keener and clearer sense of what they do and do not share. Perhaps Muslims living in the West will use Western technology and democratic institutions to revitalize the Muslim communities in their countries of origin, as well as the rest of the Muslim *ummah*. The speed of modern travel and communications may contribute to this process.

For a time it seemed that political developments might contribute to it as well. Many hoped that the end of the cold war in 1989 and the moves made in the 1990s towards ending the long and bitter conflict between Israelis and Palestinians might allow for better relations between the Western and Muslim worlds in general. But the Israeli–Palestinian conflict has only deepened, and new conflicts have emerged over the past few years.

One major factor in the latter development was the Iranian revolution of 1979. A second can be traced to the same year, when the Soviet Union invaded Afghanistan. Muslims from around the world volunteered to fight with the Afghans for their liberation, and the United States contributed heavily to their training. They were called *mujahidin* (the word is derived from *jihad*), and at the time—before the end of the cold war—they were seen as 'freedom fighters' by much of the world, including the American president, Ronald Reagan.

Among the other contributors to Afghanistan's 'holy war' was Osama bin Laden (b. 1957), the son of a wealthy Saudi Arabian family, who created Al-Qaeda ('the base') to help fund and train *mujahidin*. The Soviet troops were withdrawn in 1988. But Al-Qaeda was not disbanded. In 1996 bin Laden issued a *fatwa* (religious legal opinion) calling for the overthrow of the Saudi government and the removal of US forces in Arabia, and in 1998 he declared war against Americans generally. A series of terrorist actions followed, culminating in the attacks on the United States of 11 September 2001. In response, the United States and its allies went to war, first in Afghanistan and then in Iraq.

Muslims around the world have repeatedly condemned terrorist activity. Muslim leaders have pointed out that the use of suicide bombers violates mainstream Islamic teachings that prohibit both suicide and the killing of civilians during war, and in March

Mecca Home to the Ka'ba, the first place of monotheistic worship. Also the place where Muhammad was born and received his first revelations.

Medina The home of the first Muslim community and the place where Muhammad was buried.

Jerusalem The area of the ancient city called Haram al-Sharif (the 'Noble Sanctuary'; also known to Jews and Christians as the Temple Mount) contains two sacred buildings: the Masjid al-Aqsa—the 'farthest mosque', from a passage in the Qur'an (17:1) referring to Muhammad's miraculous journey—and the Dome of the Rock, a sanctuary built on the spot from which tradition says Muhammad made his ascent to heaven.

Karbala The city in Iraq where Imam Husayn (the third Imam and the grandson of Muhammad) was martyred; of special importance to Shi'i Muslims.

Cairo Home of Al-Azhar University, the oldest university in the Western world and an important centre of Sunni learning.

Istanbul Captured by the Turkish ruler Muhammad II in 1453, Istanbul had been called Constantinople under the Byzantines. It became the capital of the Ottoman Turkish Empire and the centre of the sultan's power. It contains many imperial buildings, including the famous Topkapi Palace and the Western-influenced Dolma Bace Palace.

2005, on the first anniversary of the 2004 Al-Qaeda train bombing in Madrid, Spanish clerics issued a *fatwa* against bin Laden himself. Unfortunately, extremists seem impervious to mainstream Muslim opinion.

Muslims can accomplish much in the West if they work with their non-Muslim neighbours to promote justice and moral consciousness. But many non-Muslims see 'Islam' and 'the West' as mutually exclusive realities, and do not recognize their shared heritage. If future generations of Muslims are to remain active as Muslims in pluralistic Western societies, it is more important than ever to change old images and ideas.

Glossary

caliph From the Arabic *khalifah* ('one who represents or acts on behalf of another'). The Caliph was the Prophet's successor as the head of the Muslim community; the position became institutionalized in the form of the caliphate, which lasted from 632 to 1924.

dhikr 'Remembering' God's name; chanted in Sufi devotional exercises, sometimes while devotees dance in a circle.

dhimmis 'Protected people': non-Muslim religious minorities (specifically Jews and Christians, as 'People of the Book') accorded tolerated status in Islamic society.

Eid al-Fitr The holiday celebrating the end of the Ramadan fast; the festival traditionally begins following the sighting of the new moon.

Fatihah The short opening *surah* of the Qur'an, recited at least 17 times every day.

fatwa A ruling issued by a traditional religio-legal authority.

fiqh Jurisprudence, or the theoretical principles underpinning the specific regulations contained in the *shari'ah*.

Hadith The body of texts reporting Muhammad's words and example, taken by Muslims as a foundation for conduct and doctrine; a *hadith* is an individual unit of the literature.

hajj The annual pilgrimage to Mecca.

halal Ritually acceptable; most often used in the context of the slaughter of animals for meat; also refers to generally to Muslim dietary regulations.

hanifs 'Pious ones'; a group of pre-Islamic Arabs who shared the ethical monotheism of Jews and Christians.

haram 'Forbidden', used especially of actions; similar in its connotations to 'taboo'.

hijab A woman's veil or head covering.

hijrah The Prophet's migration from Mecca to establish a community in Medina in 622 CE. In dates, the abbreviation AH stands for 'year of the *hijrah*' (the starting-point of the Islamic dating system).

ijma' The consensus of religio-legal scholars; one of the two secondary principles used in jurisprudence; some legal schools give it more weight than others.

ijtihad Personal reasoning applied to the development of legal opinions.

imam The person who leads the prayer when two or more Muslims pray together; Shi'a also use the term to refer to the legitimate leader of the Muslim community after Muhammad.

Imamis ('Twelvers') Shi'a who recognize twelve imams as legitimate heirs to the Prophet's authority; the last, in occultation since 874, is expected to return some day as the **Mahdi**.

Isma'ilis ('Seveners') Shi'a who recognize only seven Imams; named after the last of them, Isma'il, whose lineage continues to the present in the Aga Khan.

isnad The pedigree or chain of transmission of a *hadith*, with which each one begins.

jihad Struggle in defence of the faith; some *jihads* are military, waged in response to threats to the community's security or welfare; others are spiritual, waged to improve moral conduct in society.

kufr Rejecting belief; implies lack of gratitude for God's grace.

Mahdi The Shi'i twelfth Imam, understood in his role as the 'rightly guided one' who will emerge from hiding at some unspecified future date to restore righteousness and order to the world.

mi'raj The Prophet's miraculous night journey from Mecca to Jerusalem.

mu'adhdhin The person who calls people to prayer.

qiblah The direction of prayer, marked in mosques by a niche inside the wall nearest Mecca.

Ramadan The month throughout which Muslims fast during daylight hours.

sadaqah Alms given voluntarily, in addition to the required *zakat*.

salat The prescribed daily prayers, said five times during the day.

shahadah The Muslim profession of faith in God as the only god and in Muhammad as God's prophet.

shari'ah The specific regulations of Islamic law; see also *fiqh*.

shaykh The Arabic term for a senior master, especially in the context of Sufism.

Shi'a Muslims who trace succession to the Prophet's authority through imams in the lineage of 'Ali; the smaller of the two main divisions of Islam, accounting for about one-sixth of all Muslims today.

sunnah The 'life-example' of Muhammad's words and deeds, based mainly on the *Hadith* literature; after the Qur'an, the primary source of guidance for Muslims.

Sunni Muslims who trace succession to the Prophet's authority through the caliphate, which lasted until the twentieth century; the larger of the two main divisions of Islam, accounting for about five-sixths of all Muslims today.

surah A chapter of the Qur'an; there are 114 in all, arranged mainly in decreasing order of length except for the first (the *Fatihah*).

tafsir Commentary on the Qur'an.

taqlid Following the *ijtihad* or legal opinion of a particular jurist.

ummah The Muslim community.

zakat The prescribed welfare tax; 2.5 per cent of each Muslim's accumulated wealth, collected by central treasuries in earlier times but now donated to charities independently of state governments; see also *sadaqah*.

Further Reading

Ahmed, Leila. 1992. *Women and Gender in Islam: Historical Roots of a Modern Debate*. New Haven: Yale University Press. A frequently cited contribution on this topic.

Alvi, Sajida Sultana, et al., eds. 2003. *The Muslim Veil in North America: Issues and Debates*. Toronto: Women's Press. A good collection of essays about the issues surrounding *hijab*.

Coulson, N.G. 1964. *A History of Islamic Law*. Edinburgh: Edinburgh University Press. Traces the development of Islamic jurisprudence from its inception in the ninth century through to the influence of modern Western legal systems.

Encyclopedia of Islam, The. Rev. edn. 1963–. Leiden: E.J. Brill. (First published in 4 vols, 1913–38.) Vast and technical, but authoritative. Entries appear under Arabic head-words, sometimes in unfamiliar transliterations, and so pose a challenge for the beginner.

Esposito, John., ed. 1995. *The Oxford Encyclopedia of the Modern Islamic World*. New York: Oxford University Press. An indispensable reference.

Grabar, Oleg. 1973. *The Formation of Islamic Art*. New Haven: Yale University Press. Concentrates on Islamic art in the Middle East in the early Islamic centuries.

Haddad, Yvonne Y., and Jane I. Smith, eds. 1994. *Muslim Communities in North America*. Albany: State University of New York Press. Examines how Islamic tradition and identity are being spelled out in the modern Western diaspora.

Mottahedeh, Roy. 2002. *The Mantle of the Prophet: Religion and Politics in Iran*. Oxford: Oneworld Publications. One of the best single-volume studies of the events leading up to the Iranian revolution.

Peters, Francis E. 1994. *A Reader on Classical Islam*. Princeton: Princeton University Press. An anthology of historical source readings.

Qureshi, Emran, and Michael A. Sells, eds. 2003. *The New Crusades: Constructing the Muslim Enemy*. New York: Columbia. An excellent collection of essays on the representation of Islam and Muslim lives.

Safi, Omid, ed. 2003. *Progressive Muslims: On Justice, Gender and Pluralism*. Oxford: Oneworld. A collection of essays by Muslim scholars of Islam on these contemporary topics.

Schimmel, Annemarie. 1975. *Mystical Dimensions of Islam*. Chapel Hill: University of North Carolina Press. A survey of Sufism by one of its most respected Western interpreters.

Watt, W. Montgomery. 1962. *Islamic Philosophy and Theology*. Edinburgh: Edinburgh University Press. A masterly survey of Muslim religious intellectuals, especially in the first six centuries of Islam.

References

Arberry, Arthur J. trans. 1955. *The Koran Interpreted*. London: Allen and Unwin.

Nicholson, Reynold A. 1931. 'Mysticism'. In *The Legacy of Islam*, ed. T. Arnold and Alfred Guillaume, 210–38. London: Oxford University Press.

_____, trans. 1950. *Rumi: Poet and Mystic*. London: G. Allen and Unwin.

The Hindu Tradition

VASUDHA NARAYANAN

The earliest scriptures in the Hindu tradition are oral compositions called *shruti* ('that which was heard'); but the people who transmitted the sacred words were called *rishis* ('seers'). This dual emphasis on hearing and seeing the holy is typical of the Hindu tradition.

When Hindus make a pilgrimage or visit a temple, they go to see with devotion, to behold with faith, and to be seen (*darshana*) by the deity or holy teacher. But they also believe it is important to hear and to speak aloud. Reciting prayers, chanting, storytelling, singing devotional songs, meditating on a holy mantra: these are just some of the ways in which Hindus experience and enjoy the sacred words of their tradition. Through sight and sound, Hindus experience the divine.

'Hinduism'

It is hard to identify common denominators in Hinduism. While some texts and some deities are widely accepted, there is no single text, deity, or teacher that all Hindus would consider supremely authoritative. There is a corpus of holy works, but many non-literate Hindus may not even have heard of them. Similarly, there are many local deities with local names who may or may not be identified with pan-Indian gods. The Hindu tradition is in fact many traditions encompassing hundreds of communities and sectarian movements, each of which has its own hallowed canon, its own sacred place, and its own concept of the supreme deity.

The absence of a single authoritative text or supreme divinity reflects the fact that for most of their history the people we call Hindu did not consider themselves to belong to a single religious tradition. It was only in the colonial period, beginning in the eighteenth century, that the term 'Hinduism' came to be used to refer to the religion of the subcontinent's non-Muslim population. 'Hindu' and 'India' are both derived from 'Sind': the name of the region, now in Pakistan, of the river Sindhu (Indus).

Today Hindus make up roughly 80 per cent of India's population, and when they are asked about their religious identity they generally refer to their particular caste or community. An alternative term designating a comprehensive tradition is *sanatana dharma* ('eternal faith'), but it is normally used only in philosophical contexts and has little to do with local manifestations of the faith.

According to Indian law, the term 'Hindu' applies not only to those who belong to one of the Hindu 'denominations' such as Vira Shaiva or Brahmo Samaj, but also to 'any other person domiciled in the territories to which [the Hindu Family Act] extends who is *not a Muslim, Christian, Parsi or Jew by religion*' (italics added). In short, 'Hindu' has been a kind of default identity in India.

c. 2700 BCE	Evidence of Indus Valley civilization
c. 1750?–1500 BCE	Earliest Vedic compositions
c. 600 BCE	Production of *Upanishads*
c. 500 BCE	Production of Hindu epics begins
326 BCE	Greek armies in India under Alexander
c. 272 BCE	Accession of King Ashoka
c. 200 BCE	First contacts with Southeast Asia
c. 200 BCE–200 CE	Composition of *Bhagavad Gita*
c. 200 CE	Compilation of *Laws of Manu* and *Natya Sastra* completed
c. 500	Beginnings of tantric tradition
c. 700–900	Alvars and Nayanmars, Tamil *bhakti* poets
c. 700–800	Shankara's Advaita Vedanta
1017	Traditional birth date of Ramanuja, Vaishnava philosopher (d. 1137)
1100–1150	Angkor Wat built in Cambodia
1398	Traditional birth date of Kabir, North Indian *bhakti* poet (d. 1518)
c. 1400	Major endowments at Tirumala–Tirupati temple
1486	Birth of Chaitanya, Bengali Vaishnava *bhakti* leader (d. 583)
c. 1543	Birth of Tulsidas, North Indian *bhakti* poet (d. 1623)
1757	British rule established in Calcutta
1828	Ram Mohan Roy founds Brahmo Samaj
1836	Birth of Ramakrishna Paramahamsa (d. 1886)
1875	Dayananda Saraswati founds Arya Samaj
1893	Vivekananda attends World's Parliament of Religions in Chicago
1905–6	Vedanta Temple built in San Francisco
1926	Birth of Sathya Sai Baba
1977	Hindu temples consecrated in New York and Pittsburgh.

The very concept of religion in the Western, post-Enlightenment sense is only loosely applicable to the Hindu tradition. Hindus may consider many things—from astronomy and astrology to phonetics, music and dance, or plants—essential in the practice of their religion. While it would be impossible to do justice to all the subjects that fall under the rubric of the sacred for Hindus, the following discussion will include a number of features not usually covered by the word 'religion' in the Western world.

Origins

The origins of Hinduism have been much debated. The standard view in the early twentieth century was that it had grown from a fusion of the indigenous religions of the Indus Valley with the faith of the Aryans, an Indo-European people usually thought to have migrated there between 1750 and 1500 BCE. More recently, however, several different theories have been proposed.

The Harappa Culture

In 1926 excavations revealed the remains of several large towns on the banks of the Indus River in what is now Pakistan. Two of these towns, known today as Mohenjo Daro ('Mound of the Dead') and Harappa, were more than 480 km (300 mi.) apart. Yet archaeological evidence suggested a certain uniformity in the culture across the entire northwestern part of the subcontinent. Similar objects found in towns hundred of kilometres apart suggest continuous travel and communication between them, and although the culture is still widely identified with the Indus Valley, some scholars prefer to call it the Harappa culture because it extends well beyond the Indus basin itself.

It is believed that the towns were in existence by about 2750 BCE, though some historians push the dates back several centuries. Inscriptions on carved seals show that this culture had a written language; however, no one has yet been able to decipher the script with any assurance. What we do know is that the people of the Harappa civilization were impressive builders who lived in what appear to have been planned cities. In the citadel mound at Mohenjo Daro there is a huge swimming-pool-like structure (archaeologists call it 'the Great Bath'), surrounded by porticos and flights of stairs. The care with which the complex was built has led scholars to believe that it was designed for religious rituals of some sort. Some of the houses also appear to have included a room with a fire altar, suggesting a domestic fire ritual. Stone sculptures and terracotta statuettes of what looks like a mother goddess may have been used as icons in worship.

Approximately 2,000 flat seals and many amulets have been found in the excavations around the Indus River. A few of the seals represent a man seated on a low throne in what looks like a yoga posture. The man's headdress and the animals around him suggest that this figure may be a prototype of the deity that came to be known as Shiva. What happened to the Harappa civilization is not known. Some scholars think it was destroyed by Indo-European invaders from Central Asia around 1750 BCE. Other theories centre on flooding or epidemics. Perhaps a combination of these factors led to the

NUMBERS
Approximately nine hundred million to one billion around the world.

DISTRIBUTION
Primarily India; large numbers in the United States, Canada, and Western Europe, as well as many parts of South and Southeast Asia.

PRINCIPAL HISTORICAL PERIODS

c. 2500–600 BCE	Indus Valley civilization; composition of the Vedas
c. 500 BCE–1000 CE	Composition of epics and *Puranas*
600–1600	Devotional poetry in local languages
13th–18th centuries	northern India under Muslim rule
mid-1700s–1947	British colonial period

FOUNDERS AND LEADERS
Important early figures include Shankara, Ramanuja, Madhva, Vallabha, Ramananda, Chaitanya, Swami Narayanan, Ramakrishna, and Vivekananda. Among the hundreds of teachers who have attracted followings in the last century alone are Aurobindo, Ramana Maharishi, Maharishi Mahesh Yogi, Sathya Sai Baba, Anandamayi Ma, and Ma Amritananda Mayi.

DEITIES
Hindu philosophy recognizes one supreme being (the ineffable Brahman) who is not limited by gender and may take countless forms; classical rhetoric typically refers to 330 million. Some sectarian traditions identify the supreme deity as Vishnu, some as Shiva, and some as a form of the Goddess. The supreme being may be understood as male, female, androgynous, or beyond gender.

AUTHORITATIVE TEXTS
The Vedas are technically considered the most authoritative texts, though the epics (the *Ramayana* and the *Mahabharata*, including the *Bhagavad Gita*), the *Puranas*, and several works in regional languages have also been very important.

NOTEWORTHY TEACHINGS
In general, most Hindus recognize a supreme being, variously conceived—personal for some, impersonal for others. Most think of the human soul as immortal and believe that when it reaches liberation it will be freed from the shackles of karma and rebirth. Specific teachings vary depending on sectarian tradition, region, and community.

civilization's decline. All we can say with any certainty is that the Indo-European Vedic culture was dominant by about 1500 BCE.

The Indo-Europeans

Who were the Indo-Europeans? This question is still debated. 'Indo-European' or 'Indo-Aryan' ordinarily refers to the family of languages of which Sanskrit is one. Western scholars in the nineteenth century noted the similarities between some Indian and European languages and posited a theory of migration that would account for the resemblances. According to this theory, people from Central Asia began migrating to widely distant regions at some time between 2000 BCE and 1500 BCE. Some moved west and north into what is now Europe, from Ireland to Scandinavia. Others headed south or east and settled in the region of Iran; these people called themselves Aryans.

Other scholars think that the Indo-Europeans came from the region around modern Turkey, and that the migration may have begun as early as 6000 BCE. Still another school holds that the Indo-Europeans originated on the Indian subcontinent and moved from there into Europe. None of the evidence is conclusive, however, and some theories clearly reflect political, racial, religious, and nationalist agendas. What we do know is that the Indo-Europeans composed many poems and, eventually, manuals on rituals and philosophy. These traditions were carefully committed to memory using various mnemonic devices to ensure correct pronunciation, rhythm, and intonation, and passed from generation to generation by word of mouth.

The Vedas

The earliest surviving Indo-European compositions are the Vedas (from the Sanskrit for 'knowledge'); these are the works collectively known as *shruti* ('that which was heard'). The Vedic seers (*rishis*) 'saw' the mantras and transmitted them to their disciples, starting an oral tradition that has continued to the present.

Traditionally regarded as revealed scripture, the Vedas are now generally thought to have been composed between roughly 1750 BCE and 600 BCE. There are four Vedic collections: *Rig, Sama, Yajur,* and *Atharva*. Each of these collections in turn consists of four sections: hymns (*Samhitas*; the earliest parts), directions for the performance of sacred rituals (*Brahmanas*), 'compositions for the forest' (*Aranyakas*), and philosophical works called the *Upanishads* ('sitting near [the teacher])'.

The earliest section of the *Rig Veda* contains 1,028 hymns. The hymns of the *Sama Veda* and *Yajur Veda* are largely borrowed from the *Rig*, but the *Sama Veda* was meant to be sung in a specific manner. The *Upanishads*, composed around 600 BCE, are the most recent sections of each collection. The term 'Vedas' has been used in the Hindu tradition to denote the whole corpus: hymns, ritual treatises, and philosophical texts. Although Orientalists and Western Indologists have often used the term *Veda* to apply only to the hymns, the *Samhita* portion of each collection, this narrower sense of the term is generally not accepted by Hindus.

The Vedic Hymns

Some of the most important deities of later Hinduism, such as Narayana (Vishnu) and Sri (Lakshmi), are mentioned occasionally in the earliest hymns, but it is only in the later ones that they are directly addressed. Rather, the earliest *Samhitas* (c. 1500 BCE) are addressed to many gods (such as Varuna) who are not so familiar today. Agni, the god of fire, was seen as a messenger between human beings and the deities; thus offerings were placed in the fire to be carried to other worlds. The moon is identified as a male god called Soma, which was also the name of an intoxicating drink, extracted from plants, used in rituals. A goddess called Saraswati is also spoken of, sometimes as a river, sometimes as representing learning, but in later Vedic literature—the ritualistic sections called the *Brahmanas*—she is identified with the goddess Vac ('speech'). As Vac she is speech incarnate, the power of the word, and the mother of the Vedas. Most of the early hymns ask not for salvation or eternal bliss, but for a good and happy life on this earth.

Central to Vedic religious life was the ritual sacrifice (*yajna*). Both domestic and community sacrifices, ranging from the simple to the extremely complicated, were usually performed with a fire. We do not find any direct references to temples or temple worship in the Vedas. Sacrifices were conducted by ritual specialists and priests, who supervised the making of altars, sacrifice of animals, and recitation of hymns. Many sacrifices involved the making, offering, and drinking of *soma*.

The hymns composed around 1000 BCE include speculation on the origins of the universe and refer to a cosmic sacrifice that began creation. The *Hymn of Origins* expresses

---

| Box 5.1 | **The Creation Hymn, *Rig Veda* 10.129** |

There was neither non-existence nor existence then; there was neither the realm of space nor the sky which is beyond. What stirred? Where? In whose protection? Was there water, bottomlessly deep?

There was neither death nor immortality then. There was no distinguishing sign of night nor of day. That one breathed, windless, by its own impulse. Other than that there was nothing beyond.

Darkness was hidden by darkness in the beginning; with no distinguishing sign, all this was water. The life force that was covered with emptiness, that one arose through the power of heat.

Desire came upon that one in the beginning; that was the first seed of mind. Poets seeking in their heart with wisdom found the bond of existence in non-existence.

Their cord was extended across. Was there below? Was there above? There were seed-placers; there were powers. There was impulse beneath; there was giving-forth above.

Who really knows? Who will here proclaim it? Whence was it produced? Whence is this creation? The gods came afterwards, with the creation of this universe. Who then knows whence it has arisen?

Whence this creation has arisen—perhaps it formed itself, or perhaps it did not—the one who looks down on it, in the highest heaven, only he knows—or perhaps he does not know (Doniger O'Flaherty 1981:25-6).

wonder at the creation of the universe from nothing and ends with the statement that perhaps no one knows how it all came to be.

A delicate connection was seen between the rituals and the prevalence of cosmic and earthly order, or *rta*. *Rta* is truth and justice, the rightness of things. It makes harmony and peace possible in the earth and the heavens. Although it is an impersonal cosmic principle, it was upheld by Vedic gods like Varuna.

One set of verses that still figures in rituals today is the 'Hymn to the Supreme Person' (*Purusha Sukta*). In it the universe itself is said to have originated through a cosmic sacrifice in which the primeval man (Purusha) was offered. Straining to capture infinity in words, the composer uses the notion of 'a thousand' to denote all that cannot be measured or perhaps even imagined:

> (1) The cosmic person has a thousand heads
> a thousand eyes and feet
> It covers the earth on all sides
> and extends ten finger-lengths beyond
> (2) The cosmic person is everything
> all that has been and will be. . . .

Various elements of the universe are said to arise from this sacrifice:

> (13) From his mind came the moon
> from his eye, the sun
> Indra and Agni from his mouth
> the wind came from his breath.

> (14) From his navel came space
> from his head, the sky
> from his feet, earth;
> from his ears, the four directions
> thus the worlds were created.

In this context an idea is introduced that was to change forever the religious and social countenance of the Hindu tradition:

> (12) From his mouth came the priestly class
> from his arms, the rulers.
> The producers came from his legs;
> from his feet came the servant class.

Thus the origins of the four classes (*varnas*) of Hindu society are traced to this initial cosmic sacrifice. Though this verse is generally seen as the source of what came to be called the caste system, it is likely that the stratification of society had already taken place long before the *Rig Veda* was composed.

The Upanishads

By the time the *Aranyakas* and *Upanishads* were composed, in the seventh and sixth centuries BCE, the sacrificial world view of the early Vedic age had given way to critical philosophical inquiry. This period—a little before and perhaps during the lives of Gautama Buddha and the Jain teacher Mahavira—was a time of intellectual ferment, of questioning and rejecting authoritarian structures.

Yet the *Upanishads* do not totally reject the early hymns and sacrificial rituals. Instead, they rethink and reformulate them. Thus some rituals are interpreted allegorically, and the symbolic structures of the sacrifices are analyzed in some detail.

Most of the *Upanishads* take the form of conversations—between a teacher and a student, between a husband and wife, or between fellow philosophers. In the beginning of one study session a teacher exclaims: 'May we work with vigour; may our study illumine us both. May there be no discord between us. *Om.* Let there be peace, peace, peace' (*Taittiriya Upanishad* 11.1.1). After years of Veda instruction, a departing student receives moving advice from his guru (teacher):

> Speak the truth. Practice virtue. Do not neglect to study every day. Do not neglect truth, virtue, studying or teaching. . . . Be one to whom your mother is a god, your father is a god, your teacher is a god, a guest is like a god. . . . Give with faith . . . give liberally, give with modesty . . . give with sympathy. . . . This is the command. This is the teaching. This is the secret of the *Veda*. . . . (*Taittiriya Upanishad* 1.11.1–6).

Karma and samsara

It is in the *Upanishads* that we find the earliest discussions of several concepts central to the later Hindu tradition, among them the concept of karma. Karma literally means 'action', especially ritual action, but in these books it eventually comes to refer to a system of rewards and punishments attached to various actions. This system of cause and effect may require several lifetimes to work out. Thus the concept of karma implies a continuing cycle of death and rebirth or reincarnation called *samsara*. To achieve liberation (*moksha*) from this cycle, according to the *Upanishads*, requires a transforming experiential wisdom. Once that wisdom is attained one becomes immortal (*a-mrta*, 'without death').

A frequent theme of the *Upanishads* is the quest for a unifying truth. This 'higher' knowledge is clearly distinguished from the 'lower' knowledge that can be conceptualized and expressed in words. Its nature cannot be explained or taught: it can only be evoked, as in the question posed by the seeker in the *Mundaka Upanishad*: 'What is it that, being known, all else becomes known?' (1.1.3). The *Brhadaranyaka Upanishad* of the *Yajur Veda* reflects the quest for enlightenment in these lines:

> Lead me from the unreal to reality
> Lead me from darkness to light
> Lead me from death to immortality
> *Om,* let there be peace, peace, peace.

Significantly, in later centuries the 'higher wisdom' is not connected with any Vedic or book learning or conceptual knowledge. One is freed from the birth-and-death cycle only by the experience of enlightenment.

Atman and Brahman

At the heart of this wisdom is experiential knowledge of the relationship between the human soul (Atman) and the Supreme Being (Brahman). Brahman pervades and yet transcends not only human thought but the universe itself. Ultimately, Brahman cannot be described any more than infinity can be contained.

To know Brahman is to enter a new state of consciousness. The *Taittiriya Upanishad* associates Brahman with existence or truth (*satya*), knowledge (*jnana*), infinity (*ananta*), consciousness (*chit*), and bliss (*ananda*); elsewhere Brahman is described as the hidden, inner controller of the human soul and the frame over which the universe is woven.

The relationship between Atman and Brahman is discussed in many passages of the *Upanishads*, but invariably they suggest rather than specify the connection between the two. In one famous conversation in the *Chandogya Upanishad*, a father asks his son to dissolve salt in water and says that Brahman and Atman are united in a similar manner. The father ends his teaching with a famous dictum—*tat tvam asi* ('you are that')—in which 'that' refers to Brahman and 'you' to Atman. More than 1,000 years later, philosophers still differed in their interpretations of this passage. For Shankara in the eighth century, 'you are that' indicated that Brahman and Atman were identical. On the other hand, for Ramanuja in the eleventh century it meant that the two were inseparably united but not identical.

| Box 5.2   How Many Gods Are There?

Vidagha Shakalyah asked: 'Yajnavalkya, how many gods are there?'
He answered . . . in line with the ritual prayer, '. . . three hundred and three, and three and three thousand.'
'Yes, but Yajnavalkya, how many gods are there, really?'
'Thirty-three.'
'Yes, but really, how many gods are there, Yajnavalkya?'
'Six.'
'Yes, but really, how many gods are there, Yajnavalkya?'
'Three.' . . .
'Yes, but really, how many gods are there, Yajnavalkya?'
'One and a half.'
'Yes, but really, how many gods are there, Yajnavalkya?'
'One.'
'Yes, but who are those three hundred and three and three thousand and three?'
'They are but the powers/greatness of the gods; but there are only thirty-three gods' (*Brihadaranyaka Upanishad* 3.9.1–2; trans. Vasudha Narayanan).

We learn more of the relationship between Brahman and Atman elsewhere in the *Upanishads*. In some passages, the sage Yajnavalkya refers to Brahman as the hidden, inner controller of the human soul (Atman); in others, as the frame and the substance of the universe. In the latter analogy the reference is to a weaving loom: the universe is said to be woven over Brahman.

The *Upanishads* represent the beginnings of Hindu philosophical thought; in the opinion of some, they also represent the best. The quest for a unifying knowledge or higher wisdom is a recurring theme in various systems of Hindu philosophical reasoning, and continues to preoccupy thinkers today.

Women in the Vedas

Among the poets named in the early *Samhitas* were three women: Ghosa, Apala, and Lopamudra. Women participated in the quest for ultimate truth and sought salvific knowledge in both domestic and public forums. In the *Brihadaranyaka Upanishad*, Maitreyi, the wife of Yajnavalkya, questions him in depth about the nature of reality, and a woman philosopher named Gargi Vachaknavi challenges him in a public debate. Obviously, women like Gargi and Maitreyi, whose names appear in the *Upanishads* and elsewhere in the Vedas, were honoured and respected for their wisdom.

Other women are mentioned by name in the *Upanishads*' lists of those through whom the sacred teachings have been transmitted. In most cases it is the fathers of the

---

| Box 5.3 | Gargi Vachaknavi Questions Yajnavalkya

Then Vachaknavi said, 'Venerable Brahmanas, I shall ask him two questions. If he answers me these, none of you can defeat him in arguments about Brahman.' 'Ask, Gargi'[said he].

She said, 'As a warrior son of the Kasis or the Videhas might rise up against you, having strung his unstrung bow and having taken in his hand two pointed foe-piercing arrows, even so, O Yajnavalkya, do I face you with two questions. Answer me these.' 'Ask, Gargi.'

She said, 'That, O Yajnavalkya, of which they say, it is above the heaven, it is beneath the earth, that which is between these two, the heaven and the earth, that which the people call the past, the present and the future, across what is that woven, like warp and woof?'

He said, 'That which is above the heaven, that which is beneath the earth, that which is between these two, heaven and earth, that which the people call the past, the present, and the future, across space is that woven, like warp and woof.'

She said, 'Adoration to you, Yajnavalkya, who have answered this question for me. Prepare yourself for the other.' 'Ask, Gargi.'

She said, 'That, O Yajnavalkya, of which they say, it is above the heaven, it is beneath the earth, that which is between these two, the heaven and the earth, that which the people call the past, the present, and the future, across what is that woven like warp and woof?'

| Box 5.3 | *Continued*

He said, 'That which is above the sky, that which is beneath the earth, that which is between these two, sky and earth, that which the people call the past, the present, and the future, across space is that woven like warp and woof.'

He said, 'That, O Gargi, the knowers of Brahman call the Imperishable. It is neither gross nor fine, neither short nor long, neither glowing red (like fire) nor adhesive (like water). (It is) neither shadow nor darkness, neither air nor space, unattached, without taste, without smell, without eyes, without ears, without voice, without mind, without radiance, without breath, without a mouth, without measure, having no within and no without. It eats nothing and no one eats it.'

'Verily, at the command of that Imperishable, O Gargi, the sun and the moon stand in their respective positions. At the command of that Imperishable, O Gargi, heaven and earth stand in their respective positions. At the command of the Imperishable, O Gargi, what are called moments, hours, days and nights, half-months, months, seasons, years stand in their respective positions. At the command of that Imperishable, O Gargi, some rivers flow to the east from the white (snowy) mountains, others to the west in whatever direction each flows. By the command of that Imperishable, O Gargi, men praise those who give, the gods (are desirous of) the sacrificer and the fathers are desirous of the *darvi* offering.'

'Whosoever, O Gargi, in this world, without knowing this Imperishable performs sacrifices, worships, performs austerities for a thousand years, his work will have an end; whosoever, O Gargi, without knowing this Imperishable departs from this world, is pitiable. But, O Gargi, he who knowing the Imperishable departs from this world is a Brahmana (a knower of Brahman).

'Verily, that Imperishable, O Gargi, is unseen but is the seer, is unheard but is the hearer, unthought but is the thinker, unknown but is the knower. There is no other seer but this, there is no other hearer but this, there is no other thinker but this, there is no other knower but this. By this Imperishable, O Gargi, is space woven like warp and woof.'

She said, 'Venerable Brahmana, you may think it a great thing if you get off from him though bowing to him. Not one of you will defeat him in arguments about Brahman.' Thereupon [Gargi] Vachaknavi kept silent (*Brihadaranyaka Upanishad* 3.8; Radhakrishnan 1953:230–4).

---

teachers who are identified, but there are more forty-five instances where their mothers are identified instead. This suggests that those teachers received their early spiritual instruction from their mothers.

The Status of the Vedas

Almost all educated Hindus would point to the Vedas as their most sacred texts; yet many of them would be hard pressed to explain in any detail what they contain.

Millions of other Hindus through the centuries likely never heard of them. They are not books kept in people's houses, but ritual texts believed to have been passed down through the generations without change. A few of the Vedic hymns are recited regularly at temples and in homes, and the philosophical sections have been translated and commented upon frequently, but the rest of the Vedas are known only to a handful of specialists.

The Vedas are particularly significant to the brahmins, the priestly class that historically considered itself the 'highest' in Indian society. Commentators from some philosophical traditions considered the Vedas to represent 'eternal truth' and 'eternal sound', and to be coeval with God. All schools of medieval thought agreed that the Vedas were both transcendent and authoritative. They differed, however, on exactly what it meant to say that the Vedas were not of human origin (*apauruseya*; literally, 'superhuman'). Philosophers of the Nyaya ('logic') school believed that meant that God was the author of the Vedas and that, since God is perfect, the Vedas were infallible. Many other Hindu schools have not subscribed to this view, however. Two of them, still influential today, are the Mimamsa and Vedanta schools, which say that the Vedas are both eternal and of non-human authorship, but not created by God.

Although several works have been more popular among the masses than the Vedas, their theoretical, ritual, and epistemological significance has been unquestioned. Thus the highest honour for any Hindu religious text was to call it a 'fifth Veda'.

In the last 2,000 years this title has been accorded to several texts, including the *Mahabharata*, one of the two great Hindu epics; a collection of narratives called the *Puranas*; an important treatise on dance and performance called *Natya shastra*, composed around the beginning of the Common Era; the *Tiruvaymoli* ('sacred utterance') of Nammalvar in the ninth century; and the *Periya Puranam*, a collection of life stories of saints who were devotees of Shiva. These texts did not try to imitate the Vedas or to comment on them; rather, they were venerated because they embodied the eternal wisdom of the original four Vedas and made it accessible in a new place and time.

Crystallization

Classical Hinduism

The literature that was composed after the Vedas, starting around 500 BCE, was recognized as human in origin and loosely called *smrti* ('that which is remembered'). Though theoretically of lesser authority than the *shruti*, this material was nonetheless considered inspired, and it has played a far more important role in the lives of Hindus for the last 2,500 years. There are three types of *smrti*: epics (*itihasas*), ancient stories (*puranas*), and codes of law and ethics (*dharmasastras*). (The term *smrti* can also refer to the codes alone.)

For many Hindus the phrase 'sacred books' refers specifically to two epics, the *Ramayana* ('Story of Rama') and the *Mahabharata* ('Great Epic of India' or 'Great Sons of Bharata'). The best-known works in the Hindu tradition, these stories are told to children by their parents and invariably constitute their first and most lasting encounter with Hindu scripture.

The *Ramayana*

The *Ramayana* has been memorized, recited, sung, danced, enjoyed, and experienced emotionally, intellectually, and spiritually for the last 2,500 years. It has been a source of inspiration for generations of devotees in India and elsewhere. The epic is danced and acted in places of Hindu (and Buddhist) cultural influence throughout Southeast Asia. Its characters are well known as far away as Thailand and Indonesia.

The hero of the *Ramayana* is the young prince Rama, whose father, Dasaratha, has decided to abdicate in favour of his son. On the eve of the coronation, however, a heartbroken Dasaratha is forced to exile Rama because of an earlier promise made to one of his wives. Rama accepts cheerfully and leaves for the forest, accompanied by his beautiful wife, Sita, and his half-brother Lakshmana, who both refuse to be separated from him. Bharata, the brother who has now been named king, returns from a trip to discover that his brother has gone into exile and his father has died of grief. He finds Rama and begs him to return, but Rama refuses because he feels he must respect his father's decision to banish him. He asks Bharata to rule as his regent.

While in the forest, Sita is captured by Ravana, the demon king of Lanka. Rama, full of sorrow at being separated from his wife, sets out to search for her with the aid of his brother and a group of monkeys led by Hanuman, a monkey with divine ancestry. It is Hanuman who finds Sita and reports her whereabouts to Rama, who, with the monkeys' help, goes to war with Ravana. After a long battle, Rama kills Ravana and is reunited with Sita. They eventually return to the capital and are crowned. Rama is considered such a just king that *Ram rajya* ('kingdom or rule of Rama') is the Hindu political ideal.

Rama is also the ideal son and husband, at least in most of the story, and Sita as well has been idealized both for her own qualities and for her relationship with her husband. In a sequel to the *Ramayana*, however, Rama's subjects become suspicious about Sita's virtue following her captivity in Ravana's grove. Because there is no way of proving her innocence, and he does not want to create a legal precedent for excusing a wife who has slept outside the home, Rama banishes his own wife, who by now is pregnant.

The exiled Sita gives birth to twins. Some years later, the twins prepare to meet Rama in battle, and it is then that Sita tells them he is their father. There is a brief reunion. Rama asks Sita to prove her innocence in public by undergoing some ordeal, but Sita refuses and asks Mother Earth to take her back. She is then swallowed by the ground.

Many Hindus have seen Sita as the ideal wife because she follows her husband to the forest. Others see her as a model of strength and virtue in her own right. She complies with her husband as he does with her; their love is one worthy of emulation. Yet she is also a woman who stands her ground when asked by her husband to prove her virtue. On one occasion, in Lanka, she acquiesces, but the second time she gently but firmly refuses and so rules out any possibility of a reunion. There have been other versions of this tale called *Sita yana*, which tell the story from Sita's viewpoint. Even traditional commentators agree with the traditional saying 'Sitayas charitam mahat' ('The deeds of Sita are indeed great').

Rama is a paragon of human virtue, and in later centuries he came to be seen as an incarnation of the lord Vishnu. Temples dedicated to Rama and Sita are found in many parts of the world.

The *Mahabharata* and the *Bhagavad Gita*

With approximately 100,000 verses, the *Mahabharata* is said to be the longest poem in the world and is not found in many homes; many people, however, own copies of an extract from it called the *Bhagavad Gita*.

The *Mahabharata* is the story of the great (*maha*) struggle among the descendants of a king called Bharata. The main part of the story concerns a war between the Pandavas and the Kauravas. Though they are cousins, the Kauravas try to cheat the Pandavas out of their share of the kingdom and will not accept peace. A battle ensues in which all the major kingdoms are forced to take sides. Krishna, by this time considered to be the ninth incarnation of the god Vishnu, is on the side of the Pandavas. Though he refuses to take up arms, he nevertheless agrees to serve as charioteer for the warrior Arjuna, who in later centuries would come to be seen as symbolizing the human soul in quest of salvation.

Just as the war is about to begin, Arjuna, who has hitherto been portrayed as a hero emerging victorious from several battles, becomes distressed at the thought of fighting his relatives. Putting down his bow, he asks Krishna whether it is correct to fight a war in which many lives will be lost, especially against one's own kin. Krishna replies

---

| Box 5.4　**From the *Bhagavad Gita***

On the immortality of the soul:
Our bodies are known to end, but the embodied self is enduring, indestructible, and immeasurable; therefore, Arjuna, fight the battle!

He who thinks this self a killer and he who thinks it killed, both fail to understand it does not kill, nor is it killed.

It is not born, it does not die; having been, it will never not be; unborn, enduring, constant, and primordial, it is not killed when the body is killed. . . .

As a man discards worn-out clothes to put on new and different ones, so the embodied self discards its worn-out bodies to take on other new ones.

Weapons do not cut it, fire does not burn it, waters do not wet it, wind does not wither it. It cannot be cut or burned; it cannot be wet or withered; it is enduring, all-pervasive, fixed, immovable, and timeless. . . .

On the way of action:
Be intent on action, not on the fruits of action; avoid attraction to the fruits and attachment to inaction!

| Box 5.4 *Continued*

Perform actions, firm in discipline, relinquishing attachment; be impartial to failure and success—this equanimity is called discipline. . . .

Wise men disciplined by understanding relinquish the fruit born of action; freed from these bonds of rebirth, they reach a place beyond decay. . . .

When suffering does not disturb his mind, when his craving for pleasures has vanished, when attraction, fear, and anger are gone, he is called a sage whose thought is sure.

When he shows no preference in fortune or misfortune and neither exults nor hates, his insight is sure. . . .

On the mystery and purpose of incarnation:
Though myself unborn, undying, the lord of creatures, I fashion nature, which is mine, and I come into being through my own magic.

Whenever sacred duty decays and chaos prevails, then, I create myself, Arjuna.

To protect men of virtue and destroy men who do evil to set the standard of sacred duty, I appear in age after age. . . .

On the nature of God and the way of devotion:
Always glorifying me, striving, firm in their vows, paying me homage with devotion, they worship me, always disciplined. . . .

I am the universal father, mother, granter of all, grandfather, object of knowledge, purifier, holy syllable OM, threefold sacred love.

I am the way, sustainer, lord, witness, shelter, refuge, friend, source, dissolution, stability, treasure, and unchanging seed.

I am heat that withholds and sends down the rains; I am immortality and death; both being and nonbeing am I. . . .

Men who worship me, thinking solely of me, always disciplined, win the reward I secure.

When devoted men sacrifice to other deities with faith, they sacrifice to me, Arjuna, however aberrant the rites.

I am the enjoyer and the lord of all sacrifices; they do not know me in reality, and so they fail. . . .

The leaf or flower or fruit or water that he offers with devotion, I take from the man of self-restraint in response to his devotion.

Whatever you do—what you take, what you offer, what you give, what penances you perform—do as an offering to me, Arjuna!

You will be freed from the bonds of action, from the fruit of fortune and misfortune; armed with the discipline of renunciation, your self liberated, you will join me. . . .

If he is devoted solely to me, even a violent criminal must be deemed a man of virtue, for his resolve is right. . . .

Keep me in your mind and devotion, sacrifice to me, bow to me, discipline your self toward me, and you will reach me!

(Miller 1986:32–87)

that it is correct to fight for what is right; one must try peaceful means, but if they fail one must fight for righteousness ('dharma'). The conversation between Arjuna and Krishna, which unfolds across 18 chapters, constitutes the *Bhagavad Gita*.

One of the holiest books in the Hindu tradition, the *Gita* teaches loving devotion to the lord and the importance of selfless action as Krishna instructs Arjuna on the nature of God and the human soul, and how to reach liberation. It was probably written sometime between 200 BCE and 200 CE, and for centuries people learned it by heart. In verses that are still recited at Hindu funerals, Krishna describes the soul as existing beyond the reach of the mind and the senses, unaffected by physical nature. Just as human beings exchange old clothes for new ones, so the human soul discards one body and puts on another through the ages, until it acquires the knowledge that will free it forever from the cycle of birth and death.

Thus Arjuna is told not to grieve at what is about to take place; however, he is also warned that if he does not fight for righteousness, he will be guilty of moral cow-ardice and will have to face the consequences of quitting at a time when it was his duty (dharma) to wage a just war and protect the people.

Krishna also makes several statements about himself that mark an important shift in Hindu theology. In the *Upanishads* the sages were reluctant to describe Brahman; but in the *Bhagavad Gita* Krishna reveals himself as the ultimate deity, a personal god, filled with love for human beings, who incarnates himself periodically to protect them. Whereas the Supreme Being of the *Upanishads* was beyond human conceptualization, the deity of the *Bhagavad Gita* is loving and gracious. Krishna describes himself as the goal, supporter, lord, witness, refuge, sanctuary, and friend of the human being, as well as the origin, dissolution, and maintenance of the universe. Many of the traditions within Hinduism have retained this overtly theistic flavour. When Arjuna is unsure about Krishna's claim to be God incarnate, Krishna reveals his cosmic form. Arjuna quakes at this vision and is filled with love and awe. Trembling, he seeks forgiveness of Krishna and implores him to resume his normal form.

The Three Ways to Liberation

In the course of the *Gita* Krishna describes three ways to liberation (or, as some Hindus believe, three aspects of one way to liberation) from the cycle of births and death: (1) the way of action, (2) the way of knowledge, and (3) the way of devotion. Each way (*marga*) is also a discipline (yoga).

The way of action (*karma yoga*) is the path of unselfish duty performed neither in fear of punishment nor in hope of reward. Acting with the expectation of future reward leads to bondage and unhappiness. If our hopes are disappointed we may respond with anger or grief, and even if we do receive the expected reward we will not be satisfied for long. Soon that goal will be replaced with another, leading to further action—and fur-ther accumulation of karma, which only leads to further rebirth.

Other books of the time pointed out that even the 'good' karma acquired by per-forming good deeds is ultimately bad, because to enjoy the good karma we must be reborn. A thirteenth-century Hindu philosopher, Pillai Lokacharya, described good karma as 'golden handcuffs'. Therefore Krishna urges Arjuna to act without attachment to the consequences. Evil will not touch the person who acts according to his dharma, just as water does not stick to a lotus leaf. All actions are to be offered to Krishna. By discarding the fruits of our action, we attain abiding peace.

Krishna also explains the way of knowledge (*jnana yoga*): through scriptural knowledge, one may achieve a transforming wisdom that also destroys one's past karma. True knowledge is an insight into the real nature of the universe, divine power, and the human soul. Later philosophers say that when we hear scripture, ask questions, clarify doubts, and eventually meditate on this knowledge, we achieve liberation.

The third way—the one emphasized most throughout the *Gita*—is the way of devotion (*bhakti yoga*). If there is a general amnesty offered to those who sin, it is through devotion. Ultimately, Krishna makes his promise to Arjuna: if we surrender to the lord, he will forgive all our sins (*Gita* 18:66).

The Deities of Classical Hinduism

The period of the Gupta Empire (c. 320–540) was one of great cultural and scholarly activity. In mathematics the concept of zero was introduced along with the decimal system. Around 499 Aryabhatta established both the value of pi (3.14) and the length of the solar year (365.3586 days). He also maintained that the earth is spherical and rotates on its axis. Commerce increased contact with Greek and Roman trade missions from the Mediterranean, and coastal towns flourished, particularly in southern India.

The Gupta period also saw a renewed surge in religious and literary activity. Temple building was encouraged, pilgrimages were undertaken, and playwrights used religious themes in their dramas. Hindus, Jains, and Buddhists all composed poems and dramas that reveal a great deal about religious trends of the time. Temple architecture, literature, astronomy, and astrology received royal patronage.

From the Gupta era onward, three deities become increasingly prominent: Vishnu, Shiva, and Shiva's consort, variously known as Parvati, Devi, and simply 'the Goddess'. Devotees who give primacy to Vishnu are termed Vaishnavas, those who focus on Shiva are termed Shaivas, and followers of the Goddess are called Shaktas, in reference to her role as the *shakti* ('power') of her divine consort.

Starting around 300 BCE and continuing until a little after 1000 CE, numerous texts known as the *Puranas* (from the Sanskrit for 'old') were composed that retold the 'old tales' of the Hindu tradition, shifting the emphasis away from the major Vedic gods and goddesses in favour of other deities. In the Hindu tradition nothing is ever really discarded. Older deities or concepts may be ignored for centuries, but eventually they are discovered afresh. As we have seen, a prototype for Shiva may have existed as long ago as the ancient Harappa culture, and Vishnu was mentioned as a minor figure in the early Vedic hymns. These gods moved to the forefront in the first millennium of the Common Era. In the process, the Hindu tradition as we know it today crystallized.

Vishnu

Vishnu ('the all-pervasive one') is portrayed as coming to Earth in various forms, animal and human, to rid the world of evil and establish dharma or righteousness. In the first of these incarnations (*avataras*) he appears as a fish who saves Manu, the primeval man. This story was originally part of the Vedic literature, but is expanded in the *Puranas*.

While bathing in a lake, Manu finds a small fish in his hand. The fish speaks to him and asks him to take it home and put it in a jar. The next day it has expanded to fill the jar. Now Manu is asked to put it in a lake, and eventually, when it outgrows the lake overnight, into a river and then the ocean. The fish, who is really Vishnu, then tells him that a great flood is coming, and that he must build a boat and put his family in it, along with the seven sages and 'the seeds of all the animals'. Manu does as he is told. When the flood sweeps the earth, those on the ship survive. This story is sharply reminiscent of flood myths in other religious traditions.

Eventually, Vishnu will have ten incarnations in the present cycle of creation. Nine are said to have already happened, and the tenth is expected at the end of this age. His seventh incarnation was Rama, the hero of the epic, and according to some narratives the ninth was the Buddha, who may have diverted people from Hindu teachings but is praised by some interpreters for the emphasis he gave to non-violence.

In other texts Vishnu's ninth incarnation is Krishna, whom we have already met in the *Bhagavad Gita*. The *Puranas* tell other stories from the life of Krishna: the delightful infant, the mischievous toddler who steals the butter he loves, the youth who steals the hearts of the cowherd girls and dances away the moonlit nights in their company. Some of the later *Puranas* glorify the love of Krishna and his girlfriend Radha.

In many other incarnations Vishnu is said to be accompanied by his consort Sri (Lakshmi), the goddess of good fortune, who bestows grace in this world and the next, blessing her worshippers not only with wealth but eventually with liberation. All stores have pictures of her, and so do most homes.

Shiva

Like Vishnu, Shiva emerged as a great god in the post-Upanishadic era. Unlike Vishnu, however, he was not seen as manifesting himself in a series of incarnations. Instead, the manifold aspects of Shiva's power were expressed in what was perceived as a divine paradox: creator and destroyer, exuberant dancer and austere yogi. The wedding portrait of Shiva and Parvati is one of the dominant images in the tradition of Shiva.

The Goddess

It is also in the *Puranas* that full-fledged worship of the great Goddess first becomes evident. Though she is sometimes treated as the *shakti* of Shiva, in many other instances her independence from the male deity is stressed, and in a few *Puranas* she is even seen as the Supreme Being—not just an appendage to a male deity but the ultimate power, the creator of the universe, and the redeemer of human beings in her own right.

The Goddess, sometimes called Devi in Sanskrit literary tradition, most often appears as Parvati, the wife of Shiva. In her beneficent aspect, she is frequently called Amba or Ambika ('little mother'). But she can also appear as the warrior goddess Durga, represented in iconography with a smiling countenance and a handful of weapons, or as Kali, a dark, dishevelled figure with a garland of skulls. Even in this manifestation, how-

A temple dedicated to Mundakanni Amman, a local form of the Goddess Parvati/Durga, in Mylapore, Chennai (Vasudha Narayanan).

ever, she is called 'mother' by her devotees. Although Western scholars consider Durga and Kali to be separate entities, for many Hindus the lines between these manifestations are blurred. In rural areas local goddesses with distinctive names and histories are identified as manifestations of the Sanskritized, pan-Hindu Devi.

Festivals including the autumn celebration of Navaratri ('nine nights') are dedicated to the Goddess, and millions of Hindus continue to offer her prayers and devotional songs. The continuing importance of the Goddess is a distinctive characteristic of the Hindu tradition.

Other Popular Deities

Probably the most popular god in all Hinduism is Ganesha, the elephant-headed son of Shiva and Parvati. He is seen as a remover of obstacles, and must be propitiated with a coconut or at least a prayer before any new project or venture can begin. Another of Shiva's sons, Murukan, is popular in the Tamil region of south India. Hanuman, portrayed as a monkey, is the son of the wind god and a model devotee of Rama and Sita.

Local manifestation is an extremely important feature of Hinduism. Thus in south India Vishnu, Shiva, and Devi are frequently known by local names. The presiding deity of the Tirupati hills and Srirangam is Vishnu, but in these places he is known as

Venkateshvara ('lord of the Venkata hill') and Ranganatha ('lord of the stage'). Each manifestation has a unique personality and history linking it with a place. These myths are recorded in books called *sthala puranas* ('*puranas* about the place').

Ages of Time

The *Puranas* envision the cosmos as moving through cycles of creation and destruction known as the days and nights of Brahma: a creator god who is nevertheless a relatively minor deity, not to be confused with Brahman, the Supreme Being. Each day and each night of Brahma lasts approximately 4,320 million earthly years. One year of Brahma consists of 360 such days and nights, and Brahma lives for 100 years. At the end of this cycle—after more than 311,000,000 million years—the entire cosmos is drawn into the body of either Vishnu or Shiva (depending on which *Purana* one is reading), where it remains until another Brahma is evolved.

Secondary cycles of creation and destruction occur within the days and nights of Brahma. A day in the life of Brahma is divided into fourteen *manavantaras* of 306,720,000 years. During the long intervals between *manavantaras* the world is recreated and the human race begins again with a new Manu or primeval man.

Within each *manavantara* are 71 great eons (*maha yugas*), each of which is divided into four eons (*yugas*). A single one of these eons is the basic cycle. The golden age (*krta yuga*) lasts 1,728,000 earthly years. During this time dharma or righteousness is firmly established; to use traditional animal imagery, the bull of dharma stands on all four legs. The Treta age is shorter, lasting 1,296,000 earthly years; dharma is then on three legs. The Dvapara age lasts half as long as the golden or *krta* age (864,000 earthly years), and dharma is now hopping on two legs. During the *kali yuga*—the worst of all possible ages—dharma is on one leg, and things get progressively worse. This age lasts for 1,200 god years (432,000 earthly years). It is in this degenerate *kali yuga*, which according to traditional Hindu reckoning began around 3102 BCE, that we live today.

Morality, righteousness, life span, and human satisfaction all steadily decline through these ages, until at the end of the *kali yuga* there will be no righteousness, no virtue, no trace of justice. The *Puranas* deal with astronomical units of time; the age of the earth itself is infinitesimally small in relation to the eons of time the universe experiences. Many Hindu systems of thought maintain that human beings can escape the cycle of birth and death and attain *moksha* or liberation. For those who have not reached enlightenment, however, the cosmic cycles of creation and destruction continue.

Caste and the 'Laws of Manu'

'Caste' is used as a shorthand term to refer to the thousands of social and occupational divisions that have developed from the simple fourfold structure laid out in the 'Hymn to the Supreme Person': priests, rulers, merchants, and servants. There are more than 1,000 *jatis* ('birth groups') in India, and people regularly identify themselves by their *jati*. Underlying this hierarchical system is the idea that people are born with different spiri-

| Box 5.5   Becoming a Brahmin

Nahusha asked Yudhishthira:
'Who can be said to be a brahmin, O King?'
Yudhishthira replied:
'O lord of Serpents! The one who is truthful,
is generous, is patient, is virtuous, has empathy,
is tranquil, and has compassion—such a person is a brahmin'
(*Mahabharata Vana Parva*, 177.15, trans. Vasudha Narayanan).

tual propensities. Ritual practices, dietary rules, and sometimes dialects differ between castes, and inter-caste marriage is still relatively rare. The modern word 'caste' signifies both the four broad *varnas* and the minutely divided *jatis*, although Western scholars sometimes translate *varna* as 'class' and *jati* as 'caste'.

By the first centuries of the Common Era, many treatises on the nature of right-eousness, moral duty, and law had been written. Called the *dharmasastras*, these are the foundations of later Hindu laws. The most famous is the *Manava Dharmasastra* ('Laws of Manu'), attributed to the primordial man that Vishnu saved from the flood. These were probably codified around the first century, for they reflect the social norms of time: the caste system is firmly in place, and women have slipped to an inferior position from the relatively high status they enjoyed in the period of the Vedas.

When reading this text we have to understand that in many parts of India the rules it laid down were not followed strictly. We also have to take its pronouncements on women with a grain of salt. The upper classes were generally called 'twice born', in reference to the initiatory rite by which the males of these social groups were spiritually reborn as sons of their religious teachers. This rite, the *upanayana* (see p. 305), initiated a boy into life's first stage, that of a student.

The brahmins have been known as the priestly class of society and they retained the authority to teach and learn the Vedas. Although not all members of this community were priests, they held the power and prestige generally associated with spiritual learning.

The dharma of the *kshatriya* ('royal' or 'warrior') class was to protect the people and the country. Many kings traced their ancestry to either the sun (*surya vamsa*) or the moon (*chandra vamsa*), both going back to the primeval progenitors of humanity. Here we see classic instances of the ruling class seeking legitimacy by invoking divine antecedents; even usurpers of thrones eventually began to trace their ancestries thus. In the Hindu tradition, then and now, lines of claimed biological descent are all-important. The *kshatriya* families held the power of rulership and governance, and rituals of later Hinduism explicitly emphasized their connection with divine beings. The 'Laws of Manu' describe in detail the duties of a king. He is to strive to conquer his senses, for only those who have conquered their own senses can lead or control others. He must shun not only the vices of pleasure—hunting, gambling, drinking, women—but also the vices that arise from wrath, such as violence, envy, and slander. Members of the mercantile class (*vaisyas*) were permitted to study the Vedas but not to teach them. Rather, they were in charge of most commercial transactions, as well as agricultural work, including the raising of cattle. The power of wealth and economic decisions lay with this class.

The last class mentioned formally in the *dharmasastras* is the *shudras,* a term that has generally been translated as 'servants'. The *dharmasastras* say that it is the duty of *shudras* to serve the other classes; they would not be permitted to accumulate wealth even if they had the opportunity to do so. There was no kind of power that *shudras* could acquire, and the only *shudras* to be treated with any respect were the elderly. As the *Laws of Manu* put it, 'The seniority of brahmins comes from sacred knowledge, that of *kshatriyas* from valour, *vaisyas* from wealth, and *shudras,* only from old age.'

In practice, however, the caste system is far more complex and flexible than the *dharmasastras* suggest. For example, the Vellalas were considered a *shudra* caste technically, but they wielded considerable economic and political power in the south. They were wealthy landowners, and the *dharmasastra* prohibitions do not seem to have had any effect on their fortunes.

The caste system is such a strong social force in India that non-Hindu communities such as the Christians, Jains, and Sikhs have also been influenced by it. Nadar Christians from the south, for instance, will marry only people of the same heritage, and similar restrictions are observed all over India.

Also part of India's social fabric are various 'outcastes': groups officially excluded from the caste system either because they originated in mixed marriages in the distant past or, more often, because they are associated with occupations deemed polluting, such as working with animal hides or dealing with corpses. The English word 'pariah', for instance, comes from the Tamil for 'drummer' (drums were made with animal hides stretched taut over a frame). Until the nineteenth century the caste laws were only one factor among the many considerations in the judicial process and in society itself. Cases were decided with reference to the immediate circumstances, and local customs were no less important than written texts—sometimes more so. It was India's British colonial rulers who, assuming that the laws were binding, attributed a new authority to them.

The Stages and Goals of Life

The dharma texts of the classical period recognized four stages of life (*ashramas*) for males from the upper three classes of society. First, a young boy was initiated into studenthood, during which he was to remain celibate and concentrate on learning. Education was to be provided for all those who desired it, and families were to support students. Although the early epics suggest that girls could also become students, it is likely that this right had been withdrawn by the first century, when the 'Laws of Manu' were codified.

In the next stage the young man was to repay his debts to society and his forefathers, and his spiritual debt to the gods, by marrying and earning a living to support his family and other students. It was the householder's dharma to be employed and lead a conjugal life with his partner in dharma (*saha-dharmacarini*). Most men never went beyond these two stages, and for many the first was probably not particularly important.

Even so, the 'Laws of Manu' describes two more stages. When a man's children have grown and become householders themselves, he and his wife may retire to the forest and live a simple life devoted to recitation of the Vedas. Finally, in the last stage, an elderly man would renounce the material world altogether and take up the ascetic life of the *samnyasin*. His old personality was now dead; he owned nothing, relied on food given as alms, and spent the rest of his days seeking enlightenment and cultivating detachment from life. This kind of formal renunciation became rare with the increasing popularity of the *Bhagavad Gita*, which stresses controlled engagement with the world.

The literature of the period just before the beginning of the Common Era also recognized a number of aims that human beings strive for. These are neither good nor bad in themselves, but may become immoral if they are pursued at an inappropriate time of life or with inappropriate intensity. The aims are dharma, the discharging of one's duties; *artha*, wealth and power in all forms; *kama*, sensual pleasure of many types, including sexual pleasure and the appreciation of beauty; and finally, *moksha*, or liberation from the cycle of birth and death. The last was sometimes seen as belonging to a different category, but texts like the *Gita* made it clear that we may strive for liberation even in daily work as long as we act without attachment.

Differentiation

Vedanta

Six schools of philosophy are recognized within the Hindu tradition: Samkhya, Nyaya, Vaisheshika, Mimamsa, Yoga, and Vedanta. Elements of all six can be seen in modern Hinduism, and Yoga has attracted a wide popular following in recent years. As a philosophical school, however, Vedanta is by far the most important. Vedanta ('end of the Vedas') has engaged Hindu thinkers for more than a thousand years. Although the term 'Vedanta' traditionally denoted the *Upanishads*, in popular usage it more often refers to systems of thought based on a coherent interpretation of the *Upanishads* together with the *Bhagavad Gita* and the *Brahma Sutras*: a collection of roughly 500 aphorisms summarizing the teachings of those texts.

An important early interpreter of Vedanta was Shankara (fl. c. 800). For him, reality is non-dual (*advaita*): the only reality is Brahman, and this reality is indescribable, without attributes. Brahman and Atman (the human soul) are identical; Shankara interprets the Upanishadic phrase 'you are that' in a literal way and upholds the unity of what most people perceive as two distinct entities. Under the influence of *maya* we delude ourselves into believing that we are different from Brahman, but when the illusion is dispelled the soul is liberated by the realization of its true nature. Liberation, therefore, is the removal of ignorance and the dispelling of illusion through the power of transforming knowledge. That goal can be reached in this life; human beings can achieve liberation while still embodied (*jivanmukti*). Final release, however, will come only after the death of the body. Those liberated in this life act without binding desire and help others to achieve liberation.

Shankara also posits three levels of reality. He recognizes that human beings believe life is real, but points out that when we are asleep we also believe that what happens in our dreams is real. Only when we wake up do we discover that what we dreamt was not real. So too in this cycle of life and death we believe that all we experience is real. And it is—until we are liberated and wake up to the truth about our identity. One might argue that there is a difference: that the dream seems true only to the individual dreamer, whereas the phenomenal world seems real to millions who seem to share the same reality. But the school of Shankara would say that our limited reality is the result of ignorance and illusion. Through transforming knowledge, the higher knowledge spoken of in the *Upanishads*, we realize that we are really Brahman and are liberated from the cycle of life and death. But the cycle of life and death would go on for the other souls still caught in the snares of *maya*.

Shankara's philosophy was criticized by later philosophers like Ramanuja and Madhva. One of their principal objections is connected with the status of *maya*: if *maya* is real, then there are *two* realities: Brahman and *maya*. If *maya* were unreal, Shankara's critics argue, surely it could not be the cause of the cosmic delusion attributed to it. Shankara tries to avoid this objection by saying that *maya* is indescribable, neither real nor unreal, and his followers would say that in the ultimate state of liberation, which is totally ineffable, such criticisms are not valid in any case.

Ramanuja (traditionally 1017–1137) was the most significant interpreter of theistic Vedanta for the Sri Vaishnava community—the devotees of Vishnu and his consorts Sri (Lakshmi) and Bhu (the goddess Earth)—in south India. In his commentaries on the *Brahma Sutras* and the *Gita*, as well as his independent treatises, Ramanuja proclaims the supremacy of Vishnu–Narayana and emphasizes that devotion to Vishnu will lead to ultimate liberation. He challenges Shankara's interpretation of scripture, especially regarding *maya*, and his belief that the supreme reality (Brahman) is without attributes. For Ramanuja, Vishnu (whose name literally means 'all-pervasive') is immanent throughout the universe, pervading all souls and material substances, but also transcending them. Thus from one viewpoint there is a single reality, Brahman; but from another viewpoint Brahman is qualified by souls and matter. Since the human soul is the body and the servant of the Supreme Being, liberation is portrayed not as the realization that the two are the same, but rather as the intuitive, total, and joyful realization of the soul's relationship with the lord.

The philosopher Madhva (c. 1199–1278) is unique in the Hindu tradition in classifying some souls as eternally bound. For him there are different grades of enjoyment and bliss even in liberation. He is also one of the explicitly dualistic Vedanta philosophers, holding that the human soul and Brahman are ultimately separate and not identical in any way.

Yoga

Yoga is the physical and mental discipline through which one 'yokes' one's spirit to a god. It has been held in high regard in many Hindu texts and has had many meanings in the history of the Hindu tradition. Its origins are obscure, though some scholars have pointed out that seals from the Harappan culture portray a man sitting in what looks like a yogic position.

For many Hindus the classic yoga text is a collection of short, aphoristic fragments called the *Yoga Sutras*, finalized some time in the early centuries of the Common Era and attributed to Patanjali. We do not know who Patanjali was, but he is said to have lived in the second century BCE. It is likely that yoga had been an important feature of religious life in India for centuries before the text was written.

Patanjali's yoga is a system of moral, mental, and physical discipline and meditation with a particular object, either physical or mental, as the 'single point' of focus. It is described as having eight 'limbs' or disciplines. The first of these, *yama*, consists of restraints: avoidance of violence, falsehood, stealing, sexual activity, and avarice. (Interestingly, the same prohibitions are part of the 'right conduct' taught by the Jain tradition.) The second, *niyama*, consists of positive practices such as cleanliness (internal and external purity), equanimity, asceticism (what Patanjali calls 'heat', a kind of energetic concentration), the theoretical study of yoga, and the effort to make God the focus of one's activities. In addition Patanjali recommends a number of bodily postures and breathing techniques.

A crucial aspect of yoga practice is learning to detach the mind from the domination of external sensory stimuli. Perfection in concentration (*dharana*) and meditation (*dhyana*) lead to *samadhi*: absorption into and union with the divine. There are various stages of *samadhi*, but the ultimate stage is complete emancipation from the cycle of life and death. This state is variously described as a coming together, uniting, and transcending of polarities; empty and full, neither life nor death, and yet both. In short, this final liberation cannot be adequately described in human language.

Although Patanjali's yoga is widely considered the classical form, there are numerous variations. In the broadest terms, the word has been used to designate any form of meditation or practice with ascetic tendencies. More generally, it refers to any path that leads to final emancipation. Thus in the *Bhagavad Gita* the way of action is called karma yoga and the way of devotion *bhakti yoga*. In some interpretations of these forms, the eight 'limbs' of classical yoga are not present; *bhakti yoga* simply comes to mean *bhakti marga*, the way of devotion. In this context yoga becomes a way of self-abnegation, in which the worshipper seeks union with the Supreme Being through passionate devotion. Some philosophers, such as Ramanuja, have said that *bhakti yoga* includes elements of Patanjali's yoga, but many Hindus use the term 'yoga' much more loosely. Although its theoretical aspects have had considerable importance in particular times and traditions, Patanjali's yoga has not enjoyed mass popularity over the years, and few religious teachers have regarded it as a separate path to liberation. Recent decades have seen increasing interest in the physical aspects of yoga, especially in the West, but that interest does not always extend to the psychological and theoretical foundations of the practice.

Tantra

The 'tantric' component of the Hindu tradition is hard to define, partly because it is portrayed differently by its advocates and its detractors. Essentially tantra consists of a body of ritual practices—occasionally sexual—and the texts interpreting them, which appear to be independent of the Vedic tradition.

'Tantra' may be derived come from a root word meaning 'to stretch' or 'expand'. It began to gain importance in the Hindu and Buddhist traditions in about the fifth century. Some scholars believe it originated in the indigenous culture of the subcontinent and re-emerged more than a millennium after the Aryan conquest. Others see it as a later development outside (though not in opposition to) the Vedic tradition. A number of other movements within Hinduism, including Shaivism and Vaishnavism, incorporated elements of tantra in their own practice. For example, large geometric drawings (*mandalas*) representing gods or goddesses and the cosmos are drawn on the floor and used as objects of meditation and ritual.

Tantrism developed its own form of yoga, known as *kundalini*, in reference to the *shakti* or power of the Goddess, which is said to lie coiled like a serpent at the base of the spine. When awakened, this power rises through six *chakras* or 'wheels' within the body to reach the spot under the skull known as the thousand-petalled lotus.

The ultimate aim of this form of yoga is to awaken the power of the *kundalini* and make it unite with Purusa, the male Supreme Being, who is in the thousand-petalled lotus. When this union is achieved, the practitioner is granted visions and psychic powers that eventually lead to emancipation (*moksha*).

There are many variants of tantrism, but the main division is between the 'left-handed' and 'right-handed' schools. As the left hand is considered inauspicious, the term 'left-handed' was applied to movements that did not meet with the approval of the larger or more established schools. 'Left-handed' practices centred on the ritual performance of activities forbidden in everyday life, such as drinking liquor, eating fish and meat, and having sexual intercourse with a partner other than one's spouse. These activities were disapproved of in many other Hindu circles, so that to a large extent left-handed tantrism remained esoteric. The 'right-handed' school was more conservative.

One may also see divisions in tantra along the sectarian lines of Shaiva, Shakta, and Vaishnava, each of which has its own canon of texts called *tantras*.

Ayurvedic Medicine

Medicine made great progress in the Hindu world in the first millennium. One of the most important systems was called Ayurveda, the *veda* (knowledge) of enhancing life. The physician or *vaidya* ('one who is learned') promotes both longevity and quality of life. The prototype is a deity called Dhanavantari, sometimes identified as an incarnation of Vishnu. The south Indian parallel to Ayurveda is the Tamil system called Siddha.

At some time during the last three centuries BCE, the surgeon Sushruta and the physician Charaka presented theories that they claimed had been transmitted to them by the gods. These teachings reflected an understanding of illness as a lack of balance among three elements: air, phlegm, and bile. This analytic approach recalls Greek and Chinese medical theories of about the same period. The *Sushruta Samhita* begins by declaring that the physician's aim is 'to cure the diseases of the sick, to protect the healthy, to prolong life', while the *Charaka Samhita* includes a detailed statement of the ethics required of a physician. In these respects, the ancient roots of Ayurvedic medicine seem strikingly modern. With the growth of tantra after about 500, however, the Ayurvedic literature devoted increasing attention to ritual as a complement to treatment with medicines.

Today in India Ayurveda serves as a bridge between modern international medicine and traditional Indian religio-philosophical theories. In its clinical practice it prescribes specific remedies and therapies, just as modern medicine does, while its theory draws on elements of tantra and yoga. It shares their outlook on life and the world, but puts greater emphasis on health than on spiritual attainment.

Hinduism in Southeast Asia

Hindu culture today is associated almost exclusively with the Indian peninsula, but traces of its influence can still be found across Southeast Asia. Archeological evidence suggests that extensive trade links were established by the second century CE, and both Hindu and Buddhist texts in India refer to Southeast Asia as the land of gold (*suvarna bhumi*) and gems.

Cultural connections were also widespread. Chinese sources mention kings in Cambodia with Hindu names beginning in the third century. Many Sanskrit inscriptions and thousands of icons and sculptures portraying Hindu deities indicate that Hindu influences were pervasive in Cambodia, Thailand, Laos, Vietnam, Java, Indonesia, and Bali. One of the largest Hindu temples in the world is Angkor Wat, built by King Suryavarman II in the twelfth century CE and dedicated to Vishnu.

Even so, Hindu traditions in Southeast Asia, as elsewhere, took on distinctive local characteristics. The Khmer people in Cambodia, for instance, emphasized some stories that were not so important in India, and temples in Cambodia, Laos, and Indonesia are often quite different from their counterparts on the subcontinent.

Although the Hindu influence faded by about the fifteenth century, stories such as the *Ramayana* and *Mahabharata* still flourish in these cultures, especially in the performing arts.

Angkor Wat. At the spring equinox the sun rises directly over the central tower (Vasudha Narayanan).

South Indian Devotion (*Bhakti*)

The culture of the region south of the Vindhya mountains and Gujarat is distinct in many ways from that of the north. It was flourishing as early as the fifth century BCE, and after 600 CE gave rise to a number of historically significant changes in the Hindu tradition. Use of the vernacular language for devotion (*bhakti*)—a primary characteristic of many Hindu traditions—became established here first and then spread to other parts of the country.

A sophisticated body of literature in the Tamil language existed 2,000 years ago. The earliest works were secular poems that fell into two categories. *Puram* poetry took as its subject the 'outer' world of warfare, chivalry, valour, and kings. *Akam* poems, by contrast, dealt with the 'inner' world of love and romance: secret meetings, forbidden lovers, the anguish of separation, and the overwhelming joy of union. Although the earliest extant Tamil composition shows some similarities to Sanskrit literature, and the early poems of love and war borrowed many words from Sanskrit, Tamil literature on the whole is quite independent of any Sanskrit influence.

The earliest religious works that we have are poems addressed to Vishnu and hymns of praise to Murukan, the son of Shiva and Parvati, which probably date from the sixth century. Around the same time, poet-devotees of Vishnu and Shiva began travelling from temple to temple singing the praises of their chosen deity in their own mother tongue—the language of childhood, intimacy, tenderness, and powerful emotion. By the twelfth century 75 of these poets were recognized as saints: 63 devotees of Shiva, known as Nayanmars, and 12 devotees of Vishnu, known as Alvars.

Drawing freely from the Tamil heritage, the Alvars incorporated the symbolism of the earlier *akam* and *puram* poems in their work, depicting their lord as both accessible and remote, gracious and grand, and seeking from him both the embrace of the beloved and the protection of the king.

Many poems refer to incidents from the *Ramayana*, the *Mahabharata*, and the *Puranas*, as well as stories not found in any of these sources. Through repeated recollection of the salvific deeds of Vishnu in his various incarnations, the Alvars express their belief in the power of Vishnu (Narayana) and his desire to save all beings. In the following verse, the poet speaks of his longing to see Vishnu enshrined in the temple at Tillai (the modern city of Chidambaram):

> In the beautiful city of Ayodhya, encircled by towers,
> A flame that lit up all the worlds
> appeared in the Solar race
> and gave life to all the heavens.
> This warrior, with dazzling eyes,
> Rama, dark as a cloud,
> the First One, my only Lord,
> is in Chitrakuta, city of Tillai.
>   When is the day
>   when my eyes can behold him
>   and rejoice?
> (*Perumal Tirumoli* 10.1)

Sometimes the Alvars speak in the voices of characters in the Cankam poetry, the epics, or the *Puranas*. In the following verse from the famous *Tiruvaymoli* ('sacred

---

| Box 5.6 | **Heaven on Earth**

This is the temple of him who became
    the divine fish, tortoise, boar, lion and dwarf.
    He became Rama in three forms, he became Kanna,
    and as Kalki he will end [these worlds].
This is Srinagam, where the swan and its mate
    swing on the lotus blossoms, embrace on flowery beds,
    and revel in the red pollen strewn around the river
(*Perumal Tirumoli* 4.9.9, trans. Vasudha Narayanan).

utterance'), for example, the poet Nammalvar adopts the persona of one of the cowherd girls in the *Puranas*:

> You were gone the whole day,
> grazing cows Kanna [Krishna]!
> Your soothing words burn my soul.
> Evening tramples like a rogue elephant
> and the fragrance of jasmine buds,
> loosening my bonds, blows upon me.
> Embrace my beautiful breasts
> with the fragrance of the wild jasmine
> upon your radiant chest.
> Give me the nectar of your mouth
> and adorn my lowly head
> with your jeweled lotus hands.
> *Tiruvaymoli* 10.3.5

| Box 5.7   **From the *Tiruvaymoli***

Relinquish all;
having relinquished,
submit your life
to him who owns heaven (1.2.1).

Think for a moment:
your bodies inhabited by your souls
last as long
as a lightning flash (1.2.2).

Move to his side,
your bondage will loosen.
At the time your body falls,
think of him (1.2.9).

Being
    poverty and wealth,
    hell and heaven
Being
    enmity and friendship,
    poison and ambrosia,
The great Lord, diffused everywhere,
    is my ruler.
I saw him
    in the Sacred Celestial City,
a city of wealthy people (6.3.1).

Being
    the joys and sorrows that we see,
    confusion and clarity,

Being
    punishment and grace,
    heat and shade,
The great one, rare to behold,
    is my ruler.
His is the Sacred Celestial City;
    a good city,
    surrounded by clear waters
    and waves (6.3.2)   .

Being
    virtue and sin,
    union and separation,
    and all of these;
Being
    memory, being forgetfulness;
Being
    existence, being non-existence;
Being none of these,
The Lord resides
    in the Sacred Celestial City
    that is surrounded by lofty mansions.
See the sweet grace of Kannav,
    [Can this be] false? (6.3.4)

(Carman and Narayanan 1989: 202-23).

| Box 5.8 | The Songs of Andal

A thousand elephants circle,
as Narana, Lord of virtues,
walks through the town in front of me.
Golden jars brim with water;
Festive flags and pennants fly through this town,
eager to welcome him—
I saw this in a dream, my friend!

Drums beat happy sounds; conches were blown.
Under the canopy strung heavy with pearls,
Madhusuda, my love, filled with virtue,
came and clasped the palm of my hand
I saw this in a dream, my friend!

Those with eloquent mouths recited the good Vedas,
With mantras they placed
the green leaves and the grass in a circle.
The lord, strong as a raging elephant,
softly held my hand as we circled the fire.
I saw this in a dream, my friend!

(*Nachchiyar Tirumoli* 1.1 and 1.6–7, by Andal; trans. Vasudha Narayanan)

Tamil devotees of Vishnu consider the Alvars' poems the equivalent of the Sanskrit Vedas and recite them daily, in temples and at home. They also venerate the Alvars themselves, especially Nammalvar and Andal ('she who rules')—the group's one female member. Tradition says that Andal so longed for union with Vishnu that she refused to marry, and her passionate verses, said to have been composed in December, are broadcast over every radio station in Tamilnadu and Karnataka in that month. It seems significant that, in addition to this independent-minded woman, the Alvar saints included a number of poets from lower- and even outcaste backgrounds. The fact that the Alvars were venerated regardless of sex or caste is a clear indication that the hierarchical class system, which denied salvific knowledge to women, *shudras*, and outcastes in particular, was not necessarily respected.

Devotion to Shiva was also widespread in south India. In the tenth century, queens of the Chola dynasty contributed liberally to the building and maintenance of Shiva temples in the Tamil region. In the twelfth century, the Vira Shaiva movement emerged in what is now the state of Karnataka. The sayings of the Vira Shaiva saints made explicit their contempt for the caste system. The Vira Shaiva poets also included a woman—Akka Mahadevi—and rejected temple-based worship; instead, they showed their adoration to a stylized manifestation of Shiva in the shape of a small *linga* (see p. 299) carried by every devotee.

Classical Carnatic Music

As early as the time of the Vedas, music was a part of worship in the Hindu tradition. The mystical syllable *om* was considered the beginning of sound in the universe and a manifestation of the Supreme Being. Knowledge of the proper nature of sound and its expressions was therefore considered to be religious knowledge. The Vedas specify the different kinds of pitch and tone by which the verses were to be recited. The exalted status of the *Sama Veda* was in part a reflection of its melodious qualities.

Classical music was for the most part religious in nature. Treatises on music spoke of a divine line of teachers, frequently beginning with the deities Shiva and Parvati, and offered worship to Saraswati as the patron goddess of the fine arts. Bharata's *Natya shastra*, a classical Sanskrit text on dance and mime thought to have been written around the beginning of the Common Era, spoke of the performing arts as a spiritual path to liberation. And some later *Puranas* say that Vishnu and Sri are manifested as Nada Brahman or the Supreme Being in the form of sound. If sound was properly controlled and articulated, it could lead to a mystical experience. Thus music in itself was no less important than the lyrics sung to it. *Nadopasana*, meditation through sound, became a popular form of religious practice.

Carnatic music—the classical music of south India—evolved into its present distinctive form between the fifteenth and eighteenth centuries. Various deities were praised in ragas (a musical form, known in most regions of India, based on specific scales and connected with specific moods and times) accompanied by specific rhythmic beats. Of particular note are the intensely moving songs composed in praise of Rama by Tyagaraja (1767–1847). The most renowned poet-musician of south India, Tyagaraja is considered one of the world's greatest composers. As expressions of *bhakti* his songs are intended to bring listeners closer to the lord, but in effect the joy of the music becomes an end in itself. More than 150 years after his death, Tyagaraja's music is still played today at wedding concerts and songfests, on radio, television, and the internet, and in many homes.

North Indian Bhakti

Having begun in south India, the *bhakti* tradition gradually spread to the north, where it became very popular in the fifteenth century. North Indian *bhakti* resembled its southern counterpart both in its use of vernacular languages and in the fact that its practice was open to people of every caste, from high to low.

The two *bhakti* traditions did differ in one respect, however. In the south *bhakti* was generally addressed to a particular deity, but in the north the object of devotion could also be a less specific, even formless, divine being. One factor that may have contributed to this difference was the Islamic presence in the north, where a Muslim sultanate had been established since the early 1200s. A synergistic relationship developed between Hindus and Muslims in northern India that was reflected in the delightful, sometimes poignant works composed in the vernacular by poet-singers of the Sant ('holy person' or 'truth') tradition. Emphasizing the *nirguna* ('without attributes') Brahman discussed in the *Upanishads*, the Sants held the divinity to be without form. Hence their worship had nothing to do with physical images and they expressed their devotion either in poetry or in silent meditation. At the same time, in addition to rejecting distinctions based on caste, they rejected distinctions between religious communities.

Among the most important Sant poets was Kabir, a Hindu weaver from Varanasi whose life is said to have spanned more than a hundred years (1398–1518). A mystic who emphasized that God is beyond the particularities of any religious community, Kabir had much in common with a Punjabi mystic named Nanak (1469–1539) and a Sufi Muslim teacher named Dadu (1544–1603). All three men attracted followers. In time, the disciples of Kabir and Dadu were reabsorbed into the general populations of Hindus and Muslims respectively, but Nanak's ultimately formed a separate community—the Sikhs. As we will see in Chapter 6, Kabir became one of several Sant poets whose works form part of the Sikh scripture.

| Box 5.9 | From Kabir

Go naked if you want,
Put on animal skins.
What does it matter till you see the inward Ram?

If the union yogis seek
Came from roaming about in the buff,
Every deer in the forest would be saved. . . .

Pundit, how can you be so dumb?
You're going to drown, along with all your kin
Unless you start speaking of Ram.

Vedas, Puranas—why read them?
It's like loading an ass with sandalwood!

Unless you catch on and learn how Ram's name goes,
How will you reach the end of the road?

You slaughter living beings and call it religion:
Hey brother, what would irreligion be?
'Great Saint'—that's how you love to greet each other:
Who then would you call a murderer?

Your mind is blind. You've no knowledge of yourselves.
Tell me, brother, how can you teach anyone else?
Wisdom is a thing you sell for worldly gain,
So there goes your human birth—in vain.

(Hawley and Juergensmeyer 1988:50–1)

Two other important Sant poets were Surdas and Tulsidas. Surdas (c. 1483–1563) was a blind singer whose most famous work, the *Sursagar*, tells the story of Krishna. Evoking both the mischievous butter thief and the irresistible flute player, Surdas celebrates Radha's passion for Krishna as a model of *bhakti*. Tulsidas (1543?–1623) is perhaps best-known for his *Lake of the Deeds of Rama*, a retelling or translation of the ever-popular *Ramayana* in verses that have their own beauty and have inspired hundreds of traditional storytellers and millions of Rama devotees in Hindi-speaking areas. Large sections of Tulsidas' work are learned by heart: sidewalk vendors, shopkeepers, house-wives, and learned people can all quote from it even today.

One of the best-known religious leaders of this period was Chaitanya (1486–1583), who at the age of thirty-four took the religious name Krishna-Chaitanya, 'he whose con-sciousness is Krishna'. Many of his followers believe that in the *kali yuga*—the present degenerate age—people have little chance of fulfilling all the requirements of religious action and duty; hence the only way to *moksha* is through trusting devotion to the lov-ing and gracious lord.

For Chaitanya, in fact, the ultimate goal was not *moksha* in the traditional sense of liberation from attachment but rather the active enjoyment of an intense spiritual love of Krishna—a passionate love like the one that the cowherd girls felt for him. Chaitanya is said to have led people through the streets, singing about his lord and urg-ing others to join him in chanting Krishna's names. Eventually, many of his followers came to believe that Krishna and Radha were present in Chaitanya himself.

The Hare Krishna movement has spread this tradition abroad. A.C. Bhaktivedanta (1896–1977) launched the International Society for Krishna Consciousness in New York in 1966. Both its theology, locating divine grace in Krishna, and its devotional chanting can be traced directly to Chaitanya.

| Box 5.10 | **From Mirabai**

Mirabai (1450?–1547) was a Rajput princess in Gujarat. Left a widow when she was still a young woman, she became a devotee of Krishna and wrote passionate poetry about her love for him.

Sister, I had a dream that I wed
the Lord of those who live in need:
Five hundred sixty thousand people came
and the Lord of Braj was the groom.
In dream they set up a wedding arch;
in dream he grasped my hand;
in dream he led me around the wedding fire
and I became unshakably his bride.
Mira's been granted her mountain-lifting Lord:
from living past lives, a prize.

(*Caturvedi*, no. 27; Hawley and Juergensmeyer 1988: 137)

What has been the legacy of the *bhakti* movement? With its spread, the message of the Sanskrit scriptures was reinforced by powerful vernacular works. Overwhelming numbers of Hindus can recite devotional verses composed in their own languages. Thus the Hindi poems of Surdas or the Tamil poems of Nammalvar or Andal may function as scripture for particular communities.

These vernacular poems and songs offer the faithful far more guidance, inspiration, consolation, hope, and wisdom than the Vedas have ever done. It is not that the vernacular literature is at variance with the message of the Vedas. Rather, most Hindu communities believe that the poet-saints gathered the truth from the Vedas and made it accessible to everyone, inspiring devotion and preparing devotees to receive the shower of divine grace.

Reform and Revival

Once a sea route was opened in the late fifteenth century, expeditions from Portugal, the Netherlands, England, and France all made their way to India. Before long, foreign powers intent on establishing themselves on Indian territory became involved in local politics. When the Mughal Empire disintegrated in the early eighteenth century, many chieftains attempted to acquire parcels of land and to enlist English or French help in their enterprise. Eventually the domination of the East India Company and the British led to a loose unification of large parts of the Indian subcontinent under British control, bringing about changes in many areas. Many foreign missionaries were appalled by the caste system, the treatment of women, and what they perceived as idolatry. But the foreigners were not the only ones anxious to promote social reform.

Ram Mohan Roy and the Brahmo Samaj

Among the Hindu reformers was Ram Mohan Roy (1772–1833). Roy had become familiar with Western mores and the Christian scriptures while serving with the East India Company and had formed close ties with members of the Unitarian movement. Although he did not accept the Christian view of Jesus as the son of God, he believed that Christ's ethical teachings were compatible with Hinduism, and wrote a book on the subject entitled *The Precepts of Jesus: The Guide to Peace and Happiness*. In 1828 he established a society in Calcutta to discuss the nature of Brahman as it appears in the *Upanishads*. This organization, which came to be called the Brahmo Samaj ('congregation of Brahman'), actively promoted monotheism, rationalism, humanism, and social reform.

Although he rejected most of the stories in the epics and *Puranas* as myths standing in the way of reason, Roy drew on the *Upanishads* and sections of the *Brahma Sutras* to defend Hinduism against missionary attacks. At the same time, together with the Unitarians, he accused the missionaries who believed in the Christian Trinity of straying away from monotheism. A pioneer in the area of women's rights, including the right to education, he is also credited with the legal abolition of *sati*—the practice in which a widow would immolate herself on her husband's funeral pyre.

The Brahmo Samaj has never become very popular, but it revitalized the Hindu tradition at a critical time in its history, and Roy himself has often been called the father of modern India.

The Arya Samaj

The Arya Samaj ('society of Aryas') movement was founded in 1875 by Dayananda Sarasvati (1824–83), an ascetic who sought to return Hinduism to its ancient roots. Holding the *Samhita* sections of the Vedas to be the revealed truth, he condemned all later developments of the Hindu tradition, including idol worship, the caste system, and the exclusion of women from study of the Vedas. He thought that the early hymns of the *Rig Veda* in particular reflected a golden age, and advocated a life of vigorous work and service to humanity. Followers of this movement have introduced a ritual through which descendants of Hindus who converted to other faiths may 'return' to the tradition of *sanatana dharma*. Similar rituals have been adopted by many communities in India, allowing people of other traditions to become Hindus, including some who may not have any ancestral connection with Hinduism.

The Ramakrishna Movement

Gadadhar Chatterjee (1836–86), a Bengali raised in the Vishnuite *bhakti* tradition who took the name Ramakrishna, cultivated ecstatic trance experiences. By his account, he experienced the Divine Mother as an ocean of love that rescued him from emotional turmoil.

Following the death of Ramakrishna Paramahamsa, his disciples in Calcutta formed a monastic order and a mission to spread his ideas. Their leader, Swami Vivekananda (1862–1902), was a former member of the Brahmo Samaj who believed that Western science could help India make material progress, while Indian spirituality could enlighten the West. As a Hindu participant in the 1893 World's Parliament of Religions in Chicago, and later as a lecturer in America and Europe, he spread a new interpretation of Shankara's non-dualist (*advaita*) Vedanta. As a result of the attention he attracted, the West generally came to think of Vedanta as the definitive form of Hinduism.

The monastic wing of the movement held that renunciation of the world promotes spiritual growth. Unlike other forms of monasticism, the Ramakrishna order believed in engagement with the world. Therefore its members dedicated themselves to providing humanitarian service.

In keeping with Ramakrishna's belief that all religions are true, the Ramakrishna movement encouraged non-sectarian worship. Beginning in the early twentieth century, it opened hundreds of educational and medical institutions for the welfare of all, regardless of caste. This activity was particularly significant because until then most of India's new medical and educational institutions had been run by Christian missionaries.

| Map 5.1   Hinduism

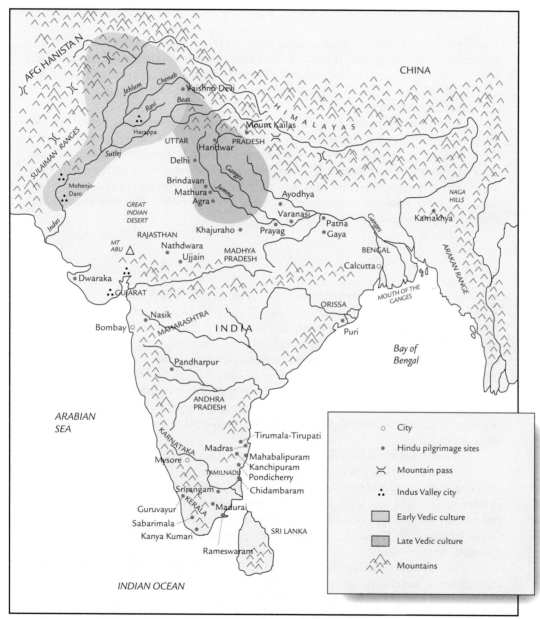

CHINA

AFGHANISTAN

Jehlum
Chenab
Vaishno Devi
Ravi
Beas
SULAIMAN RANGES
Harappa
Mount Kailas
H I M A L A Y A S
Sutlej
UTTAR   PRADESH
Haridwar
Delhi
Ganges
Mohenjo-
Daro
Brindavan
Mathura
Agra
Jumna
Ayodhya
NAGA
HILLS
Indus
GREAT
INDIAN
DESERT
Varanasi
Kamakhya
RAJASTHAN
Khajuraho
Prayag
Patna
Gaya
Ganges
ARAKAN RANGE
MT
ABU
Nathdwara
Ujjain
MADHYA
PRADESH
BENGAL
Calcutta
Dwaraka
GUJARAT
Nasik
MOUTH OF THE
GANGES
Bombay
MAHARASHTRA
I N D I A
ORISSA
Puri
Pandharpur
Bay of
Bengal
ANDHRA
PRADESH
ARABIAN
SEA
KARNATAKA
Tirumala-Tirupati
Madras
Mysore
Mahabalipuram
Kanchipuram
Pondicherry
TAMILNADU
Srirangam
Chidambaram
KERALA
Madurai
Guruvayur
Sabarimala
Kanya Kumari
SRI LANKA
Rameswaram

INDIAN OCEAN

Legend:
- ○ City
- ● Hindu pilgrimage sites
-)(Mountain pass
- ∴ Indus Valley city
- Early Vedic culture
- Late Vedic culture
- Mountains

Source: Adapted from N.C. Nielsen et al., eds, *Religions of the World*, 3rd ed. (New York: St Martin's Press, 1993):85.

Practice

The Sacred Syllable *Om*

The word *om* is recited at the beginning and end of all Hindu (and Jain) prayers and recitations of scripture, and is used by Buddhists also. It is understood to have three sounds—*a-u-m*—which yield the sound *o* when the diphthong consisting of *a* and *u* is shortened. The sound itself, beginning deep in the body and ending at the lips, is believed to be auspicious.

All Hindu philosophers and sects agree that *om* has tremendous power, but they disagree on its meaning. Some believe it represents the supreme reality or Brahman. Many have said that *om* was at the beginning of the manifest universe, and that it contains the essence of true knowledge. Some say that its three sounds represent the three worlds: earth, atmosphere, and heaven. Others say that it represents the essence of the three Vedas: *Rig*, *Yajur*, and *Sama*. Some trace the word to the Sanskrit root *av-*, meaning 'that which protects'.

Temple Worship

As we have seen, there is no reference to temples in the Vedic literature, although the ancient Harappa culture may have designated some buildings specifically for worship. When exactly temples began to figure in Hindu worship is uncertain. In the southern part of India, however, examples of temple architecture survive from as early as the seventh and eighth centuries. Temples in the north tend to be much more recent because many were destroyed during the period of Muslim rule and in the course of various invasions. But the tradition is old; architectural guides written after the fourth century specify the details of temple construction, including the towers that are an essential part of their design. In popular religion, even seeing the temple tower is said to be enough to destroy one's sins.

A central element in most—though not all—forms of Hindu worship is the image (*murti*) of the deity, which is treated like a royal guest in the temple dedicated to him or her. The *murti* (variously translated as 'idol', 'icon', 'form', or 'object to be worshipped') is adorned, carried in processions, and entertained with music and dance. Devotees believe that the god is simultaneously present in the temple, in heaven, in the world, and in the human soul. The deities are always complete, regardless of how many forms they manifest themselves in.

Some Hindus believe that the image in a temple is only a symbol of a higher reality, and some—notably, members of the recent Brahmo Samaj and the Vira Shaiva movements—reject images altogether. The Sri Vaishnava community, on the other hand, believes that once the image of Vishnu in the temple has been consecrated it becomes a piece of transcendental matter here on earth. It is not a symbol of Vishnu; it is Vishnu himself, making himself present in image form because he wants to be accessible. In this way the presence of the image in the temple is a direct analogue to Vishnu's past manifestations as Rama or Krishna. Temples to Vishnu include large shrines for the goddess Sri or Lakshmi, and temples dedicated to Shiva or Parvati usually include shrines for their consorts.

As a rule there is no congregational prayer in the style of the Sunday morning Christian worship or the Friday prayers for Muslims. Hindu priests are ritual specialists rather than counsellors, though they may be taking on a more pastoral role today in the United States. In most cases the priests offer fruit, flowers, or coconut to the deity and then give back some of the blessed objects to devotees to take home. The food thus presented is considered ennobled because it is now *prasada* ('divine favour')—a gift from the deity.

Many temples hold regular festivals commemorating events recounted in local myths. For instance, in the Minaksi-Sundaresvara temple at Madurai, one of the larger complexes in south India, Minaksi is a goddess portrayed as a princess of the local Pandyan dynasty, but she is also a manifestation of Parvati. After a military career in which she conquers minor deities who preside over the eight directions, she marries Sundaresvara, who is seen as Shiva himself. The wedding of the god and goddess is celebrated with much pomp and joy every year in the temple, and pilgrims in the hundreds of thousands attend the festival.

At the centre of the temple is the *garbha grha*, 'the womb-house', where the god or goddess is enshrined. The chamber is called a 'womb-house' because this is where spiritual regeneration or rebirth is believed to take place. The emphasis is on seeing the deity; this is as important as hearing the sacred words of Hindu scripture. In south Indian temples devotees are not permitted to go beyond the threshold of the womb-house; only the priests and ritual specialists who have been specially initiated are permitted to advance to the inner shrine. In many north Indian temples, however, devotees too may go all the way inside.

Devotees frequently walk around the temple inside one of the enclosures; this 'circumambulation' of the deity is an essential part of the temple visit. They may perform an *archana* ('formal worship') in which the priest praises the deity by reciting his or her names. Devotees also bow down before the deity. Sometimes they will go to the temple kitchen for *prasada*. In some temples devotees must buy the *prasada*; in others it is provided at no charge from endowments made by patrons in the past. Such patrons frequently earmark their donations for particular charitable deeds or functions in the temple, and their donations are inscribed on stone plaques on the temple walls. Among the inscriptions at the temple in Tirupati, for example, is one recording a donation made in the year 966 by a woman named Samavai to celebrate some festivals and consecrate a silver processional image of Vishnu.

These inscriptions represent a tangible honour for the many patrons over the centuries who have generously donated funds for pilgrims and festivals. In addition, the large amounts of money received point to the temples' power as economic institutions.

Sculptural and Pictorial Symbolism

The *Naga*

One of the earliest symbols in the Hindu tradition may be the *naga* (serpent). In many villages (as well as quiet spots in large cities) there are sacred trees surrounded with small stone images of intertwined snakes, which are venerated with spots of red powder (the same kumkum powder that is used to adorn women's foreheads). Women come to these open-air shrines to worship at particular times of the year, or when they want to make a wish regarding matters such as childbirth. *Nagas* are also important in the iconography of Shiva and Vishnu.

In Cambodia balustrades in the form of large *nagas* are an integral part of the Hindu and Buddhist temple landscape. Cambodian narratives trace the descent of the kingdom from a Hindu prince from India and a *naga* princess.

The Dance of Shiva

Iconographically, Shiva is often portrayed as a cosmic dancer known as Nataraja, the king of the dance. In this form Shiva is the archetype of both the dancer and the ascetic, symbolizing mastery over universal energy on the one hand and absolute inner tranquillity on the other.

In the classic Nataraja representation, Shiva has four hands. One of the right hands holds an hourglass-shaped drum, symbolizing sound—both speech and the divine truth heard through revelation. The other right hand is making a gesture that grants fearlessness to the devotee. One of the left hands holds a flame, symbolizing the destruction of the world at the end of time. The feet grant salvation and are worshipped to

Shiva in the form of the cosmic dancer Nataraja (Vasudha Narayanan).

obtain union with Shiva. The left foot, representing the refuge of the devotee, is raised, signifying liberation. The other left hand points to this foot.

Dancing through the creation and destruction of the cosmos, Shiva–Nataraja is the master of both *tandava*, the fierce, violent dance that gives rise to energy, and *lasya*, the gentle, lyric dance representing tenderness and grace. The entire universe shakes when he dances; Krishna sings for him, the snake around his neck sways, and drops of the Ganges River, which he holds in his hair, fall to the earth.

The *Linga*

In temples Shiva is usually represented by a *linga*: an upright shaft, typically made of stone, placed in a receptacle called a *yoni*, which symbolizes the womb. The sexual connotation is not explicit, although *linga* is generally translated into English as 'phallus'. In Sanskrit *linga* means 'distinguishing symbol' and Hindus do not normally think of it as a physical object. Rather, it serves as a reference point to the spiritual potential in all of creation, and specifically to the positive energies of Shiva. The union of the *yoni* and *linga* is a reminder that male and female forces are united in generating the universe. Although Shiva is stereotyped as the 'destroyer' in some literature, it is his creative role that is represented in the temple.

Erotic Sculpture

People from other cultures have often been shocked by temple sculptures celebrating *kama*, sensual love. Probably the most famous examples of such art are found at Khajuraho (c. 1000 CE), in the state of Madhya Pradesh southeast of Delhi, and Konarak (c. 1250), in the eastern coastal state of Orissa. Although many other temples also contain erotic sculpture, it is frequently kept in inconspicuous niches or corners.

Some art historians have speculated that the sculptures may have been intended to serve an educational purpose for young men who as students were isolated from society, preparing them for adult life in a world where *kama*—sensual enjoyment—of all kinds was considered a legitimate goal and spouses were expected to be partners in *kama* as well as dharma. Other scholars have suggested that such scenes illustrate passages from various myths and literary works such as the *Puranas*.

Forehead Marks

Perhaps the most common visual sign of Hindu culture is the forehead mark or *tilaka* ('small, like a *tila* or sesame seed'), especially the red dot (*bindi*) traditionally worn by married women. In many parts of India, however, men—ascetics and temple priests—also wear various forehead marks in the context of religious rituals. Like many elements in the Hindu traditions, forehead marks may be interpreted in various ways, depending on the gender and marital status of the person wearing it, the occasion for which it is worn, the sectarian community from which the wearer comes, and, occasionally, the caste.

At the simplest level, the forehead mark is decorative. In this spirit, unmarried and Christian as well as married Hindu women today wear *bindis*, and the traditional dot of kumkum powder has been largely replaced by stickers in a wide variety of shapes and colours. Thus many people today do not think of forehead marks as having anything to do with religion. Yet their value is more than cosmetic. Married women see the *bindi* as a symbol of the role that they play in society. Other marks indicate the wearer's sectarian affiliation. When worn correctly in ritual situations, the shape and colour indicate not only which god or goddess the person worships, but also the socio-religious community he or she belongs to (e.g., Sri Vaishnava).

The materials used to create the mark depend on the wearer's sectarian affiliation and the purpose for which the mark is worn. Marks denoting affiliation to a particular deity may be made with white clay, sandalwood paste, smoke-collyrium, flower petals, or ash. In general, followers of Vishnu, Krishna, and Lakshmi wear vertical marks; worshippers of Shiva and Parvati wear horizontal or slightly curved crescent marks made of ash or other substances with a red dot in the middle; and a combination of dots and crescents usually indicates a preference for the Goddess (Devi) in one of her many manifestations. Other variations are instantly identifiable to those familiar with India's many philosophical traditions.

Domestic Worship

One of the most significant ways in which Hindus express their devotion to a deity or spiritual teacher is through rituals performed in the home, usually called puja ('worship'). Daily puja typically consists of simple acts in which all family members can take part, such as lighting oil lamps and incense sticks, reciting prayers, or offering food to the deity. More elaborate or specialized rituals, however, may involve a priest or other specialist.

Significantly, a number of domestic rituals are specific to the women of the household. In many parts of India, women gather on certain days of the year to celebrate the goddess by fasting and feasting, and then perform what are called 'auspiciousness' rituals for the happiness of the entire family. Other women's rituals are performed only in certain geographic regions. In the south, for example, women often gather before a major family celebration (such as a wedding) to ask for the blessing of a particularly auspicious group of female ancestors: those who had the good fortune to die while their husbands were still alive. Even in death such women are believed to have immense power to determine the success of any ritual. In some communities in northern India, young virgin girls are venerated by other women who believe that they are temporary manifestations of the Goddess.

The Significance of Food

The Hindu religion is preoccupied with food: not just what kind of food is eaten, when it is eaten, and how it is prepared, but who prepares it, who has the right to be offered it first, and who may be given the leftovers. Certain dates and lunar phases require either fasting or feasting. Furthermore, there are technical distinctions among fasts: some demand abstention from all food, others only from grain or rice. According to some texts, one can win liberation from the cycle of life and death simply by observing the right kinds of fast.

Contrary to a common Western stereotype, most Hindus are not vegetarians. Nor does vegetarianism for Hindus mean abstaining from dairy products. Generally speaking, vegetarianism is a matter of community and caste. The strictest Hindu vegetarians are the Vaishnavas, devotees of Vishnu in northern India. In addition, most brahmins are vegetarian—except in Bengal and Kashmir. In the West, members of the International Society for Krishna Consciousness (the Hare Krishna movement) not only abstain from meat, fish, and fowl, but also avoid certain vegetables that are thought to have negative properties, such as onions and garlic.

These dietary prohibitions and habits are based on the idea that food reflects the general qualities of nature: purity, energy, and inertia. The properties of food include both those that are intrinsic to it and those that are circumstantial. Pure foods such as dairy products and many vegetables are thought to foster spiritual inclinations. By contrast, meat, poultry, and onions are believed to give rise to passion and action, while stale food and liquor are seen as encouraging sloth. Thus a strict vegetarian diet is prescribed for people who are expected to cultivate spiritual tranquility and avoid passion, such as brahmins, Vaishnavas, and widows.

In addition, the nature of a given food is thought to be influenced by the inherent qualities of the person who cooks it. For this reason it was common even in the mid-twentieth century for strictly observant brahmins to eat only food prepared by people of their own caste.

Food is also auspicious and inauspicious. Weddings, funerals, ancestral rites, and birthdays require the use of auspicious lentils, spices, and vegetables. What one feeds the forefathers is different from what one feeds the gods and human beings; death and life-promoting rituals involve different kinds of food. Turmeric powder, for example, is auspicious, while sesame seed is inauspicious. Similarly, food prepared for ritual use in temple and death ceremonies is restricted to traditional ingredients; innovations such as potatoes and red peppers (both hot and sweet), introduced to India by Europeans in the last few centuries, are to be avoided.

A central element in temple rituals is the offering of food to the deity, after which the 'leftovers' are served to devotees as *prasada*. Inscriptions on the walls of medieval temples show that most endowments were intended for food offerings, and in the case of the temple at Tirupati, in Andra Pradesh, include detailed instructions for the preparation of offerings. Certain pilgrimage centres eventually became famous for particular kinds of *prasada*. The cooking and distribution of *prasada* is a multimillion-dollar industry in major temples such as the one in Tirupati.

Beyond the practicalities of use or avoidance, food appears in Hindu thought as an important symbol of spiritual experience. In a well-known story about the eighth-century poet-saint Nammalvar, the Supreme Being appears as the spiritual and physical nourisher of all human beings. Nammalvar has spent the first sixteen years of his life in a yogic trance, and has never eaten or spoken. Then an elderly brahmin is guided to him by a vision of light. To test Nammalvar, this man asks him a question: 'If a little thing is born out of the stomach of a dead thing, what will it eat and where will it lie?' When Nammalvar, speaking for the first time in his life, replies, 'It eats that, and lies there,' the old man is convinced of his wisdom and becomes his disciple. This exchange is usually paraphrased as follows: If a human soul takes on a body (since flesh by itself is considered to be a 'dead' or inanimate substance), what will nourish it, and what is its support? Nammalvar answers that the sustenance and support of the human soul is the Supreme Being, in this case the god Vishnu.

Food also plays an important role in medicine. Ayurvedic medicine recommends diets based on principles derived from texts ancillary to the Vedas, while many regional systems rely on different foods to rectify imbalances of 'cold' and 'heat' accumulated in the body.

The Annual Festival Cycle

In the Hindu tradition there is a festival of some kind almost every month of the year. The most popular are the birthdays of Rama, Krishna, and Ganesha.

Some festivals are specific to certain regions. Holi, for instance, is a north Indian festival celebrated in early spring with bonfires and abandoned throwing of coloured powder. It commemorates an event in the life of Prahlada, a devotee of Vishnu. To save Prahlada, Vishnu takes his fourth incarnation, that of a man-lion. In the state of Kerala, Onam is celebrated in August or September; the fifth incarnation of Vishnu as a dwarf-brahmin is remembered in that festival.

Other festivals, like Navaratri and Deepavali (Divali in some areas) are more or less pan-Hindu. A detailed discussion of Navaratri will give us an idea of the complexities involved in explaining the origins and the practice of the festivals within the many Hindu communities.

Navaratri

The festival of Navaratri ('nine nights') begins on the new moon that appears between 15 September and 14 October and is celebrated all over India, but in different ways and for different reasons.

In the region of Tamil Nadu, Navaratri is largely a festival for women. Exquisite dolls representing the goddesses Saraswati, Lakshmi, and Parvati are arranged in tableaux depicting scenes from the epics and *Puranas*. Every evening, women and children visit one another to admire the dolls, play musical instruments, and sing songs from the classical repertoire in praise of one or another of the goddesses. It is a joyous time of music and beauty, and a glorious celebration of womanhood. On the last two days—a special countrywide holiday—large pictures of Lakshmi and Saraswati, draped with garlands of fresh flowers, are placed in front of the display of dolls and worshipped.

In the state of West Bengal, by contrast, the same nine or ten days are dedicated to the goddess Durga. During Durga Puja, Hindus make sumptuous clay statues of

Durga for her spirit to inhabit; then, after nine nights, they immerse the statues in water to symbolize her return to the formless state. In the state of Gujarat Navaratri is celebrated with two special dances. In the circular dance called *garbha*, a sacred lamp is kept in the centre of the circle as a manifestation of the goddess. The second dance, called *dandiya*, is performed with sticks and recalls the dance that Krishna is said to have performed with the cowherd girls. In many parts of northern India during Navaratri women will invite seven pre-pubescent girls to a home for veneration as representatives of the goddess Durga.

Some Hindus believe that it was during the same nine nights and ten days that Rama battled Ravana. In Ramnagar, a city near Varanasi (Banaras) on the river Ganga, people act out the story of the *Ramayana* in a play called *Ram lila* and on the tenth day celebrate Rama's victory. Little boys play the parts of Rama and his brothers in what is considered to be India's largest outdoor theatre, spanning several hectares.

Some believe that it was on the ninth day of Navaratri that Arjuna found the weapons he had hidden a year before and paid his respects to them before entering battle. Because of this story, the last two days, dedicated to Lakshmi and Saraswati, are called *Ayudha Puja* ('veneration of weapons and machines'): cars and buses are draped with garlands, while computers and typewriters are blessed with sacred powders and given the day off work. The ninth day of the festival honours Sarasvati, the patron of learning and music. All the musical instruments in the house, any writing devices, and selected textbooks are placed in front of the deity's image, to be blessed by her for the rest of the year.

In many parts of India the last day of the festival is dedicated to Lakshmi. This is a time for fresh starts: to begin new ventures and new account books, to learn new prayers and music, to acquire new knowledge, and to honour traditional teachers. On the last days of the Navaratri festival, the fortune of learning, the wealth of wisdom, and the joy of music are said to be given by the grace of the goddesses.

Deepavali

Deepa means 'lamp', and *vali* means 'necklace' or 'row'; thus Deepavali (or Divali) means 'necklace of lights'. It is a Hindu festival of lights that takes place on the new moon between 15 October and 14 November. Seen as the beginning of a new year in some parts of India, it is celebrated by decorating houses with lights, setting off firecrackers, and wearing new clothes. As in the case of Navaratri, Hindus celebrate Deepavali for many reasons. In south India it is believed that on that day at dawn Krishna killed Narakasura, the wicked demon from the nether world, thus ensuring the victory of light over darkness. Fireworks, which resemble weapons, are used in celebrations all over India.

In north India Deepavali day marks the return of Rama to Ayodhya and his coronation, while in Gujarat it is the beginning of the new year, when businesses open new account books. In many parts of India the river Ganga itself is said to be present in all the waters on Deepavali day: thus people get up at four in the morning for a purifying ritual bath. The traditional greeting in some communities is 'Have you had a bath in the river Ganga?' New clothes are worn, presents are exchanged in some communities, and it is generally a time of feasting.

Life-Cycle Rites

Every culture has its rites of passage: rituals marking a person's transition from one stage of life to another. Some of the *dharmasastra* texts begin the discussion of the life-cycle sacraments with the birth of a child. Others begin with the sacrament of marriage, since it is in this context, properly speaking, that the next generation will begin.

Two factors are important to note in discussing life-cycle rites. First, not all are pan-Hindu, and even those that are may be relatively unimportant in some communities. Second, many of the important rites, especially those that are celebrated for girls or women, are not even discussed in any classical text. One reason may be the fact that most if not all the texts were written by and for men, to whom women were simply adjuncts. It may also be that some of these rites developed only after the texts were written. We shall discuss first the normative *dharmasastra* sacraments, and then look at a few of the rites of passage that have more localized regional importance.

A central concept in Hindu life is what is usually translated into English as 'auspiciousness'. Certain kinds of people, animals, rituals, smells, sounds, and food are considered auspicious because they are expected to bring about good fortune and a good quality of existence (*su asti*). A marriage is called 'the auspicious ceremony' in Tamil, and in some north Indian contexts the word *subha* ('auspicious') always precedes the word *vivaha* ('marriage'). All sacraments must be conducted at auspicious times as determined by the horoscopes of the individuals involved, which are cast at birth.

The right hand is associated with auspicious activities such as gift-giving, eating, and wedding rituals. The left hand is associated with the inauspicious: insults, bodily hygiene, and death, including funeral rites.

Birth Rituals

The Sanskrit term for life-cycle sacraments, *samskara*, specifically refers to a process of purifying or perfecting. This process begins well before birth, since the time of conception, the rituals administered to the expectant mother, and her behaviour during her pregnancy are all believed to influence the personality of the unborn child. Thus in traditional usage there was a ritual for the proper conception of a child, and mantras were to be recited before the prospective parents came together. In addition, the *Upanishads* prescribed certain rituals to be observed if one wanted, for example, a learned daughter or a heroic son— although in later times daughters were rarely if ever desired. While the conception sacrament has now been largely discarded, it still plays a part in wedding-night rituals.

According to some *dharmasastra* literature, the man is duty-bound to have intercourse with his wife at particular times of the month. A few even go so far as to say that if a man does not do so he is guilty of abortion. But these texts apparently have little influence today; abortion is legal in India and is practised quite widely.

Many communities in India also practise prenatal rites called *pumsavana* ('seeking a male offspring') and *simanta* ('hair parting'). Originally prescribed for the fifth month of pregnancy, they are performed later now to ensure the safe birth of a child, preferably a male.

The next ceremony, *jatakarma* ('birth action'), follows the birth. In earlier days it was supposed to be performed before the umbilical cord was cut, but it is now done much later. The moment of birth is also noted, so that the exact horoscope of the child can be cast. The *jatakarma* rites include *medhjanana* ('birth of intelligence'), in which the father seeks the intellectual well-being of the child, and *ayusya*, in which he prays for longevity for himself as well as the child: 'May we see a hundred autumns, may we hear a hundred autumns.' The ceremony ends with a request for the infant's physical strength and well-being.

Initiation Rituals

The ritual that traditionally initiates young boys of the three highest castes (especially brahmins) into the study of the Vedas is called *upanayana* or *brahma upadesa*. *Upanayana* can mean either 'acquiring the extra eye of knowledge' or 'coming close to a teacher' to get knowledge. *Brahma upadesha* means receipt of the sacred teaching (*upadesha*) concerning the Supreme Being (Brahman).

The *upanayana* ritual, traditionally performed around the age of eight, initiates boys into the first stage of life, called *brahmacharya*: literally, 'travelling on the path that will disclose the Supreme Being' (that is, studenthood). In this stage the student is to concentrate on acquiring knowledge rather than wealth. Therefore he does not work for a living, but is supported by society. Often the student lived in his teacher's house and begged his food from other households, then took it home for his teacher's wife to prepare. Before 600 BCE, women may also have undergone this ceremony, but that practice was discontinued.

The *upanayana* ritual takes two days. On the first day, the boy is bathed in water that has been blessed by the recitation of sacred verses from the Vedas invoking the essence of all the sacred and life-giving waters. In a larger sense, this ritual, called *udaga shanti* ('peace brought on the waters'), seeks peace on all the waters and lands of the earth. The verses end with several repetitions of the word *shanti*: peace for the individual, the soul, the body, the divine beings, the family, the community, and the entire earth.

On the second day the boy is given a sacred thread to wear over his left shoulder. This thread may represent an upper garment that the student was to wear when he was fit to perform a sacrifice, though it has also been interpreted as representing a spiritual umbilical cord symbolic of the boy's rebirth through his spiritual parent (his teacher), who will now initiate him into the study of the sacred texts.

Then comes the central part of the ritual: the actual *brahma upadesa*, or imparting of the sacred teaching on Brahman. As the boy sits with his father and the priest sits under a silk cloth (symbolizing the spiritual womb, in some interpretations), he is given a sacred mantra that he is to chant three times a day, 108 times in each session. The mantra is short: 'I meditate on the brilliance of the sun; may it illumine my mind.' This is the *Gayatri* or sun mantra, considered the most important of all mantras. The boy is then taken outside and shown the sun, the source of light, knowledge, and immortality. He has to twine his fingers in a particular way to ward off the harmful rays while looking directly at the heart of the sun.

In Vedic times and possibly even well into the first millennium of this era, the boy then went to live with his teacher for several years. Today, however, the ceremony is primarily social and generally performed only in brahminical circles. Efforts are underway to introduce similar initiation ceremonies for young girls.

Weddings

According to the *dharmasastra* codes of law and ethics, a man is born with debts to the sages, the gods, and the ancestors that he cannot repay without marrying. By performing the correct domestic and social rituals with—and only with—his wife, a man pays his debt to the god; by having children, the debt to the ancestors is discharged. A wife is a man's partner in fulfilling dharma, and without her he cannot fully perform his religious obligations.

Perhaps no rite within the Hindu tradition shows more regional variations than the wedding ceremony. In Kerala it may take less than a half hour; in other communities it may last five days.

Before a wedding can be planned, the parents of the prospective bride seek a suitable candidate with the help of the extended family and friends. Ideally, the bridegroom will come from the same geographic region, speak the same language, belong to the same community and subcommunity, and in some cases belong to a different *gotra* or clan. He should be compatible with the bride in education, looks, age, and outlook; the families should be of similar socio-economic status.

When such a young man is finally found, the family obtains his horoscope and has an astrologer compare it with that of the prospective bride. The purpose of this reading is not only to assess character and compatibility, but also to ensure balance: to minimize adversity in the future, the bad times predicted for each partner's life should not coincide. Parents will sometimes obtain a number of horoscopes before choosing the most suitable candidate. In the past, parents relied largely on informal networks to find prospective mates, but today such searches can be conducted by marriage bureaus, on the internet, and through newspaper advertisements. If the horoscopes match, the young people and their families meet to decide whether they like each other. Sometimes the decision is based on nothing more than a brief look at one another, and either party may opt out at this point. Sometimes the young people insist on getting to know each other a little better. Obviously, arranged marriages are becoming less common now that men and women are studying and working together. Today many couples marry across caste, community, language, and geographic boundaries, with or without their parents' approval.

Nevertheless, for the marriage to be considered legal, several rituals must still be observed. These include the *kanya dana* (the gift of the virgin by the father), *pani grahana* (the clasping of hands), *sapta padi* (taking seven steps together around a fire, which is the eternal witness), and *mangalya dharana* (the establishment of 'auspiciousness'). In addition the bride and groom exchange garlands.

Some weddings include a lavish exchange of presents with friends and extended family members, processions on horseback or in antique cars, fireworks, and entertainment in addition to a lavish feast. Typically, the atmosphere is extremely festive, and everyone has a good time. The ceremony itself lasts several hours and may involve several

A bride and groom of Gujarati background exchange garlands at their wedding in Tampa, Florida (Vasudha Narayanan).

changes of elaborate clothing and jewelry for the bride. The bride's parents have an active role to play, as do the groom's sister and the bride's brother and maternal uncle, but the guests are free to come and go as they please. During the *kanya dana* or 'giving of the virgin', the father of the bride recites words from the epic *Ramayana*. The words are those spoken to Rama by Sita's father: 'This is Sita, my daughter; she will be your partner in dharma.'

The groom's family then present the bride with 'the gift of auspiciousness', a necklace or string that corresponds to a Western wedding ring. The bride will wear it around her neck for the rest of her life, or until her husband dies. There is no equivalent symbol for the groom, although in the castes in which men wear the sacred thread, a double thread is worn once the man is married. In north India the bridegroom anoints the bride's forehead with *sindura*, a red mark near the parting of her hair indicating her married status.

In the central rite of the wedding, when the couple take seven steps around the fire together, the groom says:

Take the first step; Vishnu will follow you. You will not want for food for the rest of your life. Take the second step; Vishnu will guard your health. Take the third step; Vishnu will follow you and see that you may observe all religious rituals. Take the fourth step; Vishnu, following you, will grant you happiness. Take the fifth step; Vishnu will follow and grant you cattle and kine. Take the sixth step; let Vishnu follow you and let us enjoy the pleasures of the season. Take the seventh step; Vishnu will follow you. We shall worship together.

Then, clasping the bride's hand, the groom says:

You have taken seven steps with me; be my friend. We who have taken seven steps together have become companions. I have attained your friendship; I shall not forsake that friendship. Do not discard our relationship.

Let us live together; let us think together. We have come to a right and fitting stage of our lives; let us be happy and prosperous, thinking good thoughts. Let there be no difference in our hopes and efforts; let us attain our desires. And so we join ourselves (our lives). Let us be of one mind; let us act together and enjoy through all our senses, without any difference.

You are the song (*Sama*), I am the lyric (*Rig*), I am Sama, you are Rig. I am the sky, you are the earth. I am the seed; you shall bear my seed. I am thought; you are speech. I am the song, you are the lyric. Be conformable to me; O lady of sweet unsullied words, O gem of a woman, come with me; let us have children and attain prosperity together.

Many of these statements come from sections of the *Upanishads* and Vedas that prescribe ritual. The officiating priest speaks the mantras, which the bride and bridegroom repeat after him. In these extracts from the Vedic literature, the wife is not considered a man's possession, chattel, or obedient servant. She is his partner in dharma and his companion and friend in love.

All these central rituals must take place near a sacred fire. As the eternal witness to life and its sacraments, the sacred fire burns throughout the milestone moments of growth and aging. Offerings are made to the fire not only during the wedding, but in prenatal rites, when a child is one year old, when a man reaches the age of sixty, and again if he reaches eighty. Finally, when a person dies, his or her body is committed to fire. A wedding is valid only if the couple is married with a fire as the witness.

In another ritual the bridegroom bends down and places the bride's foot on a firm heavy stone. The act itself is significant in that the man touches the bride's feet. This is an unequivocal gesture of respect in Hindu culture, for the body represents a hierarchy. He then places rings on her toes, saying, 'Stand on this stone, be firm and steady as this stone. Stand conquering those who oppose you; be victorious over your enemies.'

Later in the evening, in a ritual called *Arundhati darshana* ('the sighting of Arundhati'), the newly married couple are taken to see the stars in the sky. In Indian astrology the seven stars of the Great Bear constellation are the seven sages, one of which is Vaisistha, and a small companion star represents his wife Arundhati, a symbol of fidelity throughout India. Just as the companion stars remain close together through the years, so the husband and wife are urged to stay together forever.

Funeral Rites

Funeral rites reflect a combination of beliefs drawn from the Vedas, the *Bhagavad Gita*, and the particular philosophies of various sects. Death is associated with pollution, and the family of the deceased is considered to be polluted by it for a certain period of time (from twelve days to almost a year). Usually the body is cremated within a few hours—at most a day—of death. In most Hindu traditions the final sacrament is cremation, although in a few communities, such as the Virasaivas, and in the case of an infant or an ascetic, the body may be buried. Until the body is removed and the cremation fire is lit, no fire is to be lit or tended in the house where the death occurred.

These rituals are normally performed by the eldest son. For the first few days, the spirit of the deceased is a *preta* or ghost. To quench the thirst it is believed to suffer as a result of cremation, the spirit is offered water and balls of rice for a few days. Some of the rituals go back to the earliest Vedic times, when the dead were thought to live on the far side of the moon and thus to need sustenance for their journey.

After a designated number of days, varying among different castes, there is an 'adoption of auspiciousness', when the injunctions relating to pollution are lifted. The first anniversary of the death is marked with further ceremonies, and the family is then freed from all constraints.

Women's Rituals

Though most women's rituals are domestic, undertaken for the welfare of the family and earthly happiness, a few are intended solely for personal salvation or liberation. Many practices, such as worship at home shrines or temples, pilgrimages, and the singing of devotional songs, are similar to those undertaken by men, but some are unique to married women whose husbands are alive. Underlying many of the rites is the notion that women are powerful and that rites performed by them have potency. Though many women's rituals share certain features, the differences among the many communities, castes, and regions are so great that generalizations should be avoided.

Early History

There is some evidence in the early Vedas, beginning around 1500 BCE, that upper-caste girls may have been permitted, following initiation, to study the Vedas. The epics tell of women lighting and tending the sacrificial fire to make ritual offerings to the gods. They also refer to women ascetics, who would presumably have undergone renunciatory rites similar to those required of men. These privileges appear to have been withdrawn by the beginning of the Common Era, however.

Calendrical Rituals Today

Many traditional women's rituals are no longer practised today. Yet there are still a number of votive rituals (*vrata*) that are observed on particular days during specific lunar months. These domestic rituals involve the welfare of others—whether one's husband, extended family, or community—and only unmarried women or married women whose husbands are alive may participate in them; widows are excluded. While Sanskrit manuals say that these rites enable a woman to attain final liberation from the cycle of birth and death, most women who perform them pray either for marriage or for a long life for their husbands.

After prayers to the family deity, the women may eat a meal together and distribute emblems of auspiciousness such as betel leaves, bananas, coconuts, turmeric, and kumkum powder. The rituals may last anywhere between a few minutes and five days, with periods of fasting alternating with communal eating.

In a special worship ceremony in the month of Adi (15 July–14 August), women at the Marudeesvarar (Shiva) temple in Tiruvanmiyur, Chennai, invoke the Goddess Lalitha (a form of Parvati) into the lamps (Vasudha Narayanan).

In south India women's rituals are celebrated by many communities during the month of Adi (15 July–14 August). Married women were traditionally enjoined to stay celibate during this month. Brahmin women pray to the goddess Lakshmi for domestic happiness. Women of some non-brahminical castes carry special pots of water and other ritual items to temples of a local goddess and worship her for the benefit of the entire family. Others cook rice and milk dishes in the temples of the local goddesses and distribute the food. In the temple of Draupadi Amman, women and men alike enter a trance and walk over hot coals in a ceremony called 'walking on flowers'.

In north India many women's rites focus on the welfare of male relatives. In late summer, for example, girls tie a protective cord around the wrists of their brothers. And in October–November, women undertake two fasts for the well-being of their husbands, as well as one for the health of their sons. These daytime fasts are broken only after the stars come out in the evening.

Women's Life-Cycle Rituals

Life-cycle rituals for upper-caste women are similar to those performed for men and include those associated with weddings, funerals, and the naming of children. There are also many other sacraments associated with women that have not received scriptural ratification. Some of these rites are performed only in some regions and communities.

In the past it was common to celebrate a young girl's first menstrual period, since this 'blossoming' meant that she was ready for marriage. Urban girls now tend to consider this practice vulgar, but in rural areas the celebration can still resemble a mini-wedding, and the girl is showered with money or clothing by her family.

Special rituals may also attend pregnancy, especially the first. In south India one popular ritual is called 'bracelets and amulets'. The pregnant woman is dressed in a heavy silk *sari*, and women of all ages slip bangles and bracelets onto her arm. In earlier days a bangle-seller was invited and the woman's parents gave everyone who attended the ceremony glass bracelets that were supposed to safeguard the wearer from evil spirits.

In another rite the expectant mother's hair is adorned with flowers, to enhance the natural radiance that is often said to accompany pregnancy. In the Hindu tradition married women often wear flowers in their hair, but normally only a bride's hair is completely woven with flowers. Rituals such as these acknowledge the importance of a woman's body and celebrate its life-bearing potential.

Attitudes towards Women

On the whole, Hindu scriptures and ritual reflect contradictory views of women. An understanding of what constitutes auspiciousness may help to clarify some of the contradictions.

Auspiciousness refers to prosperity in this life. Thus married women with the potential to bear children are auspicious because they further the three fundamental human goals recognized by classical scriptures: dharma (duty), *artha* (prosperity), and *kama* (sensual pleasure).

In the classical literature of the *dharmasastras* and in practice, even today, a *sumangali*—a woman whose husband is alive—is auspicious because she can be a full partner in dharma, *artha*, and *kama*, can bear children, and can help her husband acquire both wealth and religious merit. Only a married woman can be honoured with the title Srimati ('the one with *sri* or auspiciousness'). Traditionally, the Hindu wife was to be faithful to her husband in life and faithful to his memory after his death. Some of these notions are still important. In the *Puranas*, which reflect codes of conduct (*dharmasastras*) dating back to the beginnings of our era, it was the dharma of a faithful wife to worship and serve her husband as a god. At the same time her fidelity gave the faithful wife almost limitless powers. Both the *Puranas* and the oral tradition include many stories about the power of the faithful wife to save lives and even perform miracles.

Women and Pollution

In the Hindu tradition menstruation was generally regarded as physically polluting. This attitude used to be prevalent in almost all communities except the Vira Shaiva, and it entailed the total removal of the menstruating woman from everyday life. This strict segregation is no longer observed by most people, though vestiges remain in some families. Frequently, menstruating women are prohibited from cooking even in Vira Shaiva households, and most communities do not permit menstruating women to participate in any religious ritual or even to attend a place of worship. Hindu women almost invariably have a purifying ritual bath on the fourth day.

The same concept of pollution extends to childbirth. Even though the birth of a child is a happy and auspicious occasion, it is thought to render the entire family ritually impure. For several days after the birth, the family cannot go to a temple or celebrate an auspicious event, and the mother, who may bleed for up to six weeks after giving birth, is treated as if she were menstruating.

Interaction and Adaptation

Religious Leaders

For more than 20,000 years Hindus have venerated holy men and women. The *Taittiriya Upanishad* exhorts a departing student to consider his *acharya* (religious instructor) as a god, and there have been countless other gurus, ascetics, mediums, storytellers, and *sadhus* ('holy men') who have commanded anything from obedience to veneration. It would not be an exaggeration to say that for many Hindus, the primary religious experience is mediated by someone they believe to be in some way divine.

This is no less true of modern times than of the ancient past. Followers of Sri Sathya Sai Baba (Sathya Narayan Raju, b. 1926), a charismatic teacher from Andhra Pradesh in the south, believe him to be an *avatara*. The abbots of three monasteries established by the philosopher Shankara in the eighth century exercise considerable leadership among the educated urban population, as do a number of intellectual

Vedantic commentators. In their interpretation of the ancient scriptures and their mediation of traditional values, we see the dynamic and adaptable nature of the Hindu tradition.

Like *acharyas*, gurus also attract wide followings. Whereas most *acharyas* belong to specific sectarian traditions, however, gurus are not necessarily connected to any particular lineage. In other words, all *acharyas* are gurus, but not all gurus are *acharyas*. Another difference is that many women have been gurus, while *acharyas* are almost invariably male. Unlike *acharyas*, who usually teach particular sectarian traditions, gurus, male or female, tend to emphasize more 'universal' and humanist messages, stressing the divinity in all human beings and encouraging their followers to transcend caste and community distinctions. An example is Ma Amritananda Mayi ('Ammachi'). Known as the 'hugging guru', she is one of the most popular female religious leaders in the world today, and her movement sponsors an international network of charitable, humanitarian, educational, and medical institutions.

Many charismatic teachers are called *swami* ('master') by their followers. Others may have titles derived from the name given to the composers of the Vedas: *rishi* ('seer'). An example is the founder of the Transcendental Meditation movement, popularly known in the west as TM. Maharishi ('great seer') Mahesh Yogi (b. 1911) is probably one of the most influential teachers in the Western world.

Modern Reproductive Technology

Of all the technological innovations developed in recent years, those associated with reproduction tend to be among the most controversial. Yet Hindus appear on the whole to be quite accepting of intervention in this area. In the case of assisted reproduction, this acceptance is probably not surprising: the traditional teachings on dharma have always emphasized that reproduction is a primary duty. Thus many Hindus today accept artificial insemination, for example, although the husband is generally the only acceptable donor. In particular, members of the 'higher' castes, which set great store by their lineage, are more likely to seek technological help than to adopt a child of unknown background.

In fact, many stories about supernatural or 'unnatural' means of conception and childbirth can be found in the classic literature. In the *Mahabharata*, a queen named Gandhari grows 100 sons in brass jars. In other texts, an embryo is transplanted from one woman to another, Krishna's brother Balarama is transplanted into another womb, and deities are invoked to 'fertilize' women whose husbands cannot procreate.

The ethical considerations become more complex where issues such as contraception and gender selection are concerned. For thousands of years, male children were more welcome than females, largely because of the traditional duty to the ancestors: in a patriarchal, patrilineal society, sons would continue the family line and could be counted on to look after their parents in old age, whereas daughters would be of benefit only to their husbands' families. Indeed, the cost of providing a dowry for a daughter represented a significant financial burden for many families.

Today sonograms and amniocentesis are often used for the express purpose of ascertaining the sex of the fetus early in pregnancy, so that female fetuses can be aborted. As a result, the numbers of female births have dropped dramatically in recent years.

According to the *dharmasastra* texts, the unborn fetus has life; according to popular belief and stories from the *Puranas*, the fetus is even capable of hearing conversations that take place around it and learning from them. Nevertheless abortions are legal in India and are accepted without any strong dissent from religious leaders or prolonged editorial, legislative, or judicial debate.

Thus it appears that the dharma texts do not have the compelling authority of their counterparts in some other religious traditions.

The Hindu Diaspora

When the first brahmins crossed the seas to Cambodia and Indonesia, early in the first millennium CE, it was not long before they began building temples. The process of emigration has continued. Since the 1970s Hindu immigrants have been transforming their new homes in North America into sacred places.

Places of worship were established in the United States as early as 1906 in the San Francisco area, but the first really ambitious attempt to reproduce the traditional architecture and atmosphere of a Vaishnava sacred place was the Sri Venkateswara temple in Penn Hills, a suburb of Pittsburgh, Pennsylvania, built in 1976. The Penn Hills temple enshrines a manifestation of Vishnu as Venkateswara, lord of the hill known as Venkata ('that which can burn sins') in the south Indian state of Andra Pradesh. (Other Venkateswara temples have been established in California, Illinois, and Georgia.) The Penn Hills temple was built with the help, backing, and blessing of one of the oldest, richest, and most popular temples in India, the Venkateswara temple at Tiru Venkatam.

Despite devotees' desire to maintain sacred traditions and remain faithful to the architectural forms common in India, some compromises and innovations have been necessary. As far as possible, for example, the ritual calendar has been adapted to fit the American secular calendar, since many festival organizers live far from the temple and long weekends are often the only time they can travel. Nevertheless, the land on which the temple is located is considered no less sacred than the land in India where Tiru Venkatam stands. The devotees celebrate the significance of having Venkateswara dwelling on American soil with his consort Sri (known locally as 'the lady of the lotus' or Padmavati). In a popular song that was recorded and sold to temple visitors in the 1980s, the following verse is sung in Sanskrit:

Victory to Govinda [Krishna], who lives in America,
Victory to Govinda, who is united with Radha who lives on Penn Hills,
Victory to the Teacher, Victory to Krishna.

The idea that that the Penn Hills temple is located on sacred land is not merely abstract. Devotees see the entire Pittsburgh area as geographically similar to the sacred land of India. Drawing on *Puranic* lore, the Penn Hills devotees see their temple's physical location—at the confluence of three rivers, one of them subterranean—as recalling the sacred place in India where the rivers Ganga and Yamuna meet the underground Sarasvati. As they described it in 1986:

> Pittsburgh, endowed with hills and a multitude of trees as well as the confluence of the three rivers, namely, the Allegheny, the Monongehela, and the subterranean river (brought up via the 60 foot high fountain at downtown) to form the Ohio river is indeed a perfect choice for building the first and most authentic temple to house Lord Venkateswara. The evergrowing crowds that have been coming to *the city with the thriveni Sangama* [confluence of three rivers] to worship at the Temple with the *three vimanas* reassure our belief that the venerable Gods chose this place and the emerald green hillock to reside in.

The concept of sacred land is not unique to the Penn Hills devotees. Republicans from the Hindu community in the Dallas–Fort Worth area understand the notion of *karmabhumi*—the land where actions bear fruit, where actions produce merit or demerit—in a far broader sense than the authors of the *dharmasastras* intended. An 'Asian Indian Caucus Booklet' circulated by a small group of Hindus at the Republican party convention in Dallas in 1984 underlines the importance of sacred land to many Hindus. Reporting on the convention, the writer V.S. Naipaul (b. 1932) quoted from the booklet:

> Indians immigrated to the USA to pursue their 'DREAM' to achieve fully their potentials in this land of 'Opportunities'. They came in pursuit of their dreams, visions, happiness and to achieve excellence. . . . During the last few years most of the people have changed from 'Green card holder' status to that of 'US CITIZENS', thus enabling themselves to be full participants in socio-economic and political processes. They have chosen, by their free will, the USA as the 'KARMABHUMI'—the land of karma or action.

That a place outside India could be the *karmabhumi* is a new idea in Hinduism. According to the lawmakers, the land of the Aryas where the black antelope roams was the only land that could be called *karmabhumi*. Apparently some Hindus in America have extended the concept to the big-sky rangeland where the deer and the antelope play.

Miracles and Temple-Building

Statues of Venkateswara and his consorts were carved in India, then brought to the United States, and consecration rituals were performed at Penn Hills. Although the establishment of the temple was almost a miracle in itself, given the bureaucratic red tape involved, the temple does not have an origin myth. Other temples in America do, however. An origin myth involves a dream or vision, or the 'discovery' of the form of the lord in natural formations such as mountains or caves.

Generally these origin myths are associated with Shaiva temples, especially if there is a strong connection with American devotees. Thus the Light of Truth Universal Shrine temple at Yogaville, Virginia, was established in response to a vision experienced by Swami Satchidananda (b. 1919) of the Divine Life Mission. Overlooking the temple is a mountain called Kailas, after the traditional abode of Shiva. The Iraivan/Kadavul temple on Kauai, Hawaii, was built in 1970 by Swami Shivaya Subramuniyaswami (1927–2001), who was born in America and initiated in Sri Lanka. In 1975 he had three visions of Shiva walking in the meadows near the Wailua River. Twelve years later, a rare Shiva *linga*, a six-sided quartz crystal, was discovered and taken to Kauai from Arkansas. A new Iraivan temple expected to last for a thousand and one years is now being built of stone carved in Bangalore and shipped to Hawaii.

Perhaps the most unusual temple with mythic origins is the one at Wahiawa (Oahu), Hawaii, now run entirely by Hindus from India. This temple is dedicated to Visvanatha (which they translate as 'lord of the universe'), and the organization in charge of it is called the Lord of the Universe Society. The Shiva *linga* at the Wahiawa temple, said to be a healing stone, is believed to be the embodiment of the Hawaiian god Lono, a priest-healer of ancient times whom the Hindus believe to be a manifestation of Shiva. According to another myth, this stone represents two sisters from Kauai who are turned into rocks. Classic hierophany (manifestation of the divine) is seen in this statement issued by the society:

> The Sacred Healing Stone has been discovered and rediscovered. Several people have experienced healings, visions, dreams and profound feeling of peace and well-being after coming into contact with the Healing Stone and its powers. . . . [In] March 1988, some Indians were taken to the Healing Stone by their friends and they were awe-stricken by the resemblance of the Sacred Healing Stone to Lord Shiva in the form of a Shiva Lingam. . . . In April 1988 a special Pooja was organized. It became apparent to those who attended the Pooja that this place was indeed special, sacred and holy (Sengupta n.d.).

In undertaking to build a temple, overseas Hindu communities gain more than a local place of worship with formally consecrated icons, where sacraments can be conducted and offerings of devotion made. They also acquire an institution that has self-consciously taken on the role of educating the younger American-born generation through weekly language and religion classes, frequent lectures, sponsorship of classical music and dance (which have a broad religious base in India), summer camps, and an outreach bulletin.

New temples are springing up all over the North American landscape. In many cases the community hall is built even before the shrine. This emphasis on community life is understandable at a time when Hindus are trying to assert their identity in a society where they feel culturally and linguistically marginalized. The community hall is a place where different groups can meet for classes in language, music, and dance.

Significantly, disputes arise within the North American community over which deity is to be enshrined and what mode of worship is to be adopted. Devotees of Vishnu, Shiva, the Goddess, or Ganesha, or those who worship Vishnu as Rama or Krishna, want the temple to be primarily dedicated to that deity. In this way a temple intended to unite the Hindu community in the diaspora frequently gives rise to division. The reason is clear: as we noted at the outset, Hinduism is not a unitary tradition. It is not a single identity, and it lacks a united community and central authority. Because of its

Almost every village has a locally important temple, and countless hills, mountains, rivers, and groves are considered sacred. The following list is only a very small sample.

Badrinath, Uttaranchal. An important pilgrimage site, high in the mountains, with a temple of Vishnu in the form of the sages Nara and Narayana; one of 108 sacred places for the Sri Vaishnava community.

Chidambaram, Tamilnadu. The abode of Nataraja, the Dancing Shiva, a large temple complex with shrines to both Shiva and Vishnu.

Haridwar, Uttaranchal. One of seven holy sites identified in the Puranas. Located on the banks of the river Ganga, it is one of the cities where a great festival called Kumbha Mela is held.

Guruvayur, Kerala. This temple dedicated to the youthful Krishna draws millions of pilgrims every year.

Kanchipuram, Tamilnadu. A temple town important for at least two millennia, home to dozens of temples dedicated to Vishnu and Shiva.

Mount Kailas. An important peak in the Himalayan range, said to be the abode of Lord Shiva.

Kamkhya, Assam. One of the most important Shakti *peethas* (sites where the power of the Goddess is said to be palpably felt). The temple is dedicated to the goddess Kamakhya, a form of Shakti/Parvati/Durga.

Kanya Kumari, Tamilnadu. A small temple town at the southernmost tip of the Indian peninsula, famous for its temple dedicated to Parvati.

Madurai, Tamilnadu. A large city, important for more than two thousand years and home to dozens of temples including a famous complex dedicated to the goddess Meenakshi (a form of Parvati) and the god Sundareswar (Shiva).

Mathura and **Brindavan, Uttar Pradesh.** A city and a complex of pastoral and urban pilgrimage sites nearby, all associated with incidents in the early life of Krishna.

Nathdwara, Rajasthan. Home of a celebrated temple to Krishna in the form of Srinathji, in which legend says he lifted up the mountain Govardhana. Located near Udaipur.

Pandharpur, Maharashtra. Home of a temple to Vithoba or Vitthala (a form of Vishnu) and Rukmini (Lakshmi).

Continued

Prayag, Uttar Pradesh. The holy site where the Ganga and Yamuna rivers are said to come together with a legendary subterranean river called Saraswati.

Puri, Orissa. Site of a temple dedicated to Jagannath (a form of Vishnu), his brother Balabhadra, and their sister, Subhadra. Also the site of a famous festival (Ratha Yatra) in which Lord Jagannath (the origin of the English word 'juggernaut') is taken through the streets on a huge chariot.

Sabarimala, Kerala. A temple to Ayyappan, set in the hills of Kerala and site of an important pilgrimage where millions of pilgrims, almost all male, congregate every January. Women are ordinarily forbidden to make the pilgrimage

Srirangam, Tamilnadu. An island temple-town in the Kaveri river, where Vishnu, here called Ranganatha ('Lord of the stage'), reclines on the serpent Ananta ('infinity'); one of the most important pilgrimage sites for the followers of Vishnu, celebrated in the poems of the Alvars.

Tirumala-Tirupati (also known as Tiruvenkatam), Andhra Pradesh. Probably one of the most important pilgrimage sites in India. The temple, located on seven hills, is dedicated to Venkateswara (Vishnu) and is said to be the richest religious institution in the world next to the Vatican.

Vaishno Devi, Jammu and Kashmir. Located at an elevation of more than 1580 metres, this temple is dedicated to the Goddess Vaishno Devi, who is sometimes perceived as a form of Durga and sometimes as an amalgamation of all the major goddesses.

Varanasi, Uttar Pradesh. Also known as Kasi or Banaras; one of the holiest cities in India, located on the banks of the river Ganga. After cremation, many Hindus' ashes are brought here to be ritually submerged in the waters.

diversity, reaching consensus is almost impossible. Lines are drawn along sectarian, caste, and regional lines, and debates continue as they have throughout the history of the tradition.

Conclusion: The Future of Hinduism

As the communities in the diaspora face the challenges of raising a new generation in the faith, Hindus in many parts of the world are engaging in the process of self-definition. Many of the statements made in this context are questionable and may not be historically true. Examples include statements such as 'Hinduism is not a religion, it is a way of life,' or 'Hinduism is a tolerant religion.' The difficulty of proving or disproving such claims only underscores the complexities of a religious tradition that has evolved through more than 3,000 years of recorded history—5,000 if the Harappa culture is included.

The dynamism of the many Hindu traditions is unmistakable. Vedanta is continually being interpreted. People continue to experience possession by deities, to situate their homes in auspicious directions, and to choose religiously correct times for happy events. Temples continue to be built, consecrated, and preserved. The sacred words of the Vedas and the *smrti* literature are still broadcast widely. Manuscripts are being restored, edited, and published, and new technologies are making literature more widely accessible; the tradition confining the sacred word to particular castes is gone forever. The airwaves are flooded with religious programs, horoscopes are cast and matched by computer, surgeries are scheduled for auspicious times. In short, Hinduism continues to adapt to changing times and different lands.

Glossary

acharya The leading teacher of a sect or the head of a monastery.

Advaita Shankara's school of philosophy, which holds that there is only one ultimate reality, the indescribable Brahman, with which the **Atman** or self is identical.

Alvars Twelve devotional poets in South India whose works are central to the *bhakti* tradition.

artha Wealth and power; one of the three classical aims in life.

ashramas Four stages in the life of an upper-class male: student, householder, forest-dweller, and ascetic.

Atman The individual self, held by Upanishadic and Vedantic thought to be identical with **Brahman**, the world-soul.

avatara A 'descent' or incarnation of a deity in earthly form.

Ayurveda A system of traditional medicine, understood as a teaching transmitted from the sages.

Bhagavad Gita A section of the *Mahabharata* epic recounting a conversation between Krishna and the warrior Arjuna, in which Krishna explains the nature of God and the human soul.

bhakti Loving devotion to a deity seen as a gracious being who enters the world for the benefit of humans.

Brahma A creator god; not to be confused with **Brahman**.

Brahman The world-soul, sometimes understood in impersonal terms.

Brahmanas Texts regarding ritual.

brahmin A member of the priestly class.

darshana Seeing and being seen by the deity in the temple or by a holy teacher; the experience of beholding with faith.

devanagari The alphabet used to write Sanskrit and northern Indian vernacular languages such as Hindi and Bengali.

dharma Religious and social duty, including both righteousness and faith.

Deepavali (Divali) Festival of light in October–November, when lamps are lit.

guru A spiritual teacher.

Holi Spring festival celebrated by throwing brightly coloured water or powder.

jnana Knowledge; along with action and devotion, one of the three avenues to liberation explained in the *Bhagavad Gita*.

kama Sensual (not merely sexual) pleasure; one of the three classical aims of life.

karma Action, good and bad, as it is believed to determine the quality of rebirth in future lives.

ksatriya A member of the warrior class in ancient Hindu society.

linga A conical or cylindrical stone column, sometimes considered phallic, symbolic of the god Shiva.

Mahabharata A very long epic poem, one section of which is the *Bhagavad Gita*.

mantra An expression of one or more syllables, chanted repeatedly as a focus of concentration in devotion.

moksha Liberation from the cycle of birth and death; one of the three classical aims in life.

murti A form or personification in which divinity is manifested.

Navaratri 'Nine nights'; an autumn festival honouring the Goddess.

om A syllable chanted in meditation, interpreted as representing ultimate reality, or the universe, or the relationship of the devotee to the deity.

prasada A gift from the deity, especially food that has been presented to the god's temple image, blessed, and returned to the devotee.

puja Ritual household worship of the deity, commonly involving oil lamps, incense, prayers, and food offerings.

Puranas 'Old tales', stories about deities that became important after the Vedic period.

Ramayana An epic recounting the life of Lord Rama, an incarnation of the god Vishnu.

rishi A seer; the composers of the ancient Vedic hymns are viewed as *rishis*.

sadhu A holy man.

samnyasin A religious ascetic; one who has reached the fourth of the classical stages of life for Hindu males after student, householder, and forest-dweller.

samsara The continuing cycle of rebirths.

sati The self-sacrifice of a widow who throws herself onto her deceased husband's funeral pyre.

shruti 'What is heard'; the sacred literature of the Vedic and Upanishadic periods, recited orally by the brahmin priests for many centuries before being written down.

shudra A member of the lowest of the four major classes, usually translated as 'servant', though some groups within the *shudra* class could be quite prosperous.

smrti 'What is remembered', a body of ancient Hindu literature, including the epics, *Puranas*, and law codes, formed after the *shruti* and passed down in written tradition.

tantra A esoteric school outside the Vedic and brahminical tradition, which emerged around the fifth century and centred on a number of controversial ritual practices, some of them sexual.

tilaka A dot or mark on the forehead made with coloured powder.

upanayana The initiation of a young brahmin boy into ritual responsibility, in which he is given a cord to wear over his left shoulder and a mantra to recite and is sent to beg for food for the day.

Upanishads Philosophical texts in the form of reported conversations on the theory of the Vedic ritual and the nature of knowledge, composed around the sixth century BCE.

vaisya A member of the third or mercantile class in the ancient fourfold class structure.

Vedas The four collections of hymns and ritual texts that constitute the oldest and most highly respected Hindu sacred literature.

yoga A practice and discipline that may involve a philosophical system and mental concentration as well as physical postures and exercises.

Further Reading

Baird, Robert D. 1993. *Religions and Law in Independent India*. New Delhi: Manohar. Takes up some problems of the status of various groups.

_____, ed. 1995. *Religion in Modern India*. 3rd ed. New Delhi: Manohar. Good individual chapters on nineteenth- and twentieth-century sectarian movements.

Basham, Arthur Llewellyn. 1954. *The Wonder That Was India*. London: Sidgwick & Jackson. Arguably still the definitive introduction to the pre-Muslim culture of the sub-continent.

Beny, Roloff, and Aubrey Menen. 1969. *India*. London: Thames and Hudson. Menen's text interspersed with Beny's photographs in this coffee-table book provides a lively sixty-page introduction to the culture—opinionated and provocative.

Bhattacharji, Sukumari. 1970. *The Indian Theogony: A Comparative Study of Indian Mythology from the Vedas to the Puranas*. Cambridge: Cambridge University Press. Good for tracing the shift from Vedic to other deities as the focus of devotion.

Blurton, T. Richard. 1992. *Hindu Art*. London: British Museum Press; Cambridge: Harvard University Press. A good introductory survey.

Brown, C. Mackenzie. 1990. *The Triumph of the Goddess: The Canonical Models and Theological Visions of the Devi-Bhagavata Purana*. Albany: State University of New York Press. Study of a text important for feminine manifestations of deity.

Bumiller, Elisabeth. 1990. *May You Be the Mother of a Hundred Sons. A Journey among the Women of India*. Useful insights into Indian society.

Chapple, Christopher, and Mary Evelyn Tucker, eds. 2000. *Hinduism and Ecology: The Intersection of Earth, Sky, and Water*. Cambridge, MA: Center for the Study of World Religions, Harvard Divinity School. Part of an important series in which various traditions address current environmental issues.

Chatfield, Charles, ed. 1976. *The Americanization of Gandhi: Images of the Mahatma*. New York: Garland. Includes American applications of Gandhi's ideas concerning the struggle for racial justice.

de Bary, William Theodore, ed. 1958 *Sources of Indian Tradition*. New York: Columbia University Press. The classic sourcebook: well selected, well introduced.

Dimock, Edward C., Jr., and Denise Levertov, trans. 1967. *In Praise of Krishna: Songs from the Bengali*. Garden City, NY: Doubleday. Lyrical expressions of devotion in eastern India.

Doniger O'Flaherty, Wendy, ed. and trans. 1988. *Textual Sources for the Study of Hinduism*. Manchester: Manchester University Press. A good sourcebook in a rather compressed format, covering the main phases of the Hindu tradition.

Eck, Diana L. 1981. *Darcan: Seeing the Divine Image in India*. Chambersburg, Penn.: Anima Books. Brief but authoritative, on the significance of coming into the presence of the deity.

Embree, Ainslie T., ed. *Sources of Indian Tradition*. 2nd ed. 2 vols. New York: Columbia University Press. 1988. Expands on the de Bary first edition but drops a few items in the process.

Erndl, Kathleen M. 1993. *Victory to the Mother: The Hindu Goddess of Northwest India in Myth, Ritual, and Symbol*. New York: Oxford University Press. Well focused on one region.

Felton, Monica G. 1967. *A Child Widow's Story*. New York: Harcourt, Brace & World. Brings concreteness to description of social situations.

Findly, Ellison B. 1985. 'Gargi at the King's Court: Women and Philosophic Innovation in Ancient India'. In Yvonne Y. Haddad and Ellison B. Findly, eds. *Women, Religion and Social Change*, 37–58. Albany: State University of New York Press. Shows that intellectual activity was not totally limited to males.

Harlan, Lindsey, and Paul B. Courtright, eds. 1995. *From the Margins of Hindu Marriage: Essays on Gender, Religion, and Culture*. New York: Oxford University Press. A useful collection.

Hawley, John S., and Donna M. Wulff. 1982. *The Divine Consort: Radha and the Goddesses of India*. Berkeley: Berkeley Religious Studies Series. Another useful work on feminine aspects of the Hindu tradition.

_____. 1996. *Devi: Goddesses of India*. Berkeley: University of California Press. Expands on the theme of the previous work.

Hiriyanna, Mysore. 1985. *The Essentials of Indian Philosophy*. London: Allen and Unwin. A frequently consulted, accessible introduction.

Jones, Kenneth W. 1976. *Arya Dharm: Hindu Consciousness in 19th-century Punjab*. Berkeley: University of California Press. Describes Dayananda Sarasvati's Arya Samaj and its legacy in modern India.

Kinsley, David. 1986. *Hindu Goddesses: Visions of the Divine Feminine in the Hindu Religious Tradition*. Berkeley: University of California Press. Separate chapters on individual figures.

_____. 1997. *Tantric Visions of the Divine Feminine: The Ten Mahavidyas*. Berkeley: University of California Press. Responsible approach to a controversial topic.

Leslie, Julia, ed. 1991. *Roles and Rituals for Hindu Women*. London: Pinter; Rutherford, NJ: Fairleigh Dickinson University Press. A coherent set of essays on the subject.

Lopez, Donald S., Jr., ed. 1995. *Religions of India in Practice*. Princeton: Princeton University Press. A sourcebook containing a fine range of material; strong on ritual.

Marglin, Frédérique, and John B. Carman, eds. 1985. *Purity and Auspiciousness in Indian Society*. Leiden: E.J. Brill, 1985. A useful collection, in an anthropological series.

Michell, George. 1989. *The Penguin Guide to the Monuments of India*. Vol. 1. London: Penguin. Local maps, plans, and descriptions of pre-Mughal Indian temples and other sites.

Miller, Barbara Stoler, trans. 1977. *Love Song of the Dark Lord: Jayadeva's Gitagovinda*. New York: Columbia University Press. An important *bhakti* text.

Narayan, R.K. 1972. *Ramayana: A Shortened Modern Prose Version of the Indian Epic*. New York: Viking. A useful point of access to this classic.

Narayanan, Vasudha. 1994. *The Vernacular Veda: Revelation, Recitation, and Ritual Practice*. Columbia: University of South Carolina Press. The ritual use of the *Tiruvaymoli* among India's scheduled castes as well as brahmins.

_____. 1996. '"One Tree Is Equal to Ten Sons": Hindu Responses to the Problems of Ecology, Population, and Consumption'. *Journal of the American Academy of Religion* 65 (1996), 291–332. Discusses some classic resources for addressing concerns of today.

Olivelle, Patrick, trans. 1996. *Upanisads*. New York: Oxford University Press.

_____, trans. 1997. *The Pancatantra: The Book of India's Folk Wisdom*. New York: Oxford University Press.

_____, trans. 1999. *Dharmasutras: The Law Codes of Atastamba, Gautama, Baudhyayana, and Vasistha*. New York: Oxford University Press. This and the two foregoing items are lucid translations of influential texts.

Orr, Leslie C. 2000. *Donors, Devotees, and Daughters of God: Temple Women in Medieval Tamilnadu*. New York: Oxford University Press. Provides a useful corrective to prescriptive male writings in Sanskrit on Hindu women.

Radhakrishnan, Sarvepalli, and Charles A. Moore, eds. 1957. *A Source Book in Indian Philosophy*. Princeton: Princeton University Press. Still the best anthology for philosophical texts.

Rajagopalachari, Chakravarti. 1953. *Mahabharata*. Bombay: Bharatiya Vidya Bhavan. A sampling from this vast epic.

Ramanujan, A.K., trans. 1981. *Hymns for the Drowning: Poems for Visnu by Nammawvar*. Princeton: Princeton University Press. An excellent source for Tamil *bhakti*.

Rangacharya, Adya, trans. 1986. *The Natyacastra: English Translation with Critical Notes*. Bangalore: IBH Prakashana. A text frequently considered India's fifth *Veda*, important for the role of the performing arts in modern Hindu tradition.

Renou, Louis. 1964. *Indian Literature*. New York: Walker. One of the best concise introductory surveys.

Richman, Paula, ed. *Many Ramayanas: The Diversity of a Narrative Tradition in South Asia*. Berkeley: University of California Press, 1991. Reflects the importance of the *Ramayana* in vernacular South Asian tradition.

_____, ed. *Questioning Ramayanas: A South Asian Tradition*. Delhi: Oxford University Press, 2000.

Roy, Kumkum, ed. 1999. *Women in Early Indian Society*. Delhi: Manohar. A useful collection of articles on both Hindu and Buddhist women.

von Stietencron, Heinrich. 1989. 'Hinduism: On the Proper Use of a Deceptive Term'. In Günther D. Sontheimer and Hermann Kulke, eds. *Hinduism Reconsidered*, 11–27. New Delhi: Manohar. One of the best discussions of the problem of viewing Hinduism as a single 'religion'.

Waghorne, Joanne P., Norman Cutler, and Vasudha Narayanan, eds. 1985. *Gods of Flesh, Gods of Stone: The Embodiment of Divinity in India*. Explores a range of forms in which Hindus see deity manifested.

Williams, Raymond Brady, ed. 1992. *A Sacred Thread: Modern Transmission of Hindu Traditions in India and Abroad*. Chambersburg, PA: Anima. A good description of the diaspora in the 1970s and 1980s.

Wujastyk, Dominik, intro. and trans. 1998. *The Roots of Ayurveda: Selections from Sanskrit Medical Writings*. Delhi: Penguin. Useful for the relationship between traditional Indian medicine and religion.

Zimmer, Heinrich. 1946. *Myths and Symbols in Indian Art and Civilization*. New York: Pantheon. A classic study, still often cited.

References

Carman, John B., and Vasudha Narayanan, trans. 1989. *The Tamil Veda: Pillan's Interpretation of the Tiruvaymoli*. Chicago: University of Chicago Press.

Doniger, Wendy, and Brian K. Smith, trans. *The Laws of Manu*. London: Penguin, 1981.

Doniger O'Flaherty, Wendy, ed. and trans. 1981. *The Rig Veda: An Anthology, One Hundred and Eight Hymns*. Harmondsworth: Penguin.

Hawley, John S., and Mark Juergensmeyer, trans. 1988. *Songs of the Saints of India*. New York: Oxford University Press.

India. Ministry of Education and Social Welfare. 1984. *Toward Equality: Report of the Status of Women in India.* New Delhi: Ministry of Education and Social Welfare.

Jackson, William J., trans. 1991. *Tyagaraja: Life and Lyrics.* Delhi: Oxford University Press.

Kennedy, Melville T. 1925. *The Chaitanya Movement: A Study of the Vaishnavism of Bengal.* Calcutta: Association Press.

Lipski, Alexander. 1977. *Life and Teachings of Sri Anandamayi Ma.* Delhi: Motilal Banarsidass.

Miller, Barbara Stoler, trans. 1986. *The Bhagavad-Gita: Krishna's Counsel in Time of War.* New York: Columbia University Press.

Naipaul, V[idhiadar] S. 1984. 'Among the Republicans'. *New York Review of Books* 31:16 (25 Oct. 1984), 5–17.

Radhakrishnan, Sarvepalli, trans. 1953. *The Principal Upanisads.* London: Allen and Unwin.

Sengupta, D. n.d. 'The Historic Healing Stone—L.O.T.U.S.' Kauai: Lord of the Universe Society.

Tagore, Rabindranath, trans. 1915. *One Hundred Poems of Kabir.* London: Macmillan.

Venkateswara Temple. 1986. 'Kavachas for the Deities'. Pittsburgh: Venkateswara Temple.

The Sikh Tradition

VASUDHA NARAYANAN | WILLARD G. OXTOBY

The name Sikh means 'disciple'. Sikhs are disciples of the supreme being, the ten Sikh Gurus, and the sacred scripture called the *Adi Granth*. One of the world's younger religious traditions, Sikhism originated in the Punjab ('five rivers') region of northwestern India five centuries ago, in the period when the founder of the Mughal dynasty, the Muslim emperor Babur (1483–1530), was establishing the empire that eventually stretched across most of the subcontinent.

Origins

The inspired teacher around whom the first Sikhs gathered, Guru Nanak (1469–1538), was one of the North Indian 'poet-saints' associated with the Sant tradition (p. 291). Two elements in particular flowed together in the Sants. One was *bhakti*, the devotional Hinduism of communities like the Vaishnava. Unlike the latter, however, who often directed their love for Vishnu to one of his *avataras* (incarnations), such as Krishna, the Sants disciplined themselves not to rely on tangible or worldly forms, and they expressed their love for the supreme lord inwardly only, in meditative repetition of God's name. Sants generally believed God to be both formless and beyond description, since to attribute any qualities to the supreme being would be to limit its transcendent character.

The second major element in the Sant tradition was yoga, specifically *hatha yoga*, a system of meditation involving postures and breath control based on an elaborate mapping of correspondences between the individual body and the structure of the universe. A third element that may have had some influence on the Sants was Sufism, the Islamic mystical tradition. But its contribution was probably marginal. The Sant vocabulary drew far more from Hindu than from Muslim sources.

The Sants believed that God's love is manifest in both the created world and the human heart. They rejected caste-based social distinctions and they expressed their devotion to God as the Sat Guru ('true teacher') not in the Sanskrit and formal rituals of the priests but in poetry using the vernacular language of the people.

Guru Nanak

The story of Guru Nanak's life and career is told in the *janam-sakhis* ('life testimonies'): a collection of biographical traditions that developed long after his death. According to the *Puratan Janam-sakh*, Nanak is born in Talwandi, a village 65 km (40 mi.) from Lahore, and marries young. His brother-in-law arranges a job for him as a steward for a local official at Sultanpur, southeast of today's Amritsar. But Nanak has no interest in worldly

1499	Nanak's mystical commissioning experience
1519	Establishment of the first Sikh community (Kartarpur)
1539	Nanak is succeeded by Angad
1577	Ramdas, fourth Guru, establishes the town that will become Amritsar
1603–4	Arjan, fifth Guru, oversees compilation of *Adi Granth*
1606	Martyrdom of Arjan
1675	Martyrdom of Tegh Bahadur, ninth Guru
1699	Gobind Singh, tenth Guru, organizes the Khalsa
1708	Succession of Gurus ends with the death of Gobind Singh
1799	Punjab united under Maharaja Ranjit Singh
1873	Singh Sabha movement established
1919	British kill 378 Sikhs at Jallianwallah Bagh in Amritsar
1947	Partition of the Punjab between Pakistan and India
1984	Hundreds of Sikhs are killed when the Indian army is sent to remove militants occupying the Golden Temple

pursuits and prefers the company of wandering ascetics. Finally, at the age of thirty, he disappears for three days, during which he has his first mystical experience,

God gives him a cup of the nectar of immortality (*amrit*) and commissions him to call people to awareness of God's name and to teach the practice of devotion. Nanak responds with a creedal affirmation called the *mul mantra* ('primary mantra'):

> There is one Supreme Being, the Eternal Reality. He is the Creator, without fear and devoid of enmity. He is immortal, never incarnated, self-existent, known by grace through the Guru. The Eternal One, from the beginning, through all time, present now, the Everlasting Reality.

Today the same mantra is a part of all Sikhs' morning devotions.

On returning home, Nanak proclaims the irrelevance of religious communities: 'There is no Hindu, there is no Muslim.' He gives away all his possessions and sets out on the first of four great journeys, one in each direction of the compass, in search of spiritual teachers, Hindu and Muslim alike. He wears a mixture of Hindu and Muslim clothing himself, and is often asked which community he belongs to. Visiting the great mosque at Mecca, he stretches out in a colonnade to sleep. When a local Muslim judge reproves him for pointing his feet in the direction of the Ka'bah, the house of God, Nanak replies, 'Then turn my feet in the direction where God does not dwell.'

After twenty years of travel Nanak settles with his family at Kartarpur, northeast of Lahore. A circle of disciples ('sikhs') soon gathers, seeking instruction, and he spends the remaining twenty years of his life leading them in study, *nam simaran* ('meditation on the divine name'), and *kirtan* ('singing' hymns of praise). At the same time he insists that his followers do practical labour and live a regular family life.

Roughly a century after Guru Nanak's death, more than 900 of his devotional hymns became the basis of the *Adi Granth*. Many of the religious ideas they express were shared with his Hindu milieu, including the concept of *samsara* (the cycle of rebirth) and the need for religious discipline to achieve spiritual liberation from it. Nevertheless, in their emphasis on egalitarianism and insistence on moving beyond communal boundaries, his teachings represent a significant departure from Hindu tradition.

The Ten Gurus

Before his death Nanak appointed his disciple Angad as his successor, inaugurating a spiritual lineage each of whose members was accorded the title of 'Guru' and served for life. Counting Nanak, the succession of ten Gurus would extend for two centuries, during which the Sikhs developed from an informal circle of disciples into an organized community.

At least two crucial steps in that process are attributed to Angad (1504–52): beginning the collection of Guru Nanak's hymns and standardizing the script called *gurmukhi* ('from the guru's mouth') that would eventually be used to write the Sikh scriptures. He also continued the custom, introduced by Guru Nanak, of the *langar*: an open

NUMBERS
Estimates range between 20 and 25 million around the world.

DISTRIBUTION
Primarily northern India, especially Punjab and Haryana, with minorities in many other countries, including Canada, the United States (especially California), and Britain.

FOUNDERS AND LEADERS
Founded by Guru Nanak c. 1500 CE, and developed over the following two centuries by a succession of nine more inspired teachers, the last of whom, Guru Gobind Singh, died in 1708.

DEITY
The supreme being is considered to be one and without form. Guru Nanak refers to the deity as 'Onkar', an expression of the sacred syllable 'Om'; Hindu names such as Hari and Ram are also used occasionally.

AUTHORITATIVE TEXTS
The *Adi Granth* or *Guru Granth Sahib* is a compilation of divinely inspired hymns by the ten Sikh Gurus and other poet-saints; the *Dasam Granth*, a collection made in the time of the tenth Guru, is also revered.

NOTEWORTHY TEACHINGS
There is one supreme reality, never incarnated. In addition to reverence for the ten Gurus and the sacred text, Sikhs emphasize egalitarianism, tolerance, service to others, and a righteous life in this world as the way to ultimate liberation from the cycle of rebirth.

kitchen used to prepare and serve a communal meal (also called *langar*). The *langar* has remained a central feature of Sikh practice, an expression of the moral and social principle that all people, regardless of caste, are equally welcome.

The *langar* was further institutionalized under Angad's successor, Guru Amardas (1479–74). According to some stories, he even insisted that the great emperor Akbar take part in it before meeting with him.

The fourth Guru, Ramdas (1534–81), founded the town, to the east of Lahore, that would become Amritsar ('pool of the nectar of immortality'). A leader among the people of the Punjab, Ramdas appointed his son Arjan (1563–1606) as his successor, making the office of Guru hereditary. All subsequent incumbents came from the same family.

Arjan is credited with supervising the compilation of the *Adi Granth* and beginning the construction of the temple at Amritsar. Called Harimandir Sahib—'the honoured temple of Hari (God)—it would become known as the Golden Temple after its exterior was covered with gilded copper in the early nineteenth century.

Meanwhile, however, the political context in the region was changing. The Mughal emperor Akbar had been famous for his tolerance of religious traditions other than his own, and had even exempted Hindus from the tax that Islamic rulers traditionally imposed on non-Muslim subjects. But Akbar's son Jehangir pursued a different policy. Shortly after Jehangir came to power in 1605, Guru Arjan was charged with supporting a rebellion against the new emperor. Imprisoned in Lahore, he was tortured and put to death, becoming the first Sikh martyr. As a consequence, the role of Guru acquired a new politico-military dimension, which Arjan's son Hargobind (1595–1644) made explicit when he put on two swords, one symbolizing traditional religious authority and the other the new temporal authority.

Political conditions eased under Jehangir's son Shah Jehan, the builder of the Taj Mahal. But by the time of the ninth Guru, Tegh Bahadur (1621–75), Shah Jehan's son Aurangzeb had seized power. Determined to strengthen Islam, he reinstated the taxes removed by his great-grandfather and set out to replace Hindu temples with mosques. When Guru Tegh Bahadur objected to these policies he was imprisoned, and he became a martyr for freedom of worship when he was executed for refusing to convert to Islam.

Sikh political activism reached a peak with the tenth Guru. Gobind Singh (1666–1708) redefined the core of the community as a military order when in 1699 he created the Khalsa (frequently translated as 'pure', the term is also used to refer to the entire community of initiated Sikhs). Alarmed by these developments, the Mughal regime dispatched forces against the Sikhs. Two of the Guru's sons died in battle, and the remaining two were captured and executed. But Gobind Singh himself escaped and sent the emperor a message that came to be known as the *Zafar nama* ('Victory Letter'): 'What use is it to put out a few sparks when you raise a mighty flame instead?'

The succession of Gurus ended in 1708, when Gobind Singh was stabbed by an assassin. Instead of appointing a successor, he declared that henceforth the Guru's authority would reside in the sacred scriptures and the consensus of the Sikh community.

Crystallization

The Sacred Scriptures

The principal sacred text of the Sikhs is the *Adi Granth* ('first book'), also known as the *Guru Granth Sahib* ('revered book that is the Guru'). Written in *gurmukhi*, it consists of devotional poems by the first five Gurus along with similar verses by various other North Indian poet-saints. The poems are organized according to the different ragas (musical modes) in which they are to be sung. For each raga, the *bani* (hymns) of the gurus are presented in order, beginning with those of Guru Nanak, and followed by the hymns of the non-Sikh poet-saints. Musical directions are included.

In 1603–4 the *Adi Granth* was placed in the Harimandir Sahib at Amritsar, but the editing process continued for another century as various works were added (among them hymns by the ninth Guru, Tegh Bahadur) and others, not universally accepted, were deleted. Next in scriptural rank after the *Adi Granth* is the *Dasam Granth* ('book of the Tenth'), a collection of works attributed in whole or in part to Gobind Singh. Among its devotional hymns is the long *Jap Sahib* ('master recitation'), which some Sikhs recite as a morning prayer along with the shorter *Japji* ('honoured recitation') of Guru Nanak. The *Dasam Granth* also contains Gobind Singh's autobiography and various poetic accounts not only of Sikh heroes but of some Hindu deities. The inclusion of the latter points to the fluidity of religious boundaries three centuries ago. In the early 1700s it was possible to have a particular affection for the spiritual lineage of Guru Nanak without repudiating Hindu religion and culture.

| Box 6.1 | **From the Sacred Writings of the Sikhs**

Guru Nanak exalts the divine Name:
If in this life I should live to eternity, nourished by nothing save air;
If I should dwell in the darkest of dungeons, sense never resting in sleep;
Yet must your glory transcend all my striving; no words can encompass the Name.
(*Refrain*) He who is truly the Spirit Eternal, immanent, blissful serene;
Only by grace can we learn of our Master, only by grace can we tell.
If I were slain and my body dismembered, pressed in a hand-mill and ground;
If I were burnt in a fire all-consuming, mingled with ashes and dust;
Yet must your glory transcend all my striving; no words can encompass the Name.
If as a bird I could soar to the heavens, a hundred such realms in my reach;
If I could change so that none might perceive me and live without food, without drink;
Yet must your glory transcend all my striving; no words can encompass the Name.
If I could read with the eye of intelligence paper of infinite weight;
If I could write with the winds everlasting, pens dipped in oceans of ink;
Yet must your glory transcend all my striving; no words can encompass the Name (*Siri Ragu* 2, *Adi Granth* 14–15; McLeod 1984:41).

| Box 6.1 | *Continued* |

Though the following passage has been construed as telling Muslims that they should worship at their mosque, Nanak declares that there is no need for outward religious observance:

Make mercy your mosque and devotion your prayer mat, righteousness your Qur'an;
Meekness your circumcising, goodness your fasting, for thus the true Muslim expresses his faith.
Make good works your Ka'bah, take truth as your pir, compassion your creed and your prayer.
Let service to God be the beads which you tell and God will exalt you to glory (*VarMajh* 7:1, *Adi Granth* 140–1; McLeod 1984:43).

The third Guru, Amardas, directs his words to brahmins, allegedly proud of the traditional learning that they have monopolized:

He who is truly a dutiful brahmin will cast off his burden of human desire,
Each day performing his God-given duty, each day repeating God's Name.
To such as submit God imparts divine learning, and those who obey him live virtuous lives.
He who is truly a dutiful brahmin wins honour when summoned to God (*Malar* 10, *Adi Granth* 1261; McLeod 1984:47).

The tenth Guru, Gobind Singh, praises the sword. This passage, often repeated at Sikh functions, has now come to serve as the national anthem of the Khalsa:

Reverently I salute the Sword with affection and devotion.
Grant, I pry, your divine assistance that this book may be brought to completion.
Thee I invoke, All-conquering Sword, Destroyer of evil, Ornament of the brave.
Powerful your arm and radiant your glory, your splendour as dazzling as the brightness of the sun.
Joy of the devout and Scourge of the wicked, Vanquisher of sin, I seek your protection.
Hail to the world's Creator and Sustainer, my invincible Protector of the Sword! (*Bachitar Natak, Dasam Granth,* 39; McLeod 1984:58).

Next after the *Adi Granth* and the *Dasam Granth* come the hymns of two Sikh poets, Gurdas Bhalla (d. c. 1633) and Nand Lal Goya (1633–c. 1712). So highly esteemed is their work that it is approved for recitation in the gurdwara ('gateway to the guru'; the Sikh house of worship), and in that sense it stands as a third body of scriptural material. The title Bhai ('brother'), regularly used with their names, is a mark of honour.

The centrality of the book in Sikh worship and the authority accorded to the *Adi Granth* in particular suggest comparisons with the place of the written text in Islam. At the same time, every copy of the *Adi Granth* is treated with a respect that may be best described by analogy with Hindu devotion to the deities believed to be present in their images.

In the gurdwara the sacred book is entrusted to the care of a 'reader' called the *granthi.* It has its own room and is honoured with all amenities that would be provided to a guest. On festival days it is carried through the town at the head of a procession on a

The *granthi* reads from the *Guru Granth Sahib* inside the Golden Temple of Amritsar (Willard G. Oxtoby).

wagon or truck decked with flowers. During worship services a sweet food called *karah prasad* is presented to the book and later distributed to the congregation—just as, in Hindu temples, *prasada* is first offered to the deity and then distributed to the worshippers.

Readings from the *Adi Granth* are often selected by opening the book at random and reading whatever hymn appears on the left-hand page. Similarly, at the name-giving ceremonies for a newborn child, the *granthi* opens the book and reads out the first word of the first hymn on the left-hand page to the parents, who then select a name starting with the same letter.

The Khalsa

Not all Sikhs have been members of the Khalsa. Nevertheless, the institution has come to define the image of the Sikh to outsiders and to be regarded by many within the community as the orthodox expression of its identity.

The story of the Khalsa begins in 1699, with Guru Gobind Singh calling his followers to assemble at the time of a festival in Anandpur, east of Amritsar. There he selects five followers to become the core of his disciplined force. Accounts of how the *panj piare* ('five cherished ones') were chosen all begin the same way. Gobind Singh asks for someone's head, a volunteer comes forward, and the two enter the Guru's tent; then the swish of a sword is heard, followed by the thump of a falling head. After this process has been repeated four more times, one account says that the curtain is drawn aside to reveal five brave volunteers and five headless goats. (Another account says the Guru actually decapitates the five volunteers and then brings them back to life intact.)

In keeping with the egalitarian spirit of Sikhism, the Khalsa includes women as well as men. All initiates are required to wear five items of dress at all times. The Punjabi terms for these items begin with *k*; hence they are called the *panj kakke* or 'five Ks':

- *kes*, uncut hair and beard
- *kangha*, a comb worn in the hair
- *kirpan*, a steel dagger or sword
- *kara*, a steel ring worn on the right wrist
- *kachh*, shorts

As part of the baptism-like initiation ritual, new members of the Khalsa sip a consecrated sweetened water called *amrit* that is said to resemble the sacred nectar offered to Guru Nanak at the moment of his vision and call. Hence a fully initiated or Khalsa Sikh is described as *amrit-dhari* ('nectar-bearing').

The Khalsa way of life is summarized in the *Rahit* ('path'): a set of rules governing faith and practice in four areas: doctrine regarding the deity, the ten gurus, and the sacred scripture; personal conduct, from hygiene to social behaviour; the proper observance of community rituals; and the procedures for disciplining those who violate the code.

Amrit-dhari Sikhs are an influential minority both in the Punjab and overseas. Two other categories within the community make up its principal constituency. *Kes-dhari* ('hair-bearing') Sikhs are males who keep their hair uncut but have not undergone the Khalsa initiation; they are a majority among Sikhs in parts of India and a sizable minority overseas. A Sikh male who has always shaved and cut his hair is called *sahaj-dhari*, a term that many Sikhs today translate as 'gradualist'. One sense of the word is 'instinctive' or 'innate', but scholars also interpret *sahaj* as referring to the serenity or bliss experienced in following the spiritual discipline of Guru Nanak. Many Sikhs in India and the majority overseas are *sahaj-dhari*.

Unshorn hair, then, is common to both Khalsa and non-Khalsa Sikh males. The hair is gathered in a knot on top of the head, sometimes with a handkerchief-sized white cloth, and then wrapped with a strip of cloth several metres long, usually of a solid colour, to form a turban. Some also support the beard in a hammock-like net, although others insist that the whole beard must be shown. The turban has come to be the most visible sign of Sikh identity.

Sikh women in the Indian subcontinent often wear the *salwar-kamiz*, a combination of tunic and loose trousers with a long, flowing neck scarf. But this is a common regional costume, worn by Hindus and Muslims as well. Sikh women may also wear Indian saris or Western dress.

Gobind Singh instructed that all male Sikhs should take the name Singh, meaning 'lion', as a surname, and all Sikh women the surname Kaur, 'princess'. Hence 'Singh' by itself is often a surname, although many Sikhs also follow the name Singh with another name denoting a clan, home town, or other association. Thus Sikhs who do not use 'Singh' or 'Kaur' as their surnames will have 'S.' or 'K.' as a middle initial.

Four Notions of Guruship

Sikhs recognize four centres of authority, each of which is referred to as 'Guru'. Four different manifestations of one eternal Guru, they are complementary rather than contradictory.

God as Guru

To experience the deity is to experience divine guidance. For Nanak the Guru was the divine voice speaking within the consciousness of the devotee. As in the Sant tradition, God is formless, invisible, beyond attributes or characteristics. But the transcendent nature of the supreme being does not prevent Sikhs from experiencing the divine as a personal presence, and a variety of names and attributes can be found in Sikh literature and devotion.

As Akal Purakh, the 'timeless person', God is characterized as *nirankar* or formless. He is also Sat Kartar, 'true creator', Sat Guru, 'true teacher', and Sat Nam, 'true name'. In some devotional hymns Nanak uses the Hindu names Hari and Ram for God—a usage reflected in the formal name of the Golden Temple, Harimandir Sahib. On the other hand, Nanak also refers to God as Onkar, 'the expression of om' (the sacred syllable of the Hindus). After Nanak's time, the devotional expression *Vahiguru*, 'hail to the Guru', came to be used as yet another name for God, the eternal Guru.

Theologically, *nam* represents much more than a name. It is the deity's essence and identity, his power and majesty. *Nam* is the link between absolute transcendence and worldly manifestation. Thus worship itself is understood as 'remembering the name' (*nam simaran*): making the deity the focus of one's awareness and motivation. This practice takes various forms, from the highly structured recitation (*nam japan*) of a mantra to congregational chanting and singing (*kirtan*) devotional hymns to less structured meditation and prayer.

The Teacher as Guru

Sikh doctrine holds that the spiritual guidance or guruship of the deity was vested in Nanak, who became a living embodiment of it. His religious insight provided a model for the insight that others might gain through reflection, and he personally became a model of authority in conduct that others might emulate or obey. This authority was transmitted from Nanak to the nine gurus who followed him, passing guruship like a torch from one runner to another.

Since the death of the tenth Guru, Gobind Singh, the authority of guruship has resided in the scripture (*Guru Granth*) and the collective wisdom of the community (*Guru Panth*).

The Scripture as Guru

Seen as a gift from God, the *Adi Granth* or *Guru Granth Sahib* embodies the divinity's manifestation as *sabad* or divine word. Sikhs consider the *Granth*'s hymns to be divinely inspired even though they are explicitly attributed to individual human beings (some of whom were not Sikhs themselves). Yet the *Granth*'s authority is not a matter of inspiration alone. Since Nanak and his successors are seen as embodiments of the eternal Guru, their *bani* are understood to be of explicitly divine authorship.

The Community as Guru

Sikhs often refer to their community as the *panth*—Punjabi for 'path' or 'way'. The concept of the path is nearly universal: almost all religions speak of following their precepts or traditions as one would follow a road or path. In the Sikh case, the word for path initially referred to followers of Nanak's way (the *Nanak-panth*), and eventually came to signify the entire community.

The idea that the consensus of the community or of its leadership core has some form of authority is also widespread among the world's religions. In the Sikh case, the source of that authority is traced to Gobind Singh's designation of the community's consensus as the collective embodiment of his divine mandate.

Practice

Prayer

Devout Sikhs pray three times a day: in the early morning, at sunset, and before going to sleep. Morning prayers include Guru Nanak's *Japji*, beginning with the *mul mantra* creed, and the long *Jap Sahib*. Evening prayers (*Rehiras*) consist of hymns by five of the Gurus. The bedtime prayer, *Sohila* ('Hymn of Joy'), is also recited at funerals.

Congregational Worship

The Sikh house of worship, the gurdwara, is typically a rectangular hall with a dais on which the *Guru Granth Sahib* rests during services and a side room where it is kept at night, along with a kitchen (*langar*) for preparation of the communal meal that will follow the service. There is no special day set aside for worship, though in the West the

Langar at a Toronto gurdwara (Stephen Epstein/Ponkawonka.com).

main congregational services are usually held on Sunday. Worshippers sit on the floor (men usually on one side, women on the other) and may enter and leave at any time.

In principle any adult Sikh, male or female, may conduct religious ceremonies. The main congregational activity is *kirtan*: the singing of hymns from the scriptures. A reading and sermon or talk, together with prayer, make up the rest of the service. At its conclusion, *karah prasad* is distributed; then everyone shares in the *langar* prepared and served by volunteers as part of the community service expected of all Sikhs.

The Annual Festival Cycle

In India, Sikhs observe their own rituals at the time of three seasonal Hindu festivals. Two that have been important since the time of the third Guru, Amardas, are Baisakhi (or Vaisakhi) and Divali (or Deepavali). The third Hindu festival with a special component for Sikhs is Holi, to which the tenth Guru, Gobind Singh, is said to have added a day known as Hola Mohalla.

Baisakhi, which is celebrated as New Year's day in India, follows a solar calendar and usually falls on 13 April. It began as a grain harvest festival for Hindus, but it has acquired historical associations for Sikhs. Since Gobind Singh formed the Khalsa at a Baisakhi assembly in 1699, Sikhs have celebrated the festival as their community's birth-day. Further Baisakhi assemblies have added to the deposit of historical memory, par-ticularly when a crowd in Amritsar in 1919 were fired on as political agitators by the British, with 378 fatalities.

The date of Divali, the Hindu festival of lights, varies because it follows the Indian lunar calendar, but generally falls during October or November. Sikhs too light lamps on Divali and use strings of electric lights to outline the architectural features of gurdwaras. Whereas Hindus associate Divali with the *Ramayana* and *Mahabharata* narratives, Sikhs tell a story about Guru Hargobind during his imprisonment under the Mughal emperor Jehangir. When the emperor orders that he be freed, Hargobind refuses to leave without 52 Hindu princes who are imprisoned with him. Jehangir agrees to release only as many of them as can hold on to Hargobind's clothing, whereupon Hargobind has a cloak made with tassels long enough for all to accompany him to freedom.

Hola Mohalla, the day after Holi, is celebrated in February or March. For Hindus, Holi is a time to splash coloured powder or water on everyone and everything in sight, and Sikhs follow this custom to some extent. The day after Holi is dedicated to military exercises and organized athletic and literary contests.

In addition to these holidays, Sikhs observe the birthdays of Guru Nanak and Guru Gobind Singh, as well as the martyrdom of the fifth Guru, Arjan. Occasions such as these are marked with an *akhand path*: an 'unbroken reading' of the *Guru Granth Sahib*, in which the text is read aloud in its entirety by relays of readers, each in turn reading for up to two hours. The reading, which takes two days, is scheduled to end just before dawn on the anniversary day, so that the conclusion of the reading leads into the morn-ing *kirtan* for which the worshippers have gathered. An *akhand path* can also be scheduled to accompany ceremonies such as weddings or funerals. In a private home, where non-stop reading may not be practical, the cover-to-cover reading can take seven days and is called *saptahak path* or *sahaj path*.

Life-Cycle Rituals

In India family loyalty has been considered more important than romantic love. Thus marriages have traditionally been arranged between families. In this respect Sikh wed-dings follow general Indian custom. What is distinctive about the Sikh ceremony is that it must be conducted in the presence of the *Guru Granth Sahib*.

One of the marriage hymns in the *Granth*, composed by Guru Ramdas, is called the *lavan* ('circling'). While it is sung, the couple slowly walk in a clockwise direction around the sacred book four times, once for each stanza. The first stanza affirms the Hindu conception of responsibilities in the householder stage of life, though it instructs the couple to 'sing the *bani* instead of the Vedas'. Subsequent stanzas dwell on the devo-tee's awareness of divine love as present in the fellowship of the community and in the blissful experience of mystical union.

Sikh funeral practices follow the Indian custom of cremation within a day of death on a pyre lit, if possible, by the deceased's eldest son. Preparation of the body for cremation includes washing and, often, making sure that the five symbolic articles of attire, the five Ks, are present. The ashes are generally thrown into a river, though numer-

---

| Box 6.2 | **From Sikh Hymns and Prayers**

Despite his militancy, Guru Gobind Singh shares with Guru Nanak a sense that religious boundaries are irrelevant to God:

There is no difference between a temple and a mosque, nor between the prayers of a Hindu and a Muslim. Though differences seem to mark and distinguish, all men are in reality the same.

Gods and demons, celestial beings, men called Muslims and others called Hindus—such differences are trivial, inconsequential, the outward results of locality and dress.

With eyes the same, the ears and body, all possessing a common form—all are in fact a single creation, the elements of nature in a uniform blend.

Allah is the same as the God of the Hindus, Puran and Qur'an are the same. All are the same, none is separate; a single form, a single creation (*Akal Ustat, Dasam Granth*, 19–20; McLeod 1984:57).

Bhai Gurdas likewise declares the irrelevance of external religious observances:

If bathing at tiraths procures liberation, frogs, for sure, must be saved;
And likewise the banyan, with dangling tresses, if growing hair long sets one free.
If the need can be served by roaming unclad the deer of the forest must surely be pious;
So too the ass which rolls in the dust if limbs smeared with ashes can purchase salvation.
Saved are the cattle, mute in the fields, if silence produces deliverance.
Only the Guru can bring us salvation; only the Guru can set a man free.

The Sikh prayer called the Ardas, standardized by the 1930s, contains a roll-call of the ten Gurus. Sri Hari Krishan, included in it, is the child who became the eighth Guru, and should not be confused with the Hare Krishna movement arising from Hindu Vaishnavism in Bengal:

Having first remembered God, turn your thoughts to Guru Nanak; Angad Guru, Amar Das, each with Ram Das grant us aid.
Arjan and Hargobind, think of them and Hari Rai.
Dwell on Sri Hari Krishan, he whose sight dispels all pain.
Think of Guru Tegh Bahadur; thus shall every treasure come.
May they grant their gracious guidance, help and strength in every place (*Chandi di Var, Dasam Granth*, 119; McLeod 1984:67).

Martyrdom is a frequent theme in Sikh history, motivating Sikhs to persevere in struggles today:

These loyal members of the Khalsa who gave their heads for their faith; who were hacked limb from limb, scalped, broken on the wheel, or sawn asunder; who sacrificed heir lives for the protection of hallowed gurdwaras never forsaking their faith; and who were steadfast in their loyalty to the uncut hair of the true Sikh: reflect on their merits, O Khalsa, and call on God, saying, *Vahiguru*! (*Chandi di Var*; McLeod 1984:104).

ous shrines are located at the presumed burial sites of the ashes of holy men. An oral reading of the *Granth* can follow in the days after a funeral. Sikhs understand death to be followed by rebirth unless, through faith and divine favour, the individual achieves release from the cycle.

Another major stage of life for some Sikhs is initiation into the Khalsa, which is performed at or after the age of fourteen. The officiants are five persons (men or women), recalling the *panj piare* or 'cherished five', and a *granthi*. During a recitation of hymns and prayers lasting about two hours, the five mix the *amrit* (nectar), stirring sweetened water in an iron bowl with a short double-edged sword. The initiates then come forward, sip *amrit* five times from their cupped hands, and have it sprinkled five times on their eyes and hair.

The initiates are then instructed in the rules of conduct, four of which have come to be listed as major offences against the *Rahit* or code. Some of these prohibitions involve moral issues such as adultery or profiting from an arranged marriage. Others have more to do with religious identity, such as cutting one's hair, eating meat slaughtered in the Muslim style (where the animal is bled to death), or performing ceremonies incompatible with Sikhism.

Some interpreters see the practices of the Khalsa as symbolic reversals of ascetic practices in other Indian communities. Rather than shaving their heads, Sikh initiates are unshorn. Rather than espousing pacifism, they are always armed. Rather than having a personal mantra privately whispered to them, they take their vows publicly. Perhaps these differences reflect the fact that the early Sikh leaders came not from the priestly brahmin caste but from the mercantile khatris.

Differentiation

Sikh Reform Movements

In 1799 the Punjab was unified under Maharaja Ranjit Singh (1780–1839) and for a while the Sikhs were masters of their own territory. But the political unity he achieved could not be sustained after his death, and in 1849 the Punjab was annexed by the British.

One consequence was that the boundary between Sikh and Hindu identity became increasingly difficult to draw. Sikhs and Hindus had always shared much in their outlook on human existence in the universe, in their standards of personal and social conduct, and in their ritual practices. It was not uncommon for followers of Guru Nanak to revere Hindu saints as well; the Gurus who compiled the Sikh scriptures had done so themselves. By the mid-nineteenth century, however, nearly a hundred and fifty years had passed since the death of the tenth Guru. In the absence of a central authority to articulate a single definition of Sikhism, transmission of the tradition depended on individual clan and caste groups, many of which eventually returned to Hindu practices that Guru Nanak and his successors had rejected.

The Mughals had used the term 'Hindu' primarily to refer to the non-Muslim population of India. The term acquired a different meaning under the British, who used it as an explicit religious designation for those Indians—the majority of the population—who did not belong to an identifiable minority group. (The Hindu Family Act still defines 'Hindu' this way, specifically excluding Muslims, Christians, Parsis or Zoroastrians, and Jews—but not Jains or Sikhs.)

Three Sikh reform movements emerged in the second half of the nineteenth century, each attempting to restore a sense of spiritual identity to their community. In so doing, they helped to keep Sikh identity distinct at a time when the vast array of India's religious traditions were increasingly seen as belonging to single 'Hindu' tradition.

The Nirankaris

Although he was never initiated into the Khalsa, Dyal Das (1783–1853) became the leader of a movement to renew Sikhism by rejecting Hindu practices—especially the worship of images. For that reason his followers called themselves Nirankaris ('worshippers of the Formless One').

The Namdharis

The Namdhari movement was formed in 1857, when a group of Sikhs led by Ram Singh (1816–84), a former soldier, created their own baptismal ritual and austere rule of conduct emphasizing a vegetarian diet, all-white dress, and chanting of the divine Name (the practice from which they took their name). As the number of his followers increased, Ram Singh took on an active role in public life, promoting boycotts of various kinds as a form of non-violent resistance to the British occupation. After the British gave permission for the slaughter of cattle—banned under Maharaja Ranjit Singh—to resume, a number of Muslim butchers in Amritsar and Ludhiana were killed by Namdhari extremists. The British responded by ransacking the Namdharis' headquarters, sending Ram Singh into exile, and executing more than 60 Namdharis without trial in a particularly horrifying way—tying them over the mouths of cannons and blasting their bodies to pieces. The Namdharis came to be seen as political martyrs and forerunners of the Gandhian movement for Indian independence.

The Namdharis developed a doctrine of religious authority reminiscent of the Shi'i Muslim teaching about the hidden Imam, maintaining that Gobind Singh did not die in 1708 but went into hiding, and that Ram Singh succeeded him as the twelfth Guru. Members of the Namdhari movement today still expect Gobind Singh to return some day. In the meantime, they believe that authority is vested not in the *Adi Granth* but in their founder's descendant Jagjit Singh, whom they consider to be his personal representative.

The Singh Sabha movement

The Singh Sabha movement began in 1873 as an effort to counter the Sikh community's losses to Christian missionary activity. But it soon broadened its focus to include purging Sikhism of Hindu influences and strengthening Sikh identity. Education was an important part of that project. In 1892 the Singh Sabha established Khalsa College in Amritsar. The distinguished poet and philosopher Vir Singh (1872–1937) launched the Khalsa Tract Society two years later, to further the organization's aims by publishing works on Sikh history, philosophy, and culture. And in 1897 the Tat Khalsa of Lahore (one of the elements in the Singh Sabha) published a pamphlet entitled 'We are not Hindus'. By 1900 the Singh Sabha had more than a hundred chapters across the Punjab and adjoining regions, from Delhi to the northwestern frontier.

The version of Sikhism that the Singh Sabha established as orthodox was apparently based on observance of the Khalsa *Rahit* or rule established by the tenth Guru in 1699. In this way Khalsa Sikhs—who had been only one element in the Sikh community, albeit an important one, for two centuries—eventually came to be considered the only true Sikhs.

Interaction and Adaptation

Twentieth-Century India

In 1920 a committee was formed to manage all Sikh houses of worship. The Shiromani Gurdwara Prabandhak Committee (SGPC) is the central authority to which both administrative matters and questions of religious discipline are referred. In 1947 the British withdrew and the subcontinent was partitioned to create two independent countries: the secular state of India and the Islamic Republic of Pakistan. Partition was especially hard for the Sikhs because it split the Punjab in two. Most of the 2.5 million Sikhs living west of Lahore fled Pakistan as refugees and were absorbed into the Indian portion of the Punjab, from Amritsar east.

What remained as independent India was now officially 'secular'. In practice that meant not anti-religious but multi-religious or pluralistic. Therefore it was important that the government not be perceived to favour any one group over another. When the system of electoral representation by religio-communal identity was abolished in favour of regional representation, Sikhs living in districts where they were a minority lost their representatives.

By the 1980s many Sikhs were concerned that the central government did not adequately recognize their community's status as a distinct religio-communal entity. Most did not go so far as to demand an independent Sikh homeland. But a minority did. In 1984 a group of armed militants demanding the creation of an independent 'Khalistan' occupied the Golden Temple. Hundreds were killed when government forces stormed the complex, among them the militants' leader, Jarnail Singh Bhindranwale (1947–84). Many Sikhs who had denounced Bhindranwale were appalled by this assault on their holiest shrine. A few months later, Prime Minister Indira Gandhi (1917–84) was assassinated by her Sikh bodyguards, apparently in retaliation for the Golden Temple attack. The anti-Sikh violence that followed spurred a wave of Sikh emigration.

The Golden Temple in Amritsar (Martin Gray).

The Sikh Diaspora

By the beginning of the twentieth century communications and transportation links were well established throughout the British Empire. Sikh emigrants were able to make their way to Singapore and Hong Kong, and from there by steamship across the Pacific. Between 1903 and 1907 more than 5,000 Sikhs, most of them farmers, arrived in British Columbia alone. In California the migrants found farm work in the state's interior, but in British Columbia most turned to the lumber industry. In the first decade virtually all the migrants were young men. Some had left wives and children in India; some established themselves before returning to India to find wives; and some married North American women. Canadians and Americans generally assumed all migrants from India to be Hindus.

Between 1908 and 1913, both countries imposed restrictions that made immigration virtually impossible for anyone from the subcontinent. It was only after immigration laws were relaxed in the 1950s that Sikh immigration to North America resumed. This time many Sikhs arrived in family groups.

Sikhs in North America have both contributed to and benefited from the trend towards religious pluralism in the last few decades. In general, the turban is understood and accepted in the same way that the Jewish *yarmulke* is. On the other hand, some Canadians have objected to the wearing of turbans by police officers and members of the military on the ground that government officials should not only operate on strictly secular principles but should be seen to do so. There has also been strong opposition to the wearing of the *kirpan* by students in schools that forbid their pupils to carry weapons.

Feminine Dimensions of Sikh Faith

Sikh religious literature is almost completely the work of men, and the community's institutions have been almost completely staffed by men. In this Sikhism differs little from other major religions. Furthermore, even though the Khalsa is open to women, the fact that it originated as a military brotherhood reinforces the impression that the Sikh tradition is male-centred. Recently, though, some Sikhs, especially in the diaspora, have been reinterpreting various aspects of the tradition in ways that allow more scope for women. Their insights have followed several lines.

First is the question of historical attitudes towards women. We have already noted that the Gurus emphasized social egalitarianism. Today interpreters are recruiting them as forerunners of women's liberation as well, seeing in the early Panth a community of equal spiritual access for male and female. Pivotal in such interpretations is this hymn by Guru Nanak:

> Of woman are we born, of woman conceived,
> To woman engaged, to woman married.
> Woman we befriend, by woman do civilizations continue.
> When a woman dies, a woman is sought for.
> It is through woman that order is maintained.
> Then why call her inferior from whom all great ones are born?
> Woman is born of woman;
> None is born but of woman.
> The One, who is Eternal, alone is unborn.
> (*Asa* 19, *Adi Granth* 473; Singh 1993:30)

From the beginning, Sikh women were seen as partners of Sikh men. Married family life, not celibacy, was seen as the ideal. And because both sexes took part in the *langar*—not just in eating the food but in preparing and serving it—some interpreters argue that both were equally valued in religious contexts. On the other hand, the sexes are often separated in the gurdwara even today.

A second aspect to modern thinking about women's place in the tradition is the historic value attributed to women's unique ability to give birth. The word that Guru Nanak used for 'woman' in the hymn quoted above is *bhandu*, etymologically 'vessel'. Creation pours forth from woman. On the other hand, so does the 'pollution' associated with the discharge of blood. On this point, a feminist reading of Nanak makes him a revolutionary who condemns the notion of pollution as false:

> If pollution attaches to birth, then pollution is everywhere
> (for birth is universal).
> Cow-dung [used as fuel] and firewood breed maggots. . . .
> How can we then believe in pollution, when pollution inheres within
> staples?
> Says Nanak, pollution is not washed away by purificatory rituals;
> Pollution is removed by true knowledge alone.
> (*Asa* 18, *Adi Granth* 472; Singh 1993:32–3)

Still, it is not easy to tell whether this text actually denies that bodily discharges constitute pollution or rather assumes that it does, in order to make the point that spiritual insight is of higher value than purificatory rituals.

A third line of interpretation focuses on the metaphorical or symbolic role of femininity. Here again Guru Nanak's hymns are important evidence, for they are rich in bridal imagery. The created universe is the bride and God is the groom. Modern Sikh fiction likewise finds religious analogies in various aspects of the marriage ceremony. Once again, though, the question to ask is whether the female role is truly equivalent to that of the male: is not the groom, or God as groom, the master in the relationship? On this point, Sikhs do see God as male.

In any event, if, as Sikh thought holds, divinity is truly formless—if it is beyond the categories and images that humans use to describe it—then it is beyond femininity and masculinity alike. Feminist interpretations may encourage a new awareness of the female, but classical Sikh doctrine already recognizes gender to be ultimately irrelevant.

Punjabi Sikhs and White Sikhs

Beginning as the circle of disciples surrounding a mystical teacher, the Sikh tradition developed over four centuries into a structured religio-ethnic community. In the process, the movement became one that outsiders were increasingly unlikely to join. Yet Sikhism is not without modern converts.

Harbhajan Singh Puri (1929–2004) was born in the western Punjab. After partition his family settled in Delhi, where he worked as a customs officer until 1968, when he moved to North America to work as a yoga instructor, first in Toronto and then in Los Angeles.

Instantly successful as a teacher, he organized a spiritual commune for a group of his students. He took the name Yogi Bhajan, promoted tantric yoga as 'Kundalini Yoga: The Yoga of Awareness', and taught a discipline that he described as 'the healthy, happy, holy way of life', which included vegetarianism but focused especially on the experiential and medical benefits of meditation. He incorporated his movement as 3HO—the

Healthy, Happy, Holy Organization—and new chapters or ashrams were founded in various North American cities.

Puri's background in the Sikh tradition did not come to the fore until 1971, when he took 84 of his followers to Amritsar and was welcomed at the Akal Takht—the most important of five seats of authority within Sikhism, located inside the Golden Temple complex. Having been commended for his missionary activity, he took the title Siri Singh Sahib when he returned to North America, claiming he had received it from the SGPC. In 1973 his organization was legally registered as the Sikh Dharma Brotherhood, a religious organization empowered to ordain ministers so that the marriages they performed would be valid.

The tantric yoga that Puri taught was not part of the Sikh tradition, but most of his followers were ready to be persuaded that it was the essence of Sikhism. Sikh Dharma's members ('brotherhood' was dropped with the advent of inclusive language), male and female alike, wore white turbans, tunics, and tight trousers. Members kept their first names, used Singh as a middle name, and, as a sign of their egalitarianism, all took the same last name: Khalsa. They lived and raised families in communal houses, spending long hours in chanting and meditation. With good educational backgrounds, many worked at white-collar jobs, and all presented a disciplined and diligent image to the wider public. In several American and Canadian challenges to safety and uniform requirements, the members of 3HO were recognized by government or regulatory agencies as legitimate Sikhs and granted exemptions under the freedom-of-religion provisions of the law.

But acceptance by the mainstream population has not given 3HO an entrée to the ethnic Sikh community of Punjabis in North America. In the Punjab Sikh women do not normally wear turbans, and it is a sign of mourning for anybody but a Namdhari to dress entirely in white. (In recent struggles white turbans have also been seen as a sign of sympathy with the policies of the Indian government.) Because yoga is so closely associated with Hinduism, the organization's emphasis on it alarms Punjabis still anxious to assert the distinction between Sikhs and Hindus. And though the converts memorize some hymns in order to sing *kirtan*, most lack any real ability to read the sacred texts. Harbhajan S. Puri (Yogi Bhajan, Siri Singh Sahib) is seen more as an entrepreneur than as a spiritual teacher.

At first some Punjabi Sikhs were impressed by the strict Khalsa-style discipline of the '*gora*' ('white') converts and took imitation to be a sincere form of flattery, but before long many came to see them as pseudo-Sikhs, to be kept at arm's length. Few if any white turbans were seen when the Sikh community turned out for a Baisakhi assembly in Toronto in 1992, even though it was held not far from the local 3HO ashram.

Still, the existence of converts to a faith that has historically been inseparable from a specific cultural heritage underlines the fact that religious traditions continually diversify. A community's self-definition rarely anticipates new cultural environments or challenges. No one can predict the specific form that the Sikh tradition will take, in India or elsewhere, a century from now. The only certainty is that Sikhs will still be bearing a witness of faith in the eternal creator who is beyond all forms.

Amritsar, Punjab. The holiest of all places for Sikhs, Amritsar is the site of the Harimandir Sahib (Golden Temple) and was named for the 'pool of nectar' that surrounds the shrine. Facing the temple and connected to it by a causeway is the Akal Takht ('Eternal Throne'), the most important of five seats of authority within the Sikh world. Amritsar is also the site of the Jallianwallah Bagh—the gardens where British troops massacred 378 Sikhs on Baisakhi day in 1919.

Anandpur, Punjab. The birthplace of the Khalsa; the Takht Sri Keshgarh Sahib is said to stand on the spot where Guru Gobind Singh created the panj piare in 1699.

Nanded, Maharashtra. The place where Guru Gobind Singh died and the site of the Takht Sri Hazoor Sahib.

Patna, Bihar. The birthplace of Guru Gobind Singh and the site of the Takht Sri Patna Sahib.

Talwandi Sabo, Punjab. Guru Gobind Singh is said to have stayed here for several months c. 1705; site of the Takht Sri Damdama Sahib.

Glossary

Adi Granth The collection of devotional hymns that Sikhs revere as the authoritative scripture and the successor to the ten Gurus.

Akal Purakh 'Timeless Person', a description of or name for God.

amrit-dhari 'Nectar-bearers'; full members of the Khalsa, so named because they have sipped *amrit*, the 'nectar of immortality', as part of their initiation.

Baisakhi An Indian New Year's day, observed by Sikhs around 13 May on the solar calendar (Vesak for Buddhists follows a lunar date.)

bani The hymns of the gurus collected in the *Adi Granth*.

gurdwara A Sikh house of worship.

gurmukhi The script in which the *Adi Granth* is written.

Guru One in the succession of authoritative teachers beginning with Nanak, the eleventh and last of which is the *Adi Granth*.

Guru Granth Sahib A title of respect for the *Adi Granth*.

Harimandir Sahib The 'honoured temple of Hari' at Amritsar; the original name of the building often referred to as the Golden Temple.

janam-sakhis Traditional accounts of the life of Guru Nanak.

Jap Sahib A hymn of the tenth Guru, Gobind Singh, a regular part of morning prayer.

Japji A prayer associated with the *mul mantra* or creedal statement of the first Guru, Nanak, also a regular part of morning prayer.

karah prasad A food made of whole-grain meal, sugar, and ghee or clarified butter, placed in the presence of the sacred book during prayer and then shared by the worshipping congregation.

Khalsa The 'special' core of the Sikh community, organized along the lines of a military brotherhood by the tenth Guru, Gobind Singh. Male initiates wear five marks of membership, including unshorn hair covered by a turban.

kirtan The singing of hymns from the scriptures in worship.

langar A kitchen attached to a gurdwara, producing meals in which all present are to share.

mul mantra A declaration of the eternity and transcendence of God, the creator, the wording of which is ascribed to Nanak's commissioning experience.

nam simaran 'Remembering the Name', a meditation on the character of God that together with kirtan or hymn-singing is part of worship.

Panth The Sikh community as the locus of religious commitment and consensus.

sahaj-dharis Sikh males who have always shaved and cut their hair, in contrast to *amrit-dharis*.

Sants Ascetic holy men at the time of Guru Nanak, many of whom spoke of divinity as beyond all forms or descriptions.

Singh Sabha A revival movement among the Sikhs in the latter part of the nineteenth century that succeeded in defining the tradition more explicitly and strictly.

Vahiguru 'Hail to the Guru', an expression that came to be used as a name for God.

Further Reading

Brown, Kerry. 1999. *Sikh Art and Literature*. London: Routledge. Illustrations include paintings depicting events in Sikh history.

Cole, W. Owen, and Piara Singh Sambhi. 1978. *The Sikhs*. London: Routledge and Kegan Paul. Particularly useful for aspects of Sikh life in Britain.

Fenech, Louis E. 2000. *Martyrdom in the Sikh Tradition: Playing the Game of Love*. Delhi: Oxford University Press. An important study of calls for struggle in defence of the Sikh faith and community.

Gill, Mahindra Kaura. 1995. *The Role and Status of Women in Sikhism*. Delhi: National Book Shop. Contributes to the discussion of this point as it has been developing in India.

McLeod, W. H[ewat]. 1968. *Guru Nanak and the Sikh Religion*. Oxford: Clarendon Press. The study that first established McLeod as a leading historian of the Sikh tradition.

_____. 1975. *The Evolution of the Sikh Community*. Delhi: Oxford University Press. Traces the historical development of a sense of community authority and separate identity.

_____, ed. 1984. *Textual Sources for the History of Sikhism*. Manchester: Manchester University Press. Offers a representative sampling from different genres of literature across five centuries.

_____. 1991. *Popular Sikh Art*. Delhi: Oxford University Press. Lithographs that function in traditional Sikh piety are illustrated in colour.

_____. 1995. *Historical Dictionary of Sikhism*. Lanham, MD: Scarecrow Press. Concise and authoritative; alphabetically arranged articles, all by McLeod.

_____. 1997. *Sikhism*. London: Penguin. A good general introduction.

Oberoi, Harjot S. 1993. *The Construction of Religious Boundaries: Culture, Identity, and Diversity in the Sikh Tradition*. Delhi: Oxford University Press. An important study of the nineteenth-century emergence of a sense of separate Sikh identity.

O'Connell, Joseph T., Milton Israel, and Willard G. Oxtoby, eds. 1988. *Sikh History and Religion in the Twentieth Century*. Toronto: University of Toronto Centre for South Asian Studies. Essays reflect the wide range of contemporary Sikh studies.

Singh, Harbans, ed. 1992–8. *The Encyclopaedia of Sikhism*. 4 vols. Patiala: Punjabi University. An ambitious project, with articles by a range of authors, primarily Sikhs.

Singh, Kahan, Nabha. 1984. *Sikhs, We Are Not Hindus*, trans. Jarnail Singh. Willowdale, Ontario: Jarnail Singh. The 1897 essay that galvanized a movement to assert Sikh identity as independent.

Singh, Khushwant. 1963–6. *History of the Sikhs*. 2 vols. Princeton: Princeton University Press. Readable, lively account by an influential Indian journalist and intellectual.

Singh, Nikki-Guninder Kaur. 1993. *The Feminine Principle in the Sikh Vision of the Transcendent*. Cambridge: Cambridge University Press. Makes the case for the portrayal of femininity and feminist values in the tradition.

References

Kohli, Surinder Singh. 1987. 'Dasam Granth'. In Mircea Eliade, ed., *The Encyclopedia of Religion*, 4:241–2. New York: Macmillan.

Macauliffe, Max Arthur. 1909. *The Sikh Religion*. 6 vols. Oxford: Clarendon Press.

McLeod, W.H. 1984. *Textual Sources for the History of Sikhism*. Manchester: Manchester University Press.

_____. 1989. *Who Is a Sikh? The Problem of Sikh Identity*. Oxford: Clarendon Press.

Singh, Nikki-Guninder Kaur. 1993. *The Feminine Principle in the Sikh Vision of the Transcendent*. Cambridge: Cambridge University Press.

The Jain Tradition

VASUDHA NARAYANAN

Information brochures on the Jain tradition usually sum it up in one Sanskrit phrase: *Ahimsa paramo dharmah* ('Non-violence is the highest form of religious conduct'). Commitment to this principle translates into preservation of all forms of life on this earth and, ultimately, preservation of the earth itself. Jains today see non-violence as central not only to individual spiritual and physical well-being but to environmental protection and global peace as well.

Ahimsa: Non-Violence

The great Jain teacher of the present age, Vardhamana Mahavira, is believed to have been only the most recent in a succession of holy people through many ages who have taught the same principles. Having transcended the suffering of life and attained enlightenment, these teachers are called *jina*, 'victors'. Thus the followers of Mahavira—born around the beginning of the sixth century BCE, and thus roughly contemporary with Gautama Buddha—came to be called Jain(a)s, 'followers of the Victorious One'.

In time Buddhism was largely displaced from its Indian homeland, but the Jain tradition has continued without interruption for 2,500 years. Although a tiny minority in India, the Jains have not only maintained their own distinctive identity but had considerable influence on various Hindu traditions in their practice of vegetarianism and non-violence.

For Jains the universe is pulsating with life in countless forms, and any violence done to that life, even unintentionally, is a stain on the soul. Thus the doctrine of non-violence governs virtually every aspect of a Jain's life: diet, manner and times of eating, movements, travel, and choice of career. No other religion in the world has paid such close attention to the theory, practice, and propagation of non-violence. Only by avoiding violence in any form, including thought and word as well as deed, and practising 'right conduct' can the translucent, luminous nature of the soul be restored and liberation from the cycle of life and death achieved. Ultimately, it is through our own spiritual practice—not the grace of a divine being—that we achieve liberation.

Jains and Hindus both believe in karma and the immortality of the soul. They also share some practices in common, such as fasting, going on pilgrimages, and worshipping in temples. As we will see, though, two groups differ in the ways they understand some of these concepts and practices.

NUMBERS
Estimates range from five to eight million worldwide.

DISTRIBUTION
Primarily India; smaller numbers in East Africa, England, and North America.

PRINCIPAL HISTORICAL PERIODS
599–527 (or 510) BCE	Traditional dates of Mahavira
c. 310 BCE	Beginning of the split within the Jain community
2nd century BCE	Possible composition of *Kalpa Sutra*
6th century CE	Crystallization of Svetambara sect
17th century	Emergence of the Svetambara Sthanakvasi subsect
18th century	Emergence of the Svetambara Terapanth subsect

FOUNDERS AND LEADERS
The 24 *jinas* or *tirthankaras*: a series of 'ford-builders' who achieved perfect enlightenment and serve as guides for other human beings. The most important *tirthankaras* are the two most recent, Parshva and Mahavira.

DEITIES
None in philosophy; a few minor deities in popular practice; some Jains also worship Hindu deities such as Lakshmi. Although the *tirthankaras* are not gods, their images are revered by many Jains.

AUTHORITATIVE TEXTS
All Jains agree that the earliest texts were lost long ago. The Svetambara sect reveres a collection called the *agama*, consisting of various later treatises known as the *angas*, as well as the *Kalpa Sutra,* which contains the life stories of the *tirthankaras*. The Digambara sect believes that the original *angas* were lost as well and focus instead on a set of texts called *prakaranas* (treatises).

NOTEWORTHY TEACHINGS
The soul is caught in karmic bondage as a result of violence, both intended and unintended, done to other beings. Non-violence is the most important principle, in thought, word, and deed. Freed from karma, the soul attains crystal purity.

Origins

The Enlightened Teachers

According to the Jain tradition, Mahavira was the most recent of the 24 *jinas*. Each of these enlightened teachers is honoured as a *tirthankara*: one who creates a ford so that others can make their way through a body of water to the other side. It is *tirthankaras* who enable the faithful to cross through the river of life to the shore of enlightenment. At the same time, the four components of the Jain community—monks, nuns, laymen, and laywomen—are called *tirthas*.

The first *tirthankara*, Rishabha, is said to have lived in an era not far removed from the golden age, when the ideal society was just beginning to decline. To bring order in a time of increasing chaos, Rishabha and his son Bharata—the legendary first emperor of the subcontinent, which many Indians call 'Bharata varsha'—introduce the basic elements of the society, culture, and values that we know today. Twenty-two more *tirthankaras* appear over the ages that follow before Mahavira is born.

Mahavira

Accounts of Mahavira's life differ in many details, largely because a schism developed among his followers roughly two centuries after his death. Over time, the Digambara ('sky-clad') and Svetambara ('white-clad') Jains diverged in several areas of doctrine and practice (see p. 362). They agree, however, that Mahavira was born near the city of Patna in northern India, that his parents were members of the *kshatriya* (warrior) class, and that his given name was Vardhamana ('one with increasing prosperity'; 'Mahavira' is a title or epithet meaning 'great hero'). The traditional date for his birth is around 599 BCE. Early texts portray Mahavira as almost divine. As with so many other spiritual teachers, his birth was associated with unusual omens: his mother Trisala is said to have had fourteen wonderful dreams before he was born.

In the Svetambara narrative, Mahavira marries and has a daughter before renouncing secular life; the Digambaras maintain that he never married. In either case, he embarks on his quest for spiritual enlightenment at the age of thirty. Many celestial beings attend his renunciation of the world, an event that he marks by pulling out all the hair on his head. (To this day, those who join Jain orders, both monks and nuns, follow his example; this practice serves a double purpose, reminding novices of the pain that others suffer while showing their disregard for their own bodies.)

At some point Mahavira also renounces clothes as a sign of attachment to modesty or shame and hence of selfhood. Finally, after twelve years of arduous and extreme ascetic practices, he achieves enlightenment. According to the Svetambaras, he gives his first sermon on the importance of non-violence and then spends several seasons travelling and spreading his teaching through northern India.

The Digambara Jains, by contrast, maintain that upon his enlightenment Mahavira ceases all worldly activity. His body becomes like crystal, free of all impurities; he neither eats nor sleeps; and far from travelling and teaching, he spends the remaining thirty years of his life in a kind of celestial hall called the *samavasarana*—'the refuge of all creatures'—where, without speaking, he transmits his teachings in the form of a sacred sound resembling 'om'. This sound is interpreted by his chief disciple, Indrabhuti, who then records his interpretations as the sermons of Mahavira.

All Jains agree that Mahavira attained liberation or nirvana at the age of seventy-two, and that Indrabhuti in turn received enlightenment within a few hours of his teacher's death. They celebrate Mahavira's attainment of nirvana on the new moon that occurs between 15 October and 14 November—the same new moon that begins Deepavali (the Hindu festival celebrating the victory of light over darkness and good over evil).

Five 'auspicious' events (*panca kalyanaka*) in Mahavira's life are celebrated as representative of the life of all *jinas*: his conception, birth, renunciation, enlightenment, and final release from life. These events are portrayed in art and architecture, in rituals at temples and at home, in festivals, and in the performing arts. They may also be re-enacted when a new image of Mahavira is enshrined in a temple. Such ceremonies are usually underwritten by patrons, who may then enjoy the honour of portraying Sakra (also known as Indra) and his wife Indrani, the king and queen of the celestial beings who rejoice at the birth of a potential *jina*. Sponsoring such activities is thought to produce an abundance of good karma.

India, Rajasthan, Sirohi School, *Digambara Jain manuscript page: Jina and worshippers*; 18th century; ink, opaque watercolour, and gold on paper; 29 cm × 18.8 cm (11⁷⁄₁₆ in. × 7⅜ in.).

Gift of Dr and Mrs Leo S. Figiel and Dr and Mrs Steven J. Figiel. University of Michigan Museum of Art, Accession no. 1975/2.180.

| Box 7.1 | The Sakra Stava (Hymn of Indra) |

'Sakra' is an alternative name for the god Indra. This hymn, in which the god praises the jinas, is recited by observant Jains.

[Indra, the god of the celestial one, spoke thus]:

'My obeisance to my Lords, the Arhats, the prime ones, the Tirthankaras, the enlightened ones, the best of men, the lions among men, the exalted elephants among men, lotus among men.

Transcending the world they rule the world, think of the well-being of the world.

Illuminating all, they dispel fear, bestow vision, show the path, give shelter, life, enlightenment.

Obeisance to the bestowers of *dharma*, the teachers of *dharma*, the leaders of *dharma*, the charioteers of *dharma*, the monarchs of the four regions of *dharma*,

To them, who have uncovered the veil and have found unerring knowledge and vision, the islands in the ocean, the shelter, the goal, the support.

Obeisance to the Jinas—the victors—who have reached the goal and who help others reach it.

The enlightened ones, the free ones, who bestow freedom, the Jinas victorious over fear, who have known all and can reveal all, who have reached that supreme state which is unimpeded, eternal, cosmic and beatific, which is beyond disease and destruction, where the cycle of birth ceases; the goal, the fulfillment,

My obeisance to the *Sramana Bhagvan Mahavira*

The initiator, the ultimate Tirthankara, who has come to fulfill the promise of earlier Tirthankaras.

I bow to him who is there—in Devananda's womb from here—my place in heaven.

May he take cognizance of me.'

With these words, Indra paid his homage to *Sramana Bhagvan Mahavira* and, facing east, resumed his seat on the throne (*Kalpa Sutra* 2; Lath 1984:29–33).

Crystallization

The Jain View of the Universe

Space

The Jain universe has three principal realms, some with multiple subdivisions. The underworld, occupied by demons and demigods, consists of coloured layers with the darkest at the bottom. The earth's surface forms the middle world. On top of all this, beyond the heavens, is the crescent-shaped apex of the universe, a region permanently occupied by souls who are already liberated. Jain texts describe in great detail the specific characteristics of various tiers in this unique physical arrangement.

In the middle, or terrestrial, layer, there are many worlds, only a few of which are conducive to human life. They are arranged in an infinite number of concentric rings, each separated from the others by water. The land in which Mahavira was born is called Bharata (India). It is located on the continent or island of the Jambu Tree (Jambudvipa). Jambudvipa and two of its adjacent worlds are the only places that may be called *karma-bhumi*, the land of action. Only in these worlds do human actions lead to merit and demerit (karma), and only there may one reach the supreme goal of liberation.

Time

Like Hindus, Jains believe in cycles of time divided into units of progressively increasing happiness or unhappiness. For the Jains, each half-cycle of time consists of six 21,000-year stages in which world civilization and individual happiness are either increasing or decreasing. The present half-cycle of declining values and happiness began millions of years ago, and we are now in the fifth stage of decline.

After tens of thousands of years, when civilization has passed through the sixth stage of decline and reached rock bottom, the quality of life will slowly improve through six progressively happier stages lasting millions of years. When the apogee of that prosperous age has been reached, decline will begin again. Twenty-four *tirthankaras* appear in each full cycle of time. Mahavira lived near the very end of the fourth stage in the descending cycle.

There are also other worlds with cycles of time quite different from ours. In some worlds the conditions are always similar to our third and fourth ages. *Jinas*, it is believed, can only be born in the third and fourth stages of the cycle, when there is neither extreme unhappiness nor extreme happiness. Thus no more teachers will appear in this world until there is an upward swing in civilization. But even now there may be *jinas* living in other worlds where the conditions are more felicitous than those on this earth.

Physical Existence

With logical perseverance, Jains have sought to understand how we obtain and verify information about the world we live in. The remarkable system of knowledge they have developed is studied under two headings: *anekanta* ('many-sidedness') and *syadvada* ('assertion with qualification').

Jains believe that when we observe an object, we should be simultaneously aware of both its unchanging unified nature and its changing manifold modes. Anything that exists is said to have three aspects: substance, quality, and mode. Any substance (*dravya*) is the abode of inherent qualities (*gunas*). Qualities constantly undergo changes, losing and acquiring modes (*paryayas*).

For example, if we observe a flower for several minutes or even hours, we may not notice any significant change. Yet the flower is constantly changing, and in time those changes will show. It is the simultaneous recognition of the enduring entity and the changing variety of its being that is called *anekanta*.

Jains also take great care to avoid making absolute statements. Virtually every statement can—indeed must—be qualified. To say simply that a glass of water is cold, for instance, would not be acceptable, because it might seem warm to someone who has just come in from the cold; even the fact that the glass exists should not be stated without acknowledgement that in the future it may not exist. The principle behind this insistence on the relative nature of our perceptions is known as *syadvada*. In effect, Jains believe that every statement should be accompanied by the phrase 'in some ways'.

Categories of Reality

Jain philosophers recognize three basic categories of reality: matter (*pudgala*), sentient beings, and that which is neither material nor sentient, namely space, time, movement, and rest.

Matter is formed from atoms, which in themselves have no extension in space but begin to form shapes when combined with other atoms. In the Jain tradition, karma also is material and accounts for the bondage in which the souls of sentient beings are held.

Jains believe that there are four types of sentient beings: celestial beings or gods, humans, inhabitants of the underworld, and plants and animals. Every sentient being has a soul, which adapts to the dimensions of the body it occupies. While the soul itself is in one sense unchanging, its qualities do undergo change. Indeed, the universe is populated by souls in a constant process of embodiment and transmigration. That is, they are born, they die, and they are born again into this universe.

Within the lowest category of life (plants and animals), the very lowest level is occupied by an almost imperceptible creature called a *nigoda*. *Nigodas* are born in clusters and die within milliseconds. They are found in every part of the universe, including the bodies of human beings, plants, and animals, and have only one sense: that of touch. Matter—including the elements of earth, water, fire, and air—is made up of slightly larger single-celled creatures. Thus every time a lamp is lit and the flame is put out, fire bodies come into being and are extinguished. Plants too are considered to be creatures with only the sense of touch. Animals are categorized by the number of sense organs they are believed to have. Animals are not considered much lower than human beings; Mahavira himself is said to have been a lion in one of his previous births. Embodiment takes place when a soul becomes entangled and entrenched in karmic matter.

Karma and Bondage

The Jain understanding of karma differs from its Buddhist and Hindu counterparts in one important way: Jains consider karma to be material in nature, consisting of undifferentiated particles that become attracted to the soul whenever the sentient being thinks, speaks, or acts in any way. Karmic matter seems to be especially attracted to souls that are 'moist' with desires; drier, more dispassionate souls are not so easily polluted. Particles of karmic matter stick to the soul and keep it in a state of bondage. Over successive births, the soul becomes coloured by the particular type of karma that pollutes it; the darker the soul, the more soiled it is with negative karma. This is a far cry from the crystalline purity of the liberated soul.

| Box 7.2 | Dharma |

Dharma [religious and social duty] is the most important principle in the world. It is the main cause for all happiness. It comes from human beings and through it, human beings attain what is good (*Kalpa Sutra* 2).

Intentions are just as important as actions and determine the quality of the karma that attaches itself to the soul. It makes a significant difference if a particular action is planned rather than accidental. The intention to hurt or harm a being is the most violent and entails the worst karma. A tenth-century book, the *Yashatilaka*, describes the harm that befalls a prince who sacrifices a rooster made of dough. Even though no living bird was harmed, the intention to kill was present in the act. Such intentions darken the soul and prevent it from being liberated.

A well-known Jain story explains how the soul falls into deeper layers of bondage. In it, the soul is represented by a man who falls into a well. Before hitting the bottom, he manages to clutch at the branch of a tree growing from the side of the well. As he hangs on, he sees two mice, one black and one white, gnawing at the branch. He realizes that when the mice chew through the wood, he will fall. Glancing down at the pit, he sees poisonous serpents waiting for him. At this moment, a beehive on the tree above is shaken and drops of honey fall near the man. Forgetting his predicament, he reaches out for the honey and loses his grip on the branch.

The man in the well is the soul, which can at any moment fall into deeper trouble. The mice represent our lives; the white mouse symbolizes the days and the black mouse the nights. Time is eating away at our lives. Yet instead of concentrating our energies on getting out of the predicament that we find ourselves in, we risk everything, even our ultimate happiness, for the sake of a fleeting pleasure. If we miss our chance to get on the right path, we will be reborn again and again. Still, the situation of the man in the well is not entirely hopeless. He is not necessarily doomed to revolve endlessly in the cycle of birth and death, for he can attain liberation.

Jain Symbolism

The Sanskrit word *svastika* means 'well-being'. In the symbol of the swastika, Jains read not only the human predicament but the means of overcoming it. Its four spokes represent the four stages of this existence in the wheel of samsara, the cycle of life and death.

The swastika can seen on everything from Jain temples and household doorways to wedding invitations and greeting cards. It is also used in Jain meditation; practitioners may sometimes use grains of rice to create a swastika on the floor or ground.

The swastika used in meditation is a special one, with additional marks. There are three dots above the swastika and a little crescent on top of all this, with a dot in the middle. The four arms represent the four realms of possible births: human, heavenly, infernal, and plant or animal. The crescent and dot symbolize the land of the perfected

One of the five Dilwara temples at Mount Abu in Rajasthan, built between the eleventh and thirteenth centuries (Willard G. Oxtoby).

soul, which cosmographical texts describe as resembling an inverted umbrella. The three dots represent the hope for final emancipation from the cycle of life and death by way of the 'three jewels', or *ratna traya*: : right insight, viewpoint, or faith (*samyak darshana*), right knowledge (*samyak jnana*), and right conduct (*samyak charitra*).

Right faith implies a moment of spiritual insight, a glimpse of the truth from a right viewpoint; this flash of insight is enough to start the soul on the path to eventual liberation. Right knowledge leads the way along that long and arduous path, while right conduct consists in adherence to five basic principles (*mahavrata*) of practice: non-violence, truthfulness, non-stealing, sexual purity, and non-possession.

Differentiation

The fundamental split in the Jain tradition appears to have taken place in the fourth century BCE, after a council held at Patna failed to reach agreement on what should constitute official Jain doctrine. According to those who eventually became the Digambaras, it was soon after this that a leader named Bhadrabahu, predicting a serious famine, led many Jains south to the region that is now Karnataka. Several years later, when the southern group returned to the north, they found that those who had stayed behind had not only broken with the Jain tradition of absolute renunciation and begun wearing clothing, but had adopted as scripture a number of texts that the Digambaras did not accept.

After a series of councils beginning in the fourth century, the Svetambara movement crystallized in the sixth century with the fixing of a scriptural canon that the Digambaras rejected because they believed many of the ancient teachings had been lost. In time the Digambaras wrote their own sacred texts, and the two groups never did reach agreement.

Two Scriptural Canons

A vast body of Jain literature, both Digambara and Svetambara, has been composed in a variety of languages over the last 2,000 years. Some texts are overtly religious, while others present Jain moral teachings in the context of narrative or poetry. Interestingly, books considered canonical are not always important in the liturgy, and books that are popular in worship and ritual are not necessarily a part of either canon.

Both the Digambaras and the Svetambaras maintain that the earliest Jain texts—known as the *purvas*—were lost long ago. In addition, the Digambaras believe that two other collections of books, the *angas* ('limbs' or ancillaries) and *anga bahya* ('outside the *angas*'), had been lost by the second century CE. Other texts, called the *prakaranas* ('treatises'), date from the beginning of the Common Era. The principal sacred collection of the Svetambaras, called the *agama* ('tradition'), contains between 32 and 45 treatises grouped into 12 *angas*.

One particularly important text is the *Kalpa Sutra*, which is thought to date from the second century BCE. A chapter from one of the *anga bahya* texts, it is normally published (with two appendices) as a separate book, just as the Hindu classic the *Bhagavad Gita* is extracted from the much larger *Mahabharata* epic. Recitation of the *Kalpa Sutra* is a central part of the festival of Paryusan in September (see p. 368). Various episodes in the life of the *jinas* are highlighted.

On the whole, Jains have discouraged study of the sacred texts without active guidance and instructions from a teacher because the individual reader may misinterpret the sacred word. Nor is the study of scripture by itself, without ascetic practice, recommended, since it cannot be efficacious in the quest for liberation.

Two Views of Women

As the division of the community into four *tirthas*—monks, nuns, laymen, and laywomen—indicates, the distinction between male and female is no less fundamental to the Jain tradition than the distinction between ascetic and householder. And just as the tradition accords more respect to ascetics than to householders, so it, like other ancient traditions, seems to confer special privilege on men. Nevertheless, Digambara and Svetambara Jains differ significantly in their views regarding women.

Apparently Mahavira himself willingly ordained women. At a time when Hinduism restricted ordination to men, thousands of Jain women became nuns under the leadership of a holy woman named Chandana. Svetambara Jains have continued to ordain women to the present day. They consider women no less capable than men of attaining liberation. They believe that the first person to attain liberation in the present cycle of time was Rishabha's mother, Marudevi, and even consider the nineteenth *tirthankara*, Malli, to have been a woman.

The Digambaras, however, insist that Malli must have been a man, for only true ascetics can attain enlightenment, and only those who renounce everything—including clothes—can be true ascetics. Since nakedness is impractical for women, in the Digambara view they are excluded from enlightenment; the only chance for a woman to attain liberation is to be reborn in a male body. Although women are not refused entry to Digambara orders, the few who do become nuns are regarded as high-status householders rather than ascetics. All nuns, whatever their seniority, must show respect to monks, however young or inexperienced.

Subsects

Some Svetambara Jains, known as Murtipujaks, worship in temples, where they revere icons of *tirthankaras* and minor deities. Others have rejected this practice. The latter group in turn is divided between two subsects, Sthanakvasi and Terapanthi, both of which are extremely rigorous in their observance of the *ahimsa* principle. The Digambara movement also has several subgroups.

Caste Divisions

Jains are divided socially along caste lines. Although Mahavira rejected the idea that only members of the higher castes could attain liberation, we see a strong awareness of the caste system in Jain literature.

In regions where the same castes exist in both the Hindu and Jain communities, caste allegiances can override religion. Thus a higher-caste Jain will often choose to marry a Hindu from a similar caste rather than a lower-caste Jain. In Rajasthan, for example, a Svetambara Jain and Vaishnava Hindu who are both members of the Oswal caste can have a good deal in common, since Vaishnavas are often strict vegetarians and, like Jains, may be part of the business community. Compatibility in these areas of life often outweighs other considerations.

Practice

The Five Principles (*Mahavrata*)

Non-violence

Non-violence or not harming (*ahimsa*) is the first and most important principle. Jains find even the thought of harming others abhorrent. The principle of non-violence is applied in all areas of Jain life, but is perhaps most perceptible in dietary habits. Non-violence automatically means that all Jains are vegetarians.

The taking of animal life is prohibited, and one must be as sparing as possible in the destruction of plant life for food. Many periods of fasting are required for lay Jains as well as monks and nuns. Many monks do not eat more than one meal a day. Digambara monks use their cupped hands as begging bowls and eat as sparingly as possible. Among laypersons, women tend to observe more fast days than men and are frequently stricter about avoiding foods perceived to entail violence to plant life.

Meat, fish, and fowl are always out of bounds. In addition, certain non-animal foods, including honey, alcohol, and eggplant, are prohibited on the grounds that they abound in life forms and the potential for life, and several other vegetables are also normally prohibited for various reasons, although they may be permitted under extenuating medical circumstances. Because many Jains, especially those living outside India, find it impractical to avoid all the prohibited vegetables, they are frequently included in the diet today.

Water is to be strained or boiled before drinking, so that one will not inadvertently consume any micro-organism that might grow in it. In the past, evening meals were eaten before sunset specifically to avoid lighting lamps that would attract insects and thus inadvertently do violence to their souls.

All Jain monks ritually sweep the ground before them as they sit down, to avoid harming any life form. In addition, monks and nuns of the Terapanthi and Sthanakvasi subsects wear a small scarf or plastic screen around their mouths, to avoid harming organisms in the air either by breathing them in or by breathing out hot air onto them.

Work that might cause any harm to life is generally discouraged, although rural occupations such as farming were inescapable for some Jains. Because the practice of business did not appear to involve doing harm, many Jains have worked as merchants. Ironically, in a roundabout way, a choice of work motivated by altruistic concern for other beings had the effect of contributing to Jains' economic prosperity.

Non-violence was the principal instrument used by the Hindu socio-political leader Mohandas K. Gandhi (1869–1948) in his struggle to gain India its independence from Britain. Gandhi had known Jains in Gujarat in his youth, and there is no doubt of Jain influence on his thought.

Truthfulness

Adherence to truth (*satya*) is also important for Jains. They are encouraged not to hide the truth and not to lie. The only exceptions permitted are those occasions when telling the truth might result in violence.

Non-stealing

Non-stealing in most circumstances means avoiding taking what does not belong to one; in many cases it is interpreted as not taking what has not been voluntarily given.

Sexual Purity

Until the nineteenth century, polygamy was accepted by all the many religions of India. Thus sexual purity for the Jain laity meant fidelity to one's spouse or, in the case of men with more than one wife, to their spouses. Today laypersons are exhorted to lead as celibate a life as possible, or at least to limit their activities to those permissible in traditional Jain society. Monks and nuns are required to give up any thought of sexual activity.

Non-possession

The Jain ideal is to renounce not only possessions themselves but the desire for possession that distracts us from the pursuit of knowledge and impels us to act in ways that may cause harm to others. Jains are supposed to own as little as possible and to give away whatever is not necessary. In addition, laymen are asked to observe 14 principles of renunciation; these involve abstaining from or limiting quantities of food, clothes, decorations, and so on. Those who become monks or nuns formally give away all their belongings, in emulation of Mahavira.

Vows for Ascetics and Householders

All Jains, laypersons ('householders') as well as ascetics, are expected to practise the five principles, and all take vows to that effect. The five 'minor' vows taken by householders are called *anuvratas* and mirror the vows taken by ascetics, although they are much less stringent. In the case of sexual purity, for instance, ascetics must renounce all sexual activity, whereas householders are not expected to be celibate: they need only restrict their sexual activity to their spouses and exercise self-control regarding sensuality generally.

Similarly, whereas ascetics are required to give up all possessions, householders are required only to limit themselves to what is genuinely needed. Specifically, they must place a limit on purchases of real estate, gold, silver, jewellery, cash, cars and other vehicles, equipment, and all consumer goods. Austerity in every form is strongly encouraged.

Six additional actions are obligatory for ordained monks and nuns:

- cultivating equanimity (a tranquil, meditative state of mind);
- singing a short hymn in praise of the *tirthankaras*;
- showing formal respect and reverence for their teachers;
- showing repentance (at least twice daily) after thorough introspective examination of personal behaviour and faults;
- meditating while standing motionless for long periods of time in a position called *katyosarga* ('abandonment of the body'); and
- refraining from various specific transgressions involving violence.

Sallekhana (Fasting unto Death)

A unique feature of Jainism is the ritual called *sallekhana*: a fast unto death that is considered the ideal and is reserved for the wisest and most holy. While the taking of one's own life is condemned as an act of passion and violence, *sallekhana* is not considered suicide: rather, it is death with dignity and dispassion, undertaken in a meditative state of mind, with total control over one's faculties, and is idealized as the ultimate expression of restraint from violence to living beings.

Devotion and Images of the Revered *Jinas*

Jains have frequently been represented as considering asceticism and struggle to be the only paths to liberation, but in fact ritual devotions and worship are an integral part of Jain piety. The majority of Jains revere images (*murtis*) of Mahavira and other *jinas*, whether in temples or at home shrines. This tradition goes back a long way: an inscription from the first century BCE in a cave in the state of Orissa refers to an image of a *jina* in connection with a king who lived three centuries earlier. In the Mathura region, temples built between the second century BCE and the third century CE all seem to have

The image of Mahavira in a posture of meditation (Vasudha Narayanan).

| Box 7.3 | The Great Mantra of Adoration

I bow to the victors, those who have attained perfection, those who have attained liberation, to religious leaders, to religious teachers [preceptors], and all the monks. This fivefold adoration that destroys all sins is the most important and the most auspicious of all.

included images of the *jinas*. And the state of Bihar has several standing images of *jinas* believed to date from the first century.

While some images are only a few centimetres in size, one colossal statue near Mysore in Karnataka is 21 m (68 ft) tall. Carved from a single block of stone, it depicts Rishabha's younger son, Bahubali, in the pose of standing meditation for which he is known. According to Jain tradition, Bahubali became an ascetic after fighting his brother Bharata for the title of universal emperor: just as he was about to win the duel, he saw the futility of worldly life and renounced it. Thereafter he stood for years in a meditation so intense that no part of his body moved. Vines grew on his body, and snakes, lizards, and even a scorpion made their nests there, believing it to be inanimate.

Erected and consecrated in the late tenth century, the statue was first bathed and then anointed with various substances. Every twelve years or so, the Digamabaras repeat this *mahamastabhiseka* ('grand head anointing'). The image is drenched with fragrant liquids, flowers are strewn from helicopters, and hundreds of thousands of people witness the ceremonies.

Unlike most Hindus, Jains do not believe that consecration brings such images to life, and many teachers maintain that images are not 'inhabited' by the *jinas* they represent. Rather, most believe that the images serve mainly to remind all human beings that the state of liberation is available to all and that all should work towards attaining it.

The most famous Jain mantra is the *namaskara* ('Great Mantra of Adoration'), which pays obeisance to the omniscient beings, the other perfected beings, the ascetic teachers, the ascetic preceptors, and all Jain mendicants. Simply reciting this mantra of praise is believed to be such a holy deed that it destroys all bad karma.

In addition Jains venerate and build temples for a number of celestial beings called *yakshas* (feminine *yakshis*) whose stories are told in myths and legends. One of the most popular *yakshis*, Padmavati ('she who resides on the lotus'), resembles the Hindu goddess Lakshmi, the bestower of worldly fortune and divine grace.

The Ritual Calendar

Jains observe many rituals involving food, both fasts and feasts, through the year. Almost all are associated with the phases of the moon, practised on a particular day in the cycle of a waxing or waning moon. As in the Hindu tradition, the lunar calendar is regularly adjusted to catch up to the solar one.

Fasting is practised on many days of the month, especially by women. Some fasts involve total abstention, even from water, while some require only avoidance of certain foods. In the Svetambara fast called *ayambil*, foods are prepared in a common kitchen with particular care and flavourful ingredients such as salt and oil are avoided. Fasts are undertaken for both personal liberation and the well-being of the family.

Fasting is not necessarily a private domestic affair; some difficult fasts are undertaken in public places of worship and culminate with pomp and ceremony. Participants in these fasts gain a certain prestige from their public display of piety. Some fasts involving large groups may be accompanied by activities such as the narration of edifying stories. Frequently, the fasting may be followed by a *pratikramana*, a ritual of confession and repentance.

Ritual giving is also an important part of Jain life. As an exercise of non-possession, Jains give away part of their riches in elaborate ceremonies. Like the act of fasting, ritual donation is a sign of the piety and prestige of an entire family.

The period of Chaturmas ('four months') coincides with India's hot, rainy monsoon season—roughly June through September. This is a time of special observances for ascetics of all three traditions, Buddhist, Hindu, and Jain, and is generally a period of retreat for monks. Many people avoid travel in order to prevent the accidental killing of the many insects and other small forms of life that tend to come out during the rainy season. Many Jain laypeople are also involved with their religious institutions during Chaturmas and undertake frequent fasts.

An eight- to ten-day period in the fall called Paryusan is particularly sacred for Jains. The entire *Kalpa Sutra* is read aloud, and the final day is devoted to ritual confession and seeking of forgiveness from one's family and associates; letters and sometimes printed cards seeking pardon are mailed to friends and relatives. Digambaras hold a similar festival called Dasa Laksana Parvan ('the time of the ten characteristics') around the same time as Paryusan.

Jains also celebrate the festival of Divali (or Deepavali), though for different reasons than Hindus. Jains believe that on this day Mahavira reached nirvana. During Divali Jains join with Hindus in worshipping the goddess Lakshmi, who as the bestower of wealth and good fortune is especially important to Jain business people. This time (which usually falls in October–November) also marks the Jain new year, when new account books are started.

All Jains celebrate Mahavira's birth on the thirteenth day after the new moon occurring between mid-March and mid-April. On the third day of the next waxing moon a holiday called Aksaya Trtiya commemorates an incident in the life of the first *tirthankara*, Rishabha. In this story, Rishabha has been fasting for a long time and a holy man gives him sugar-cane juice to break the fast. Many Svetambaras fast during this time at Mount Satrunjaya in Gujarat, where Rishabha is enshrined. Rishabha's attendant, a goddess called Chakresvari, protects pious Jain women, especially those who undertake voluntary fasts

Pratikramana

One of the central rituals of the Jain tradition is *pratikramana* ('turning back'). For some, the term means returning the soul to its original pristine state, restoring virtues like compassion, peace, and equanimity. For others, it means turning away from one's transgressions.

| Box 7.4   From the *Bhaktamara Stotra*

The Bhaktamara stotra *is one of the most beloved Jain texts. It is addressed to Adinatha—another name for Rishabha, the first* tirthankara.

In the fullness of faith
I bow
to the feet of the Jina,
shining as they reflect the gems in the
crowns of the gods
who bow down in devotion,
illuminating the darkness
of oppressive sin,
a refuge in the beginning of time
for all souls
lost in the ocean of birth (1)

. . .

Praising you
instantly destroys
the sinful karma that binds
embodied souls
to endless rebirth
just as the sun's rays
instantly shatter
the all-embracing
bee-black
endless dark night (7)

. . .

Gods like Hari and Hara
don't have your shining knowledge.
Light is glorious
in a glittering jewel
but not in a piece
of even the best glass.

I think it is good
that after seeing
Hari, Hara, and the rest of the gods
my heart is pleased

only with you.
I have gained so much in this world
by seeing you
o lord.
None other can steal my mind,
not even in my next life (20-1)

. . .

Praise to you,
o lord,
remover of the pain
of the three worlds.
Praise to you,
stainless ornament
of the earth's surface.
Praise to you,
supreme lord
of the triple world.
Praise to you,
o Jina,
you dry up
the ocean of rebirth (26)

. . .

O Jina King
Laksmi comes quickly to Manatunga,
who forever wears around his neck
your garland of praise,
woven from the qualities
of my bhakti
and adorned by the multihued flowers
of radiant color (44)

(*Bhaktamara Stotra, Manatunga*, 1, 7, 20-1,
26, 44; Cort 2004:95-8).

In this ritual the faithful confess their transgressions of omission and commission and then seek forgiveness. Ideally, it should be performed twice a day, because the longer one goes without making peace—with oneself as well as others—the more difficult it becomes to remove the clinging karma. In practice, since the whole ritual, carefully executed, can take as long as three hours, some perform it only once every two weeks or once every four months. It must be performed at least once a year; the Svetambaras perform it on the last day of Paryusan.

The complete *pratikramana* ritual has six essential parts, each of which must be performed in its entirety. In the first stage devotees seek to free themselves of passions such as anger, greed, and arrogance and enter a state of equanimity (*samayika*). They begin by reciting the Great Mantra of Adoration and bowing down before the teachers who have achieved liberation; then they adopt the motionless posture of the ascetic and meditate on the nature of the human soul. Curtailing physical activity in this way helps to establish tranquillity.

The next two stages of the ritual focus on veneration of the *tirthankaras*, monks, and nuns. Then comes the central *pratikramana* act of seeking forgiveness. Householders reaffirm their vows, including the commitment to non-violence. Then they formally express the hope that they will have the faith and courage to perform a religious fast unto death in the future. After the recitation of each vow, worshippers speak ritual words seeking forgiveness from all.

The last of the six essential acts is called the *pratyakhyana*. Devotees vow to renounce activities that cause violence or harm in any way. Having worshipped all worthy souls, and humbly sought pardon from all beings for their sins against them, devotees emerge cleansed and purified.

Interaction and Adaptation

Jains in Hindu Society

Relations between Jains and Hindus in India have generally been very cordial. In some regions men and women from the two traditions may intermarry, and in North America some temples accommodate both faiths. Historically, however, there have also been times of conflict and tension.

The relationship between the Jain and Hindu traditions has been somewhat ambiguous in post-independence India. Although the religious identity of the Jains has not been compromised, their legal and social identities have become somewhat blurred. Since India does not have a uniform civil code, Jains (and Sikhs) are included under the Hindu family law. Thus marriage, divorce, and inheritance are all governed by a law grounded in Hindu tradition. Legal texts point out that, in the absence of a Jain custom that directly contradicts the Hindu law, Indian courts have always applied the Hindu law to Jain cases.

The Jain Diaspora

It is only since the 1960s that significant numbers of Jains have immigrated to Canada and the United States. More than two-thirds of the Jains in North America reportedly come from the western Indian state of Gujarat. It is estimated that there are now approximately 25,000 Jains in the United States, 10,000 in Canada, and another 25,000 in

Jain nuns at Palitana in Gujarat, where a mountain covered with Jain temples is a major pilgrimage site (Ashish Mehta).

Britain. As in India, many overseas Jains are business people and bankers. About 40 per cent are engineers, and perhaps 20 per cent are physicians. The Jain emphasis on austerity has evidently contributed to the community's economic stability, and philanthropy is zealously practised.

There are numerous Jain centres in North America. The umbrella organization for many of them is called Jain Associations in North America, with the felicitous acronym 'JAINA'. Although there are sectarian, linguistic, and geographic differences within the diaspora, such organizations work to bridge them, emphasizing the transmission of Jain traditions to a generation born and raised outside India. In addition, such organizations frequently hold devotional rituals and sponsor lectures by scholars and visiting religious specialists.

Because of the rigour of the vows they take, ascetics do not travel great distances, and they never leave India. Thus one of the most striking features of Jainism as it is practised in other countries is the absence of ascetics to guide, bless, and gently encourage devotees.

Many Jain leaders today seek to translate traditional concepts and practices into terms relevant to the concerns of the younger generation. Although traditional asceticism may be impossible overseas, the principle of *ahimsa* is clearly applicable in many areas of personal and social life. Vegetarianism is encouraged not only as a way of minimizing harm to other creatures but as a healthful way of living. Similarly, traditional Jain ideals are clearly in harmony with efforts to protect the environment, conserve resources, and reduce waste. The preface to an edition of the *pratikramana* ritual published in the United States notes that 'For the sake of Ahimsa to trees, we have used recycled paper. Hopefully, we have spared some trees.' The same publication is printed with soybean-based ink.

Activists from various 'green' organizations attend JAINA conventions and distribute information about causes that Jains sympathize with. These include the magazines *In Defense of Animals* and *The Compassionate Shopper*, which speak out against the use of animals for clothing and medical experimentation and also list companies that avoid using animal products for cosmetics and cleaning materials. While traditional Jain teaching emphasized austerity and non-possession as preconditions for liberating the soul, those principles are no less essential for preserving the physical environment on which all life depends.

Jain conventions and festivals invariably include a large feast and entertainment, particularly demonstrations of classical and folk dances. Occasionally, though, traditional messages are also conveyed in modern forms, including rap. In form and content, the Jain message is being made relevant to a new generation.

The Jain population in England is concentrated in urban areas. In Canada and the United States Jains live mainly in Ontario, New York, New Jersey, and California. In some places where their numbers are relatively small they share facilities with Hindus from northern India, whose cultural background is similar. Examples include joint Hindu–Jain cultural centres and temples in Pittsburgh and Allentown, Pennsylvania, and there is a close relationship between the Jain Center of Northern California and the Hindu Temple and Cultural Center of Fremont, in the San Francisco Bay area. In these temples, images of Hindu deities share space with Mahavira and other *tirthankaras*. Although these arrangements allow both communities to make the most of the available land, money, and cultural resources, some Jains worry that Hindu priests may not be sufficiently knowledgeable to render the *jinas* the service they require.

Conclusion

The last century has given both a new impetus and a new direction to the traditional Jain emphasis on moral principles, beginning with non-violence. In the twenty-first century, it is no longer enough to refrain from eating certain foods: larger issues of environmental responsibility and social justice are now emphasized.

Many Jains are now working to extend the principle of non-violence to a broader range of issues, from human rights to national security and modern warfare. They see their tradition as one that offers a vision not just for the liberation of the individual soul, but for the very survival of life on this planet.

Sravanabelagola, Karnataka. This important pilgrimage site is located 100 km from Mysore. Pilgrims climb 614 steps to reach the top of the hill where the colossal image of Bahubali (also known as Gomateshwara) is carved out of the rock.

Dilwara temples, Rajasthan. Five strikingly beautiful marble temples, the earliest of which were built c. 1100 CE; a very important pilgrimage destination for Jains and also a tourist attraction.

Palitana, Gujarat. Located in the Shatrunjaya hills, this temple complex is said to consist of more than 863 shrines spread over 3.5 kilometres. Some of the temples have been dated to the eleventh century.

Ranakpur, Rajasthan. About 60 km from Udaipur in the Aravali Mountain range is a beautiful temple complex that has been dated to approximately the fifteenth century. The central temple is dedicated to the first *tirthankara*, Rishabha.

Udayagiri and Khandagiri, Orissa. Two sandstone hills near Bhubaneswar where Buddhist and Jain monks carved cave temples in roughly the first century BCE.

Glossary

agama 'Tradition'; the Svetambara scriptural corpus of ancient texts in Sanskrit, comprising up to 45 treatises.

ahimsa Non-violence, a goal pursued to remarkable lengths and applications in Jain tradition.

anekanta 'Many-sidedness'; the notion that the objects of our knowledge are seen under varied and changing modes.

anga bahya 'Outside the *angas*'; the texts that are not part of the *angas* but are included in the Svetambaras' canonical *agama* literature.

angas 'Limbs'; the twelve core divisions of the Svetambara *agama* or scriptural tradition.

Chaturmas A four-month period of retreat, fasting, and religious discipline, usually coinciding with the hot, rainy summer monsoon season.

Digambaras The 'sky-clad' branch of Jains, stronger in southern India, who as part of their ascetic practice have traditionally rejected clothing.

gunas In the Jain theory of knowledge, the changeable qualities that attach to the substance of things that we perceive, affecting their appearance to us.

jina 'Conqueror', one who has achieved an exemplary spiritual victory over the afflictions and conditions of life.

Kalpa Sutra An anthology of scriptural material, composed somewhat later than the *anga* texts, but more widely used in ritual and cited in popular Jain devotion.

nigoda The smallest, simplest form of living creature, believed to have only one sense perception: touch.

sallekhana The ritual of voluntary fasting to death, normally undertaken only by deeply spiritual people who have already achieved a ripe age.

samyak charitra Right conduct, implemented through the 'five practices' of non-violence, truthfulness, non-stealing, sexual purity, and non-possession.

samyak darshana Right faith, seen as an insight into truth from the right viewpoint.

samyak jnana Right knowledge, proper comprehension of the nature of the world and our existence in it.

Svetambaras 'White-clad' Jains, ascetics who wear clothing; based mainly in northern and western India.

swastika The four-spoked wheel or four-armed cross symbolizing the cycle of rebirths.

syadvada The core of the Jain theory of knowledge; the principle requiring that any statement of 'fact' be qualified to take into account the relative nature of human perception.

tirtha A ford or crossing of a river; in the Jain context, a crossing from this existence to the 'other side', liberation; also used to refer to the fourfold structure of the Jain community.

tirthankara 'Ford-maker', a title used of the great spiritual teachers in each age.

yaksha, yakshi Celestial beings figuring in Jain mythology; *yakshas* are masculine; *yakshis* are feminine.

Further Reading

Babb, Lawrence A. 1996. *Absent Lord: Ascetics and Kings in a Jain Ritual Culture*. Berkeley: University of California Press.

Carrithers, Michael, and C. Humphrey. 1991. *The Assembly of Listeners: Jains in Society*. Cambridge: Cambridge University Press.

Cort, John E. 2004. *Jains in the World: Religious Values and Ideology in India*. New York: Oxford University Press.

Dundas, Paul. 2002. *The Jains*. New York: Routledge.

Granoff, Phyllis. 1996. *Forest of Thieves and the Magic Garden: An Anthology of Medieval Jain Stories*. Harmondsworth: Penguin.

Jaini, Padmanabh. 2001. *The Jaina Path of Purification*. 2nd edn. Columbia, MI: South Asia Books.

_____. 1991. *Gender and Salvation: Jaina Debates on the Spiritual Liberation of Women*. Berkeley: University of California Press.

Kelting, M. Whitney. 2001. *Singing to the Jinas: Jain Laywomen, Mandal Singing, and the Negotiations of Jain Devotion*. New York: Oxford University Press.

Laidlaw, James. 1996. *Riches and Renunciation: Religion, Economy, and Society among the Jains*. New York: Oxford University Press.

Umasvati. *That Which Is: Tattvartha Sutra*. Translated by Nathmal Tatia.

Vallely, Anne. 2002. *Guardians of the Transcendent: An Ethnography of a Jain Ascetic Community*. Toronto: University of Toronto Press.

References

Jacobi, Herman, trans. 1884. *Jaina Sutras*, Part I (F. Max Müller, ed., *Sacred Books of the East*, 22). Oxford: Clarendon Press.

_____, trans. 1895. *Jaina Sutras*, Part II (Sacred Books of the East, 45). Oxford: Clarendon Press.

Lath, M., trans. 1984. *Kalpa Sutra*, ed. V. Sagar. Jaipur: Prakrit Bharati.

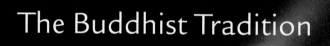

The Buddhist Tradition

ROY C. AMORE | JULIA CHING

When the continuing-education division of an American university organized a one-day Buddhist retreat, more than a hundred students signed up within a few hours. What is the appeal of Buddhism, especially Buddhist meditation, for Westerners? Why do people who still identify themselves as Christians or Jews flock to Buddhist meditation sessions? What is it that has attracted so many Hollywood celebrities to Buddhism? To attempt to answer these questions, we need to review the 2,500-year history of Buddhism, its varieties, and its spread—first throughout Asia, then throughout the world.

Overview

With his last words to his disciples, 'Everything that arises also passes away, so strive for what has not arisen,' the Buddha passed into everlasting nirvana some 2,500 years ago. After a deep enlightenment experience at the age of 35, he had spent the remaining 45 years of his life teaching that all worldly things are transient phenomena, caught up in a cycle of arising and passing away. He set the wheel of **dharma** (teaching) in motion, established a community (*sangha*) of disciples, and charged his followers to carry the dharma to all regions of the world. The missionary effort succeeded. Today there are Buddhists in nearly every country, and Buddhism is the dominant religion in many parts of East, South, and Southeast Asia.

Buddhism has three main traditions or 'vehicles', all of which originated in India. The earliest is **Theravada** (also known as **Hinayana**), which spread to Southeast Asia; the second is **Mahayana**, which became the principal school in East Asia; and the third is **Vajrayana**, which developed out of Mahayana and became closely associated with the Himalayan region. All three traditions also have followers in Europe and North America.

Buddhists say they 'take refuge' in the 'Triple Gem': (1) the Buddha, (2) the dharma, and (3) the *sangha*. As they progress along the path to enlightenment, they seek to become more compassionate, more generous, more detached from desire and hatred, more focused mentally, more pure of mind, and more spiritually wise.

Origins

Religious Life in Ancient India

The area along the Ganges River was a hotbed of economic activity in the seventh and sixth centuries BCE. Agriculture flourished on large estates owned by ruling-class landlords and worked by commoners; a thriving caravan trade crossed the region from east

c. 531 (or 589 or 413) BCE	Shakyamuni's enlightenment
c. 496 (or 544 or 368) BCE	His *parinirvana* or passing
c. 395 BCE	First Buddhist council
c. 273 BCE	Accession of King Ashoka
c. 225 BCE	Mahendra takes Theravada Buddhism to Sri Lanka
c. 100 CE	Emergence of Indian Mahayana
c. 200	Nagarjuna, Madhyamika philosopher
c. 350	Asanga and Vasubandhu, Yogacara philosophers
372	Buddhism introduced to Korea from China
c. 500	Emergence of tantra in India
604	Prince Shotoku, Japanese regent and patron of Buddhism, issues Seventeen-Article Constitution
c. 750	Padmasambhava takes Vajrayana Buddhism to Tibet
806	Shingon (tantric) Buddhism introduced to Japan
845	Persecution of Buddhism in China
1173	Birth of Shinran, Japanese Pure Land thinker (d. 1262)
1222	Birth of Nichiren, Japanese sectarian Buddhist leader (d. 1282)
1603	Start of Tokugawa regime, Japanese state control of Buddhism
c. 1617	Dalai Lamas become rulers of Tibet
c. 1900	Beginning of Buddhist missionary activity in the West
1956	B.R. Ambedkar (1891–1956) converts to Buddhism, leading to the conversion of 380,000 other Dalits and re-establishing Buddhism in India.
1959	China takes over Tibet; the Dalai Lama and other Tibetans flee to India
1963	Thich Quang Doc immolates himself in protest against persecution of Buddhists in Vietnam

Table 8.1	Buddhist vehicles and schools

1. Theravada (sometimes called Hinayana, the 'Lesser Vehicle'), now dominant in Sri Lanka and Southeast Asia: the only survivor of the 18 sects that existed in the third century BCE
2. Mahayana (the 'Greater Vehicle'), now dominant in East Asia and Vietnam:
   - Madhyamika in India, Sanlun in China
   - Yogacara in India, Faxiang in China
   - Tiantai in China, Tendai in Japan
   - Huayan in China, Kegon in Japan
   - Zhenyan in China, Shingon in Japan
   - Pure Land, Jingtu in China, Jodo in Japan
   - Chan in China, Son in Korea, Zen in Japan
     - Linji in China, Rinzai in Japan
     - Caodong in China, Soto in Japan
   - Nichiren in Japan
3. Vajrayana (the 'Diamond Vehicle'), now dominant in Tibet and elsewhere in the Himalayas, in Mongolia, and in the Republic of Kalmykia, Russia:
   - Gelugpa ('Yellow Hats')
   - Kargyu ('Red Hats')
   - Karma-pa ('Black Hats')
   - Nyingma ('Ancient' school)

to west; and the emergence of a money economy led to the establishment of one of the world's first banking systems.

The new money economy also created a new class of urban merchants and bankers whose wealth and financial power far outstripped their social status. The conservative brahmins—the priestly class—disapproved of the bankers as money-lenders, and both they and the ruling warrior class looked down on the merchants because they did not own land. Perhaps the most important cultural tension, however, was religious, between the Hinduism of the brahmins and the indigenous religious traditions of the region, out of which Buddhism and Jainism developed.

It would not be accurate to say that Buddhism developed 'out of Hinduism' in the same way that Christianity developed out of Judaism. It is true that Buddhism explicitly rejected the authority of the brahmin scriptures (the Vedas) and the hereditary authority of the brahmin class. But this does not mean that it arose in reaction against Hinduism. Rather, like Jainism, Buddhism represented a continuation of the traditional religion of India, and claimed to reach back hundreds or even thousands of years before the time of the Buddha himself. A more accurate way to understand its relationship with Hinduism is to recognize that both evolved out of ancient Indian spirituality: Hinduism from the brahmin tradition and Buddhism from the non-brahmin ascetic tradition that flourished in the region of the Ganges.

Along the banks of the river were camps that served as centres for the study of the various religious traditions. Each camp had its spiritual master, who laid down a

NUMBERS
Most estimates range between 200 and 500 million.

DISTRIBUTION
South, Southeast. and East Asia, plus minorities in Europe and North America.

PRINCIPAL HISTORICAL PERIODS

5th–1st century BCE	Early Indian Buddhism; the roots of the Theravada tradition, which eventually spread to Sri Lanka and Southeast Asia
1st century CE	Mahayana emerges and begins spreading to Southeast and East Asia
5th century CE	Vajrayana emerges and begins spreading to Himalayan region.

FOUNDER
Shakyamuni Buddha, who taught in northern India 2,500 years ago.

DEITIES
The Buddha is worshipped not as a god but as a fully enlightened human being. Regional variants of Buddhism have often incorporated local gods and spirits. Mahayana developed a theory of three bodies of the Buddha, linking the historic buddhas to a cosmic force.

AUTHORITATIVE TEXTS
Theravada has the *Tripitaka* ('Three Baskets'): *Vinaya* (monastic rules), Sutras (discourses), and *Abhidharma* (systematic treatises). Mahayana has a great number of texts, in Chinese, Japanese, and Tibetan. Vajrayana has the *Kanjur* (Tantric texts) and *Tanjur* (commentaries).

NOTEWORTHY DOCTRINES
The Three Characteristics of Existence are suffering, impermanence and no-soul. The Four Noble Truths are suffering, origin of suffering, cessation of suffering, and the Eightfold Path. Other teachings include karma, rebirth, and nirvana. Mahayana and Vajrayana stress the emptiness (non-absoluteness) of all things. All schools stress non-violence and compassion for all living beings.

discipline (*vinaya*) and a set of teachings (dharma). Rival masters competed for followers, while students (like their counterparts today) shopped around for the teacher who seemed most advanced spiritually, most astute philosophically, or perhaps least demanding in discipline.

These religious training camps were the forerunners of Buddhist monasteries. Students—all men, though Buddhist orders would eventually be established for women as well—were required to take a vow of celibacy. There were also dietary restrictions, the most common being avoidance of meat because killing animals caused them suffering. Most masters required their disciples to rise early and spend part of the day doing physical work to sustain the camp, in addition to studying and meditating.

Students were expected to deny themselves bodily pleasures for the sake of spiritual development. Some of the ascetic practices required—standing for hours at a time, fasting on full-moon days, or sleeping on the ground—were relatively mild by the standards of the time. But some were quite harsh: exposing themselves to the rain and cold, standing naked in the sun for hours in summer, piercing their skin, going without food or water for long periods of time.

The ethical values of the masters were rooted in the concept of *ahimsa* (non-harming or non-violence). Many non-brahmin masters took this ethic so seriously that they denounced the ritual sacrifice of animals, and some even required their disciples to mask their noses and mouths and strain their drinking water in order to prevent inadvertent harm to insects.

Leaving the everyday life of the 'householder' behind to follow the path of spiritual development, students 'departed the world', took vows of celibacy and poverty and became *shramanas* (disciples). Apart from the creator god Brahma and the storm god Indra, deities played a surprisingly small role in the life of the *shramanas*. Students were expected to develop through their own efforts, without relying on the grace bestowed by a god. As the twentieth-century Zen Buddhist master D.T. Suzuki put it, 'If there is anything to take hold of, you must take hold of it for yourself' (1991:49). The spiritual master shows the path, but the disciples must walk it themselves. One verse of the *Dhammapada*—a popular collection of the Buddha's teachings—puts it this way: 'You must strive for yourselves. The Tathagatas [buddhas] are only your guides. Meditative persons who follow their path will overcome the bonds of Mara [death]' (*Dhammapada*, no. 276).

Among the students who made their way to the Ganges was one named Siddhartha Gautama. A prince from a small kingdom of Shakya people in what is now southern Nepal, he would come to be known as Shakyamuni ('Shakyan sage') and 'the Buddha': the most recent in a succession of fully enlightened teachers who have come to earth through the ages.

The First Gem: The Buddha

The Buddhist view of the cosmos is that universes arise and pass away in endless succession. Within each universe, various eras come and go. The law of **karma** means that living creatures are reborn again and again, for better or worse depending on their moral conduct in previous lives. Whenever dharma teachings have declined, a new buddha for that era arises. (Similarly in the *Bhagavad Gita*, Krishna explains that he comes to earth to save it when dharma has declined.)

No God is needed to mastermind this system. The new buddha is aware of the needs of the world and knows when to be reborn. There have been buddhas in previous eras and there will be other buddhas in the eras to come. We shall see later that one school of Buddhism venerates a buddha of a previous age, named Amida, and that all Buddhists look forward to a future buddha known as Maitreya. Although each era is considered to have only one fully enlightened, teaching buddha, there are numerous beings in each era who are thought to have achieved some degree of enlightenment. There are several types of these spiritually advanced beings, including *Arhats* ('worthy ones' or 'saints'), Pratyeka Buddhas (hermit buddhas) and Bodhisattvas (those who have vowed to become buddhas).

All Buddhist traditions agree that Shakyamuni lived to the age of eighty, although they do not agree on the dates. In Sri Lanka and Southeast Asia he is said to have lived from 624 to 544 BCE. Scholars who correlate the Buddhist chronicles with Greek evidence prefer slightly later dates—either 566–486 BCE or 563–483 BCE—while Japanese scholars relying on Chinese and Tibetan texts place him later still, from 448 to 368 BCE.

Shakyamuni is venerated for having achieved enlightenment (perfection of spiritual wisdom) and liberation (*moksha*) from *samsara* (the cycle of rebirths) after striving through hundreds of previous lives to perfect his 'mind of enlightenment'. This marks a significant difference between Buddhism and traditions that stress the manifestation of deity in a human form. Unlike Krishna or Jesus, the Buddha is not an incarnate god but a human being who has fulfilled his spiritual potential.

The story of Shakyamuni Buddha begins in an earlier age, with a young man who is part of a crowd of villagers filling mud holes in the road in preparation for the arrival of the buddha of that era. When the buddha comes and one hole is still unfilled, the young man offers himself as a stepping-stone. Instead of stepping on him, the buddha pronounces that the young man will become a buddha in the future.

The young man takes the startling prophecy to heart and vows to work towards full enlightenment. In so doing he becomes a bodhisattva: one who has vowed to become a buddha. After the young man dies, his karma complex—the matrix of his past actions—gives rise to a new being who in turn will die and be reborn again and again. A collection called *Jataka*, 'Birth Stories', recounts more than 500 lives lived by Shakyamuni as he progresses towards the final purification of his mind. The last *Jataka* story tells of a prince named Vessantara who, in keeping his vow of generosity, gives away everything, including his kingdom, his wife, and his children—though in the end they are restored.

Siddhartha's Birth and Childhood

When Vessantara dies, the bodhisattva is reborn in the heavens, where he waits until the earth needs a new buddha to set the wheel of dharma (*dharmachakra*) in motion once again. Then he makes several 'determinations', deciding where and when to be born and who his mother and father shall be.

| Box 8.1 | From the *Dhammapada* |

Many of the Buddhist Sutras include one or more verses that sum up the teaching. These memory verses were eventually collected as a separate work called the Dhammapada, *'fundamentals of Dharma'. The verses from Chapter One concern the pure mind.*

1. The mind is the source of all mental actions [dharmas],
   mind is the chief of the mental actions, and they are made by the mind.
   If, by an impure mind, one speaks or acts,
   then suffering follows the mind as a cartwheel follows the footprint of the ox.
2. The mind is the source of all mental states,
   mind is their leader, and they are made by the mind.
   If, by a pure mind, one speaks or acts, then happiness follows the mind like a shadow.
3. 'I was abused.' 'I was beaten.' 'I was hurt.' 'I was robbed.'
   Those who dwell excessively on such thoughts never get out of their hating state of mind.
4. 'I was abused.' 'I was beaten.' 'I was hurt.' 'I was robbed.'
   Those who leave such thoughts behind get out of their hating state of mind.
5. In this world hatreds are never ended by more hating.
   Hatreds are only ended by loving kindness.
   This is an eternal truth [dharma].
6. Some people do not know that we must restrain ourselves.
   But others know this and settle their quarrels.
7. One who dwells on personal gratifications, overindulges the senses, overeats, is
   indolent and lazy,
   that person is overthrown by Mara [Death] like an old, weak tree in a windstorm.
8. One who dwells in meditation on the bodily impurities, keeps the senses under
   control, eats moderately, has faith and disciplined energy,
   that person stands against Mara like a rocky mountain.
9. Whoever puts on the ochre robe but lacks purity, self-control, and truthfulness,
   that person is not worthy of the robe.
10. Whoever puts on the ochre robe and is pure, self-controlled, and truthful,
    that person is truly worthy of the robe.
11. Mistaking the unessential for the important,
    and mistaking the essential for the unimportant,
    some persons, dwelling in wrong-mindedness,
    never realize that which is really essential.
12. Knowing the essential to be important,
    and knowing the unessential to be unimportant,
    other persons, dwelling in rightmindedness,
    reach that which is really essential.

As the story has it, one afternoon the queen of the Shakya people, Mahamaya, is taking a nap when she dreams that the four world protectors (minor gods who look after the earth) carry her to a pleasant grove of trees. There a spiritual being in the form of a white elephant descends from the heavens, miraculously enters her body through her right side, and becomes the embryo of the bodhisattva. Ten lunar months later the child is born through her right side as she holds on to a tree branch at a roadside park called

A Theravada *bhikshu* with a palm-leaf umbrella (Roy C. Amore).

Lumbini. Most Buddhist traditions hold that the birth occurs on the full-moon day of the rainy month called Vaishakha, which usually falls in May. That night a bright light illuminates the world, marking the holy event. (In the ancient world, the birth of special persons was often thought to be marked by astral events, such as a bright light or an auspicious alignment of a constellation with the planets.)

It is interesting to compare the birth stories of Buddha and Jesus. Both are conceived miraculously, without sexual intercourse. Buddha's mother is married to King Shuddhodana but is under a vow of celibacy, while Mary is said to be an unwed virgin. Both infants are born outside the house, Buddha in a grove and Jesus in a stable. Both births are announced by a bright light in the sky, and sages foretell the infants' future greatness. In both cases the births are announced by angels—to a meditating sage in one case, to shepherds in the other.

The child is presented to the king, who names him Siddhartha, 'successful one'. The court brahmins then examine the child's body for signs predicting his future. They find the 32 signs of the Great Person (*mahaparusa*)—including unusually long ear lobes (a sign of great spiritual wisdom), a golden complexion (a sign of inner tranquillity), and wheel patterns on the soles of his feet (indicating that he will be a wheel-turner)—and predict that if he stays 'in the world' he will become a great emperor. If he 'departs the world', however, he will reach the highest achievement of a monk, becoming a fully enlightened buddha. A hermit sage named Asita, 'Blacky', who is more spiritually advanced than the others, correctly foresees that the baby will become a Buddha.

But the king wants Siddhartha to become a great emperor, so he orders that no evidence of sickness, old age, or death be allowed near the boy, lest the knowledge of life's inevitable suffering lead him to abandon the world and follow the spiritual path. Thus the child is raised as a pampered prince, sheltered from life's problems:

> I was delicate, most delicate, supremely delicate. Lily pools were made for me at my father's house solely for my benefit. Blue lilies flowered in one, white lilies in another, red lilies in a third.

> I had three palaces; one for the Winter, one for the Summer and one for the Rains (*Anguttara Nikaya* iii.38; Nanamoli 1972:8).

Only a few childhood events are recorded. In one story the boy amazes his first teacher with his knowledge of several alphabets. In another he wins a martial arts tournament even though he has shown little interest in war. The most significant story tells how he enters a meditational trance state (*dhyana* in Sanskrit; *jhana* in Pali, the scriptural language of early Indian Buddhism) while sitting in the shade of a rose-apple tree.

The Four Sights and the Great Departure

Despite the king's efforts to protect him from life's sorrows, the prince finally learns the truth when he is nearly thirty. By then he has married and has a son named Rahula. During a chariot ride through the royal park, the prince sees four great sights that will alter the course of his life. The first three sights—of a sick man, a suffering old man, and a dead man—awaken him to life's problems. When he asks what is wrong with these men, his chariot driver answers honestly, revealing to him for the first time the harsh realities of life. The Buddha will later explain to his disciples his response to the reality of sickness:

> When an untaught ordinary man, who is subject to sickness, not safe from sickness, sees another who is sick, he is shocked, humiliated and disgusted; for he forgets that he himself is no exception. But I too am subject to sickness, not safe from sickness, and so it cannot befit me to be shocked, humiliated and disgusted on seeing another who is sick. When I considered this, the vanity of health entirely left me (*Anguttara Nikaya* iii. 38; Nanamoli 1972:8).

The bodhisattva's fourth sight is a monk whose calm detachment from the world suggests a path to overcoming suffering. To this day, Buddhist monks often say that what first attracted them to the monastic life was seeing, as children, the calmness and serenity of the monks and nuns on their daily alms-seeking rounds.

That night, with the help of the world protectors, the bodhisattva takes his horse and servant and flees the palace. Buddhist temples often have murals depicting this event, called the Great Departure.

Eventually dismissing his servant and horse, the bodhisattva exchanges his princely clothes for those of a poor hunter, obtains an alms bowl, and embarks on the life of a wandering student seeking spiritual truth. He travels towards the Ganges, where he studies under a yoga teacher, then another yogi. But even when he achieves the deep tranquillity of yoga trance, he is not satisfied, so he leaves the teacher and seeks another approach. With five others he undertakes a very strict ascetic practice that includes standing in the cold rain and hot sun. Above all, he excels in the discipline of fasting, living on only one palmful of water and one of food per day. He becomes extremely thin and loses consciousness, but the four world-protectors look after him (as the angels help Jesus during his fasting time in the wilderness). Later on, he will denounce such severe practices as unhelpful.

Enlightenment

Frustrated by his failure to achieve a spiritual breakthrough despite years of striving, the bodhisattva is now at a loss. He leaves the cave where he has been living and goes to a pleasant town now called Bodh Gaya ('bodh' being short for 'enlightenment'). There he resumes eating and drinking, but he still needs a method. Then he remembers the wakeful meditational trance he experienced spontaneously as a child:

> I thought of a time when . . . I was sitting in the cool shade of a rose-apple tree: quite secluded from sensual desires, secluded from unprofitable things I had entered upon and abided in the first meditation, which is accompanied by thinking and exploring with happiness and pleasure born of seclusion. I thought: Might that be the way to enlightenment? Then, following up that memory there came the recognition that this was the way to enlightenment (*Majjhima Nikaya*; Nanamoli 1972:21).

He decides to try this approach. Choosing a pleasant spot beside a cool river, under a *pipal* tree (a large fig tree thereafter known to Buddhists as the Bodhi tree and considered sacred in India as far back as the Harappa civilization), he sits to meditate, vowing that he will not get up until he has achieved nirvana.

It is at this point, just before dusk on the evening of the full-moon day in the month of Vaishakha, that Mara, the lord of death, arrives. Mara plays a role in Buddhism not unlike that of Satan in Christianity. His main function is to come for people's souls at death and oversee their rebirth in an appropriate place. But he knows that the bodhisattva is sitting at a special place on a decisive occasion. To tempt the bodhisattva to give up his mission, Mara first summons his daughters, whose names suggest psychological forces such as greed, boredom, and desire. When that fails, Mara offers to grant any worldly wish if only he will go back home and live a life of good karma (merit) as a householder. The bodhisattva refuses.

Now Mara becomes violent. He calls for his sons, whose names suggest fear and anger, to attack. The bodhisattva's spiritual power serves as a force field to protect him.

Mara then challenges the bodhisattva to a debate, claiming that he, Mara, is the one worthy to sit on the Bodhi Seat (the place of enlightenment) on this auspicious night. With his sons and daughters cheering for him, Mara seems to have the upper hand. But the bodhisattva has the power both of his great merit and of having truth on his side. He replies that he is the one with generosity, courage, wisdom, and so forth, perfected through countless previous lives. Calling on the Earth herself to bear witness to the truth of his claim, the bodhisattva works a miracle: the earth quakes and Mara is driven away. Many Buddhists today understand the exchange with Mara as symbolizing the surfacing of the last remnants of the mind's deep impurities, which the bodhisattva must overcome. Whatever its meaning, many temples celebrate this event with a depiction of the Buddha in a pose called 'touching the earth' or 'calling the earth to witness'.

Having defeated Mara, the bodhisattva begins to meditate in his own way—the reverse of the way he has been taught by the yoga masters. A traditional yogi seeks to shut out the world and move deeper and deeper into unconsciousness, drawing in the conscious mind as a turtle draws in its head and limbs. By contrast, the bodhisattva meditates to become more conscious, more aware, more mindful.

During the first watch of the night, the bodhisattva remembers his own past lives. During the second watch, he sees the working of the law of karma, observing the past lives of various people and recognizing that evil deeds in one life will have evil consequences in the next one. During the third watch, he understands how to put an end to suffering and comes to see the Four Noble Truths (p. 389 below).

Just before dawn, the bodhisattva enters a state of complete awareness, of total insight into the nature of reality; this state is called *bodhi*. After hundreds of lives, he has fulfilled his bodhisattva vow. He is no longer a *sattva* (being, person) striving for *bodhi*; he is now a buddha, a 'fully enlightened one': 'I had direct knowledge. Birth is exhausted, the Holy Life has been lived out, what was to be done is done, there is no more of this to come' (*Majjhima Nikaya*; Nanamoli 1972:25).

Having completed the path to full enlightenment, he has earned the title Tathagata ('thus-gone one'). He uses this title to refer to himself: 'Whatever a Tathagata utters, speaks, and proclaims between the day of his enlightenment and the day he dies, all that is factual, not otherwise, and that is why he is called "Tathagata"' (*Anguttara Nikaya* ii.22; Dhammika 1989:50).

Another term for the state of enlightenment that the Buddha has reached is 'nirvana'. This state has two aspects, negative and positive. In its negative aspect nirvana represents freedom from worldly evils such as greed, hatred, and delusion. In its positive aspect it represents transcendent happiness. A poem by Patacara—one of the early ordained Buddhist women—suggests how the positive and negative aspects of nirvana (*nibbana* in Pali) come together in that perfect happiness arrives when evil desires have been extinguished.

> One day, bathing my feet, I sit and watch
> The water as it trickles down the slope.
> Thereby I set my heart in steadfastness,
> As one doth train a horse of noble breed.
> Then going to my cell, I take my lamp,
> And seated on my couch I watch the flame.
> Grasping the pin, I pull the wick right down
> Into the oil . . .
> Lo! the Nibbana of the little lamp!
> Emancipation dawns! My heart is free!
> (C. Rhys Davids 1964:73)

The Buddha reflects on whether or not enlightenment is teachable. The answer is yes, and so at the age of thirty-five he begins a teaching career motivated by his great compassion for all living beings.

Setting the Wheel in Motion

The newly enlightened Buddha's first concern is to seek out and instruct his two former yoga teachers, but through his psychic powers he perceives that both have died. So he decides to find and teach the five ascetics with whom he used to practise. Again using clairvoyance, he determines that they are staying at Sarnath, a deer park near Varanasi (Banaras).

On the way there two merchants offer him food, setting the pattern whereby laypeople offer material support (food, medicine, robes), while ordained Buddhists offer spiritual gifts (the dharma, advice, chanting). This pattern of reciprocal giving is central to all forms of Buddhism.

Upon arriving at the deer park, the Buddha is at first shunned by his five friends because he has abandoned the rigorous ascetic discipline they so value. But when they see his aura they realize that he has attained nirvana and ask to know how he did it. The reply is his first Sutra (discourse, sermon), known as the 'Wheel-turning Discourse' because it marks the moment when the wheel of true dharma is once again set in motion.

The Buddha begins by telling the five to follow a path of moderation between self-indulgence and asceticism (for this reason the discourse is also known as the 'Instruction on the Middle Path'). He says that as long as he lived the life of a pampered prince, he did not develop spiritually. At the other extreme, however, asceticism left him too weak to make any significant progress. Only after he began to eat, drink, and sleep in moderation was he able to reach enlightenment. This principle of moderation eventually became the basis for a general ethic of the 'Middle Way', according to which in material matters, 'enough is better than too much'. The principle was also applied to Buddhist philosophy. Some refer to Buddhism itself as 'the Middle Way'.

The rest of the discourse is devoted to the Four Noble Truths about the causes of suffering and the Eightfold Path to overcoming it. The five students become disciples and begin spreading the dharma to others.

Entering *Parinirvana*

For the next 45 years the Buddha travels throughout the Middle Region, ordaining disciples and teaching thousands of lay followers, including members of his own family and local kings. Finally one day he and his disciples are invited to dine with the leader of a local tribal group. When a smelly mushroom dish is brought to the table, he tells his host to serve it only to him and not to his disciples. The dish makes him ill, and when it becomes apparent that he is dying, the Compassionate One tells his disciples not to blame the host, who meant well. They ask whom they should follow if he dies, and he tells them to follow the dharma. Thus in Buddhism no individual has absolute authority, although there are senior authorities in particular traditions (the Dalai Lama, for example).

On his deathbed—in a grove of trees at Kushinagar—the Buddha meditates through the yoga stages. Then, at the moment of death, he experiences *parinirvana*: the final end of the cycle of rebirth, the total cessation of suffering, the perfection of happiness. Until that moment he has been in the state known as nirvana 'with remainder'—the highest level of nirvana possible for one still living. Buddhism does not elaborate on the nature of *parinirvana*—'nirvana without remainder'. Nevertheless, it seems clear that to say the Buddha became extinct or ceased to exist would be a distortion of the Buddhist position.

Crystallization

The Second Gem: Dharma

> Avoid doing all evil deeds, cultivate doing good deeds,
> and purify the mind—this is the teaching of all buddhas.
> (*Dhammapada* 183)

The Sanskrit term 'dharma' is related to the Latin *firma*; thus we could understand 'dharma' (and its Pali equivalent, *dhamma*) to refer to teachings that are firm or lasting. Among those eternal truths are the laws of nature, the reality of spiritual forces such as karma, and the rules of moral conduct.

The Buddha and his followers often used short numbered lists to summarize dharma teachings. We will use the same approach here.

The Four Noble Truths and the Eightfold Path

At the core of the Buddha's first sermon in the deer park were the Four Noble Truths about suffering and Eightfold Path to overcoming it:

1. Noble Truth of Suffering: No living being can escape suffering (*duhkha*). Birth, sickness, senility, and death are all occasions of suffering, whether physical or psychological.
2. Noble Truth of Origin: Suffering arises from craving (*trishna*), from excessive desire.

| Box 8.2 | **From the *Itivuttaka*** |

The Itivuttaka *('So I heard') is a collection of the Buddha's teachings said to have been made by Khujjuttara, a lay woman of the servant class who used it to teach other women. Each section begins with the expression 'So I heard' ('Itivuttaka').*

Even if one should seize the hem of my robe and walk step by step behind me, if he is covetous in his desires, fierce in his longings, malevolent of heart, with corrupt mind, careless and unrestrained, noisy and distracted and with sense uncontrolled, he is far from me. And why? He does not see the Dhamma, and not seeing the Dhamma, he does not see me. Even if one lives a hundred miles away, if he is not covetous in his desires, not fierce in his longings, with a kind heart and pure mind, mindful, composed, calmed, one-pointed and with senses restrained, then indeed, he is near to me and I am near to him. And why? He sees the Dhamma, and seeing the Dhamma, sees me (Dhammika 1989:49–50).

3. Noble Truth of Cessation: Suffering will cease when desire ceases.
4. Noble Truth of the Eightfold Path: It is possible to put an end to desire and hence to suffering by following the Eightfold Path: right view or understanding (specifically of the Four Noble Truths), right thought (free of sensual desire, ill-will, and cruelty), right speech, right conduct, right livelihood, right effort, right mindfulness, and right meditation.

The Three Characteristics of Existence

According to the dharma, existence has three characteristics: suffering, impermanence, and 'no-soul'. Suffering here includes all the aspects outlined above, in the first Noble Truth. Impermanence refers to the passing nature of all things, the fact that all earthly things are in process, constantly changing. Finally, 'no-soul' (*anatman* in Sanskrit, meaning without Atman, the eternal self or soul) underlines the implications of impermanence for human life. Philosophically, no-soul means that there is nothing absolute or unchanging about us. Psychologically, no-soul means that 'I' should not think of anything as 'mine', for there is no absolute 'me'. As Buddhadasa of Thailand stresses, in meditation one learns to get beyond 'me and mine' egotism. Wise people are detached from both material goods and images of themselves.

The concept of no-soul does not mean that Buddhism denies the existence of personality or the sense of self. Rather, the dharma emphasizes that personality is the product of shifting, fluid circumstance. In that respect, the Buddhist understanding of personality has more in common with modern psychological theory than with religious notions of an eternal soul.

The Three Instructions

In the fifth century CE a monk named Buddhaghosa wrote a famous commentary on the dharma called *The Path of Purity*. In it he explains that the first stage of training or instruction consists in following moral principles.

At the second stage of instruction the goal is concentration: the development of a mental state in which one is focused, tranquil, and alert. This *samadhi* state of mind is helpful in every aspect of life, but it is essential if one is to acquire the wisdom necessary to reach nirvana.

That wisdom—the third stage of instruction—involves insight into things such as causality, including karma.

Dependent Origination and the Twelve-spoked Wheel

Like Western science, Buddhism teaches that everything is conditional: everything originates in dependence on other factors. This doctrine of 'dependent origination' reflects the understanding that all things are constantly changing and that the changes they go through in turn cause other things to change. Buddhism depicts this state of flux as a wheel with twelve spokes representing the twelve interconnected stages of dependent origination.

The twelve links in the chain of dependent origination may be divided into three stages, reflecting the movement from a past life through the present one and on to the future:

Past	1.	Ignorance, leading to
	2.	karma formations (the state of the individual's karma complex at death) leading to
Present	3.	a new individual 'consciousness', leading to
	4.	a new body–mind complex, leading to
	5.	the bases of sensing, leading to
	6.	sense impressions, leading to
	7.	conscious feelings, leading to
	8.	craving, leading to
	9.	clinging to (grasping for) things, leading to
	10.	'becoming' (the drive to be reborn), leading to
Future	11.	rebirth, leading to
	12.	old age and death

The process does not stop with the twelfth link, of course, since old age and death lead to yet another birth. All living beings are in process and will be reborn over and over again until they realize nirvana.

Tripitaka: The Three Baskets of Sacred Texts

Shakyamuni did not write down his dharma teachings or rules of discipline. At the first council Ananda, who had been his travelling companion, recited the Sutras (discourses on the doctrine), and Upali recited the *vinaya* (the monastic rules). Later, another disciple recited the systematic treatises (*abhidharma*) that were composed after Shakyamuni's death. The teachings were finally put into writing by Theravada monks in Sri Lanka in the first century CE, after a famine had so reduced the *sangha* there that the oral tradition was in danger of disappearing. Written on palm leaves strung together and bundled like Venetian blinds, the texts were sorted into three baskets. As a result, the Theravada tradition refers to the scriptures collectively as the *Tripitaka* ('three baskets').

The *Sutra Pitaka*, or 'discourse basket', contains the talks on dharma attributed to Shakyamuni or his early disciples. The discourses often take the form of responses to questions. The following opening of the 'Discourse on the Lesser Analysis of Deeds' is typical:

Thus have I heard: At one time the Lord was staying near Savatthi in the Jeta Grove in Anathapindika's monastery. Then the brahmin youth Subha, Todeyya's son, approached the Lord; having approached, he exchanged greetings with the Lord; having conversed in a friendly and courteous way, he sat down at a respectful distance. As he was sitting down at a respectful distance the brahmin youth Subha, Todeyya's son, spoke thus to the Lord:

'Now, good Gotama, what is the cause, what the reason that low-
ness and excellence are to be seen among human beings while they are in
human form?' (Horner 1967, 3:248–9).

Subha, addressing Buddha by the respectful title 'Lord' ('Bhagavan', meaning
'respected one' rather than 'god'), has asked the timeless question of why bad things happen to apparently good people. Shakyamuni explains to Subha how karma accounts for
the fact that some people suffer short, unhappy lives while others enjoy long, blessed lives.

The *Vinaya* ('discipline') *Pitaka* contains the rules of monastic discipline and stories about how Shakyamuni came to institute each rule, while the *Abhidharma* ('further
discourses') *Pitaka* contains seven books by early Buddhists who systematically analyzed
every conceivable aspect of reality from the standpoint of various principles. For example, the first book of *abhidharma* classifies all mental phenomena according to whether
they are good, bad, or neutral karmically. The development of *abhidharma* is associated
with Sariputra, one of the brightest of the Buddha's disciples.

The Third Gem: The *Sangha*

The third part of the Triple Gem has two components: the monastic community of
ordained men (*bhikshus*) and women (*bhikshunis*), and the broad community of all the lay
people who follow the Buddha's path.

Theravada monks in Laos collecting alms (Euan White).

Bhikshus and *Bhikshunis*

Shakyamuni began accepting disciples from the time of his first sermon. An ordination ritual took shape in which new disciples recited the Triple Refuge, took vows of chastity, poverty, obedience, and so on, and put on the distinctive robes of a monk. (In early Indian Buddhism monks' robes were usually dyed with saffron, which produces a bright orange-yellow. Most Theravada monks still wear saffron robes, but in East Asia other colours came into use, such as red and brown. There is no special meaning to the colour, although all members of a particular branch of Buddhism wear the same one.)

Ordination practices vary. In Theravada, each novice (*shramanera*, meaning 'one gone forth') is assigned both a demanding teacher and a supportive spiritual guide. After completing his or her studies the novice is eligible for ordination as a *bhikshu* or *bhikshuni*. The ordination ritual is performed only in certain designated areas, marked off with 'boundary stones', and because seniority plays an important role in monastic life, careful attention is paid to the exact time and date of the ordination. Friends and relatives attend the ceremony and pay their respects to the new *sangha* members, who give presents to their teachers and counsellors in gratitude for their assistance.

Controversies, Councils, and Sects

Sectarian divisions first developed within the *sangha* early in the fourth century BCE, when a *bhikshu* criticized the monks of Vaishali for accepting donations of gold and silver. A meeting, called the Vaishali Council, was called and it was decided that *vinaya* rules forbade the acceptance of such donations. Although it seems that only a minority disagreed with this decision, more troubling issues soon arose. A certain monk listed five points of controversy, mostly having to do with the level of perfection possible for Buddhists in this life. At a council called to deal with the issue, some monks dissented from the majority opinion, and a division arose between the 'Great *Sangha*' (*Mahasangha*) sect and the 'Elders' ('Theravada') sect. By the third century BCE Buddhism had split into 18 distinct ordination lineages. Despite their differences on some matters of doctrine or practice, all had similar versions of the teachings, the *vinaya* rules, and the ordination ritual. Monks of different sects sometimes lived together in one monastery, especially at the major training centres.

King Ashoka's Conversion

The golden age of Buddhism began approximately two centuries after the Buddha's death, when King Ashoka (r. c. 273–232 BCE) renounced violence and converted to Buddhism. Appalled at the blood shed in the war of conquest he had waged with the kingdom of Kalinga, Ashoka devoted himself to a 'dharma conquest', erecting pillars and large stones at crossroads throughout his empire with messages intended for the moral instruction of his subjects. On the rock at Kalinga he expressed his remorse for the death and suffering he had caused:

> When the king, Beloved of the Gods and of Gracious Mien, had been consecrated eight years Kalinga was conquered, 150,000 people were deported,

100,000 were killed, and many times that number died. But after the conquest of Kalinga, the Beloved of the Gods began to follow Righteousness [dharma], to love Righteousness, and to give instruction in Righteousness. Now the Beloved of the Gods regrets the conquest of Kalinga, for when an independent country is conquered people are killed, they die, or are deported, and that the Beloved of the Gods finds painful and grievous. . . . The Beloved of the Gods will forgive as far as he can, and he even conciliates the forest tribes of his dominions; but he warns them that there is power even in the remorse of the Beloved of the Gods, and he tells them to reform, lest they be killed (*Thirteenth Rock Edict*; de Bary 1958:146).

Ashoka then laid out his ideals for governing his new subjects, saying that he desired security, self-control, impartiality, and cheerfulness for all living creatures in his empire. He claimed that his dharma conquest was spreading not only within the Indian continent but westward among the various Alexandrian kingdoms, and noted that the only real satisfaction for a ruler lies in persuading his people to follow dharma:

Thus he achieves a universal conquest, and conquest always gives a feeling of pleasure; yet it is but a slight pleasure, for the Beloved of the Gods only looks on that which concerns the next life as of great importance. I have had this inscription of Righteousness engraved that all my sons and grandsons may not seek to gain new victories, . . . that they may consider the only [valid] victory the victory of Righteousness, which is of value both in this world and the next (*Thirteenth Rock Edict*; de Bary 1958:147).

Dharma Ashoka, as Buddhists call him, was prepared to sentence criminals (and rebels) to punishment and even death. But he pledged to be just and moderate in punishment, and remained committed to non-violent practices in other matters, encouraging his subjects to abstain from meat and give up occupations such as hunting. In this he became a model for later Buddhist rulers.

Buddhism and the State

The King as Wheel Turner

Traditionally in India, a great king was described as a Wheel Turner (*chakravartin*): a ruler with the spiritual wisdom to perceive order and the political power to bring it into effect. When Buddhists referred to the Buddha as a *chakravartin*, they were according him an honour normally reserved for a king.

Buddhism understood the king to have special duties with regard to the dharma. In addition to providing for the basic welfare of his subjects by establishing food distribution centres and medical clinics, he was to set a good example and support the teaching of dharma by sponsoring lectures and literature on the subject.

As Buddhism spread throughout Asia, so did its social and moral ideals for kingship. A Zen Buddhist story tells how, in the sixth century, a Chinese ruler named Wu had

| Box 8.3   King Milinda Questions Nagasena

The military campaigns of Alexander the Great in the late fourth century BCE left a number of Greek-derived regimes in eastern Iran and northwestern India. These may have been the 'Yavanas' (presumably 'Ionians') to whom the Buddhist King Ashoka reported sending missions. The following extract recounts a meeting, real or imagined, between a foreign king and a Buddhist sage.

Now Milinda the king went up to where the venerable Nagasena was, and addressed him with the greetings and compliments of friendship and courtesy, and took his seat respectfully apart.

And Milinda began by asking, 'How is your Reverence known, and what, Sir, is your name?'

'I am known as Nagasena, O king. But although parents, O king, give such a name as Nagasena . . . [it] is only a generally understood term, a designation in common use. For there is no permanent individuality (no soul) involved in the matter.'

'If, most reverend Nagasena, there is no permanent individuality (no soul) involved in the matter, who is it, pray, who gives to you members of the Order your robes and food and lodging and necessaries for the sick? Who is it who enjoys such things when given? Who is it who lives a life of righteousness? . . . You tell me that your brethren in the Order are in the habit of addressing you as Nagasena. Now what is that Nagasena? Do you mean to say that the hair is Nagasena?'

'I don't say that, great king.'

'Or is it the nails, the teeth, the skin, the flesh, the nerves, the bones . . . or any of these that is Nagasena?'

And to each of these he answered no.

'Is it the outward form then (*rupa*) that is Nagasena, or the sensations, or the ideas, or the confections, or the consciousness, that is Nagasena?'

And to each of these he answered no.

'Then is it all these *skandhas* [physical and mental 'heaps' or processes] combined that are Nagasena?

'No! great king.'

'But is there anything outside the five *skandhas* that is Nagasena?'

And he still answered no.

'Then thus, ask as I may, I can discover no Nagasena. Nagasena is a mere empty sound. . . .'

[*Now Nagasena asks the king how he travelled to their meeting. When the king says he came in a chariot, the sage asks him to explain what a chariot is.*] 'Is it the pole that is the chariot?'

'I did not say that.'

'Is it the wheels, or the framework . . . ?'

'Certainly not.'

'Then is it all these parts that are the chariot?'

'No, Sir.'

'Then . . . I can discover no chariot. Chariot is a mere empty sound.'

'It is on account of its having all these things—the pole, and the axle . . .—that it comes under the generally understood term, the designation in common use, of "chariot".'

'Very good! Your Majesty has rightly grasped the meaning of "chariot". And just even so it is on account of all those things you questioned me about . . . that I come under the generally understood term . . . "Nagasena". For it was said, Sire, by our Sister Vajira in the presence of the Blessed One: "Just as it is by the condition precedent of the coexistence of its various parts that the word 'chariot' is used, just so is it true that when the *skandhas* are there we talk of a 'being'."'

'Most wonderful, Nagasena, and most strange. Well done, well done, Nagasena' (abridged from Rhys Davids 1890:40–55).

converted to Buddhism and dedicated himself to doing all the things expected of a good Buddhist king, apparently in the hope of earning a long and pleasant rebirth in heaven. When he learned that an Indian monk named Bodhidharma had taken up residence in his kingdom, Wu summoned him to court and proudly showed off his good Buddhist works: an altar, rice kitchens for feeding the poor, a new wing of the palace filled with scribes translating and copying Buddhist texts. After the tour, King Wu asked Bodhidharma, 'How much merit do you think I have made from all this?' 'None whatsoever!' was the famous response. Bodhidharma then explained that true merit comes only from activities that increase one's wisdom and purify the mind. King Wu, it seems, had been doing all his good deeds for the wrong reason.

Non-violence as a Public Ethic

Ideally, Buddhist rulers were expected to embrace non-violence. Unnecessarily harsh punishments were forbidden, and justice was to be administered both quickly and fairly, whatever the social status of the accused. A pious king of ancient Sri Lanka is remembered for instructing his staff to wake him even in the middle of the night if a citizen came seeking justice. Prisoners were often released from jail as part of festival celebrations. Although the Buddhist king was expected to maintain an army and a police force for security, force was not be used for purposes of conquest, and Buddhism itself was spread by missionary conversion rather than by force of arms.

Differentiation

By Ashoka's time, as we have seen, Buddhism had split into 18 distinct sects. Over the following centuries all but one of these disappeared. The survivor, Theravada, became one of the three major vehicles (*yana*) or schools of Buddhism that exist today. The second school, which emerged around the first century CE, called itself Mahayana, 'Great Vehicle', in contrast to what it called the Hinayana, 'Lesser Vehicle', of Theravada and its contemporaries. The third school, Vajrayana, emerged some five hundred years later and considered itself the third turning of the wheel of dharma.

Theravada

Theravada means 'Way of the Elders' in Pali. As the name suggests, Theravada Buddhism was—and remains—conservative. Claiming to preserve Buddhism in its original form, it does not recognize as scripture anything written after the formation of the *Tripitaka*.

In the third century BCE Theravada was taken to Sri Lanka by the son of King Ashoka, a monk named Mahinda. According to the island's 'Great Chronicle' (*Mahavamsa*), Mahinda and his assistant *bhikshus* travelled through the air by psychic power and arrived on a large hill near the island's capital. There they were discovered by the king of

Sri Lanka and his hunting party, who were immediately converted. The next day, Mahinda entered the capital and converted the king's court. On the following day, the largest building available—the king's elephant stable—was cleaned and put into service as a dharma hall, where everyone else was converted. Mahinda and his colleagues established their community on the hill where they landed ('Mahinda Hill' remains an important site for monks and lay pilgrims today). A proper stupa, temple, and dharma hall were built, a Bodhi tree sapling was brought from India by a *bhikshuni* (Ashoka's daughter), and the king was re-ordained in the Indian fashion.

In reality, the conversion of Sri Lanka probably took a little longer than the legend suggests. Accepting Buddhism may have appealed to the Sri Lankan king as a way of allying himself with the powerful emperor on the mainland. The island of Sri Lanka became a cultural extension of Ashoka's empire while maintaining its sovereignty. And the union of spiritual and temporal leadership in the person of the king set the pattern for the spread of Buddhism in mainland Southeast Asia, where the various rulers became the lay leaders and chief supporters of Buddhism in their kingdoms.

Theravada Buddhism is still the main religion of Sri Lanka, even though there were two periods when it almost disappeared. In the eleventh century, famine so reduced the numbers of the Sri Lankan *sangha* that it could not ordain any new members. Since a minimum of five senior monks were required to officiate at an ordination, *bhikshus* from Burma had to be imported to ensure continuation of the Sri Lankan lineage. A similar appeal to Siam (Thailand) in the eighteenth century led to the establishment of a new ordination lineage, appropriately named the Siam (Siyam) Nikaya. Although Shakyamuni taught that a person should be judged by character rather than birth (caste), and the *sangha* was open to anyone, regardless of social group, the Siam Nikaya accepts only members from the Goyigama, a landowning caste. Other orders in Sri Lanka, however, accept members from all castes.

Theravada in Southeast Asia

The spread of Buddhism into Burma, Cambodia, Siam, and Laos took place in stages over many centuries. By the year 1000 various sects of early Indian Buddhism as well as the Mahayana and Vajrayana schools were competing for support in the region. Theravada's emergence as the dominant form was assisted by local rulers' efforts to regularize and consolidate religion in their domains by establishing the Theravada ordination lineage as the standard one. This created a certain cultural unity across Southeast Asia. Today Buddhist culture remains dominant on the mainland, although the islands are largely Islamic.

The area most easily reached from India was Burma (now known as Myanmar). What was then called the kingdom of Pagan developed ties with the Theravada rulers of Sri Lanka by the eleventh century. A temple enshrining a tooth alleged to be from the Buddha became the guardian and legitimizer of the kingdom. Although the region that corresponds to modern Cambodia was influenced by several forms of Indian Buddhism before the fifteenth century, since then Theravada has established itself as the dominant school.

Theravada's influence in Siam (now Thailand) also dates from the fifteenth century, when Thai monks ordained in the Theravada tradition in Sri Lanka returned home and gained favour with King Tiloraja. Four centuries later, two of the country's most important kings played active roles in reforming the Thai *sangha*. King Mongkut (r. 1851-68) is revered by Thais under the name Rama IV but is best known in the West as the king portrayed in the film 'The King and I'—which has never been shown in Thailand because its portrayal of him is thought to be disrespectful. Having been a *bhikshu* himself for more than twenty years, Mongkut set out to restore discipline and direction to the *sangha* after he became king. The result was a new ordination lineage called the Thammayut ('Dharma-adherents') Nikaya. This reform movement set the tone for modern Theravada not only in Thailand but elsewhere as well: the king of Cambodia, for example, arranged for the establishment of the Thammayut Nikaya in his country before the end of the century.

Following in his father's footsteps, King Chulalongkorn (Rama V; r. 1868-1910) united the various ordination lineages under a central administrative authority and standardized the training given to novices. In the modern period, every Thai crown prince has spent time in a monastery in preparation for his role as lay head of the *sangha* and leader of Thai cultural life.

Although there is inscriptional evidence that Sri Lankan *bhikshus* took Theravada orthodoxy to Laos more than 500 years ago, proximity and a common language gave Thai Buddhism more influence there.

Mahayana

The Mahayana ('Greater Vehicle') movement appears to have emerged around the first century CE. Although its origins are unclear, we know that its members were dismissing older forms of Buddhism as Hinayana ('Lesser Vehicle') by the third or fourth century, and that around the same time it was becoming the dominant form of Buddhism across the region traversed by the Silk Road, from Central Asia to northern China.

Mahayana differed from Theravada in everything from the scriptures it emphasized, its rituals and meditation practices, to its central doctrines. Whereas Theravada saw the discipline of the *bhikshu* as a precondition for enlightenment and liberation, Mahayana offered laypeople the opportunity to strive for those goals as well. Whereas Theravada focused on the historical Shakyamuni, Mahayana developed a framework in which he represented only one manifestation of buddhahood. Furthermore, whereas Theravada emphasized that the only way to enlightenment and liberation was through personal effort—that there was no supernatural grace on which human beings could call—Mahayana populated the heavens with bodhisattvas dedicated to helping all those who prayed to them for assistance.

Yet despite their differences, Mahayana and the earlier forms of Buddhism share a common core of basic values and moral teachings, practices (such as meditation, chanting, scripture study, and veneration of relics), and forms of monastic life and buildings. In short, Theravada and Mahayana are different vehicles (*yanas*) for travelling the same path to enlightenment.

Mahayana Doctrine

Lay Spirituality

The practice of venerating Shakyamuni at the stupas enshrining his relics had begun soon after his death. In time, many lay people began making pilgrimages to stupas with major relics, and new ones were built in all Mahayana countries. (The veneration of sacred relics was an important part of several religions in this period, including Hinduism and Christianity.) Lay Buddhists came to believe that they could earn valuable karmic merit by making a pilgrimage.

This development marked a major shift away from early Buddhism, in which the religious role of laypeople had been somewhat subordinate, limited to providing material support for the *sangha*. Anyone who wished to seek enlightenment was expected to 'depart the world' and become a *bhikshu* or *bhikshuni*. Mahayana Buddhism, by contrast, offered laypeople the possibility of pursuing spiritual development and even attaining enlightenment while living in the world.

Doctrine of the Three Bodies (Trikaya)

To account for the various ways in which one could experience or refer to buddhahood, Mahayana developed a doctrine of 'three bodies' (*trikaya*). The earthly manifestation body of a buddha is called the Appearance Body or Transformation Body (*nirmanakaya*). The heavenly body of a buddha that presides over a buddha-realm and is an object of devotion for Mahayana Buddhists is called the Body of Bliss (*sambhogakaya*). These are supported by the buddha as the absolute essence of the universe, called the Dharma Body (*dharmakaya*).

The Three Bodies doctrine calls attention not only to the oneness of all the buddhas that have appeared on earth, but also to the unity of the buddha-nature or buddha-potential in all its forms. That is, the *trikaya* doctrine envisions one cosmic reality (Dharma Body) that manifests itself in the form both of heavenly beings (Body of Bliss) and of humans such as Shakyamuni (Appearance Body). By connecting the earthly Buddha to the Dharma Body or Absolute, the doctrine of the three bodies also moved Mahayana Buddhism in the direction of theistic religion—in sharp contrast to the Theravada school, which continued to revere the Buddha as an exceptional human being.

The Lotus Sutra

From its early days, Buddhism recognized the importance of tailoring its teachings to suit a particular audience's capacity to grasp them. As the Mahayana tradition developed, it came to emphasize that all doctrine is temporary, provisional, and expedient. The popular Mahayana text called the *Lotus Sutra* treats many previous Buddhist teachings as provisional, as steps towards a more complete understanding. To illustrate this point, the *Lotus Sutra* tells a story about a father whose children are inside a burning house. He persuades them to come out by promising them chariots—a lie of sorts, but a 'skillful means' to get them out quickly. Similarly, temporary formulations hide the ultimate truth from those just starting on the path, but spiritual advancement makes it possible to see the purpose of the earlier stages.

Bodhisattvas

Early Buddhism taught that every individual makes his or her own karma: there is no supernatural source of grace. The Mahayana school, however, proposed that grace was available in the form of merit transferred to humans from bodhisattvas. Mahayana cosmology envisions a multitude of spiritually advanced beings, all of them prepared to share their great merit with anyone who prays for help.

Bodhisattvas were not unknown in early Indian Buddhism: in a previous life Shakyamuni himself had become a bodhisattva when he vowed to attain buddhahood one day, and he remained a bodhisattva until the night of enlightenment. For most Buddhists, however, the highest goal was to reach the status of an *Arhat*. The Mahayana school sharply criticized this goal as self-centred, focused solely on achieving personal liberation. They maintained that those who take bodhisattva vows are dedicating themselves first and foremost to the salvation of all living beings. All Mahayana Buddhists were therefore encouraged to take the bodhisattva vow, pledging not only to attain buddhahood themselves but also to work towards the liberation of all beings.

The corollary of this innovation in Buddhist thought was the introduction of prayer. Early Indian Buddhism had considered Shakyamuni, after his *parinirvana*, to be beyond the realm of direct involvement with human lives, and therefore had no tradition of appealing to him for assistance. In some forms of Mahayana Buddhism, by contrast, worshippers not only venerate the bodhisattvas but petition them for blessings, much as Roman Catholics venerate the saints and ask them for help.

Some important bodhisattvas have special functions. For example, Bodhisattva Manjusri is the guardian of Buddhist wisdom, and novices entering Buddhist training often call on him to guide and inspire them. The bodhisattva known especially for compassion, Avalokiteshvara ('the Lord who looks down') is popular in all Mahayana countries. Originally Avalokiteshavara was masculine, but in China he came to be venerated in female form under the name Guanyin. This change of gender is an example of the bodhisattva's power to take any shape necessary in order to benefit believers (a famous *Lotus Sutra* chapter lists 33 examples of such 'shape shifting'). Known as the 'Bodhisattva of Compassion', Guanyin is the most venerated bodhisattva in Buddhist history, and has been called the 'virgin Mary of East Asia' by Westerners, since graceful statues of her are found everywhere. Many Mahayana women feel especially close to her because she is believed to bring children to those who lack them and to care for infants who die, as well as aborted fetuses.

Bodhisattva Maitreya (the 'Friendly One') is expected to be the next buddha, the one who will turn the dharma wheel once again after the wheel set in motion by Shakyamuni has stopped. Some Mahayana Buddhists pray to Maitreya requesting that they be reborn when he comes, for it is easier to become enlightened when there is a living buddha to follow.

The heavens in which the buddhas and bodhisattvas reside are known as 'fields' or 'realms'. The belief in such 'Buddha realms' is another characteristic of the Mahayana school. If one venerates a certain buddha, one may be reborn into that buddha's heaven. As we shall see, this is a central belief of the Pure Land movement, which has been especially popular in East Asia.

Meditation and Visualization

Mahayana Buddhism's belief in various buddhas and bodhisattvas, each with his or her own heaven, gave rise to a practice known as 'vision meditation'. The aim of vision practice was to focus so intensely on a particular bodhisattva or buddha that the meditator would be granted a vision of that figure. In the process, the practitioner hoped to achieve a heightened state of consciousness and develop a special rapport with that particular bodhisattva or buddha. The Vajrayana school, discussed later, also came to emphasize visualization.

Mahayana Schools in India

The above overview suggests some substantial differences between Mahayana and Theravada Buddhism, especially regarding scriptures, the nature of the Buddha, and the efficacy of prayer. But in fact the various schools that developed within the Mahayana tradition vary widely among themselves. The Chan (Zen) school, for example, downplays the veneration of Buddha and has much in common with Theravada, whereas the Pure Land school seems more theistic—more like Christianity in some ways. In this section we will introduce some of the more important Mahayana schools.

Madhyamika

The Mahayana movement gave rise to several specific schools of Buddhist philosophy. One of the earliest and most important was Madhyamika, the 'Middle Way'. Early Buddhism taught that there were six 'perfections', the last and most important of which was the perfection of wisdom in the sense of highly developed consciousness or awareness (*prajna*). Mahayana Buddhists put great emphasis on the development of *prajna* and wrote a number of texts on the subject, including the lengthy *Perfection of Wisdom in Eight Thousand Verses* and two popular later works known as the *Heart Sutra* and the *Diamond Cutter Sutra*. In these texts the highest form of spiritual wisdom is attained through awareness of the emptiness (*shunyata*) of all things.

Sometime in the latter part of the second century, a brahmin converted to Buddhism and took the ordination name Nagarjuna. He wrote Buddhist devotional hymns and ethical guides, but his fame is based on philosophical works such as the *Mulamadhyamaka-karika* ('Fundamentals of the Middle Way'). Nagarjuna's philosophical position is called the 'Middle Way' because it refuses either to affirm or to deny statements about reality on the grounds that all realities ('dharmas', the plural of the word for teaching or doctrine) are equally 'empty' of absolute truth or 'self-essence'. At the centre of Nagarjuna's doctrine of emptiness is the idea that everything in the phenomenal world is ultimately unreal. In fact, he goes so far as to claim that emptiness itself is unreal, although it may be experienced in meditation. Nagarjuna sums up this paradox in a famous eightfold negation:

> Nothing comes into being,
> Nor does anything disappear.

Nothing is eternal,
Nor has anything an end.
Nothing is identical,
Or differentiated,
Nothing moves hither,
Nor moves anything thither.
(Ch'en 1964:84)

For Madhyamika and the later Mahayana schools it influenced, including Zen, enlightenment involves the realization of the emptiness (*shunyata*) of all dharmas. The concept of *shunyata* is also translated as 'the Void' or 'Nothingness'.

Realizing that ultimately his own thinking must be as empty as any other teaching, Nagarjuna made it his philosophical 'position' to refuse to take a position. A modern Japanese Buddhist professor reports that when, as a graduate student, he expressed his uncertainty in relation to the various Buddhist philosophical schools, his teacher said, 'Your position is to have no position.' This anecdote points to the continuing influence of Nagarjuna.

Through a process of paradoxical reasoning, Nagarjuna finds that nirvana, Emptiness, is logically identical to *samsara*, the phenomenal world. Each is present in the other: '*samsara* is nirvana, and nirvana is *samsara*'. This is the most characteristic and most puzzling Madhyamika teaching. Early Buddhism had understood the two to be opposites, *samsara* being the temporal, worldly process of 'coming to be and passing away', and nirvana being the eternal, unchanging goal of one's spiritual quest. Madhyamika accepted that conventional wisdom might distinguish between them, but argued that from the perspective of higher wisdom no distinction was tenable.

By the sixth century, a split in the Madhyamika school developed around two teachers, each of whom considered himself to be the true follower of Nagarjuna. The school of Bhavaviveka (or Bhavya, c. 490–570) was willing to talk about levels of reality and degrees of insight, as long as it was understood that the distinctions applied only to the realm of conventional truth. This school was also known by the name Svatantrika because, unlike its rival, it accepted the validity of knowledge arrived at by independent (*svatantra*) inference.

The rival Madhyamika school, founded by Buddhapalita (c. 470–550), rejected independent inference and the other positions taken by Bhavya. It was called the Prasangika school because it maintained that all statements of knowledge, or theories, were ultimately self-contradictory (*prasanga*).

Chinese Madhyamika: Sanlun

The Chinese extension of Madhyamika was called the Sanlun ('Three Treatises') school because it was introduced to China with the translation of three treatises in the early fifth century. Its chief teaching was that everything is empty (*shunya*), because nothing has any independent reality or self-nature. The Sanlun school survived until the ninth century and then quickly declined, in part because of a state-sponsored campaign against Buddhism that began in 845.

| Map 8.1   The spread of Buddhism

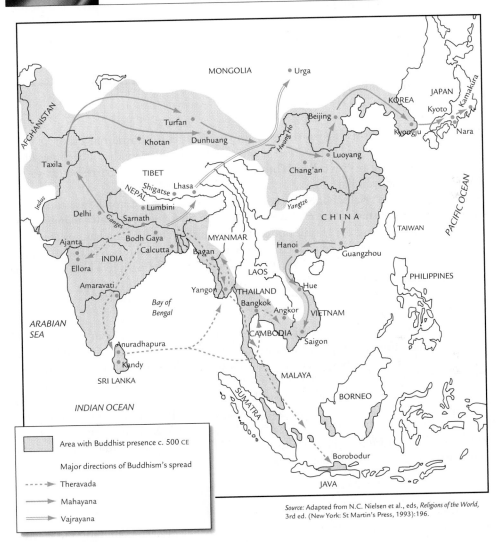

Area with Buddhist presence c. 500 CE

Major directions of Buddhism's spread

- - - ► Theravada

——► Mahayana

═══► Vajrayana

Source: Adapted from N.C. Nielsen et al., eds, *Religions of the World*, 3rd ed. (New York: St Martin's Press, 1993):196.

Yogacara or 'Consciousness Only'

In the late fourth century, three Indian *bhikshu*s named Maitreyanatha, Asanga, and Vasubandhu founded a new Mahayana school that rivalled Madhyamika. Though usually called Yogacara ('Practice of Yoga') because it stresses meditation, it is also known as 'Consciousness Only' (Vijnanavada), because it argues that we cannot truly know either the external world or ourselves: apparent realities are nothing more than ideas and images taken from a 'storehouse consciousness' (*alaya-vijnana*).

For Yogacara, the universe and the perceiver exist only in the process of perceiving. Even our 'selves' and our karma are merely reifications of momentary awareness. Impressions are 'seeds' that lead to acts or thoughts:

> A seed produces a manifestation,
> A manifestation perfumes a seed.
> The three elements (seed, manifestation, and perfume) turn on and on,
> The cause and effect occur at the same time.
> (Ch'en 1964:323)

According to this theory, the only way to avoid false substantialization is to so exhaust the consciousness, through yoga and spiritual cultivation, that it becomes identical to the ultimate reality called 'Thusness' (*tathata*), which also corresponds to the Emptiness of Madhyamika.

Critics from rival schools claimed that the concept of the storehouse consciousness seemed to contradict the traditional Buddhist doctrine of no-self (*anatman*) and come close to affirming the Hindu notion of Atman that the Buddha had rejected. The Yogacara writers, however, were careful to point out that although, like the Atman in Hinduism, the storehouse consciousness transmigrates from birth to birth, unlike the Atman it has no eternal, unchanging substance.

Faxiang: Chinese Yogacara

Yogacara's most important contribution to later Mahayana Buddhism in China and Japan may have been its emphasis on meditation. The Chinese version of the Yogacara school also has two names, Weishi ('Consciousness Only') and Faxiang ('Dharma Character'). First introduced into China in the sixth century, the school grew up around Asanga's *Compendium of Mahayana*. It was his perplexity over the meaning of this work that spurred the famous monk Xuanzang to set out for India to find more scriptures, and upon his return the Big Wild Goose Pagoda was built in Xian in the seventh century to house those scriptures. Like the Sanlun school, the Faxiang was hard hit by the ninth-century persecution of Buddhism.

Pure Land Buddhism

In the first century a new Mahayana school developed around the veneration of a celestial buddha of 'infinite life' and 'infinite light' known in Sanskrit as Amitayus or Amitabha and eventually in Japanese as Amida. In English this buddha is usual known by the Japanese name.

The **Pure Land** school took its name from two Sutras in which Shakyamuni tells the story of Amida: an earlier buddha who before his enlightenment, as a young prince named Dharmakara, took 48 bodhisattva vows detailing his intention to achieve higher enlightenment, to help others and to establish a heaven called the 'Pure Land'. In the important eighteenth vow, Amida promises to establish a heaven for those who express their desire to be reborn there by thinking of him (i.e., through faith in his compassionate power):

> If, after my obtaining Buddhahood, all beings in the ten quarters should not desire in sincerity and trustfulness to be born in my country, and if they should not be born by only thinking of me for ten times, except those who have committed the five grave offences and those who are abusive of the true *Dharma*, may I not attain the Highest Enlightenment (Bloom 1965:2–3).

Amida vows that he will strive to become a completely enlightened buddha, but only on the condition that he can actively work to help all living beings towards liberation. To this end, he vows to establish a Buddha-realm called the Western Paradise into which all his followers can be reborn. In that Pure Land or Happy Land (*sukhavati* in Sanskrit), the streets and buildings will be made of jewels. Suffering, old age, and death will be unknown, and the followers of Amida Buddha will be so uplifted by his merit that their progress towards nirvana will be easy.

This idea of paradise represents a remarkable change. In early Buddhism, worthy persons might hope to enjoy rebirth in paradise for a time, but eventually their merit would be exhausted and they would have to return to earth, since only earthly humans could accumulate merit and develop the higher wisdom required to move towards the final goal of nirvana. In Amida's Pure Land, by contrast, one would be able to learn from Amida, and therefore go on perfecting one's mind, eventually moving directly to nirvana without having to return to earth.

Practice in the Pure Land tradition focuses on opening oneself to Amida's grace. The *Shorter Sutra on the Pure Land* spells out what is to be done to benefit from his great store of merit. One who has recollected and repeated Amida's name before death will, upon dying, be reborn in his Pure Land. This rebirth is not earned by meritorious works and wisdom, as was the case with the path laid down by Shakyamuni. Rather, one is granted rebirth in the Pure Land through the infinite merits of Amida. Another Pure Land text, the *Meditation on Amitayus Sutra*, is a manual explaining 16 ways of meditating to achieve a vision of Amida. It is an example of a Mahayana vision text, which teaches how to meditate on a certain bodhisattva or buddha until he or she appears to the practitioner in a vision. The promise of the *Meditation sutra* is that whoever achieves such a vision will be reborn in the Pure Land.

Chinese Pure Land

The Pure Land school spread to East Asia, where it remains the most popular of all forms of Buddhism. In China Pure Land is known as Jingtu and Amida Buddha as Omitofo. He is assisted by two bodhisattvas (*pusa* in Chinese), one of which is Guanyin, the Bodhisattva of Compassion.

The *Shorter Sutra on the Pure Land* teaches that the only condition for rebirth in the Pure Land is faith in the infinite compassion of Amida, shown through prayerful and meditative repetition of his name. This reliance on an external power, called 'other power', stands in sharp contrast to the self-reliance emphasized in early Buddhism. In India such 'other-reliance' is described as 'cat grace', as opposed to the 'monkey grace' of self-reliance—the idea being that a mother cat carries her babies while they remain passive, whereas a baby monkey has to reach up and hold on to its mother.

The recitation of praise to Amida is called *nianfo* in Chinese. During the recitation the devotee usually fingers a string of beads. Thus Pure Land Buddhism parallels some forms of Christianity in several ways, with a God-figure (Omitofo), a mediator (Guanyin), a doctrine of faith and grace, and a form of devotion not unlike the rosary.

In China Pure Land Buddhism has especially appealed to the masses of people who seek not only ultimate salvation but also a power that will assist them in everyday life. The bodhisattva Guanyin is particularly important in this respect, especially for women. This 'goddess of mercy' soon came to symbolize the 'giver of children'—an adaptation that underlines the more worldly focus of Chinese Buddhism, compared with its Indian counterpart. Guanyin is associated with the medieval legend of the Chinese princess Miaoshan, who was killed by her parents to prevent her from becoming a nun. Sometimes seen holding a child, Guanyin recalls the Christian figure of the Madonna with child, and it has been suggested that this pose reflects the presence of Christian missionaries in China in the late seventeenth and early eighteenth centuries.

Japanese Pure Land

In Japan Pure Land is called Jodo (from Chinese Jingtu), its Buddha is called Amida (from Omitafo) and the female bodhistattva is called Kannon. Most Buddhists in Japan belong to the Jodo school.

Pure Land Buddhism was introduced to Japan by the monk Honen (1133–1212). A man of saintly reputation, Honen wanted to provide a simpler way to salvation for those unable to undertake the rigorous meditation techniques prescribed in the *Meditation on Amitayus Sutra*. The devotional practice that he taught relied entirely on faith in Amida's power of salvation, and consisted in chanting a phrase meaning 'Homage to Amida Buddha'. Repeated chanting of this phrase, called the *nembutsu* in Japanese, leads to a spiritual state of consciousness. During services, the chanting often starts slowly and then quickens to a feverish pace.

| Box 8.4 | **Pure Land Buddhism: Honen on the Nembutsu**

The method of final salvation that I have propounded is neither a sort of meditation, such as has been practised by many scholars in China or Japan, nor is it a repetition of the Buddha's name by those who have studied and understood the deep meaning of it. It is nothing but the mere repetition of the 'Namu Amida Butsu', without a doubt of his mercy, whereby one may be born into the Land of Perfect Bliss. The mere repetition with firm faith includes all the practical details, such as the three-fold preparation of mind and the four primordial truths. If I as an individual had any doctrine more profound than this, I should . . . be left out of the Vow of the Amida Buddha (Tsunoda 1958:208).

Honen's disciple Shinran (1173–1262) further developed Pure Land Buddhism in Japan, underlining the need for the 'other-power' of Amida's grace in an age that he considered degenerate and not conducive to spirituality. Condemning the magical and syncretic tendencies that he saw in other schools, Shinran taught the *nembutsu* as an act of faith and thanksgiving. In a moving passage about the salvation of the wicked, Shinran says:

> People generally think . . . that if even a wicked man can be reborn in the Pure Land, how much more so a good man! This latter view may at first sight seem reasonable, but it is not in accord with the purpose of the Original Vow, with faith in the Power of Another. The reason for this is that he who, relying on his own power, undertakes to perform meritorious deeds, has no intention of relying on the Power of Another and is not the object of the Original Vow of Amida. Should he, however, abandon his reliance on his own power and put his trust in the Power of Another, he can be born in the True Land of Recompense. . . . Amida made his Vow with the intention of bringing wicked men to Buddhahood. Therefore the wicked man who depends on the Power of Another is the prime object of salvation (*Tannisho*; Tsunoda 1958:217).

Both Honen and Shinran met with opposition from rival schools and were exiled by the authorities, but found wide support among the masses. Shinran founded a new sect called Jodo Shinshu ('True Pure Land') or Shin Buddhism. He also did something revolutionary: like Martin Luther in Europe, he chose to marry, maintaining that husband and wife are to each other as the bodhisattva Avalokiteshvara (in Japanese, Kannon) is to the believer. In so doing he laicized Buddhism. Although this break with the tradition of monastic celibacy was widely opposed, today most Buddhist priests in Japan are married, and temples are usually passed down through their families; the oldest son is typically called the 'temple son' and expected to train for the priesthood so that he can continue the family tradition.

Shin Buddhism grew significantly under the fifteenth-century patriarch Rennyo (1415–49), who wrote pastoral letters to the faithful and rebuilt the Honganji temple in Kyoto. Today it remains the largest Buddhist sect in Japan.

Mahayana Schools Originating in China

Chan (Zen)

Chan Buddhism is better known in the West by its Japanese name: Zen. Its founder was Bodhidharma—the same sixth-century Indian monk who told King Wu that all his good works had earned him no merit at all. In sharp contrast to the Pure Land sect, Chan emphasized 'self-power' and the attainment of personal enlightenment through rigorous practice of meditation. Although there is no evidence that a similar school existed in India, Chan tradition traces Bodhidharma 's lineage to the Buddha's disciple Kashyapa, whose intuitive insight is celebrated in the story of the 'Flower Sermon'.

This story begins with the disciples asking the Buddha for a dharma talk. He agrees, but when they gather to hear him speak, he simply holds up a lotus flower. All are dumbfounded except for Kashyapa, who in that moment experiences an intuitive flash of enlightenment. The Buddha acknowledges his understanding, and Kashyapa the Great (Mahakashyapa) becomes the first Patriarch in a lineage that stresses the achievement of the state of mind called *dhyana* in Sanskrit and *jhana* in Pali—the state reached by the young bodhisattva Shakyamuni while meditating under the rose-apple tree.

The Chinese pronounced the word *dhyana* or *jhana* as *chan*, and Bodhidharma is seen as the first patriarch of the Chan school in China. Bodhidharma taught what he called a 'mind to mind, direct transmission' of enlightenment, with 'no dependence on words'. Just as the Buddha relied on a single enigmatic gesture to deliver his 'flower sermon', so Bodhidharma and later Chan masters used surprising, shocking, paradoxical, or even violent actions to bring about the state of mind best known in the West by the Japanese term *satori*.

The Shaolin monastery in the valley below Bodhidharma's cave became a centre of Chan training not only in meditation but in what are now called the martial arts. The story is that Bodhidharma began teaching the students self-defence exercises as an antidote to their long hours of sitting meditation. Whether it is true or not, all the East Asian martial arts traditions trace their roots to the Shaolin monastery. Today the mountain town of Shaolin remains a centre of martial arts training.

One day a young Chinese man showed up at Bodhidharma's cave, begging to study under him. Bodhidharma refused, but when the man cut off his arm and presented it as a proof of his sincerity, he was accepted as a disciple. The one-armed man went on to become the patriarch after Bodhidharma's death. The lineage of patriarchs continued and the Chan school spread to other areas, but typically preferred higher altitudes, which are more conducive to meditation. For this reason Chan Buddhism has been called the 'mountain school'.

During the era of the fifth Chan patriarch, a young boy from southern China named Huineng arrived at the Chan monastery, asking to be admitted as a novice. He was not accepted, but stayed to work in the kitchen. When it came time for the aging patriarch to choose his successor, candidates were asked to compose a poem (*gatha* in Sanskrit) expressing their state of enlightenment. The most senior disciple wrote this verse on the wall:

> This body is the Bodhi-tree;
> The soul is like the mirror bright;
> Take heed to keep it always clean,
> And let no dust collect upon it.
> (Suzuki 1991)

That night, Huineng wrote a counter-poem on the wall nearby:

> The Bodhi (True Wisdom) is not like the tree;
> The mirror bright is nowhere shining:
> As there is nothing from the first,
> Where does the dust itself collect?
> (Suzuki 1991)

The patriarch called Huineng into his room, acknowledged his deep understanding, and awarded him the robe and staff of the office of patriarch— but with the advice that he should go back to the South. This he did, and though still a layman began teaching about the deep state of intuitive wisdom known as *satori*. Eventually he was ordained and recognized as the true Sixth Patriarch. It was Huineng who spread Chan to the masses and into southern China, from which it later spread to Korea and Japan, where it came to be known as Zen.

Today in Japan there are two main Zen schools, Rinzai and Soto. The first is named after Linchi, a famous Chinese Chan monk who is said to have entered training as a shy young boy. After he had trained diligently for more than a year, it was time for him to meet with the master, Huang-po. When the master asked why he had come, Linchi humbly requested instruction in enlightenment, whereupon the master hit him hard with his stick.

When Linchi told the novice trainer what had happened, the trainer suggested he try again, which led to a second beating. After three such beatings, Linchi decided to leave training, thinking he was not worthy. The master allowed him to leave, but requested that he first visit an old hermit monk. The hermit, upon hearing Linchi describe being hit hard three times by his master, exclaimed, 'Poor old Huang-po, he must have nearly exhausted himself hitting you.' This lack of sympathy so shocked and angered Linchi that he experienced a breakthrough and burst out laughing. 'Why the sudden change?' demanded the hermit. 'There's not so much to old Huang-po's Zen after all' was the reply. Upon returning to Huang-po, Linchi threatened to hit the master with his own stick. 'Just get back to your training,' said the master. The school that Linchi ('Rinzai' in Japanese) eventually founded stresses exactly the kind of 'sudden

---

| Box 8.5   **Zen Buddhism: Extracts from the *Platform Sutra***

The *Platform Sutra is said to have been written by the sixth Chan patriarch, Huineng (638–713), as instruction to his disciples who were to spread the Chan teachings.*

On meditation and wisdom
Good friends, how then are meditation and wisdom alike? They are like the lamp and the light it gives forth. If there is a lamp there is light; if there is no lamp there is no light. The lamp is the substance of light; the light is the function of the lamp. Thus, although they have two names, in substance they are not two. Meditation and wisdom are like this (*The Platform Sutra of the Sixth Patriarch*, sec. 15; Yampolsky 1976:137).

On sudden and gradual enlightenment
Good friends, in the *Dharma* there is no sudden or gradual [enlightenment], but among people some are keen and others dull. The deluded commend the gradual method; the enlightened practise the sudden teaching. To understand the original mind of yourself is to see into your own original nature. Once enlightened, there is from the outset no distinction between these two methods; those who are not enlightened will for long kalpas be caught in the cycle of transmigration (*The Platform Sutra of the Sixth Patriarch*, sec. 16; Yampolsky 1976:137).

enlightenment', or *satori*, that he experienced as a result of his struggle to understand what seemed to be Huang-po's irrational behaviour.

At the centre of this approach is the **koan**: a paradoxical anecdote or riddle that is specifically designed to defy rational understanding and force the student out of normal 'heady' (reason- or word-centred) mode into a more intuitive, body-centred state of mind.

The other Zen sect in Japan is the Soto school, which prefers the 'gradual enlightenment' brought about by hours and hours of zazen (sitting meditation). Both schools use koans and zazen, so the differences lie mainly in emphasis and tradition. The numbers of people in Japan who practise Zen are not large, but the tradition has had a great influence on Japanese culture.

Mahayana in Korea

Physical proximity created close links between China and Korea. The Han dynasty conquered the northern part of the peninsula in the late second century BCE and Buddhism was introduced roughly two centuries later, spreading from the northern kingdom of Koguryo first to Paekche in the southwest and then to Silla in the southeast. It became most influential after Silla conquered the other two kingdoms and united the country (668–935).

The new religion expanded on an unprecedented scale during the Silla period. Among the major schools of Buddhism introduced from China were the Theravada tradition of the *vinaya* (monastic discipline) and the Faxiang (Yogacara) school, which eventually developed into a syncretic tradition. The most influential school, however, was Chan (Son in Korean), introduced in the early seventh century. Nine Son monasteries, known as the Nine Mountains, were eventually established.

In the late twelfth century the Son and the scholastic schools were united by a charismatic monk named Chinul (1158–1210) to create the Chogye sect, which became the orthodox form of Buddhism in Korea and remains the largest denomination today. It was also Chinul who introduced the paradoxical exercise called *gongan* in Chinese but more familiar in the West in its Japanese form, koan.

Buddhist influence withered for several centuries after the Yi dynasty (1392–1910) adopted Confucianism as Korea's state ideology. Confucian scholars petitioned the court to restrict the number of Buddhist temples, supervise the selection of monks, and reorganize the ecclesiastical system while reducing the number of sects to facilitate state control. In the fifteenth century, temple properties were confiscated, the serfs retained by monasteries were drafted into the army, and Buddhist monks were banned, especially in Seoul, the capital.

Mahayana in Japan

Buddhism was first introduced to Japan from Korea in the mid-sixth century. It had taken almost 900 years to reach the extremities of East Asia, and it had been transformed along the way. Japanese Buddhism takes many forms, but is primarily Mahayana.

An important landmark for Buddhism in Japan was the warm reception it received from the regent, Prince Shotoku, who in 604 issued a set of moral guidelines for the ruling class (the 'Seventeen-Article Constitution') that extolled the value of harmony and urged reverence for the Three Gems. Welcoming Buddhism (as well as Confucianism) for its civilizing benefits, the prince became the centre of a Buddhist cult that still endures. The state offered protection for Buddhism, even building its temples, and Japanese monks travelled to China to pursue further study.

It was during the Nara period (710–94), under the influence of Buddhism, that Japanese culture experienced its first golden age. Eventually, however, the monks' close ties with the state led many to become increasingly secularized and in some cases corrupt. The state limited the number of monks and forbade them from proselytizing among the general populace. As a result, the practice of Buddhism was for a time mainly restricted to the aristocracy.

Tendai

The most influential Buddhist sect during the Heian period (794–1185) was Tendai, founded by the monk Saicho (766–822). After studying in China, Saicho returned home determined to reform Japanese Buddhism. Breaking with the increasingly secularized older sects established in the Nara period, he made Mount Hiei, northeast of the new capital of Kyoto, his base of operations. The temple complex on Mount Hiei eventually became a kind of fortress with its own monk-soldiers.

Japanese Tendai believed in the universal attainment of buddhahood or salvation, as taught in the *Lotus Sutra*, and the harmonization of Buddhist teachings. Tendai also incorporated a number of esoteric beliefs and rituals associated with certain forms of Vajrayana. Like the Shingon sect (p. 413), Tendai taught that anyone can attain buddhahood, and focused on life in this world rather than the next. Both sought the favour of the court and the support of the nobility, and both practised magical rites intended to secure material prosperity and earthly happiness. Shingon and Tendai became the prototypes of all later Japanese Buddhist sects.

Nichiren

Nichiren Buddhism was founded by a controversial monk with the religious name Nichiren ('Sun and Lotus'; 1222–82). He had studied on Mount Hiei but left because he believed that Tendai had abandoned the teachings of its central scripture, the *Lotus Sutra*. His own message was very simple. Whereas the Pure Land school placed its trust in Amida, Nichiren placed his in the power of the *Lotus Sutra* itself.

Like the Pure Land Buddhists who invoked the power of Amida simply by calling on his name, Nichiren sought to invoke the power of the *Lotus Sutra* by repeating the words *Namu myoho renge kyo* ('Homage to the *Lotus Sutra*') as a chant or mantra. Nichiren inscribed this formula, called the Daimoku, on a calligraphic scroll, the *Gohonzon*, kept at the temple of the Nichiren Shoshu sect at Taisekiji, near Mount Fuji. Each disciple has small *Gohonzon* for personal devotional use.

Starting out as a reformer, Nichiren established a new, characteristically Japanese form of Buddhism that became associated with Japanese nationalism at a time when the country feared a Mongol invasion. In the fifteenth century, with the collapse of political order during the 'warring states' period, Nichiren Buddhists rose up in arms.

Nichiren was aggressive in attacking other Buddhist sects, especially Pure Land and Zen, and for this he was sentenced to death; but an apparent miracle intervened, so instead he was exiled to an island, where he wrote extensively. For him Japan was a sacred land, the land of the *Lotus Sutra*. The Soka Gakkai movement, discussed in Chapter 10, is a twentieth-century offshoot of Nichiren Buddhism.

Ji

Ji ('time-sect') Buddhism was founded by an itinerant monk named Ippen (1239–89) who preached simple sermons, taught the *nembutsu*, and incorporated a number of Shinto deities (see Chapter 10) into his practice. With no fixed abode and no consolidated organization, Ippen and his followers travelled from place to place, gathering groups of local people and teaching them the *nembutsu*.

Vajrayana

'Vajrayana'—from *vajra*, meaning both 'diamond' and 'thunderbolt'—is just one of several names for the third vehicle of Buddhism. The image of the diamond suggests something that cannot be broken or split. *Vajra* is also the name of a small ritual sceptre that is held in the hand during Vajrayana ceremonies. Shaped somewhat like an hourglass with curved prongs at each end, it symbolizes the enlightened awareness: unbreakable itself and capable of shattering spiritual obstacles.

Followers also refer to Vajrayana as the 'Third Turning' of the wheel of dharma, representing the culmination and completion of the two earlier schools. This view is reflected in a system of Vajrayana training that unfolds in three stages: from basic moral discipline (Hinayana) through basic Buddhist doctrines (Mahayana), to advanced doctrines and practices (Vajrayana).

Arising in India around the fifth century, Vajrayana was eventually taken to virtually every part of the Buddhist world, but it became the principal form of Buddhism in the Himalayan region (Tibet, Bhutan, Nepal). For this reason it is sometimes called Northern or Tibetan Buddhism.

Another name, 'Mantrayana', reflects Vajrayana's use of mantras—sacred chants believed to evoke great spiritual blessing when properly intoned. The meanings of the mantras are passed on as secret teachings from master to pupil. Because of these secret teachings, Vajrayana is also described as 'esoteric' Buddhism.

Finally, Vajrayana is often called 'tantric' Buddhism. Like Hindu tantrism, Buddhist tantrism envisions cosmic reality as the interplay of male and female forces and teaches a set of practical techniques for tapping into the spiritual energy produced by that interplay.

Thus a central component of tantric Buddhism is the concept of sexual union. Some tantric texts suggest that since the world is bound by lust, it is to be released by lust. While the 'right-hand' school understood this symbolically, the 'left-hand' school understood it in a more literal fashion, practising ritual unions in which a man and woman visualized themselves as divine beings. Such practices, properly undertaken, would confront lust, defeat it, and transcend it. The texts that lay out such techniques are termed *tantras*. The Tibetan canon includes a vast library of *tantras* under the heading *Kanjur* and various commentaries under the heading *Tanjur*.

The Vajrayana *tantras* classify the many buddhas and bodhisattvas in various families, which are often depicted in a sacred geometric design called a **mandala**. For example, the 'head' of the family will occupy the place of honour in the centre of the design, surrounded by the other members of the family, each of which occupies a specific position.

Practitioners meditate on a particular buddha or bodhisattva in order to achieve a vision that will help them along the path to enlightenment. The Vajrayana guru initiates the disciple into the symbolic meanings of the various members of the family and their relationships, as well as the rituals required to develop inner wisdom.

Having built up a visualization, practitioners begin to identify with that buddha or bodhisattva and tap his or her energies. Visualizing oneself as identical with that figure, one senses several *chakras* or centres of power within one's own body and may perceive oneself to be at the centre of a sacred space defined by a mandala. At the culmination of this process of gradual enlightenment, the initiate aspires to dissolve slowly into Emptiness (*shunyata*), liberated from ego attachment.

A classic mandala pattern reflects tantric Buddhism's emphasis on the *Mahavairocana* ('Great Sun') *Sutra*. For example, a mandala might centre on Mahavairocana, surrounded by the buddhas of the four directions: Aksobhya in the east, Amitabha in the west, Amoghasiddhi in the north, and Ratnasambhava in the south, all of whom together represent the various emanations of buddhahood itself. It is also characteristic of tantric Buddhism to give female counterparts not only to the buddhas but to the bodhisattvas who accompany them; as a result, mandalas often include numerous figures.

These deities have dual aspects, pacific and angry, depending on their functions (e.g., to assist in beneficial activities or to repel evil forces). The union of wisdom and compassion, considered the key to enlightenment, is represented by the father–mother image evoked by the embrace of deities and their consorts.

Vajrayana in East Asia

Introduced to China in the eighth century under the name Zhenyan ('true word' or 'mantra'), tantric Buddhism enjoyed only a brief period of popularity as a novelty there. In 806, however, a Japanese monk who had been studying in China introduced Zhenyan to his homeland. Shingon Buddhism, as it came to be known, flourished in Japan and is still practised there today.

Shingon tantrism is of the 'right-handed' type. For the Shingon school, enlightenment consists in the realization that one's own Buddha-nature is identical with the Great Sun Buddha, Mahavairocana, and can be achieved in this life, in this world, through the esoteric doctrine of Shingon.

Vajrayana in Tibet

Vajrayana is said to have been established in Tibet in the eighth century by a *bhikshu* named Padmasambhava. Revered as *Guru Rinpoche* ('precious teacher'), he combined instruction in dharma with magical practices involving the world of the spirits. The figure of Padmasambhava is claimed particularly by a school of Tibetan Buddhism known as the Nyingma, the 'ancient' school that dates back to his time. The indigenous religion of Tibet in that period, Bön ('truth' or 'reality'), appears to have combined and inter-acted with Buddhism, and elements of it have continued to the present day.

Tibetan Buddhism is divided among three main ordination lineages or orders. The best-known, the Gelugpa, was founded by the reformer Tsongkhapa (1357–1419). On ceremonial occasions, members of this order wear large yellow hats, whereas members of the Kargyu and Karma-pa orders wear red and black hats respectively.

Tibet and China

To understand the office of **Dalai Lama** ('Ocean of Wisdom') and the controversial Chinese claim that Tibet is a part of China, we need to understand the historic relationship between Tibet and the Mongols. As the rulers of China from 1222 to 1368, the Mongols did not invade Tibet. They did, however, appoint the head of the Shakya monastery to serve as their viceroy for the region. Some two centuries later, a Gelugpa missionary named Sonam Gyatso (1543–88) went to Mongolia and converted its ruler, Altan Khan, who created the title Dalai Lama and gave it to Gyatso's two predecessors retroactively, designating Gyatso the third in the succession of Dalai Lamas. With the sponsorship of the Mongol princes, the Gelugpas soon became the dominant sect in both Mongolia and Tibet.

The Dalai Lamas became the rulers of Tibet from the time of the fifth Dalai Lama, Ngawang Lobsang Gyatso (1617–82). With Mongol aid he subdued the challenge of the rival Karma-pa lineage and constructed the famous Potala palace in Lhasa. He

A Tibetan monk in the throne room of the early Dalai Lamas, Drepung Monastery (Kate Brunn).

recognized his teacher, Lobsang Chögye Gyaltsen (1569–1662), as an incarnation of the bodhisattva Amitabha and gave him the title Panchen Lama. The position of the Panchen Lamas still exists, but has become controversial because the Dalai Lama and Chinese government now recognize different people as the legitimate Panchen Lama.

The Fifth Dalai Lama also established diplomatic relations with the Manchu (Qing) dynasty, which came to power in China in 1644. As a result, Tibet became embroiled in the eighteenth-century rivalry between the Manchus in Beijing and the Oirots of Mongolia, and became a Manchu protectorate. Inner Mongolia came into the Chinese orbit too, while Outer Mongolia was torn between Chinese economic influence and Russian political protection. These old Tibetan ties with Mongolia and China are the basis of modern China's claim to Tibet.

Practice

Shakyamuni himself had little use for rituals. He disapproved of the rituals conducted by the brahmins of his day, especially those involving animal sacrifice. He also recognized the potential for ritual and doctrine alike to become objects of attachment and warned his followers against becoming dependent on them. To make his point, he told a parable about a man who builds a raft to cross a flooded river during the rainy season and then, because it has been so useful, decides to carry it with him over dry land. Doctrine and rituals, he said, are like rafts: they can be useful, but should not become a burden on the journey towards mental purification and nirvana.

Despite the Buddha's teachings, however, all forms of Buddhism soon developed their own rituals. Four places associated with Shakyamuni himself became important pilgrimage sites—Lumbini (birth), Bodh Gaya (enlightenment), Sarnath (first sermon), and Kushinagar (*parinirvana*)—and as Buddhism spread, a number of places in other countries also became pilgrimage destinations.

Theravada Practice

The most common Theravada ritual is the Buddha-puja, which pays respect to the Buddha. Typically, when visiting a temple, Buddhists pay respect to the guardian spirit at the entrance and place flowers on altars near the stupa and Bodhi tree before proceeding into the temple to place flowers on the altar(s) there. They may also put coins into an offering box. Then they say prayers expressing their dedication to living according to the dharma. In front of the main altar, they perform the Buddha-puja chanting praise to the Buddha and vowing to observe the 'five precepts'. Unlike the 'commandments' of the Judeo-Christian tradition, these precepts are moral rules that Buddhists voluntarily undertake to follow. The Buddhist vows to refrain from

- taking life
- taking that which is not given
- sensual misconduct (sexual immorality)

- wrong speech (lying, slander and the like) and
- intoxicants leading to the loss of mindfulness.

On holy days lay persons may undertake additional precepts.

Theravadins also perform a number of more elaborate 'merit-making' rituals specifically designed to produce good karma. Of these, three of the most important are almsgiving, the *dana* ritual, and the Buddha Day (Vaishakha) festival.

Almsgiving

Traditionally, members of the *sangha* would leave the monastery early each morning carrying bowls to collect their daily food. As they moved slowly through the streets without speaking, their eyes downcast to maintain a tranquil, composed state of mind, laypeople would come out of their houses, put cooked food into the alms bowls, then bow low or prostrate themselves as a sign of respect.

The practice of going for alms is increasingly rare in most countries. In Sri Lanka, however, there has recently been an effort to revive the practice with the assistance of some *bhikshus* from Thailand, where it is still current. In other countries, such as Malaysia, the ritual is performed in the vicinity of the temple on important Buddhist occasions. People bring rice and food packets from home and put their offerings in the alms bowls as the *bhikshus* proceed along the road near the temple.

The *Dana* Ritual

The practice of giving food and other necessities to the *sangha* has developed into a ritual called *dana*, from the Sanskrit word for 'giving'. A *dana* might be held at a temple or a pilgrimage site, but is often held by a family in their home to celebrate some important occasion. The following description of a *dana* as held in a Sri Lankan home offers a glimpse of several other Buddhist rituals as well.

As the monks arrive at the door, their feet are washed by the men of the family. (If the guests were *bikshunis*, the women of the family would perform this hospitality ritual.) Upon entering the home, the *bhikshus* first bow before the Buddha altar. Then they seat themselves on the floor around the room and conduct a Buddha-puja, after which they chant from a collection of scriptures called *paritta*. After the chanting, the *bhikshus* conduct a merit-transfer ritual, in which the merit made by all present through their participation is transferred 'to all living beings': 'May the merit made by me now or at some other time be shared among all beings here infinite, immeasurable; those dear to me and virtuous as mothers or as fathers are, . . . to others neutral, hostile too. . . .'

Somewhat like the traditional Roman Catholic practices of performing penance or purchasing 'indulgences' for the benefit of deceased relatives, the Buddhist merit transfer is intended to help one's ancestors, and others, in the afterlife. Although the concept might seem to violate the early Buddhist principle that everyone must make their own karma, according to the scriptures Shakyamuni himself advocated this practice.

Preparations for the next ritual are made before the chanting begins and involve running a string from the Buddha image on the home altar to a pot containing water, then to the monks, and finally to all the laypeople. The monks and laypeople hold the string in their right hands during the chanting and dharma talk. The water and the string become sacred objects through the power of the chanting. After the merit-transfer ritual, the *bhikshus* cut the string into short pieces, which they tie around the right wrist of each male. A layperson ties a string around the wrists of the women, because monks and or nuns are not supposed to come into contact with members of the opposite sex. The string is left on the wrist until it falls off.

Buddha Day Festival

Many Buddhist festivals developed out of earlier seasonal festivals, and there are variations from country to country. However, Buddhists in most countries celebrate the day of the full moon in the 'rains' month, known in Theravada countries as Vesak (Sanskrit Vaishakha). In English-speaking countries this festival is often called 'Buddha Day'. According to Buddhist tradition, three major events in the life of Shakyamuni occurred on that day: his birth, his enlightenment, and his passing (*parinirvana*).

One of the rock inscriptions recounting King Ashoka's accomplishments and pronouncements, from 259 BCE, states that he organized a procession to be held annually on Vaishakha day. In contemporary Sri Lanka, the custom is for Buddhists to travel from place to place to see special paintings depicting scenes from the life of the Buddha. Talks are given on Shakyamuni's life, and special Buddha-pujas are performed.

Life-cyle and Death Rituals

Early Indian Buddhists did not have any special rituals marking the various stages of the life cycle: they simply continued to follow the life-cycle rituals of what we now call Hinduism. As Buddhism spread to other countries, the new converts similarly continued to celebrate their own traditional life-cycle rituals. Thus there are no specifically Buddhist wedding or childhood rituals. It is in part for this reason that Buddhism has co-existed with the traditional belief systems of each country where it has established itself: Sri Lankan Buddhists continue to observe Indian rituals; Thai Buddhists still worship the traditional spirits; and Japanese Buddhists still visit Shinto shrines.

There is a Buddhist funeral ritual, however, based on the ancient Indian cremation ceremony. The Theravada funeral includes a procession, ritual prayers, a water-pouring ritual, the cremation, final prayers, and a communal meal. But the pattern varies from country to country. Cremation is not mandatory, for example, and so burial is practised where the cost of wood is prohibitive.

A traditional Buddhist funeral in Sri Lanka illustrates the principal features of the ceremony. On the day of burial, the corpse is taken in a procession to the cemetery along a route prepared in advance by filling in potholes, cutting the grass and weeds beside the road, and placing flowers along the way. These preparations reflect traditions that have parallels in many parts of the ancient world (Christians may recall the preparations made for Jesus' procession into Jerusalem on Palm Sunday).

At the cemetery the body is placed in a temporary wooden structure above a funeral pyre. A brief service is then held that includes chants, prayers, and a ritual in which family members and friends take turns pouring holy water out of a container while a long prayer is chanted. After the service the pyre is lit, ideally by the eldest son of the deceased. In the event that a crematorium is used instead of a funeral pyre, some aspects of the traditional ceremony, such as the water-pouring ritual, are postponed until the *dana* held on the seventh day after the death, but one or more *bhikshus* will still come to recite prayers over the body.

The loss of a loved one is always a difficult experience, but Buddhists prepare for it through years of prayer and meditation on the inevitability of death. One of Buddhism's strengths is the way it helps its followers to be realistic about the end of life through rituals that remind the living of how all things pass away. Also, Buddhist death rituals do not end with the burial. On the sixth night after the death, a dharma talk is held at the home, followed by a *dana* on the seventh day. Other memorial *dana* rituals are held at the home of the deceased after three months, on the eve of which *bhikshus* may be invited to chant all night long, and after one year.

Vipassana Meditation

Theravada Buddhists practise a simple form of meditation called *vipassana* ('insight' or 'mindfulness'). While sitting in a meditational posture, practitioners concentrate on their breathing, focusing either on the sensation of air passing through the nostrils or on the rising and falling of the abdomen. Although the breaths are usually counted (in cycles of ten), the point is not to keep track of the number but to focus the mind. Unlike some forms of yoga, *vipassana* does not require practitioners to slow the rate of breathing. Practitioners may also cultivate mindfulness of other parts of the body, personal emotions, or relationships with others. The goal is to live in a totally mindful way.

Mahayana Practice

In Mahayana countries, the three anniversaries of the Buddha—his birth, his enlightenment, and his *parinirvana*—are remembered on separate days, determined by the lunar calendar. Festivals honouring other buddhas and bodhisattvas are also observed, especially Guanyin's birthday. Different sects also celebrate the anniversaries of their patriarchs (for example, Nichiren in Japan).

Under the influence of the ancestor cult in China and Japan, the dead are honoured by an 'all souls' day'. In China this day is celebrated by burning paper boats to free the *preta* ('hungry ghosts') who have perished in violence. In Japan, at the feast called the Obon, two altars are built, one for offerings to the dead ancestors and the other for the 'ghosts'. Traditionally, Chinese avoided non-essential outside activity during the 'ghosts month', to lessen the chance of encountering a ghost.

Buddhism has also adopted local customs surrounding occasions such as New Year. In China pilgrimages are made to the four sacred mountains, each dedicated to a different bodhisattva. In Japan the temple gong is struck 108 times on New Year's Eve, symbolizing forgiveness of the 108 kinds of bad deeds.

Vajrayana Practice

The use of mandalas in Vajrayana meditation has already been outlined. In addition, this tradition makes ritual use of mantras and ritual gestures. Mantras do not need to be spoken to be activated; they can be written on banners or slips of paper and hung on trees or lines, or rotated in cylindrical containers called prayer wheels.

The best-known mantra is the phrase *Om mani padme hum*. Vajrayana Buddhists interpret this phrase in various ways. The words are Sanskrit: *om* and *hum* are sacred syllables, not words per se; *mani* means 'jewel'; and *padme* is 'lotus'. So in English we might say 'O the Jewel in the Lotus', or simply 'Om jewel lotus hum'. But Vajrayana Buddhists offer several interpretations. Some see the jewel and lotus as symbolic of the male and female principles, and understand their union to represent the harmony of the male and female cosmic forces. Others understand it to refer to the bodhisattva Avalokiteshvara in feminine form as the 'jewelled-lotus lady'. Some count its six syllables as referring to six realms of rebirth or six spiritual perfections. Whatever the interpretation, the mantra evokes a cosmic harmony.

A unique feature of Tibetan Buddhism is the text called the *Bardo Thodol* ('Liberation by Hearing on the After-Death Plane'), better known as *The Tibetan Book of the Dead*. A set of written instructions concerning the afterlife, the *Bardo Thodol* is meant to be read aloud to dying persons in order to help them achieve liberation during the three stages of the *bardo* state between death and subsequent rebirth.

During the first stage the dying person loses consciousness, experiences a transitional time of darkness, and then emerges into a world filled with strange objects unknown on the earthly plane. A brilliant light then appears. If the person recognizes the light as the Dharma Body of Buddha, he or she will attain liberation and experience nirvana rather than rebirth. More often, however, bad karma prevents people from recognizing the true nature of the light, and instead they turn away in fear. Thus most people then pass on to a second *bardo* stage in which some consciousness of objects is regained. One may be aware of one's own funeral, for example. Peaceful deities appear for seven days, then wrathful deities appear for seven more days. These are all the Buddha, in the Body of Bliss form, and those who meditate on them as such will experience liberation. Those who do not recognize them will gradually assume a new bodily form within a few weeks of death. Liberation is possible right up to the moment of rebirth, but karma keeps most people in the grip of *samsara*, the wheel of death and rebirth. In the third stage one experiences judgment according to one's karma, and rebirth.

Choosing a New Dalai Lama

Considered to be a manifestation of the bodhisattva Avalokiteshvara, each Dalai Lama is said to be the reincarnation of the previous one. When a Dalai Lama dies, a complicated search is undertaken to find a young boy who shows signs of being his reincarnation. The candidate must display intellectual qualities and personality characteristics similar to those of the deceased, and various objects are presented to the boy to see if he chooses ones that were his favourites. Finally, the State Oracle goes into a trance in order to

| Box 8.6   The Fourteenth Dalai Lama

When the thirteenth Dalai Lama died in 1933, his head was turned to the northeast. This was a sign that his successor would come from that region. After a senior monk had a vision in which he saw the first letter of a northeastern province's name, a monastery, and a house with distinctive guttering, a search party found a candidate in a peasant farming village.

Lhamo Thondup was just three years old, born on 6 July 1935. It is said that he called one of the selection party by name, and that when shown a collection of toys he picked out the ones loved by the thirteenth Dalai Lama. Recognized as the reincarnation of the late leader, he was taken to Lhasa, where he was renamed Tenzin Gyatso, made the spiritual leader of Tibet, and ordained as a novice in 1940. His long course of Buddhist studies was interrupted in 1950, when an earthquake and threats of a Chinese invasion led to his installation as the polit-ical leader of Tibet at the age of 15. To avoid arrest or worse from the Chinese, he went into exile in northern India, where he continues to lead a government in exile from Dharmsala.

The Dalai Lama travels extensively and has written numerous books on Tibetan Buddhism, meditation, and philosophy as well as an autobiography, *Freedom in Exile*. Politically, he con-tinues to advocate for the well-being of the Tibetan people while stressing non-violence. Although negotiations with the Chinese government have so far not been fruitful, he is greatly respected around the world, and in 1989 he was awarded the Nobel Peace Prize.

contact the spirits to confirm the selection. The fourteenth and current Dalai Lama, Tenzin Gyatso (b. 1935), was chosen in this way from a family of Tibetan descent living in China. A senior monk's dream played a key role in locating the boy.

Cultural Expressions

Because Buddhism has been the principal religion of many Asian countries, cultural expressions of its influence are widespread.

Stupas and Pagodas

Before his death, the Buddha was asked how he ought to be buried. He answered that the remains of a Tathagata should be enshrined in a memorial stupa of the kind built for great rulers. In the Indo-Aryan culture, the remains of rulers were traditionally placed in an above-ground crypt, which was then covered with earth to form a large bur-ial mound. Tables or platforms for offerings were then constructed in each of the four cardinal directions near the mound.

After the *parinirvana* of the Buddha, several kings requested the honour of enshrining his cremated remains in their kingdoms. Accordingly, the remains were divided and nine memorial mounds were built over them. As Buddhism spread to other parts of India, additional stupas were built over other sacred objects, such as the cremated remains of Shakyamuni's major disciples, or portions of the Buddhist scriptures.

Each portion of ashes was placed in a small casket about the size of a shoe box, richly decorated with jewels. The casket was then interred in a stone crypt, which was covered over with a large mound of earth and a layer of bricks, then plastered and finally whitewashed.

On top of the mound, over the crypt, a pole representing the central mountain of early Buddhist cosmology was run through a series of wooden disks symbolizing the layers of heaven. There were often nine such layers, in keeping with Indian astrology and cosmology. (These wooden elements were later built of stone because wood was too difficult to maintain.)

There are several terms for these white memorial mounds. The Sanskrit *stupa* is cognate with the English word 'tomb'. Another name is *caitya*, 'shrine'. And the term in East Asia is 'pagoda'. Nearly every Buddhist temple precinct in the world has one of these structures, many of which are said to enshrine relics of the Buddha himself; important stupas in Sri Lanka, Myanmar, and China, for example, all claim to enshrine one of his teeth.

In addition to the large main stupa, a temple complex will often include smaller stupas that serve as memorial crypts for people associated with that particular temple. These small votive stupas add to the beauty and spiritual atmosphere of the temple grounds. Buddhists sometimes strew flower petals around them while vowing that they too will some day overcome death and achieve nirvana.

The construction of small stupas was especially popular as a merit-making devotional practice in Myanmar. Some, such as the ones near the ancient Burmese city of Pagan, were built to last, but others were not. Since the merit associated with building a stupa came not from the structure itself but from the mental purification experienced in the process of building it, there was no need for the structure to endure.

The shape of the stupa changed over the centuries, especially when Buddhism spread to East Asia. There the structure eventually developed into an elegant five- or seven-storied stone or wooden tower—a pagoda— that devotees could either walk around or climb up. The many storeys of the Chinese or Japanese pagoda derive from the various levels of the heavens symbolized by the wooden disks of the original Indian stupa. This pagoda architecture exaggerated the 'heavenly' upper levels at the expense of the lower parts of the original stupa, including the mound itself. In Korea, by contrast, most pagodas are scarcely taller than a single-storey house. Although their exterior form replicates in miniature the architectural details of their prototype, the multi-levelled tower with tiled roofs at each level, they are made out of solid stone and cannot be climbed.

Temples

Buddhist monasteries grew out of the simple refuges in which early monks lived during the rainy season—usually a collection of thatched huts located on the outskirts of a city. Weathy devotees would earn merit by paying for the construction of permanent buildings,

A temple in Laos (Euan White).

and over time a temple complex would take shape consisting of living quarters, a small shrine, and a meeting hall. Eventually, to accommodate large numbers of lay worshippers, the small shrine developed into a large temple housing images of the Buddha. Today, besides the stupa and temple, the grounds usually contain a Bodhi tree, dharma hall, monastery, library, and refectory, and are usually surrounded by an ornamental wall with elaborate entrances.

In some regions of India, cliffside cave complexes were developed that included all the essentials of a temple complex, with shrine caves, living area caves and even large dharma hall caves. Similar complexes can be found in China and elsewhere.

In China, the rectangular wooden buddha hall reflected the influence of the tile-roofed imperial hall of state, with the buddha statue enshrined in the posture of an emperor. This style made its way to Japan, the best-known example being the Todaiji, the

Great East Monastery in Nara, which houses a bronze image of Vairocana, the cosmic buddha, more than 16 metres (52 ft) high.

Images of the Buddha

The earliest Buddhist icons were symbols such as footprints, the dharma wheel, the Bodhi Tree, or an empty seat. It was not until the first century CE, when the devotional aspects of Mahayana Buddhism were becoming increasingly popular, that stone images depicting Shakyamuni himself were erected (it is possible that these were preceded by wooden carvings that have not survived). As in the Hindu tradition, images of the Buddha show him in a variety of poses: standing, sitting, seated in the lotus position of yogic meditation, or reclining, either asleep or entering *parinirvana*.

Hand gestures or **mudra**s became an important feature of Buddhist art. In one, Shakyamuni touches the earth with the fingers of his right hand, 'calling the earth to witness', as he did during his encounter with Mara on the eve of his enlightenment. Another popular image shows him in a posture of teaching. Sometimes the Buddha's right hand is raised, palm outward and fingers upward, in a gesture signifying 'granting of protection'. This *mudra* is usually combined with 'fulfilling a wish', in which the left hand is extended downward with the palm outward and fingers pointing down. Buddhist iconography also includes the 32 major signs of Shakyamuni's status, the most obvious of them being the *usnisa* (the protuberance on the top of his head that was supposed to be the locus of his supernatural wisdom) and elongated ear lobes. Some art historians think that these features were associated with royalty (elaborate hair styles, earlobes stretched by heavy earrings), but Buddhists see them as signs of Shakyamuni's supernatural nature. Other signs include wheel images on the soles of his feet and fingers all the same length.

Buddhist iconography in China typically shows the Buddha encircled by his company like an emperor surrounded by his court. The Buddha is seated in a serene posture, flanked by two monks, Kashyapa and Ananda. Nearby stand the bodhisattvas and stern-looking *Arhats* (*lohans* in Chinese). The Four Heavenly Kings (World Protectors) often stand guard at the entrance or along the sides of the hall.

Story Illustrations

Many paintings and relief carvings serve a narrative purpose, illustrating scenes from the Buddha's life (or previous lives). Temple fences and interior walls are often decorated with such scenes, arranged in chronological order.

As Buddhism spread, other cultures developed their own distinctive iconography. In China, images of Shakyamuni gradually took on a more Chinese appearance, and the figure of Guanyin developed into the graceful, standing feminine form now found throughout East Asia. There is a distinctive Korean representation of Maitreya as a pensive prince with one leg crossed over the other knee. This kind of image also spread to Japan at the time of Prince Shotoku. An example is the famous wooden statue of

Maitreya—the greatest of all national treasures—in Koryuji temple, Kyoto, which was founded in 622 for the repose of the prince.

Zen Art and the Tea Ceremony

The highly ritualized tea ceremony was introduced by Zen monks and spread from monasteries to become one of the most familiar symbols of Japanese culture, expressed in everything from special tea bowls to distinctive tea houses. The Zen influence is also reflected in the minimalism of Japanese painting, in which empty space plays a central role, and the raked-sand gardens (the space accented only by the occasional boulder) typically found in the courtyards of Zen temples such as Ryoanji in Kyoto. Another cultural expression of Zen values is the Japanese art of flower arranging, which originated in the practice of creating floral offerings for altars and special ceremonies.

Interaction and Adaptation

China

Chinese converts interpreted a number of Buddhist ideas in ways that served to harmonize them with indigenous teachings, especially those associated with Daoism (see Chapter 10). An example is what happened to the doctrine of no-soul (*anatman*) or emptiness. East Asian Mahayana Buddhists equated emptiness with nothingness (in Chinese, *wu*; in Japanese, *mu*), which in turn was interpreted in terms of fullness or the absolute.

The Buddhist concept of the afterlife was also adapted to conform to Chinese tradition. Chinese Buddhists extended the vague notion of the underworld and a home with their ancestors into a system of many-layered heavens and hells, with a variety of saviour figures. Among them are Guanyin and the bodhisattva Dizang ('earth-store'; in Japanese, Jizo), who relieves the suffering of those reborn in hell. Similarly, the scripture *Yulanpenjing* tells the story of a monk named Mulian, who after his enlightenment sought to rescue his mother from hell. This Buddhist expression of filial piety forms the basis for the 'all souls' day'—the fifteenth day of the seventh month of the year—in China, Korea and Japan, where it is known as Obon. Buddhism in turn had some influence on Chinese Daoism and folk religion, which incorporated the Buddhist idea of rebirth on a higher or lower level of life into the traditional system of retribution for good and evil.

The Buddhist tradition of monasticism was particularly alien to a social system based on kinship and veneration of ancestors. Not only were monks required to shave their hair, given by ancestors, but the practice of celibacy put the family lineage in jeopardy. Furthermore, endowments and donations enabled monasteries to acquire large areas of land and use serf labour to work the fields. Whereas Indian society respected the monks who begged for their living, Chinese society looked down on those who did no work. In time, therefore, Chinese monks incorporated labour into their discipline, growing their own food. As a Chinese Zen master proclaimed, 'A day without work is a day without eating.'

Imperial officials saw Buddhism as a direct threat to the state's authority, as this seventh-century memorial to the first Tang emperor shows:

> Thus people were made disloyal and unfilial, shaving their heads and discarding their sovereign and parents, becoming men without occupation and without means of subsistence, by which means they avoided the payment of rents and taxes. . . . I maintain that poverty and wealth, high station and low, are the products of a man's own efforts, but these ignorant Buddhist monks deceive people, saying with one voice that these things come from the Buddha. Thus they defraud the sovereign of his authority and usurp his power of reforming the people (Hughes and Hughes 1950:77).

Two centuries later, in 845, the Chinese state launched a campaign of persecution against Buddhism that led to the destruction of more than 40,000 temples and the laicization of 260,500 monks and nuns.

Folk Buddhism and the Milo Cult

Maitreya, the future Buddha, has more than once been the focus of political rebellions in China, including one that led to the founding of the Ming dynasty (1368).

The image of Maitreya underwent a transformation not unlike that of the Indian Avalokiteshvara into the Chinese Guanyin. Before the seventh century, Maitreya was a heroic figure, but he reappeared in the fifteenth century as Milo, a laughing monk with a pot-belly, carrying a hemp bag and accompanied by small children. According to the legend, Milo used to travel from village to village, putting interesting objects into his sack along the way. Then, on arriving at the next village, he would give them out as presents for the children, like Santa Claus. With his happy-go-lucky nature (in Sanskrit, *maitri* means friendly), his large belly, and his affinity for children, Milo, the 'Happy Buddha', reflects the importance that Chinese culture attached both to children and to worldly prosperity. His image is still popular today on altars and as an artistic decoration, especially in Chinese restaurants.

Korea

As in other countries, new cults emerged in Korea that owed their inspiration to Buddhist teachings. The best-known is Won Buddhism, which was founded in the early twentieth century. This new religion seeks to modernize the old religion by translating the sutras into modern Korean, emphasizing social service, especially in the cities, and permitting monks to marry. Its meditation object is an image of a black circle on a white background, representing the cosmic body of the Buddha, the *dharmakaya*. In South Korea today Buddhist practice may include elements from a wide range of traditions: in a single monastery, some monks will worship Buddha Amitabha of the Pure Land while others practise Son (Zen) meditation or recite sutras.

Japan

Dual Shinto

The introduction of Buddhism did not oblige the Japanese to choose between competing systems of beliefs and rituals. Instead, a syncretistic system developed called Dual Shinto that combined elements of both traditions.

Shinto shrines were built within Buddhist temples, and Buddhist sutras were chanted at Shinto shrines. Eventually *jingu-ji*, the 'shrine–temple' system arose, in which a Buddhist temple would be located within a larger Shinto shrine. The famous red gateways called *torii* were erected at the entrances to Buddhist temples as well as Shinto shrines. Shinto gods were worshipped alongside buddhas and bodhisattvas as their Japanese 'incarnations'. A rationale for this fusion was the concept of *honji suijaku*, or 'original site and local manifestations', referring to the Buddhist deities as original and the Shinto deities as their local forms (see also Chapter 10).

Tokugawa 'Temple Buddhism'

By the late sixteenth century, its great monasteries and armed warrior-monks had made Buddhism a sufficiently important political and military force to represent a challenge to the shoguns. Although the Tokugawa shogunate (1603–1867) preferred Confucianism as a source of ideological guidance, it eventually required that each household be registered with a Buddhist temple, partly to discourage the spread of Christianity.

Following the restoration of imperial rule in 1867–8, Buddhism again fell into disfavour, partly because of its institutional identification with the shogunate and partly because of its foreign origins. The Meiji government greatly favoured Shinto, and it ordered that Buddhist images be removed from Shinto shrines.

Women in Buddhism

Unlike many other religious traditions, Buddhism never defined women as the 'property' of men. Nevertheless, the early texts in particular indicate a profound ambiguity about the status of women in Buddhism. Shakyamuni himself is said to have cautioned the *bhikshus* against allowing themselves to be distracted by women:

> 'How are we to conduct ourselves, Lord, with regard to womankind?'
> 'Don't see them, Ananda.'
> 'But if we should see them, what are we to do?'
> 'Abstain from speech, Ananda.'
> 'But if they should speak to us, Lord, what are we to do?'
> 'Keep wide awake, Ananda'
> (Rhys Davids 1881:91)

Shakyamuni is also said to have resisted the formation of an order for women, the *bhikshuni sangha*, and to have predicted that its existence would shorten the life of his teachings. On the other hand, he did agree to its establishment, and encouraged close relatives, including his stepmother, to join it, maintaining that women were no less capable than men of becoming *Arhats*, and that the way to nirvana was the same regardless of gender:

> And be it woman, be it man for whom
> Such chariot doth wait, by that same car
> Into Nirvana's presence shall they come.
> (Horner 1930:104)

Other early Buddhist texts are similarly ambiguous about women. On the positive side, they describe approvingly the important role played by some rich women who were early benefactors of Buddhism. One book of the Pali canon, the *Therigatha*, even contains poems by early *bhikshunis*.

On the negative side, there was a distinct difference in status between monks and nuns. The male *sangha* officially outranked its female counterpart, and *bhikshunis* were not allowed to teach *bhikshus*. Furthermore, over time the *bhikshuni sangha* was allowed to die out in many Buddhist countries. The specific reasons may have varied, but in general the female order was simply more vulnerable than the male because it was smaller and less well connected to political power. In Sri Lanka, for instance, when both *sanghas* were devastated by famine, a king imported a number of monks from Siam to revive the male

Nuns chanting morning prayers in Lhasa (Roy C. Amore).

| Box 8.7   A Woman's Compassionate Wisdom

Once, while the Lord was staying among the Bhaggis on the Crocodile Hill . . . , the good man Nakulapita lay sick, ailing and grievously ill. And his wife Nakulamata said to him: 'I beg you, good man, do not die worried, for the Lord has said that the fate of the worried is not good. Maybe you think: "Alas, when I am gone, my wife will be unable to support the children or keep the household together." But do not think like that, for I am skilled in spinning cotton and carding wool, and I will manage to support the children and keep the household together after you are gone.

'Or maybe you think: "My wife will take another husband after I am gone." But do not think that, for you and I know that for sixteen years we have lived as householders in the holy life [that is, as celibates].

'Or maybe you think: "My wife, after I am gone, will have no desire to see the Lord or to see the monks." But do not think like that, for my desire to see them shall be even greater.

'Or maybe you think: "After I am gone, my wife will not have a calm mind." But do not think like that, for as long as the Lord has female disciples dressed in white, living at home, who gain that state, I shall be one. And if any doubt it, let them ask the Lord.

'Or maybe you think: "My wife will not win a firm foundation, a firm foothold in this Dhamma and discipline. She will not win comfort, dissolve doubt, be free from uncertainty, become confident, self-reliant, and live by the Teacher's words." But do not think like that, either. For as long as the Lord has female disciples dressed in white . . . I shall be one.'

Now, while Nakulapita was being counselled thus by his wife, even as he lay there his sickness subsided and he recovered. And not long after, he got up, and leaning on a stick, Nakulapita went to visit the Lord and told him what had happened. And the Lord said: 'It has been a gain; you have greatly gained from having Nakulamata as your counsellor and teacher, full of compassion for you, and desiring your welfare' (adapted from Dhammika 1989:111–13).

order, but there is no evidence of any effort to revive the female *sangha*. Recently, some effort has been made to revive the practice of *bhikshuni* ordination in Theravada countries.

Theravada laywomen practise devotions at home as well as at temples. Some women join orders, living a pious life, serving others, and in some cases taking vows of poverty and service even though they are not officially ordained. Some of these women are not interested in ordination because they feel they have more freedom to serve others if they are not bound by the *vinaya* rules.

In one Mahayana text, a princess named Jewel Brocade cleverly uses the Mahayana doctrine of the emptiness of all things to refute the patriarchal arguments of a monk. No distinction between male and female spiritual abilities is valid, she points out, because all distinctions are ultimately invalid:

You have said: 'One cannot attain Buddhahood within a woman's body.' Then, one cannot attain it within a man's body either. What is the reason? Because only the virtuous have eyes of Emptiness. The one who perceives through Emptiness is neither male nor female. The ears, nose, mouth, body, and mind are also Empty (Paul 1979:236).

Buddhism in the Modern World

India

After the tenth century, under pressure from both Hinduism and Islam, Buddhism declined in most parts of India. Muslim armies overran and destroyed many Buddhist universities, and some scholars, facing death if they did not convert to Islam, fled to Tibet. With its centres of learning gone and most of the population converting to Islam or Hinduism, Buddhism largely disappeared in India, except in the Assam region of the far northeast.

Only in the twentieth century did Buddhism begin to develop new roots in India. One catalyst was Dr Bhimrao Ambedkar (1893–1956), the lead author of the Indian constitution. Of low-caste background himself, Dr Ambedkar was a passionate advocate for the Dalits ('oppressed people'; formerly known as 'untouchables'), and in 1956 he publicly converted to Buddhism, encouraging many Dalits to do the same. Buddhism appeals to the 'Ambedkar Buddhists' because it is an indigenous Indian religion that does not advocate discrimination according to social or birth status. As the Buddha taught, 'Ask not about one's caste, ask about one's character.'

A second factor that has contributed to the revival of Buddhism in India is the fact that many Tibetans fleeing Chinese oppression have migrated to northwest India, where the Dalai Lama's government in exile has its headquarters. Tibetan monks and monasteries are now a common sight, especially in the hill regions of the northwest and at Bodh Gaya. Tibetans there tend to live in separate communities, but mingle freely with Hindus and Muslims in public.

A third factor is the work of the Mahabodhi Society, which since the 1950s has taken charge of restoring and running the main Buddhist pilgrimage sites in India and provides monasteries for visiting monks. As a result, increasing numbers of Buddhist pilgrims and tourists have been attracted to India. At the same time there has been a growing appreciation among Indian scholars of Shakyamuni's place in Indian history.

Sri Lanka

In the period of European expansion after the fifteenth century, Sri Lanka was colonized first by the Portuguese, then by the Dutch, and finally by the British. During the 500 years of rule by Christian Europeans, Buddhism declined in prestige but survived as the religion of most of the Sinhalese people, who take pride in their island's history as a stronghold of Buddhism.

The symbolic centre of Sri Lankan Buddhism is the temple in Kandy that holds what is said to be one of Shakyamuni's own teeth. The tooth is kept in the temple's shrine room under several miniature gold stupas. Celebrations at Kandy illustrate the cross-fertilization of Hindu and Buddhist custom in Sri Lanka. At the full moon in August, one of the miniature gold stupas that house the tooth is paraded on an elephant through the streets of Kandy for several nights. Each night the parade becomes larger and grander, and on the final night the sacred relic is given a ritual bath in a nearby river. Three other Buddhist temples and one Hindu temple participate in the Kandy Perahera, as the event is called. This torchlight procession, in which more than a hundred richly costumed elephants parade in groups of three, interspersed by musical and dancing groups, ranks as one of the world's most famous religious festivals.

Since independence in 1948, there has been a revival of Buddhist influence in Sri Lanka's ruling political parties, which draw support from the Sinhalese Buddhist majority. Feelings of oppression among some of the Tamil minority, who are mostly Hindus, led to the emergence in the 1970s of a separatist movement dedicated to creating an independent Tamil area in the northern and northeastern parts of the island. Since then the island has experienced recurring violence and bloodshed that has strained the relationship between Buddhists and Hindus and provoked many members of both religious communities to take up arms, despite the doctrine of non-violence taught by both. In 2004, for the first time in their history, monks formed a "National Heritage' political party and several were elected to parliament.

Southeast Asia

Theravada Buddhism also remains strong in mainland Southeast Asia, but there are challenges to be met. European colonial rule in the nineteenth and twentieth centuries brought heavy Christian influence to much of Southeast Asia: Protestant in Burma and Roman Catholic in Cambodia, Laos, and Vietnam. (The exception was Thailand, which was never colonized by a European power.) Although most Southeast Asian Theravadins resisted conversion, Christianity did make inroads among some non-Buddhist tribal peoples in Burma.

In modern Cambodia, the overthrow of Prince Norodom Sihanouk in 1955 marked the end of Buddhist kingship and the ideal of a government that provides the basic human needs for all citizens. The turmoil that followed—civil war, dominance by Vietnam, and in particular the period of Khmer Rouge rule under Pol Pot (1975–9)—seriously weakened the Cambodian *sangha*.

In Thailand Buddhism still has some political influence. The tradition of monastic training for the king continues, and at the beginning of each season the king still changes the clothing on the Buddha image in the famous Temple of the Emerald Buddha. These rituals symbolize the close connections between Thai Buddhism, the Thai monarchy, and Thai nationalism.

Several Buddhist reform movements have emerged in Thailand. For example, retreat centres have been established to reintroduce meditation among laypeople. The Thai reformer *bhikshu* Buddhadasa (1906–93) inspired many Thais to be more diligent in meditation and study. The Thai intellectual and social critic Sulak Sivaraksa (b. 1932) criticizes the culture of consumerism and argues for a Buddhist vision of society in which the means of development are harnessed for the good of everyone rather than the profit of multinational companies. He has helped found several Buddhist organizations dedicated to this 'middle path' toward development, including the International Network of Engaged Buddhists.

In Laos communist rule has cut the country's previous close ties with Thailand, and Buddhism has lost its political influence, but the traditional relationship of *bhikshus* and lay Buddhists survives in the villages.

Vietnam

Some Vietnamese Buddhists have turned to Theravada because they see it as purer than the Mahayana schools that Chinese settlers took with them when they immigrated. But Thien (Zen) and Tinh-do (Pure Land) remain the dominant sects. These two have influenced each other to the extent that all Thien monasteries also teach Pure Land practices. As in Korea and China, the Pure Land and Zen schools work closely together despite their philosophical differences (Pure Land relying on 'other-power' and Zen on 'self-power').

Although Vietnamese Buddhists have little public presence under communist rule, they attracted the world's attention in 1963. As a protest against the persecution of Buddhists under the Roman Catholic ruler Ngo Dinh Diem, a monk named Thich Quang Duc assumed the meditational position on a busy street in Saigon and had gasoline poured over him. Then he calmly struck a match and became a human torch, maintaining his meditative composure until he expired. Today a monument marks the intersection, and the car he arrived in is kept in a museum at his home temple. Several other monks soon followed suit. For the Vietnamese intellectual Thich Nhat Hanh, the self-immolations of 1963 were not suicides but acts of self-sacrifice intended to call attention to the suffering of the Vietnamese people. For him, changing the world requires that we first change our awareness of ourselves and the world, especially through meditation and the 'art of mindful living'. Commenting on the *Heart Sutra*, he says:

> If you are a poet, you will see clearly that there is a cloud floating in this sheet of paper. Without a cloud, there will be no rain; without rain, the trees cannot grow; and without trees, we cannot make paper. If we look even more deeply, we can see the sunshine, the logger who cut the tree, the wheat that became his bread, and the logger's father and mother.... We cannot just be by ourselves alone; we have to inter-be with every other thing (Nhat Hanh 1988:3).

China

After the invasion of Tibet by the army of communist China, the fourteenth Dalai Lama fled to India in 1959. A warm and approachable personality, he has emerged as a world figure, becoming a spokesman not only for Tibetan Buddhism but for Buddhism in general, and was awarded the Nobel Peace Prize in 1989. His acceptance by world leaders remains a sore point with the Chinese government, which does not like having attention called to his government in exile or to Chinese policies in the 'Tibetan Autonomous Region'. In 2004 the Dalai Lama's meetings with the prime minister of Canada and the president of the United States led China to threaten trade reprisals.

Buddhism has been steadily declining in China since the ninth century, and, despite all its efforts at renewal it has generally been regarded as peripheral to Chinese society and even irrelevant to modern life. Yet despite persecution, especially during the Cultural Revolution (1966–76), it continues to resurrect itself, adapting as necessary. Although leaders are appointed only with the approval of the Communist Party, today some Buddhist temples are once again attracting worshippers, albeit mostly of an older generation.

North and South Korea

In North Korea the communist regime has surpressed Buddhist activities. In South Korea, however, Buddhism experienced a renewal following the country's liberation from Japan in 1945. The more conservative Chogye sect struggled against the married monks of T'aego but won official support for their Son school in 1954, regaining control over virtually all the major monasteries. Korean Son is known for its strict discipline.

Japan

So closely is Buddhism associated with the ancestor cult that the Japanese term for the family shrine is *butsudan*: literally, the Buddhist altar. Buddhism is frequently called the religion of the dead because of its role in funerals, burials and memorial rituals, whereas Shinto is called the religion of the living because of its association with happy events such as childhood rituals and weddings.

In keeping with Japanese Buddhism's emphasis on remembering the dead, some temples have special areas where the memory of aborted fetuses is honoured. Grieving parents offer children's toys, appropriate to whatever the current ages of the 'children' would have been, to bring happiness to their spirits.

Buddhism remains a very important part of the Japanese culture, although it has little influence on political or economic policy.

Mongolia and Kalmykia

Mahayana Buddhism had been practised in Mongolia long before the thirteenth century, when Mongolia took control of Tibet. But Altan Khan's appointment of the first Dalai Lamas, in the late sixteenth century, sparked a revival of Tibetan-style Buddhism among Mongolian-speaking tribes. In the course of the next century, some of those tribes migrated as far west as the region of the Caspian Sea, where they eventually came under Russian control. Their descendants, the Kalmyks, still form the majority of the population in what is now the Republic of Kalmykia. In the twentieth century the Tibetan Buddhist traditions of the Mongolian and Kalmyk peoples were nearly wiped out by their communist states; most of the monasteries in Mongolia were destroyed, as were all the monasteries in Kalmykia. In 1990, however, Mongolia's communist regime was peacefully overthrown, and since then many people have been returning to their Buddhist roots. Similarly, the collapse of Soviet communism opened the way for a Buddhist revival among the Kalmyks.

The West

For Westerners, Buddhism was initially very difficult to comprehend. It had rituals, scriptures, and priests, but did not have the focus on God that Westerners expected of a 'religion'. European scholars first began studying Buddhist texts in the 1840s. The publication in 1879 of Edwin Arnold's *The Light of Asia*, a moving poetic account of the life of the Buddha, brought widespread attention to Buddhism. The book became so popular that one Christian writer countered with a book about Jesus entitled *The Light of Asia and the Light of the World*.

First-hand accounts of Buddhist meditational practices were not available in Western languages until the beginning of the twentieth century. By the 1930s, however, Buddhist study and meditation societies had been established in Great Britain, France, and Germany.

North America

Buddhism established its presence in North America in two ways: through immigration and through conversion. Its popular appeal in North America dates from the World's Parliament of Religions meeting in Chicago in 1893. Among the delegates to the Parliament was a Japanese Zen monk named Shaku Soyen (1856–1919), who later returned to the United States to spread Buddhism. His young translator, Daisetsu T. Suzuki (1870–1966), made two extended lecture visits to North America and wrote many popular books sprinkled with stories of Zen masters and the koans with which they challenged their disciples.

Westerners—including priests, artists, and therapists—have been especially interested in zazen (sitting meditation). Early zazen training centres were established by Japan-trained Zen masters Philip Kapleau (1912–2004) in Rochester, New York, and Robert Aitken (b. 1917) in Honolulu. In the 1950s Japan's Soka Gakkai movement brought its Nichiren practice of chanting homage to the *Lotus Sutra* to the West as well (see Chapter 10).

Since the 1960s, two lineages of Tibetan Buddhism have also gained converts in North America, usually under the guidance of a Tibetan *rinpoche*. The Kargyu lineage is represented both by the Naropa Institute in Boulder, Colorado, and by a community of Tibetans and converts based in Halifax, Nova Scotia, while the Dalai Lama's Gelugpa lineage has centres in New York and elsewhere.

Ethnic Congregations

Chinese and Japanese Buddhists began immigrating to Hawaii, California, and British Columbia in the late 1800s. As in Asia, Pure Land temples are the most common. The Buddhist Association of America (and of Canada) serves mainly Buddhists of Chinese background, while the Buddhist Churches of America (and of Canada) represents the followers of the True Pure Land tradition, who are mainly ethnic Japanese. Smaller ethnic networks exist as well.

With acculturation over time, some ethnic Buddhists have adopted Christian styles of worship, with pews, hymnals, and leaders who take on the roles expected of North American clergy. Some congregations have purchased older Christian church buildings and others have built new sanctuaries in contemporary architectural styles. There are Buddhist Sunday schools, Buddhist cemeteries, and Buddhist wedding rituals. Ethnic Buddhist temples in North America have not attracted many non-ethnic converts, but Buddhist meditation centres have been very successful in this regard. Without necessarily becoming Buddhists, many Westerners have adopted modified versions of Buddhist meditational practices in order to calm or focus their minds (athletes and performing artists in particular have found meditation to be helpful), and Buddhist (and

Hindu) values such as non-violence and notions of rebirth and karma have been widely influential. Some Buddhist centres have successfully combined traditional services, attended mainly by ethnic Buddhists, with meditation sessions.

Buddhist–Christian Dialogue

A lively Buddhist–Christian dialogue has emerged since the 1970s. One dimension of this dialogue focuses on meditation and spiritual practices. The Roman Catholic Trappist monk Thomas Merton is perhaps the most famous of the Christians who have written about Buddhist, especially Zen, meditation. In addition there have been numerous academic and theological discussions.

A second dimension of this dialogue has been reflected in several books comparing the lives or teachings of the Buddha and Jesus. Many writers have identified parallels between the two masters, despite their very different worldviews. Parallels between the birth stories, for example, have led some scholars to speculate that Buddhist traditions might have influenced the gospel accounts of Jesus. Other writers have called attention to the similarities between the Dharmapada teachings and the Sermon on the Mount, wondering whether the former might have influenced the latter. Well-known Christians, such as Hans Kuhn, have written favourably about the Buddha, and the Dalai Lama has written admiringly about Christ, describing him as a great person, 'of good heart'.

Buddhism Today

Some Buddhist leaders today feel a renewed sense of mission to teach a Buddhist alternative to modern schemes of economic development. Not surprisingly, they call for a middle path between the environmental and social disasters of overdevelopment on the one hand and underdevelopment on the other, advocating local-level, low-tech, people-oriented projects that will improve the economic prospects for everyone. They criticize megaprojects that uproot humans or animals and all activities that serve to make the rich richer and the poor poorer. Other Buddhists are dedicated to sharing a spiritual lifestyle based on non-violence and meditation, as an alternative to self-centred consumerism.

There is a growing spirit of cooperation among the various branches of Buddhism in most countries, and networks of Buddhists from various countries are being formed. Many now identify themselves first as Buddhists and only secondarily as Zen Buddhists or Theravada Buddhists. This tendency is strengthened by the willingness of many Buddhist periodicals now to publish articles by writers from various Buddhist traditions.

The sense of common purpose among Buddhists has been reinforced by the international exposure of the Dalai Lama, who has travelled widely and is recognized by most Buddhists around the world as their spokesperson. His forced exile is seen as a loss for Tibet, but in the long run it may provide the impetus that Buddhism needs to regain its traditional role as one of the world's most vigorous religions.

For 2,500 years, from Shakyamuni to the Dalai Lama, Buddhism has challenged the minds and enriched the spiritual lives of many millions of people. It has enjoyed imperial patronage and inspired rich artistic expression. It has spread far beyond the land of its origin.

Lumbini Park in southern Nepal preserves the sacred area where the Buddha was born, with old stupas, the pond where Mahamaya bathed, a Bodhi tree, and a park surrounded by monasteries for visiting monks.

Kathmandu There are two great Buddhist temples in the Kathmandu area. Svayambhunath, nicknamed the 'monkey temple', sits high on a hill, its Nepali-style 'eyes' overlooking the countryside. Bodhanath is a Tibetan-style stupa surrounded by shops and cafés.

Bodh Gaya in northeastern India preserves the area where the Buddha was enlightened. There is the huge Bodhi tree, a temple, and a park surrounded by temples and monasteries representing different schools of Buddhism. Many Tibetans come here in the winter for a festival that is usually attended by the Dalai Lama.

Sarnath is the deer park near Varanasi in northern India where the Buddha preached his first sermon. Sights include a new temple, several old stupas and temples, and a museum.

Kushinagar It was in a grove of trees near this town in northeastern India that the Buddha is said to have entered *parinirvana*.

Maharashtra state in west central India has two famous cave complexes. The Ajanta Caves, carved into a long, curving cliffside, are filled with sculpture and paintings. Similar caves are found at Ellora.

Kandy The Temple of the Tooth in Kandy is the most important Buddhist site in Sri Lanka. The midsummer Perahera festival is a spectacular parade of elephants, musicians, and dancers.

Bangkok On the grounds of the Grand Palace is the temple housing a famous jade sculpture known as the Emerald Buddha.

Angkor Thom in Cambodia is one of the world's great Buddhist temples. Nearby is the Hindu temple called Angkor Wat.

Lhasa is the site of the Potala Palace, the traditional home of the Dalai Lamas before the Chinese occupation of Tibet led the fourteenth Dalai Lama to relocate his headquarters in Dharmsala, India, as well as many famous temples such as the Jokhang and the surrounding Barkhor pilgrimage circuit.

Shaolin, in central China, is the home of both Zen Buddhism and the martial arts. The monastery has many buildings and statues of the early Zen patriarchs, and the town has dozens of martial-arts high schools. A two-hour hike up a mountain path leads to Bodhidharma's cave.

Nara, Japan's first capital, has beautiful wooden temples set in a deer park. Todai-ji is a tall wooden temple housing a huge bronze Buddha statue.

Kyoto, the second capital, has many famous temples as well, including the 'rock gardens' at Zen temples such as Ryoan-ji.

It has also experienced losses and setbacks. In India it was overshadowed and partially absorbed into Hinduism, and then was suppressed with the coming of Islamic rule. The disappearance of Buddhist kingship in much of Southeast Asia has weakened its political support in that region. And the spread of atheistic communism in several formerly Buddhist regions has been even more devastating.

Like other religions, Buddhism has also been challenged and called into question by modern, secular ways of life. Buddhists do not consider the scientific world view to represent a serious challenge, for the Buddha himself taught that everything is in process and subject to causation. Still, the concepts of karma and rebirth do not fit comfortably into the standard scientific world view. It is also true that *bhikshus* are no longer the main educators, social workers, dispute settlers, and advisers to the people in Buddhist countries, especially in the major cities. Their role has been reduced to that of ritual leaders and directors of religious education. Yet Buddhism has met these modern challenges and is not only surviving but attracting new followers, and Buddhists are not converting in any significant numbers to the other religions.

What gives Buddhism its energy? The answer may lie in the continuing power of the Triple Gem to shape spiritual life. Buddhists still feel confident in 'taking refuge' in the Buddha as a wise and compassionate teacher, in the dharma as a living set of teachings that go to the heart of reality, and in the *sangha* as a community of people on the path to enlightenment.

In the Buddhist countries of modern Asia, Buddhism will likely continue to be respected as the highest expression of spiritual wisdom—at least until the dharma wheel set in motion by Shakyamuni ceases to turn and the next buddha, Maitreya, turns the wheel once again.

Glossary

anatman 'No-soul', the doctrine that the human person is impermanent, a changing combination of components.

Arhat/lohan A worthy one or saint, someone who has realized the ideal of spiritual perfection in Theravada Buddhism.

bhikshu, bhikshuni An ordained Buddhist monk and nun respectively.

bodhisattva In Theravada, a being who is on the way to enlightenment or buddhahood but has not yet achieved it; in Mahayana, a celestial being who forgoes nirvana in order to save others.

Chan/Zen A tradition centred on the practice of meditation and the teaching that ultimate reality is not expressible in words or logic, but must be grasped through direct intuition; see also **koan** and **zazen**.

dana A 'giving' ritual, in which Theravada families present gifts of food, at their homes or a temple, to *bhikshus* who conduct rituals including chanting and merit-transfer.

dharma In Buddhist usage, teaching or truth concerning the ultimate nature of things.

duhkha The suffering, psychological as well as physical, that characterizes human life.

Hinayana 'Lesser Vehicle'; the pejorative name given by the Mahayana ('Greater Vehicle') school to earlier Indian Buddhist sects, of which Theravada became the most important.

karma The energy of the individual's past thoughts and actions, good or bad; it determines rebirth within the 'wheel' of *samsara* or cycle of rebirth that ends only when *parinirvana* is achieved. Good karma is also called 'merit'.

koan/*gongan* A paradoxical thought exercise used in the Chan–Zen tradition to provoke a breakthrough in understanding by forcing students past the limitations of verbal formulations and logic.

lama 'Wise teacher'; a title given to advanced teachers as well as the heads of various Tibetan ordination lineages.

Mahayana 'Greater Vehicle'; the form of Buddhism that emerged around the first century in India and spread first to China and then to Korea and Japan.

mandala A chart-like representation of cosmic Buddha figures that often serves as a focus of meditation and devotion in the Mahayana and Vajrayana traditions.

mudra A pose or gesture in artistic representations of Buddha figures; by convention, each *mudra* has a specific symbolic meaning.

nirvana The state of bliss associated with final enlightenment; nirvana 'with remainder' is the highest level possible in this life, and nirvana 'without remainder' is the ultimate state. See also *parinirvana*.

pagoda A multi-storey tower, characteristic of Southeast and East Asian Buddhism, that developed out of the South Asian mound or **stupa**.

parinirvana The ultimate perfection of bliss, achievable only on departing this life, as distinct from the nirvana with the 'remainder' achievable while one is still in the present existence.

prajna The spiritual wisdom or insight necessary for enlightenment.

Pure Land The comfortable realm in the western region of the heavens reserved for those who trust in the merit and grace of its lord, the celestial buddha Amitabha (Amida).

rinpoche A title of respect for Tibetan teachers or leading monks.

samadhi A higher state of consciousness, achieved through meditation.

sangha The 'congregation' or community of Buddhist monks and nuns. Some forms of Buddhism also refer to the congregation of lay persons as a *sangha*.

Shakyamuni 'Sage of the Shakya clan', a title used to refer to the historical figure of Siddhartha Gautama, the Buddha.

shunyata The Emptiness that is held to be ultimately characteristic of all things, according to Madhyamika doctrine.

stupa Originally a hemispherical mound built to contain cremation ashes or a sacred relic; in East Asia the stupa developed into the tower-like **pagoda**.

sutra A discourse attributed either to Shakyamuni himself or to an important disciple.

Theravada 'Teaching of the elders', the dominant form of Buddhism in Sri Lanka and Southeast Asia.

Tripitaka/Tipitaka 'Three baskets'; the collection of early sacred writings whose three sections consist of discourses attributed to the Buddha, rules of monastic discipline, and treatises on doctrine.

Vaishakha/Vesak A Theravada festival held at the full moon around early May, marking Shakyamuni's birth, enlightenment, and *parinirvana*.

Vajrayana The tantric branch of Buddhism that became established in Tibet and the Himalayan region, and later spread to Mongolia and eventually India.

vinaya The rules of practice and conduct for monks; a section of the Pali canon.

vipassana 'Insight' or 'mindfulness' meditation practised by Theravada Buddhists.

zazen Sitting meditation in the Chan–Zen tradition.

Zen See **Chan**.

Further Reading

Amore, Roy C. 1978. *Two Masters, One Message*. Nashville: Abindgon. Compares and contrasts the figures of Buddha and Jesus.

Batchelor, Martine. 2006. *Women in Korean Zen: Lives and Practices*. Syracuse: Syracuse University Press. A good account based on ten years of Zen practice in Korea.

Dalai Lama. 1990. *Freedom in Exile: The Autobiography of the Dalai Lama*. New York: HarperCollins.

Dalai Lama, His Holiness The. 2002. *How to Practice: The Way to a Meaningful Life*. Trans. and ed. by Jeffrey Hopkins. New York: Pocket Books.

Fisher, Robert E. 1993. *Buddhist Art and Architecture*. London: Thames & Hudson. An overview of South and East Asian developments.

Gross, Rita M. 1993. *Buddhism after Patriarchy: A Feminist History, Analysis, and Reconstruction of Buddhism*. Albany: State University of New York Press. Material for provocative debate.

Lopez, Donald S., Jr. 2002. *The Story of Buddhism: A Concise Guide to its History and Teachings*. New York: HarperCollins.

Queen, Christopher S., and Sallie B. King, eds. 1996. *Engaged Buddhism: Liberation Movements in Asia*. Albany: State University of New York Press. Twentieth-century activism from India and Thailand to Tibet and Japan.

Seager, Richard Hughes. 2000. *Buddhism in America*. New York: Columbia University Press, 2000.

Shaw, Ronald D.M., trans. 1961. *The Blue Cliff Records: The Hekigan Roku [Pi yen lu] Containing One Hundred Stories of Zen Masters of Ancient China*. London: M. Joseph. Koans especially prized by the Japanese.

Sivaraksa, Sulak. 2005. *Conflict, Culture, Change: Engaged Buddhism in a Globalizing World*. Somerville, MA: Wisdom Publications. A recent book by an important Thai Buddhist social critic.

References

Bloom, Alfred. 1965. *Shinran's Gospel of Pure Grace*. Tucson, AZ: University of Arizona Press.

Chen, Kenneth. 1964. *Buddhism in China: A Historical Survey*. Princeton: Princeton University Press.

de Bary, William Theodore, ed. 1958. *Sources of Indian Tradition*. New York: Columbia University Press.

Dhammika, Sravasti, ed. 1989. *Buddha Vacana*. Singapore: Buddha Dhamma Mandala Society.

Horner, I.B. 1930. *Women under Primitive Buddhism: Laywomen and Almswomen*. New York: Dutton.

_____, trans. 1967. *The Collection of the Middle Length Sayings (Majjhimanikaya)*. vol. 3. London: Luzac.

Hughes, Ernest R., and K. Hughes. 1950. *Religion in China*. London: Hutchinson.

Nanamoli [formerly Osborne Moore], trans. 1972. *The Life of the Buddha as It Appears in the Pali Canon, the Oldest Authentic Record*. Kandy: Buddhist Publication Society.

Nhat Hanh, Thich. 1988. *The Heart of Understanding: Commentaries on the Prajñaparamita Heart Sutra*. Berkeley: Parallax Press.

Paul, Diana Y., ed. 1979. *Women in Buddhism: Images of the Feminine in Mahayana Tradition*. Berkeley: Asian Humanities Press.

Rhys Davids, Caroline A. 1964. *Psalms of the Early Buddhists*. vol. 1 (Psalms of Sisters). London: Luzac, for the Pali Text Society.

Rhys Davids, Thomas W., trans. 1881. *Buddhist Sutras* (F. Max Müller, ed., *Sacred Books of the East*, 11). Oxford: Clarendon Press.

_____, trans. 1880. *The Questions of King Milinda*, Part I (sbe, 35). Oxford: Clarendon Press.

Suzuki, D.T. 1991. *An Introduction to Zen Buddhism*. New York: Grove Press.

Tsunoda, Ryusaku. 1958. *Sources of Japanese Tradition*. New York: Columbia University Press.

Chinese Religions:
Confucianism and Daoism

ROY C. AMORE | JULIA CHING

In 2004 an Oregon woman starts a website offering advice on relationships, furniture-arranging, and child-rearing, among other things, based on ancient Chinese numerology and feng shui. The site receives so many hits that the service has to be upgraded, and the story makes the television news across the country. Meanwhile, in certain regions of North America, some builders and realtors are consulting feng shui experts to learn what kinds of designs will appeal to the growing number of clients who want homes consistent with feng shui guidelines for good energy flow. What is feng shui and why is it so intriguing for people outside the Chinese community? Why are there dozens of books on Daoism for sale in North America? What accounts for the continuing Western interest in the *I Ching* (*Book of Changes*)? A better understanding of China's spiritual traditions may help us to answer these questions.

Introduction

At the centre of Chinese spirituality is the figure of the sage. Like the guru or *muni* (spiritual guide) in the Indian tradition, the sage is someone whose wise teachings and outstanding character make him a model for others to follow. There is no exact equivalent in the West, which has traditionally revered various prophets in the belief that they speak on behalf of God. By contrast, China has revered the sages whose own lives are in harmony with what Confucius called **Tian** ('Heaven', or the divine) and Laozi called the **Dao** (the 'Way'). Typically, a sage would himself look back to earlier sages with whom he generally agreed, resulting in the development of several traditions or schools of thought. By the time of the Han Dynasty (206 BCE–220 CE) two main traditions had emerged: Confucianism and Daoism.

The Confucian tradition takes its name from the sage known in the West as Confucius and in Chinese as Kongfuzi (the 'zi' ending is an honorific meaning 'master', conferred on Kong and other sages after their deaths). Starting with the Han court, the Confucian tradition served as the basis of political thought for many centuries, and anyone who wanted to be a civil servant ('mandarin') had to pass exams on Confucian texts. Although Buddhism and Daoism were more influential at the court of the Tang dynasty (618–907 CE), Confucianism was revived in a form known as Neo-Confucianism during the Song dynasty in the eleventh and twelfth centuries.

The Daoist tradition goes back to the sage Laozi, who taught a spirituality based on harmony with nature and a politics that might be summarized as 'the less government, the better'.

c. 1766 BCE	Beginning of the Shang dynasty
552? BCE	Birth of Confucius (d. 479); Laozi may have been a contemporary
c. 470 BCE	Birth of Mozi (d. 391), founder of the rival school known as Moism
c. 343 BCE	Birth of Mencius (d. 289); the Daoist philosopher Zhuangzi is thought to have been a contemporary
213 BCE	Confucian books burned by the first emperor, Qin Shi Huangdi, who favoured the Legalist School
125 BCE	Confucian classics are made the basis of the state examination system
142 CE	Zhang Daoling founds the Daoist Heavenly Masters sect
c. 450	Daoist canon organized in three 'Caverns'
1130	Birth of Zhu Xi, Neo-Confucian metaphysician (d. 1200)
c. 1300	Perfect Truth sect of Daoism founded
1313	The Neo-Confucian Four Books are incorporated into the examination curriculum
1472	Birth of Wang Yangming, Neo-Confucian philosopher of mind (d. 1529)
1851	Taiping rebels establish their capital in Nanjing, China
1919	Anti-traditionalist May Fourth movement emerges
1921	Chinese Communist party formed
1949	Chinese Communist party establishes the People's Republic of China
1966–76	All forms of religion suppressed during the Cultural Revolution

The Chinese refer to the 'three philosophies'. The third major tradition, besides Confucianism and Daoism, is Buddhism, which introduced to China the Indian concepts of karma and rebirth as well as practices such as celibacy, vegetarianism, and monasticism. These Indian ideas and practices, discussed at length in Chapter 8, influenced both Confucianism and Daoism. In addition we will discuss one other ancient tradition (Mohism) and several more recent religious movements, including Falun Gong.

The transliteration system used in China and in this book is called pin-yin. Readers should keep in mind that it has two special letters that are not pronounced in the usual English way: Q is pronounced something like the English 'ch', and x makes a soft 'sh' sound that does not exist in English. Thus the name of the city X'ian is pronounced something like 'shi-an' and that of the town Qufu is pronounced 'chu-fu'. Another complication is that many English sources use a second transliteration system called Wade-Giles, in which many words, including the names of the sages, are spelled quite differently. For example, the capital of China is Beijing in pin-yin but Peking in Wade-Giles.

Confucianism

Origins

'Confucianism' is the Western designation for the ideology developed by Confucius (552?–479 BCE). The Chinese have usually preferred the term *Rujia* or *Rujiao*, meaning the school or teachings of the scholars. Etymologically, it has been claimed that the word *ru*, 'scholars', is related to the word for 'weaklings' or 'cowards'. It is supposed to have referred originally to those aristocrats of antiquity who were neither landlords or warriors but lived off their knowledge of rituals, history, music, numbers, or archery.

Eventually, 'the school of *ru*' came to designate both the ancient ethical wisdom that Confucius passed on to his contemporaries and the tradition as it developed after his time. Confucius and the school named after him offered an ethical answer to questions regarding life's meaning and order in society, an answer that dominated Chinese philosophical thinking for more than 2,000 years.

Many of the source materials regarding the period in which Confucius lived are coloured by Confucian ideas, and were either composed or edited later. Given the scarcity of solid historical evidence and the abundance of legend, what can we say about Confucius's life?

His name was Kong Qiu, but after death he was called Master Kong (Kongfuzi in one transliteration system and K'ung fu-tze in the other). Jesuit missionaries latinized his name, giving us 'Confucius' in English. He was a native of the small state of Lu, born near modern Qufu, Shandong, in an era when the country was divided among feudal lords under the rule of the Zhou dynasty (1022 BCE–226 CE). His parents' circumstances were far from comfortable, but the family were said to be direct descendants of the Shang royal house (the predecessors of the Zhou, c. 1600–1000 BCE).

NUMBERS
Confucians: Estimates range from 6 to 20 million.
Daoists: Estimates range up to 30 million.
Chinese popular religion: Estimates range from 100 to 300 million.

DISTRIBUTION
Both Daoism and Confucianism are found throughout East Asia, with minorities elsewhere.

PRINCIPAL HISTORICAL PERIODS
6th century BCE	Beginning of era of the sages and early texts
2nd century BCE	Beginning of classic period of influence under the Han Dynasty
12th century CE	Beginning of Neo-Confucian era of influence

FOUNDERS AND LEADERS
Confucians revere the sages Confucius, Mencius, and Xunzi. Daoists revere the sages Laozi and Zhuangzi.

DEITIES
The sages are not gods. But the Confucian concept of Heaven represented a form of ancient deity, and Daoism has a pantheon of gods, headed by the Jade Emperor.

AUTHORITATIVE TEXTS
For Confucianism, the Five Classics and Four Books. The Daoist canon, the *Daozang*, comprises more than 1,000 books, the most important of which are the *Daodejing* and the *Zhuangzi*.

NOTEWORTHY TEACHINGS
Confucianism emphasizes social harmony and the five relationships. Its central principles are *ren* (goodness, benevolence, humanity) and *li* (ritual, propriety); the concept of the 'Mandate of Heaven' was also important in political contexts. Daoism emphasizes living in harmony with nature and the Dao; its essential teachings involve the concepts of the Dao within and the cosmic Dao.

According to one legend, when Kong"s mother was pregnant, a unicorn came to her with a gold tablet in its mouth that said she would give birth to a king without a kingdom, who would help the Zhou dynasty. Another legend says that when he was five, he would get his friends to pretend they were court officials, bowing to one another and performing rituals.

Kong described his own situation as humble. The highest public office he occupied was that of a police commissioner in his home state—a job that lasted scarcely a year. It is said that he quit his position in protest over corruption in the civil service. He then spent at least ten years travelling from village to village, recruiting and training young men as potential civil servants. A modern equivalent might be a professor of political science or public administration, someone who may have little or no direct experience in government work but nevertheless has the theoretical knowledge required to prepare others for it. He may not have made much of an impact during his lifetime, and the ruthless unifier of China, Qin Shi Huangdi (r. 221–210 BCE) denounced his school and burned its books. Yet the theories and principles that Kong taught eventually became the basis of China's formal civil-service training system.

The entrance courtyard of the Confucian Academy in Nanjing, where aspiring mandarins studied for the civil-service examination. The colourful decorations in the foreground were part of a children's festival (Roy Amore).

The most important of those principles is known in China by a phrase that has been translated as 'rectification of names'. Expressed by Confucius himself in eight cryptic words—'Ruler, ruler, minister, minister; father, father; son, son'—what it means is that names should represent realities, and that the person appointed to a position must live up to his job title. Thus civil servants should be recruited not just from the ruling class but from among the brightest and most ethical candidates, regardless of their social class. In modern terms, this means appointing officials on the basis of training and talent rather than family connections.

Ideally, for Confucius, there would be an 'aristocracy of merit' rather than an 'aristocracy of money': the best-qualified candidates would get the government jobs. At a time when rich families regularly bribed high officials to appoint their sons to positions in which they in turn would have the power to demand bribes, such reforms were not widely embraced. It took several centuries, but Kongfuzi's 'aristocracy of merit' was eventually established. While most other countries continued to be administered by sons of the aristocracy until the modern era, China was administered by mandarins (bureaucrats) recruited from the brightest young men—though not women—regardless of social class.

Although Kong was literate, he did not write down his teachings. They were not recorded until after his death, when his students recalled their sessions with the master, along with what they knew of his encounters with others, and collected them in a book called the *Analects of Confucius*. The *Analects* reveal a great teacher who used a question-and-answer approach similar to the one pioneered in the West by Socrates. One of Kong's favourite tactics was to ask students what they would do if they were placed in a particular administrative position. One student said that he if were the top administrator he would first secure the state's borders; then he would turn his attention to feeding the people; and when that was done, he would see to the arts and music. In other words, his priority ranking put military security first, economic development second, and high culture third.

This attention to culture marks a striking difference between Confucian thought and the modern school of political thinkers who regard arts and culture as irrelevant to political life. Kong really did believe that music and court rituals were an essential part of an ordered state, and he expected high officials to promote cultural activities. He himself played the zither (a stringed instrument), and after teaching students in a village he would bring it out and learn to play the local music. It is said that if necessary he would stay awake all night learning a difficult piece, but that once he had learned it, he never forgot how to play it.

The *Analects* show the human side of Confucius as well. When he asked his students what they would do if put into a civil-service position that very day, one student was reluctant to answer. Kongfuzi insisted, and the timid student confessed that on such a fine spring day he would like to get some of his male and female friends together, find a pleasant spot in the woods, and pass the time talking and playing music. 'Ah,' said Confucius, 'now that's a man after my own heart.'

In his later years he stayed closer to home and devoted more time to pursuits such as reading and music. Some legends say that he edited the five classic texts (see p. 450) during this period. He lived to roughly seventy, and became historically influential only after his death. He did not develop any systematic doctrinal structure with separate categories for manners, morals, law, philosophy, and theology. His teachings were systematized only by his successors Mencius (372–289 BCE) and Xunzi (c. 312–238 BCE).

A passage from the *Analects* offers some insight into Kong's thinking. The reference to not 'overstepping the line' suggests his high regard for propriety. At the same time, his profound reverence for the will of Heaven underlines the basically religious orientation of his life and character:

> At fifteen I set my heart on learning [to be a sage].
> At thirty I became firm.
> At forty I had no more doubts.
> At fifty I understood Heaven's Will.
> At sixty my ears were attuned [to it].
> At seventy I could follow my heart's desires, without overstepping the line.
> (*Analects* 2:4; adapted from Waley 1938:88)

The reference to ears 'attuned to Heaven's will' is of particular interest, since the pictograph for 'sage' was made up of a large ear and a small mouth. While Kong consistently exalted the sages of the past, we might infer that he also recognized himself as a wise man.

It is difficult to know how Kong understood the term 'Tian'. Was Tian a person-like god of the sky, like Indra, Zeus, or Yahweh, or an impersonal force like the Brahman of the Hindu *Upanishads* or the 'Way' of Daoism? This account of his spiritual development seems to suggest that Kong saw Tian as representing both a personal god and a higher power, order, and law that displaced the many ancestral gods such as Shangdi, the 'Lord-on-high' of the Shang dynasty. In fact, the word 'Tian', which occurs 18 times in

---

| Box 9.1 | **From *The Analects of Confucius***

In periods of purification, [Confucius] invariably wore a house robe made of the cheaper sort of material . . . he invariably changed to a more austere diet and, when at home, did not sit in his usual place (*Analects* 10:7, Lau 1979:102).

Chi-lu asked how the spirits of the dead and the gods should be served. The Master said, 'You are not able even to serve man. How can you serve the spirits?'
'May I ask about death?'
'You do not understand even life. How can you understand death?' (11:12, Lau, 107).

The Master was seriously ill. Tzu-lu asked permission to offer a prayer. The Master said, 'Was such a thing ever done?' Tzu-lu said, 'Yes, it was. The prayer offered was as follows: pray thus to the gods above and below.' The Master said, 'In that case, I have long been offering my prayers' (7:35, Lau, 91).

When Yen Yuan [Confucius's best disciple] died [at the age of thirty], the Master said, 'Alas! Heaven has bereft me! Heaven has bereft me!' (11:9, Lau, 107).

the *Analects*, is mentioned only once in association with Shangdi. Whatever Kong's interpretation of the term, his main point was that people, especially rulers, should obey Heaven: 'He who offends against Heaven has none to whom he can pray' (*Analects* 3:13; Legge 1893, 1:159).

Kong sought to understand and follow Heaven's will. He lived in an age of turmoil, during which the ancient religious beliefs, with their emphasis on divination and sacrifice, were thrown into question. He idealized the sage kings of the early Zhou dynasty and was critical of the way their legacy and high principles had been allowed to fade in his day. Was he, then, a conservative or a reformer, or perhaps a revolutionary?

'I am a transmitter,' he said, 'not an innovator; I believe in antiquity and love the ancients' (*Analects* 7:1; Waley 1938:123). His rhetoric was conservative and, as we will see, so was his approach to family relations. But he does not seem to have been conservative or pious about the religious practices of his day. Despite his insistence on respect for the gods and spirits, he also advised human beings to keep a distance from them. In short, the fact that he transmitted ancient culture did not mean that he admired everything in that culture equally.

Kong's political teachings were often reformist or even revolutionary. By putting the nobility of virtue ahead of the nobility of birth, he laid the groundwork for a social revolution. Opening up civil-service positions to bright young men from any class was not a Marxist-style revolution, in which the lower class overthrows the rulers, but it was radical all the same. His social teachings eventually led to reforms as well. His general preference for education and philosophy over military service was eventually reflected across Chinese society, which came to admire scholars above all others, while treating soldiers as virtual outcasts. (A disdain for military service persisted in Chinese families until modern times, when the communist government tried to raise the prestige of soldiers.)

The German philosopher Karl Jaspers (1883–1969) considered Confucius to be one of the great philosophers of what he called the axial age, a 'paradigmatic individual' comparable to figures such as Socrates, Jesus of Nazareth, and the Buddha. Each of these men lived in a time of social crisis to which he sought to respond with teachings aimed at all people. Each attracted and accepted disciples regardless of their social backgrounds. And in each case, Jaspers argues, the teachings concerned not abstract metaphysics but the higher order of things. Each offered his own interpretation of this higher order, emphasizing ethical principles in opposition to external conformism and hypocrisy. All made clear moral demands, and all lived what they preached.

Crystallization

The Confucian Virtues

The great merit of Confucianism, it has sometimes been said, is its discovery of the ultimate in the relative—that is, in the moral character of human relationships. Confucius himself taught a doctrine of reciprocity and neighbourliness: 'to regard every one as a very important guest, to deal with the people as one would assist at a sacrifice, never do to others what you would not like them to do to you' (*Analects* 12:2 and 15:23; adapted from Waley 1938:162,198). The last part of this quotation offers what has come to be called the 'negative Golden Rule' or 'Silver Rule'.

Confucianism characteristically speaks of '**Five Relationships**', each of which comes with a particular set of norms and duties. The relationships are those of ruler and minister, father and son, husband and wife, elder and younger brother, and friend and friend. Three of these are family relationships, while the other two are usually understood in terms of relations within a family. For example, the ruler–minister relationship resembles the father–son, while friendship resembles brotherliness. For this reason Confucian society regards itself as a large family: 'Amidst the four seas all men are brothers' (*Analects* 12:5; adapted from Waley 1938: 163–4).

The responsibilities implied by these relationships are reciprocal. A minister owes loyalty to his ruler, and a child owes filial respect to a parent, while the ruler must care for his subjects and the parent must care for the child. At the same time, each of the Five Relationships is clearly hierarchical. Even in the horizontal relationship between friends, seniority of age demands a certain respect. And although today it might seem more natural to see the husband–wife relationship as paralleling the one between siblings, in the past it was usually compared to the ruler–minister relationship, with the husband as ruler of the family.

The idea of filial respect or **filial piety** has been particularly important in Chinese society and is closely connected to what has often been called the 'ancestor cult'. Thus it was the filial duty of each new generation to have progeny in order to continue performing the rituals for the ancestors so that they might be fed and happy in the afterlife—a duty that in turn served for centuries as the ethical justification for polygamy. The obligations of filial piety have also promoted a strong tradition of mutual help within the extended family, among more distant clan members and even people from the same town, or people who bear the same surname and are therefore presumed to be descendants of the same ancestor. The central teaching of Confucius, and his main legacy, is the virtue of *ren*—a word written with the component 'human' and a component that may be read as either 'two' or 'above'. It is pronounced the same as the word for human being and is translated variously as 'goodness', 'benevolence', 'humanity', and 'humanheartedness'; essentially, *ren* means proper behaviour between persons.

In the past *ren* had been a virtue expected only of gentlemen, similar to the concept of 'noblesse oblige'—the idea that nobility came with obligations, and that it was the duty of the superior person to treat his inferiors with generosity and consideration. Confucius transformed *ren* into a universal virtue, one of the qualities that can make a human being a sage. The later application of his teachings drew from this a social implication: that moral merit, not noble birth, should be the criterion for status as a gentleman. Like many moral philosophers, Confucius offers both a description of human nature and a standard to aspire to. Descriptively, *ren* is rooted in human sentiment. Prescriptively, it is a fundamental pattern for life.

Ren is associated both with loyalty (*zhong*) to one's own heart and conscience and with reciprocity (*shu*)—respect and consideration for others (*Analects* 4:15). It is also related to *li*, a term that is often translated as 'ritual propriety' in the context of social behaviour rather than religion.

While the natural feelings underlying kinship call for special consideration, the natural feelings aroused by a neighbour's need for help are also recognized. To help a

| Box 9.2 | Confucius on the Gentleman

Tzu-kung asked about the gentleman. The Master said, 'He puts his words into action before allowing his words to follow his action' (*Analects* 2:13; Lau 1979:64).

The Master said, 'The gentleman devotes his mind to attaining the Way and not to securing food. Go and till the land and you will end up by being hungry, as a matter of course; study, and you will end up with the salary of an official, as a matter of course. The gentleman worries about the Way, not about poverty' (15:32, Lau 136).

The Master said, 'There are three things constantly on the lips of the gentleman, none of which I have succeeded in following: "A man of benevolence never worries; a man of wisdom is never in two minds; a man of courage is never afraid."' Tzu-kung said, 'What the Master has just quoted is a description of himself.' (14:28, Lau 128)

Tzu-lu asked about the gentleman. The Master said, 'He cultivates himself and thereby achieves reverence.'
'Is that all?'
'He cultivates himself and thereby brings peace and security to his fellow men.'
'Is that all?'
'He cultivates himself and thereby brings peace and security to the people.' (14:42, Lau 131)

neighbour is to act with the kind of empathy and universal love illustrated in the Christian parable of the Good Samaritan.

Family relations provide a model for behaviour in the wider society. Respect others' elders as you would respect your own; be kind to the children and younger relatives of others as you would be to your own. This philosophy is reflected in both the strong sense of solidarity in the Chinese family and the family-like solidarity of Confucian social organizations in overseas Chinese communities.

Many customs rooted in filial piety are still practised today. For example, adult children will often 'pay' part of their salary to their parents even when the latter do not need help, and many modern Chinese still expect the oldest son to live with his parents. Even grown children with their own homes are often expected to refer to their parents' house as 'home', as if they were still living there, and to 'go home' for dinner regularly—if not every night, at least on weekends. In addition, male grandchildren are taken 'home' for visits every week, often for Sunday lunch. Female grandchildren may not receive as much attention because they will not 'carry the family name'.

The Confucian Classics

The primary texts of early Confucianism are known as the **Five Classics**. Their diverse contents—from divination to history to love songs—offer a broad picture of the subjects of interest in the era of Confucius. They also suggest a clear sense of the authority of past tradition.

- The *Book of Changes* (*Yijing* or *I-ching*) is a divination manual attributed to the sages of old. It consists of short oracles arranged under 64 **hexagrams**—symbols made up of combinations of broken and unbroken lines in groups of six—with commentaries that reflect early cosmological and metaphysical speculation on concepts such as yin-yang. This book has become quite popular in the West, usually under the title *I Ching*.
- The *Book of History* (*Shang shu*, literally 'ancient documents') is mainly a collection of speeches by royalty and chief ministers, along with narrative accounts of royal achievements and principles of government, arranged chronologically. Some of the allegedly older chapters have been discredited.
- The *Book of Poetry* or *Odes* (*Shijing*) is essentially a collection of 305 verses in various genres, from hunting and love songs to banquet songs and state hymns. For many centuries the love songs were interpreted as political allegories; it took the twelfth-century philosopher Zhu Xi to recognize their actual meaning.
- The *Classic of Rites* is an entire corpus. It includes the *Ceremonials* (*Yili*), an early manual for the nobility, detailing the etiquette for everything from marriages, funerals, and sacrifices to archery contests. There is also the *Book of Rites* (*Liji*), which contains treatises on education, rituals, music, and philosophy as well as ritual and government regulations. Another component, the *Institutes of Zhou* (*Zhouli*), appears to be an idealized description of government offices in early Zhou times.
- The *Spring–Autumn Annals* (*Chunqiu*) are essentially a chronicle of the state of Lu, Kong's native state, purporting to explain the decline of the ancient political and moral order. The annals cover the period from 722 to 481 BCE, a period accordingly known as the 'Spring–Autumn Period'.

All five of these texts have in the past been attributed to Confucius, either as editor or, in the case of the *Spring–Autumn Annals*, as author. He is also said to have added the 'Appendices' to the *Book of Changes* and to have purged the *Book of Poetry* of its more licentious contents. But modern scholars no longer take these claims seriously. It is true that the core of many of these classic texts goes back to the time of Confucius and even earlier; the antiquity of the texts shows the ancient lineage of the school of *ru* ('scholars'). But each of them underwent a long period of evolution and includes material added after the time of Confucius. There was also a sixth classic on music, though it has been lost.

The textual situation was complicated by the ruthless emperor Qin Shi Huangdi, the unifier of China, whose clan name—Qin, formerly spelled Chin—may be the source of the English word 'China'. (It was near Qin's tomb that the famous army of life-sized terracotta warriors and horses was found in 1974 near modern Xian.) Qin surrounded himself with officials of the Legalist school (see p. 465) who strongly opposed Confucian thought, and under their influence he had many Confucian books burned in 213 BCE. He also unified the writing system, making it possible for all Chinese to read the same text; as a result, however, later scholars would have great difficulty deciphering older scripts when ancient texts that had survived in hiding were unearthed.

The Confucian texts came back into favour under the Han rulers who replaced the Qin, but the process of restoration was complicated by forgeries and the diverse schools of transmission that had developed since the time of Confucius. In 125 BCE the Five Classics were made the basis of examinations in the imperial college. The requirement that aspiring scholar-officials master their contents established the supremacy of the Confucian school. To ensure proper transmission, the classical texts were more than once inscribed literally on stone. In time a corpus of commentaries developed, establishing various traditions of textual exegesis.

Three other works are also considered important early Confucian texts. The *Classic of Filial Piety* (*Xiaojing*), written in the form of a dialogue between Confucius and a disciple, teaches filial piety as the foundation of all knowledge and action. The *Analects of Confucius*, as we have already seen, is a collection of his teachings as remembered by students. Finally, the *Book of Mencius* presents the teachings of the second Confucian sage; more eloquent than the *Analects*, it includes passages of lofty idealism and even mysticism.

Mencius and Xunzi

The school founded by Confucius was further developed after his death by a number of followers, most notably Mencius and Xunzi. Although these two men differed with Confucius on certain issues, and disgreed even more strongly between themselves, they had enough in common with him that they are credited with building the Confucian tradition.

The name Mencius, like the name Confucius, is a form with a Latin ending; it gained currency in Europe after Roman Catholic missionaries made contact with China beginning in the seventeenth century. He was born Meng Ko, but after his death was given the title Mengzi ('Master Meng'). Born roughly two centuries after Confucius, in the small northern state of Zhao (adjacent to the latter's home state of Lu), he too travelled from one feudal state to another, looking for a ruler who would accept his advice. At a time when might was making right in the struggle for political survival, feuding lords considered his emphasis on benevolence and righteousness to be hopelessly impractical.

Xunzi ('Master Xun') was originally named Xun Kuang or Xun Qing. Born roughly half a century after Mencius, he too was a native of Zhao. He served as a magistrate in the powerful state of Qi for a short period. The work known by his name, the *Xunzi*, consists of 32 sections organized around specific topics, such as the nature of Heaven and the wickedness of human nature. Some of the *Xunzi* may have been written by his disciples.

Mencius and Xunzi on Human Nature

The Chinese word for human nature, *xing*, is written with a compound character that includes the terms for mind or heart and life or offspring. Philological scholars have associated this etymology with early religious worship. A human being receives from

---

| Box 9.3 | Mencius on Human Nature and Virtue

Mencius said: 'No man is devoid of a heart sensitive to the suffering of others. . . . Suppose a man were . . . to see a young child on the verge of falling into a well. He would certainly be moved to compassion, not because . . . he wished to win the praise of his fellow villagers or friends, nor yet because he disliked the cry of the child. . . .

'The heart of compassion is the germ of benevolence; the heart of shame, of dutifulness; the heart of courtesy and modesty, of observance of the rites; the heart of right and wrong, of wisdom. Man has these four germs just as he has four limbs' (2A:6; Lau 1970:82–3).

Heaven the gift of life and all the innate endowments of human nature, especially the shared faculty of moral discernment. Mencius says that the sense of right and wrong is common to all (2A:6) and is what distinguishes humans from animals. A related belief is that all are equal because all share a common moral capacity, regardless of social hierarchy or distinctions between the 'civilized' and the 'barbarian'.

The Confucian tradition has sometimes been criticized for not explaining the role of evil in human existence. But in fact Confucian thought does address this question: Mencius explains evil as the product of contact between an originally good nature and its wicked environment, while Xunzi believes that it is inherent in human nature. (Contemporary Marxist scholars in China have tended to emphasize Xunzi's view in order to justify the state's control of political and social life.) However, the two thinkers agree that human nature is perfectible. Mencius declares that everyone has the potential to become a sage. Xunzi maintains that we can be educated to seek goodness:

> Man's nature is evil; goodness is the result of conscious activity. The nature of man is such that he is born with a fondness for profit. . . . Therefore, man must first be transformed by the instructions of a teacher and guided by ritual principles. . . . It is obvious . . . that man's nature is evil, and that his goodness is the result of conscious activity (Watson 1963a:157).

In the Han dynasty (206 BCE–220 CE) and generally in early Confucianism, Xunzi was more influential than Mencius. The situation changed after the tenth century with the development of Neo-Confucianism (see p. 456). When Christian missionaries arrived in China, they discovered that Confucian scholars usually followed Mencius in upholding the basic goodness of human nature. Evil was explained as a deflection from the good, a perversion of the natural.

The Europeans were confused by the absence of a Chinese word for the Christian concept of 'sin'. The closest Chinese equivalent is *zui*, which also means 'crime'. For this reason, some people have mistakenly assumed that the Chinese concept of morality was based not on an internal consciousness of moral evil, or guilt, but only on an external sense of shame rooted in the superficial desire to be respected by others. But in fact Confucian education sought to instill a strong sense of moral responsibility, inseparable from consciousness of guilt.

For Mencius the perfectibility of human nature is rooted in the union of heart and mind, a concept expressed in Chinese by the word *xin*. Usually translated as 'heart-mind', *xin* was originally written using a pictograph of fire. The heart-mind comes to us from Heaven (Mencius 6A:15) and leads us back there. The best example of what Mencius saw as the perfection of human nature is the heightened moral faculty of the sage, in whom the union of mind and heart is fully realized.

Mencius and Xunzi on Heaven and Ritual

The *Book of Mencius* suggests an evolutionary shift in the understanding of the divine. Whereas Confucius may or may not have regarded 'Tian' as representing a personal deity, Mencius seems to suggest that Heaven is immanent, present within the human heart; to know one's own heart and nature is to know Heaven (Mencius 7A:1).

The term 'Tian' also increasingly refers to the source and principle of ethical laws and values. Yet this shift in emphasis towards the ethical does not seem to detract from the importance of ritual. Mencius continues to respect the tradition of offering sacrifices to the Lord-on-high and the ancestors. 'Though a man may be wicked, if he adjusts his thoughts, fasts and bathes, he may sacrifice to the Lord-on-high' (Mencius 4B:25).

Xunzi, by contrast, sometimes appears to reduce Heaven to the laws of nature: 'Heaven does not suspend the winter because men dislike cold; earth does not cease being wide because men dislike great distances . . .' (Watson 1963a:82). At a time when the upper class was beginning to move away from practices such as divination, he also emphasizes the difference between the rationality of the educated gentleman and the superstition of the common people who believe in fortune and misfortune:

> You pray for rain and it rains. Why? For no particular reason, I say. It is just as though you had not prayed for rain and it rained anyway. . . . You consult the arts of divination before making a decision on some important matter. But it is not as though you could hope to accomplish anything by such ceremonies. They are done merely for ornament. Hence the gentleman regards them as ornaments, but the common people regard them as supernatural (Watson 1963a:85).

Even so, Xunzi too maintains the importance of rituals, defending the Confucian approach against the criticisms of Mozi (see p. 486 below):

> . . . if a man concentrates upon fulfilling ritual principles, then he may satisfy both his human desires and the demands of ritual; but if he concentrates only upon fulfilling his desires, then he will end by satisfying neither. The Confucians make it possible for a man to satisfy both; the Mo-ists cause him to satisfy neither (Watson 1963a:91).

The *Book of Rites* shows evidence of Xunzi's influence. It extols music as a path to tranquillity and inner equilibrium. Together, music and rituals promote an inner harmony that is a reflection of the harmony between Heaven and earth. The mystical dimension of this correlation between the microcosm and the macrocosm, between the inner workings of a person's mind and heart and the creative processes of the universe, is obvious. Here we touch the heart of the Chinese meaning of harmony, on which Mencius and Xunzi would agree.

Differentiation

We now turn to the most important developments during the Han and later dynasties. Neither Confucianism nor Daoism was the kind of ideology that emphasizes central authority or doctrinal orthodoxy. Thus they were free to evolve in response to changes in political thought and in competition both with one another and, especially, with Buddhism. Having survived its persecution under the first emperor and become the dominant state ideology under the Han dynasty, Confucianism experienced another period of decline, only to revive in a new form that we know as Neo-Confucianism.

Confucianism in the Han Era

The period of the Han dynasty, like its contemporary the Roman Empire, was one of important developments in the relationship between religion and the state. Confucianism became a state orthodoxy—some would say the state religion. (In the same period Daoism became an institutional religion, and Buddhism was introduced into China.) In Han China 'all under Heaven' was unified under one emperor, who ruled by Heaven's mandate with the help of Confucian orthodoxy. The similarity to Christendom under Constantine and his successors, with their 'political theology' of one God, one *logos*, one emperor, and one world, is striking. That monotheistic ideology underpinned the monarchical order for centuries, and the prestige and authority of Rome long outlasted the empire itself. Perhaps it is not surprising that the name Han is still used to identify the majority population of China in contrast to the country's ethnic minorities.

Among Han scholars, the one reputed to be most influential in consolidating Confucian gains was Dong Zhongshu (179–104 BCE). With philosophical arguments he sought to persuade the ruler to govern benevolently. Systematizing traditional thought, he established Heaven, earth, and humans as a horizontal triad or trinity, with kingship as the vertical link among them:

> Those who in ancient times invented writing drew three lines and connected them through the middle, calling the character 'king'. The three lines are Heaven, earth and man, and that which passes through the middle joins the principles of all three. . . . Thus the king is but the executor of Heaven. He regulates its seasons and brings them to completion (Chunqiu fan-lu; de Bary 1960:179).

The Han Confucians also incorporated ideas from two other independent and ancient schools of philosophical speculation. The ideas of the Yin-Yang and Five Agents schools gradually fused with one another and were absorbed into both Daoism and Confucianism.

The Yin-Yang and Five Agents Schools

According to the Yin-Yang school, there are two pervasive forces in the universe, opposing yet complementary. There is a duality between yin and yang; yin is feminine, shadowy, soft, moist, passive, and so on, while yang is masculine, bright, hard, dry, aggressive, and so on. But this is not the kind of 'dualism' that envisions a cosmic struggle between good and evil in which one side must prevail. This is not Satan versus God. What is desirable or beneficial is the proper harmony and balance of the yin and yang elements.

The Five Agents school identified five primal elements—water, fire, wood, metal, and earth—as cosmic agents engaged in interaction and change. Each has power over another: water over fire, fire over earth, earth over metal, metal over wood, and wood over water. Unlike its Greek and Hindu counterparts, both of which identify four elements—earth, fire, air and water—the Chinese group includes wood and metal and excludes the all-pervasive air. But in fact air (*qi*) had always been regarded as fundamental.

Together with yin and yang, the Five Agents were seen as working to integrate life and the universe. For example, each of the agents was associated with a dynasty: metal with the Xia, water with the Shang, wood with the Zhou, and so on. The agents were also associated both with cyclical signs designating years, days, and hours and with the Chinese zodiacal cycle of twelve animals (see p. 491).

The religious discourse of Han Confucianism was tolerant of exaggeration and superstition. Many apocryphal texts were accepted, together with legends on subjects such as the supposedly miraculous birth of Confucius. Belief in omens and portents was widespread, supported by a broad array of prognostication and divination texts. Even Dong Zhongshu appears to have believed in portents and omens:

> The creatures of Heaven and earth at times display unusual changes and these are called wonders. Lesser ones are called ominous portents. . . . Portents are Heaven's warnings, wonders are Heaven's threats. . . . If we examine these wonders and portents carefully, we may discern the will of Heaven (Chunqiu fan-lu; de Bary 1960: 187).

Neo-Confucianism

During and after the Han dynasty, many commentaries were written on the classical Confucian texts, which had become the core of the civil-service curriculum. Much of this activity was the work of scholars engaged in detailed literary and linguistic analysis of the ancient material. This activity continued into the Tang dynasty of the seventh, eighth, and ninth centuries, when Buddhism became prominent in Chinese intellectual life.

The period between the Han and the Tang dynasties was dominated first by Daoism and then by Buddhism. Thereafter, during the Song dynasty (mid-tenth to late thirteenth century), commentary on the Confucian texts resumed under a succession of influential philosophers who were not only literary and linguistic philologists but innovators and synthesizers. Their goal was to find answers in the classical heritage to a number of questions that had been raised during the centuries of Daoist and Buddhist dominance. They then attributed to Confucius the new thinking that they themselves had developed in response to Daoism and Buddhism.

These thinkers are known as the Neo-Confucians. We will consider two of them, the synthesizers Zhu Xi (1130–1200) and Wang Yangming (1472–1529).

The Four Books

The challenges of Buddhism and Daoism led the Confucian scholars to look for the spiritual legacy within Confucianism itself. But relatively little of the varied material that made up the Five Classics lent itself to philosophical and religious commentary. Therefore the Neo-Confucians reformulated Confucian philosophy on the basis of a smaller corpus that they believed to teach a legacy of the mind and heart. These **Four Books** were:

- The *Analects of Confucius*: the Master's teachings as recalled by his students, probably compiled about a century after his death;
- The *Book of Mencius*: a similar collection, including lively anecdotes about the master and his disciples as well as conversations between them.
- The *Great Learning*: a chapter from the 'Book of Rites' that makes moral and spiritual cultivation the beginning of good rulership; and
- The *Doctrine of the Mean*: another chapter from the 'Book of Rites', focusing on the inner life of psychic equilibrium and harmony.

In giving these texts pre-eminence, the Neo-Confucian philosophers oriented Confucian scholarship towards the kinds of metaphysical and spiritual questions addressed by the dominant religious tradition of their day: Buddhism. But their speculation about the nature of ultimate reality was clearly influenced by Daoism as well. The result was a new synthesis, a *Weltanschauung* (world view) that gave the old moralist answers to questions about life and the world both a new metaphysical framework and a greater spiritual profundity. Eventually, Neo-Confucian texts and ideas would greatly influence Korean and Japanese thought.

The Contributions of Zhu Xi

Zhu Xi was the most prolific author among the Neo-Confucians and was probably the greatest mind. Though he was not accepted as an orthodox thinker in his own lifetime, his commentaries on the Four Books were integrated into the curriculum of the civil-service examinations beginning in 1313, with the result that his philosophy became the state orthodoxy for the following six centuries.

Zhu Xi's philosophy and understanding of human nature draw from Daoism and Buddhism as well as his Confucian background. For Zhu Xi, as for the mainstream of Chinese philosophy, the human being and the cosmos mirror one another as microcosm and macrocosm; thus the evil in the universe is counterbalanced and rendered insignificant by the reality of human perfectibility as expressed in the person of the sage. He stressed the importance of knowing and purifying the mind's intentions in a practice he called 'investigation of things', meaning the study of moral knowledge through Confucian literature.

Zhu Xi's most important contributions concerned the philosophy of the Great Ultimate (**Taiji** or **T'ai-chi**), which emphasizes the interrelatedness of humans and the cosmos. Central to his interpretation of the Taiji is the concept of *li*, the 'principles' that constitute all things. (This *li* is a different word, written with a different character in Chinese, from the one defined earlier in terms of ritual propriety.) *Li* may be defined as a set of forms or essences, of organizing and normative principles, belonging to the metaphysical realm, 'above shapes'. Its metaphysical coordinate, to which it is logically (though not chronologically) prior, is *qi* (or *ch'i*), translated sometimes as 'ether' or 'matter-energy', which belongs to the physical realm, 'within shapes'. All things are constituted of both *li* and *qi*, which are something like Aristotelian form and matter, except that *li* is passive and *qi* is dynamic. The dynamic nature of *qi* (or *chi*) is easy to grasp if we realize that it is the same energy that practitioners of the martial arts, such as Taiji, draw on to perform amazing feats of strength and endurance.

Zhu Xi describes the Great Ultimate as the most perfect *li*, a kind of primal archetype. It is also the sum total of the principles (*li*) of everything. It serves the same function in Chinese philosophy that the Form of the Good does in the thought of Plato, and that God does in the writings of Aristotle. The Absolute that Zhu Xi envisioned was not a personal deity, but he clearly identified it with both Heaven and the Lord-on-high. As he wrote, it would not be correct to say there is a ruler in heaven who is lord of the world; but it would be equally wrong to say that there is no such ruler. In effect, he affirmed the presence of a higher power while removing the personal, anthropomorphic element associated with terms such as 'Heaven' and 'Lord-on-high'.

Human Nature

In Zhu Xi's metaphysics, the human being represents the summit of the universe and is part of the excellence of the Great Ultimate, and human nature—the result of the interaction of yin and yang and the Five Agents—is originally good, or 'sincere'. Where, then, does evil come from?

The explanation is that *li*, though wholly good in itself, loses its perfection through its relationship to *qi*, without which it cannot be actualized. Everything—physical things as well as human beings—is affected by the limitations of its *qi*. The quality of *qi* varies: people with pure or translucent *qi* are endowed with a natural inclination towards the good, while those who have impure *qi* are more attracted to evil.

The remedy for the imperfection of existence as Zhu Xi explains it is self-cultivation: maintaining an attitude of reverence (*jing*) towards one's own inner nature and its capacity for goodness, while developing knowledge about oneself and the world. This prescription was disputed, however, by his contemporary and rival Lu Jiuyuan (1139–93), and Lu's spiritual heir Wang Yangming (1472–1529). They point out that in making intellectual effort the cornerstone of moral striving, this doctrine of cultivation demands that sages be intellectuals and makes sagehood inaccessible to those for whom such development is not possible. Accordingly, these thinkers emphasized the potential for greatness in every human being and the power of the mind and heart to perfect themselves by choosing the good and practising virtue. They regarded intellectual pursuits as a useful but unnecessary component of cultivation, and preferred the dynamism of moral action as the expression of the whole personality, oriented to the highest good.

Meditation

A clear indication of the Buddhist influence in Zhu Xi's thought is his emphasis on the practice of meditation as a way of returning to our original nature, recapturing the source of our being, and allowing the original equilibrium of nature and the emotions to permeate our daily life. This kind of meditation differs from the Buddhist practice of visualization, in which the meditator imagines the presence of buddhas or bodhisattvas, but is similar to the more common Buddhist meditational practice of emptying the mind and heart of concepts and feelings. Where Confucian meditation differs from all forms of Buddhist meditation is in its focus on improvement of the individual's moral–spiritual nature rather than mystical experience, enlightenment, and liberation.

The Contributions of Wang Yangming

Wang Yangming lived three centuries after Zhu Xi, in an era when the latter's philosophy had become established as the state orthodoxy. Wang's own philosophy may be seen as one of protest against both Zhu Xi's teachings—in particular, his emphasis on *li*—and the use that the state was making of them through its examination system. Whereas Zhu Xi's emphasis on *li* as an objective principle could be—and was being—used to justify and maintain state orthodoxy and social control, Wang Yangming believed that the mind cannot be so easily controlled.

Whereas Zhu Xi speaks of the Great Ultimate as an objective reality present in both the world and the self, Wang Yangming begins with the self and speaks of ultimate reality in terms of a subjectivity that infuses all objectivity. This approach has been described as the school of mind (*xin*), in contrast to Zhu Xi's school of *li*, which is sometimes translated as 'principle'.

The Chinese character for *xin* is derived from a flame symbol. As a philosophical concept, it occurs frequently in the *Book of Mencius* and Buddhist scriptural texts, where it refers to ultimate reality. The Neo-Confucian thinkers had returned *xin* to its earlier meaning, pertaining to the deep psyche, while retaining the overtones of Buddhist metaphysics. Whereas Zhu Xi had associated *xin* with *qi*, Wang's spiritual master Lu Jiuyuan had associated it with *li*:

> Sages appeared tens of thousands of generations ago. They shared this mind; they shared this *li*. Sages will appear tens of thousands of generations to come. They will share this mind; they will share this *li* (*Xiangshan quanshu*, ch. 22, adapted from Chan 1963:580).

Wang Yangming continued the process of internalizing this metaphysical principle. In his view, the concept of the deep mind, or true self, is what connects the world and humans to the ultimate:

> The original substance (*benti*) of the mind is nothing other than the heavenly principle (*Tianli*). . . . It is your True Self. This True Self is the master of [your] physical body. With it, one lives; without it, one dies (*Chuanxi lu*, part 1, adapted from Chan 1967:80).

We do not find terms such as 'original substance', 'heavenly principle', or 'True Self' in Confucius or Mencius because they come from Buddhist and Daoist vocabulary. In using them, Wang Yangming was integrating Buddhist and Daoist insights into the Confucian tradition. For him, it was essential to take good care of the True Self, always keeping its original substance intact. As we dismantle the barricades erected by the 'false self'—the ego—that we hide behind, we clear away the selfishness that hinders the inner vision and discover the innermost core of our own being. This in turn leads to the realization of perfect goodness, which is the ultimate revelation of the Absolute in the self.

There is also a very pragmatic dimension to this philosophy, which makes sagehood accessible to all and opens the possibility of perfection to everyone, including those without any education. This may have been necessary to compete with the Buddhist assurance that everyone has an inner buddha nature and is capable of attaining enlightenment and liberation.

Practice

Rituals, Alchemy, Scholars and Priests

In addition to formal religious rites, Confucian practices include a wide range of rituals governing family, social, and other interactions. Thus Confucianism also became known as the 'ritual religion' (*lijiao*).

At the same time, however, Confucius emphasized that without the right inner disposition, ritual propriety becomes hypocrisy (*Analects* 15:17). He insisted that sacrifice must be performed with an awareness of the presence of the spirits (*Analects* 3:12), and pointed out that the importance of the rites does not reside in their external observance: 'What can rites do for a person lacking in the virtue of humanity (*ren*)?' (*Analects* 3:3).

Confucian teachings also helped to sustain the ancient cult of ancestors (using the term 'cult' in the scholarly sense of a system of rituals of worship) and perpetuated the formal worship of Heaven practised by China's imperial rulers. But he strongly disapproved of the symbolic representation of human sacrifice in the form of the wooden servant figures buried with rulers to assist them in the world of the dead (probably as substitutes for the burial of real servants in an earlier period). Confucius is reported to have said that whoever made such figures did not deserve to have posterity (Mencius 1A:4).

The Cult of Heaven

The worship of Heaven before Confucius included annual sacrifices conducted by the emperor. The site in Beijing where these rituals took place during the Ming dynasty (1368–1661) can still be visited today. The building complex of the Temple of Heaven is situated in a spacious park to the southeast of the former Imperial Palace, often called the 'forbidden city' in English. It includes a blue-tiled circular Hall of Prayer for Good Harvests (blue being the colour of the sky). Even more impressive are three concentric circular marble terraces, open to the sky itself, that served as the altar for the cult of Heaven. The middle of the topmost terrace is the place where once a year, at the time of the winter solstice, the emperor would offer sacrifices to Heaven (the Lord-on-high). Nearby is the Temple of Earth where the emperor presided over sacrifices at a different time in the yearly cycle.

China was not the only the ancient culture that marked the new year by sacrificing animals as burnt offerings. In the Chinese case, attendance was strictly limited, and

The restored Hall of Prayer for Good Harvests at the Temple of Heaven complex in Beijing (Roy Amore).

individual citizens would be guilty of high treason should they attempt to perform such a ritual. Sacrifice to the highest gods was the unique privilege and sacred duty of the Son of Heaven, the emperor in whom political and religious powers were united. In effect, the office of emperor was a continuation of the ancient office of the priest-shaman-king.

Other State Rituals

During the Han dynasty the state adopted an elaborate cycle of rituals that, rightly or wrongly, has been attributed to Confucian teachings. The rituals incorporated some very ancient beliefs in a supreme deity and in natural powers as deity symbols, as well as in the intercessory powers of various deceased heroes. The great rituals performed by the emperor himself honoured Heaven, earth, and the imperial ancestors. There were also intermediate rituals for the worship of the sun, moon, and numerous spirits of earth and sky. And there were the lesser sacrifices to minor gods, such as deities of mountains, lakes, and rivers.

Well-known historical figures—in particular, wise and honest magistrates—were honoured as 'city gods'. Confucius himself, along with his disciples and later worthies, became the centre of an elaborate cult that very likely would have been repugnant to him. Though not deified, he was venerated (especially by the scholarly class) as the teacher par excellence, and official sacrifices were offered to him. A temple dedicated to Confucius at the mandarin training academy in Nanjing, for example, conducted formal rituals on his birthday and other key dates in the academic year. In sum, the emphasis on rituals ensured continuity with the past and at the same time provided the ritual as well as moral education that young men aspiring to become gentlemen would need, whether as mandarins or in some other leadership capacity.

All state cults came to an end with the end of imperial rule and the establishment of a republic in China in 1912, but the memory of them remains as evidence of a theistic belief at the heart of traditional Chinese religion. This basic religiosity persisted throughout the ages, despite changes in philosophical formulation and interpretation.

The Ancestor Cult

The traditional Confucian understanding of the hereafter posited that every human being has two 'souls'. The upper, or intellectual, soul, called the *hun*, became the spirit (*shen*), and ascended to the world above, while a lower, or animal, soul, called the *po*, became the ghost (*guei*) and descended with the body into the grave. Tomb paintings from the Han period depict the heavenly realm where the ancestors were believed to reside.

The main ritual of the ancestor cult was a memorial service conducted annually first at ancestral temples and eventually at grave sites or in the home. Wine and food libations were usually offered, with silent prostrations in front of tablets representing the ancestors. The ancestors were believed to taste the food before the whole family partook of the meal.

The cult of ancestors goes back to the dawn of Chinese history and thus likely antedates the cult of Heaven. Although it was originally restricted to the nobility, it came to be very much a family practice—an expression of a community that included the beloved dead alongside the living—and its practice was strongly supported by the state. While the ancestor cult may be regarded as a religion in itself, its persistence has also been considered another indication of the religious character of Confucianism. Ancestor shrines are still found in some Chinese homes in Hong Kong, Taiwan, and Southeast Asia, and similar practices survive in Korea and Japan as well.

Family Rituals

The centrality of the ancestors to family life was reflected in other rituals as well. An important part of the ceremony marking the male adolescent's entry into adult life, for example, was the presentation of the young man to his ancestors. In this 'capping' ceremony, held sometime between the ages of fifteen and twenty, the young man received a ceremonial hat and gown, as well as his formal name.

Similarly, the marriage ceremony began with the announcement of the event to the ancestors in the temple, accompanied by a wine libation. The *Book of Rites* emphasizes the importance of the marriage ceremony:

> The respect, the caution, the importance, the attention to secure correctness in all the details, and then [the pledge of] mutual affection—these were the great points in the ceremony, and served to establish the distinction to be observed between . . . husband and wife. From that righteousness came the affection between father and son; and from that affection, the rectitude between ruler and minister. Whence it is said, 'The ceremony of marriage is the root of the other ceremonial observances' (Legge 1885, 2:430).

The Mandate of Heaven

A number of traditional Chinese political principles included implicit religious sanctions. For example, the Chinese believed that Heaven bestows on rulers a mandate to govern, which they forfeit if they become tyrants. Each ruler, as custodian of the '**Mandate of Heaven**', functions as a kind of high priest, mediating between the human order and the divine.

Originally formulated as advice for rulers themselves, Confucian teachings in time came to be taught to the rulers' advisers or ministers as well. The problem for the latter was what to do if the ruler was unwise (as most rulers were) or even tyrannical (as some turned out to be).

According to Mencius, 'The people come first; the altars of the earth and grain come afterwards; the ruler comes last' (Mencius 7B:14). Therefore killing a tyrant is not regicide, since the tyrant no longer deserves to rule (Mencius 1B:8). In fact, Mencius offers a doctrine of justified rebellion or revolution, based on the mandate of Heaven, popularly known as 'removal of the mandate' (*geming*). Not surprisingly, the fourteenth-century founder of the Ming dynasty sought to delete from the *Book of Mencius* the passages that approve of tyrannicide.

| Box 9.4 | Confucius on Good Government |

In the first of these extracts we find the Confucian principle known as the 'rectification of names': that each element in society should exemplify the conduct ideally ordained for it.

Duke Ching of Ch'i asked Confucius about government. Confucius answered, 'Let the ruler be a ruler, the subject a subject, the father a father, the son a son.' The Duke said, 'Splendid! Truly, if the ruler be not a ruler, the subject not a subject, the father not a father, the son not a son, then even if there be grain, would I get to eat it?' (*Analects* 12:11, Lau 1979:114).

The Master said, 'Guide them by edicts, keep them in line with punishments, and the common people will stay out of trouble but will have no sense of shame. Guide them by virtue, keep them in line with the rites, and they will, besides having a sense of shame, reform themselves' (2:3, Lau 63).

The Master said, 'If a man is correct in his own person, then there will be obedience without orders being given; but if he is not correct in his own person, there will not be obedience even though orders are given' (13:6, Lau 119).

Chi K'ang Tzu asked Confucius about government, saying, 'What would you think if, in order to move closer to those who possess the Way, I were to kill those who do not follow the Way?'
  Confucius answered, 'In administering your government, what need is there for you to kill? Just desire the good yourself and the common people will be good. The virtue of the gentleman is like wind; the virtue of the small man is like grass. Let the wind blow over the grass and it is sure to bend' (12:19, Lau 115–16).

In the Confucian classics, the phrase 'the one man' is sometimes used by the emperor to refer to himself as the sole holder of his exalted office. The emperor was Son of Heaven, governing by a mandate from above and mediating between the powers above and the people below. His high position and awesome responsibilities set him apart from all others; yet in another sense he was the collective man, guilty of fault whenever his people offended Heaven. The Confucian tradition bridged the two ends of China's political spectrum, from conservatives to radical reformers. Most Confucian scholars were activists, whether serving the government and advising the ruler, promoting reform, or resisting and protesting against tyranny.

Interaction and Adaptation

Rethinking Confucius

Neo-Confucianism has been the official philosophy in China for much of the last thousand years. The textual commentaries written or compiled by neo-Confucian scholars have also served as the basis of the civil-service examination system. The Jesuit missionaries such as Matteo Ricci (1522–1610) who travelled to China in the sixteenth century preferred classical Confucianism and objected in particular to the metaphysical aspects of Neo-Confucian philosophy, which bore the pantheistic imprint of Buddhist influence. But as recent scholars have pointed out, the Jesuits overlooked the rich spiritual dimension of the Neo-Confucian tradition.

When China was shaken, politically and psychologically, by Western intrusion in the late nineteenth century, Chinese intellectuals began to question their cultural heritage. Many regarded Confucianism as a weight and a burden—an intellectual shackle that was preventing the country from modernizing. Its strongest critic was probably the writer Lu Xun (1881–1936), whose short stories attacked the 'cannibalistic' ritual religion that stifled human freedom and individual initiative in the name of passive, conformist virtues.

These anti-traditionalist, anti-Confucian voices of the 1919 May Fourth movement gave birth to the Chinese Communist party in 1921. What began as a search for intellectual freedom led to a repudiation of the monopoly of tradition, including that of the Confucian social structure. With the communist takeover of the mainland in 1949, the advantages and disadvantages of the Confucian tradition were vigorously debated.

While mainland Marxist scholars were criticizing the entire traditional legacy, a group of philosophers and scholars in Taiwan and Hong Kong expressed concern for the survival of Chinese culture, which they identified with Neo-Confucianism. A plea for a return to Neo-Confucian sources was made public in 'A Manifesto for the Reappraisal of Sinology and Reconstruction of Chinese Culture'. Drafted by a group of Chinese philosophers in Hong Kong and Taipei in 1958, it referred to the harmony of the 'way of Heaven' (*tiandao*) and the 'way of man' (*rendao*) as the central legacy of Confucianism. It also challenged Western sinologists to give greater attention to Confucian spirituality as the core of Chinese culture. It is interesting that these scholars agreed with mainland scholars that Neo-Confucianism in particular possesses an undeniably spiritual and religious character.

The philosophers associated with this movement for Confucian revival examined traditional Chinese ideas from the perspective of European philosophers such as Immanuel Kant (1724–1804). Their legacy remains important for Chinese intellectuals outside the mainland, especially those interested in Confucian–Western dialogue.

Confucianism and the Legalist School

In China the term 'Legalism' (*fajia*)—not to be confused with the rule of law—refers to an ancient school of thought, almost as old as Confucianism itself, that advocated the use of harsh legal penalties to deter political opposition and enhance and maintain power. Its leading thinker was a prince known as Han Feizi (d. 233 BCE), whose name became the title of a work attributed to him and his school.

Legalism does not address questions about the meaning of life. Rather, it offers a political answer to the problem of order in society. Devoid of any religio-moral belief, it focuses exclusively on *Realpolitik*, political power. Assuming that a ruler's goal justifies all means, Legalist writings taught rulers how to manipulate people and circumstances to keep themselves in power. In this respect, the text *Han Feizi* has frequently been compared to *The Prince*, Niccolò Machiavelli's Renaissance-era handbook for European rulers.

The followers of Legalism were great cynics who recognized no power higher than that of the state or ruler. They subordinated all human relations to the one between ruler and minister, and divested it of any moral significance. They also recommended that the ruler use a system of rewards and punishments to ensure the loyalty of his subjects. The ruler was to take no one into his confidence, not even members of his immediate family, lest they become foes.

For much of the communist period Legalism has been regarded as 'progressive' while Confucianism has been described as 'reactionary'. Mao Zedong was frequently and approvingly compared to Qin Shi Huangdi, the ruler who unified China in 221 BCE and made Legalism the state ideology. Chinese communists described Legalism as engaged in a life-and-death struggle with Confucianism and praised it for its materialist outlook and modernizing potential.

A particularly vituperative phase of the Cultural Revolution of 1966–76 was the campaign of 1973–4, in which the fallen defence chief Lin Biao was linked with Confucius. The former head of state (1959–68) Liu Shaoqi, who had praised Confucian and Neo-Confucian ideas in a 1951 address called 'How to Be a Good Communist', became enemy number one for Mao, and the writings that Liu praised came under heavy attack. In the anti-Confucius campaign, Legalism was exalted as the heroic ideology. As recently as the 1990s, Legalism continued to be reflected in China's policy of using the judicial system to impose severe punishments for crimes large or small, real or imagined.

The excesses of the anti-Confucius campaign were discredited in the late 1970s, and Confucianism has since been restored to a degree of respectability. Because it is concerned with the state and society, however, it is still seen more as a political and philosophical ideology than as a religion. Modern China gives official status to only five religious traditions: Daoism, Buddhism, Islam, Protestantism, and Catholicism. Note that only one of these traditions is of Chinese origin, and that there are two branches of Christianity on the list.

Women and Confucianism

However relevant some Confucian and Neo-Confucian ideas may be to modern life, there are areas where obvious problems arise. In the Confucian social order, human relationships tended to be hierarchically fixed and rigid, with the superior partners—rulers, fathers, and husbands—enjoying more rights and privileges than the inferior partners, who were expected to submit to their control. Historically speaking, this structure was the product of Confucian philosophy, the Legalist theory of power, and the yin-yang philosophy, with its correlation of cosmic forces and human relationships.

Confucian ideology was used to consolidate the patriarchal family system and assign an increasingly subordinate role to women. To ensure continuation of the ancestor cult, it became women's sacred duty to provide male heirs. The same obligation also offered an excuse for husbands to marry secondary wives.

It appears that women, especially noble women, had much more freedom in Shang than in Zhou times, and in Zhou than in later times. In other words, the more Confucian the society became, the less freedom women enjoyed. The Appendices to the *Book of Changes*, with their yin-yang ideas, represent the male–female relationship in terms of the superiority of Heaven over inferior earth. The ritual texts sum up woman's place in the family—and hence society—in the 'Three Obediences': she is to obey her father while at home, her husband when married, and her son if widowed. (This is similar to the traditional Hindu view of women's role.) A woman's loyalty to her husband was equivalent to political loyalty, or a man's commitment to one dynastic government.

Only in modern times, and especially with the May Fourth movement of 1919, which espoused Western concepts of science and democracy and attacked the Confucian order for stifling individual freedom, did women begin to be liberated from some of society's harshest rules.

| Map 9.1   Indigenous Chinese religions

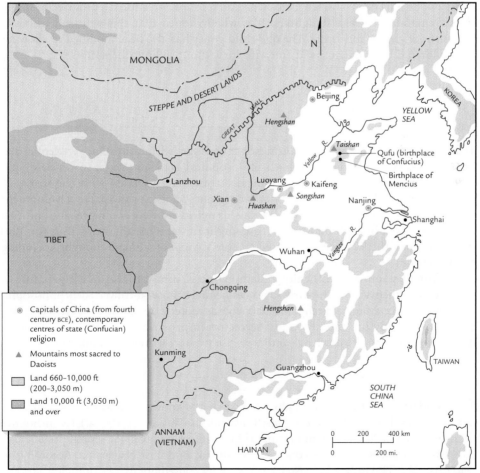

Adapted from: I. al Faruqi and D.E. Sopher, eds, *Historical Atlas of the Religions of the World* (New York: Macmillan, 1974):111.

The 'one child' family planning policy adopted in 1979 has helped to bring China's population growth under control, but at great cost. The policy has been enforced by a system of fines and denial of privileges for those who do not comply, together with perks for those who do. Many families want their one and only child to be a boy, who traditionally would remain in the family home, contributing to the family income and well-being. This is especially important when the older generation needs help with the farm or business. A girl, by contrast, would be expected to marry and move away to become a part of a different household, leaving her parents without day-to-day support in their declining years.

The preference for boys means that female fetuses are often aborted, and many infant girls are abandoned at birth, to be raised in orphanages. Some of these baby girls are adopted by Western families, but many others have died of neglect. The gender ratio in the population of marriageable age is now dramatically skewed, and for the next two decades it will be hard for many young men to find female partners. In 2004 the government of China officially recognized this problem and introduced a program of incentives for families to raise daughters. It is widely hoped that this will lead to better treatment of girls in the future. The one-child policy has also been modified to allow for two children if both the husband and wife are without siblings themselves.

Daoism

There is no single definition of Daoism (sometimes spelled Taoism). One problem is that English uses the same word for both philosophical Daoism (*Daojia* in Chinese) and religious Daoism (*Daojiao*). Philosophical Daoism is associated with the works of Laozi and his follower Zhuangzi, while religious Daoism was a later development involving deities, priests, temples, and rituals, as well as a variety of physical and spiritual techniques resembling Indian yoga. To complicate matters, the word Dao (or Tao) itself, meaning 'the Way', has been used by every school of Chinese thought, including Confucianism.

Another source of difficulty in defining both forms of Daoism is the nature of the teachings themselves. The early sages deliberately chose to convey their philosophical teachings in riddles, and religious Daoism was esoteric, reserving its secrets for initiates. Only recently has this shroud of secrecy been penetrated, as some initiates have begun to publish their knowledge and expertise to share with a wider audience.

Philosophical Daoism

The foundation of Daoist philosophy is a text that is known both as the *Laozi*, after its author, and as the *Daodejing* (*Tao-te ching*; 'Classic of the Way and its Power'). Its author has been cited by Karl Jaspers as an original thinker in the company of several pre-Socratic Greek philosophers and the second-century Indian Buddhist Nagarjuna. According to tradition, Laozi (literally, 'old master') was an older contemporary of Confucius; one legend adds that Confucius went to him for advice. Recent scholarship, however, suggests that his text may have been composed somewhat later (around 350 BCE). Among other problems, the best 'biography' we have, written in the first century BCE, is a composite life of three persons.

We are not even certain whether his surname was Lao or Li. He was allegedly a native of Chu, in southern China, and a court archivist for the Zhou house who used to teach students after work in his home. Then one day he abruptly quit his position and left the country, riding westward out of China on an ox. At the exit gate, the story says, he encountered one of his students, who begged him to fulfill his promise to write down his teachings before leaving. Reluctantly, he paused long enough to write a short poetic work about living a life in touch with the inner *dao* and its energy. Then he resumed his journey and disappeared, never to be seen again.

The *Daodejing* contains only about 5,000 words (roughly one-fifth as many as the present chapter), presented in poetic stanzas. One of the most widely translated texts in the world, it can be approached as a work of mysticism, political theory, or humanistic philosophy.

The first line of the text is famous play on words: 'The Way (Dao) that can be spoken of is not the constant Way (Dao).' In fact it is a double play, since *dao* is also a verb meaning 'to speak'. Thus what Laozi means is that 'The Dao that can be articulated ('*daoed*'), is not the constant Dao.' Like Western mystics, he warns us that the real God is beyond human understanding (or, as the poet Ogden Nash put it, 'Whatever the mind comes at, God is not that'):

> There is a thing confusedly formed,
> Born before heaven and earth.
> Silent and void
> It stands alone and does not change,
> Goes round and does not weary.
> (Lau 1963:82)

Here the Dao is described as existing before the universe came to be, as an unchanging first principle, even the ancestor of all things, by which all things come to be. This appears to be a philosophical attempt to conceptualize an earlier religious belief, recasting what was once seen as a 'personal' deity in terms of an 'impersonal' force. For Laozi, god is energy. But even if the Dao no longer represents a personal deity, it remains a model for human behaviour.

The *Daodejing*, in contrast to most traditional texts, often favours the feminine over the masculine. If forced to describe the Dao, Laozi turns to feminine imagery. He describes the Dao as the mother of all things. Following the inner Dao means abandoning egoism and masculine aggression. We need to learn to be like water, which can be forced into various shapes but still maintains its own nature:

> Know the male,
> But keep to the role of the female
> And be a ravine to the empire.
> (Lau 1963:85)

| Box 9.5 | From the *Daodejing* |

The first of these passages clearly shows the Daoist preference for unstructured naturalness over Confucian ritual correctness and formalism.

Banish wisdom, discard knowledge,
And the people will be benefited a hundredfold.
Banish human kindness, discard morality,
And the people will be dutiful and compassionate.
Banish skill, discard profit,
And thieves and robbers will disappear.
If when these three things are done they find life too plain and unadorned,
Then let them have accessories;
Give them Simplicity to look at, the Uncarved Block to hold,
Give them selflessness and fewness of desires.
(*Daodejing* 19, Waley 1934:166)

The highest good is like that of water. The goodness of water is that it benefits the ten thousand creatures; yet itself does not scramble, but is content with the places that all men disdain. It is this that makes water so near to the Way.
And if men think the ground the best place for building a house upon,
If among thoughts they value those that are profound,
If in friendship they value gentleness,
In words, truth; in government, good order;
In deeds, effectiveness; in actions, timeliness—
In each case it is because they prefer what does not lead to strife,
And therefore does not go amiss.
(*Daodejing* 8, Waley 1934:151)

On wuwei *(non-action):*
Without leaving his door
He knows everything under heaven.
Without looking out of his window
He knows all the ways of heaven.
For the further one travels
The less one knows.
Therefore the Sage arrives without going,
Sees all without looking,
Does nothing, yet achieves everything.
(*Daodejing* 47, Waley 1934:200)

The disposition that Laozi recommends is expressed in Chinese by the term *wuwei*. Although in literal terms *wuwei* means 'non-action', what it signifies is not the absence of action but rather action without overaction, without attachment to action, without artificiality. This is the practical part of Laozi, the way of living according to the Way. Emphasizing the power of the natural, the simple, even the weak, it teaches how to survive in a time of disorder while keeping one's integrity. This is the most important practical lesson of Daoist philosophy, which has had immense importance in the development of Daoist religion.

The text suggests a measure of asceticism, of withdrawal from the world and its pleasures, even its cherished values. For the person seeking the Dao, the senses are distractions:

> The five colours blind man's eyes.
> The five notes deafen his ears.
> The five tastes deaden his palate.
> Riding and hunting make his mind go wild.
>   (Adapted from Lau 1963:68)

In the light of the Dao, even the civilized virtues preached by the Confucians, such as humanity and righteousness, are undesirable if they lead one away from one's own nature.

Another way of understanding the difference between Daoism and Confucianism is in terms of yin and yang: Daoism's preference for peace and quiet aligns it with the yin force, in contrast to the Confucian emphasis on action (yang). At the same time, both as a philosophy and as a religion, Daoism gives women a higher status than Confucianism does. The claim is supported by numerous passages in the *Laozi* that admire or give privilege to yin.

Laozi also offers political advice, once again advocating *wuwei*. Not only will the sage-ruler avoid imposing too many prohibitions, prescriptions, and ethical rules of the kind taught by Confucius; he will also protect the people from the excesses of knowledge that promote inflated egos and lead people to value the artificial over the natural. People who follow the Dao, according to Laozi, do not need government regulation.

The Philosophy of Zhuangzi

Zhuangzi (or Chuang-tzu) is presumed to have been a contemporary of Mencius. Scholars know little of his life, not even his dates, but have often speculated that, like Laozi, Zhuangzi came from a different part of China than Confucius and Mencius, and that this explains why their perspectives were different from those of the classical Confucian thinkers. The Confucians are generally seen as rational and systematic northerners, whereas the classical Daoist thinkers are regarded as nonconformist southerners who prefer imagination and fantasy to strict reason and moderation.

As in the *Laozi*, the Dao is seen in the *Zhuangzi* as the principle underlying and governing the universe. On the other hand, the work shows a hermit's distaste for politics. The *Zhuangzi*, which is ascribed to a thinker presumably of the fourth or third century BCE, resembles a collection of essays that draw freely on parable and allegory, as well as paradox and fanciful imagery. It makes an ardent plea for spiritual freedom: not merely the freedom of the individual from social conventions and restraints, but a self-transcending liberation from the limitations of one's own mind—from self-interested inclinations and prejudices. According to Zhuangzi, such freedom can be achieved only by embracing nature itself, in the Dao.

| Box 9.6 | From Zhuangzi

On reality and illusion (Chuang Tzu is the Wade-Giles transliteration of Zhuangzi's name):

Once Chuang [Tzu] dreamt he was a butterfly flitting and fluttering around, happy with himself and doing as he pleased. He didn't know he was Chuang [Tzu]. Suddenly he woke up and there he was Chuang. . . . But he didn't know if he was Chuang . . . who had dreamt that he was a butterfly, or a butterfly dreaming he was Chuang. . . . Between Chuang . . . and a butterfly there must be *some* distinction! This is called the transformation of things (Watson 1968:49).

On the price of freedom:

Once when Chuang Tzu was fishing in the P'u River, the king of Ch'u sent two ministers to go and announce to him: 'I would like to trouble you with the administration of my realm.'

Chuang Tzu held on to his fishing pole and, without turning his head, said: 'I have heard that there is a sacred tortoise in Ch'u that has been dead for three thousand years. The king keeps it wrapped in cloth and boxed, and stores it in the ancestral temple. Now would this tortoise rather be dead and have its bones left behind and honored? Or would it rather be alive and dragging its tail in the mud?'

'It would rather be alive and dragging its tail in the mud,' said the two officials.

Chuang Tzu said, 'Go away! I'll drag my tail in the mud!' (Watson 1968:187–8).

On naturalism:

Lord Yuan of Sung wanted to have some pictures painted. The crowd of court clerks all gathered in his presence, received their drawing panels, and took their places in line, licking their brushes, mixing their inks, so many of them that there were more outside the room than inside it. There was one clerk who arrived late, sauntering in without the slightest haste. When he received his drawing panel, he did not look for a place in line, but went straight to his own quarters. The ruler sent someone to see what he was doing, and it was found that he had taken off his robes, stretched out his legs, and was sitting there naked. 'Very good,' said the ruler. 'This is a true artist!' (Watson 1968:228).

Zhuangzi's Mysticism

Both Laozi and Zhuangzi have been termed mystics. Whereas the *Daodejing* was addressed to rulers and contains political teachings, the *Zhuangzi* defines true happiness as a mystical union with nature that presupposes withdrawal from politics and society. The blissful trance state that it describes recalls what Western traditions have often referred to as the mystic experience.

Zhuangzi teaches that absolute happiness comes with transcending the distinctions between the self and the universe by uniting perfectly with the Dao. This requires a higher level of knowledge, a wisdom that goes beyond the distinctions among things, including that between life and death. This may be called mystical knowledge, since it is intuitive and not acquired by ordinary rational means. Indeed, it comes only with 'forgetting' the knowledge of all things—especially that of the self. The text refers to 'sitting and forgetting' (*zuowang*), as well as a 'fasting of the mind' that requires emptying the senses and even the mind itself: 'Let your ears and your eyes communicate with what is inside. . . . Then even gods and spirits will come to dwell' (Watson 1968:58).

Zhuangzi even attributes words to Confucius to give expression to Daoist teachings and ideals. The practice of 'sitting and forgetting' as well as the 'fasting of the mind' are thus explained in an imaginary conversation between Confucius and his favourite disciple:

[Yen Hui said:] 'May I ask what the fasting of the mind is?'
   Confucius said: 'Make your will one! Don't listen with your ears, listen with your mind. No, don't listen with your mind, but listen with your spirit. Listening stops with the ears, the mind stops with recognition, but spirit is empty and waits on all things. The Way gathers in emptiness alone. Emptiness is the fasting of the mind' (Watson 1968:57–8).

As in all forms of mysticism, the experience involves moving beyond discursive knowledge and even beyond distinctions of good and evil. On another occasion, the disciple and Confucius have the following conversation:

Yen Hui said, 'I'm improving!'
   Confucius said, 'What do you mean by that?'
'I've forgotten benevolence and righteousness.'
   'That's good. But you still haven't got it.'
Another day, the two met again and Yen Hui said, 'I'm improving!'
   'What do you mean by that?'
'I've forgotten rites and music!'
   'That's good. But you still haven't got it!'
Another day, the two met again and Yen Hui said, 'I'm improving!'
'What do you mean by that?'
   'I can sit down and forget everything!'
   Confucius looked very startled and said, 'What do you mean, sit down and forget everything?'
   Yen Hui said, 'I smash up my limbs and body, drive out perception and intellect, cast off form, do away with understanding, and make myself identical with the Great Thoroughfare. This is what I mean by sitting down and forgetting everything.'
   Confucius said, '. . . So you really are a worthy man after all! With your permission, I'd like to become your follower' (Watson 1968:90–1).

When one lives according to nature one must respect its laws, including the inevitability of death. But a superior wisdom frees the sage from the emotional vicissitudes of life and the world. He has not lost his feelings, but he has risen above them. His acceptance of the natural enables him to regard life and death with equanimity and frees him from the desire to prolong life. On the other hand, some passages in Zhuangzi —in particular the lyrical descriptions of the Perfect Man who has become 'immortal'— may be interpreted as suggesting that to conquer death and help others to overcome sickness are not undesirable goals.

| Box 9.7 | Zhuangzi on the Sage |

The sage penetrates bafflement and complication, rounding all into a single body, yet he does not know why—it is his inborn nature. . . .

When people are born with good looks, you may hand them a mirror, but if you don't tell them, they will never know that they are better looking than others. Whether they know it or don't know it, whether they are told of it or are not told of it, however, their delightful good looks remain unchanged to the end, and others can go on endlessly admiring them—it is a matter of inborn nature. The sage loves other men, and men accordingly pin labels on him, but if they do not tell him, then he will never know that he loves other men. Whether he knows it or doesn't know it, whether he is told of it or is not told of it, however, his love for men remains unchanged to the end, and others can find endless security in it—it is a matter of inborn nature (Watson 1968: 281–2).

There were men who followed what is called the Way that is not a way, and this exchange of theirs is what is called the debate that is not spoken. Therefore, when virtue is resolved in the unity of the Way and words come to rest at the place where understanding no longer understands, we have perfection. The unity of the Way is something that virtue can never master; what understanding does not understand is something that debate can never encompass. To apply names in the manner of the Confucians and the Mo-ists is to invite evil. The sea does not refuse the rivers that come flowing eastward into it—it is the perfection of greatness. The sage embraces all heaven and earth, and his bounty extends to the whole world, yet no one knows who he is or what family he belongs to. For this reason, in life he holds no titles, in death he receives no posthumous names. Realities do not gather about him, names do not stick to him—this is what is called the Great Man (Watson 1968:272).

Yet another dimension in Zhuangzi goes beyond the self-effacing and quietist connotations of 'nature' mysticism. There are passages that evoke more ancient customs involving ecstasy and shamanism. These 'shamanic' passages include a lyrical description of the holy or Perfect Man, who has also been called an immortal:

> There is a Holy Man living on the distant Ku-she Mountain, with skin like ice or snow. . . . He does not eat the five grains, but sucks the wind, drinks the dew, mounts the clouds and mist, rides a flying dragon, and wanders beyond the four seas. By concentrating his spirit, he can protect creatures from sickness and plague and make the harvest plentiful (Watson 1968:33).

Crystallization

The Daoist Pantheon and Great Peace

Daoism can be called a 'salvation' religion. Salvation implies a 'fallen' state, from which one is to become 'whole' again, or healed. In some traditions this healing requires the help of a saviour or healer; in others it comes about through one's own efforts. The desire for physical immortality may seem rather earthly, but it contains within itself a quest for transcendence. To become godlike—powerful like the gods, or immortal like the gods—has always been the deepest of human longings. From this perspective, the Daoist religion echoes the Latin phrase *eritis sicut Deus*: 'you shall be like God'. In its quest for wholeness, religious Daoism tends to associate human weakness and sickness with sin. Daoists consider such ills to offend against both the conscience and the deity, and believe that they can be healed through the confession of sin and the forgiveness and help of higher powers.

Daoism evolved a pantheon of innumerable spiritual beings, gods, or celestials and immortals, as well as deified heroes and forces of nature. Together these make up a divine hierarchy that functions much like a state bureaucracy. At the top of the hierarchy were three gods that assumed different names in different periods. In early Han times they were known as the 'Great One' (Taiyi), the 'Heavenly One' (Tianyi) and the 'Earthly One' (Diyi). They are sometimes interpreted as the supreme deity (a direct emanation of the Dao itself), his disciple, the Lord Dao (the Dao personified), and his disciple, the Lord Lao (Laozi deified). Thus Laozi appears as the third in a hierarchy of gods, and many believe that he revealed all the principal texts in the Daoist canon.

Later, the Daoist trinity received other names, such as the 'Three Pure Ones' (*Sanqing*), who were the lords of the Three Life Principles or 'Breaths' (*qi*). Their names were the Primal Celestial One (*Yuanshi tianzun*), the Precious Celestial One (*Lingbao tianzun*), and the Way-and-Its-Power Celestial One (*Daode tianzun*). They each represented some aspect of the ineffable Dao, transcendent and yet capable of becoming 'incarnate', especially through Laozi's revelation. More recently, the supreme deity has been called the Jade Emperor and, in Taiwan, Lord Heaven (*Tiangong*).

Scholars have noted a resemblance between the Daoist and Christian trinities: the Primal Celestial One, controlling the past, has been compared to God the Father; the Precious Celestial One, controlling the present, to God the Son; and the Way-and-Its-Power Celestial One, controlling the future, to God the Holy Spirit. But the Daoist trinity was well established by Tang times, when Christians first became active in China, so it seems unlikely that it reflects any Christian influence.

Daoism also identifies a messiah figure. The *Taiping jing* ('Classic of the Great Peace') looks forward to a future epoch when a ruler of high virtue will govern in accordance with the teachings contained in a celestial book possessed by the saviour or divine man. This messiah figure will pass its teachings on to a prophet figure called the 'true man' (*zhenren*), who in turn will transmit them to the ruler. Following the Dao, the latter will govern with the help of his ministers and the people at large, careful to maintain harmony within the realm but slow to exercise coercion or punishment.

Perhaps this text originated with the Daoists who attempted to influence the ruler in the direction of reform during the Han dynasty. Their failure led to the Yellow Turbans revolt of 184–215 (named for the yellow kerchiefs worn by the Daoist rebels), which also failed. Nevertheless, Daoist messianism became the inspiration for later movements of political protest. This is one reason why the religion has been regarded with suspicion by Chinese governments even today. It has been severely persecuted in communist China and carefully supervised in Taiwan.

The Daoist Canon

Over fifteen centuries the Daoist tradition accumulated a huge body of scriptures—more than 1,000 volumes, including the *Laozi*, *Zhuangzi*, and *Book of Changes*—known as the **Daozang** ('Daoist canon'). At the heart of this canon are three texts said to consist of divine revelations received by Daoist adepts in a trance state. None bears the name of the author or the date of composition, and much of their language can be understood only by initiates.

The structure of the Daoist canon, which comes from the fifth century, reflects the main divisions within Daoism. There are seven sections, the first three of which, known as the Three Caverns, each developed around a particular scripture or group of scriptures:

• The First Cavern (Dongzhen) has as its nucleus the Shangqing scriptures. It is associated with the Mao-shan movement, which originated near Nanjing in southern China.
• The Second Cavern (Dongxuan) has as its nucleus the Lingbao scriptures, which also originated in the south. These show a strong Buddhist influence and have been associated with the Lingbao sect.
• The Third Cavern (Dongshen) has as its nucleus the Sanhuang ('Three Sovereigns') scriptures. Their origins are less clear; they may have come from the Daoist masters who served at court, and they include exorcism texts, which have been connected with the Heavenly Masters sect (p. 478).

These texts are known as 'caverns' (*dong*) because they were said to have been revealed or discovered in caves. Each of the Three Caverns is placed under the protection of one of the three members of the Daoist trinity.

The central texts of the Four Supplements are actually older than the Three Caverns texts, and may have been added to the latter in an effort to counterbalance Buddhist influences on Daoism:

• The Taixuan is a supplement to the First Cavern. Its central text is the *Laozi* (which shows the curiously subordinate place of this treatise).
• The Taiping is a supplement to the Second Cavern. Its central text is the well-known *Taiping ching* (*Classic of the Great Peace*), a utopian and messianic text.
• The Taiqing is a supplement to the Third Cavern. Its central texts deal more directly with alchemy.
• The Zhengyi is a supplement to all three caverns. It consists of the canonical texts of the Heavenly Masters sect.

Daoist Movements and Schools

Like Confucianism, Daoism did not emphasize central authority. It developed so many branches—centred on everything from meditation and alchemy to longevity practices and new forms of political thought—that Daoism itself became difficult to define.

Neo-Daoism

The legacy of Daoist philosophy is ambiguous. This ambiguity is evident in the commentaries on Laozi and Zhuangzi. Some of these are very important, not only for the insight they offer into the original texts but also for what the commentators themselves have to say (as in the case of Confucius, a great deal can be said by creative thinkers who attribute their ideas to the ancients). The commentaries also ask important questions about the original texts. For example, is Zhuangzi's Dao the same as Laozi's? The answers can be diametrically opposite, depending on the commentators and the chapters considered.

The term 'Neo-Daoism' refers to the period from the third to sixth centuries, when the country was politically divided and in turmoil after the order imposed by the Han dynasty had collapsed under the pressure of barbarian raids from the north. Ideas associated with the Daoist tradition were both a force in and an expression of the general unrest. Daoism had a tradition of protest in that Laozi and Zhuangzi had both criticized Confucius. Rulers sometimes made use of Daoist tenets in their government, and ordinary people also appealed to Daoist ideas in revolts and rebellions. (This has remained the case into modern times: for example, the Daoist religion has been associated with the Taiwanese independence movement.)

Neo-Daoism had both a 'rationalist' side, centred on textual interpretation and philosophical discussions, and an 'aesthetic' side centred on poetry and art. It also had an iconoclastic aspect reminiscent in some ways of the hippie and student protest movements of the 1960s. Respect for authority, including the principle of the Five Relationships, was collapsing. Children were calling their parents by their personal names, while poets and philosophers found solace in drink and unstructured conversation.

Neo-Daoist Protest

One notable example of Neo-Daoist protest was Wang Bi (226–49), whose commentary on the *Daodejing* reflected his iconoclastic attitude towards the social authority of the past. Another was the group who came to be known as the Seven Worthies of the Bamboo Grove. Opposed to the 'names and doctrines' (*mingjiao*) school that represented the intellectual establishment of the day, they also revived interest in an ancient school of logic called *mingjia*. Their blend of Daoist and Confucian ideas embraced both Daoist-inspired anti-establishment protest and Confucian-inspired devotion to public service. They reinterpreted Confucius as a sage united with the Dao, and even placed him above Laozi.

The Seven Worthies of the Bamboo Grove were known for their non-conformist behaviour. One of them, Liu Ling, chose to go naked in his house. When some visitors found this strange, he responded: 'I take heaven and earth for my pillars and roof, and the rooms of my house for my pants and coat. What are you gentlemen doing in my pants?' (Mather 1976:374). Ruan Ji (210–63) and his nephew Ruan Xian were renowned as drinkers who liked to sit by a large container of wine, which they sometimes shared with their pigs.

The Seven Worthies exemplify what we might call romantic spontaneity, an aesthetic attitude towards life and the universe traditionally expressed by the phrase 'wind and stream' (*feng-liu*). This characteristic of Daoism has had a profound influence on many aspects of East Asian culture, inspiring creativity in art and poetry, and its aesthetic fascination with the grotesque, especially gnarled trees and oddly shaped rocks, greatly influenced the East Asian Buddhist aesthetic it expressed in Zen gardens. At the same time the Daoist emphasis on insightful awareness no doubt contributed to the domestication in China of ideas drawn from Indian Buddhism.

Sects: Heavenly Masters and Perfect Truth

Sectarian distinctions in Daoist religion had more to do with practice than doctrine. Some emphasized alchemy, others sexual hygiene or meditative exercises. For example, the Lingbao tradition gave special attention to rituals at court, whereas the Mao-shan tradition focused on meditation. The establishment of the Daoist canon brought these groups together in one large eclectic tradition. Although Daoism has declined steadily since the seventeenth century, two sects have survived.

The **Heavenly Masters** (or Zhengyi) sect is quite old, and its founding is often identified as the formal beginning of the Daoist religion as an institution. In later Han times (second century), a significant religious movement developed in the southern state of Sichuan under Zhang Ling (or Zhang Daoling), who claimed that Laozi had appeared to him in a mountain cave in 142, complaining that the world lacked respect for the true and the correct, and that people were worshipping pernicious demons. In this alleged revelation, Zhang was made the Heavenly Master and told to abolish the influence of the demons and establish true orthodoxy. The Heavenly Masters sect became a hereditary institution and eventually moved its traditional base from Sichuan to the Dragon-Tiger Mountain of Jiangsi. It was especially popular in southern China and has continued there to the present, although its headquarters were moved to Taiwan after the communist takeover in 1949.

The other sect is of the northern school and is known as **Perfect Truth** (*Quanzhen dao*) or 'Way of Complete Perfection'. It was founded by Wang Zhe (1113–70) and became the major monastic form of Daoism. One of Wang Zhe's disciples was influential in the court of the famous Mongol Chinggis (Genghis) Khan. Having developed in a period of religious blending, the Perfect Truth sect shows the greatest Buddhist influence. Its monks are celibate, observe frequent fasts, abstain from alcohol, and practise inner alchemy and meditation.

Practice

Rituals, Alchemy, Scholars and Priests

Although the Daoist religion revered Laozi and Zhuangzi (both the men and their texts), it radically reinterpreted their teachings. The Daoism of the early sages is only one of several intellectual strands that converged in later Daoism. The religion also incorporates ideas from the Yin-yang school, which regards the natural order as operating under two complementary yet antithetical aspects of the Dao. There is also a discernible influence of the Five Agents school, which pursued proto-scientific theories and experiments.

In early Han times, Daoism was known as the cult of Huang-Lao (that is, the Yellow Emperor Huangdi and Laozi). In ascribing its teachings to these earlier figures, its proponents did what so many others, including Confucius, have done, attributing authority to the distant past. Daoist practice includes the chanting of passages from the *Daodejing*, and interpretations of these passages are among the texts that new Daoists study. Thus later Daoists used the writings of the sages the way Buddhists and Christians use their scriptures: as sacred writings to be read aloud during services and as sources of inspiration for living in each era.

Over time, religious Daoism developed some characteristics associated with religions of salvation. It instructs the faithful in healthy living and seeks to guide them beyond this transitory life to a happy eternity. It professes a belief in an original state of bliss, followed by the present fallen human condition. It relies on supernatural powers for help and protection. Some of these features may represent Buddhist influence in Han times and later.

Practices of the Heavenly Masters Sect

The Heavenly Masters sect opposed the bloody sacrifices that were offered to the spirits of the deceased and substituted offerings of cooked vegetables. To heal the sick, it instituted the confession of sins: priests prayed for the sick, who wrote down their sins in documents that were then offered to heaven (on mountain tops), to earth (by burial), and to the rivers (by 'drowning'). The sect levied and collected a tax of five pecks (about 35 kg) of rice from the members of its congregation. For this reason it was also known as the Five Pecks of Rice sect.

Interestingly, the Heavenly Masters sect accepts women as clergy but excludes them from higher office as well as certain rituals. It has always been known for its good organization: hereditary instructors are assisted by parish councils of Daoist notables, including men and women who take part in various ceremonies, and there are secular patrons of the organization as well.

Rituals and Priests

Rituals and liturgical activities have always been the soul of Daoist religion, reflecting a quasi-sacramental regard for ritual initiation, purification and renewal in the life cycle, and cultivation of the human being. Already under development in Han times, Daoist liturgy was further transformed with the emergence of the Mao-shan cult in the later fourth century.

Buddhist literature influenced the early collection of ecstatic scriptural texts, which contained visions and inspired writings. New hymns were introduced, together with Buddhist customs like the circumambulation of sacred objects and the chanting of texts called 'sacred treasures' (*lingbao*). This literature gives assurances of salvation to the initiated at the time of expected cataclysms. It also expresses the eschatological hope that Laozi, like a messiah, will return to establish a reign of peace and equality for the elect, the very 'pure'.

Courtyard of the Temple of the Eight Immortals (Daoist Perfect Truth sect) in Xian (Kate Brunn).

Daoist priests are licensed by the Heavenly Master to perform particular rituals. Exorcism rituals are often used to cure the sick by driving out the evil spirits afflicting them. Many other rituals are performed regularly throughout the year. The best-known ones take place around the lunar New Year, when dragon dances and firecrackers are used to chase away the demons, and prayers are offered to the stove god—a very important Daoist deity who can be traced to ancient religion. There is also the rite of cosmic renewal, performed at the winter solstice to celebrate the sun's return. Some of the priests who conduct the rituals are also shamans, soothsayers, or spirit-mediums. They assist the faithful with advice and fortune-telling, explain the influence of the stars, and communicate with the spirits of the beloved dead.

Incense and the sacrificial offering of sacred writings, such as the burning of paper talismans, are central to Daoist ritual. Sometimes the papers sacrificed bear the prayers of the faithful, their names, and the purpose for which the service is being performed. The faithful who participate in such rituals are usually urged to prepare for them by fasting and cultivating a spirit of forgiveness and reconciliation.

People set up little shrines to the Daoist deities at the base of trees, on the ground near the doorway to a home, and in the kitchen (up high and down on the ground). In Hong Kong police stations, even under the British, every department has had its own small shrine. Many people keep a whole pantheon of ceramic gods in their living rooms, to ensure that no deity who might be helpful is neglected.

The Search for Immortality

As we have seen, Daoists look forward to the survival of the whole person, including the body. The unity of spirit and matter is the authentically Chinese core of the Daoist religion.

According to another central doctrine there are three life principles: breath (*qi*), vital essence or semen (*jing*), and spirit (*shen*). Each of these principles has two dimensions: microcosmic in the human being and macrocosmic in the cosmos. These cosmic principles are also manifested in the Daoist trinity.

Daoist techniques have been developed for healing and breath circulation, meditation, and sexual hygiene (a combination of sex and yoga). Many of these teachings are transmitted in secret from master to disciple, as in tantric Buddhism. They gave rise to Chinese healing techniques and the martial arts, as well as herbal medicine. This is a truly holistic healing system, based on the ancient text called the Inner Classic of the Yellow Emperor (*Huangdi neijing*), which goes back to the sixth century BCE. It gives a clear list of priorities for maintaining health—first treatment of the spirit, then proper nutrition, and finally healing.

China's belief in immortals can be traced at least as far back as the third century BCE and was elaborated after Daoism became an institutional religion. 'Heavenly immortals' are said to roam the sacred forests and mountains. There are also some human beings who appear to die, but actually only leave behind their physical frames (*shijie*).

Daoist Alchemy

The Western term 'alchemy' refers to a mystical tradition of chemical experimentation practised throughout Europe as well as Asia. In Europe the most frequent goal was to transmute base metals into gold, but in China it was to prolong life and attain immortality. Daoists have described alchemy as an effort to 'steal the secret of heaven and earth', that is, to wrest from nature the mystery of life. They may not have found the elixir of immortality, but, like the medieval European alchemists, they became pioneers of scientific experimentation. Treating the body as a kind of 'furnace' in which the elixir of immortality could be made, they developed a knowledge of physiology, chemistry, and pharmacology that has been reflected in several fields, including Chinese medicine.

In fact, alchemical information and experimentation did contribute to the preservation of the physical body. Metallic components like mercury and lead can be fatal when swallowed, but they also have preservative powers. Well-preserved bodies from Ming times and earlier have been discovered with perfumed mercury in their abdomens. Perhaps Chinese aristocrats swallowed mercury to ensure that their physical bodies would be preserved, so that their 'souls' and bodies would eventually attain immortality

Pilgrims climb Daoism's most sacred mountain, Taishan (Martin Gray). In ancient times it was the custom for emperors, on ascending the throne, to perform sacrifices to the gods of heaven at the peak of Taishan. Mao Zedong made the climb as well; watching the sunrise from the top of the mountain, he joked that, in the East, even the sky is red.

together. Pools of preserving chemicals may also have been placed in the tombs of ancient royals.

In 1972, near Changsha, Hunan, archaeologists discovered the remains of an approximately fifty-year-old noblewoman from the second century BCE. The condition of the body was remarkable—like that of someone who had been dead only a week or two. Tests found that it had been immersed in a liquid containing mercuric sulphide. Might she have died of elixir poisoning in an effort to gain immortality? With the body, archaeologists also found various talismans designed to conduct the deceased to her eternal destination after burial, into the presence of the Lord-on-high. Such finds are invaluable evidence for those seeking to reconstruct ancient beliefs.

Daoist Meditation and Inner Alchemy

It may have been in response to the physical dangers of experimenting with chemical elixirs that a different kind of alchemy developed during Tang and Song times. Based on various techniques of meditation and yoga, this 'inner' alchemy sought to nourish the yin and the yang of the body and unite them in an effort to recover the primordial energy (*qi*) that permeates and sustains all life.

| Box 9.8 | Seeking Longevity and Immortality |

In the fourth century the *Shenxian zhuan* ('Biographies of Immortals') recounted the legend of Wei Boyang. Allegedly, he had made an elixir in the mountains, and decided to try it first on his dog, which died instantly. He turned then to his disciples, and said, 'I have abandoned worldly ways and forsaken family and friends. . . . I should be ashamed to return without having found the Dao of the Immortals. To die of the elixir is no worse than living without having found it.' And so he, too, took the elixir and fell dead. On seeing this, one disciple commented, 'Our teacher is no ordinary person. He must have done this with some reason.' So he followed the master's example, and also died. The other two disciples said to each other, 'People prepare elixirs for the sake of gaining longevity. But this elixir has brought on death. It would be better not to take it, but live a few more decades in the world.' So they left the mountains to procure coffins for the burial of their master and fellow disciple. After they were gone, however, both Wei Boyang and the loyal disciple, together with their dog, revived, became real immortals, and went away! They left behind a message for the other two, who were then filled with remorse (*Shenxian zhuan* [Biographies of Immortals], fourth century).

In theory, the human body is divided into three '**cinnabar fields**': head, chest, and abdomen. (The term associates inner alchemy with the function of cinnabar—mercuric sulphide—in outer alchemy.) Each field is inhabited by many gods operating under the supervision of a member of the Daoist trinity. Methods of meditation include visualizing light, which represents energy or *qi*, and conducting it through the three cinnabar fields in a 'microcosmic orbit' or extending this circulation to the extremities of the limbs in a 'macrocosmic orbit'.

By doing Qigong exercises and meditating, the Daoist practitioner seeks a vision of the gods—there are thousands of them—and contact with them within the body. Through such contact, the Daoist may obtain their help in curing illness by ridding the body of toxins or 'evil spirits'. One might even acquire an inner elixir through spiritual illumination and produce an ethereal and immortal body within oneself. Similar exercises are still taught today.

'Embryonic respiration' was an advanced technique involving conscious imitation of the fetus in the mother's womb. It was also linked to the quest for inner peace and the integration of the personality. Daoists speak of finding the 'True Self' within and achieving greater harmony with the rhythm of the external cosmos. This 'True Self' is often envisaged as a new birth within.

Daoist practice also includes an ethical dimension. The emphasis on good works and ritual penance for wrongdoing shows the historical interaction between Daoism and Confucianism.

The Eight Daoist Immortals

An interesting group of 'deities' are the **Eight Immortals** who collectively signify happiness. All said to have been historical individuals, they are eight men and women of different ages and stations in life: the crippled Li, holding an iron crutch, who is the patron of pharmacists; the imperial relative Zao, a military commander and patron of actors; the androgynous-looking Lan, formerly a street singer and now the patron of florists; the fairy maid He, daughter of a storekeeper; Zhongli Quan, a stout man who holds a peach in one hand and a feather fan in the other and is the patron of silversmiths; Old Man Zhang, carrying a fish drum; the famous Lu Dongbin, carrying a sword and a fly whisk; and his disciple, the young Han, carrying a basket of flowers and a jade flute, who is a patron of musicians. This diversity gives them a broad appeal.

As patrons of particular groups, especially in the various trades, the Eight Immortals are similar to the Christian saints. They are not so much deities as individuals of merit, role models, and protectors. Like the ancestors, the Eight Immortals represent the close ties between the living and the dead, and their spirits are always within reach when help is needed.

Cultural Expressions

Several types of art and architecture might be considered 'Daoist'. There are sculptures of sages beginning with Laozi, dating from the third century. There are also steles and particular building forms that came to be favoured for Daoist shrines, temples and monasteries.

Besides art in which the subjects are Daoist figures or symbols, there is what might be called a Daoist spirit that runs through much Chinese art, especially in the Zen Buddhist tradition. This spirit is easier to see in the work than to characterize in words, but nature, especially the seasons of the year, is a common theme. Daoist painting and poetry often evokes not only a particular place but a particular season, and celebrates simple things such as fishing or warming by a campfire.

The techniques used in Daoist art are sometimes minimalist: a painting of the moon over water may consist of only a few brushstrokes. Working in black ink on porous paper means that the strokes must be both spontaneous and sure. Therefore it is essential that the artist work with complete concentration, in a meditative state of mind.

Because most temples in China, regardless of tradition, were built in the style of a palace complex, Daoist temples often resemble their Buddhist counterparts. There is a quick way to tell them apart, however. Whereas Buddhist temples have a warrior on either side of the entry gate, Daoist temples have a dragon and a lion. The altar in the main hall usually has statues of the three main gods, whereas Buddhist temples have a similar grouping of three Buddhist figures. Daoist temples typically have up-turned eaves as well.

Interaction and Adaptation

The communist era in China has been difficult for Daoism. Like other religions, it fared badly after 1949 under the state's anti-religious policies. During the infamous Cultural

Revolution, gangs of youth called Red Guards were encouraged to eliminate all traces of old forms of culture, with the result that Daoist temples and art collections were largely destroyed. Since the end of the Cultural Revolution in 1976 Daoism has begun to re-establish itself, but recovery has been slow.

The good news is that during this same period Daoism has spread beyond East Asia. Daoist temples have been established in some large Western cities. Many Westerners are learning Daoist-inspired spiritual and martial exercises such as Qigong and Taiji, and books such as the *Daodejing* and *Zhuangzi* have become quite popular.

Some modern writers perceive several points of agreement between ancient Daoist thought and modern physics. Others look to the Daoist tradition for ideas on everything from ecology to sexual practices.

Buddho–Daoist Hells

Daoism is primarily concerned with life on earth, Buddhism with life after death. Thus popular beliefs in the rewards and punishments to come in the afterlife reflect Buddhist influences. The Daoist belief in a series of hells, derived from Chinese Buddhism, is particularly evident in the scrolls depicting them that are hung during funeral services.

The exact number of hells varies, but most accounts say there are ten. They are sometimes said to be situated under a high mountain in Sichuan, in southwest China. Each is ruled by a king who serves as judge, surrounded by ministers and attendants who carry out his decisions. Justice is meted out impartially. Most punishment is corporal, inflicted with instruments of torture. Supposedly, the soul of the deceased moves through the series of hells until it is ready for rebirth; thus—like the Catholic purgatory—the Chinese hells are not final. As in Catholic belief, offerings and prayers for the dead can mitigate the punishments they suffer after death.

Syncretism: The 'Unity' Sect

Yiguandao is an ethical society devoted to the salvation of all humankind. The term means 'Unifying Dao' and is sometimes translated simply as 'Unity Sect'. A fine example of syncretism, Yiguandao claims to embrace Daoist, Buddhist, and Confucian teachings, as well as the cult of the Daoist goddess known as Eternal Venerable Mother. Its adherents chant and meditate, study scriptures, including morality books, do *taiji* or *qigong* exercises, and abstain from meat.

The syncretic character of the Unity sect can also be seen in its texts, which include spirit-writing tracts and scriptural texts borrowed from Confucianism, Daoism, and Buddhism as well as other small sects. They deal with doctrine, ritual, and the important issue of lineage or apostolic succession. Like the Neo-Confucian thinkers, members of the Unity sect believe that the true line of transmission of ancient doctrine, through Confucius and Laozi, ceased with the death of Mencius. But they maintain that this Dao blended with Buddhism in India and proceeded through Chan in China to the Sixth Patriarch Huineng (see p. 409), after which it was once again lost, only to be recovered by the 'common people', who continue the process of transmission.

Chinese Popular Religion and Other Movements

Besides the 'Three Religions' (Confucianism, Daoism and Buddhism), China has a folk tradition known to scholars as 'popular religion', the roots of which go far, far into the past, as well as many smaller religious traditions. We will start with a discussion of the tradition started by Mozi, the breakaway follower of Confucius mentioned earlier. Then, after an introduction to some elements of popular religion, including feng shui, tombs, and the calendar, we will discuss two more recent movements: the Taipings who almost took control of China in the mid-1800s, and Falun Gong, the contemporary *qigong* movement now banned in China but spreading around the world.

Mozi on Universal Love and Pacifism

Mozi, Master Mo, lived roughly a century after Confucius (c. 470–391 BCE). His school of philosophy, Moism, had strong moral and religious overtones. Mozi was initially a student of the Confucian school. Whereas Confucius was a moderate, however, Mozi tended to extremes. He became a severe critic of the Confucian school as he knew it and developed the independent philosophy outlined in the work called *Mozi*, which is believed to have been composed by disciples of his school. The text *Mozi* is organized around a vast range of topics, from ghosts and spirits to military strategy to non-aggression and even militant pacifism.

Confucius was criticized by religious conservatives for not talking much about Heaven and the afterlife, but Mozi has a good deal to say about religion. He believes in Heaven as the Supreme Being and in the will of Heaven as the guide to human existence. He also believes in a hierarchy of spirits and ghosts, like those popular in ancient China. For this reason, he is sometimes said to be the direct heir to early Chinese religion.

As a believer in Heaven and spirits, Mozi would spare no expense for sacrificial rituals to honour the gods. When it came to the ancestor cult and funerary rituals, however, he criticized the Confucians' re-enactment of ancient practices such as searching for the spirit of the deceased before preparing the body for burial (presumably to call the spirit to return to life):

> When a parent dies, the Confucians lay out the corpse for a long time before dressing it for burial while they climb up onto the roof, peer down the well, poke in the ratholes, and search in the washbasins, looking for the dead man. If they suppose that they will really find the dead man there, then they must be stupid indeed, while if they know that he is not there but still search for him, then they are guilty of the greatest hypocrisy (Watson 1963b:125).

Confucius taught the virtue of humanity (*ren*), which has sometimes been called 'graded' love, since it begins with the family and extends outward. Mozi, by contrast, taught universal love, equal love (*jianai*) for all, on the grounds that Heaven loves all equally:

> How do we know that Heaven loves the people of the world? Because it enlightens them universally. How do we know that it enlightens them universally? Because it possesses them universally. How do we know that it possesses them universally? Because it accepts sacrifices from them universally (Watson 1963b:81–2).

Mencius rejected this idea of Mozi's on the grounds that it undermined family values.

Mozi believed in authority even more fervently than Confucius and Mencius, and like them, he considered it a duty to offer advice to rulers. Unlike them, however, he actively devoted himself to the cause of maintaining peace and opposing war. He was a militant pacifist who did his homework: he became a specialist in weaponry and military strategy precisely in order to use that knowledge to bring about peace. For example, when Mozi heard that the state of Ch'u was planning an attack on the smaller state of Song, he walked for ten days and ten nights to the capital of Chu. There he persuaded the ruler to call off the expedition, after providing his disciples with weapons to help protect the smaller state. This story illustrates Mozi's tireless devotion to his causes. It also suggests a high degree of organization on the part of his disciples, who are sometimes described as knights religiously devoted to their leader.

Over time, the Chinese people preferred Confucius to Mozi as a teacher. Mozi was a great man, but perhaps excessive in virtue. Zhuangzi criticized him as follows:

> Mo-tzu [Mozi] wrote a piece 'Against Music', and another entitled 'Moderation in Expenditure', declaring that there was to be no singing in life, no mourning after death. With a boundless love and a desire to insure universal benefit, he condemned warfare. . . . His views, however, were not always in accordance with those of the former kings, for he denounced the rites and music of antiquity. . . . A life that is all toil, a death shoddily disposed of—it is a way that goes too much against us (Watson 1968:365–6).

Although important in Mozi's own time, Mohism was eventually overshadowed first by Confucianism and later by Daoism and Buddhism. Interest in Mozi was renewed, however, with the introduction of Christianity, which recalled his teachings on Heaven and universal love. In modern times some scholars in mainland China have praised certain aspects of his thought, but the Marxist legacy has made it impossible to approve of his religious teachings.

Popular Religion

'Popular religion' is the faith and practice of the common people, as opposed to the sophisticated doctrines and institutional structures of Confucianism, Daoism, and

Buddhism. Popular religion is not a formally boundaried tradition with a centralized authority or official doctrine. In fact, borrowing from other traditions is one of its distinguishing characteristics.

The survival of native traditions in combination with foreign elements, known as syncretism, is possible because popular religion is less self-conscious or doctrinal than the established traditions and has little need to defend its own orthodoxy. China's ancient religious beliefs and practices have never been entirely assimilated into the doctrinal systems of institutional Confucianism, Daoism, or Buddhism. The people's expressions of piety have proved to be remarkably long-lasting. Thus popular or folk religion integrates an apparently amorphous mass of accumulated tradition from the past with current beliefs and practices. Popular religion crosses the boundaries between

---

| Box 9.9   Teachings of Master Chuang

A twentieth-century Daoist master from Taiwan teaches the proper use of the 'Dao of the Left', a form that can be used to do harm but needs to be learned in order to counter those who might use it in that way.

Chuang began to repeat his injunctions about preserving the secrets he was going to reveal and never using the feared Tao of the Left except to help one's fellow man. Orthodox Taoists like himself and his sons were never permitted to use such techniques except in the most extreme conditions. . . .

In a brief few sentences, Chuang got to the point. There were three preliminary warnings, he said. The heart must first be made to control the impulses and the phantasms which entered the mind. Before such a dangerous doctrine was imparted to the disciples, the master must assure himself that their hearts were pure and their motives simple. Anyone learning these secrets who intended to use them for gross profit or for harming others needlessly would be punished drastically by the spirits. The second warning had to do with self-discipline. The spirits will only obey those who are upright and who have practised the rubrics so thoroughly that not the slightest detail is missing. The third point concerned the method of bringing the power of the spirits into one's own body. The mind had to be emptied of all cares and worries and the body purified in all respects before the power could be brought into the microcosm of the body. . . .

A hundred days before beginning the rite for enfoeffing the spirits, the disciple must begin by regulating his mind and senses. The exercise of breath control and meditation on the purest of the heavenly spirits must be practised daily upon arising and before going to bed. The Taoist must envision the three principles of life in the centre of the microcosm, the Yellow Court within his own body, and see himself contemplating before the eternal, transcendant Tao. When the Three Principles of Life—Primordial Heavenly Worthy, Ling-pao Heavenly Worthy, and Tao-te Heavenly Worthy—are present, then mystic contemplation on the eternal Tao is possible. As the time for beginning the ritual approaches, the Taoist must abstain from meat and practise celibacy. He must be particularly careful to give good example to his neighbours, by acts of benevolence and mercy towards the poor, loyalty to his friends, and filiality to his parents. Only then will it be possible to perform the Tun-chia rites; if at any time during the period of preparation or of ritual enfeoffment the Taoist fails to act virtuously, the spirits will immediately refuse to obey him (Saso, 1978:131–2).

Confucianism, Daoism, and Buddhism, and has no single sacred text or set of documents. Its basic ideas and values are those that pervade the culture as a whole, with particular emphasis on those most important to personal and communal survival: health, children, education, finance, violence, even war and peace. Popular religion and mainstream Confucianism and Daoism share the belief that even though the spirits have power over this life, they require sustenance from those who are alive; thus offerings are made to them in return for their help, and may be withheld if help is not forthcoming. The 'ghosts', in their turn, may harass the living and demand propitiation.

Religious ritual and practice on the folk level are often reminiscent of the ancient religion. The understanding of priesthood changed with the historical development of Confucianism, Daoism, and Buddhism, and the state religion based on divination, shamanism, and sacrifice lapsed centuries ago with the Shang dynasty, but divination, trances, and sacrificial offerings of cooked food, especially to the ancestors, persist in popular religion.

In Taiwan today, the country's prosperity is reflected in the abundance and wealth of its temples and popular shrines, which are the supposed earthly palaces of the deities and spirits. Often the temple is the only architectural structure in a modern town or village that still follows the traditional style of roofs with curved eaves. It is a rectangular tile-roofed structure, usually with its longer sides aligned across a north–south axis. The image of the deity faces south, enthroned like a ruler or emperor in a Chinese palace centuries ago. The entrance is usually a three-arched gate.

Large temples are situated in walled compounds with many courtyards. The central structure that contains the images of the deities is flanked or surrounded by courtyards or long halls. With their green roof tiles and red pillars, these temples are easily recognizable when they are well maintained. The statues of deities, especially of buddha figures, are often gilded. Even in communist China, there are so many temples today that one wonders how the Chinese could ever have been described as an irreligious people. Shrines in the form of miniature temples, the dwellings of more humble deities such as the local earth god, are even more common.

Feng Shui and Numerology

Feng shui—literally, 'wind and water'— is based on the belief that unseen energies flowing through the world influence our lives for better or worse. It provides a set of guidelines for avoiding the bad energy that brings loss, illness, injury, and failure, and drawing on the good energy that brings wealth, health, and success.

These guidelines are often used in laying out a house or a business. For example, a feng shui expert pointed out that the reason a certain restaurant—at a busy intersection in a popular nightlife area of Singapore—kept losing money was that it was located uphill, above a sloping road: in feng shui terms, this meant that all the money would run out the front door and down the road.

The three basic principles studied in feng shui are yin-yang, the five phases or elements (wood, fire, earth, metal, water) and the *bugua*: eight trigrams, or three-line combinations, of broken (yin) and solid (yang) lines arranged around an octagon, with the centre being a ninth sector. Each trigram relates both to a specific part of the body and to a specific area of life. For example, one of the nine sectors controls wealth. Other sectors control career, relationships, and fame. There are two main schools of feng shui, the East/West System and the Nine Floating Stars system.

Feng shui is an intrinsic part of Chinese culture. Around the world, feng shui principles are a frequent subject of conversation in Chinese homes. Meals are planned so that they balance yin and yang foods, and feng shui masters do on-site consultations to check for stagnant energy and balance the elements. Many of the simpler teachings of good feng shui—a house located at a T-junction, or with a blue roof, is to be avoided; it isn't good to engage in 'yin' activities like doing laundry or washing hair at night—are common knowledge among Chinese people.

Chinese numerology also plays an important role in traditional decision-making. Certain numbers are considered unlucky or lucky, in part because they sound like other Chinese words for bad or good things. The numbers vary with the dialects of Chinese, which differ widely. Cantonese speakers love the number eight because it sounds like 'abundance' or 'prosperity', and double 8 is especially good. (In fact, 8 is even more popular now, since Feng Shui maintains that in 2004 we entered a twenty-year cycle in which 8 is the dominant lucky number.) They also like the combination 28, which sounds like 'easy to get abundance'. They don't like 5 before 8 because it sounds like 'no wealth', and they don't like 6, which sounds like 'descent', 'decline', or 'decrease'. On the other hand, Hokkien (Fukkien) speakers like six because it sounds to them like 'luck' in English! No one likes 4 because it sounds like 'die' or 'death'. People pay a lot for licence plates and phone numbers with 'lucky numbers'. Western real-estate agents are sometimes puzzled that Chinese clients have no interest at looking at certain homes simply because of their street numbers or because their location or layout violates feng shui guidelines.

Tombs

The rulers of old China expended great effort and resources on ensuring that they would have magnificent tombs. Many of these tombs have been excavated and some are open to visitors. The most famous is the tomb of the first emperor, with its terracotta warriors, but some tombs survive from the Ming and other dynasties as well. They are laid out in careful conformity with feng shui. For example, they are always located on a hill, with protecting higher hills behind the tomb and a valley in front. The entrance road runs through the valley, but is not completely straight. It is usually lined with stone pillars representing spirits, and so is sometimes called the 'spirit way' or 'spirit road'. Nearing the tomb, the road crosses a stream—crossing moving water is good in feng shui terms—and leads to a shrine, where offerings to the dead can be made. Up the hill from there lies the underground room, or in some cases the underground palace, containing the crypt, along with food, clothes, and other supplies.

Confucian and Buddhist Influences

Over the centuries Confucian influences have been passed on through osmosis, especially through the institution of the family. Families have generally urged their children to work and study hard and to behave according to the Confucian rules of propriety in order to uphold the family's good name. This kind of moulding has been supported by the state through its own emphasis on political loyalty and civil obedience. Some popular sects have called themselves Confucian. In Taiwan there is a salvation religion with shamanic features called 'Confucian lineage spirit religion' (Ruzong Shenjiao). Introduced from the mainland, it honours, among other figures, the Daoist Jade Emperor and General Guan Gong, a historical figure who became a Daoist divinity. Its scriptures are believed to have been revealed from above, sometimes through a form of spirit writing in which the medium is a heavenly bird.

Certain buddha and bodhisattva (*pusa*) figures are prominent in the popular cult. These include the historical Buddha himself and also Omitofo (Amitabha), the buddha of the Pure Land; the future buddha Maitreya, also known as Milo, the Laughing Buddha; and the famous Guanyin. This female bodhisattva ranks ahead of Milo, Omitofo, and even the historical Buddha in popular devotion. There is also a Healing Buddha called Yaoshi.

The Compassion Society

A number of sects believe themselves to be under the special protection of the Eternal Venerable Mother, also called 'Golden Mother' or 'Queen Mother'. Yiguandao is one, and another is the 'Compassion Society', founded on the east coast of Taiwan in the mid-1950s. The Canadian scholar Daniel Overmyer has described a chapel of this sect. There are six images on an altar, arranged in two transverse rows of three. In the front, the Jade Emperor is flanked by Guanyin on his right and the Earth Mother on his left. The back row has the Queen Mother in the centre, with two female figures flanking her: on the right, the Mysterious Woman of the Nine Heavens from Daoist mythology and on the left the ancient creator goddess Nuwa. This appears to be a faith-healing sect that also relies on spirit-mediums. Members, both male and female, are considered adopted children of the goddess Mother.

Popular religion is still part of life for ethnic Chinese communities in Taiwan, Hong Kong, Singapore, Southeast Asia, and beyond. Even in China itself, religious freedom is guaranteed. at least in theory, although implementation of those guarantees has varied from time to time and from place to place. Here and there one can find evidence that expressions of religious beliefs formerly dismissed as 'superstitions' are re-emerging.

The Chinese Religious Calendar

The Chinese religious calendar reflects the syncretic character of popular religion. Years are designated by animals, in a twelve-year cycle: mouse (or rat), ox, tiger, hare, dragon, snake, horse, sheep, monkey, cock, dog, and boar (or pig). These animals are the constellations of the ancient Chinese zodiac.

The calendar follows a lunar cycle, the first of the moon or month coinciding with the new moon and the fifteenth coinciding with the full moon, with an additional month added periodically to catch up with the solar year. The lunar calendar ties in with the agricultural cycle. Even with the official adoption of the solar calendar, the traditional Chinese almanac remains an important book. The cycle begins with preparations for the lunar New Year, which usually arrives in late January or early February. About a

week before the New Year, on the first day of the first moon, the stove god, whose portrait decorates the kitchen, has to be sent off to heaven with his report on the family
members. After bribing him by smearing his lips with honey or sticky candy, the family
then removes his picture and burns it. He returns on New Year's eve when a new picture
is pasted over the stove. New Year rituals originally included worship of various deities
as well as the ancestors. Today they include dragon dances (to encourage rain and fertility) and firecrackers (originally to chase away demons). The New Year's celebrations usually extend to the fifteenth day of that month, which is called the Feast of the Lanterns.

'Double Two'—the second day of the second moon—is celebrated as the birthday
of the local earth god, to whom incense, candles, and paper offerings are made. He is
considered the local registrar for births, marriages, and deaths. The birthday of
Guanyin is celebrated on the nineteenth of the same moon. She is sometimes
represented as having a thousand eyes and a thousand hands, the better to hear and
respond to prayer.

The next important event in the calendar is Qingming, the 'clear and bright' festival, which falls fifteen days after the spring equinox. This is the time for visiting and
repairing family tombs. People take picnics to family grave sites, where they burn incense
and paper representations of things the dead might want, such as a cell phone, a
Mercedes Benz, or a maid, and sometimes offer sacrifices of cooked food. Attendance is
an important family obligation.

Shakyamuni's birthday is celebrated on the eighth day of the fourth moon,
which usually falls in May. The principal rite is the 'bathing of the Buddha', in which a
small Buddha image is cleansed with scented water in a temple ritual of Indian origin.
In late spring, a popular custom honours the ancient poet and minister Qu Yuan (c.
343–289 BCE), who drowned himself in a river. This is the dragon boat festival on
'Double Five', the fifth day of the fifth moon. It is said to be a re-enactment of the search
for the dead poet's body, sometimes as an effort to placate dragons living in the waters.
Cooked rice, wrapped in leaves, is eaten in commemoration of the custom of offering
food to the spirit of the drowned man. This has become a mainly secular celebration.

A feast special to women is 'Double Seven'—the seventh day of the seventh
moon—commemorating the love story of a cowherd and the weaving maid who is the
youngest daughter of the stove god. Granted only one reunion a year with her husband,
she meets him on a bridge of magpies over the Milky Way. Also in the seventh moon is
the Buddhist Pudu ritual, a kind of 'All Souls' Day'. Its name (literally, 'ferrying across
to the other shore') refers to the spirits of all the departed in their next abode.

In the eighth moon there is a harvest festival similar to the North American
Thanksgiving. Since it coincides with the harvest moon, round moon cakes are eaten.
Traditionally, women made offerings to the moon, but the day has now become mainly
a secular family feast. The ninth day of the ninth moon is reserved for remembering the
deceased and climbing heights; many families spend the day picnicking and flying kites.

In the tenth moon, the ancestors are remembered once more with ritual visits to
their tombs. Mock paper money and paper clothing are burned, representing what is
needed for the cold season. After that, during the eleventh moon, comes the winter solstice.
Traditionally, thanksgiving offerings were made at the family altar to Heaven and earth,
the household gods, and the ancestors, and then the family enjoyed a sumptuous dinner.

Soon after that, preparations for the lunar New Year begin the whole cycle once again. While many people do not observe all the events in this liturgical calendar, most families take part in at least some of them, especially the New Year's festival. The calendar evokes the rhythm of nature's seasons and of human life, giving meaning and fulfillment to life itself. A comparison can be made with the post-Christian West and its own yearly cycle. Even though Christmas has been secularized, the observance of seasonal festivals points to the importance of traditions that inspire peace and generosity.

The Taiping Rebellion

The ideal of *taiping* ('Great Peace'), which comes from a Confucian text and refers to a golden age of the past, has served as a rallying point for Daoist and Buddhist popular movements with a messianic emphasis. The movement behind the Taiping rebellion of 1850–65, however, included Protestant Christian as well as traditional Chinese elements.

Under the leader Hong Xiuquan (1813–64), who called himself the younger brother of Jesus Christ, the Taiping rebels from southern China took over a large part of the country and established their capital in Nanjing in 1851, calling their theocratic domain the Heavenly Kingdom of Great Peace.

In some respects the Taiping movement was revolutionary for its time. Like many Protestant fundamentalist denominations, it prohibited smoking, drinking, and extramarital sex. It also advocated compulsory education for both boys and girls, and demanded monogamy of its members—although some of its leaders exempted themselves from the general rule. The movement's rejection of Chinese traditions provoked the enmity of the Confucian gentry, who, with some Western help, came to the aid of the Manchu rulers and defeated the rebels. But its syncretism is reflected in other cults found in China even today, where Christian beliefs sometimes blend with faith healing and other traditional practices.

Today there is a Taiping museum in Nanjing. The historical descriptions there are written from the point of view of the communist government. Describing the Taipings as peasants who dared to stand up against imperialism, they portray the uprising as a precursor of the communist revolution. But they make no mention of the pro-Western, pro-Christian nature of the Taiping leaders. In fact, they make no reference at all to the religious nature of the movement.

Falun Gong

Ambiguity continues to surround phenomena deemed to be religious in China, even today. Take the case of Chinese yoga or Qigong. Is this a religious practice? The answer depends on the practitioner. Some people practise Qigong strictly for health reasons, explaining the exercise in purely physiological terms, but others take a more religious approach.

An example of the latter is the spiritual–physical purification movement called Falun Dafa (loosely, 'Buddhist Law'), better known as Falun Gong. Founded by a former soldier named Li Hongzhi (b. 1952), Falun Gong preaches the moral principles of truth,

In April 2006 thousands of Falun Gong practitioners in Taipei, Taiwan, marched in protest against China's suspected persecution of Falun Gong members (AP Photo/Chiang Ying-ying).

compassion, and forbearance, and practises a combination of meditation and yoga-like exercises. Falun Gong neither teaches nor practises violence. Although it affirms Buddho-Daoist influences, it does not call itself a religion (probably because the Chinese constitution acknowledges only five religions).

Falun Gong first attracted world-wide attention in April 1999, when it responded to government criticism by mounting a number of silent demonstrations in Beijing. One of the aims of this action was to reassure the government that Falun Gong was peaceful and non-aggressive. But it had the opposite effect. The government banned Falun Gong and in October 2000 launched a campaign of brutal suppression. Since then, international supporters have claimed that many Falun Gong members in China are long-term prisoners in labour camps.

Although the government declared Falun Gong an 'evil cult' (xiejiao), comparable to Aum Shinrikyo in Japan and the Jonestown cult, the real reason for the ban was probably the movement's popularity: according to the government, there were two million members, and the movement itself claims 40 million. Whatever the true figure may be, it seems that many Chinese people under communism have experienced a spiritual vacuum needing to be filled. Western Christianity has also experienced a revival in recent years, as have other belief systems.

Beijing The Imperial Palace complex (known in the West as the Forbidden City) includes the Temple of Heaven, where the emperor performed the grandest sacrifices. Beijing's most important Daoist site is the White Cloud Temple, which houses an old statue of Laozi. One of the best-restored sections of the Great Wall is found outside Beijing.

Qufu The city in Shandong province where Confucius was born, Qufu has a very large Confucius Temple modelled on the Imperial Palace.

Nanjing The Confucian Academy where mandarins were trained includes a ceremonial gateway and a grand hall honouring Confucius. The Jinghai Temple is dedicated to the goddess of the Sea, in honour of China's great seafaring admiral Zhenghe.

Suzhou The Temple of Mystery in Suzhou is dedicated to the four protectors of the Daoist Law. It features a hall with statues of Daoist gods.

Taishan (Mount Tai) One of the five sacred mountains of China, in Shandong province, Taishan is the site of several Daoist temples, including the Tai Temple (the third largest complex in China) and the Rosy Temple.

Xian Outside Xian is the tomb of the first emperor, with its famous terracotta warrior guardians.

Taiwan A large Confucius Temple in the old city of Tainan was a Confucian training academy. The Confucius Temple in the current capital, Taipei, is also impressive, with an Altar of Heaven, an echo hall, and a Vault of Heaven.

California The Bok Kai Temple in the Sacramento Valley was built in the 1880s by Chinese involved in the gold rush and is dedicated to a Daoist Water God who controls flooding. The Temple of Five Gods in San Jose dates from the same era.

Conclusion

The Chinese have an ancient civilization that is rich in both institutionalized and popular religious beliefs and practices. Instead of adhering to a single religion, most Chinese have embraced a variety of traditions, turning from one to the other depending on their particular concerns. They have in general looked to Confucianism for political theory and guidance in family and social life; to Daoism for meditation, health, artistic inspiration, and a spirituality based on living in harmony with one's nature; and to popular religion for many other things.

Today this complex religious culture is attracting interest in Europe and North America, but it first spread beyond China many centuries earlier. Its influence in Korea and Japan will be discussed in the next chapter.

Glossary

cinnabar fields Three regions of the body (head, chest, abdomen) in Daoist 'inner' or spiritual alchemy; cinnabar (mercuric sulphide) was an important ingredient in Daoist 'outer' or physical alchemy.

Dao/Tao 'Way' in Chinese; for Daoists, the idea of the way at once describes the dynamic flow of nature and prescribes naturalness as a guiding principle in human affairs.

Daozang/Tao-tsang The Daoist canon of of texts and commentaries, comprising more than a thousand volumes organized in three 'Caverns' and four supplementary collections.

Eight Immortals Daoist deity figures, allegedly historical individuals, who function as patrons of various professions and crafts.

filial piety The principle of respect for one's parents in the Chinese tradition, especially Confucianism.

Five Classics A corpus of texts considered authoritative by the early Confucians, including poetry, historical speeches, chronicles, and instructions regarding ritual and divination.

Five Relationships The five reciprocal relationships—ruler to minister, father to son, husband to wife, elder to younger brother, and friend to friend—central to Confucianism, in which each role has specific norms and duties of moral conduct.

Four Books Earlier texts promoted as a canon by the Song dynasty Neo-Confucians: *The Analects, The Book of Mencius, The Great Learning*, and *The Doctrine of the Mean*.

Heavenly Masters sect A lineage of Daoist teachers originating with the Heavenly Master Zhang Daoling, who claimed that Laozi appeared to him in a vision in 142.

hexagrams Sixty-four combinations of six solid and broken lines that are consulted as an aid to divination, especially by Daoists.

I Ching The *Book of Changes*; a divination manual, one of the Five Classics, interpreting the 64 **hexagrams**.

li In early Chinese thought, the concept of ritual, including propriety in behaviour towards others. In Neo-Confucian thought, a second term, also spelled *li* but represented by a different Chinese character, refers to the metaphysical or formal principle or pattern in everything, a coordinate of *qi* (matter or energy).

Mandate of Heaven The ancient Chinese concept of a divine right to rule that is nevertheless subject to forfeiture (and hence justifies rebellion) if the king is a tyrant.

Perfect Truth sect A Daoist sect whose monks are celibate, dating from the thirteenth-century era of Mongol rule.

qi/chi Air or ether, regarded as the material component that together with *li* constitutes all things in the metaphysics of the Neo-Confucian Zhu Xi.

Qigong/Chigong Breath control exercises, used especially by Daoists.

ren The Confucian virtue of humaneness.

Taiji/T'ai-chi The Great Ultimate, viewed in Song Neo-Confucianism as a macrocosm equivalent to the structure of the human body; also the name of a set of breathing and exercise routines practised by Daoists.

Taiping A future age of Great Peace, envisioned in a classic text that spurred Daoist and Buddhist messianic movements; also the name adopted by a Christian-inspired rebel movement in 1851.

Tian The term for Heaven or God in the first millennium BCE, when Confucius lived; 'Tiananmen' means 'Gate of Heaven'.

wuwei Non-action; the path of least resistance, of allowing things to run their natural course, preferred by Daoism.

xin The aspect of personality comprising both 'heart' and 'mind'; an important concept for Mencius and for the Neo-Confucians.

yang The masculine principle, the complement of **yin**, that is characterized as aggressive, hard, dry, and bright.

yin The feminine principle that is the complement of **yang** and is characterized as accommodating, soft, moist, and dark.

Further Reading

Berthrong, John H., E.N. Berthrong, and E. Nagai-Berthrong. *Confucianism: An Introduction*. Oxford: Oneworld Publications, 2000. Introduces Confucianism as lived by Chinese, including rituals, beliefs and interaction with other traditions.

Ching, Julia. 1993. *Chinese Religions*. London: Macmillan; Maryknoll, NY: Orbis. Covers all the religions of China.

Fung Yu-lan. 1958. *A Short History of Chinese Philosophy*. New York: Macmillan. Still a good short introduction to the subject.

Levenson, Joseph R. 1968. *Confucian China and Its Modern Fate: A Trilogy*. Berkeley: University of California Press. A masterful assessment of twentieth-century challenges.

Lopez, Donald S., Jr, ed. 1996. *Religions of China in Practice*. Princeton: Princeton University Press. A worthwhile sourcebook providing ample coverage of ritual and illustrating the interrelatedness of China's traditions.

Miller, James. 2003. *Daoism: A Short Introduction*. Oxford: Oneworld Publications. An introduction focusing on the way Daoism has evolved through the centuries.

Saso, Michael. 2001. *Taoist Master Chuang*. Netherland, CO: Sacred Mountain Press. The life and teachings of a twentieth-century Daoist master from Taiwan, written by a disciple.

Silvers, Brock. 2005. *The Taoist Manual: An Illustrated Guide Applying Taoism to Daily Life*. Netherland, CO: Sacred Mountain Press. A very practical introduction to Daoist practice.

Yao, Xinzhong. 2000. *An Introduction to Confucianism*. Cambridge: Cambridge University Press. Broad coverage, including ethics, politics and relations with other religions in China.

References

Chan, Wing-tsit, trans. 1967. *Instructions for Practical Living*. New York: Columbia University Press.

Ching, Frank. 1988. *Ancestors: Nine Hundred Years in the Life of a Chinese Family*. New York: Morrow.

de Bary, William Theodore, ed. 1960. *Sources of Chinese Tradition*. New York: Columbia University Press.

Lau, Dim C., trans. 1963. *The Tao Te Ching*. Harmondsworth: Penguin.

———, trans. 1979. *Confucius: The Analects*. Harmondsworth: Penguin.

Legge, James, trans. 1885. *Li Ki*. In F. Max Müller, ed., *Sacred Books of the East*, 28. Oxford: Clarendon Press.

———, trans. 1893. *The Chinese Classics*. 2nd ed. 5 vols. Oxford: Clarendon Press.

Liu Shaoqi. 1951. *How to Be a Good Communist*. Beijing: Foreign Languages Press.

Mather, Richard B., trans. 1976. Liu I-ch'ing, *Shih-shuo Hsin-yü: A New Account of Tales of the World*. Minneapolis: University of Minnesota Press.

Saso, Michael. 1978. *The Teachings of Taoist Master Chuang*. New Haven and London: Yale University Press.

Watson, Burton, trans. 1963a. *Hsün Tzu: Basic Writings*. New York: Columbia University Press.

———, trans. 1963b. *Mo Tzu: Basic Writings*. New York: Columbia University Press.

———, trans. 1968. *The Complete Works of Chuang Tzu*. New York: Columbia University Press.

Waley, Arthur. 1934. *The Way and its Power: A Study of the Tao Te Ching and its Place in Chinese Thought*. London: Allen & Unwin.

———, trans. 1938. *The Analects of Confucius*. London: Allen & Unwin.

Wolf, Arthur P. 1974. 'Gods, Ghosts and Ancestors'. In Arthur P. Wolf, ed., *Religion and Ritual in Chinese Society*, 131–82. Stanford: Stanford University Press.

Korean and Japanese Religions

ROY C. AMORE   JULIA CHING

In 2001, at a time when many universities in North America were struggling financially, Soka University opened the doors at a new multi-million-dollar campus in southern California. It is operated by an American branch of Soka Gakkai, a new religion that originated in Japan shortly before the Second World War as a movement of lay Buddhists concerned about an apparent lack of values among young people. How did a few Japanese laypeople give rise to a new religion that is spreading around the world? Why have so many other Japanese turned to new religions? To answer such questions, this chapter will consider the non-Buddhist religious traditions of Korea and Japan, with special attention to the new religions of Japan.

The Korean peninsula and the Japanese islands lie along the eastern edge of Asia and were historically on the receiving end of many cultural influences from China, including trends in religion as well as art, architecture, writing, and politics. The primary religious influences were Buddhism and Confucianism, but Daoism also had some impact, especially in the form of the Daoist art and ideas that were incorporated into Chan (Zen) Buddhism.

In each case we will begin with shamanism—the foundation of most Asian religions. Following a discussion of 'popular religion', we will conclude with a look at the many ways in which Korean and Japanese religions have interacted with foreign traditions as well as Western ideas generally.

Korea

The modern name Korea has its roots in the name of the Koryo dynasty (935–1392 CE), but the country's traditional name was Cho-sen ('morning dew')—a reference to the country's geographical position on the eastern border of China, which called itself the 'Middle Kingdom'. When Confucianism, Daoism, and Buddhism arrived from China, beginning around the fourth century, Korea was divided into three independent kingdoms: Koguryo in the north, Paekche in the southwest, and Shilla (or Silla) in the southeast.

Korean Shamanism

Indigenous Korean religion has three main deities: the god of earth, the god of ancestors, and—above all—the personal deity known as the god of heaven. In addition there is a pantheon of lesser deities.

Timeline

125 BCE	Chinese culture begins to influence Korea
604 CE	Japan's Prince Shotoku issues the Seventeen-Article Constitution
645–50	Taika reforms strengthen Confucianism in Japan
1192	Establishment of the Kamakura shogunate, which rules Japan until 1333
1274	The first of two attempts to invade Japan from China fails, supposedly driven back by *kamikaze* ('divine winds')
1501	Birth of Yi T'oegye, Korean Neo-Confucian (d. 1570)
1603	Establishment of the Tokugawa shogunate, which rules Japan until 1868
1728	Kada petitions the emperor of Japan to establish a centre for National Learning
1730	Birth of Motoori Norinaga, advocate of Shinto revival (d. 1801)
1837	Miki Nakayama experiences the possession trance that leads her to found Tenrikyo
1859	Konko Daijin becomes a mystic healer and founds Konkokyo
1868	Meiji Restoration ends shogunate rule, brings State Shinto into prominence, and begins to modernize Japan
1892	Deguchi Nao has the mystic experience that leads her to found Omoto
1937	Soka Gakkai founded by Tsunesaburo Makiguchi
1945	Japanese surrender leads to end of State Shinto
1948	Korea divided to form communist North Korea and secular South Korea
1995	Aum Shinrikyo members release poison gas in Tokyo subway

According to one myth, the country was founded in 2333 BCE by a descendant of the god of heaven, a shaman-king named Dangun (or Tangun) who was also known as the 'Sandalwood Prince'. The son of a bear-woman, he ruled over the tribes of Dragon, Horse, Deer, Crane, Eagle, and Egret, and mediated between them and heaven. (In another myth, an ancestral figure of the Shilla royal house emerged from a 'cosmic egg'.)

Box 10.1	The Birth of Tangun, Korea's First Ruler

From the late thirteenth-century account Samguk yusa: Legends and Histories of the Three Kingdoms of Ancient Korea.

In those days there lived a she-bear and a tigress in the same cave. They prayed [to the heavenly king] to be blessed with incarnation as human beings. The king took pity on them and gave them each a bunch of mugwort and twenty pieces of garlic, saying, 'If you eat this holy food and do not see the sunlight for one hundred days, you will become human beings.'

The she-bear and the tigress took the food and ate it, and retired into the cave. In twenty-one days the bear, who had faithfully observed the king's instructions, became a woman. But the tigress, who had disobeyed, remained in her original form.

But the bear-woman could find no husband, so she prayed under the sandalwood tree to be blessed with a child. [The son of the heavenly king] heard her prayers and married her. She conceived and bore a son who was called Tangun Wanggom, the King of Sandalwood.

. . . [Sometime before 2000 BCE] Tangun came to P'yongyang [now Sogyong], set up his royal residence there and bestowed the name Chosun upon his kingdom (Ha and Mintz 1972:32–3).

Some scholars believe that the Korean language belongs to the same family as that of the Siberian Tungus—the people from whom English borrowed the term 'shaman' for a ritual expert who specializes in communicating with the spirit world. Koreans also share with the Tungus a long tradition of shamanism, although they call its practitioners by a different name: *mudang*. Shamanism is still practised in modern Korea, and the majority of *mudang* today, as in the past, are women (see also p. 508).

Shamanic communication can take a variety of forms, but the two most common are soul travel and spirit possession. Both begin with a self-induced trance. In the first type, the shaman's soul travels to the spirit world. In the second, the spirit takes possession of the shaman and speaks through her mouth. In Western terms, shamanic soul-travel has a parallel in the mystic journey undertaken by the Prophet Muhammad, while spirit-possession recalls the prophetic tradition, in which deities use individual humans to deliver their messages.

Confucianism in Korea

The Confucian influence is more evident in Korea than in Japan. Confucianism arrived in Korea from China around 125 BCE and was taught in schools and practised in gov-

The Tradition at a Glance

NUMBERS
Shinto: Estimates range from a low of 4 million self-described adherents to
100 million or more if all Japanese influenced by traditional Shinto culture are
included.
Tenrikyo: Estimated at approximately 2 million worldwide.
Soka Gakkai: Estimates range from 9 to 30 million worldwide.
Korean Shamanism: Estimates range from 1 to 3 million.
Unification Church: Estimates range from 1 to 3 million worldwide.
Choendogyo: Estimated at approximately 1 million.

DISTRIBUTION
Traditional religions are practised wherever people of Korean and Japanese background live. New religions from both regions have recently begun to spread and
attract followers from different backgrounds.

FOUNDERS
Neither Korean nor Japanese traditional religions have founders as such, but
many charismatic leaders have founded new sects.

DEITIES
Korean religion has three main gods, headed by the God of Heaven. Shinto has a
pantheon of deities (*kami*), led by the Sun Goddess, Amaterasu.

AUTHORITATIVE TEXTS
Neither Korea nor Japan has any equivalent to the scriptures of more institutional traditions. The earliest evidence of religion is provided by collections of
ancient narratives: for Korea, the *Samguk Sagi* ('Records of the Three Kingdoms')
and *Samguk Yusa* ('Stories of the Three Kingdoms'), compiled in the twelfth and
thirteenth centuries, and for Japan the *Kojiki* ('Record of Ancient Matters') and
Nihongi ('Chronicles of Japan'), both of which date from the early eighth century.

NOTEWORTHY TEACHINGS
Shamanism emphasizes contact with the spirits through trance possession.
Shinto emphasizes ritual purity and harmony with nature. Most new religions of
Japan and Korea emphasize chanting, 'healing hands', or other rituals said to
improve daily life and health.

ernment even during periods when Buddhism was the dominant religion. The Royal Academy instituted official examinations during the Shilla period (668–935), and its influence as a vehicle of Confucian learning continued during the Koryo dynasty.

Confucianism became the official ideology of the Korean state and society during the Yi dynasty. The Four Books and Five Classics became the basis of the civil-service examination and the curriculum of the Royal Academy.

The Neo-Confucian philosophy propounded in China by Zhu Xi came to be known in Korea as the 'learning of human nature and principle' (*songni hak*). The relationship between human nature and the emotions became the subject of intense debate among Korean thinkers. Different views led to the development of separate philosophical schools and were even reflected in political divisions that affected the course of the country's politics over several centuries.

The subject that most interested Korean philosophers was the nature of the emotions, usually referred to as 'the Four and the Seven'. The former were what Mencius (2A:6) called the Four Beginnings of Virtue (commiseration, shame, modesty, and moral discernment, from which come the virtues of humanity, righteousness, prosperity, and wisdom); and the latter were what the Book of Rites called the Seven Emotions (joy, anger, sadness, fear, love, repulsion, and desire).

The Chinese Neo-Confucian Zhu Xi had distinguished in a general way between the two categories, maintaining that although the Four Beginnings of Virtue are also emotions, they manifest *li* (principle) whereas the Seven manifest *qi* (energy). But Korean philosophers devoted several centuries to debating the distinctions, if any, between the Four and the Seven, and whether such distinctions are real or arbitrary.

The best-known of these Korean philosophers, Yi Hwang (also called Yi T'oegye; 1501–70), adhered strictly to the thought of Zhu Xi, especially Zhu's dual teaching of *li* and *qi*. Yi Yi (also called Yi Yulgok; 1536–84) rejected this dualistic view, and instead concentrated his attention on human nature itself. In general, however, Korean intellectuals were so faithful to Zhu Xi that the work of his important Chinese successor Wang Yangming was seldom read or discussed, and a small Yangming school in Korea survived only as an underground current. The writings of Chong Hagok (1640–1736), a Yangming scholar and important court official, were not published until the late twentieth century.

By the late nineteenth century increasing contact with the West meant that Korean Confucian scholars, like their counterparts in China and Japan, confronted a number of challenges. While some were unable to adapt to the changing times, others issued a call for understanding Western learning. This entailed putting Neo-Confucian principles like Zhu Xi's 'investigation of things' (seeking moral knowledge through study of Confucian literature) into practice in the modern world. Confucianism is stronger than Daoism and even Buddhism in Korea today.

Daoism in Korea

Daoism was introduced to Korea in the seventh century, during a period of heavy Chinese influence. Since Daoism itself had been shaped in part by the ancient religious traditions of China, including shamanism, it also overlapped in many ways with the indigenous folk religion of Korea. Together with Confucianism and Buddhism, Daoism constituted one leg of the 'tripod' of religions in Korea. Even during the fourteenth-century unification of Korea under the Yi dynasty, which preferred Confucianism, Daoism suffered less than Buddhism. Its followers, particularly the common people, continued to worship Daoist deities. Korean Daoism is basically of the Heavenly Masters sect, with a married clergy. Because of its affinities with shamanism, Daoism is still practised in Korea today, and its influence can be seen in some of the newer cults that have emerged over the last two centuries.

Korea's New Religions

It is interesting to note that Christianity has attracted a significantly higher proportion of converts in Korea than in either China or Japan. The only country in eastern Asia with a more substantial Christian population is the Philippines, where Christians are the majority.

Christian missionary activity in Korea has been mainly Protestant, especially Presbyterian, although Catholics have also made inroads. Today there are more than 7 million Christians in Korea, with Protestants outnumbering Catholics by about four to one.

At the same time Korea, like Japan, has been fertile ground for the formation of 'new religions'. These movements typically arise within an existing tradition, under a charismatic leader who claims to offer new knowledge or powers. In the first example below, the new religion arose out of Buddhist and Daoist traditions. In the second, it developed out of Christianity.

Choendogyo

Choendogyo (or Chundogyo or Chondogyo), the 'religion of the heavenly way', was founded by Choe Suun (1824–64) in 1860 under the name Donghak (or Tonghak; 'eastern learning') and acquired its present name in 1905. Although its founder was killed by a government suspicious of his political intentions, his two successors made Choendogyo a major force in the country, and the writings of all three form its scriptural canon.

Reflecting both Confucian and Daoist influences, Choendogyo proclaims faith in a heavenly lord called Hanullim or Chonju ('lord of heaven'). It sees human nature as a reflection of divinity (a bowl of clear water is placed on its altars to reflect heaven to the faithful) and enjoins its followers to treat human beings as God, with respect and consideration.

The practice of Choendogyo includes purification rituals and rice offerings. Sunday worship consists of hymns, prayers, scriptural readings, and a sermon. Its teachings emphasize moral discipline, sincerity, and respect for others, especially within the family:

There is nothing that is not the Way in daily activities. The divine spirit of the universe moves together with all things. Therefore, practise the principle of respecting people and things. . . .

> If a guest comes to your house, think that God has arrived.

> The peaceful harmony of husband and wife is the heart of our way, and therefore, if a wife is disobedient, bow before her with all earnestness. If one bows once, twice and repeatedly, even the wife who has the hardest heart will be reconciled. . . .

> Do not strike a child, for striking a child is striking God.

> Especially respect your daughter-in-law like God (Kim 1977:243).

These instructions are remarkable in light of the low position traditionally accorded to women in Korea—especially wives in relation to their husbands and parents-in-law, who often live under the same roof.

Choendogyo was behind the Donghak revolution of 1894, a popular uprising that contributed to the modernization of Korean society. It also played an important role in the 1919 movement for independence from Japanese rule. Based in Seoul, Choendogyo currently has approximately a million followers.

The Unification Church

Founded by Sun Myung Moon (b. 1920) in 1954, the Holy Spirit Association for the Unification of World Christianity has Christian (especially Presbyterian) roots and a larger following in the West than in Korea itself. The word 'unification' has powerful connotations in Korea, which has been divided between North and South since the end of the Second World War. But in this case it refers to the coming together of all Christians, or all humans, under the new revelations given to the Reverend Moon. Though the name suggests ecumenical reunion, Moon's book *Divine Principle* proposes to unite all religions on the basis of an interpretation of the Bible currently espoused only by the 'Moonies' themselves.

The Unification Church grew rapidly after its founding in the mid-twentieth century, but it has been dogged by controversy because of financial scandals and its aggressive recruitment methods.

Korean Popular Religion Today

Besides the mainstream religions there are many traditional beliefs, rituals, and customs that have been an important part of life in Korea. As in China, folk religion still plays a significant role today. Also as in China, ancestor worship is practised according to the Confucian model, and Korean folk deities share many names with their Chinese counterparts (stove god, Dragon King god, and so on)—although unlike the latter they are not organized into a vast supernatural bureaucracy.

In fact, the one major difference between Korea and China in the area of folk religion is that the shamanic tradition is still alive and well in Korea today. There are two types of professional *mudang*: those who have been called to the profession following personal experience of spirit possession and those who come from shamanic families. The first type, the most numerous, gain their authority as a result of their own ecstatic experience and their ability to repeat it, while the second type inherit their authority from ancestors who presumably experienced possession themselves some time in the past. Both perform rituals, but only the possessed *mudang* seek to communicate with the spirits on behalf of their clients, who make offerings of food to the spirits in hopes of securing either their guidance or some special favour, such as ensuring the welfare of the household, the recovery of sick family members, or the safe conduct of the deceased to a happier existence. Both types of *mudang* play an important role in divination by serving as mouthpieces for supernatural beings. For example, a *mudang* will often be hired to perform a ritual for a newborn. After chanting and doing a ceremonial dance to ward off evil spirits, the *mudang* will suggest a name for the infant and foretell its future.

A Korean shaman in California (Kayte Deioma).

Korean Art and Architecture

Small shrines of various types are common in rural areas of Korea. One type, associated with the shamanic tradition, is dedicated either to various traditional gods or to the spirits of great leaders, especially military heroes. A typical shrine honouring a mountain god consists of a modest complex of buildings in traditional wooden style with ribbed roofs, located on a mountain slope.

There are also ancestral shrines, usually located in the home area of an extended family, honouring the founders of the clan, who function as spirit protectors of the family. These shrines may include a stele (an upright stone sitting on a stone turtle base) inscribed with the accomplishments of the dedicatee. Another type of shrine honours local Confucian sages.

Map 10.1   Japan and Korea: Major cities and religious sites

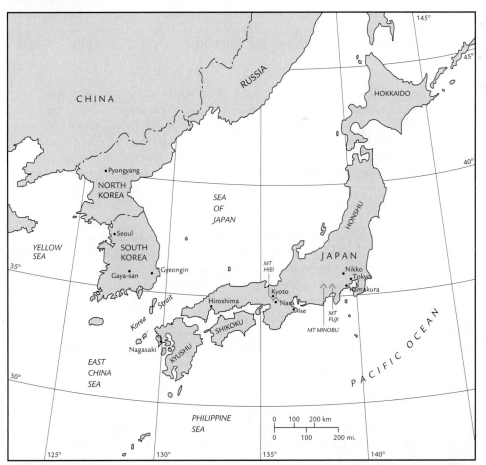

Source: Adapted from W.A. Young, *The World's Religions* (Englewood Cliffs: Prentice-Hall, 1995):211.

Like the royals of ancient China, the Korean kings were buried in large circular mounds in mountain valleys at sites determined by feng shui. Their tombs, like those of their counterparts in China, include many grave goods such as gold belts, bejewelled swords, and of course containers of food and drink to nourish the soul in the afterlife. One tomb from the Shilla era has a painting of a mythic animal that may have been envisioned as carrying the soul to the heavenly realm.

Japan

Japanese Shamanism

In Japan, as in Korea, rulership in ancient times was associated with both divinity and shamanic powers. Presumably these rulers served the *kami*—the gods and spirits—and functioned as their mouthpieces. Interestingly, the position of ruler was not reserved for men. The best-known female ruler was the charismatic Queen Himiko, who ruled the Yamato state during the late second and early third centuries. Her story is told in a Chinese chronicle:

> [The people of Wo] elected a young girl as their queen who was then named Himiko [literally, 'child of the Sun']. She attended and rendered service to the gods or spirits [literally, the way of the ghosts] and had a special power that bewitched the people. She never married even in her youth and her brother helped her administer the affairs of the Kingdom. After she was enthroned only a few persons were able to see her. Only one man always attended her, served her meals, transmitted her words, and had access to her dwelling (*Chronicle of Wei*, ch. 30; Hori 1968:188).

This charismatic queen reigned for 68 years. Her personality and character appear typical of a shamanic queen. Some historians have even identified her with **Amaterasu**, the great sun goddess and reputed ancestor of the imperial family. Today the rituals associated with the imperial family, especially the heir to the throne, are reminders of the shamanic character of the royal institution.

But shamanic powers have not been limited to queens in Japan. Other women have also been greatly respected for their shamanic powers, and several founders of new religions in modern Japan have been women alleged to have shamanic powers.

Shinto: The Way of the *Kami*

Shinto is the term normally used in English to refer to the indigenous religious heritage of Japan, in contrast to the traditions imported from mainland Asia, especially Confucianism and Buddhism. It means 'the way of the gods' and reflects the Japanese pronunciation of the Chinese term *shendao*, meaning 'the way (dao) of the spirits (*shen*)'. A second term for the same tradition, widely used in Japan, consists of the same phrase in the Japanese language: *Kaminomichi* (or *kami no michi*), the 'way of the gods (*kami*)'.

As with other ancient religions, much of Shinto seems to have arisen from nature worship. Thus many of the *kami* are nature spirits associated with features such as rivers, seas, islands, forests, and (in particular) mountains, as well as certain animals. Others are deified clan ancestors, especially the sun goddess Amaterasu, and spirits of deceased emperors, saints, and heroes.

Most Japanese today take part in a variety of spiritual traditions—Shinto, Confucian, and Buddhist—depending on the sphere or phase of life involved. For example, most practise Shinto birth rituals, but look to Confucian teachings for moral principles and turn to Buddhism for funerals, burials and memorials. Traditionally, most Japanese married at Shinto shrines, though today many weddings are held in Christian churches, even if the couple are not Christians themselves.

Japan borrowed many religious beliefs and practices from China, integrating them with the indigenous Shinto heritage in a distinctive synthesis that came to be known as Dual Shinto. Yet in many ways Japanese religion has remained uniquely Japanese. It gives a high priority to ritual purity, which does not have such an important place in Chinese religion. Some also say that Japanese culture is distinct in its more martial spirit, its aesthetic leanings, and its predisposition for ritualized behaviour. In any case, the uniqueness of Japan cannot be ascribed to any single factor or practice.

Shinto's Narratives of Origins

Myths play a much more important role in Japanese than in Chinese culture. The earliest historical accounts of Japan, the 'Land of the Rising Sun', date from around the seventh century—much later than the recorded history of China and Korea. Accounts of Japanese mythology are similarly late. The *Kojiki* ('Record of Ancient Matters') and the *Nihongi* ('Chronicles of Japan') both date from the early eighth century. Their narratives concern the origins of Japan, the Japanese people, and the Japanese state.

In the beginning, heaven and earth are not separate but a single inchoate mass containing the life principle. The purer and clearer part then rises to become heaven, while the grosser and heavier part settles down as earth. Scholars who see this part of the narrative as an account of abstract principles believe it reflects the influence of ancient Chinese cosmological theory.

The birth of the gods, however, is much more concrete. Something resembling a sprout of vegetation, also referred to as the 'pillar of the land', springs up as an island between heaven and earth and becomes a god known as the one who established the eternal land. Eventually it gives rise to the primal couple, who introduce male–female reproduction.

These first parents are Izanagi, the male principle, and Izanami, the female principle, who descend from heaven to the island and then set out in different directions to walk around it. The narrative underlines the connection between correct gender behaviour and the notion of purity so important to Shinto, for when they meet it is Izanami who speaks first. For the female to initiate the courtship conversation is a ritual offence,

| Box 10.2 | The Marriage of Izanagi and Izanami |

Now the male deity turning by the left, and the female deity by the right, they went around the pillar of the land separately. When they met together on one side, the female deity spoke first and said: 'How delightful! I have met with a lovely youth.' The male deity was displeased, and said: 'I am a man, and by right should have spoken first. How is it that on the contrary thou, a woman, shouldst have been the first to speak? This was unlucky. Let us go round again.' Upon this the two deities went back, and having met anew, the male deity spoke first and said, 'How delightful! I have met a lovely maiden.' . . . Hereupon the male and female first became united as husband and wife (Aston 1896:12–13).

and therefore bodes ill for their first offspring, which turns out to be a leech. They set it adrift and start over. Now it is Izanagi, the male, who speaks first. Having observed the correct procedure this time, Izanami gives birth to the Japanese archipelago, its animals and mountains, and all the rest of creation, including the *kami*.

In the *Kojiki*'s account, Izanami dies of burns suffered in giving birth to the fire spirit. Izanagi then goes to the underworld to look for her. Finding putrid decay and maggots, he turns back and goes to cleanse his body by diving deep into the sea. In the process he gives rise to another generation of deities. Washing his left eye, he produces the sun goddess, Amaterasu; washing his right eye, he produces the moon god, Tsukiyomi. And rinsing out his nostrils, he generates the god of the hot summer wind, Susano-o.

Central to the narrative, and to Shinto, are the notions of purity and pollution. In general, the sun is associated with life, fertility, and good fortune. The narratives refer to heaven as a higher region reached by a bridge from Japan. Purification brings humans closer to the realm of the divine.

Another ritual taboo incorporated in the origin story involves Susano-o, the hot summer wind that can damage crops. His fiery nature expresses itself in a series of offences against his sister, the sun goddess Amaterasu. Not only does he block the irrigation channels and break down the dividing ridges in her rice paddy, but he removes the hide from a colt and tosses it at her, then deposits excrement under her throne.

Angered by these insults, Amaterasu withdraws to the Rock Cave of Heaven and bars its door. To coax her out, the spirits decide to have the ancestors of two Japanese clans set up an evergreen *sakaki* tree outside her cave. A mirror is hung high on the tree and jewels on the middle branches, while white and blue ribbons decorate the lower branches. The 'Terrible Woman of Heaven', from whom ritual dancers are descended, then performs a lewd dance. When the noise of the spectators lures Amaterasu out of her cave, the clan ancestors string up a rope to prevent her from going back.

The image of the sun hiding in a cave has been interpreted as representing a solar eclipse—a mysterious and terrifying occurrence in ancient times. Some scholars have also identified connections between Shinto practices and some of the narrative's details. For example, a tree festooned with white—though not blue—paper ribbons is a characteristic feature of Shinto shrines. The mirror and jewels form part of the regalia of the emperor, who according to tradition is a descendant of the sun goddess. And the

Box 10.3	The Birth of the Sun Goddess

A different account of the birth of Amaterasu, this one from the Nihongi.

After this Izanagi no Mikoto and Izanami no Mikoto consulted together, saying, 'We have now produced the Great-eight-island country, with the mountains, rivers, herbs and trees. Why should we not produce someone who shall be lord of the universe?' They then together produced the Sun Goddess, who was called [Amaterasu no Oho kami]. . . .

The resplendent lustre of this child shone throughout all the six quarters. Therefore the two Deities rejoiced, saying: 'We have had many children, but none of them have been equal to this wondrous infant. She ought not to be kept long in this land, but we ought of our own accord to send her at once to Heaven, and entrust to her the affairs of Heaven.'

At this time Heaven and Earth were still not far separated, and therefore they sent her up to Heaven by the ladder of Heaven (Aston 1896:18).

sakaki tree is still the sacred tree of Shinto. Recently, Michael Witzel (2005) has noted a connection between the body of myth surrounding Amaterasu and the mythology of ancient India, suggesting that the two may have developed out of a common ancestral culture that he calls Laurasian (after the name of an early land mass that eventually separated to form North America, Europe and Asia).

Japan's first emperor, Jimmu, the Yamato ruler traditionally dated to 660 BCE, was said to be descended from the sun goddess, who by extension is also the ancestor of the Japanese people. In effect, Amaterasu is the supreme Shinto deity. The three insignia of the imperial throne—the mirror, the jewel, and the sword—are her gifts to the Yamato rulers. As Japan prepared for an Allied invasion near the end of the Second World War, the emperor was particularly concerned with the safekeeping of these imperial objects.

Dual Shinto

As Buddhism spread outside its Indian homeland, it did not demand the exclusive allegiance of its followers. The monotheistic religions of the West labelled the traditional deities of other cultures as 'pagan', 'false', or 'of the devil', but Buddhism did not. Thus the Japanese were not obliged to choose between competing systems of belief.

Instead, Buddhist elements were incorporated into Shinto, and a new syncretic tradition developed that came to be known as Ryobu (Dual) Shinto. The Western assumption that there can be only one true religion simply does not apply in East Asia, thanks mainly to the accommodating nature of Buddhism and the East Asian love of harmony in all things.

Under imperial patronage, Shinto shrines honouring local *kami* were built inside Buddhist temples, Buddhist sutras were chanted at Shinto shrines, and eventually large Shinto shrines were built with Buddhist temples inside them. The use of different words for Shinto and Buddhist places of worship is conventional in Japanese as well as English. The Dual Shinto religious centres are known in Japanese as the *jingu-ji* ('shrine and temple') system. The distinctive red *torii* (gateways) associated with Shinto shrines can also be found at many Buddhist temples.

The 'floating torii' at Miyajima, which is surrounded by water during high tides (David Grisham).

As Shinto gods were worshipped alongside buddhas and bodhisattvas, Buddhists came to see the *kami* as manifestations of universal Buddhist powers, and in 937 two *kami* were declared to be incarnations of bodhisattvas. Eventually all the important *kami* were identified with a particular buddha or bodhisattva. (In the same way, many Christian saints originated as regional spirits and folk heroes—the European equivalents of *kami*.)

The principle behind this process is referred to in Japanese as *honji suijaku* ('original site and local manifestations'). In a sense, Shinto was represented as a Japanese manifestation of Buddhist truths. As the many Shinto deities came to be regarded as manifestations of buddhas and bodhisattvas, the two religions converged to the point where it became difficult to tell them apart. We might say that Shinto was absorbed into

Buddhism, as Buddhism adapted itself to Shinto. The *kami* were *avataras* (incarnations) of the bodhisattvas, and buddha figures were treated as guests of the *kami*.

In merging with Shinto, different Buddhist sects incorporated the *kami* in different ways. In Tendai Shinto the *kami* are part of the Buddha-nature—the reality behind all phenomena. In Shingon Shinto—whose central figure, the cosmic Buddha Mahavairocana, is symbolized by the sun and unites the masculine and the feminine principles—the sun goddess Amaterasu represents the feminine aspect. Shinto developed particularly intimate ties with Shingon, which recognizes thirteen buddhas. A number of *kami* came to be seen as local manifestations of these figures.

At the same time Shinto priests developed some doctrines of their own. In 1274 and 1281 the Mongols attempted to invade Japan but were frustrated by storms at sea. Interpreting the storms as 'winds of the gods' (*kamikaze*), sent by the *kami* to protect Japan, some began to assert the superiority of Japan's indigenous traditions over influences imported from the mainland. The consequence was a strengthened claim for the place of Shinto. (The term *kamikaze* would take on a new meaning seven centuries later, towards the end of the Second World War, when there was not enough fuel for bomber pilots to return from their missions: ordered to sacrifice themselves along with their aircraft, pilots were expected to strike like the 'wind of the gods' in defence of Japan.)

Nor were all Japanese happy with the merger of Buddhism and Shinto. The Shinto leader Yoshida Kanetomo (1435–1511) reversed the earlier Ryobu Shinto position and asserted the primacy of Shinto over Buddhism. For him the *kami*—not the bodhisattvas—were the 'original site'. Yoshida's interpretation also took into account the other major import from the mainland, Confucianism:

> Prince Shotoku stated in a memorial that Japan was the roots and trunk [of civilization], China its branches and leaves, and India its flowers and fruit. Similarly, Buddhism is the flowers and fruit of all laws, Confucianism their branches and leaves, and Shinto their roots and trunk. Thus all foreign doctrines are offshoots of Shinto (Tsunoda 1958:271).

For Yoshida, the bodhisattvas were indeed the guests of the *kami*.

Shinto and National Identity

Yoshida's efforts notwithstanding, it was not until the seventeenth century that the cultural emphasis really began to shift. Some patriotic scholars abandoned the Chinese classics in favour of ancient Japanese poetry and mythology. This movement, known as Kokugaku ('National Learning'), sparked a Shinto revival that blossomed in the eighteenth century and played a role in the Meiji Restoration of 1868.

A precursor of the Kokugaku movement was Yamazaki Ansai (1618–82), a Neo-Confucian scholar who established a new school of Shinto incorporating the ethics of Zhu Xi (see p. 522 below). Among the leading figures in the National Learning movement itself was Kada no Azumamaro (1669–1736), who is often credited with persuading the shogunate to establish a school dedicated to the study of Japanese literature.

Box 10.4	Petition for a Centre of National Learning

In 1728 the Shogun received a petition requesting the establishment of a centre for National Learning. Often attributed to Kada no Azumamaro, it argued that Buddhist and especially Confucian teachings from China had been harmful to Japan.

Respectfully submitted, craving your bountiful favour in promoting the creation of a school of National Learning. I bow my head in awe and trepidation; vile and base as I am, I abjectly offer my words.

. . . The people's manner of living has benefited by great advances, but our National Learning is gradually falling into desuetude. Cultivated fields are being abandoned steadily and possessions are being exhausted by contributions to Buddhism. Most lamentably, however, the teachings of our Divine Emperors are steadily melting away, each year more conspicuously than the last. Japanese learning is falling into ruin and is a bare tenth of what it once was. The books of law are disappearing: who is there to ask about studies of the old learning? The way of the *waka* [poetry] is falling into oblivion; what can revive the great refinement of the old styles? . . .

Prostrate, I here make my humble request: that I be given a quiet tract of land in Kyoto where I can open a school for studies of the Imperial Land. I have collected since my youth many secret and obscure writings, and have collected since becoming aged numerous old records and accounts. I propose to store them at this school to provide for the researchers of future days. . . .

Japan in ancient days was governed in accordance with the natural laws of Heaven and earth. There was never any indulgence in such petty rationalizing as marked China, but when suddenly these teachings were transmitted here from abroad, they quickly spread, for the men of old in their simplicity took them for the truth. In Japan, there had been generation after generation, extending back to the remote past, which had known prosperity, but no sooner were these Confucian teachings propagated here than . . . a great rebellion occurred. . . .

Confucianism made men crafty, and led them to worship the ruler to such an excessive degree that the whole country acquired a servant's mentality. . . . This occurred because the country had become infected with Chinese ideas. Some people speak ill of Buddhism, but since it is a teaching which makes men stupid, it does not represent a grave evil; after all, rulers do not prosper unless the people are stupid.

Just as roads are naturally created when people live in uncultivated woodlands or fields, so the Way of the Age of the Gods spontaneously took hold in Japan. Because it was a Way indigenous to the country it caused our emperors to wax increasingly in prosperity. However, the Confucian teachings had not only repeatedly thrown China into disorder, but they now had the same effect in Japan. . . . (Tsunoda, 1958:510–12).

Kamo Mabuchi (1697–1769) wrote in Japanese and openly rejected both the Chinese language and Chinese literary influences, while Motoori Norinaga (1730–1801) criticized earlier efforts to link Shinto with Buddhism and Confucianism and made the study of the Japanese classics, the *Kojiki* and the *Nihongi*, central to the agenda of the National Learning movement; he also gave special veneration to the sun goddess

Amaterasu. In time, the success of the National Learning movement led to a revival of Shinto.

State Shinto

In 1868 State Shinto was established as the official cult of Japan. Created for political and ideological purposes, it was declared to be more than a religion. It centred on veneration of the emperor as the descendant of the sun goddess, and its practice consisted of rituals performed by the emperor himself and devotions performed in his honour.

The Golden Pavilion in Kyoto; a modern reconstruction of the original, built c. 1400 as a residence for the retired shogun Ashikaga Yoshimitsu (David Grisham). After his death it served as a Zen Buddhist temple until 1950. Both the interior and the exterior are covered with gold leaf.

In fact, the emperor cult had existed in principle for many hundreds of years before the creation of State Shinto. But it had rarely been practised since the late twelfth century, when the emperor was effectively replaced by the first in a long series of military rulers known as shoguns. Different clans within the warrior class held power at different times. Two important shogunates were the Kamakura (1192–1333; named for the city that was the capital in that period) and the Tokugawa (1603–1868; named for the ruling clan). For more than five hundred years the shoguns controlled the armies and made the laws, and although the emperor remained the titular ruler, his power was only symbolic. Following the 'restoration' of governing power and authority to the young emperor Meiji in 1868, the imperial family was raised to new heights; the ruler of Japan was even described as the ruler of the universe by divine mandate.

State Shinto was abolished following Japan's defeat in the Second World War (1945), when the emperor was forced to renounce his divinity under the terms of surrender to the Allied forces. Even so, the distinction between religion and the state has only gradually gained acceptance in Japan.

Contemporary Shinto

The Shinto tradition is a grab-bag of elements that mean different things to different people and in different social milieus. Beyond the rituals still practised by the imperial household, there are three main currents of Shinto today: Shrine Shinto, Folk Shinto, and Sect Shinto.

Shrine Shinto

Shrine Shinto is the oldest and most prevalent form, practised throughout Japan at shrines dedicated to various nature spirits. The best-known is the shrine dedicated to the sun goddess at Ise, south of Nagoya. For centuries the shrines had been under the control of the individual families that served them as hereditary priests, but under the State Shinto law that control was transferred to the government. This action 'secularized' the shrines, although it was reversed after 1945. Shinto shrines can be found all over the countryside today.

Worship at Shinto shrines is divided into four main parts: purification, offering, prayer, and a symbolic feast. Devotees usually pause at the ablution basin to wash their hands and rinse their mouths before removing their hats and coats and entering the gate to the inner precincts. Facing the main sanctuary from outside, worshippers bow, throw a coin into the offering box, clap their hands twice to attract the attention of the *kami*, and pause in brief prayer. Before leaving they usually make an offering to a priest, who gives each one a branch (sometimes real, sometimes a paper replica) of the sacred *sakaki* tree. Besides money, offerings may take the form of food or drink, flowers, or perhaps a tree sprig.

At specific rituals or ceremonies, the prayers recited by the priests are usually in classical rather than vernacular Japanese. They praise the spirits and make reference to the ritual involved. The ritual concludes with a sacred feast, though this may consist of nothing more than a symbolic sip of sake (rice wine), served by a priest or attendant. Shinto shrines receive many visitors on feast days, especially New Year's (Japan adopted the Western calendar in 1873).

Box 10.5	A Korean Critique of the Western Calendar

The Western (Gregorian) calendar was known in Asia as early as the mid-1600s, but both Japan and Korea continued to use calendars based on the Chinese lunar model until 1873 and 1896 respectively. Yi Hangno (1792–1868), a Korean Confucian scholar, explained his objections to the Western calendar as follows.

The Western methods of calendrical calculation are certainly precise and detailed. However, they lack a solid foundation. Why do I say that? In the time of Yao, calendars took as their only basis the clarification of human relationships by revering the will of heaven. So there was nothing they said to do that was not prescribed by the Five Human Relationships and the Five Constant Virtues. You can see this in the *Yüeh-ling* (Monthly Ordinances) and in the *Hsia Hsiao-cheng* (Little Calendar of the Hsia). Sacrificial rites, rituals for local deities and for the end of the year, marriage rites, and other rites and ritual music, daily tasks, and monthly recitations are all listed in those calendars so that they will be performed assiduously and unflaggingly.

In the West, however, people totally avoid any discussion of the important principles and fine points behind the celestial order and its seasonal variations. All they do all day is look up toward heaven and beg for forgiveness of their sins and the bestowal of blessings. So what use do they have for a calendar telling them how to correlate their actions with seasonal changes?

In the time of Yao, calendars took as their only basis the clarification of human relationships by revering the will of heaven. The Western calendars take disdain for the will of heaven and rejection of human relationships as their only focus. Whether that Western calendar is more exact or not is irrelevant (Lee 1996:114).

Shrine Shinto also includes family worship in the home. Many ordinary Japanese maintain a small shrine called a *kamidana* that serves as an family altar, on which they place sacred tablets from Shinto shrines, candles, and other offerings.

Although the cult of the emperor was abolished in 1945, along with the political ideology centred on his divinity, the imperial family continues to mark special occasions such as weddings and funerals with special rituals at four palace shrines associated with deities such as the sun goddess as well as imperial ancestors. The Japanese public is divided on the value of these ceremonies, but many still appreciate the continuity of tradition that they represent.

Folk Shinto

'Folk Shinto' is a kind of umbrella term covering a variety of folk beliefs in deities and spirits and the practices connected with them. In many ways it reflects the interaction between indigenous and foreign elements. Some practices, such as divination, spirit possession, and shamanic healing, represent the survival of ancient local customs. Some, such as chanting of the Buddhist *nembutsu*, are borrowed from the other religious traditions that established themselves in Japan many centuries ago. Others, such as the worship of sacred mountains, or practices involving abstinence and purification, are more closely associated with the foundations of Shinto itself.

Sect Shinto

The Sect Shinto category consists of thirteen disparate groups formed since the mid-1800s, some of which have little to do with traditional Shinto. These groups do not have shrines, and meet in congregational halls. In the Meiji period they came under the supervision of a government office. Later, most of the principal groups became independent religious bodies, and for this reason they were officially classified as 'Sect Shinto'. Some 'new religions' have also been considered part of the Sect Shinto group.

Some of the sects grew out of older traditions such as the cult of Mount Fuji. Others focus on activities such as faith-healing or traditional purification rituals. There are also Revival Shinto sects, based on the National Learning movement, and sects combining Revival Shinto and Confucianism.

Shinto Practice

Unlike institutional religions such as Buddhism or Christianity, Shinto has no historical founder, no official scriptures, and no organized teachings, although it does have hereditary priests who specialize in conducting rituals and facilitating communication with the *kami*. The range of activities associated with Shinto is extraordinarily broad, embracing everything from ascetic disciplines to social-service activities. Basically, Shinto is a way of life inextricably woven into Japanese thought and culture.

According to Shinto, the *kami* are present in every aspect of nature, but some of their manifestations are particularly noticeable. Storms and high winds demonstrate their power, and their presence is often felt in the vicinity of outstanding geological features such as mountains. These places are prime locations for shrines; but it is also possible to acknowledge the presence of *kami* simply by tying a straw rope to a rock or tree.

Ancient Shinto had a positive attitude towards nature and life. What must be cleansed is pollution, especially the pollution associated with decay and substances separated or discharged from the human body. Spilled blood is a defilement—but the ritually guilty party is the victim who bleeds, not the person who inflicts the wound. The physical, ritual impurity that Shinto focuses on is different from moral guilt; there is no concept of sin in classical Shinto. The offences emphasized in the ancient myths and rituals hardly ever involve what we would consider morality, though in time Shinto did come to teach the importance of purifying the heart and keeping it true.

If pollution is a physical problem to be addressed through ritual, it follows that the outward action is more important than the internal attitude of the petitioner. For a purification ritual to be effective, therefore, it must be conducted correctly by a qualified practitioner. As in the recitation of a charm or mantra, it is the correctness, precision, and beauty of the ritual that are thought to impress the *kami*. This aspect of Shinto was particularly compatible with Shingon ('true word' or mantra) Buddhism, which shares roots with Tibetan and Mongolian tantrism. Before presiding at rituals, Shinto priests typically purify themselves by bathing and abstaining from sex and certain foods. As we noted earlier, a number of the objects used in Shinto ritual are mentioned in the sun-goddess myth. The purpose of Shinto ritual is to ensure harmony between human beings and nature.

A fundamental assumption in Shinto is that all humans receive life from *kami*; therefore all are the children of *kami*. This understanding is reflected in the Shinto emphasis on the family (including ancestors) and community, of which the individual is only one small part. Communication with the spirits or *kami* takes place during seasonal festivals called *matsuri*, some of which probably originated in fertility rituals (young girls carry phallic objects in ritual processions). Food, drink, and entertainment such as music and dance are offered to the *kami* in return for their blessings and protection. When the spirits have received these gifts, the priest dips a branch from a sacred *sakaki* tree in holy water, waves it over the people, and sprinkles them with the *kami*'s blessings. Together, everyone then partakes of the meal prepared for the *kami*.

Another way of communicating with the *kami* is through female mediums called *miko*, who are often blind. The fact that this function is reserved for women recalls the shamanic role of early women rulers. The *miko* are called on to transmit the spirits' advice in times of crisis such as sickness, war, or natural disaster, or when important decisions have to be made regarding things like marriage. Although this practice is rare in most parts of Japan today, it is still important in the rural areas of northeast, where shamanic rituals also survive.

The practice of asceticism is also a remnant of ancient Shinto. Ascetics, male and female, living alone or in groups, typically spend their days making pilgrimages on foot to various holy places and using the ancient techniques of trance and exorcism to heal the sick and resolve spiritual problems for those who consult them. Although asceticism was part of the Shinto tradition, many ascetics are now ordained Buddhist priests of the Tendai, Shingon, or Nichiren sects.

Shinto's animistic beliefs and magical practices were reinforced with the introduction of Daoism, which arrived in Japan from Korea in the seventh century. Daoism's yin-yang and Five Agents (metal, wood, water, fire, and earth) theories are reflected in the myths and legends recorded in the *Kojiki* and *Nihongi*. These theories made a lasting impact on the Shinto practice of divination. Daoist influences are less readily distinguishable from indigenous shamanism, for Shinto has strong affinities with Daoism in shamanism and nature worship.

Confucianism in Japan

If Shinto provides a mythology and aesthetic, and Buddhism offers a view of the afterlife, Confucianism provides an ethical basis for Japanese society. Japanese chronicles say that Confucianism was first introduced near the end of the third century, when a Korean from the southwestern realm of Paekche took the *Analects of Confucius* to the Japanese court. Whether or not that date is correct, the Confucianism that the Japanese learned about was clearly an already evolved form, reflecting the influence of both yin-yang and Daoist teachings.

Confucian teachings became important at the time of Prince Shotoku (573–621), who was also a patron of Buddhism. His Seventeen-Article Constitution, emphasizing harmony and administrative efficiency, reflected the Confucian cosmology in which the hierarchy of humans, earth, and heaven should function as a harmonious system.

Confucianism was further strengthened after Shotoku's death by the so-called Taika reforms (645–6), which introduced a legal and administrative system modelled on that of Tang China. Over time, Confucianism encouraged the spread of ancestor worship from the aristocracy to the common people and provided a system of ethics that became the basis of Japanese feudalism, especially in the Tokugawa era.

Yet Confucian teachings were not always in harmony with Japanese ways. Whereas the Chinese emphasized the parent–child relationship and filial piety above all, the Japanese gave priority to the ruler–minister relationship and the commitment of absolute loyalty from generation to generation. Japanese society was more hierarchical than its Chinese counterpart, rigidly distinguishing vassal from lord and woman from man. Thus the Confucian doctrine of the Mandate of Heaven, with its implicit approval of rebellion against tyranny, did not sit well with a society that demanded unquestioning loyalty to a divine imperial house. Moreover, the feudal character of traditional Japanese society, where the **samurai** were the dominant class, differed from the traditional Chinese society dominated by the scholar gentry. In China and Korea Confucianism was developed and taught mainly by scholar-officials. In Japan, by contrast, many Confucian thinkers came from the samurai class. The famous **bushido** code of the samurai reflects the fusion of warrior ideals and Confucian principles.

Neo-Confucian ideas were introduced to Japan around the beginning of the seventeenth century by Buddhist monks who had gone to China for training. They gradually became entrenched as Japan's official ideology through the efforts of a single family of scholars who persuaded the Tokugawa shoguns that Neo-Confucianism supported a strong central government. Originally a Zen scholar, Hayashi Razan (1583–1657) admired Zhu Xi's combination of rationalism and humanism, ethics focused on human relationships, and emphasis on patriotism and good government. Hayashi's son, who shared these inclinations, became a noted historian, and his grandson was eventually named head of the school for training officials—a position that became hereditary.

Zen practitioners were particularly well prepared to grasp the Neo-Confucian concepts of reverence (*kei* in Japanese) and meditation (quiet sitting; *seiza* in Japanese). As teachers to the military aristocracy and sometimes lecturers to *daimyos* (prefecture leaders), Zen monks helped to spread these and other Confucian ideas in Japan. That spread was encouraged by the Tokugawa shoguns, who were eager both to preserve social order and to halt the spread of Christianity, which had gained many followers in Japan since the first missionaries arrived in the mid-1500s.

Another influential follower of Zhu Xi was Yamazaki Ansai (1618–82), the scholar whose new Suiga Shinto school integrated Zhu's ethics with Japan's indigenous religious tradition. Stressing reverence, purity of mind, prayer, and loyalty to the emperor, Suiga Shinto gave the indigenous tradition an ethical dimension, related Shinto creation legends to Chinese cosmology, and connected the Shinto pantheon and Neo-Confucian metaphysics. Yamazaki's fondness for Chinese sages did not dampen his love of Japan. He once said that should Confucius and Mencius lead a Chinese invasion into Japan, he himself would take up arms against them—though he would fight to capture them alive, since that was 'what Confucius and Mencius teach us to do'.

Unlike Zhu Xi, Wang Yangming had been a soldier as well as a philosopher, and his teachings emphasized action. Perhaps for those reasons, Wang proved particularly attractive to intellectuals from the lower strata of the samurai class, who tended to be less attached to the shogunate establishment than those higher up the social ladder.

A prominent member of the Yomeigaku (Yangming) school was Nakae Toju (1608–48), a religious teacher who considered filial devotion to his mother more important than service to his feudal lord. His doctrine of innate or intuitive knowledge came directly from Wang Yangming, but he combined it with a strong personal theism rooted in Shinto as well as Chinese thought.

Nakae's disciple Kumazawa Banzan (1619–91) was a samurai who served in government and dared to suggest that officials should be chosen on the grounds of merit and qualifications rather than hereditary class. This teaching did not, needless to say, endear him to the shogunate, and he was forced to resign his position.

More than a century later, in 1837, a Yomeigaku scholar and bureaucrat named Oshio Heihachiro (1793–1837; also called Oshio Chusai), led a peasant rebellion in response to a famine. The uprising failed, but it attracted attention for its defiance of the shogunate in the name of conscience. As Oshio put it:

> In face of a crisis, a hero certainly transcends considerations of fortune or disaster, life or death. But even when [the crisis is over and] the work is accomplished, he should still question [the importance of] fortune or disaster, life or death. This is the same with the gentleman whose learning has become refined and genuine (Ching 1976:252).

Interestingly, it seems that scholars leaning towards the Yangming school also played a part in the shaping of modern Japan. Once Japan had been opened to foreign trade, in 1858, Sakuma Shozan (1811–64) and his disciple Yoshida Shoin (1830–59) called for the study of Western science and its integration with Eastern ethics. Presumably it was Yangming's emphasis on protest that inspired them to defy the isolationist policies of the shogunate.

The Neo-Confucians had their rivals, however, in the Kogaku (Ancient Learning) school. Among the scholars who returned to the teachings of Confucius and Mencius was one of the founders of bushido, Yamaga Soko (1622–85). Ito Jinsai (1627–1705), who emphasized philology (the study of language and texts) over philosophy in his approach to the early classics, focused on *ren* (in Japanese, *jin*), which he interpreted as 'love', including in its meaning the virtues of loyalty, good faith, reverence, and forgiveness.

Another eminent scholar of ancient Chinese texts was Ogyu Sorai (1666–1728), who turned to early Confucianism for inspiration on social ethics and political institutions. Ironically, the Kogaku school's emphasis on ancient Chinese thought inspired other scholars to take a closer look at ancient Japan. The result was the rise of the Kokugaku movement that did so much to revive Shinto.

Popular Religion in Japan

Simultaneous or alternating adherence to a variety of religious traditions is common in Japan. Three-quarters of all Japanese households have either a *kamidana* (Shinto household shrine) or a *butsudan* (Buddhist household altar)—and nearly half have both. Even people who profess no attachment to religion will visit both Shinto shrines and Buddhist temples, though they may not always distinguish clearly between the two: many people observe the Shinto custom of hand-clapping when they enter Buddhist temples.

In Japan as elsewhere, one central function of the household shrine or altar is to make offerings to the ancestors, whose spirits need to be placated lest they become angry and inflict misfortune on the living. Other living creatures are also believed to have spirits that may be offended if they are not properly honoured for their services. For example, a restaurant that serves eels will periodically engage the local Buddhist temple to perform memorial rites for the souls of the eels sacrificed for humans. Keeping the eel spirits happy is an investment in the restaurant's continued prosperity and also helps to support the temple.

Utilitarian objects are treated similarly. A time-honoured custom is to cremate worn-out implements in a ritual resembling a funeral. The spirits of these objects are thanked for the wear and tear they have suffered in giving benefit to humans. It may be hard today to think of steel and plastic as animate, but in pre-modern times most household items were made of wood, bone, or straw—materials that were once alive.

In recent years, similar ceremonies have been performed for obsolete or worn-out electronic gear in urban Tokyo. Since burning materials like plastic would contribute to air pollution, however, what is cremated is not the equipment itself but a photograph of it.

Shugendo

Literally 'the way of mastering religious power', Shugendo is an age-old ascetic tradition that combines native Shinto and imported (especially Buddhist) elements. It is difficult to place Shugendo in any category other than that of popular or folk religion. It is a mountain cult, some of its practices involve magic, and its semi-legendary seventh-century founder, En no Gyoja, is associated with various miracles.

The main practitioners of shugendo, the *yamabushi* ('mountain monks'), follow a strict ascetic discipline (fasting, going without sleep, standing under cold waterfalls) that is believed to give them extraordinary power as healers and exorcists. To demonstrate their power, they sometimes walk barefoot through the hot embers of a ritual bonfire.

By the thirteenth century Shugendo was already a highly organized tradition with many local variations. There were pilgrimages to the sacred mountains, where purification and other rituals were enacted. The Shugendo fire ritual, in which five kinds of grain are put into a fire of cedar wood, may have originated in Japanese folk religion, but it is also related to esoteric Shingon or Tendai Buddhism.

Typically, the *yamabushi* dispenses charms and blessings, especially for healing illness. An example is a woman ascetic who is a professional healer and exorcist. She lives in her own home, which is also a temple to her tutelary deity, and makes occasional visits to the Buddhist temple with which she is formally affiliated. Her clients are people who believe they are possessed by malignant spirits.

Sometimes she performs fire rituals, even indoors, before a Buddhist altar honouring a guardian figure named Fudo. Wooden sticks with her clients' prayers written on them are burned and thus dispatched to the deities. The flames rise dangerously close to the paper decorations that hang from the ceiling (the Japanese word for paper, *kami*, sounds like the word for spirits). While she petitions the spirits for a cure, some piece of the sick person's clothing is passed quickly through the fire. The ritual may be attended by close to a hundred people and can take more than an hour to complete.

Shugendo was banned by the Meiji government in 1872, which was intent both on restoring Shinto to a 'pure' state, free of Buddhist influence, and on uprooting what it took to be superstition. Since 1945 some Shugendo traditions surviving in Shinto and Buddhism have been revived, and new forms of Shugendo have developed. Even so, many of those who in the past might have looked to Shugendo for spiritual healing are turning to new religions.

New Religions in Japan

More than a hundred new religions have emerged in Japan since the mid-nineteenth century. Though many of them sprang from Shinto or Buddhist roots, they are distinct organizations and are recognized as such.

Much of their success can be attributed to urbanization and the restructuring of Japanese life after the Second World War. In 1942 Japan controlled an empire that stretched from Manchuria almost as far as Australia. Four years later its industrial cities had been reduced to rubble, its economy was in ruins, and its American occupiers had drafted a new constitution that marked a dramatic break with the past. Under the constitution of 1946, which mandated the separation of religion and the state, freedom of religion was guaranteed. Now any marginal religion could register with the Ministry of Education and receive official recognition.

Practically none of the new religions claims exclusive possession of the truth. Each accepts the others on the basis of equality, and they do not require their followers to abandon any traditional faith. Generally, they represent an effort at doctrinal simplicity and appeal mainly to people who are not interested in excessive intellectual sophistication. Most are lay organizations without a complex hierarchy.

The new religions tend to attract people facing stressful situations: illness or death in the family, trouble in a marriage, problems with a job or business, or the pressures of school admission and examinations. Much of the help they offer, whether meditation, self-discipline, shared activities, or counselling, would have been readily available from the extended family or the community in premodern Japan, but such support is not so easy to find in large modern cities.

Some of the new religions are of mainly Shinto inspiration. Like Shinto itself, they tend to be preoccupied with purification rituals, and to emphasize Japanese culture and nationhood. Many offer faith healing based on what they claim to be the shamanic powers of their founders. Several were founded by women, although in most cases men eventually took over.

Tenrikyo

The founder of Tenrikyo ('religion of the heavenly principle') was a woman from a Pure Land Buddhist background named Miki Nakayama (1798–1887). In 1837 she apparently experienced a possession trance and declared her body to be the temple of God, saying, 'I am the True and Original God. I have been predestined to reside here. I have descended from Heaven to save all human beings, and I want to take Miki as the Shrine of God and the mediatrix between God and men' (Thomsen 1963:34). When she began giving away the family's possessions, many thought she was mad, but in time her apparent success in spiritual healing and in reducing the pain of childbirth gained her a following.

Miki and her nineteenth-century followers were harassed by the government, partly because their exuberant dancing attracted attention at a time of peasant unrest. Dancing, now more ritualized, has continued to be a feature of Tenrikyo worship, dramatizing aspects of Miki's thought, especially the notion that we have allowed strife and greed to settle on our minds like dust. Dancing helps to sweep the mind clean of such impurities.

Although Miki herself urged her followers to give up personal possessions, the religion she founded has acquired considerable wealth. With its headquarters in Tenri city, not far from Kyoto, it has built libraries, hospitals, and even a university, and has more than 1.5 million followers today.

Konkokyo

Konkokyo ('religion of golden light') was founded by Akazawa Bunji (1814–83), a peasant farmer who fell seriously ill around the age of forty. Believing that he must have offended a malevolent mountain deity named Konjin, he prayed to Konjin, and when he recovered, he declared Konjin to be the one true God of the universe, Tenchi-Kane-no-kami. He said he had received instruction and guidance in a revelation from the deity, with whom he began to communicate on behalf of others who asked for his assistance. He gave up farming in 1859 and spent the next two decades at an altar in his house, praying for the people who came in search of help and healing. His followers called him Konko Daijin, the mediator between the divine and the human, sent by God.

Konko Daijin's spiritual healing earned him the resentment of the Shugendo ascetics who had been the principal healers in the region and saw him as a threat to their income. Thus for protection he registered under Shinto auspices, even though the one god he recognized was not a traditional Shinto deity.

Although Konko Daijin denied that his movement was a form of Shinto, his successors and disciples succeeded in having it recognized as one of the Meiji government's thirteen official Shinto sects. Some became active supporters of State Shinto and adopted its militaristic trappings. The sect's leaders since 1945, however, have eliminated Shinto ritual and costume.

Konkokyo has developed an extensive organization, produces publications, and conducts missionary activity, teaching the interdependence of God and humans; its followers believe that our suffering is God's suffering, and that our salvation is God's joy.

Omoto

Like Tenrikyo, Omoto (the great 'root' or 'foundation') was founded by a woman. Deguchi Nao (1837–1918) led a life of misfortune and poverty, working as a maid by the age of eleven and bearing eight children before being widowed and becoming a rag-seller at thirty. Of her children, three died in infancy, two sons ran away from home, and two daughters went mad.

In 1892, driven to despair by her favourite daughter's mental illness, Deguchi Nao reportedly received from Tenchi-Kane-no-kami (the god of Konkokyo) a trance vision of the end of the world, the coming of a messiah figure, and the ushering in of a new day. The Scripture of Omoto describes this renewal:

> The Greater World shall be reconstructed and transformed into an entirely new world. After going through a complete cleaning-up, the Greater World shall be changed into the Kingdom of Heaven, where peace reigns through all eternity. Be prepared for it! The Word of God given through Deguchi Nao shall never fail (Thomsen 1963:129).

In 1898 Nao met a young man named Ueda Kisaburo. A student of literature and a dedicated follower of ascetic practices and spiritualism, he claimed that in a mountain cave experience, his soul had taken leave of his body and travelled to heaven, where he learned all the mysteries of the universe and became aware of his mission as the saviour of humanity. Nao declared him to be the expected messiah and adopted him. He took the name Deguchi Onisaburo (1871–1948), married her youngest daughter, and collaborated with Nao to systematize the Omoto movement.

The chaos in the present world, according to Omoto, is the result of strife among the primordial *kami*. The original rulers of Japan—the summer wind, Susano-o, and the *kami* Kunikotachi-no-Mikoto—have been driven out by evil *kami*, and must be restored. This teaching was a clear challenge to the national ideology based on the emperor's descent from Amaterasu. In addition, Onisaburo opposed capitalism and the Russo-Japanese war: as he wrote, 'Armament and war are the means by which landlords and capitalists make their profit, while the poor must suffer. There is nothing in the world more harmful than war and more foolish than armament' (Thomsen 1963:130).

By 1921 Onisaburo was writing his name in a form reserved for kings and princes. After he bought an influential Osaka newspaper the police raided Omoto's headquarters near Kyoto, destroyed its main sanctuary, and imprisoned its leaders on a charge of lèse-majesté (contempt for the ruler's dignity).

Onisaburo was freed after four months, thanks to a general amnesty on the emperor's death, but he jumped bail and went to Mongolia. Calling himself a living buddha and the saviour of the world, he set out to form a state but ran afoul of the local warlord. On his return to Japan, he travelled with an imperial-style motorcycle escort and renamed the rooms of his headquarters with palace room names. By 1935 the government had again had enough: the Omoto buildings were dynamited and Onisaburo was sentenced to life imprisonment for lèse-majesté. Released in 1942 on condition that his family restrain his activities, Onisaburo again spoke in the name of the divine will, criticizing Japan's participation in the Second World War and predicting defeat.

During the 1920s and 1930s, Omoto enjoyed worldwide visibility. It preached an internationalist message, urged the adoption of Esperanto as a world language, and asserted the common origin and essential unity of religions. Onisaburo established international contacts with like-minded movements, such as the Baha'i Faith, and organized the Universal Love and Brotherhood Association. After the Second World War, Onisaburo claimed that the *kami* had preserved Omoto as the basis for world renewal.

Seicho no Ie

Spiritual healing was important to the founder of Seicho no Ie ('House of Growth'), Taniguchi Masaharu (1893–1985). When he contracted venereal disease, he consulted a hypnotist, and though he was actually cured by standard medicine, he denied the principle of contagion and relied on positive thinking to prevent others from catching the disease.

In the 1920s Taniguchi argued that the material world is only the shadow of the mind and that one can eliminate suffering by concentrating on positive thoughts. This view attracted attention at a time when Japan was in economic distress following the Tokyo earthquake of 1923. For the next several years he explored the power of mind over matter, listened to spiritualists, practised self-help cures, and read the newly translated psychological writings of Sigmund Freud. Launching a magazine (later reissued as a series called 'Truth of Life'), he argued that the material world does not exist; the only reality is the divine life of the mind:

> This manifest world, visible to the naked eye and felt with the five senses, is not God's creation. I was greatly mistaken in accusing and judging God. This world, as perceived with the five senses, is merely a production of our minds. God is love and mercy. The Real World, created by God's infinite wisdom, love, and life, is filled with eternal harmony (Thomsen 1963:154).

In 1930 Taniguchi's publishing enterprise became the basis of Seicho no Ie as an organized religion. At first he maintained that it was above the other religions and that its mandate was to help each religion to be true to its essence. In time it became an eclectic religion itself, one that claimed to be the fundamental essence of the others. Seicho no Ie amalgamates teachings from Shinto, Buddhism, and Christianity, including

Christian Science, and considers the Buddha and Christ along with the Shinto *kami* to be incarnations of the supreme deity. During the Second World War it was strongly nationalistic, identifying the emperor with the ultimate being. Consequently its publishing activity was suspended during the American occupation of 1945–52, but it resumed thereafter, reaching a more middle-class audience than most of Japan's other new religions.

PL Kyodan

PL (standing for 'perfect liberty') Kyodan ('Church' or 'Group') is another example of Western influence. Founded under the American occupation in 1946 by Miki Tokuchika (1900–83), it worships the supreme deity and venerates ancestral spirits. Misfortunes are taken to be divine admonitions, interpreted to the believer through counselling. PL holds that life is art, and it urges its followers to cultivate appropriate self-expression in art and sports. A number of its centres have golf courses.

Mahikari

Mahikari ('true light') was founded in 1959 by Okada Kotama (1901–74), a scion of a samurai family who claimed to have received a revelation from the 'Su' god, creator of the human race, entrusting him with the task of purifying the world and repairing its ills. His principal successor is his daughter, Okada Sachiko. The movement counted 50,000 adherents in 1980.

Like most of Japan's new religions, Mahikari believes in miracles performed by a deity who cares for people and, with the help of true believers, intervenes to provide for their welfare. Mahikari healers raise their hand over the subject to direct healing light where it is needed. This healing practice has spread to several parts of the world.

Followers often believe themselves to be possessed by spirits—especially those of deceased samurai—and there are regular exorcism sessions for the possessed, who first therapeutically 'act out' their spiritual dramas. An interesting tenet of this movement is that Jesus Christ was never crucified: instead, he went to Japan, where he married, raised a family, and was buried. Mahikari followers believe they can point out his gravesite.

Reiyukai

Reiyukai (society of spiritual friendship) is one of several new religions that began as offshoots of Nichiren Buddhism. Founded in 1925 by Kubo Kakutaro (1892–1944) and Kotani Kimi (1901–71), his sister-in-law, it emphasizes the *Lotus Sutra* and daily ancestor worship.

Rissho Kosei Kai

Reiyukai in turn gave rise to Rissho Kosei Kai ('society for the establishment of righteous and friendly relations'). Founded in 1938, it relies on repentance to break the chain of karma and practises shamanism. Today it has over two million members. As we saw in Chapter 8, Nichiren has a long tradition of Japanese nationalism, but Rissho Kosei Kai has moved away from that heritage; its co-founder Niwano Nikkyo (1906–99) became active in initiatives to promote interreligious understanding and international peace in the 1950s and 1960s.

Soka Gakkai

Then there is the controversial Soka Gakkai ('value-creating study group'). Founded in 1937 as a lay organization by a schoolteacher, Makiguchi Tsunesaburo (1871–1944), it follows the tradition of Nichiren Shoshu, the small Nichiren branch that venerates the Gohonzon scroll. Like many of its counterparts, its main goal is to achieve happiness in this world, and it values profit, goodness, and beauty. Unlike other new religions, however, it has used aggressive recruitment tactics called *shakubuku* ('break and subdue'), which have drawn criticism.

After the Second World War, Soka Gakkai gained political influence through its association with a political party called the Komeito, which attracted attention because of its rapid growth in the 1950s and 1960s. During those years Soka Gakkai, under the name Nichiren Shoshu, or True Nichiren Buddhism, spread all over the world.

In 1991, however, financial scandals and other problems led to Soka Gakkai's 'excommunication' from the Nichiren parent body. It was the most dramatic event in recent Japanese religious history and the climax of a long power struggle between the sect's priests, who insisted on their absolute authority in matters of doctrine and practice, and its largest lay organization (claiming 16 million members), whose leaders called for reform of a priestly hierarchy they believed to be stuck in the past. After the priests cut their ties with Soka Gakkai, they even tore down and replaced a 'Grand Hall' at their headquarters designed and funded by the organization.

Although it is no longer part of Nichiren Shoshu, Soka Gakkai continues to play an important role in Japanese politics through its party, the Komeito, which has sometimes been part of the governing coalition. In North America Soka Gakkai has worked actively to spread the Buddhist message, and founded Soka University as part of this missionary endeavour.

Agonshu

After a lifetime of illness, poverty, business failure, and crime, Tsutsumi Masao (b. 1921) was about to commit suicide when the rope he had thrown over a beam dislodged a book on the mercies of the Buddhist goddess Kannon (Guanyin), which he paused to read. Believing he had been chosen for salvation, he took up meditation and asceticism and was ordained as a lay member of the tantric Shingon Buddhist sect under the name Kiriyama Seiyu. In 1970 he had a vision of Kannon informing him that he had 'cut his karma': removed the hindrance of unhappy spirits of his deceased ancestors that had caused his failures. Now he was to help others.

Kiriyama began to write extensively; his 1971 book *Henshin no genri* ('Principles of Transformation') sold widely. In it he credits esoteric Buddhist practices for his power and offers to guide others to similar self-realization. In 1978 he renamed his group Agonshu ('the Agama sect') after claiming to discover in the early discourses (*agama*) of the Buddha a route to buddhahood that is effective not only for the living but for the unhappy ghosts among their ancestors, whose spirits can be liberated through elimination of their karmic hindrances.

It matters little that this is not how ancient India understood the Buddha's discourses, nor that turning the spirits of the dead into buddhas is not what classical Buddhism was all about. The focus of the Agama movement is not the content of the texts but the supposed inner meaning discovered by Kiriyama. Agonshu's followers believe that making the spirits of the dead happy produces comfort and happiness for the living, and therefore fulfills the purpose of Buddhism in general.

The site at Yamashima, near Kyoto, that Agonshu acquired in 1976 is believed to have been spiritually validated by the subsequent appearance of various Buddhist deities in visions. In 1986 the president of Sri Lanka, Junius Jayawardene, presented Agonshu with a casket said to contain a bone relic of the Buddha. To adherents, this confirmed Agonshu's acceptance in the wider Buddhist world. Veneration of the reliquary has become their central ritual, and they use models of it for personal devotion.

Agonshu, like other new religions, is media-conscious and uses the latest technology to broadcast its supposedly ancient doctrines. The biggest spectacle takes place annually on 11 February at Yamashima, when two gigantic pyres are lit, one containing hundreds of thousands of sticks and chips of wood inscribed with prayers for the ancestral spirits contributed by adherents from all over Japan, and the other containing wishes and petitions to benefit the living. The traditional and the modern are combined as the volunteers who place these prayers on the fire, dressed in the clothing of *yamabushi*, coordinate their movements by cell phone.

Aum Shinrikyo

The most violent new religion in Japan is Aum Shinrikyo, which combines a version of Hindu yoga and some Buddhist elements with a fervent millenarianism (the belief that the world is approaching its end). 'Aum' is a variant of the Hindu mystic chant *om*, and Shinrikyo means 'supreme truth'. It was founded by Asahara Shoko (Matsumoto Chizuo, b. 1955), a nearly blind yogi, in 1984, and it now has more than ten thousand followers in Japan and perhaps thirty thousand in Russia. The sect's numbers in Japan are thought to be growing, despite the sarin gas attack it carried out on the Tokyo subway system in 1995, in which twelve died and thousands were injured. Police investigations eventually uncovered other criminal activities, including kidnapping and murder.

Media reports described cult members who had given all their wealth to the organization and were living in poverty, practising meditation and yoga, and passively obeying Asahara's orders. The cult's headquarters at the foot of Mount Fuji were raided, its leaders, including Asahara, were imprisoned, and the government no longer recognizes the group as a religion. But it continues to thrive. Interestingly, many followers, both before and after the cult's violent activities became known, have been university-educated people looking for meaning in life.

Cultural Expressions

Japanese Art and Architecture

In Japan, Chinese and Korean styles in art and architecture combined with the indigenous aesthetic tradition to produce a highly distinctive visual culture. This aesthetic may be seen in everything from the simple bowls used in the tea ceremony to the carefully sculpted 'naturalness' of a Shinto or Zen garden.

Meditators at the 'rock garden' of the Ryoanji Zen Temple, Kyoto (Kate Brunn).

Shinto shrines come in many shapes and sizes, and are typically constructed of unpainted wood using traditional hand tools. The wood ages at a different rate toward the top of the shrine, creating a range of shades that highlights a central aspect of the Japanese aesthetic: variation is more beautiful than uniformity. A piece of pottery, for instance, should vary subtly but perceptibly in both colour and texture. A related insight is that natural objects such as rocks and trees are not symmetrical: thus asymmetry is a fundamental part of the beauty of an artistic creation such as a flower arrangement.

Another aspect of the Japanese aesthetic is expressed in the term *wabi sabi*. Impossible to translate exactly, it has connotations of poverty, incompleteness, and impermanence. Perhaps this minimalist aesthetic has something to do with the limitations of the natural landscape, much of which is mountainous and does not lend itself easily to cultivation. In any event, it is obviously compatible with the emphasis on simplicity in both Zen and Daoist thought.

The Japanese honour the most respected practitioners of various traditional arts by naming them 'living treasures'. One elderly 'living treasure', a master potter who was already rich, famous, and greatly respected, was so dedicated to his craft that he continued to get up at 4:00 every morning to fire the kiln and resume work on a particular piece that he was determined to perfect before he died.

Interaction and Adaptation

The modernization of Japan began when political control of the country shifted from the shoguns to Emperor Meiji in 1868. Western-style factories were built to support heavy industry and a modern military, along with the railways needed for transport. In effect, Japan adopted Western technology and began the process of industrialization almost overnight, without any large-scale adoption of Christianity or related Western social norms. It is not possible to modernize without coming under the influence of the values associated with modernity, but Japan has proudly insisted on the uniqueness and superiority of its own culture. Westerners coming to discuss joint business ventures soon learn to follow and respect Japanese approaches to business relations.

When Christianity reached Japan in the mid-sixteenth century, it was at first regarded as a form of Buddhism. One reason for the confusion was that Buddhist terms were used to explain Christian concepts. Another was the Jesuit missionaries themselves, who resembled Zen monks in their learning and discipline. This misconception no doubt contributed to Christianity's initial success in Japan, but Japanese rulers eventually turned against it, fearing foreign political encroachment.

Japan adopted a European-style parliamentary system of government beginning in 1890: it calls its legislature by the German name 'Diet', and the emperor's powers are exclusively ceremonial. Yet the emperor remains a symbol of the state, and Confucian values (especially the 'work ethic') continue to dominate daily life.

Since 1945, uneasiness over Japan's defeat and the US military occupation has been reflected in a tendency to downplay the idea that the West might have contributed in any way to the process of modernization. Instead, most commentators have emphasized the influence of forces that had been part of the Japanese tradition for many centuries before the modern era began. Of these forces the most prominent is Neo-Confucian rationalism, the dominant school of thought in the cultural circle that also includes China and Korea. The earliest Japanese 'modernizers', in the late nineteenth century, were usually from the samurai class, steeped in the Confucian classics and motivated by a nationalistic desire to (as Meiji policy put it) 'enrich the country and strengthen the armed forces'. This desire, combined with the Confucian work ethic, has been the moving force behind the country's economic success.

Religion and Work

For many years religion played an important role in the Japanese workplace. Much of Japan's economic success was attributed to the Buddhist and Confucian emphasis on values such as harmony, duty, and cohesion, and even today employers may send new employees to Zen temples to deepen their understanding of concepts such as discipline and loyalty. Some companies have their own shrines to Inari—the Shinto rice god who has become the god of business—at which rituals are performed regularly. Other companies have shrines to the *kami* of their own deceased founders. Many businesses also sponsor memorial rites for deceased employees, and there may even be company graves.

Increasingly, though, the concept of lifelong loyalty is losing ground. Now that business faces international competition, many employers are prepared to lay workers

Part of a shrine to Inari, the kami of rice, in Kyoto (Kate Brunn).

off in bad times. Similarly, many employees no longer feel obligated to stay with the company that gave them their first position.

Conclusion

Shamanism and ancient folk traditions are the foundations of religion in both Korea and Japan, and they continue to be practised across the region. In addition, three major traditions were imported from China to Korea beginning in the second century and to Japan from the sixth century on. Buddhism—the first formal, institutional religion in the region—has had an impact on nearly every aspect of life, from art and architecture to concepts of the hereafter. Confucian thought, especially as developed by the neo-Confucian school, has profoundly affected both political thought and social values, and has been particularly influential in the workplace. Daoism is a formal religion in Korea but not in Japan (although it has made its influence felt through its contributions to Buddhism). The many forms of Shinto developed out of traditional Japanese religion, but over through the centuries have also incorporated elements from both Buddhism and Confucianism. Modern Japan has been an especially fertile ground for new religious movements, many of which originated in existing traditions such as Buddhism and shamanism. Western values have become more evident in Japanese society in recent years, but so far they do not appear to have displaced traditional values.

Glossary

Amaterasu The sun goddess in Japanese tradition.

bushido The 'Way of the Warrior', a code emphazing obedience, loyalty, frugality and other samurai values.

Choendogyo A Korean religion founded in 1860 that regards human nature as a reflection of divinity and refers to God as Hanullim or Chonju, 'lord of Heaven'.

honji suijaku 'The original site and the local manifestations', a Japanese formula characterizing Shinto as derived from Buddhism; see also *Ryobu Shinto*.

kami The gods and spirits of Japanese religion, believed to be present in countless natural phenomena.

Kojiki 'The Record of Ancient Matters', a collection of Japanese narratives including myths regarding the origins of the world and of Japan.

Kokugaku 'National Learning'; the movement that, beginning in the sixteenth century, promoted a return to indigenous Japanese thought and sparked the revival of Shinto.

miko Japanese female shamans, often blind, who transmit the spirits' advice on important matters.

mudang Korean shamans, often women, who conduct rituals and in some cases communicate with the spirits through soul travel or possession.

SOUTH KOREA

Gaya-san The Haein-sa Temple houses the Tripitaka Koreana—the Buddhist scriptures carved onto 81,340 wooden blocks—as well as a nice three-storied pagoda.

Gyeongju The Gyeongju area was the centre of the Shilla dynasty. Among the royal tombs in its Tumuli Park is one known as the 'Flying Horse'. The Bulguk-sa ('Buddha Land') Temple was built in the sixth century, destroyed by the Japanese in the sixteenth, and restored in the twentieth. Nearby is Golgul-sa: a cave temple carved in rock that is a centre for training in the Sonmudo style of martial arts. The Samjeon Grotto Temple features an image of Vairocana, the Buddha of Light, carved into a rock cliff.

Seoul One of many temples in Seoul, the Hwagye-sa—home of the Seoul International Zen Center—is noted for its Zen garden.

JAPAN

Ise Site of the main shrine to the sun goddess, Amaterasu.

Kyoto Home to the Imperial Palace and Nijo Castle, the second capital also abounds in temples and shrines. Toji is a Buddhist temple with the country's tallest pagoda. Ryoanji is a Zen temple with a famous rock (sand) garden (p. 532). The picturesque Kinkakuji, or Golden Pavilion, was built as a shogun's palace overlooking a lake and is now a Zen temple (p. 517).

Nara Nara Park in Japan's first capital has many famous buildings. The Todaiji Temple, said to be the world's largest wooden building, houses an enormous Buddha image. The Kofukuji Temple features a five-storied pagoda. The Kasuga (Shinto) Shrine is home to a famous lantern festival in late summer. Another festival is dedicated to the park's deer.

Nikko Rinnoji is a Buddhist temple founded by the famous monk Shonin. Nearby is the Futarasan Shrine, built by Shonin in the eighth century and dedicated to the *kami* of the surrounding mountains. The Toshogu, the tomb of first Tokugawa Shogun, has a beautiful ceremonial bridge and a famous carving of the three monkeys who 'see no evil, hear no evil and speak no evil'.

Tokyo Among the many historic sites throughout Tokyo are the Meiji Shrine, the Senkakuji Temple, and the Yasukuni Shrine, dedicated to Japan's war dead.

Nihongi The 'Chronicles of Japan', a second collection of ancient Japanese myths.

Ryobu Shinto A syncretic tradition in which elements of Shinto were incorporated into Buddhist worship and vice versa, and the principal *kami* were equated with bodhisattvas; see also *honji suijaku*.

sakaki A sacred tree found at Shinto shrines.

samurai The warrior elite in the feudal society of premodern Japan.

Sect Shinto Thirteen groups that were recognized as new sects by Japan's Meiji regime in the late nineteenth century.

Seicho no Ie 'House of Growth', one of Japan's twentieth-century 'new religions', founded as a publishing enterprise in 1930.

shogunate The institutional form of government under the **shoguns**; different periods in the shogunate era are identified by the name of the capital or the ruling clan during each one.

shoguns The military leaders, members of the warrior class, who ruled Japan from 1185 to 1868.

Shrine Shinto The worship of *kami* or nature deities and spirits, practised at shrines throughout the Japanese countryside since ancient times.

Shugendo A Japanese popular tradition that includes magical and ritual techniques and is associated with sacred mountain regions; its principal practitioners are the *yamabushi* or 'mountain monks'.

Taika reforms New regulations, based on Confucian values, issued in 646 by Japan's Emperor Taika to centralize power.

Tenrikyo A 'new' Japanese religion that seeks to purify the mind of the spiritual 'dusts' that pollute it; founded by Miki Nakayama, who claimed to have experienced spirit possession in a trance in 1837.

Further Reading

Blacker, Carmen. 1975. *The Catalpa Bow: A Study of Shamanistic Practices in Japan*. London: Allen & Unwin. Excellent on Japanese popular religion; written from the viewpoint of a scholarly eyewitness.

Bowring, Richard, and Peter Kornicki, eds. 1993. *The Cambridge Encyclopedia of Japan*. Cambridge: Cambridge University Press. A good general reference for geography, history, and culture.

Buswell, Robert. 2003. *Korean Religions in Practice*. Princeton: Princeton University Press. Good information on practices.

Kim, Chongho. 2003. *Korean Shamanism: The Cultural Paradox*. Aldershot: Ashgate Publishing. Suggests that Koreans look down on shamanism and yet continue to use it.

Kitagawa, Joseph M. 1987. *On Understanding Japanese Religion*. Princeton: Princeton Univesity Press. Good introduction to Shinto and Japanese Buddhism.

Lee, Peter H., and William Theodore de Bary, eds. 1997. *Sources of Korean Tradition*. vol. 1. New York: Columbia University Press. Representative texts for Korean cultural history through the sixteenth century.

Reader, Ian T. 1991. *Religion in Contemporary Japan*. Basingstoke: Macmillan; Honolulu: University of Hawai'i Press. An engaging view of diverse attitudes towards and practices of religion in Japan.

Tanabe, George J., Jr, ed. 1999. *Religions of Japan in Practice*. Princeton: Princeton University Press. A fine sourcebook, highlighting the complexity and interrelatedness of practices and institutions.

Tsunoda, Ryusaku, ed. 1958. *Sources of Japanese Tradition*. New York: Columbia University Press. A companion volume to de Bary's Indian and Chinese sourcebooks in a still valuable series.

References

Aston, W.G., trans. 1896. *Nihongi: Chronicles of Japan from the Earliest Times to A.D. 697*. Kegan Paul/Charles E. Tuttle Co., Inc.

Ching, Julia. 1976. *To Acquire Wisdom: The Way of Wang Yang-ming*. New York: Columbia University Press.

Hori, Ichiro. 1968. *Folk Religion in Japan: Continuity and Change*. Chicago: University of Chicago Press.

Kim, Yong-Choon. 1977. 'Ch'ondogyo Thought and Its Significance in [Modern] Korean Tradition'. In Chai-shin Yu, ed., *Korean and Asian Religious Tradition*, 237–47. Toronto: Korean and Related Studies Press.

Lee, Peter H., ed. 1996. *Sourcebook of Korean Civilization*. Vol. 2. New York: Columbia University Press.

Thomsen, Harry. 1963. *The New Religions of Japan*. Rutland, VT: Tuttle.

Tsunoda, Ryusaku, ed. 1958. *Sources of Japanese Tradition*. New York: Columbia University Press.

The Nature of Religion

ALAN F. SEGAL | WILLARD G. OXTOBY

Suppose someone asks you: 'Aren't religions all pretty much the same?' The question looks simple enough. Presumably what the questioner means is that all religions resemble each other in certain essential respects, and that any differences in the details can be dismissed as secondary.

To answer responsibly, though, we should start by unpacking the question. The questioner could be asserting that all religions accomplish some common result in their practice, or share some essential core in their teachings. On the other hand, the questioner could be talking about the value of the world's diverse traditions in relation to one another. Questions of value are almost inevitable when we compare faiths, especially when we include our own in the comparison. For the moment, though, let us consider the matter of diversity itself.

The diversity of the world's religions is nowhere more evident than in their representations of supernatural power. Some localize the divine in tangible objects; others claim it to be beyond form altogether. We can marvel not only at the divine itself but at the bewildering array of its manifestations. Still, some groupings do emerge when we begin to sort those manifestations into categories.

The Nature of the Divine

Monotheism and Polytheism

The terms 'monotheism' (from the Greek for worship of only one god) and 'polytheism' (worship of many gods) first appear in European writing in the seventeenth century: a time of absolute monarchy when a single God functioned to justify a single monarch on the throne. Sometimes these terms were used in an intra-Christian context; for example, by Protestants who condemned the Roman Catholic veneration of saints as polytheistic. Then as now, however, they referred principally to the contrast between the Hebraic model of exclusive devotion to one god and the Hellenic model of devotion to many. Furthermore, then as now, the concept of monotheism included an implicit judgment not only on polytheism—by far the more common system around the world—but on diversity itself.

Western civilization owes to ancient Israel the idea that there is only one god. Well before the word 'monotheism' was coined, the idea was a distinctive characteristic of the three principal religions in the West: Judaism, Christianity, and Islam. This monotheism is exclusive. It declares that the faithful should worship only the one God, that the worship of any other deity is an abomination to God, and that no other gods even exist. The deity's exclusive status tends to be matched by exclusivity in the communities of followers. Christians and Muslims, as members of missionary religions, tend to draw clear boundaries between themselves and outsiders, and then encourage those on the other side of the line to cross over and join them.

Jews, on the other hand, think of themselves as a family community. They allow others to join the community if they are truly motivated, but have rarely attempted to attract converts. Instead, Jews proclaim that the righteous of all nations will enter paradise in the world to come. Christians and Muslims, when they have come into contact with Eastern traditions whose communities are less clearly demarcated, have tended to describe those traditions as if they too followed the boundaried model. But neither Chinese nor Indian religions need to be defined in those terms, and even Judaism does not fit the 'boundaried' definition very well.

Scholars have often tried to identify the forces that produce monotheism in a society. Guy E. Swanson, in his famous book *The Birth of the Gods: The Origin of Primitive Beliefs*, maintains that monotheism is associated with social complexity, reflecting the establishment of a multi-layered hierarchy. From another perspective, though, multiple gods may simply represent the attribution of human motivations to natural phenomena, and in that case the movement towards monotheism could just as easily be seen as marking a society's repudiation of this primitive understanding of causation.

Perhaps scholars should pay more attention to the principles that a society considers important. Polytheistic Greek society eventually adopted the family principle, arranging all the gods into a large extended family. The Greek philosophers also attempted to reduce the complexities of the world to one single, overriding element or principle, whether water, fire, change, time, love, or knowledge. Contemporary cosmological physicists seek a theory of everything—one that will unify gravity, electromagnetism, and the forces that keep atoms together. So far that theory has been elusive.

On the other hand, the search for single causation may be a product of the human mind itself. Some great Eastern religious systems like Hinduism and Buddhism identify a single principle of salvation in which animals, humans, and gods all participate. For them, monotheism and polytheism are not the polar opposites that Jews, Christians, and Muslims tend to consider them.

Dualism: Zoroastrianism, Gnosticism, Manichaeism

'Dualism' in religion postulates two ultimate principles opposing each other and more or less evenly matched. These principles are usually (though not always) personified as a good god and an evil devil.

Zoroastrianism

Zoroastrianism is a nominally monotheistic religion with dualistic overtones. It developed in Persia (Iran) sometime before the mid-sixth century BCE; it was the state religion of the Sasanians, Iran's last great pre-Islamic empire; and it is still alive today in India and Iran, in small remnant communities that have preserved the tradition over the past fourteen centuries.

The supreme creator god of the Zoroastrians is called Ahura Mazda ('Wise Lord'). In ancient times Zoroastrians called themselves Mazda worshippers and their tradition 'the Good Religion'. 'Zoroastrianism' came later, from the Greek name for the tradition's priestly and prophetic teacher, Zarathushtra. The time, place, and details of his life are unknown. All we can say with any assurance is that he lived somewhere in Iran before the beginning of the Achaemenian era (559–331 BCE). The scholarly consensus credits him only with 17 psalms, called the *Gathas*, that form part of the sacred book called the *Avesta*. (The rest of the text consists mainly of ritual hymns and a work on priestly purity regulations.)

The religious thought of Zoroastrianism places it among the great religious traditions of human history. Five features are of particular interest. One is its emphasis on ethics: morality is central, both as an ideal and as an achievement. Another is its eschatology, centred on the expectation of a world to come both for the individual and for the world as a whole, when this life will be overhauled and a new utopian age ushered in. A third notable characteristic is the Zoroastrian tradition's vivid personification of evil as a demonic antagonist who, like Satan in the Christian and Muslim traditions, seems beyond the good deity's control. Fourth, Zoroastrians traditionally dispose of their dead by exposing the remains to birds of prey in 'Towers of Silence'. Fifth and finally, there is its historical influence: although this remains more a question than a fact, it is possible that Zoroastrian ideas about evil and the soul contributed to the development of comparable ideas in Judaism, Christianity, and Islam.

Most Zoroastrians today consider themselves monotheists, perhaps in part because their tradition was maintained under Islamic rule in Iran and under Christian rule in British India. Yet their monotheism is not exclusive: Zoroastrians revere a host of divine entities (some corresponding to deities in the Hindu Vedas) that they consider to function as agents and deputies of Ahura Mazda. In the early parts of the Zoroastrian scripture, the *Avesta*, there are statements suggesting that two gods hold sway over the universe. The good god, Ahura Mazda, is the one to whom all praise and thanks are due. His evil counterpart, known first as Angra Mainyu and later as Ahriman, is the god who controls evil and must be exorcised.

The devil is a much more elusive figure in Judaism, Christianity, and Islam, perhaps because theologians wanting to affirm God's purpose and power have been reluctant to make room for a second locus of ultimate power. Nevertheless, he is a visible presence in the art and narratives of the Christian Middle Ages and continues to figure in the folklore and popular piety of all three Abrahamic traditions today.

The devil or Satan is mentioned in both the New Testament and, as Shaytan or Iblis, the Qur'an. But he does not figure in Old Testament narrative. The snake of Genesis 2–3 is never described as anything more than a snake. Satan makes no appearance in the Hebrew creation story, and even the book of Job refers only to 'the satan'—a Hebrew word meaning 'adversary' and apparently designating a court official; it is not a personal name. The few other references to 'satan' in the Hebrew Bible are best understood in the same way.

After the Muslim conquest of Persia many Zoroastrians fled to India, where their descendants came to be known as Parsis ('Persians'). Here four Parsi priests perform a fire ceremony at a gathering in Bombay. The cloths covering their mouths are intended to prevent any spittle from coming into contact with the fire (Willard G. Oxtoby).

When did 'the adversary' become 'Satan'? Most scholars today would place the transition sometime between the completion of the Old Testament and the beginning of the writing of the New Testament. That is because there is no statement in the Old Testament that can unambiguously be applied to a figure in opposition to God. Yet Satan is a fully developed power independent of God in the New Testament, and this same characterization is also present in a series of books composed after the Old Testament and before the New Testament, which are not included in either the Jewish or the Christian Bible. In fact, the devil appears to emerge in Jewish and Christian tradition just at the moment when Persian influence was at its height. There seems no doubt that the image of Satan as he appears in the Christian and Muslim traditions, and to a lesser extent in Jewish folklore, owes something to Persian depictions of Ahriman.

Gnosticism and Manichaeism

Westerners tend to see monotheism as the culmination of religious development—the final stage in an evolutionary progression away from polytheism. For them dualism thus represents an intermediary stage. Historically, though, dualism appears to have arisen only after monotheism had established itself. In fact, dualism seems to represent a kind of strategic retreat necessitated by the difficulty of explaining evil in a monotheistic system. The scope of God's power is, in principle, limited by whatever the demonic adversary can control. If God is both physical creator and moral sovereign, then the religious narrative must answer two questions regarding the force of evil. First, how was it that the creator's power permitted the introduction of evil? Second, given the present force of evil, how may we be assured that good will triumph in the end?

An influential narrative response to these questions came in the movement we call Gnosticism. Spreading mainly among Hellenized Jews and Christians living in an atmosphere of popularized Platonic thought, Gnosticism suggested that humanity could be released from its primal entrapment in the sinful cosmos only through divine redemption. Since pure spirit was seen to have fallen into an evil material existence, it was the task of the faithful to renounce physical satisfaction and seek an ascetic's release from entrapment in matter. Jewish communities were particularly receptive to the Gnostic message because of early Jewish mysticism, in which adepts of meditation could ascend to heaven to discover hidden truths. Gnostic mythological systems proliferated in the first few centuries of our era, each with a different story of how the evil world came into being and how the saviour beyond it was to be reached. The Gnostic literary enterprise tended towards stories of origins, but implicitly it was no less concerned with salvation. The awakened person was duty-bound to escape the evil universe, and the only guide consisted in the special redeeming knowledge called *gnosis* in Greek. In many Gnostic systems the spiritually awakened person was called a 'pneumatic', from the Greek *pneuma*, meaning spirit.

In the third century a Syrian Christian named Mani (c. 216–c. 274) organized his own new religion, Manichaeism, on a largely Christian Gnostic base. It attracted many of those who cherished individual Gnostic systems and melded them into a new world religion. Manichaeism spread westward across the Mediterranean world, where its narratives of conflict between good and evil lingered into the Middle Ages in the Balkans and southern France. It also spread across Central Asia to China, where it survived for centuries before dying out. In the course of its Central Asian dispersion it came into Buddhist territory, where both its emphasis on a saving message and its program of asceticism appear to have landed on fertile soil. But the question to which Manichaeism offered an answer was not one that troubled Buddhism. The monotheistic religions of the Middle East and Mediterranean might see the problem of suffering and evil as a reason to question divine power, but Buddhism does not. Whereas the Western traditions ask why a good God allows suffering, Buddhism (especially the Mahayana school) sees the celestial powers as helping humans along the path to liberation from suffering.

Mani was active in Syria and later Persia, where the Zoroastrian tradition was rooted, and it was just after his time that Zoroastrianism became the established religion of Persia's Sasanian dynasty (r. 226–51). The Sasanian Zoroastrians' vision of the universe, from the creation to the final judgment and renewal, drew on earlier Persian ideas that may have underlain the biblical and Gnostic–Manichaean narratives as well. Still, Zoroastrian and Manichaean interpretations of the struggle between good and evil differ in one crucial respect. For Gnostics and Manichaeans, spirit is good and material existence is inherently evil. For Zoroastrians, however, the material world is simply the context within which the moral forces of good and evil operate: in itself, that world is morally neutral. Only at certain times in its history, principally in the Sasanian era, has the Zoroastrian tradition seriously explored the philosophical idea that the ultimate power of Ahura Mazda, the Wise Lord, is in any substantial way compromised by the activity of the evil spirit.

Both the ethical struggle of the Zoroastrians and the spirit–matter opposition of the Gnostics and Manichaeans have been termed dualistic. The word 'dualism' was coined in 1700 by the Englishman Thomas Hyde (1636–1703), writing on Zoroastrianism, to refer to a system of thought in which an evil being is set over against the being who is the source of good. For Hyde, then, the spirit–matter contrast of the Gnostic traditions was not a defining characteristic of dualism. But within a generation the term came to be used in other contexts, and as a result it acquired additional connotations. The German philosopher Christian Wolff (1679–1754), for instance, applied it to the contrast between mind and matter in the philosophy of René Descartes.

Since then, the term has been applied to such a variety of dualities that it has lost almost all useful meaning. To call Daoism dualistic, for example—as some have done on account of its opposition between yin and yang—is not helpful, since Daoists, while privileging yin in conduct, see goodness in the universe as inhering in an ideal dynamic balance of the two. Even so, to the extent that 'dualism' refers explicitly to a struggle between good and evil as ultimate powers, it does offer a useful alternative to monotheism, and may have flourished precisely as a response to one of the most difficult problems raised by monotheism.

Missionary Religions

The idealized questioner imagined at the beginning of this chapter proposed that all religions are pretty much the same. Missionary religions, to the contrary, believe not only that they are all different, but that the differences are so consequential that they cannot be dismissed: therefore those who know the truth are obliged to spread it. Missionaries' motives are often profoundly altruistic. They may spend long years far from their homes, living a frugal and sometimes dangerous life, simply in order to help others understand a message that will save their souls. Any worldly fame or otherworldly merit gained through such dedicated service is generally secondary.

No one can say how many religions there have been in the world, for the boundaries distinguishing them are sometimes fluid or arbitrary at best, and new religions emerge all the time. Yet a mere three traditions account for half the world's population, thanks to their worldwide diffusion. Buddhism, Christianity, and Islam have all succeeded as missionary religions. Interestingly, all three have presented their messages as 'universal', intended for all humans, not merely for specific groups defined by heredity or descent.

In the early phase of Buddhism's development, a sense of India's geographical nationhood may not have been very firmly established, but Indian society was already stratified into four broad social classes. Buddhism set these caste distinctions aside as irrelevant to the achievement of liberation.

Christianity began as a sect of Judaism, a religion that, although it did proselytize early in its development, emphasized the special national destiny and responsibility of the Jewish people. Judaism developed universalism by admitting that all righteous persons, regardless of ethnic or religious identity, will achieve God's kingdom. Hence it saw no need for missionary activity. Instead Judaism concentrated on moral teachings meant for everyone, and as a result Jews were able to survive as guests in cultures where other religions predominated. An early decision that steered Christianity on its missionary course was that converts did not need to become Jews first in order to become Christians. At the same time Christian rhetoric appropriated the divine promises made to Israel and claimed them for the new Israel represented by the ethnically inclusive Christian Church. Early Christian preaching promoted a universal spiritual and moral interpretation of the ideas of community and kingship received from Judaism. Paul's repudiation of the difference between Jew and Greek in Galatians 3 and Romans 10 reverberates through the centuries in the Christian community's consciousness: 'There is no longer Jew or Greek, there is no longer slave or free, there is no longer male and female; for all of you are one in Christ Jesus' (Gal. 3:28). This is a universal declaration of striking generality; yet others have noted that it makes no reference to pluralism. There is only the one faith, to which all must adhere.

The Qur'an maintains that God has used different prophets to deliver his message to different peoples. But Muhammad did not think that monotheism was intended for the Arabs alone, and the message of *islam* ('submission') was inherently universal. Indeed, *islam* functionally connotes conversion for Muslims, though it also describes life in community thereafter. Describing its own message, specifically addressed to the population of Arabia, as clear, reasonable, even self-evident, the Qur'an invites comparison with the revelations given earlier to Jews and Christians. But the purpose of the comparison is not so much to show the previous revelations to be false as to proclaim them incomplete. The words that God has been sending to particular communities are seen as parts of an overall word to humanity at large. It is not their ethnic identity but their devotion and obedience that renders humans acceptable in the sight of God.

In principle, the community that was established among the Arabian followers of Muhammad had the potential to expand beyond Arabia, and Islam became a world empire within a century of the Prophet's death. An essential component of the missionary effort was the idea of free choice between one tradition and another; the Qur'an explicitly says: 'Let there be no coercion in religion' (Q. 2:256). In virtually every society, people have the choice either to accept or to reject the society's prescribed path of conduct. It has been much less common for people to be offered a choice between different paths. In fact, missionary religions are very careful to define the content of their faith and must often combat alternative understandings that develop in the course of their spread. Christianity grew out of Judaism (specifically an early form that attributed a great deal of power to God's predominant angel, called the 'Angel of the Lord, the 'son of man,' or the 'Glory of the Lord'). Islam grew out of the Judeo-Christian tradition, defining itself in contradistinction to Christianity's mediated monotheism.

Protestantism too can be understood as a new religion, formed in response to the critiques of the Roman Catholic Church put forward by reformers like Martin Luther, even though it saw itself as a renewal movement. Many new religious traditions have grown out of reform movements within an existing tradition, especially under the influence of a charismatic leader or prophet. A relatively recent example of this phenomenon is the Baha'i Faith (see Box 11.1).

| Box 11.1 | The Baha'i Faith

In comparision with its closest relative, the Baha'i Faith is undoubtedly a 'new religion': Islam was already more than 1,200 years old when Baha'i emerged in the mid-1800s. On the other hand, certain writings of its founders have made the transition from current literature to scripture. The Baha'i community, formerly governed by the lineal descendants and living companions of early leaders, is now run by elected assemblies. And though it was once composed largely of Iranians, the Baha'i Faith now has a worldwide diffusion rivalling that of Christianity.

The Baha'i Faith arose as an explicit rival to Islam. Although the Baha'is shared the Muslims' faith in the one God, they disagreed on the possibility of further prophetic revelations. Whereas Muslims assert the finality of Muhammad as the 'seal' of the prophets sent by God to various peoples, Baha'is leave the door open for more.

The roots of the Baha'i Faith are in the particular eschatology of Iranian Shi'ism. Ever since the disappearance into hiding of the last imam, in 874, Twelver Shi'a had been waiting for a figure known as the Bab ('gateway') to appear and reopen communication with the hidden imam. After ten centuries, most people no longer expected this to happen anytime soon, but seeds of messianic expectation germinated in the soil of political unrest.

In 1844 Sayyid 'Ali Muhammad (1819–50) declared himself to be the Bab: the intermediary who would transmit a new prophetic revelation to the Twelver community. Four years later, his followers, the 'Babis', repudiated the shari'ah law and the Bab proclaimed himself to be the hidden imam. He was executed by a firing squad in 1850, but left behind a number of writings considered scriptural.

The momentum then passed to Mirza Husayn 'Ali Nuri (1817–92), known as Baha'u'llah, 'Glory of God', who was banished first from Iran to Baghdad and eventually to Istanbul. This forced transfer expanded the sphere of his spiritual activity. The horizons were no longer Shi'i or Iranian; now Baha'u'llah could address the religiously diverse population of the entire Ottoman Turkish Empire. Baha'u'llah wrote prolifically, and Baha'is consider his work to be God's inspired revelation for this age. After his death in 1892 the authority to interpret the Baha'i tradition was passed down through his family. In the 1950s his great-grandson appointed an International Baha'i Council, and in 1963 leadership was vested in an elected body of representatives called the Universal House of Justice. Baha'i teachings on human nature are in line with the traditions of the Middle East and Mediterranean. Each person has a body and a soul. The soul is independent both of the body and of space and time, and it can never decay. It is eternal but becomes individuated at the moment of the human being's conception. Personal spiritual cultivation is encouraged, and the use of drugs and alcohol is forbidden.

The Baha'i House of Worship in Wilmette, Illinois. Construction began in 1920 and the temple was formally dedicated in 1953 (Andrew Leyerle).

Likewise traditional is the Baha'i notion that various prophets have been sent by God to diagnose spiritual and moral disorder and prescribe the appropriate remedies. But whereas Islam maintains that the prophets' messages have been intended for specific communities, Baha'is believe that the prophets speak to the entire world. They also believe that the line of prophets has not come to an end: according to their doctrine of 'progressive revelation', there will be more prophets in future ages.

Baha'u'llah himself wrote that he came to 'unify the world', and Baha'is believe that— as the inscription over doorway to one Baha'i house of worship puts it— 'All the Prophets of God proclaim the same Faith.' In addition to teaching the doctrine of unity, Baha'is actively advocate economic, sexual, and racial equality. World peace is to be achieved through disarmament, democracy, and the rule of law, and international education and human rights are to be promoted. Though these goals are compatible with modern secular values, they have a spiritual quality for Baha'is, who cite Baha'u'llah's saying that human well-being is unattainable until unity is firmly established.

Many liberal Jews, Christians, and Muslims could certainly support the principles encapsulated by the Baha'i Faith. But support and sympathy are not enough for the Baha'i religion: it also wants converts. This is true of most monotheistic religions. They innovate by hiving off into new sects or cults, which then seek converts, especially when the prophets of the innovations face significant opposition from authorities within the society. This pattern is true of religion in general, but it is particularly characteristic of monotheistic and missionary traditions.

Missionary Expansion

With the imperial support of Constantine, the missionary religion that was Christianity became a state religion as well. Islam was both a missionary and a state religion from the start. A comparison of their expansion processes may be instructive.

Christianity frequently saw entire populations convert following the conversion of their rulers. If a mission to a particular people could succeed in gaining the ruler's favour, an entire nation could be incorporated into the Christian fold. That approach succeeded in the case of the Slavs and some northern European peoples, but failed in the cases of the Chinese and Japanese.

In its earlier centuries, Islam likewise succeeded in persuading a significant number of nations to convert. (Part of its appeal may have been the juridical status and tax exemption it offered to those who accepted Islam.) The Mediterranean from Iraq to Gibraltar became Muslim and adopted the Arabic language. Iran and Central Asia also became Muslim, although they retained Persian as their language. The third great wholesale conversion was that of the Turkish people, who also continued to speak their own language. Nevertheless, both the Persians and the Turks used the Arabic script for writing their languages until the twentieth century, and this became an important mark of their Islamic identity.

Christianity's spread after the 1490s was closely connected with European military and cultural expansion. Priests accompanied soldiers in Mexico and Peru, and the sponsoring Spanish and Portuguese regimes took it as their responsibility to save the various Native peoples' souls even as they were enslaving their bodies. The cultural-religious imperialism of Catholic countries in the sixteenth century was matched in the nineteenth when Protestant Britain extended its influence in Africa.

Muslim rule in northern India began with the establishment of the Delhi sultanate in the thirteenth century. This was the first case in which Islam did not succeed in converting the entire population of the land it had taken over. Only in the Indus Valley, Bengal, and the mid-southern interior did Muslims become the majority; the rest of the subcontinent remained predominantly Hindu.

In the later centuries of its expansion, Islam grew not so much through military conquest as through trade and the missionary activity of the Sufis in particular. The Sufi devotional life resonated with the Hindu and Buddhist meditational piety already present in Southeast Asia and gave Islam an entrée to the region, in which it became dominant. Similarly in Africa south of the Sahara, traders and Sufis were the principal vehicles for Islam.

In general, missionaries for the major religions have been more successful in recruiting converts from the traditional religions of small-scale tribal societies than from the other major religions. The reasons may have something to do with the material culture and technology of the major civilizations, whose writing systems and scriptural literatures have given the major traditions a special authority among cultures that are primarily oral. As a result, it has been relatively easy for them to use the content of their scriptures to shape the target societies' values.

The credit for the early spread of Buddhism goes to the missionary effort undertaken by King Ashoka. We do not know enough about the indigenous traditions in the lands converted by his missionaries to understand why their Theravada teachings was so effective. We have a clearer idea in the case of China, where the Daoist interest in magic and healing techniques likely gave Buddhism, especially Mahayana, its initial foothold.

Can we evaluate missionary activity in general? Some missionaries have been ardent advocates for their host peoples, working to defend them against colonial or entrepreneurial exploitation. Missionaries have also produced some of the ablest linguistic, ethnographic, and historical studies of indigenous traditions. On the other hand, missionaries have often been intrusive and invasive, blind or insensitive to the inner dynamics of their target cultures. Some have imposed alien customs and cultural values from their own homelands—values not necessarily central to the messages of the traditions they were preaching. And some have been pawns of their home countries' geopolitical interests. In short, the missionary record has been mixed at best, with some very disturbing undertones.

In the twentieth century some Christian denominations reassessed and began to curtail their missionary activity, partly out of an increasing respect for other communities and traditions. But the retreat may also be attributed in part to the judgment that the returns are too small to justify the investment required. After the mid-twentieth century, much of Africa gained independence from European colonial rule. European Christian missionaries suffered from identification with colonial interests, particularly in West Africa, where Europeans had dominated the slave trade. Increasingly, Christian missionaries in Africa were replaced by an emerging generation of indigenous church leaders.

Missionaries were often more welcome for their social contributions than their theology. Some countries that denied visas to Westerners for evangelistic missionary activity continued to grant them for agricultural development, education, and medical work. The schools and hospitals operated by Christians were an important influence in many parts of Asia, but that influence declined as government support for educational and medical institutions increased.

Pluralism

Since the middle of the twentieth century, the term 'pluralism' has often been used to mean both the fact of diversity in itself and the evaluation of that diversity as desirable. This double sense of pluralism reflects a convergence of developments in many areas of life.

The fact of diversity has been reinforced by increasingly close contact between cultures. Today tens of thousands of people cross the Pacific by jet every day, and even without travelling we can be instantly in touch with almost any part of the world. Migration has also increased significantly. Since the end of the Second World War, the demographic profile of European and North American cities has been transformed by the arrival of immigrants who have brought their Muslim, Hindu, Buddhist, and other traditions with them. Though apprehensive at first, Western societies have made some progress towards recognizing and appreciating these traditions.

Change in the evaluation of diversity is reflected in many details of contemporary life, large and small. In some cases institutions that were originally religious have been given new secular rationales. Sunday, for instance, the Christian day of religious observance, remains the day for reduced business activity in many jurisdictions. But the main arguments for legislation preserving Sunday store closing have shifted from religious observance to reasons involving fairness, family time, and opportunity for recreation.

We should distinguish pluralism from secularism. Secularism is the exclusion in principle of all religious groups, institutions, and identities from public support and participation in public decision-making. Pluralism is the granting of equal support, acceptance, or decision-making roles to more than one religious group. Whereas recreational arguments for Sunday closing are secularist, arguments for school holidays at the Jewish New Year and Passover, or at the Ramadan fast, are pluralist. Up to a point, secularism and pluralism go hand in hand in the West because both propose limiting Christianity's role in setting society's standards. Where they differ is in what they propose to replace it with.

Pluralism places a parallel and a positive value on the faith and practice of different communities. It often does so on the assumption that the practice of any religion is beneficial to society as long as it does nothing to harm others. It can also presume that the act of understanding our neighbour's religion—whatever it may be—is beneficial to society. Essentially, pluralism downplays the specific commitments of individual religions and concentrates instead on shared values. In its scale of priorities, it subordinates the differences between religions to the value of harmony in the society as a whole.

Responding to Difference

For three decades the 1978 Jonestown tragedy, in which 914 people committed mass suicide, has stood as a challenge to any categorical acceptance of religious diversity. An agricultural commune established in Guyana in 1972, Jonestown was populated by American followers of the Reverend Jim Jones (1931–78), about 70 per cent black and 30 per cent white. For the study of religion the task is twofold: to understand how and why the Jonestown community came to take such a drastic action, and to decide the grounds on which such an action should be accepted or condemned.

Jim Jones was a charismatic leader, a messiah to his followers. He founded the Peoples Temple in Indianapolis, Indiana, in the 1950s, and moved with some of his group in the mid-1960s to establish a rural settlement in Redwood Valley, California. In time they also established an urban following in San Francisco. Jones's eschatological goal—an overhaul of the existing world order—was compatible with a reformist and utopian strand in Protestant (and Marxist) thought, but he also sought from his followers an uncritical dedication to his personal leadership that frightened many observers. When the political climate in the United States shifted to the right in the early 1970s, Jones moved his base to rural Guyana. The mass suicide was carried out after a number of investigations convinced Jones and his followers that evil forces were closing in on them and that the only honourable escape was death.

History repeats itself. Suicide has been embraced as martyrdom more than once by members of various religious traditions. In 1993, for example, 85 members of the Adventist sect called the Branch Davidians perished with their leader, David Koresh (Vernon Wayne Howell, 1959–93), rather than escape from the flames that engulfed their commune outside Waco, Texas, when it was stormed by US government agents investigating firearms violations.

Martyrdom operations have become associated with Muslim extremists in particular, though Muslims are not the only ones to undertake them. Israel has reported that failed suicide bombers it has captured have been motivated in part by the hope of heavenly reward and in part by the political aim of establishing a Palestinian state. But other motives are just as significant: the hope of obtaining heavenly dispensations for family and friends is also important when economic and political conditions prevent young people from becoming honorable wage-earners supporting their families.

The social context in which a martyrdom operation takes place is also important. Those who volunteer for such missions are celebrated with posters and parades praising their courage and devotion. The valorization of prospective martyrs by family and friends is also important. People who feel powerless to help their loved ones on earth may look forward to gaining the power to provide for them in heaven.

But our own right to practise a religion or invite others to join us is limited by the right of others to know what we are offering and to refuse it if they so choose. Religious groups forfeit their right to acceptance in a pluralistic society if, in order to maintain themselves, they engage in illegal activities (such as tax fraud or trafficking in narcotics or firearms) or use psychological or physical coercion. Critics of the new religious movements that have flourished since the 1960s often refer to them as 'cults'. In this context the word 'cult'—originally meaning worship—is used disparagingly, often with the implication that the movements are fraudulent, coercive, or both, and that their leaders demand an excessive and uncritical dedication from their followers. Critics find it particularly alarming when such movements tell their recruits to sever all ties with their families, although there have been parallels to such demands in many other religious traditions, including early Christianity.

The new religious movements spurred an anti-cult reaction. As large numbers of young people left their families and friends for the Unification Church (the 'Moonies') or the International Society for Krishna Consciousness (the Hare Krishna movement), or paid large fees to the Church of Scientology, families intent on 'rescuing' them often resorted to a coercion that matched or even outdid that of the movements themselves. Young people kidnapped by their parents might be subjected to intense 'deprogramming', which was justified as a matter of fighting fire with fire—in this case, using psychological influence to fight psychological influence. In the same period, sociological and psychological researchers sought to understand why such movements appealed so strongly to the children of well-to-do families. One answer was that, for young people whose parents gave them practically everything they wanted, the new religions offered precisely what their parents did not: a strict and demanding discipline, with structured goals to be achieved.

In the last decades of the twentieth century, some new religions achieved a degree of institutional maturity and public acceptance. Most of these organizations were compatible with mainstream religions in that they helped their members cope with their lives and encouraged good citizenship. In effect, like mainstream religions, in one way or another they addressed the human condition.

The last point is important. Religions are not all the same, but many may be humanly acceptable if they in fact benefit human beings; an appropriate test is suggested by Jesus' words in the Sermon on the Mount: 'you shall know them by their fruits' (Matthew 7:16). On some occasions, when they have lived up to their ideals, all the major traditions have passed that test; on other occasions, when they have fallen short of their ideals, the same traditions have failed. Typically, though, the various traditions see their distinguishing features as eminently valuable in themselves. If all religions were of equal worth, if there were no fundamentally important differences, why would anyone choose one of them over another? Most Christians, for instance, would assert that salvation through Jesus Christ is different from the Hindu or Buddhist models of liberation. Though pluralism is socially desirable, it poses a serious theological challenge. Does it really require us to modify our own ritual or devotional practices and alter our own doctrinal claims?

We are convinced that it does. In the past, statements of religious truth tended to be absolute and universal: claiming to explain the entire material universe and report past events exactly as they happened. But modern philosophers of religion and theology have shifted the force of such statements. Today affirmations of religious truth are often perspectival—true 'for me', not necessarily for everyone. Thinkers in several traditions now present their heritages as symbolic accounts of the physical world and metaphorical narratives of past events. What is more, they now contend that this is the way the various traditions should always have been understood, and that literalism has been a mistake through the centuries.

It is not our task here to say how different religions should or will change in the future. That challenge is one for the religious communities themselves to face. What is certain is that, as human society becomes ever more interconnected, the opportunities to see one another in action and to engage in open dialogue will be far greater than they ever were in the past. Observers of religion will want to be alert to the new forms and formulations that emerge.

Defining 'Religion'

One way to approach the question of whether or not all religions are essentially 'the same' is to look at the words we use to talk about the subject. There is, after all, a substantial body of discourse about 'religion'. Bookstores and libraries have sections on religion, schools and universities offer courses and conduct research on it, the Saturday newspaper may devote a page to it, and there are laws that guarantee its freedom.

Yes, people do seem to have an idea of what they mean by 'religion'. Some find it in historical uses of the term. Others find it in the characteristics shared by a 'short list' of the traditions that are generally agreed to constitute religions. Still others define the concept by contrasting it with what it does not include, refining it through the discussion of borderline cases. We will consider each of these approaches in turn.

'Religion' in the West

The Euro-American West in general has defined the concept of 'religion' primarily by reference to the West's principal religion, Christianity. During the European Middle Ages, the Latin word *religio* and its derivatives had a meaning internal to Christianity: it meant piety, or the faith and action incumbent on a practising member of the Christian community. Even today, 'a religious' is someone who is a member of a Christian religious order.

This is not to say that European Christians were unaware of other traditions. Early Christian writers referred to rival teachings. The medieval Christians knew of the Muslims as a major challenge to the south and east of Europe, the Jews as a distinct minority within medieval Christendom, and 'pagans' as rivals in the classical Mediterranean region and in pre-Christian northern Europe. But they did not refer to those other traditions as 'religions' until after the fifteenth century.

When the Christian West looked at other traditions, it sought to define them in terms parallel to the terms in which it understood Christianity. The Christian historical self-understanding imposed three of its own tendencies on what it described.

First, it insisted on pinning things down as affirmations of belief. One identified oneself as a Christian by stating a creed, by declaring such-and-such a belief about God, Jesus, or the world. Therefore one expected adherents of a different tradition to have a corresponding set of creedal beliefs, which it would be the observer's task to formulate. Some of Asia's great traditions, such as Buddhism, do present substantial, sophisticated, and challenging doctrines; but in traditions such as Shinto, statements of doctrine are virtually non-existent. Thus to expect every religion to have a systematic doctrine is to exclude a vast and important range of religious activity from view. So 'religion' defined as 'belief' is not a descriptive definition of the spectrum of phenomena, but a prescriptive restriction to the narrow band within the spectrum that fits the observer's stipulations.

Second, Christianity tended to impose on all religions its own institutional distinction between the sacred and the secular. Having survived for three centuries as a minority before receiving state patronage, Christianity was quite accustomed to the idea that some things belong to God and others to Caesar. Even the medieval Latin Church, at the height of its influence, took conspicuous note of this principle in its struggles over authority with various European rulers. One of the chief characteristics of modernity in the Euro-American West is a secularity that puts both intellectual and institutional limits on the sphere allocated to religion.

Islam, however, did not share Christianity's formative experience of 300 years as a minority. From the beginning, it was a total value system governing every aspect of life, including commerce and even warfare. In the case of Islam, virtually every aspect of culture and civilization is relevant to religion.

The sacred–secular contrast is also unhelpful when we consider Chinese thought of 2,500 years ago, though for different reasons. The principal contribution of Confucius and his early successors was a humane social ethic: what in the West we might consider moral philosophy. Admittedly, Confucius made rhetorical references to Heaven, but he seems to have been rather agnostic about much of the traditional religion and ritual in his day. Perhaps the closest parallel to Confucius in the West is Socrates, who represents the more secular Hellenic part of the Western cultural heritage, as distinct from the part that is rooted in the religion of the ancient Hebrews. Still, the tradition stemming from the teachings of Confucius became more religious in later centuries, when the Neo-Confucians cultivated an inner personal spirituality and speculated on the ultimate nature of things.A third Christian expectation concerning 'religion' is the notion of exclusive membership. That God should demand loyalty and tolerate no rivals is part of Judaism and was passed on to Christianity and Islam. Each of these three has been at pains to demarcate the boundaries of its community. In southern and eastern Asia, however, following one tradition has rarely if ever meant that one can't follow another as well.

This point is doubly relevant in the case of the Sikh tradition. The early Sikhs were disciples of a teacher who saw God as transcending all forms, including the boundaries of human communities—boundaries made all the more visible with the arrival of Islam in India. Four centuries after Guru Nanak, however, some Sikh leaders were seeking strenuously to define their community in contrast to a Hindu population with whom they had a great deal in common. And five centuries after his time, Sikhs contend that full recognition of their identity has been denied them.

Do boundaries help us to understand Japan? Studies report that only a small percentage of Japanese see themselves as belonging to any religion. Yet when surveys ask whether they follow Buddhist or Shinto or other rituals and practices, the positive answers add up to more than the total population of the country.

The Roster of Religions

Perhaps we can arrive at a definition or characterization of religion in general by looking at the most commonly cited examples. As eighteenth- and early nineteenth-century handbooks show, Europe was content for three centuries after the 1490s to recognize just four religions: Christianity, Judaism, Islam, and paganism. But the 'pagan' category expanded dramatically as new 'discoveries' were made in Asia, Africa, and the Americas. As with stress building up along an earthquake fault, a realignment would have to come sooner or later. What brought it about was probably the rapid increase in the information available regarding doctrines. One of the first books in English to devote a chapter to each of half a dozen major traditions was written in 1846 by a versatile Anglican theological scholar named Frederick Denison Maurice. The idea of the 'great' or 'living' or 'world' religions was launched. To be included on that short list, a religion is required to be both historically influential and still alive today. In addition, it has been expected for the past century and a half that each short-listed tradition will have a well-developed literature or body of doctrine.

As with any canon, there have been some undisputed nominees, and many more marginal cases. Consensus always lists the three great missionary religions (Buddhism, Christianity, and Islam). It has often included the national religious heritages of Israel (Judaism), Persia before Islam (Zoroastrianism), India (Hinduism), and Japan (Shinto). It can also include two distinct communities in India (the Sikhs and the Jains) and two distinct sets of teachings in China (Confucian and Daoist).

If we consider the traditions omitted from that core consensus, we find three kinds. One consists of the religious traditions of indigenous peoples. Despite some overall resemblances, they are fragmented and diverse, and their traditions are oral rather than textual. A second type includes the traditions that, no matter how sophisticated their doctrine or rich their mythology, have essentially died out. Manichaeism is one example; others include the religions of ancient Greece and Rome, Mesopotamia and Egypt, Mexico and Peru. The third type consists of movements too recent for inclusion in the nineteenth-century canon, such as Japan's new religions and the Baha'i Faith. All these traditions have tended to receive scant coverage in textbooks. But this situation may well change in the future. As some of the new religions endure and gain historical and doctrinal depth, the canon will need reassessment. It is also conceivable that a pan-tribal synthesis of Native American, African, Polynesian, or Melanesian religion could take shape and gain recognition as a 'new' religion.

If we could identify the characteristics that all the 'world' religions share, it might be possible to define an essence of religion. But when we look at the candidates for inclusion on an 'essential' list, it seems there are always exceptions:

- Belief in a personal god or spirits: Early Buddhist doctrine—as distinct from southern Buddhist folk religion and East Asian Buddhist doctrine—lacks this feature. And for Hindu Vedanta, ultimate reality is not personal.
- A path to personal experience of altered consciousness: There is only a little in contemporary Zoroastrian tradition that offers such a path.
- A cohesive worshipping community: Confucianism seems to be deficient in this regard.
- Divinely sanctioned morality: It's hard to see much of this in Shinto.
- A promise of life after death: Classical Hebrew religion offered no such assurance.

In fact, it seems impossible to identify any feature that is absolutely essential in order for a tradition to qualify as a religion. The short list is more about standard examples than any essence that those examples might share.

If we cannot expect all religions to share any single feature, perhaps a 'syndrome' approach would be more appropriate. As in clinical medicine, perhaps we should identify as a religion whatever displays a majority of the symptomatic features listed above. Such a fuzzy characterization is unsatisfactory from a logical and philosophical standpoint. All the same, it seems to be what Western civilization has meant by 'religion' for 500 years now.

Defining by Exclusion

Another way of demarcating the sphere of religion is to consider things that look like religion but are commonly agreed to be something different. By examining these other phenomena, perhaps we can identify some distinguishing feature of religion that they lack.

The modern Protestant theologian Paul Tillich characterized religion as 'ultimate concern', concern for what ultimately matters most in this world, this life, and beyond. His view has sometimes been distorted to suggest that religion is whatever we hold as our highest priority, however mundane; for some people, golf might be a religion. For Tillich, though, such mundane concerns do not qualify; validly ultimate concerns must have something to do with the overall meaning of the universe and of life in it.

For more than seventy years after the Russian revolution of 1917, many thought that the communist system, built on the atheistic socialism of Karl Marx, posed a worldwide threat to religion. As implemented after the mid-twentieth century all the way from Czechoslovakia to China, it repressed traditional religious institutions while bearing some curious resemblances to religion itself. These resemblances are particularly noticeable *vis-à-vis* the monotheistic Western religions. Like Judaism, Christianity, and Islam, communism seeks to liberate the poor from exploitation; finds direction, meaning, and significance in history; and idealizes a future moment when evil will be overthrown and justice will prevail. A new order will be ushered in, the classless society corresponding to the kingdom of heaven.

Marx critiqued all religion and politics before his time on the grounds that they had failed morally and materially to improve the lot of humanity. But communism too can be judged by Marx's standards, and eventually it too was found wanting. Communism like traditional religions, wants to state an 'is' and derive from it an 'ought'. There is a huge philosophical difference between descriptive laws of nature, which must be modified to conform to the behaviour of phenomena, and prescriptive laws of society, which demand that individuals modify their behaviour to conform and which threaten punishment for failure to do so. Yet both communism and religion seek the benefits of description and prescription simultaneously. Each sees the order of things as a description of the way things necessarily are, and at the same time proposes to derive from that description a prescription for the way individuals should voluntarily behave.

Furthermore, communist ideologues have resembled missionaries in their zeal to spread their teachings. Members of the community of the committed take part in group rituals that reinforce solidarity. Intense pressure is applied to persuade individuals to confess and publicly disavow their faults and shortcomings. In the case of China's Mao Zedong, the cult of the leader even had its own scripture—a pocket-sized anthology of his quotations, bound in red. Yet communism has not thought of itself as a religion, and in practice it has often has shown active hostility towards religion. In addition, a crucial difference emerges if we ask whether a power may exist above or beyond humankind. Religion characteristically says yes: the way or power of the universe governs us. Communism has said no; history is human history, and controllable by humans. This postulation of a transhuman power is sometimes termed faith in transcendence. When communism is disqualified as a religion, it is generally because it lacks that essential ingredient.

It remains to consider one further alternative to 'religion'—namely, philosophy. Are there not philosophies that, like religions, contemplate ultimate reality? When we look at the Chinese moral teachers in their cultural setting, it is not easy to draw a clear line between philosophy and religion. Don't both seek to map out the good that people should seek in their conduct?

If we form a view of the universe or a set of prescriptions for thought and action, we may have stated a personal philosophy, but we have not created a religion in the sense intended in this book. If with a circle of friends and disciples we discuss these views, subjecting them to rational criticism and argument, we may have participated in a philosophical movement, but we have not formed a religion. If our group meets regularly, repeating the same activities each time, we may have ritualized our conduct, but we still may not have become a religion. Where do we cross the line?

Part of the difference is that philosophy is an intellectual, rational pursuit, while religion seeks a commitment of the will and the emotions as well. Philosophy's decisions are by nature decisions for an individual mind to make; many of religion's decisions are made by groups. The rituals of philosophers are seldom essential to the force of their arguments, but the rituals of religion are often seen as creating or confirming centrally important states of affairs.

A Provisional Definition

We can now sum up these efforts at characterizing religion. We have looked at the evolution of our vocabulary, at standard religions as examples, and at communism and philosophy as important counter-instances. In so doing, we have been circling our prey. No single line of definition seems able to trap it, but we can weave a net. Religion is a sense of power beyond the human that is

- apprehended rationally as well as emotionally,
- appreciated corporately as well as individually,
- celebrated ritually and symbolically as well as discursively, and
- transmitted in conventionalized forms as a tradition that offers people
  - an interpretation of experience,
  - a view of life and death,
  - a guide to conduct, and
  - an orientation to meaning and purpose in the world.

Some Twentieth-Century Analyses

An often-cited article by the American anthropologist Clifford Geertz expands on each dimension of the previous observations about religion:

> A *religion* is: (1) a system of symbols which acts to (2) establish powerful, pervasive and long-lasting moods and motivations in men by (3) formulating conceptions of a general order of existence and (4) clothing these conceptions with such an aura of factuality that (5) the moods and motivations seem uniquely realistic (Geertz 1966:4).

Some of the wording here seems elastic (what is an 'aura' of factuality? how do symbols, rather than people, 'act'?). Nevertheless, many have found Geertz's article a useful mainstream example of twentieth-century social theory of religion.

In focusing on the social function of religion, social scientists like Geertz stood back from the theories of religious origins contributed by their discipline's nineteenth-century pioneers. Yet most shared with their predecessors the conviction that religion can be treated as a social and psychological phenomenon and analyzed with conceptual tools from outside religion itself.

The Role of the Participant

After the middle of the twentieth century, anthropologists increasingly questioned the usefulness, if not the validity, of describing cultural structures in terms alien to the culture in question. Sometimes for intellectual reasons, sometimes for political ones, investigators sought to give voice in cultural description to terms or concepts internal to a tradition or community. They were trying to bridge the classic gulf between participant and observer.

But are the participants in a system always consciously aware of what the system relies on? A common-sense answer must be no. In researching many aspects of human affairs, investigators have repeatedly identified cases where the observer can detect patterns, relationships, and similarities of which the participant is unaware. A Siberian indigenous people, for instance, may be very familiar with shamanism as they practise it without being aware of shamanism as a cross-cultural phenomenon.

The Perspective of the Observer

From the 1960s through the 1980s, 'structuralist' approaches were popular in several fields of cultural studies. The specific meaning of 'structuralism' depended on the field, whether anthropology, developmental psychology, linguistics, or literary studies. One common feature of such efforts, however, was to point out that all religions are structured in similar ways and that the structures are accessible to scholarly or scientific observation even if the adherents of those religions do not recognize them. As the French anthropologist Claude Lévi-Strauss (b. 1908) explained it:

Science has only two ways of proceeding: it is either reductionist or struc-turalist. It is reductionist when it is possible to find out that very complex phenomena can be reduced to simpler phenomena on other levels. For instance, there is a lot in life which can be reduced to physiochemical processes, which explain a part but not all. And when we are confronted with phenomena too complex to be reduced to phenomena of a lower order, then we can only approach them by looking to their relationships, that is, by trying to understand what kind of original system they make up. This is exactly what we have been trying to do in linguistics, in anthropology, and in other fields (Lévi-Strauss 1978:9–10).

The structures so identified had validity if they made sense in the mind of the investi-gator, regardless of whether they were understood by the populations under study. In short, structuralists assumed that they knew better than their subjects themselves what the latter were doing.

Post-structuralist, deconstructionist, and postmodern writers took that 'We know better' assumption and turned it on the investigators themselves. Twentieth-century scholarship has undergone a kind of politicization, in which the motives of the investigator are considered to be socially and economically determined. Intellectuals are seen as slaves to their political, racial, class, and gender affiliations. Scholars are por-trayed as career-driven rather than thirsting for understanding. Where we might have assumed a kind of free will in the history of ideas, we are now confronted with a kind of determinism in the sociology of knowledge. To overstate the development only slightly: scholars do not seek truth, but work in their own self- or group interest.

Recent discussions along these lines may seem new, but the issues are long-standing. In every age, people have striven to comprehend the world. In every age, peo-ple have called for fairness in action and fair criteria in judgment. And the determinists are to a considerable extent right: in every age, people have been conditioned to interpret the world in the light of the assumptions current within their own class or community. As debates continue, people will continue to disagree, while seeking (according to dif-ferent understandings) to do justice to the data. Meanwhile, we must all continue work-ing to recognize and challenge our own parochial assumptions.

Religious Theories of Religion

Adherents of the world's religions have generally believed that their own tradition's mes-sage was divinely constituted. The idea that all religions might be equally God-given is a relatively modern phenomenon.

We can see this religion-in-general stance as, in part, a reaction to European social-scientific theories that emerged in the late nineteenth century. Theories such as Tylor's animism or, later, Durkheim's totemism attributed religion to human causes, describing it as the product of cultural circumstances, or psychological needs, or the human imagination. Religious people were understandably alarmed at such interpretations, for while many might have been willing to dismiss other people's religions as merely human artifacts, they were alarmed at the thought of explaining away their own faiths.

Theologians have a term for this explain-it-away spirit: reductionism. Religion is 'reduced' to the factors claimed to cause it, explained in terms other than its own. Many scholars of religion reject reductionist explanations. Yet before writing them off completely, we should consider what other kinds of explanations, if any, might be more acceptable.

The German philosopher of religion Rudolf Otto was profoundly disturbed by the turn-of-the-century tendency to explain religion as socially conditioned. In 1910 he wrote an article criticizing the cultural-evolutionist perspective of a work on ethnic psychology by the German Wilhelm Wundt—a work that Durkheim admired greatly—and in 1917 he published *The Idea of the Holy*, which became a theological best-seller. Building on Schleiermacher's view of religion as intuitive feeling, Otto described a sense of mystery—at once overpowering and fascinating—that he called the numinous:

> We are dealing with something for which there is only one appropriate expression, *mysterium tremendum*. The feeling of it may at times come sweeping like a gentle tide, pervading the mind with a tranquil mood of deepest worship. . . . It may burst in sudden eruption up from the depths of the soul with spasms and convulsions, or lead to the strangest excitements, to intoxicated frenzy, to transport, and to ecstasy. . . . It may become the hushed, trembling, and speechless humility of the creature in the presence of—whom or what? In the presence of that which is a *Mystery* inexpressible and above all creatures (Otto 1923:12–13, italics in original).

Otto believed that the sense of the numinous was a common feature of all religions, although he gave a privileged place to Christian examples of it.

In 1933 a theologian and historian of religions named Gerardus van der Leeuw published a wide-ranging survey whose English title is *Religion in Essence and Manifestation*. Like Otto, van der Leeuw treated religion as a response to a divine stimulus:

> Many ancient peoples were familiar with the idea of a World-course, which however is not passively followed but rather itself moves spontaneously, and is no mere abstract conformity to Law such as are our Laws of Nature, but on the contrary a living Power operating within the Universe. *Tao* in China, *Rata* in India, *Asha* in Iran, *Ma'at* among the ancient Egyptians, *Dike* in Greece:—these are such ordered systems which theoretically, indeed, constitute the all-inclusive calculus of the Universe, but which nevertheless, as living and impersonal powers, possess *mana*-like character (Van der Leeuw 1938:30).

Also like Otto, van der Leeuw found his definitive examples in the Christian tradition.

Another important figure in this line of thought was the Romanian Mircea Eliade, whose extensive work in the area of comparative religion drew particularly on Hindu and tribal traditions. Like Otto, who spoke of religion as a response to the holy, Eliade saw religion as a response to a transcendent reality—a reality that he called 'the sacred'. For Durkheim the sacred might have been nothing more than a human social construct, but for Eliade it originated somewhere else entirely:

> Man becomes aware of the sacred because it manifests itself, shows itself, as something wholly different from the profane. To designate the *act of manifestation* of the sacred, we have proposed the term hierophany. . . . It could be said that the history of religions—from the most primitive to the most highly developed—is constituted by a great number of hierophanies, by manifestations of sacred realities. . . . In each case we are confronted by the same mysterious act—the manifestation of something of a wholly different order, a reality that does not belong to our world, in objects that are an integral part of our natural 'profane' world (Eliade 1959:11).

Do all religions ultimately say the same thing? In the view of these theorists, the answer seems to be yes. The sacred or holy is what the religions all point to, despite their vast diversity.

Similarities and Differences

Another way of approaching the question of unity is by way of the contexts in which claims have been made for the fundamental similarity of all religions and for crucial differences between them.

We do not have to look far for situations in which religions are treated as different. Every community that undertakes missionary activity is implicitly declaring that its religion stands apart from the rest. Not only must the difference be large enough that prospective converts can be expected to perceive it, but it must be important enough that, ultimately, the missionaries' efforts will be worth the sacrifices they may entail.

Non-proselytizing communities can also assert fundamental differences among religions. Shinto, for instance, is closely linked with Japan's national identity. Given Japan's traditional insistence on the unique character of its heritage, practitioners of Shinto are not likely to see all religions as essentially the same. At the same time, many Japanese practise more than one religion, recognizing distinctive benefits in each one.

Philosophers in particular have been interested in identifying instances of disagreement on specific issues. In cases where two religions have become established in geographic isolation from one another, we might be able to dismiss any philosophical differences between them as circumstantial. Any differences between Confucian and

Christian notions of duty and morality, for example, might be attributed to the different cultural vocabularies in which they are expressed. It might even be possible to harmonize the Shinto and Hebrew narratives of creation if we were to understand their details as metaphorical.

Sooner or later, though, we must face up to outright disagreements. For instance, the various Hindu traditions all assert the reality of the self; even in Vedanta, where individual identity is seen as illusory, it merges with reality in a cosmic self. Early Buddhism, by contrast, clearly repudiated the idea of the human self as a persisting reality. Buddhism and Hinduism share many features, among them monastic asceticism and the notion of cyclical rebirth. But their difference over the self is so fundamental that it poses a serious problem for any attempt to argue that religions are fundamentally the same.

An equally significant difference exists between Christianity and Islam on the subject of divine incarnation. For Christians, Jesus is the son of God and a manifestation of God's very nature in a human life. For Muslims, the absolute otherness of God forbids the association of any other being with God at God's level. The Qur'an (112:3) explicitly states that God does not beget and is not begotten. There is even a charming passage (5:116) that imagines God asking Jesus at the day of judgment, 'Did you tell them you were to be worshipped as divine?' and Jesus replying, 'No; why would I ever tell them such a thing?'

Yet even in the face of such disparities, people still assert the fundamental unity of religion. There is a Hindu saying: 'Truth is one; the sages call it by different names.' We need to consider how this statement should be understood. Is it rhetoric, meant to persuade, or an apologetic defence against some criticism? Is it a moral necessity? Or a matter of revelation? Is it a conclusion that can be substantiated?

Conclusion

Earlier in this chapter we noted that all the major religious traditions seek in one way or another to benefit human beings. Another fundamental similarity can be seen in the ways their adherents have found to live out their religion.

As late as the 1950s, two things were expected of practising Christians. One was 'faith', generally understood as belief in a particular set of doctrines. The other was 'works' in the sense both of ritual activity and of ethical behaviour. In the 1960s, however, the consciousness revolution gave rise to a new emphasis on what we might call 'experience'. Some sought religious ecstasy in drugs, though most soon found this route a dead end. Others looked to 'exotic' cultures—Zen, Sufism, yoga—for depths of experience that they considered the Western traditions to lack. By the early 1970s charismatic movements were gaining ground in some previously staid denominations, tapping sources of 'feeling' in the Western tradition that, although they were not new, had been largely forgotten by the mainstream. Today experience stands alongside faith and works as an essential dimension of their religion for many Christians.

A similar development took place in the Hindu tradition approximately 2,000 years ago with the composition of the *Bhagavad Gita*. The *Gita* is a remarkable text, not only for its literary beauty and its religious depth, but for its skilful synthesis of three alternative 'ways' in religion. The way of works, *karma marga*, includes both ethical and ritual dimensions, as in the Christian tradition. The way of knowledge, *jnana marga*, parallels the doctrinal or 'faith' component in Christianity. Finally, the way of devotion, *bhakti marga*, is presented in the *Gita* as the climax and fulfillment of the other two ways. This experiential and devotional element has been central to Hinduism ever since.

Islam suggests a similar triad of paths, though it does not identify them as such. They are the *shari'ah*, the law governing ritual and conduct; philosophical theology; and Sufism, the mystical, devotional tradition that gave Islam its entrée to the Hindu and Buddhist cultures of Malaysia and Indonesia and provided a basis for understanding between the Muslim ruling minority and the Hindu majority population of medieval northern India.

It may be tempting to see these broad similarities as reason enough to agree with the proposition that, ultimately, the world's religions are much the same. But the differences are significant too, as we have seen. Perhaps it is less important to answer the question of unity in diversity than to recognize its fundamental moral, political, and intellectual significance for the world we live in.

Further Reading

de Vries, Jan. 1967. *The Study of Religion: A Historical Approach.* New York: Harcourt, Brace & World. Reviews theories of religion, with particular attention to European interpretations of myth.

Hallencreutz, Carl F. 1970. *New Approaches to Men of Other Faiths, 1938–1968: A Theological Discussion.* Geneva: World Council of Churches. Traces the emergence of ecumenical Christian interest in interreligious dialogue as a wider ecumenism.

Hick, John H. 1995. *The Rainbow of Faiths: Critical Dialogues on Religious Pluralism.* London: SCM Press. (Also published as *A Christian Theology of Religions: The Rainbow of Faiths.* Louisville: Westminster John Knox Press, 1995.) By a leading investigator of the philosophical implications of religious pluralism.

Laymen's Foreign Missions Inquiry, Committee of Appraisal. 1932. *Re-thinking Missions: A Laymen's Inquiry after One Hundred Years.* New York: Harper. A landmark study challenging older missionary assumptions, by a committee chaired by the Harvard philosopher William Ernest Hocking.

Lessa, William A., and Evon Z. Vogt, eds. 1979. *Reader in Comparative Religion: An Anthropological Approach.* 4th edn. New York: Harper & Row. A superb anthology with substantial extracts from nineteenth- and twentieth-century ethnographic and theoretical literature, well introduced. The four editions vary in their content, but some classics survive in all of them.

Oxtoby, Willard G. 1983. *The Meaning of Other Faiths.* Philadelphia: Westminster Press. An appeal to a Christian readership for greater openness toward various religions.

Pals, Daniel L. 1996. *Seven Theories of Religion.* New York: Oxford University Press. Perhaps the best introduction to modern views on religion, especially social-scientific ones.

Segal, Alan F. 2005. *Life After Death: A History of the Afterlife in Western Religions*. New York: Doubleday.

Sharpe, Eric J. 1975. *Comparative Religion: A History*. 2nd edn. La Salle, IL.: Open Court. Very good on nineteenth- and twentieth-century shifts in attitudes regarding the study of religion.

Ziolkowski, Eric J., ed. 1993. *A Museum of Faiths: Histories and Legacies of the 1893 World's Parliament of Religions*. Atlanta: Scholars Press. A useful appreciation of the influence of the parliament.

References

Durkheim, Émile. 1915. *The Elementary Forms of the Religious Life*. London: Allen & Unwin.

Eliade, Mircea. 1959. *The Sacred and the Profane: The Nature of Religion*. New York: Harcourt, Brace.

Geertz, Clifford. 1966. 'Religion as a Cultural System'. In Michael Banton, ed. *Anthropological Approaches to the Study of Religion*, 1–46. London: Tavistock.

Van der Leeuw, Gerardus. 1938. *Religion in Essence and Manifestation*. London: Allen & Unwin.

Lévi-Strauss, Claude. 1978. *Myth and Meaning*. Toronto: University of Toronto Press.

Otto, Rudolf. 1923. *The Idea of the Holy: An Inquiry into the Non-rational Factor in the Idea of the Divine and Its Relation to the Rational*. London: Oxford University Press.

F. BOWIE AND O. DAVIES. Extract from *Scivias*, translated by Robert Carver, in *Hildegard of Bingen: Mystical Writings*, edited by Fiona Bowie and Oliver Davies (New York: Crossroad Publishing Co. Inc., 1990). This work is protected by copyright and it is being used with the permission of Access Copyright. Any alteration of its content or further copying in any form whatsoever is strictly prohibited.

CAMBRIDGE UNIVERSITY PRESS. Extracts from the *New English Bible*. © Oxford University Press and Cambridge University Press 1961, 1970.

JOHN CARMAN AND VASUDHA NARAYANAN. Extract from *The Tamil Veda: Pillan's Interpretation of the Tiruvaymoli*, translated by J. Carman and V. Narayanan, from *The Tamil Veda: Pillan's Interpretation of the Tiruvaymoli* (Chicago: University of Chicago Press, 1989), 202-23. © 1989 by The University of Chicago.

D.C. LAU. Extracts from *The Analects* (Harmondsworth: Penguin Classics, 1979): 63, 64, 91, 102, 107, 114, 115-16, 119, 128, 131, 136. Copyright © D.C. Lau, 1979. Reproduced by permission of Penguin Books Ltd. Extracts from *Mencius* (Harmondsworth: Penguin Classics, 1970): 82-3. Copyright © D.C. Lau, 1970. Reproduced by permission of Penguin Books Ltd.

W.T. DE BARY. Extracts from *Sources of Indian Tradition*, edited by William Theodore de Bary. Copyright © 1958 by Columbia University Press. Reprinted with permission of the publisher.

SRAVASTI DHAMMIKA. Extract from *Buddha Vacana* (Singapore: Buddha Dhamma Mandala Society, 1989). Reprinted by permission of the publisher.

WENDY DONIGER O'FLAHERTY. Extracts from *The Rig Veda: An Anthology of One Hundred and Eight Hymns* (Harmondsworth: Penguin Classics, 1981). Copyright © Wendy Doniger O'Flaherty, 1981. Reproduced by permission of Penguin Books Ltd.

I.R. AL FARUQI AND D.E. SOPHER. The map 'Expulsion and Migration of Jews from European Cities and Regions, Eleventh to Fifteenth Centuries CE' from *Historical Atlas of the Religions of the World*, edited by I.R. al Faruqi and D.E. Sopher (New York: Macmillan, 1974). Reprinted by permission.

T. HA AND G.K. MINTZ. Extracts from *Samguk Yusa: Legends and Histories of the Three Kingdoms of Ancient Korea*, translated by T. Ha and G.K. Mintz (Seoul: Yonsei University Press, 1972). Reprinted by permission of the publisher.

F.C. HAPPOLD. Extract from *Mysticism* by F.C. Happold. Reprinted by permission of Dr David Happold.

JOHN STRATTON HAWLEY AND MARK JUERGENSMEYER. Excerpts from *Songs of the Saints of India*, translated by J.S. Hawley and M. Juergensmeyer (New York: Oxford University Press, 1988). By permission of Oxford University Press Inc.

567

MARTIN LUTHER KING, JR. Extract from *Why We Can't Wait* by Martin Luther King, Jr. Reprinted by arrangement with the Estate of Martin Luther King, Jr, c/o Writers House as agent for the proprietor New York, NY. Copyright 1963 Martin Luther King Jr, copyright renewed 1991 Coretta Scott King.

MUKUND LATH. Extract from *Kalpa Sutra of Bhadrabahu*, edited by Vinay Sagar, English translation by Dr Mukund Lath. Reproduced with permission of Prakrit Bharati Academy, Jaipur.

PETER H. LEE. Extract from *Sourcebook of Korean Civilization*, Vol. 2, ed. P.H. Lee. Copyright © 1996 Columbia University Press. Reprinted with permission of the publisher.

W.H. MCLEOD. Extracts from *Textual Sources for the Study of Sikhism*. Reprinted by permission of W.H. McLeod, University of Otago.

BARBARA STOLER MILLER. Extract from the *Bhagavad-Gita*. Translation copyright © 1986 by Barbara Stoler Miller. Used by permission of Bantam Books, a division of Random House, Inc.

NANAMOLI. Extracts from *The Life of the Buddha*. Reproduced with the permission of the Buddhist Publication Society Inc, 54 Sangharaja Mawatha, Kandy, Sri Lanka.

VASUDHA NARAYANAN. Extracts from *Hinduism: Origins, Beliefs, Practices, Holy Texts, Sacred Places*, translated by V. Narayanan. By permission of Oxford University Press Inc. and Duncan Baird Publishers.

C.A. RHYS-DAVIDS. Excerpt from *Psalms of the Early Buddhists* (Pali Text Society). Reprinted by permission of the publisher.

NIKKI-GUNINDER KAUR SINGH. Extracts from *The Feminine Principle in the Sikh Vision of the Transcendent*. © Cambridge University Press 1993. Reprinted with the permission of Cambridge University Press.

R. TSUNODA. Extracts from *Sources of Japanese Tradition*, edited by R. Tsunoda. Copyright © 1958 by Columbia University Press. Reprinted by permission of the publisher.

ARTHUR WALEY. Extracts from *The Way and its Power: A Study of the Tao Te Ching and its Place in Chinese Thought*. By permission of John Robinson.

BURTON WATSON. Extracts from *Hsun Tzu: Basic Writings*, translated by B. Watson. Copyright © 1963 by Columbia University Press. Reprinted with permission of the publisher. Extracts from *Mo Tzu: Basic Writings*, translated by B. Watson. Copyright © 1963 by Columbia University Press. Reprinted with permission of the publisher. Extracts from *Chuang Tzu: Basic Writings*, translated by B. Watson. Copyright © 1968 by Columbia University Press. Reprinted with permission of the publisher.

PHILIP YAMPOLSKY. Extracts from *The Platform Sutra of the Sixth Patriarch*, translated by P. Yampolsky. Copyright © 1976 by Columbia University Press. Reprinted by permission of the publisher.

Every effort has been made to determine and contact copyright owners. In case of omissions, the publisher will be pleased to make suitable acknowledgement in future editions.